PUERTO RICO
and
PUERTO RICANS

i

PUERTO RICO
and
PUERTO RICANS:

Studies in History and Society

Edited by
Adalberto López and James Petras

A Halsted Press Book

Schenkman Publishing Company

JOHN WILEY & SONS

New York - London - Sydney - Toronto

Copyright   1974 by Schenkman Publishing Company
3 Mount Auburn Place, Cambridge, Mass. 02138

Distributed solely by Halsted Press, a Division
of John Wiley & Sons, Inc. New York.

Library of Congress Cataloging in Publication Data
López, Adalberto.
Puerto Rico and the Puerto Ricans.
"A Halsted Press book."

Bibliography: p.
1. Puerto Rico—Social conditions—Addresses,
essays, lectures. 2. Puerto Rico—Economic conditions
Addresses, essays, lectures. 3. Puerto Ricans in the United
States—Addresses, essays, lectures. I. Petras,
James F., 1937-   joint author. II. Title.
233.L66   309.1'7295   74-8796
ISBN 0-470-54493-7
ISBN 0-470-54494-5 (pbk.)

To the new generation
of Puerto Ricans on the mainland and in Puerto Rico
that is leading the struggle for independence and social justice,
and to the older militants who have kept the faith.

v

Contents

Part III: Puerto Ricans on the Mainland

Bibliographical Essays

Chronology of Puerto Rican History   486

ACKNOWLEDGEMENTS

We would like to thank our students and colleagues, both at the State University of New York at Binghamton and elsewhere, who encouraged and challenged us to produce a book on Puerto Rico and Puerto Ricans. We especially would like to thank Angel Quintero Rivera.

The Editors

ADALBERTO LÓPEZ is Director of the Latin American and Caribbean Area Studies Program and Assistant Professor of History at the State University of New York at Binghamton. He was born in Cidra, Puerto Rico, and lived for many years in New York City. In addition to several reviews and essays on Puerto Rico, he has written several articles on the colonial history of southern South America.

JAMES PETRAS is Professor of Sociology at the State University of New York at Binghamton. He is co-editor of *Latin America: Reform or Revolution?*, co-author of *Peasants in Revolt*, editor-contributor of *Latin America: From Dependence to Revolution*, and author of several other books and numerous articles on Latin America.

The Contributors

ANGEL G. QUINTERO RIVERA is Research Associate and Instructor at the Social Science Research Center, University of Puerto Rico. He was born in San Juan, Puerto Rico. Among his works are *Lucha Obrera en Puerto Rico* and *El liderato local de los partidos y el estudio de la politica puertorriqueña*.

DIANA CHRISTOPULOS is a doctoral candidate in the Department of History, State University of New York at Binghamton.

ISABEL PICÓ is Instructor of Political Science at the University of Puerto Rico. Her articles and reviews have appeared in *La Escalera*, *Caribbean Monthly Bulletin*, and other publications.

MORRIS MORLEY is a doctoral candidate in the Department of Sociology, State University of New York at Binghamton.

EDUARDO SEDA is Associate Professor in the Graduate School of Planning, University of Puerto Rico. He was born in Cabo Rojo, Puerto Rico, and is the author of *Los derechos civiles en la cultura puertorriqueña, Réquiem para una cultura, Social Change in a Puerto Rican Agrarian Reform Community* and several other books and articles on Puerto Rico and Puerto Ricans on the mainland.

MARY K.VAUGHAN teaches history at the University of Illinois, Chicago Circle. She currently is working on a book about Mexico.

MANUEL MALDONADO-DENIS is Professor of Political Science at the University of Puerto Rico. He was born in San Juan, Puerto Rico, and is the author of *Puerto Rico: A Socio-Historic Interpretation* and other books and numerous articles on Puerto Rico.

HERBERT HILL is Labor Director of the National Association for the Advancement of Colored People and a member of the New School for Social Research. He is editor of *Anger and Beyond: The Negro Writer in the United States* and co-editor of *Employment, Race and Poverty.* Some of his land articles have appeared in *The Nation, New Politics.*

PEDRO PIETRI, IRIS MORALES, and FELIPE LUCIANO all are young Puerto Rican militants and among the founders of the Young Lords Party (now Puerto Rican Revolutionary Workers Organization).

PEDRO JUAN SOTO is Instructor in the Department of Spanish, University of Puerto Rico. He was born in Cataño, Puerto Rico, lived in New York City for many years, and is recognized as one of Puerto Rico's major literary figures. Among his works are *Spiks, Usmail* and *Ardiente suelo, fria estación.*

FRANK BONILLA is Director of the Centro de Estudios Puertorriqueños of The City University of New York and Professor of Political Science. He is author of *The Failure of Elites,* co-author of *Student Politics in Chile,* and co-editor of *Structures of Dependency.*

GORDON K. LEWIS teaches in the Department of Social Sciences at the University of Puerto Rico. He is author of *Puerto Rico: Freedom and Power in the Caribbean, The Growth of the Modern West Indies,* and numerous articles and reviews on Puerto Rico and the West Indies.

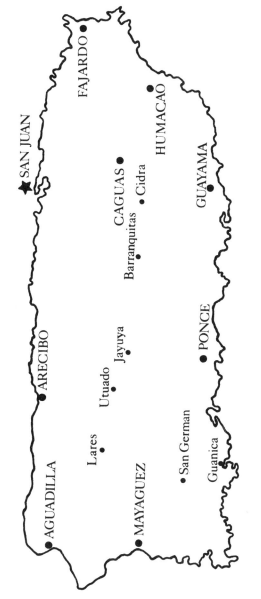

ATLANTIC OCEAN

CARIBBEAN SEA

★ SAN JUAN

FAJARDO ●

HUMACAO ●

CAGUAS ●

● Cidra

GUAYAMA ●

Barranquitas

ARECIBO ●

Jayuya ●

Utuado ●

● PONCE

Lares ●

● San German

AGUADILLA ●

MAYAGUEZ ●

Guanica

Note: This map is from a government publication and is therefore public property.

xi

Introduction

A survey of the social science and historical literature on Puerto Rico over the last 10 years is disappointing: What is lacking in quality is found in quantity. On the one hand there are the discursive and poorly researched exhortatory essays; on the other, there are empirical studies anchored in faulty analytical frameworks.

Among contemporary U.S. social scientists there has been a systematic avoidance of key theoretical issues such as dependency and imperialism. Few empirical studies have critically examined the longer term structural impact of dependence on labor, migration and squalor: Rather, so-called development sociologists and economists have fallen all over themselves in developing quantitative indicators of social and economic expansion in Puerto Rico. In a country as thoroughly penetrated by foreign firms as Puerto Rico it would seem obvious that aggregate growth figures would best be used as measures of *foreign* expansion. The question that should be faced is, for whom is growth? The emphasis on growth of per capita income fails to take account of the gross disparities of income between the foreign rich and their local counterparts and the mass of poor: The averages are highly deceptive. The fundamental problem with all economies being exploited ("developed") from above and the outside lies in determining the effect of investments on jobs and living standards for the mass of laborers, regional and sectoral disparities, social and educational services, stability of social life, coherence and efficacy of primary and secondary groups. The essays in this volume are attempts to rectify some of these deficiencies. This volume makes no claim to being in any sense a definitive study—rather, the essays through their explicit and implicit emphases stake out new areas of inquiry and cast old problems in a new light.

1

The perennial question of why there was no major independence movement in 19th century Puerto Rico is examined in essays by López and Quintero, who argue that the type of colony, an administrative-military center, retarded the development of a landed-commercial bourgeoisie; the immigration of pro-Spanish ruling classes reinforced the colonial ideology pervasive among the islanders; the late-developing planter class and the colonial emigrees (and local allies) defined politics within the autonomist—anti-autonomist framework. The efforts of a national agro-capitalist elite to develop in the 19th century were aborted by the massive entrance of U.S. capital; the socio-economic formations that hegemonized Latin American independence movements (an expanding "free trade", landed commercial elite) were not sufficiently crystallized to direct Puerto Rico's political independence. Pre-and semi-capitalist social formations and colonial institutions tied to Spanish bureaucratic-military institutions were fragile obstacles to the elephantine movements of U.S. imperialism. U.S. penetration of Puerto Rican society at a moment of 'transition' (facilitated by the enormous material resources at the disposal of U.S. officials) resulted in an effort at total cultural penetration. Earlier studies discussed "how" U.S. domination was imposed; that discussion is necessary to understanding the attitudes and behavior of Puerto Ricans and U.S. officials of a later period. The behavior of contemporary Puerto Rico and Puerto Ricans can be explained in part by the long term totalizing nature of U.S. domination. The study of contemporary Puerto Rican families, slum-neighborhoods, sugar workers, migration, local leadership, "criminality", political parties, primary groups, mediating structures and organizations and "deviant" behavior (subjects that have most attracted North American empirical scientists) cannot be understood apart from a historical study of the mutli-faceted impact of U.S. imperialism on Puerto Rican society. Problems may be experienced at the level of face to face groups, but the source of the problem as well as the solution may be distant and embedded in impersonal processes and networks of relationships. At best some of the studies of Puerto Rico and Puerto Ricans are studies of symptoms—consequences of larger exploitative relationships cultivated and institutionalized over time. The lack of a world-historic view among U.S. social scientists blinds them to the causes of Puerto Rican problems. Their causal explanations of what are euphemistically described as "societal maladjustments" frequently are nothing more than circular arguments or question-begging formulas that end up by blaming the poor for being poor ("non-achievers"), the dominated for being dominated ("docility"), the "criminal" for crime (drug addiction, etc.). The weaknesses of these studies are not merely that they fail to take account of some key factors in an otherwise sound analysis, but rather that the theoretical-conceptual framework from which they design their research eliminates the most critical dimensions of the problem.

There are of course a few studies that are critical of aspects of Puerto Rican society and U.S. relations with Puerto Rico and that point to inadequacies in the process of development. Nevertheless these studies frequently have concluded that while conditions are found wanting, they are improving. It is worthwhile to stop and examine the basis for these assertions. Most such assertions are derived, implicitly or explicitly, from some kind of comparison. Rural migrants to the slums of San Juan or South Bronx, we are told, are "relatively better off". The base line for measurement, arbitrarily selected, is the migrants' *past* situation; more relevant to understanding his position, however, would be his *present* location in the urban class structure. To argue otherwise is to amalgamate units of analysis: the rural migrant moves from one lower class position to another. In the city the urban slum dweller is on the lowest level of the social ladder. The unhealthy fascination of social scientists in counting the minor acquisitions of the poor does not leave them time to deduct the unattainable goods that the wealthy urban classes possess. On the national level, Puerto Rico's per capita income is favorably compared to Latin America rather than to states within the United States. Given the degree to which the United States controls all aspects of Puerto Rican life, including a large chunk of its earnings, there is every reason to argue for comparison within the United States rather than to Latin America. Once this "minor" adjustment is made, it turns out that Puerto Rico is last among the states—apparently not a pleasant finding for our cheery social scientists, who view the diffusion and assimilation of U.S. "know how" and experiences as a prerequisite for modernization.

These invidious comparisons, the ideological assumptions that underlie them, and the political purposes to which they are put highlight the "value-laden" nature of all research that has been done. The problem is not of discovering a value-free solution, but of determining which value directed paradigms are best suited to understanding and interpreting the development of society. For those who swim on the beaches and lounge in the hotels it is convenient to believe that they are not only enjoying themselves but helping others "to develop". The self-serving nature of most of the comparisons of progress is evident; and it is precisely this complacent posture that is most evidently absent in this volume.

No doubt on the micro-level some individuals can provide testimonials of success stories to anthropologists or sociologists who, in their presumed innocence, will count this as part of the "other side"—thus giving the appearance of a balanced account. It is not our purpose to quarrel with these studies: It is indeed not our purpose to deny individual nuances or even individual feelings of improvement. But it is an abdication of the responsibility of the social scientist to shed the historical study of society's structural development in favor of the study of opinion. More to the point, opinions change according to events outside of the control of the opinion-holder; and it is our sense of the movement of history that it is no longer moving toward the enrichment of the western imperial countries. On that assumption the critical problems dealt with in this volume include:

1) The emergence of imperialism and its impact on the Puerto Rican class structure. What classes developed or failed to develop? What kind of "political class" emerged to direct the process of externally based growth?

2) The economic and social significance of "industrialization" through dependency. What was its impact on the labor force, social welfare, income distribution and development?

3) The rise and fall of working class militancy. What were the conditions, structural and geographical, that were conducive to social solidarity and class anchored politics?

4) Tourism as an ingredient in the development equation. What are the costs and benefits of tourism? How does tourism contribute to or detract from the growth of skills, employment, welfare and the national allocation of resources? Can vertical and horizontal monopolies be integrated into national development?

5) The expansion of urban slums through the importation of cheap labor from the colony and the incapacity of the economy to "absorb" the new labor force in meaningful and remunerative work. To what extent is U.S. capitalism degenerating into a stagnant administrative state capable of providing only subsistence allowances and menial employment in decaying cities?

6) The growth of revolutionary nationalist and militant working class movements among Puerto Ricans. What are the appeals and what are the institutional restraints?

These problems and issues are of interest to scholars and students. These questions, however, are hardly confined to the academic world: Their answers will have a profound effect on the development of society both on the mainland and the island.

James F. Petras

PART I

Puerto Rico From 1493 to 1900

Introduction

Spanish imperialism, in common with other instances of European expansion, reshaped and transformed the island of Puerto Rico to fit its imperial needs. The long and short-term effects of imperialism and a colonial economy adversely affected the underlying population and the possibilities for developing a self-sustaining economy capable of meeting the needs of the Puerto Rican people in an equitable and efficient manner.

For the original indigenous population Spanish economic expansion and exploitation meant death, migration, disruption of their society and economy, disease, exploitation and domination by external forces — leading to the total destruction of its culture. Subsequently the island's development within the empire was tied to the production of foodstuffs and raw materials and to the defense needs of the Spanish colonial metropolis. This prevented the settlers from developing an economy capable of taking advantage of the world markets of the industrial nations and from developing a more balanced economy. Defined by the Spanish officials as a strategic outpost of the larger empire, Puerto Rico and its society became administratively and militarily top-heavy at the cost of internal economic development. The stunting of economic growth and the subsidization of these critical noneconomic activities increased Puerto Rico's dependence on Spain. The development of a large stratum of Spanish clients (civil and military officials concerned with defense of the empire) within the island who were not tied to productive economic activity for their livelihood heightened their allegiance and loyalty to their external benefactors. The reduction of Puerto Rico to a strategic defense outpost of the empire weakened the economic basis for the development of an expansionist indigenous landowning and commercial elite that could have become the basis for an independence movement. The bureaucratic officials, lacking an autonomous economic base, were quick to mobilize the settlers against the intrusions of rival imperialist powers—whose hegemony might have led to greater economic activity but certainly would have displaced the Spanish appointees from their government posts. Contrary to the assertion of some "development" theorists, western contact with the third world (and in this case Puerto Rico) was not in the interests of both dominated and dominant peoples but rather was a very one-sided relationship in which the dominated contributed to the welfare of the dominant imperial nation.

The nineteenth century witnessed the transformation of Puerto Rico from a primarily colonial military base to an economic colony. The growth of agricultural export products within a cash-crop economy was based on the expansion of large landed estates. The forcible transformation of subsistence farmers into part and full-time agro-workers and the later abolition of slavery created the basis for a colonial-capitalist society—one in which the main indigenous classes and governing elite were closely linked to the Spanish empire. The migration of colonial officials and classes from post-independence South America strengthened the colonial segments of Puerto Rican society, thus inhibiting the development of an "autonomous" bourgeois political class with a nationalist project. Lacking such a class, the political movements of the nineteenth century were largely attuned to elaborating new forms of colonial rule (autonomists) or reinforcing colonial ties. The insertion of the Puerto Rican economy into the world capitalist system was the major stimulus for internal development and it shaped the nature of the productive system, the goods produced, as well as political relations: Events in Europe and North America created the economic and political conditions for internal development. But as López's essay on the nineteenth century demonstrates, the capitalist mode of production adapted many precapitalist forms of social relations in order to secure an adequate labor supply in a situation of labor scarcity and land abundance. The emergence of an indigenous entrepreneurial group within Puerto Rico, as Quintero Rivera argues, was severely limited by the process of imperial expansion during the latter half of the nineteenth century. However, in his discussion, Quintero Rivera focuses on internal class relations and describes the Puerto Rican economy as essentially precapitalist—notwithstanding the world-wide process of capitalist reproduction, expansion and accumulation of which Puerto Rico was an integral part. The forms of expropriation of the economic surplus (slavery, the *agregado* system) become the core of his analysis rather than the ends to which that surplus was directed—reproduction of the means of production. The advantage of Quintero Rivera's approach, however, is not in his formal theoretical discussion but in his analysis of the specific manner in which class formation occurred in Puerto Rico as well as the process of incorporation of the island to the U.S. empire. The lateness in the development of the bourgeoisie, its external linkages and internal fragmentation contributed toward weakening its class consciousness—its sense of having a "nationalist entrepreneurial vocation." The precapitalist labor relations in turn hindered the development of class consciousness among the laboring population and left the society with neither a hegemonic class nor a class aspiring to a hegemonic position. The intrusion of U.S. imperialism within Puerto Rican society thus assumed the so called peaceful penetration not evidence in Cuba and later resisted in Puerto Rico.

The Beginnings of Colonization:
Puerto Rico, 1493-1800

Adalberto López

Five hundred years ago there were no Puerto Ricans. There were an Indian people whom the Spaniards called Tainos and who lived on an island they knew as Boriquén (Land of the Noble Lord). The Tainos were members of the Arawak linguistic family. Long before the arrival of the Europeans in the Caribbean, they had migrated from northern South America to Boriquén by way of the Lesser Antilles. From Boriquén they went on to occupy Hispaniola (today Haiti and the Dominican Republic) and Cuba. There, as in Boriquén, they supplanted a more primitive people who had originally migrated to the islands from the Florida Peninsula and who we know as the Archaics or Ciboneys.

Unlike the Ciboneys—who were fishermen, hunters and gatherers of wild fruits and roots—the Tainos were an agricultural people. They grew cotton from which they wove *naguas* (a small cotton wrap used by married women to cover the lower part of their bodies) and thin ropes for *hamacas* (hammocks); *achiote*, red coloring seeds used to make paint for their bodies; corn, which was often used to make an alcoholic beverage; tobacco, ordinarily used during religious ceremonies; sweet potatoes, and *yuca*, the main crop of the Boriquén Tainos. Out of the *yuca* Taino women made a dried flour that was baked into an unleavened bread known as *casabe*. In pre-Columbiam times a typical Taino meal probably consisted of *casabe*, some corn, sweet potatoes and perhaps a little fish or bird meat. Fish abounded in the island's rivers, but meat was hard to come by. When the Spaniards arrived in Boriquén, there were no domesticated animals on the island save a species of small dogs that the newcomers called *perros mudos* (mute dogs) because they did not bark.

On the eve of the Spaniards' arrival, Boriquén must have been an idyllic place. Both the mountain chain of the interior (the *cordillera central*) and the coastal plains of the north and south were covered by lush vegetation that abounded in bird life. The rivers were clear and rich in fish. The climate was mild and the land fertile. Also, the island was sparsely populated. At the time of Christopher Columbus's arrival there were in Boriquén between 30,000 and 50,000 Tainos. They were a handsome people, described by the Spaniards as short, strong, copper-colored and with straight black hair. They were also an extremely clean people who ordinarily went about naked and who bathed themselves in the rivers several times a day.

Like agriculturalists throughout the New World, the Tainos lived in villages (*yucayeques*) whose average population was probably between 300 and 600. In these villages there were no great temples or stone buildings as found among the more advanced peoples of Meso-America and the Andean region. Each *yucayeque* was simply a collection of large dwellings (*bohíos*) built of forest materials and spread around a large plaza-like space called by the Tainos the *batey*. Most of the *bohíos* were circular and accomodated several families. Rectangular *bohíos* were less common and were reserved for the village chief and other village notables. From the poles that supported the *bohíos*, hammocks were hung at night for sleeping and removed in the morning to make room for the women to do the cooking, weaving and other household chores. The *bohíos* were crowded places. Lovemaking and other private activities probably took place in the bush.

Taino society was a male-dominated society. The women took care of children, made *casabe*, and did the weaving, cooking, and other household chores as well as the bulk of the agricultural work. The men made weapons, went hunting and fishing, built the houses and made the simple stone carvings that are characteristic of Taino culture. For both men and women life was relatively easy. The land was fertile and there was plenty of it; a little work went a long way. During their leisure time the Tainos went swimming, played a sort of balley-ball game in the *batey*, or danced. Religious festivals were frequent. During these, the villagers smoked tobacco, drank, and danced in groups to the accompaniment of drums, *güiros*, maracas and flutes. During these ceremonies vomiting was encouraged, for it was seen as a means of ridding the body of evil substances and thus purifying the individual before the gods.

Taino religion was based on belief in a supreme deity known as

Tocahú who was perfect, invisible and could not be represented in the form of idols. He was the creator of the universe, the unmoved mover. Below Tocahú and closer to mankind were Yukiyú, the god representing the forces of good, and Jurakán, who represented the forces of evil and who, according to Taino beliefs, resided somewhere in the Lesser Antilles. Below these two antagonistic gods there were dozens of spirits (*zemis*) who were worshipped constantly, since they were believed to be always present and directly involved in the affairs of man. There were *zemis* for rain, the earth, the stars, the moon, the birds and trees and all other living things with which the Tainos were familiar.

At the top of Taino social structure were the chief (*cacique*) and the shaman (*bohiqué*). Among the privileges of the chief were a large rectangular *bohío*, many wives and exemption from all forms of labor. Upon his death a chief was ordinarily succeeded by his eldest son, but a chief who proved weak or incompetent could be removed and replaced by another chosen by the adult males of the village. The shaman served the functions of priest and medicine man. He presided at religious ceremonies, acted as an intermediary between man and his gods and took care of the ill. It was he who was responsible for preserving and adding to the tribe's knowledge of medicinal herbs and passing that knowledge on to his successor—usually his eldest son.

Below the chief and the shaman was a small aristocracy (*nitaynos*) whose members were usually related by kinship ties to the chief and who, like him, enjoyed certain privileges such as the right to have more than one wife and exemption from certain kinds of labor. Below this aristocracy were the commoners (*naborías*) and below these the slaves, whose number was small and whose sources, role and status in Taino society are not yet clear to historians.

Most chiefs ruled over one village, a few ruled over several. At the time of the Spanish arrival in Boriquén there were some 20 *cacicatos* (areas ruled by *caciques*) on the island. Of these the most important was Guainía, which stretched along the southern coast. The relations among the various chiefs is not clear, but it appears that they were autonomous of each other and that only in times of emergency did they come together under one leader, usually the chief of Guainía who was a sort of *primus inter pares*.

The Tainos of Boriquén were not a warlike people, but neither were they passive military pushovers. In the latter part of the fifteenth century they were locked in a perennial war with the Caribs, an aggressive, brutal and cannibalistic people who, like the Tainos, had originated in northern South America and had overwhelmed and wiped out the Tainos of the Lesser Antilles. In the 1490s southeastern Boriquén was the frontier between the Taino Caribbean and the Carib Caribbean. Against the Caribs the Tainos fought with bows and arrows and the *macana*, a short wooden club favored by them but, like the assagais of the Zulu, useful only in close combat. The Tainos fought well and tenaciously. But the Caribs, whose existence centered on warfare and who enjoyed the use of poisoned arrows, had the upper hand. Just before the arrival of the Spaniards, Taino villages on the coast of southern and eastern Boriquén were being abandoned and moved inland. It is probable that had the Europeans arrived later than they did, Boriquén would have been eventually conquered by the Caribs and the Spanish occupation of the island would not have been as easy as it was.

In 1492 Columbus sailed into the Caribbean, discovered the Bahamas and Hispaniola and returned to Spain with tales of strange peoples and wealth. In the following year he returned to the Carribbean. During this voyage he came upon the Lesser Antilles and, while on his way to Hispaniola upon Boriquén. Columbus and some members of his crew landed on the island, took possession of it for the Crown of Castile, and named it San Juan Bautista in honor of Prince Juan, heir to the throne. Columbus then went on to Hispaniola, where three years later the city of Santo Domingo was founded. For many years that city (the oldest permanent European settlement in the New World) remained the center of Spanish governmental activity in the Caribbean area.

For over a decade after Columbus's discovery of Boriquén, the Spaniards in the Caribbean made no effort to occupy the island. It was in 1508 that Juan Ponce de León, an impoverished Castilian nobleman who had accompanied Columbus during the latter's second voyage, under-took the occupation of Boriquén for the glory of his Church, his king and himself. Unlike the Caribs of the Lesser Antilles, who from the beginnings of their contacts with the Europeans refused to have any dealings with them, the Tainos of Boriquén proved friendly and hospitable. When Ponce de León and about 50 Spaniards who accompanied him from Hispaniola landed on the southern coast of the island, they were welcomed by the *cacique* of Guianía, Agüeybana I. Agüeybana not only provided the newcomers with food and lodging, but also became Ponce de León's blood brother and encouraged other Taino chiefs to do the same. In the weeks that followed the Spaniards' arrival, the Indians helped them explore the island and build houses in the settlement that Ponce de León founded in 1509. The new town was named Caparra and was located on the northern shore of a large bay on the northern coast of the island that was baptized by the Spaniards as Puerto Rico. Soon thereafter another Spaniard, Cristóbal de Sotomayor, founded the settlement of San Germán on the southern coast. For years Caparra remained the center of Spanish activity in Boriquén. Many of its settlers, however, complained that the site was unhealthy and no good for a town, and pressured Ponce de León to remove it to a more favorable spot. In 1519 Ponce de León gave in to these demands and ordered the evacuation of Caparra, an evacuation that had been completed by 1521 (the same year that Ponce de León died in Habana de Cuba after a fruitless expedition to the Florida Peninsula). The new site chosen for the settlement was on the tip of a small island at the mouth of the bay and separated from the rest of the island by a narrow stretch of water. The settlement was at first known as Puerto Rico. But as the years passed, it became known as San Juan and Boriquén as Puerto Rico.

Ponce de León and those who had accompanied him in 1508 went to Boriquén primarily to find gold. And they were not disappointed. There existed on the island alluvial gold deposits that in pre-Columbiam times had been exploited by the Tainos to make simple jewelry. It was this jewelry that provided the Spaniards with their first gold. In the months following their arrival on the island, the Spaniards bartered the Tainos's simple jewelry for hawks' bells, pieces of colorful cloth and all sorts of cheap trinkets that drew the curiosity of the Indians. But this curiosity died quickly, and as the months passed fewer and fewer Indians were willing to barter with the Spaniards. Fewer still were the Indians who were willing to work voluntarily for the Spaniards in the gold fields and in other activities. Since the Spaniards were not about to do their own work, they introduced the *repartimiento de indios*, by virtue of which the Indians were required to provide wage-free labor for the European newcomers in return for "protection" and the blessings of the Christian faith.

With the *repartimiento* system in operation, gold production on the island grew rapidly. Between 1509 and 1515 alone, output was over 400,000 pesos. But if gold production was the mainstay of the island's economy during those early years of Spanish rule, it was by no means the only economic activity. The Spaniards learned from the Indians the use of *yuca* and corn, but they liked neither. Consequently, in the years after they occupied Boriquén they introduced a variety of Old World crops and forced the Indians to grow them for them. Rice, sugar, bananas, plantains, ginger, yams, oranges, lemons and many other fruits and vegetables were introduced into the island by the whites. So were cows, horses, mules, chickens, sheep and pigs. The date and coconut palm trees, too, were introduced by the Europeans during those years. Slowly not only did the subsistence economy of the island become more diversified, but the landscape began to take on a new look. The palm tree slowly spread over the white sandy beaches and the banana and plantain trees unnoticeably crept up the mountain slopes of the interior.

For the Indians—who had welcomed the Spaniards to their land as guests—life in the years following Ponce de León's arrival became a continuous nightmare. They were forced to work for the Spaniards from dawn to dusk, every day of the week, except for the few hours when they were permitted to work on their own agricultural fields. The Spaniards, who brought with them very few of their own women, went among the Taino villages and grabbed whatever Indian maidens caught their fancy. In the meantime Christian priests who had followed their countrymen into the island almost immediately after the Spanish occupation had begun, busied themselves wiping out all vestiges of the Indians' religion and practices that they deemed uncivilzed, diabolical, or both. The Tainos were forced to give up their relative nakedness and were even discouraged from taking too many baths, a practice which smacked of the work of the devil to the foul-smelling Europeans. A few sensitive Spanish friars spoke against the inhuman exploitation to which the Indians were subjected, but their voices went unheard. As the months passed the entire fabric of Indian society was torn to shreds.

The Indians reacted to the brave new world in which they found themselves in several ways. Many committed suicide (sometimes in groups); others killed their children so as not to see them grow up to be brutalized by the Spaniards. Young couples often refused to have children. Many ran away to the forests of the interior or left the island altogether. Many of these exiles migrated to nearby islands and to the Lesser Antilles, where they made peace with their former Carib enemies. The majority of the Tainos, however, remained on their island, and whenever they thought the time opportune they rose up in arms against their European oppressors.

The first and most important Indian rebellion against the Spanish presence in Boriquén took place in 1511 and was led by Agüeybana II, the *cacique* of Guainía and a nephew of the chief who had welcomed Ponce de León in 1508. During the rebellion, dozens of Spaniards were killed (including Sotomayor, the founder of San Germán). Ponce de León and the other Spaniards in Caparra learned of the rebellion before the Indians had had time to march against them and immediately took the offensive. The army that Ponce led into the interior defeated the Indians in a series of battles, in the course of which Agüeybana was killed. The rebellion was crushed with merciless brutality. Hundreds of Indians were killed and many of their villages burned to the ground. In spite of this defeat, however, Indian resistance did not end. In 1513 and in 1518 there were Indian rebellions on the island. These too, were easily put down by the Spaniards. The latter's weapons were far superior to those of the Indians; the Indians were never able to take the Spaniards by surprise, and invariably there were many Indians who either refused to get involved at all or who actively collaborated with the Spaniards against their copper-skinned brothers.

After each rebellion, hundreds of defeated Indians fled from Puerto Rico and joined those who had fled earlier to the Lesser Antilles and the small islands in the vicinity of Puerto Rico. Together with the Caribs, these exiles periodically returned to Puerto Rico to raid Spanish settlements and burn down their agricultural fields. San Germán was attacked and so were Spanish households near San Juan itself. Partially as a result of these raids and the ever-present possibility of Indian rebellion the construction of La Fortaleza was begun in 1533. In 1576 the small fortress became the official residence of the governor of Puerto Rico and has remained so to the present.

The last Indian rebellion against the Spaniards in Puerto Rico took place in 1565. It was a minor affair, primarily because at that time the Indian population of the island was on its way to extinction. Of the 30 to 50,000 Indians who lived on the island when the Spaniards arrived, only a few thousand remained by the early 1530s. Several decades later, in 1582, the governor of Puerto Rico wrote to his king that there were almost no Indians left. Although there is evidence that suggests that Indians survived on the island into the eighteenth century, there is no question that between 1508 and the middle of the sixteenth century, the Indian population underwent a demographic decline of major proportions and that henceforth Indians would play an insignificant role in the social, cultural and economic development of the island.

The disappearance of the Indian population of Puerto Rico was not a unique development in the New World. The same happened in Cuba and Hispaniola and in those parts of the American mainland occupied by the Spaniards. It is infantile to claim, as some have, that the Indians of Puerto Rico disappeared because it was the policy of Spain to exterminate them. The Spaniards who conquered and settled in Puerto Rico were certainly brutal, but they were not fools who would have deliberately destroyed their major source of labor. Hundreds, perhaps thousands of Indians died because of the maltreatment and extreme hard labor to which they were subjected under Spanish rule. But there were other factors that help us explain the demographic catastrophe that overcame the Tainos of Boriquén: infanticide, suicide, refusal to have children, escape from the island and death during Indian uprisals. Perhaps most important of all, however, was epidemic disease, the major killer of Indians in the New World in the sixteenth century. Like Indians everywhere in the Americas, the Tainos of Puerto Rico had no natural defenses against common European diseases such as measles and smallpox. In Puerto Rico these diseases alone killed far many more Indians than died at the hands of the Spaniards.

Because Indian society disappeared so early in the history of Puerto Rico as a colony of Spain, the Indian component of Puerto Rican culture will not be as marked as the Indian component of, for example, Mexican and Peruvian culture. But it will be there. The Taino *bohío* continued to decorate the Puerto Rican landscape into the twentieth century. Some of the crops that the Tainos grew are still grown in Puerto Rico today (e.g. *achiote* and *yuca*). From the Indians the Puerto Ricans inherited the use of the *güiro* and the *maraca*. Finally, the language of Puerto Rico today is full of Taino words (*huracán, batey, mabí, enagua, canoa, hamaca,*) and there are literally hundreds of names of towns and rivers of Indian origin (Cayey, Caguas, Utuado, Humacao). Nevertheless, it would be misleading to overemphasize the Indian contribution to Puerto Rican culture, a culture that remains essentially Hispanic in character.

For the Spaniards in Puerto Rico, the decade of the 1530s was a difficult one. Carib-Taino bands were stepping up their raids against coastal settlements and so were French privateers. The gold deposits were almost exhausted and the Indians who had provided labor in the past had almost disappeared. A critical shortage of labor combined with a rapidly declining output of gold led many Spaniards to seek their fortunes elsewhere in the New World. Many left for Cuba, others went to Mexico, and others left to join the Spaniards in Peru who under the command of Francisco Pizarro were plundering the Inca empire. The exodus of Spaniards from Puerto Rico reached such proportions that Governor Francisco Manuel de Lando concluded that unless it was checked all the Spaniards would eventually leave and the island would be lost to Spain. He issued an order that no one was to leave the island without written permission from him and he brought his point home by publicly cutting off the legs of two Spaniards who tried to disobey him.

Since gold production was no longer a viable activity, the Spaniards who remained in Puerto Rico and the few who migrated to the island later turned to agriculture and stock raising. A variety of crops were grown for internal consumption, and a few for both internal consumption and to pay for the commodities (such as olive oil, wine, dried codfish, wheat and manufactured goods) that the European inhabitants of the island deemed necessary to civilized living. Of these exports, sugar had become the most important by the middle of the sixteenth century. The crop had been introduced into the island soon after the Spanish occupation of 1508 and by the late 1520s there were several small sugar mills (*trapiches*) in operation. Sugar farms were relatively small, usually family-run operations, and were concentrated on the northern coastal plain. Sugar remained one of the most important exports during the almost 400 years of Spanish rule in Puerto Rico. Other exports were cacao and ginger, which briefly surpassed sugar in importance in the first part of the seventeenth century, and tobacco, cotton and coffee, all of which became important only in the eighteenth century. Another export of importance in the second half of the sixteenth century and throughout the seventeenth was cattle hides. Like sugar growing, cattle raising was concentrated on the coastal plains. When the traveler Antonio Vázquez de Espinosa visited Puerto Rico in the first quarter of the seventeenth century he reported that many cattle ranches could be found throughout the coastal plains and that large quantities of leather were being exported to Spain.

Since Indian labor was rapidly disappearing by the 1530s and since there were too few Spaniards available and willing to supply the necessary labor in the sugar farms and cattle ranches, Spanish landowners on the island turned to the importation of black slaves to meet their labor needs. Permission to import black slaves into its American possessions had been granted by the Spanish Crown in 1503, and in the years immediately following the Spanish occupation of Boriquén some slaves were brought to the island. However, it was not till the late 1520s and the 1530s, as a critical shortage of Indian labor developed, that black slaves assumed an economic importance on the island. By 1530 there were in Puerto Rico close to 1,500 black slaves out of a population of slightly over 3,000. As the years passed more blacks were imported into the island, but their number grew slower than that of the non-slave population and, consequently, their proportion of the population declined. In 1765, for example, there were 5,037 slaves out of a total population of 44,883.

For the black slaves, life in Puerto Rico was short, nasty and brutish. True, out of the Spanish metropolis there emerged a code of law that treated the slaves as rational human beings capable of salvation and that was designed to protect them against the rapacity of their masters. Spanish legislation, as many historians have pointed out, was more humane than either Anglo-Saxon or French legislation concerning slaves. But in the Spanish American world there was a wide gap between the letter of the law and the way people actually behaved. In Puerto Rico, as in most societies where slavery has existed, the slaves were seen as chattel by their masters and were brutalized (physically and psychologically) as they were in the plantations of St. Dominque, Brazil and the Anglo-Saxon colonies of North America. As slaves elsewhere in the New World, those in Puerto Rico did not accept their lot in life as meekly as they were encouraged to do by the priests and friars who sought to impose their religion on them. Like the Indians, the slaves resisted the brutalization to which they were subjected. There were individual acts of violence against slave owners. Alone or in groups, slaves often ran away into the forests and mountains of the interior, and once in a while they rebelled. These rebellions ordinarily were local affairs that involved small numbers of slaves and were, therefore, easily put down by the authorities.

In spite of the growing importance of sugar production and cattle raising, Puerto Rico after the 1530s and until the end of the eighteenth century was of little economic value to Spain. The population of the island remained relatively small. Exports grew slowly; and the economy as a whole, though seldom really stagnant, was often described as such. Although a handful of sugar producers and cattle ranchers profited from commercial relations with Spain, Spain itself did not profit (in monetary terms) at all. The revenues generated by the island for the Crown remained insignificant and by the second half of the sixteenth century were not enough to cover the cost of administering and holding on to the island. In spite of this, Spain committed itself to maintaining control of Puerto Rico; for if economically the island was a liability to Spain, strategically it was of tremendous importance.

In 1494, little less than two years after Columbus's momentous first voyage to the Caribbean, the governments of Spain and Portugal signed the Treaty of Tordesillas, which was blessed by the papacy and which divided the New World into two spheres of influence and control. England, France and other European powers refused that division, and by the 1530s Spain's European enemies were harassing Spanish settlements and commerce in the Caribbean area. As French and English privateers commanded by men such as Francois LeClerc, John Hawkins, and Francis Drake enlarged their operations in the Caribbean, Spain began to take steps to protect its settlements and commerce in the area. By the 1560s Admiral Pedro Menéndez de Avilés, better known for securing Spain's hold on the Florida Peninsula and founding the settlement of St. Augustine there, had organized a fleet system by virtue of which all ships sailing from Spain to the colonies did so in one of two great fleets which, accompanied by warships, departed from the port of Seville in southern Spain every year. After entering the Caribbean one fleet sailed to the Isthmus of Panama, where it unloaded the commodities destined for the markets of the Viceroyalty of Peru and where it took aboard large quantities of silver brought from the mines of Potosi in what today is the Republic of Bolivia. The other fleet sailed to the port of Veracruz on the Gulf Coast of Mexico. There silver from northern Mexico was put aboard and a variety of commodities were unloaded for distribution throughout the Viceroyalty of New Spain, as Mexico was known then. Both fleets sailed to Havana, and from there they sailed together to Spain.

To protect this commercial system, Spain fortified the American terminals of the great fleets as well as the port of Havana. Because the two fleets sailed into the Caribbean in the vicinity of Puerto Rico, the island assumed an already-predicted strategic importance. In the 1530s, decades before the organization of the fleet system, Governor Lando had described the island as "the entrance and the key to all the Indies," a sentiment which was to be expressed many times in the future both by the kings of Spain and their representatives in the Caribbean. It was imperative that Spain hold on to the island, for should it fall into the hands of the enemies of Spain it could serve as a base of operations that could disrupt and even paralyze the entire Spanish-American commercial system.

Spain was not the only power aware of the strategic importance of Puerto Rico. In 1528 and 1538 the French raided San Germán. During those years they even threatened San Juan. It was as a result of growing foreign interest in Puerto Rico that the insular authorities began in 1539 to construct the fortress of San Felipe del Morro at the entrance of San Juan Bay and to establish there a permanent garrison of Spanish troops. The construction of the fortress, whose final form was the result of plans drawn by the Italian architect Bautista Antonelli, was a costly affair. At first funds were provided by Spain and by the more affluent Spanish American colonies. In 1586 Spain decided to formalize the subsidization of its administration and defense establishment in Puerto Rico and created the famous *situado mexicano*, a subsidy which was paid annually to the Spanish authorities on the island by the royal treasury of Mexico City.

By the end of the sixteenth century the defenses of San Juan were strong enough to foil an English attempt (1595) to wrest Puerto Rico from Spain. Commanded by the aging Francis Drake and John Hawkins (two men who in the past had made their reputations in England by raiding Spanish American settlements and ships), a large English fleet tried to sail into San Juan Bay. The artillery of El Morro drove it off. Hawkins died during the attempt; Drake sailed away and died off the coast of Panama after raiding Spanish settlements on that isthmus. Three years later the English tried again to take San Juan. This time they were temporarily successful. Led by Sir George Clifford, the Count of Cumberland, the English fooled the Spanish defenders of the city into thinking that the English fleet would try, as Drake and Hawkins had, to sail directly into San Juan Bay. Instead they landed on the coast east of San Juan and, to the consternation of the Spaniards, attacked the city from the interior. The capital was captured, but the English did not hold it for long. The Spaniards in the interior of the island organized guerrilla bands and made it difficult for the English to get supplies from the interior. This, an epidemic of dysentery that decimated the English troops and news that a powerful Spanish fleet carrrying 3,000 troops was on its way to Puerto Rico led Cumberland to evacuate San Juan. Twenty seven years later (in 1625) when Spain and the Netherlands were at war, the Dutch duplicated Cumberland's feat of capturing San Juan. Like the English, however, the Dutch were not able to hold on to their prize. Once again local resistance and disease forced the invaders to evacuate the city, but not before they burned most of it to the ground. Not till 1898 was the island capital again occupied by foreign troops.

At the time of the English and Dutch attacks, Puerto Rico was little different from what it had been in the 1530s. Sugar and leather were still the main exports. Commercial contacts with the outside world were infrequent and, by law, limited to Spain. Economically, the island was still a liability to the Spanish treasury. Administratively, it was under a governor who was appointed by and reported directly to, the king of Spain. With his official residence in the Fortaleza, the governor was commander-in-chief of all military forces on the island, enforcer of royal laws, legislator and a judicial officer as well. Below him were the two lieutenants who administered the two *partidos* (San Juan and San Germán) into which the island was divided for administrative purposes. The town councils of San Juan and San Germán, the only officially recognized towns on the island at that timme, enjoyed some autonomy over purely municipal affairs but were otherwise under the careful eye and control of the governor and his lieutenants. In Puerto Rico, as in other parts of the Spanish American world, Spain would not tolerate the development of independent town councils as those which evolved in the Anglo-Saxon colonies of North America. Neither would the Crown permit any participation by the local population in the administrative system. Ordinarily, the administration of the island was totally in the hands of Spanish-born bureaucrats whose powers were tremendous because of the lack of any written or unwritten constitutional restraints. The local population was expected, to use Lord Tennyson's phrase, to do and die, never to question why.

Juridically, Puerto Rico fell under the jurisdication of the high court (*audiencia*) of Santo Domingo in Hispaniola. Ordinarily local suits were brought before the head of the town councils (the *alcalde*) or before the governor himself. Rare were the cases that were brought before the *audiencia* of Santo Domingo. Rarer still were the cases that were taken before the Council of the Indies, whose offices were in Madrid and which enjoyed overall supervision over Spanish American affairs.

Parallel to the civil administration, there existed an ecclesiastical administration. From the beginning of the Spanish presence in Puerto Rico, Catholicism was the only religion tolerated in the island. Priests and monks arrived there almost immediately after Ponce de León's occupation and set about destroying the religion of the Indians, converting them to Christianity, and looking after the spiritual needs of the Spaniards. In 1511 the diocese of San Juan was created and in 1513 its first bishop

(Alonso Manso) arrived. Nominally, he was under the jurisdiction of the archbishop of Santo Domingo; in fact he was under the control of the civil authorities. By virtue of a series of privileges granted to the Spanish Crown by the papacy—privileges that were collectively known as the *real patronato*—the Church in Puerto Rico, as everywhere else in the Spanish empire, was kept subservient to the crown and its representatives in the colonies. It was the king, for example, who, at the recommendation of the Council of the Indies, decided who was to be bishop of Puerto Rico. Like the governors, the bishops were invariably Spaniards. The only native of the island who held the post of bishop during the almost four centuries of Spanish rule in Puerto Rico was Juan Alejo de Arizmendi, who was born in San Juan in 1757.

Under the supervision of the bishop there worked on the island the monks, nuns and priests who looked after the day-to-day spiritual needs of the island's inhabitants. Concentrated for the most part in San Juan and San Germán and periodically going into the rural areas to baptize the newborn, marry couples and give the last sacraments to the dying, the several dozen members of the clergy also ran the only health facilities (*hospitales*) available on the island. Rather than hospitals in the modern sense of the term, the *hospitales* were places where people went after all home remedies had failed, usually with the belief that death was close at hand. Even then, these primitive health facilities were only available in the towns. In the rural areas people took care of themselves when ill or went to local *curanderos*, rural medicine men whose knowledge of medicinal herbs was often surprisingly advanced.

The clergy also provided the bulk of Puerto Rico's teachers at the beginning of the seventeenth century. Educational facilities were limited and the curriculum backward even by the standards of the time. Still, only the children of the privileged few received the rudamentaries of reading and writing. Fewer still were those who received a higher education. They had to study in Santo Domingo, other Spanish American universities, or in Spain itself, for at no time under Spanish rule did Puerto Rico have a university of its own. In the first decades of the seventeenth century there were very few on the island who could read and write, a situation which did not improve significantly till the nineteenth century.

In Puerto Rico the Catholic Church was culturally and socially of tremendous importance and in the realm of religious dogma it was supreme. But unlike the Church in the more affluent colonies of Spain's

American Empire, the Church in Puerto Rico was poor and remained poor throughout Spanish colonial rule on the island. The main sources of revenue for the Church were the ecclesiastical tithe (*diezmo*), which, by virtue of the *real patronato*, was collected by the civil authorities, and voluntary contributions by the faithful. It was this poverty that placed the Church in Puerto Rico far more at the mercy of the state (which often provided badly-needed revenues) than of the Church in areas such as Mexico and Peru, where by the end of the eighteenth century it was immensely rich. In Puerto Rico the Catholic Church was in fact another branch of the colonial government, used by it to keep the populace in line and justify its arbitrary rule.

At the beginning of the seventeenth century, the population of Puerto Rico was still relatively small—no more than 3,000 people. Ethnically it was made up of several hundred whites, close to a thousand black slaves and over a thousand free blacks and mulattoes. Geographically it was still concentrated on the northern coastal plain, especially in or in the vicinity of San Juan, the administrative, ecclesiastical and commercial capital of the island. The capital was a small and unimposing place, culturally, politically and commercially in the periphery of the empire. The city did not have more than a hundred houses, the majority of which were crowded on the western tip of San Juan island, not far from the massive walls of El Morro. Its elite was small and, compared with the elites of cities such as Mexico, Lima, Panama and Potosi, poor. It included the governor, the bishop, the officers of El Morro's garrison, the heads of the few monasteries in the city, the members of the town council, a few local landowners affluent enough to own houses in the city and a handful of merchants—almost all of them born in Spain—who controlled the import-export trade. Below this elite were the artisans who made furniture, hats, shoes, leather goods and other goods in their household shops, and a few retail merchants. At the bottom of the city's social structure were the handful of full-time municipal workers, the common soldiers of the city's garrison and the slaves who served in the households of the well-to-do. Ships carrying royal dispatches to the island's authorities, supplies for the garrison, and a variety of manufactured goods that were exchanged for sugar, hides and a few other agricultural commodities, arrived in the port of San Juan infrequently—sometimes every few years—and must have been the cause of excitement and celebrations.

Besides San Juan, the other municipality on the island at the beginning of the seventeenth century was San Germán on the southern coastal plain. Compared with San Juan, it was a sleepy rural village with a few dozen houses and a small church run by a couple of resident priests. The official residents (*vecinos*) of the municipality numbered only a few hundred and lived in the rural areas within the jurisdiction of the town. Periodically, these rural residents rode into the town to hear mass, exchange gossip, drink and participate in civil and religious celebrations such as the birth of the heir to the throne, the king's birthday, or Holy Week. Most of the time the permanent population of San Germán was small.

Outside San Juan and San Germán, the island's population was either dispersed over the coastal plains in small, subsistence farms or clustered in small groups in the sugar and cattle establishments that dotted the rural areas. These farms and ranches were usually on the banks of rivers that, in the absence of roads, served as the most important means of communication between the interior of the plains and the coast. Contacts between the rural population and the towns were infrequent. Between the towns and the countryside there existed a wide cultural and psychological gap which did not begin to be closed until the last decades of the nineteenth century.

There was a small population and plenty of arable land, so conflicts over land were rare in Puerto Rico at the beginning of the seventeenth century. At the top of the rural social structure were the owners of the sugar farms and cattle ranches and their families. Below them were the workers. Most were black slaves imported through San Juan and brought there by Portuguese slave traders. But already by the beginning of the seventeenth century there were non-slaves working full time on the farms and cattle ranches. Outside these establishments were hundreds of subsistence farmers who lived isolated in the rural areas and who seldom had any contact with the sugar farms and cattle ranches or with the towns. Some of these subsistence farmers were the descendants of runaway slaves (*cimarrones*), deserters from El Morro's garrison, fugitives from the law and sailors who either had been shipwrecked off the coast or had taken advantage of their ships' stops on the coast for water and other supplies and fled from the nightmarish conditions of ship life to seek refuge in the forests of the plains. They concentrated on the production of subsistence crops such as plantains, bananas, yams and *yuca*, and on the raising of a few domestic animals such as chickens and pigs. The subsistence farmers of the interior were the ancestors of the latter-day *jíbaro*, who has gone down in Puerto Rican literature as the true representative of the Puerto Rican nation.

Much of the population of Puerto Rico at the beginning of the seventeenth century was overwhelmingly poor, illiterate and isolated from the urban centers. The people were all nominal Catholics. But priests were few, and the majority of the inhabitants of the rural areas seldom saw them. Also, the beliefs of the black slaves imported into the island had their impact on the religious beliefs of the islanders. Rural Christianity was characterized by superstition and the belief in good and evil natural forces that only the *curanderos* could understand and control. The societies of the towns and of the rural areas were male-dominated societies in which the woman's proper role was that of a good daughter, a good wife and a good mother. As a rule, the degree of control over her own life enjoyed by a woman depended on her social status: The more affluent and "respectable" she was, the greater the limitations on her social and economic activities. Among the poor, the family structure was more amorphous and flexible than among the elite. Prestige and family honor were not as important concerns as they were among the well-to-do. Within the more informal atmosphere of lower class families women enjoyed greater freedom from the restraints placed on their upper class counterparts and often assumed a relatively authoritative position within the family that carried over into the external society.

For Spain the seventeenth century was one of economic, political and military decline brought about primarily by excessive taxation of industry, lack of interest in agriculture, inefficient and free-spending monarchs, internal political dissentions and disastrous involvements in European conflicts. The weaknesses of Spain explain for the most part why in the course of the seventeenth century its enemies (England, France and the Netherlands) were able to establish permanent footholds in the Caribbean and in other parts of the New World claimed by Spain. In the first half of the seventeenth century the French and the English occupied several of the Lesser Antilles, and the Dutch occupied the small islands of Aruba and Curaçao, off the northern coast of South America. In 1655 the English occupied Jamaica. And by the end of the century the eastern half of Hispaniola (St. Domingue) had been lost to the French.

In spite of the major changes that were taking place in the Caribbean area, Puerto Rico did not change much during that century. The population remained small and grew slowly, and although there was a gradual movement of people into the mountains of the interior, the bulk of the population remained concentrated on the northern plain. A few new towns were founded (Ponce, Coamo and Arecibo), but San Juan maintained its political and commercial supremacy and San Germán continued to be the second most important town on the island. Nothing in government administration changed save that by the end of the century five new administrative *partidos* had been created. The governor continued to enjoy tremendous powers, and the local population continued to be kept from any participation in the colonial administration. As in the past, defense remained one of the major concerns of the governor and his lieutenants. In the course of the seventeenth century the defenses of San Juan were strengthened as a result of the growing English, French and Dutch presence in the Caribbean. The fortress of El Morro was expanded, the massive fortress of San Cristóbal was built, and a massive wall was constructed to surround the entire city. In addition, the number of regular Spanish troops was increased and the island's population was organized into militias. By 1700 there were on the island 14 infantry and two cavalry militia companies. Already distrustful of the local population, the Spanish authorities made sure that the militias were under the command of Spanish officers and issued ordinances forbidding militia members to be equipped with fire arms. In spite of the distrust of the Spanish authorities, however, the local population remained loyal to Spain, and the militias proved valuable in keeping the island in Spanish hands. In 1702 the English landed an expedition near Arecibo and were forced to withdraw by the fierce resistance put up by the local populace. The same happened in 1703 when the Dutch landed near Guadianilla.

Throughout the seventeenth century, Puerto Rico's economy remained based on the production of a variety of subsistence crops and the production of sugar and hides for exportation. For a few years ginger and cacao became important exports, but these never supplanted sugar and hides in importance. Because Spain was economically stagnant, it could not supply the island with the manufactured commodities and a few food products that were in demand on the island, nor could it absorb the few commodities that the island had available for export. As a result many of the landowners and cattle ranchers on the island turned to the enemies of Spain for commerce. The local population resisted efforts by England and France to wrest the island from Spain, but it was more than willing to trade with their merchants. Thus, in the course of the century there evolved a very lively contraband trade in which even the very officials charged by the metropolitan authorities with ending it participated. Some of the illegal trade took place in San Juan itself, but the bulk was carried on in isolated spots, especially along the southern coast. There the place that the settlers called Ponce became the center of a lively exchange in commodities between local farmers and cattle ranchers and English, French and Dutch traders. By the end of the century the town of Ponce was rapidly becoming one of the most important on the island.

The contraband trade of the seventeenth century, like the legal trade of the sixteenth, profited only a handful of local producers, merchants and governmental officials who often combined their official duties with illegal involvement in commercial activities. The majority of the population remained totally uninvolved in commercial relations with the outside, poor and devoted to the production of subsistence crops. Royal revenues generated by the island were never sufficient to cover the costs of administration and defense and, therefore, the governmental and military structure remained dependent on the Mexican *situado*. In years when that subsidy did not arrive on the island, a clamor of complaints would arise from civil administrators and regular soldiers whose salaries were not being paid.

In contrast with the seventeenth century, the eighteenth century was for Spain a period of recovery, economic expansion and national prosperity. In 1700 the last Hapsburg king of Spain died and willed Spain and all its possessions to Philip of Anjou, grandson of Louis XIV of France. In an attempt to prevent Spain and its overseas possessions from becoming a French sphere of influence, England, Austria, Portugal and the Netherlands went to war against Philip and France. The resulting War of the Spanish Succession was long and bloody, but Philip held on to his inheritance, and Bourbon kings sat on the Spanish throne until the declaration of the Spanish Republic in 1931.

The main goal which the Bourbons set for themselves in the eighteenth century was to turn Spain once again into the power it had been in the sixteenth century; to reverse the trends that had set in the seventeenth. To achieve this they needed military power; to build their army and navy they needed revenues; and to get these revenues they needed a centralized monarchy and a prosperous economy both in Spain and in the colonies. In pursuit of their goals the Bourbons and the able ministers who served them introduced in the course of the eighteenth century a series of administrative, military and economic reforms which in the long run had their desired results. By the time that the French revolution got under way Spain was enjoying an unprecedented economic expansion, the power of the monarchy was absolute, and abroad Spain commanded a respect that it had not enjoyed since the days of Philip II in the second half of the sixteenth century.

Bourbon policy towards the Spanish American colonies was designed primarily to generate economic growth there, to stimulate commerce between the colonies and the metropolis and to increase the amount of revenues collected in the colonies. To accomplish their ends, the kings of Spain and their ministers in the eighteenth century introduced a series of administrative changes whose goal was to bring the Spanish American world under greater royal control. They made economic reforms designed to increase mining and agricultural output in the colonies and trade between them and Spain, tax reforms to squeeze more revenues out of the colonies and military reforms designed to keep the increasingly prosperous colonies from falling into the hands of England and France. By the end of the reign of Charles III (1759-1788), the Spanish American world was better defended, better administered, and, on the whole, more prosperous than it had ever been in the past.

In the eighteenth century, Puerto Rico, too, drew the attention of the Bourbon monarchs and their ministers. In that century Spanish policy towards the island was based primarily on Spain's determination to hold on to the island and on its desire to have the island pay its own way in the empire. The Spanish government was aware that to realize these goals men of unusual energy and ability were needed to govern the island for Spain. Spaniards of military background who had proven themselves loyal, tireless and efficient servants of the crown were appointed as governors. As a group, the men who governed Puerto Rico in the eighteenth century were of a higher caliber than those who had governed in the sixteenth and seventeenth centuries. Like their predecessors, governors in the eighteenth century dedicated much of their efforts to strengthening the defenses of the island. Control of Puerto Rico was important to Spain not only because if it fell into foreign hands the Spanish commercial system in the New World would be endangered, but also because in times of war with England—Spain's major antagonist in the eighteenth century—the island served as an excellent base of operations to harass and disrupt the flourishing English commerce in the West Indies. It was not surprising, then, that in the course of the eighteenth century England tried several times, through war and diplomacy, to wrest the island from Spain.

In addition to defense, another major concern of the representatives of the Bourbon dynasty in Puerto Rico was the economic development of the island. The goal of official efforts was not to increase the material well being of the island's inhabitants (for whom royal officials showed little concern), but to generate sufficient revenues to cover the cost of administration and defense. Aware of the importance of agriculture and of the decline in leather exports in the latter part of the seventeenth century, Spanish governors in Puerto Rico did their best to drive cattle ranchers out of areas that were considered best for agricultural development. In many parts of the northern coastal plain pasture lands were turned into sugar fields. Where cattle ranchers could not be driven out, they were required to fence in their pastures to allow for agricultural development in their vicinity.

Sugar, the island's most important export in the first half of the eighteenth century, received special attention from royal officials. Tax laws were changed to facilitate the importation of machinery needed in the sugar mills, the immigration of sugar experts to the island was encouraged and efforts were made to improve communications and means of transportation between the sugar-producing areas and coastal towns such as San Juan and Ponce. In spite of this emphasis on sugar production, however, the cultivation of other commercial crops was not ignored. Cotton, for which there was a growing demand in the textile mills of Catalonia in northeastern Spain, became an export of some consequence in the eighteenth century. So did tobacco and coffee. Puerto Rican tobacco, however, found it difficult to compete with the cheaper and better quality Cuban product, and as a consequence tobacco production in the island grew slowly. Coffee production underwent a rapid expansion. Introduced into Puerto Rico from the French Antilles in 1726, the coffee tree did well on the island. Puerto Rican coffee found a ready market in Spain and, through Spain, in other European countries. Coffee production took place in relatively small, family-run farms. Because the coffee tree grew particularly well on mountain slopes, the expansion of the coffee economy generated an important migration of people from the coastal plains to the interior. Slowly, the valleys and mountains of the *cordillera central* began to assume an economic importance which they had not enjoyed in the past and which became greater in the future.

To encourage more trade between Puerto Rico and Spain and to try to put an end to the contraband trade between the islander's and English,

French and Dutch merchants, the royal authorities in Puerto Rico reduced some export-import taxes and eliminated some of the restrictions which in the past had hindered trade between the island and the rest of the empire. A further step was taken in 1756 when the Crown approved the creation of the Real Compañía de Barcelona, a Catalan charter company that was given a series of special privileges over the commerce of Puerto Rico and Hispaniola. In return for these privileges, the company was to take steps to provide some capital and machinery to encourage greater agricultural output in those two islands.

For all economic activities on the island in the eighteenth century, black slaves continued to constitute a major source of labor. As the economy grew, so did the number of slaves imported into the island. Slaves, however, were not the only laborers in Puerto Rico. By the middle of the eighteenth century non-slave labor had assumed great importance in certain activities, and in some sugar and coffee farms non-slave laborers often outnumbered the slaves. These free laborers, however, constituted an unstable labor force since many of them would work only for part of the year, and others often left their employers and settled as subsistence farmers in the interior. By the end of the eighteenth century some local landowners were already complaining of this and eventually (in the first decades of the nineteenth century) enlisted the support of the royal authorities to insure that free laborers remained attached to the sugar, coffee and tobacco farms.

The results of the efforts made by the Spanish authorities in Puerto Rico in the first half of the eighteenth century to stimulate economic growth on the island were not particularly impressive. Agricultural output grew, but slowly. So did commerce with Spain and other parts of the empire. After a promising beginning, the Catalan company discovered that contraband trade was profitable and established illegal commercial relations with the French and the English in the Caribbean. These activities brought upon the company the wrath of the Spanish government, which eventually withdrew from it the privileges it had previously granted the company and thereby brought about its demise. Commerce was also hindered by Spain's commitment not to allow Puerto Rico to carry on commercial relations with any other countries but Spain and its possessions. As a consequence of this and of the continuing lack of capital and the failure of the authorities to attract immigrants to the island, by the middle of the eighteenth century Puerto Rico was still poor, backward, sparsely populated and unable to generate the revenues necessary to pay for its administration and defense.

When he arrived in Puerto Rico in 1765 to prepare a report for his king on the state of the island, Alejandro O'Reilly was both disappointed and shocked by what he found. O'Reilly was an authoritarian, no-nonsense Irishman who, like a few other Irishmen in the eighteenth century, had entered the service of Spain and had served its monarch loyally and efficiently. At the time of his visit to Puerto Rico he enjoyed the rank of field marshall in the king's army. His mission to the island was to study the military and economic situation there and to make appropriate recommendations for change. Upon his arrival, O'Reilly was dismayed by the state of Puerto Rico's defenses. In spite of the efforts of governors since the beginning of the century, the fortifications of San Juan were in need of repairs, the artillery of the forts was antiquated and the regular Spanish troops were poorly equipped, undisciplined and badly paid. He also was shocked by the overall economic situation of Puerto Rico, whose inhabitants he described as "the poorest in America." After more than 250 years of Spanish rule there still were no roads on the island, few schools and poor sanitation facilities. O'Reilly found agricultural techniques backward and inefficient and commented on the lack of capital and agricultural experts, both of which he deemed necessary to bring the sugar industry up to date. He discovered that contraband still flourished and that in spite of past efforts by the Crown and its representatives on the island trade with Spain and the rest of the empire was still of little significance. He was particularly disturbed by the small population of the island, a situation which he considered one of the major explanations for the economic backwardness of Puerto Rico. After conducting the first island-wide census in the history of the island, O'Reilly reported a total population of 44,883. Of these 5,037 were black slaves. Of the remaining 39,846 only several hundred were Spaniards, several hundred more were creoles (locally born whites), and the remainder free blacks, mulattoes and mixtures of the latter two.

O'Reilly recommended that to strengthen the island's defenses additional funds should be made available to repair and expand the fortifications of San Juan. He also recommended that the size of the Spanish garrison in the capital be enlarged and that the regular troops stationed on the island be better paid, better equipped and more rigorously trained. He recommended that immigration from other parts of the empire and Catholic countries be encouraged to stimulate the island's economy and that state lands be made available to those

immigrants who were willing to settle in Puerto Rico. He also recommended that remaining barriers to trade between Puerto Rico and the rest
of the empire be abolished, that taxes be lowered and that roads be
constructed to facilitate the movement of people and goods between the
coast and the interior. In his report, O'Reilly emphasized the importance
of sugar production. He recommended that greater steps be taken to
curtail cattle raising in areas suitable for agricultural development and
that efforts be made to introduce into the island better agricultural
methods and technology. The Irishman also indicated the need for more
educational facilities. A man of the enlightenment, he believed that a
literate and educated population would also be an economically more
productive population.

In the years following O'Reilly's visit to Puerto Rico, efforts were
undertaken to put into practice many of the recommendations made by
him. Most of his recommendations dealing with defense were followed
almost to the letter, and by the end of the century the island was better
defended than at any other time in the past. The island's defense system
was put to the test soon after England and Spain went to war in 1796.
Early in the following year an English expedition of some 10,000 men
commanded by General Sir Ralph Abercromby landed on the coast a few
miles east of San Juan and set out towards the capital. They never took it.
The English met fierce opposition both from the regular Spanish troops
on the island and from the local militias that had been reorganized in the
years following O'Reilly's visit and that were now mobilized for the
occasion by Ramón de Castro, the able and energetic Spanish governor.
After several weeks of constant fighting the English position became
untenable, and in early May the humiliated Abercromby ordered his
troops back to their ships to sail away. It was the last time that the English
attempted to take Puerto Rico by force.

Not only was Puerto Rico's defense system at the end of the eighteenth
century in better shape than it had ever been in the past, but the island's
economy was undergoing a slow but unpreceented rate of expansion.
Following the recommendations made by O'Reilly, the Spanish authorities after 1765 launched a systematic campaign to attract Catholic
immigrants to the island. Several incentives, including free state lands,
were offered. Partially as a result of growing immigration, the population
of Puerto Rico between 1765 and 1800 grew from 44,883 to 155,000, an
increase of almost 300 per cent. Hand in hand with this expansion in
population (and primarily as a result of it) went the founding of new

towns, both in the interior and the coastal plains. Between 1750 and 1800 alone, 18 new towns were officially founded on the island. Among these was the town of Mayagüez, founded in 1763 and by 1800 one of the most important ports in Puerto Rico.

By creating greater demand for a variety of commodities, a growing population stimulated economic growth on the island. It facilitated that growth by making more labor available to work on the sugar, coffee, tobacco and cotton farms. Royal efforts also were important in bringing about a higher rate of economic growth. Beginning in the 1770s the Spanish authorities in Puerto Rico took a series of steps to stimulate growth. To facilitate internal and external commercial transactions paper money was introduced into the island in 1779. In 1787 a royal company was set up to stimulate the sale of Puerto Rican tobacco in Europe. Several taxes were lowered, a few restrictions on trade abolished (though trade outside the Spanish empire was still forbidden), and new and more efficient agricultural methods and technology introduced. As in the past, governmental efforts were concentrated on stimulating agricultural growth and trade between the island and Spain. Industrial activities, except for the production of cheap rum in the sugar farms, were discouraged by Spain, which like most countries with colonies, tried its best to prevent in the colonies the development of industrial activities (e.g. textile manufacturing) that might compete with metropolitan industries and thus preserve the colonial market for home industries. As a result of this policy, industrial activity in Puerto Rico was almost nonexistent at the end of the eighteenth century. A variety of goods were made within the island by local artisans, but the bulk of the manufactured commodities used on the island was imported from Spain which in turn imported a great deal from England and France.

As a result of population growth and governmental efforts, Puerto Rico entered the decade of the 1790s with an expanding agricultural sector and trade with the outside. Both agriculture and trade received a major boost from developments arising from the international crisis that overwhelmed Europe and the Caribbean in the years following the beginning of the French Revolution in 1789. When that revolution began the most important colony in the French Empire was St. Domingue, on the eastern part of Hispaniola. It was a prosperous sugar colony ruled by a small elite of white planters and made productive by a large mass of brutalized black slaves. In 1791, the slaves took advantage of the disruptions created in France and in the colony by the revolution and launched the first successful black rebellion in the New World. It was a violent and bloody affair, and the colony's sugar economy was destroyed. Many whites were killed and many others driven into exile. In spite of Napoleon's efforts to bring the slaves under control again, the blacks maintained their freedom from white rule, and in the first decade of the nineteenth century created the black independent state of Haiti.

The destruction of St. Domingue's sugar industry stimulated the expansion of the sugar industries of Cuba and Puerto Rico, whose sugar producers now sought to supply the European markets previously supplied by the more efficient planters of St. Domingue. In Puerto Rico, new lands were brought under sugar cultivation and more slaves imported to work them. The expansion of sugar production was facilitated by governmental policies and by the presence of French planters who had fled to Puerto Rico from St. Domingue during the black rebellion there. These families—most of whom settled permanently on Puerto Rico with the assistance of the Spanish authorities—not only brought with them badly needed capital but also knowledge about sugar production that was more advanced than that possessed by sugar producers in Puerto Rico.

As the Puerto Rican sugar industry expanded in the 1790s, so did the island's commerce with the outside. In the years following the fall of the Bastille, Spain tried to curb the excesses of the French Revolution, and after the execution of the king of France by the revolutionary government went to war against France in 1792. The war went badly for Spain, and by the mid 1790s the Spanish government pleaded for peace. The price demanded by the victorious French regime was high. By virtue of treaties signed in 1795 and 1796, Spain became a virtual economic and military satellite of France. Since at that time France and England were at war, England declared war against Spain. For Spain, the war with England was disastrous. English sea power not only disrupted Spanish commerce in Europe, but also paralyzed Spain's commerce with its American colonies. In an attempt to cope with the economic crisis that the disruption of trade with Spain created in Puerto Rico and in other Spanish American colonies, the Spanish government issued in 1797 a decree allowing neutral powers to trade with its colonies in the New World. The chief beneficiary of the decree was the United States, whose ships now sailed to Spanish American ports in unprecedented numbers. After 1797 the presence of North American ships in San Juan and other Puerto Rican ports became common, and the island and the U.S. began a lively and profitable commerce. To the United States Puerto Rico exported sugar, molasses, rum and some coffee and tobacco. To Puerto Rico the United States exported wheat, hog products and a variety of manufactured goods. As the trade between Puerto Rico and the United States grew, Spain became increasingly concerned about losing a good share of the island's commerce to the North Americans and in 1799 revoked the decree of 1797. The war with England, however made it impossible for Spain to enforce the new decree and the trade went on, often with the participation of Spanish officials on the island. In the first few years of the nineteenth century the Spanish government concluded that the trade between Puerto Rico and the United States could not be halted and that so long as it remained illegal import-export taxes could not be collected on it. As a result, in 1804 Spain once again opened Puerto Rican ports to legal trade with neutral powers. From then on commercial relations between the United States and the island grew steadily and by the end of the nineteenth century the United States had become one of Puerto Rico's major trading partners.

At the end of the eighteenth century, Puerto Rico was in several ways quite different from what it had been when the Bourbon dynasty came to the throne of Spain in 1700. The population was over 150,000 and a significant proportion of it was now concentrated in the mountain chain of the interior. There were several dozen towns; Ponce and Mayagüez were expanding commercial centers, and San Germán had a population of several thousand. Town life throughout the island was livelier than in the past; contact between the towns and the rural areas was greater. More merchants now traveled through the interior and more people lived year round in the towns. San Juan, which still remained the commercial, administrative and ecclesiastical capital, was a bustling community of over 10,000 people. Some of the capital's more affluent families, including the governor's, now had summer houses among the lovely gardens and orchards of a place known as Rio Piedras, not far from San Juan.

Commercial relations with the outside were expanding, as was agricultural output, both to meet the food demands of a growing population and for exportation abroad. Leather was no longer an export of significance. The main exports were sugar, coffee, tobacco and cotton, in that order of importance. The bulk of these exports left the island through the ports of San Juan, Ponce and Mayagüez, which were also the main centers of distribution for commodities imported into the island.

The revenues generated by Puerto Rico's economy and commerce were increasing and realization of the hopes of Spanish monarchs to have the island cover the costs of its own administration and defense seemed close at hand. In 1810 the Mexican *situado* was abolished permanently.

But if the differences between Puerto Rico at the beginning and at the end of the eighteenth century were important, the similarities were perhaps more significant. Impressive population growth had taken place in the second half of the century. Dozens of new towns had been founded, and more people now lived in the interior. But at the end of the century the island was still sparsely populated, and its population remained overwhelmingly rural and concentrated on the coastal plains. In spite of governmental efforts, the island still had no roads at the end of the century. A little progress had been made in education, and more of the sons of the elite now went abroad to study; but at the end of the century the island still had no university of its own, few schools, no printing press, and over 90 per cent of its people could neither read nor write. In the towns health and sanitation facilities were primitive; in the rural areas they were nonexistent. Life expectancy was short, the annual death rate high, and throughout the island *curanderos* continued to take care of most of the sick.

In the second half of the eighteenth century Puerto Rico had witnessed an unprecedented economic expansion that enriched a handful of landowning families and merchants and brought more revenues into the royal treasury. Yet, by the end of the century the vast majority of the island's inhabitants still remained as poor as they had been when O'Reilly had described them as "the poorest in America." The economy as a whole was backward and underdeveloped, and, in spite of growing commercial relations with the outside, relatively isolated from the mainstream of world trade. In general, sugar, coffee and tobacco farms remained relatively small. There still existed a critical shortage of capital in the sugar industry, whose technology, some improvements notwithstanding, remained primitive when compared with the technology in other sugar-producing islands in the Caribbean. In years when Spain was at peace with its European neighbors, the colonial metropolis continued to control the bulk of the island's trade. Spanish policy toward the island at the end of the century was still designed to increase governmental revenues, to prevent the development of industrial activities which might compete with home industries, and to stimulate the production of a few commercial crops that were in demand in Spain or could be channeled through Spain to other European markets.

At the end of the eighteenth century political power was still concentrated in the hands of a small elite of Spanish administrators appointed by the monarchy and responsible only to it. Not only the civil administration, but also the ecclesiastical organization still remained in the hands of Spaniards whose main concern was to maintain Puerto Rico within the Spanish empire and, with royal approval and encouragement, to keep the local population out of both administrative and ecclesiastical positions. Isolated and dispersed throughout the rural areas, the majority of the islanders showed no concern over this policy and therefore voiced no opposition. But among members of the landed elite born and raised on the island—an elite which had become increasingly well-off in the latter part of the century—there were objections to a policy that kept them from playing any role whatever in shaping the destiny of the land of their birth. These objections were not formalized in any sort of program for change. They took the form of a growing antagonism towards Spaniards, an antagonism which the historian Abbad y Lasierra had already described in 1782 when he wrote that among the islanders, Spaniards were known as "men of the other band." At the end of the eighteenth century there were still no Puerto Ricans in Puerto Rico; but the foundations for the future emergence of the Puerto Rican nation had been set during the first three centuries of Spanish rule, and the genesis of the development of a national consciousness was already appearing.

Through conquest and military domination Spanish imperialism was able to fix upon Puerto Rico its language and to shape its predominant form of economic activity: agriculture for subsistence and export. A dependent economy and a hierarchical class structure emerged that at its highest levels meshed landowners, and ecclesiastic and military officials with civil administrators. The slow rate of colonization of the island and the larger interests of the empire precluded rapid economic development and social change. The relatively large number of military and civilian officials linked to Spain, along with a lack of a political role on the part of local landowners, commercial groups, subsistence farmers and urban craftsmen, weakened the basis for indigineous political movements for self government. The process of internal migration left the administrative and commercial centers in the hands of those classes and individuals most loyal to Spain and most immune to the currents of nationalism that were to emerge in the rest of the Spanish American world in the first decades of the nineteenth century. Despite poverty and exploitation in the midst of commercial opportunity and a potential bountiful land, the combined forces of Spain and local officialdom early denied the Puerto Rican people the only framework in which these economic possibilities could be realized: a national movement.

NOTES

Most of the data and factual information in this essay was obtained from the following sources:

Abbad y Lasierra, Iñigo, *Noticias de la historia geográfica, civil y política de la Isla de San Juan Bautista de Puerto Rico.* (Madrid, 1788).

Alegria, Ricardo, *Descubrimiento, conquista y colonización de Puerto Rico, 1493-1599* (San Juan, 1969).

Brau, Salvador, *Historia de Puerto Rico* (San Juan, 1956).

Brau, Salvador, *La colonización de Puerto Rico* (San Juan, 1966).

Córdoba, Pedro Tomás de, *Memorias geográficas, históricas, económicas y estadísticas de la Isla de Puerto Rico*, Vol. I (Madrid, 1831).

Cuesta Mendoza, Antonio, *Historia eclesiastica del Puerto Rico colonial, 1508-1700* (Santo Domingo, 1948).

Díaz Soler, Luis M., *Historia de la esclavitud negra en Puerto Rico* (San Juan, 1965).

Fernández Méndez, Eugenio (ed.), *Crónicas de Puerto Rico*, Vol. I (San Juan, 1957).

Figueroa, Loida, *Breve historia de Puerto Rico*, Vol. I (Rio Piedras, 1968).

Herr, Richard, *The Eighteenth Century Revolution in Spain* (Princeton, 1958).

Ledru, Andree Pierre, *Viaje a la Isla de Puerto Rico* (1797), Trans. Julio L. Vizcarrondo (San Juan, 1863).

Miyares González, Fernando, *Noticias particulares de la Isla y Plaza de San Juan de Puerto Rico* (1775) (Rio Piedras, 1954).

Morales Carrión, Arturo, *Historia del pueblo de Puerto Rico* (Rio Piedras, 1968).

Morales Carrión, Arturo, "Origenes de las relaciones entre los Estados Unidos y Puerto Rico, 1700-1815," *Historia*, II, No. 1 (April 1952).

Morales Carrión, Arturo, *Puerto Rico and the Non-Hispanic Caribbean* (Rio Piedras, 1952).

O'Reilly, Alejandro, "Memoria," in Alejandro Tapia y Rivera (ed.), *Biblioteca Histórica de Puerto Rico*, 2nd. ed. (San Juan, 1945).

Parry, John H., *The Spanish Seaborne Empire* (New York, 1966).

Sanz, Vicente M., *Historia documental de Puerto Rico* (Rio Piedras, 1961).

Sauer, Carl Ortwin, *The Early Spanish Main* (Berkeley, 1966).

Vázquez de Espinoza, Antonio, *Compendium and Description of the West Indies* (1620s), Trans. Charles Upson Clark (Washington, D.C., 1942).

Socio-Politico Developments in a Colonial Context: Puerto Rico in the Nineteenth Century

Adalberto López

For Spain the first decade of the nineteenth century was a period of political chaos and military upheaval that eventually brought an end to its American empire. Since 1796 Spain had been a commercial and military satellite of revolutionary France, a situation that brought the country into conflict with England, then locked in a fierce was with France. Between 1802 and 1804 Napoleon Bonaparte (who was then the power among the French) brought a temporary peace with England, and Spain enjoyed a temporary respite from the burdens of war. In 1804, however, soon after Napoleon crowned himself Emperor of France, the bitter war resumed, as Napoleon sought to impose his will on continental Europe. For Spain the war with England was an unmitigated disaster. At Trafalgar the cream of the Spanish navy went down with the French fleet under the eyes of a joyous and arrogant Lord Nelson. Once again English sea power disrupted communications between Spain and its American colonies and brought commercial relations between the two to a standstill.

The collapse of trade with the Americas and the growing financial burden of the war created in Spain an economic and political crisis that was made worse by some of the steps taken by the Spanish government in an attempt to increase the necessary revenues to finance the war against England. Under the control of Manuel Godoy—a young, intelligent and hard working army officer who had risen to power because he had caught the fancy of Queen Maria Luisa and the friendship of her husband Charles IV (1788-1808)—the Spanish government expropriated some ecclesiastical properties and brought upon itself the wrath of the powerful Catholic Church. In an already inflationary situation caused by a drastic shortage of imported goods, Godoy introduced large quantities of paper money, which fed the inflation and increased popular anger against Godoy and his monarchs. By 1808 a conspiracy of nobles and churchmen took place. Centered on the figure of Ferdinand, heir to the throne, the goal of the conspiracy was to get rid of Godoy and force Charles to abdicate in favor of his son. In March the conspirators came out in the open while the royal family was in the summer palace of Aranjuez, and in the midst of a popular riot Godoy quit and Charles gave up the throne. Ferdinand VII was now the legitimate king of Spain.

Napoleon was concerned about the political squabbles then raging in Spain and angered by what he considered Spain's insignificant war effort against England. He decided to get rid of the Spanish Bourbons and place one of his brothers on the throne of Spain. At about the same time that the enemies of Godoy were acclaiming Ferdinand as their new king, French armies invaded Spain. By the end of the year Charles IV_ Maria Luisa and Godoy were in exile in Italy, Ferdinand was in luxurious imprisonment in France, Joseph Bonaparte had been declared by his brother king of Spain, and most important Spanish cities were occupied by French troops.

In spite of Ferdinand's own statements that Joseph was the legitimate king of Spain, the vast majority of the Spanish people refused to recognize Napoleon's brother as their king or to tolerate the French in Spain, and thousands of Spaniards were up in arms against the invaders. Between 1808 and 1814 guerrilla armies, often led by peasants and priests, led an effective fight against the French presence in Spain. England, now the ally of the Spanish people, provided arms and money and eventually sent to the Peninsula a large army commanded by the future Duke of Wellington. By 1814 the French position in Spain had become untenable, and the French armies of occupation were flowing across the Pyrenees back into France. In that year Napoleon freed Ferdinand, and, after getting from him a promise that Spain would declare its neutrality in the war between England and France, allowed him to return to Spain and regain his throne.

In the Spanish American colonies the French occupation of Spain and the imprisonment of Ferdinand VII opened the door to political autonomy for the creole colonial elites who had grown tired of excessive taxation, restrictions on trade with powers other than Spain and the official policy of keeping them out of administrative positions. With Spain in the midst of a bloody war of resistance against the French and with commercial relations between the colonies and the colonial metropolis at a standstill, the colonial elites throughout the Spanish American mainland made a bids for political and economic autonomy that quickly developed into full-fledged wars of independence. By 1810 rebellions had broken out in Mexico, Venezuela, Colombia and a few other areas of the Spanish American world. These rebellions continued even after the French had been forced out of Spain and Ferdinand, back on his throne, was able to send more troops and supplies to the colonies. By the mid 1820s the colonies in the mainland had won their independence, the Spanish section of Hispaniola had been occupied by black forces from the independent nation of Haiti and all that remained of what had once been an extensive and rich American empire were the islands of Cuba and Puerto Rico.

Puerto Rico was deeply affected by events in Spain and the mainland Spanish American colonies after 1808. Unlike the creole elites in the mainland colonies, however, the island's creole elite did not make a bid for independence. True, among the members of the creole elite in Puerto Rico there were a growing awareness of themselves as being different from Spaniards and a growing attachment to the land of their birth. There was also present among them a general discontent with the policies that Spain had followed and was still following towards the island. But there were too many factors that militated against the emergence of an independence movement among the Puerto Rican creole elite as a group. Many of its members still had a strong psychological and sentimental attachment to the mother country, which did not prevent them from desiring changes and reforms but certainly kept them from taking the radical step of desiring independence. Even among those who were psychologically prepared for a complete break with Spain there was the realization that for Puerto Rico to make a successful bid for independence the island's masses would have to be mobilized, something which they saw as difficult to do and which, in any case, most of them were reluctant to try. At the beginning of the nineteenth century the Puerto Rican masses (poor, illiterate and exploited) remained apathetic toward the issue of the status of the island within the Spanish empire. At the same time, the island's native elite was afraid of getting the masses involved in any sort of armed political struggle. In the aftermath of the black rebellion in St. Domingue (Haiti) many of the French planters who escaped the anger of the black masses fled with their families to Puerto Rico. In the island these families quickly assumed a certain economic and social importance. Extremely conservative, these families not only instilled fear in Puerto Rico's elite about the dangers involved when the masses (especially the slaves) were mobilized for political ends, but also joined the island's Spanish authorities in doing whatever was necessary to prevent Puerto Rico from following in the footsteps of the mainland colonies. The French royalists and the vigilant authorities in Puerto Rico were joined after 1810 by thousands of Spaniards fleeing from the wars of independence on the mainland colonies. These royalist exiles also brought with them tales of horror about what happened when the masses were involved in political struggles, and once settled in the island, they, too, made every effort to see that Puerto Rico remained a colony of Spain.

Fear of the slaves and of the masses as a whole by the creole elite and the presence of large numbers of French and Spanish loyalist exiles were not the only deterrents to the emergence of an independence movement in Puerto Rico. There were large numbers of Spanish troops, which although concentrated in San Juan, were also stationed throughout the island. Spanish troops had been present in Puerto Rico since the sixteenth century, but the Spanish military presence there became greater after 1810. Hundreds of Spanish troops that had been defeated in the mainland colonies by the patriot armies were reassigned to the garrisons of Puerto Rico. Also, after 1814 Ferdinand VII ordered more troops to the island directly from Spain to forestall any disruptions there. Finally, another factor militating against the emergence of an independence movement on the island was the political situation in Spain, which after 1808 opened before the Puerto Rican creole elite the vision of reforms and of some participation in the politics of the empire and the administration of Puerto Rico.

In the months following the beginning of the Spanish people's resistance against the French, some of those involved in the anti-French struggle demanded of the Junta Central a meeting of the traditional Spanish parliament or Cortes. Since the beginning of the sixteenth century the Cortes had rarely met except to give official recognition to the heir to the throne and to rubber stamp certain important royal decrees. Given that reputation, the conservative Junta Central concluded that no harm could come out of calling for a meeting of the Cortes and gave in to the demands for such a meeting. Among the deputies who met in the port of Cádiz—an easily defensible city still free of French control—there were some, however, who believed that the situation in which Spain found itself was partially the result of an irresponsible monarchy and who concluded that in the future the actions of the monarchy should be restrained by a written constitution. In spite of bitter opposition from conservative elements who argued that the Cortes should direct itself solely to the issue of fighting the French, the radical deputies (later known as *liberales*) carried the day and managed to turn the Cortes into a sort of constituent assembly. The radical deputies believed that in the formulation of a constitution for Spain the Spanish American colonies should have a voice, and they invited the colonies ·(most of which were at the time in the midst of wars of independence) to send delegates to Cádiz.

The Puerto Rican creole elite welcomed the invitation from the Cortes of Cádiz with joy and optimism. In June of 1809 the municipalities of the island voted to elect the representative the island had been asked to send to Spain. It was an election in which the masses did not play any role whatever, but it was the island's first election nevertheless. The man chosen to represent Puerto Rico's interests (or more accurately, the interests of the Puerto Rican colonial elite) was Ramón Power y Giralt, a native of San Juan who had been educated in Spain, visited France and had been a navy officer in the service of Spain in the Caribbean. A close friend of Power y Giralt was Juan Alejo de Arizmendi, also a native of San Juan and the first and last native of Puerto Rico to hold the post of bishop of the island during Spanish colonial rule. Bishop Arizmendi was overjoyed by the turn of events in Spain and counseled his friend Power y Giralt "to protect and uphold the rights of our Puerto Rican compatriots, as I will do until I die." Like most members of the creole elite, Arizmendi was socially and politically conservative, sharing the elite's fear of and contempt for the masses. But his counsel to Power y Giralt is indicative of a growing national consciousness that was already having its impact on the island's elite.

Upon his arrival in Cádiz, Power y Giralt was elected vice president of the Cortes. To the deputies of the Cortes he presented 22 propositions that delineated the economic aspirations of his merchant and landed countrymen. In addition to making demands for more schools, a university and more roads, he also made demands for the distribution of royal lands to those who were willing to develop them, more freedom of trade with nations other than Spain, the abolition of certain insular taxes and greater participation for the island's elite in the administration of the island. He requested, for example, that natives of the island be given preference for appointments to the insular administration, that the heads of the *partidos* be popularly elected by the municipalities, and that Puerto Rico be given effective and permanent representation in the Spanish Cortes.

The demands made by Power y Giralt and by other deputies from Spanish America were given a sympathetic hearing by those who met in Cádiz. The group, however, was more interested in providing Spain with a written constitution. By 1812 a constitution that provided for a powerful monarchy but placed some important restrictions on the monarchy had been drafted and promulgated. The new constitution declared Puerto Rico and the rebellious Spanish American colonies provinces of Spain and gave them the right to elect representatives to the Spanish Cortes. The constitution also provided for restraints on the powers of the provincial governors and included certain provisions that gave the Puerto Rican elite the hope of eventually having some sort of island assembly through which they could exercise some control over insular affairs. The constitution of 1812, however, was short lived. The war against the French was still the primary concern of the Spanish people who either did not understand what the constitution was all about or who rejected it as too radical for the country. Ferdinand had learned of the new constitution while still in prison in France and did not approve of it. Once he was back on his throne in 1814, he immediately set out to destroy that constitution. Assured of the support of the bulk of the army, Ferdinand declared the constitution null and void and issued orders to arrest and imprison or exile those who had met in Cádiz and who had dared to dream of a constitutional monarchy. Dozens of liberals were exiled or imprisoned; a few others were executed. Power y Giralt did not experience the anger of the arch-conservative Ferdinand. He had died in 1813, still arguing on behalf of greater power in Puerto Rico for the island's creole elite.

Ferdinand was too conservative to tolerate a written constitution or any sort of representation for the colonies in the Spanish government or electoral system in the colonies themselves. But he was intelligent enough to realize what was going on in the Spanish American world and to take steps to prevent Puerto Rico from following in the footsteps of the rebellious mainland colonies. After 1814 he not only enlarged the

Spanish military presence in Puerto Rico and provided the island with governors of whose loyalty he seemed assured, but he also took steps to meet some of the demands of the island's creole elite. In 1815 he issued the famous *Cédula de Gracias* designed to meet some of the economic demands of the Puerto Rican elite and to stimulate internal economic growth. The *Cédula* abolished many of the existing restrictions on trade between the island and countries other than Spain, permitted the importation of sugar-processing machinery tax free, and invited Catholics from all nations to settle in Puerto Rico. To stimulate Catholic immigration several incentives were offered. Royal lands were to be given free to these immigrants, six acres for each member of the family and three acres for each slave the family brought to the island. In addition, the *Cédula* exempted immigrants from taxation for a period of ten years after they arrived in the island and offered them Spanish citizenship after residing in Puerto Rico for five years. To make easier the implementation of the provisions of the *Cédula*, the island was divided into six *partidos* (San Juan, San Germán, Humacao, Coamo, Arecibo, and Aguada), each under a trained Spanish bureaucrat appointed by the governor.

The Ferdinandian reaction that set in in 1814 was welcomed in Puerto Rico by army commanders, civil administrators, the church and the majority of the French and Spanish merchants and landowners who resided there. To the members of the creole elite, the end of constitutional procedures in Spain and the return of Puerto Rico to a blatant colonial status run by and primarily for the benefit of the colonial masters was a source of disappointment and bitterness. A few were placated by the provisions of the *Cédula de Gracias*. The majority of them, however, continued to argue on behalf of reforms and some sort of official representation for the island in Spain in spite of fierce local conservative opposition to these demands. To those who dreamed of reforms, the opportunity once again appeared in 1820 when Spanish troops in southern Spain mutinied against the reactionary government of Ferdinand VII and against duty in the rebellious Spanish American colonies, and forced the king to recognize the constitution of 1812 as the law of the land. The Spanish authorities in Puerto Rico were concerned about developments in Spain and feared that the king had become a prisoner of radical reformers. Nevertheless, they reluctantly decided to obey the liberal government that was organized in Spain in the aftermath of the military mutiny and called for elections of representatives to the Cortes as provided in the constitution of 1812. Once again the members of the Puerto Rican elite got together and chose as their representative José Maria Quiñones, a former colleague of Power y Giralt. Upon his arrival in Spain, Quiñones established contacts with the representatives from Cuba and together launched a campaign on behalf of reforms for the two islands. Many of the demands made by Quiñones before the Cortes in Madrid were identical to those made previously by Power y Giralt in Cádiz. Quiñones, however, went one step further and demanded a degree of political participation by the island's elite which Power y Giralt had not dared mention eight years earlier. Quiñones not only asked for greater autonomy from the governor for the Puerto Rican municipalities, but also demanded greater restrictions on the powers of the insular governor and the creation of an insular assembly whose members were to be elected by the Puerto Rican creole elite.

The Overseas Commission of the Liberal government in Spain considered and accepted many of the proposals that had been submitted by Quiñones and his Cuban colleagues. Yet the degree of political autonomy and participation that Quiñones and other Puerto Rican creoles expected did not materialize. By 1822 the Liberal government in Spain was weakened by factions, personal quarrels and intrigues, and was faced by a growing Catholic-conservative rebellion whose goal was to "liberate" Ferdinand from the liberals. Secretly, Ferdinand had appealed to the Holy Alliance to come to his aid and destroy the constitutional government to which he had paid lip service. The Holy Alliance listened and encouraged France, one of its members, to intervene. In 1823 a French army of 100,000 (*Los cien mil hijos de San Luis*) invaded Spain and with the assistance of Spanish conservatives destroyed the liberal regime. Once again, Ferdinand was absolutist king of Spain. And once again, he set out to persecute those who had dared to impose a constitutional government on Spain. The constitution of 1812 was for the second time in its history declared null and void, all laws issued by the liberal governments of 1820-1823 were similarly annulled, and both Puerto Rico and Cuba were returned to their previous status. In Spain thousands of liberals were forced into exile; hundreds were jailed; dozens were executed. And while Ferdinand busied himself persecuting reformers in Spain, his representatives in Puerto Rico clamped down on the activities of the more liberal-minded among the members of the insular creole elite.

In spite of the events and crises which had shaken Spain and the

Spanish American world during the first quarter of the nineteenth century, Puerto Rico in the mid 1820s remained a colony of Spain still governed by a powerful Spanish governor who answered to the king and no one else, and with an administrative, ecclesiastical, and economic organization still dominated by Spaniards. Yet, during that quarter century the island had experienced many changes. Thousands of Spanish loyalists migrated from the rebellious Spanish American colonies and settled in Puerto Rico. Hundreds of French families from St. Domingue did the same. And later, Spanish families migrated to the island from Louisiana and Florida as these territories were lost by Spain to the French and the United States respectively. Partly as a consequence of this migration, partly as the consequence of the migration of European Catholics who were attracted to the island by the provisions of the *Cédula de Gracias*, and partly due to natural internal population growth, between 1800 and the mid 1820s the population of Puerto Rico grew by over 100,000 and San Juan became a thriving community of close to 15,000 residents. The vast majority of those who migrated to the island went into agricultural activities—primarily coffee and sugar production. Output of both commodities increased and so did output of tobacco, cotton and cheap rum.

Although by the mid 1820s Spain continued to be Puerto Rico's main commercial partner, trade with the United States was becoming increasingly important. In 1797 and again in 1804 Spain had allowed neutral powers to carry on commercial relations with the island. The United States took advantage of this and by the 1820s dozens of North American ships sailed every year to San Juan and other Puerto Rican ports carrying a variety of agricultural and manufactured commodities in demand in the island. In spite of the demands of certain Spanish merchants that trade with powers other than Spain be prohibited, the Spanish government concluded that such trade was bringing revenues into the royal treasury and that it was not harmful as long as it was restricted to commodities that did not hurt Spanish industries or Spanish consumers. To protect Spanish industries, tariffs were used to make certain non-Spanish commodities noncompetitive in Puerto Rico. In 1824 the expanding trade between the island and the United States was once again sanctioned by the Spanish government. Five years later Spain issued another law that allowed friendly powers to establish consular officers in Puerto Rico. Among the first countries to take advantage of the new law was the United States.

A growing population and more freedom of trade stimulated economic growth in Puerto Rico, a growth that was encouraged by the Spanish authorities in the island. In the first two decades of the nineteenth century, Puerto Rico was governed by men who in spite of their political conservatism were concerned about the economic conditions in the island and eager to promote growth. Of these administrators probably the most effective was Alejandro Ramírez who had been named to his post in 1813 by the constitutional government of Cádiz and who remained in that post when Ferdinand returned to Spain in 1814. During the previous administration of Governor Toribio Montes, a printing press had been introduced into the island. Montes had used that press to print the first publication to appear in Puerto Rico, *La Gaceta Oficial.* During his administration Ramírez used it to put out the *Diario Economico de Puerto Rico*, which was designed primarily to disseminate information on market potentials, new agricultural methods, technology and fertilizers. It was also during the administration of Ramírez that the Puerto Rican *Sociedad económica de amigos del pais* was created. Like the *sociedades económicas* in Spain, it was made up of affluent and "enlightened" Spaniards and Puerto Ricans dedicated to the promotion of "useful" knowledge and educational facilities. Ramírez did his best to improve the educational system on the island, to improve methods of transportation and to bring into the island more capital and technology for the sugar industry. To raise additional revenues he established the first lottery in Puerto Rico's history. During the last years of his administration he devoted a great deal of his efforts to the enforcement of the provisions of the *Cédula de Gracias* of 1815.

Much of the progress that was made in the island during the second decade of the nineteenth century must be attributed in part to the efforts of Alejandro Ramírez. He was without question one of the most efficient and progressive administrators ever sent to Puerto Rico by Spain. Spain benefited from his administration, since during that period governmental revenues increased from 70,000 to 200,000 pesos. Spanish and Puerto Rican merchants and landowners also benefitted from his efforts. Yet, those efforts had their negative effect since Ramírez's emphasis on the development of the sugar industry strengthened the trend towards a single-crop economy increasingly dependent on imports of manufactures and certain foodstuffs.

During the first quarter of the nineteenth century, then, Puerto Rico experienced an impressive population growth, an expansion of commercial relations with the United States and a modest expansion in commercial agriculture. But probably the most significant change experienced by the island during that period was political. In 1809-1814 and in 1820-1823, Spain had enjoyed constitutional governments, and those governments had invited Puerto Rico to send representatives to the Spanish Cortes. Those two brief periods of constitutional rule had whetted the appetite of the Puerto Rican creole elite, which, in spite of its fear and contempt of the masses and its refusal to follow the rebellious path of the mainland Spanish American colonies, was becoming more conscious of its separate identity and interests. The elite chafed under the arbitrary rule of Spanish governors and resented its exclusion from the civil administration and the ecclesiastical hierarchy, the taxes to which it was subjected and the limitations that still existed on trade with countries other than Spain. The first quarter of the nineteenth century witnessed the birth of Puerto Rican liberalism. Elitist in character, it was essentially a reformist movement that initially kept the issue of political autonomy low key but that eventually came to emphasize it. In the decades that followed, the Puerto Rican liberal elite split into groups, each committed to a different solution to the problem of Puerto Rico's status under Spanish colonial rule. At no time, however, did these groups develop a program of socio-economic reform beneficial to the masses to go along with their political demands.

In the decades following the overthrow of the Spanish Liberal regime in 1823, the Spanish administration in Puerto Rico changed, but not significantly. In 1828 the island was divided into seven judicial districts, each with a *justicia mayor*, and in 1832 the Real Audiencia de Puerto Rico was created. For many years the Real Audiencia, with its seat in San Juan, enjoyed jurisdiction over both criminal and civil cases. Later on, however, two audiencias were set up—one in Ponce, the other in Mayagüez—to deal with criminal cases within their jurisdictions. Aside from these changes, the administrative arrangements remained more or less as they had been at the end of the eighteenth century. The municipalities enjoyed some autonomy over purely local affairs, but were otherwise under the careful eye and control of the governor and his representatives throughout the island. The powers of the governors remained great, and ordinarily they behaved with unpredictable arbitrariness. Most were military men dedicated to preserving the colonial status of the island and keeping the populace in line. Among the most notorious governors of the nineteenth century was Miguel de la Torre, who decided to indulge the populace in "bread and circuses." He encouraged the islanders to enjoy themselves to the point where they would not possibly want to rebel. His administration became known as the regime of the three B's (*baile, botella, baraja*—dance, drinking, and gambling.) Another abusive governor was Juan Prim, who once declared that "to govern this island all that is needed is a whip and a violin." In the nineteenth century each governor usually brought his own ideas as to how best to govern the island. Some were intelligent and brutal; others were brutal and stupid. What one governor did during his administration, his successor often undid during his. But on one thing they all agreed: Any demands for political participation or autonomy for the island on the part of the Puerto Rican creole elite were treasonous and, unless the authorities in Spain ordered otherwise, to be destroyed by any means.

To back up the arbitrary rule of the generals and marshals who governed the island in the course of the nineteenth century, the Spanish government strengthened the Spanish military presence in Puerto Rico. The large garrison of Spanish regulars in San Juan was strengthened and other garrisons set up throughout the island. In 1869 the notorious *Guardia Civil* was introduced into Puerto Rico. The *Guardia* had been founded in Spain during the archconservative regime of General Narváez and was designed primarily to maintain law and order in the rural areas of Spain. In Spain the *Guardia Civil* quickly earned a reputation for discipline, efficiency and brutality, and was primarily used to protect the great landowners of southern Spain against periodic violence on the part of the land hungry and exploited peasantry of that region. In Puerto Rico the *Guardia Civil* was also used by the Spanish authorities to maintain law and order in the rural areas, a law and order designed to protect the economic interests of the landed elite, both Spanish and Puerto Rican.

To facilitate the movement of troops from one part of the island to another the Spanish authorities on the island began in 1852 the construction of a *carretera militar* (military road) that eventually connected San Juan to Ponce and that by the end of the nineteenth century was the only surfaced highway on the island. Other roads were mere dirt trails that often became impassible during the rainy season. In addition to the construction of the *carretera militar*, the Spanish authorities opened in 1880 a short railway line connecting San Juan to Rio Piedras a few miles away.

In health, sanitation and education, little progress was made in the course of the nineteenth century. The overall state of medical facilities improved a little and the number of doctors in the island increased. There were also efforts to introduce vaccination programs against such diseases as smallpox. But in spite of these improvements, health and sanitation facilities remained inadequately financed and backward. The cities were dirty; doctors and hospitals were usually found only in the main urban centers and with a few exceptions catered primarily to the needs of the members of the elite. Even after the cholera epidemic that swept the island in 1855 and killed over 30,000 people, private and governmental efforts to improve health and sanitation facilities were not substantial. By the end of the century the average life span was 35 years and the death rate approximately 31 per 1,000. In the rural areas the vast majority of people usually turned to home remedies or local *curanderos* when ill.

In education some improvements were achieved. Because of both governmental and private efforts, the number of elementary schools on the island increased after the 1830s and by the end of the century schools were to be found in many of the towns of the interior. In 1832 a theological seminary (which in 1858 was transformed into the College of Secondary Education under Jesuit control) was established. In the decades that followed a few technical schools to train students in agricultural science, navigation and commerce were founded. A few secondary schools that offered courses in biology, chemistry and a few other sciences also were created in the second half of the century. Foreign languages, especially French, began to receive some attention from those in charge of shaping educational policies. On the whole, however, the Puerto Rican masses benefitted little from these improvements. Although an occasional lower class boy was lucky enough to receive some sort of education, the majority of those attending schools were the sons and daughters of the Spanish and Puerto Rican elite of the island. Furthermore, Puerto Rico remained without a university in spite of the persistent demands of the insular elite. Ordinarily the sons of those who could afford it went for university degrees to Europe, to South American countries and, by the latter part of the century, occasionally to the United States. By the end of the nineteenth century the Puerto Rican educational system remained backward and poor. In the late 1890s only 4.5 per cent of the insular tax income was devoted to education. By the end of that decade only 8 per cent of school-age children were attending school and the illiteracy rate was almost 85 per cent.

Although the main reason for the lack of progress in communication and transportation facilities, health, sanitation and education was the reluctance of the Spanish government to spend on the island more than was necessary to hold on to it, part of the blame must be attributed to the local governors and their subordinates who often put into their own pockets funds provided by the Spanish government for the construction of roads, hospitals and schools. In nineteenth-century Puerto Rico the Spanish administration was not only arbitrary and often brutal but also exceedingly corrupt.

There were a few sensitive churchmen who sympathized with the plight of the Puerto Rican masses and who periodically complained about the arbitrariness and corruption of the local administration and petitioned for more hospitals and schools. However, the Church as a whole remained throughout the nineteenth century a conservative institution run by Spanish bishops who invariably supported the civil authorities in their efforts to maintain Spanish control of the island. Through the priests who worked under them, the Church authorities sought to convince the masses that it was God's will to accept passively Spanish rule. Temporal life, they said, was brief and unimportant. Men's business was to prepare themselves for the afterlife. In the schools run by the Church, children were taught to read and write, but they were also infused with the dogma of the Church and with an unquestionable respect for the established authorities and for imperial "law and order." Economically impoverished, the Catholic Church in Puerto Rico (like the Catholic Church in Spain) remained in the nineteenth century simply another branch of the government, loyal to, controlled by and dependent on it for a good proportion of its income. Catholicism was the religion of the state and the only religion officially tolerated on the island.

In spite of a high death rate and short life expectancy, the population of Puerto Rico grew impressively in the course of the nineteenth century because of a high birth rate. In 1800, the total population was 155,000. By 1860 it had grown to 583,000. When U.S. troops occupied Puerto Rico in 1898, the population was close to 950,000. The major cause of this population growth was natural increase among the island's inhabitants. Also, in the course of the century the island continued to attract immigrants from several parts of the world. Between 1822 and 1844, for example, when the Haitian Republic ruled what later became the Dominican Republic, thousands of Spanish-speaking families migrated to Puerto Rico. Immigrants also came from Spain and its possessions, such as the Canary Islands. Immigration was encouraged and facilitated by Spain and its representatives on the island who, following the policies originally included in the *Cédula de Gracias* of 1815, continued to do their best to offer all types of incentives (including state lands and tax exemptions) to those who were interested in immigrating to Puerto Rico.

Puerto Rico in the nineteenth century also experienced important economic changes that had a substantial impact on the island's society and politics. Probably the most important development was the expansion of commercial agriculture in the course of the century. Natural population growth, the immigration of families who often brought with them capital and agricultural know how, the abolition of many limitations on external trade (which got under way in the 1790s and was embodied in the *Cédula de Gracias* and governmental efforts to make the island more productive are all part of the explanation for the gradual expansion of commercial agriculture. Until the latter part of the nineteenth century, Puerto Rico's most important commercial crop and export was sugar, the production of which began in the first part of the sixteenth century and which was given an important boost by the destruction of the flourishing sugar economy of St. Domingue in the 1790s. Between 1830 and 1896, the amount of land devoted to sugar production grew by almost 300 per cent and sugar production rose from 17,000 to 62,000 tons. Accompanying this expansion in sugar output there were some important technological changes. Earlier the bulk of the sugar was produced in primitive *trapiches*. By the last quarter of the nineteenth century, however, large and more modern mills (*centrales*) had made their appearance. Some of these *centrales* were established by French capitalists, others by local businessmen who were organizing on a corporate basis. Although these *centrales* were not as technologically advanced as those established in Cuba around the same period, they did represent a major change in the Puerto Rican sugar industry and were producing by the end of the century a sizeable proportion of total sugar output. To be economically profitable, these *centrales* required increasing amounts of sugar cane land to be cultivated in order to keep the mills busy. Thus, concurrently with the appearance of the *centrales* there was a growing concentration of sugar cane land in the hands of fewer people. In 1882 the Puerto Rican observer José Ramón Abad wrote:

> There have been established in the island factories known as *centrales* . . . which
> have become centers for the absorption of lands and have thus reduced the number

of landowners. . . . Property, before distributed in small holdings, is being accumulated in fewer hands.

This process of concentration of sugar cane land in fewer and fewer hands gained momentum after the U.S. occupation of 1898.

Sugar remained Puerto Rico's most important export during most of the nineteenth century. By the end of the century, however, it lost its preeminence to coffee, whose cultivation began in the eighteenth century and expanded rapidly in the course of the nineteenth. Part of the reason for this was the introduction of hulling machinery and the flow of capital, mostly Spanish, into the coffee sector of the economy. Between 1830 and 1896 the acreage devoted to coffee cultivation increased by almost 600 per cent, and by the 1890s coffee had become Puerto Rico's main export. The nature and growth of the coffee economy in nineteenth century Puerto Rico still remains to be studied. It can be said, however, that as in the sugar sector of the economy there was in the coffee sector a growing concentration of land in fewer hands as the more capitalized coffee plantations absorbed more and more of the smaller coffee farms.

In addition to the expansion of sugar and coffee production, Puerto Rico in the nineteenth century also experienced growth in the production of tobacco. Tobacco exports, however, never reached the importance of sugar and coffee during that century. Unlike sugar and coffee, however, tobacco production stimulated (as shall be described below) the development of some important manufacturing activities in the urban centers.

Throughout the first three centuries of Spanish colonial rule in Puerto Rico the bulk of the acreage under cultivation was devoted to the production of subsistence crops (plantains, bananas, rice, peas and yams). In spite of the growth of sugar, coffee and tobacco production in the course of the eighteenth century and first decades of the nineteenth, the subsistence nature of agriculture did not change radically in many areas. In the second half of the nineteenth century, however, the rapid expansion of commercial agriculture brought about a decline in the proportion of cultivated land devoted to subsistence crops. By the 1890s the acreage devoted to commercial crops exceeded the acreage devoted to subsistence crops (41 per cent devoted to coffee production, 15 per cent to sugar, 1 per cent to tobacco, and 32 per cent to subsistence crops). So during the latter part of the Spanish regime, the Puerto Rican economy increasingly developed away from subsistence farming, while the importance of commercial agriculture grew and the island became more dependent on overseas trade. This development and an increasing population explain why by the 1890s the island was importing a considerable proportion of the foodstuffs it consumed. By the time the U.S. army moved into the island in 1898, the Puerto Rican economy had already taken the classical mold of a dependent colonial economy.

The Spanish government made efforts to restrict in the colonies the development of manufacturing activities that might compete with metropolitan industries and the displacement of capital abroad and in speculation and consumption. Because of this the "industrial" sector of the Puerto Rican economy in the course of the nineteenth century grew very slowly and by the 1890s remained insignificantly small. One of the major manufacturing activities in Puerto Rico at the end of the century was rum distilling, which was tied to the sugar sector of the economy. In the cities the only major industrial activity was the production of cigars, which grew as a consequence of an expanding tobacco output and which took place in large factories and was based on wage labor. Aside from the cigar industry, there were in the cities other small shops producing a variety of commodities (mostly for internal consumption) which were also based on wage labor. But these were relatively unimportant, and the urban proletariat (though restless and already making organizational efforts) constituted at the end of the century a very small proportion of the island's population. At the end of the century, as in the past, the bulk of the manufactured commodities in Puerto Rico were imported from Europe and the United States.

Until the end of the eighteenth century, Spain monopolized the legal foreign trade of Puerto Rico. It was as a consequence of the military and political crisis that overwhelmed Spain in the late 1790s and the first decade of the nineteenth century that the colonial metropolis allowed other nations to trade with the island, a policy not reversed during the rest of the nineteenth century. But although Spain permitted other nations to trade directly with Puerto Rico, she retained preferential trade advantages for herself. Puerto Rican tariffs were generally highest on articles which originated in countries other than Spain. This policy placed some limitations on trade between Puerto Rico and countries other than Spain, but did not prevent it. On the contrary, in the course of the nineteenth century Puerto Rico became increasingly incorporated into the world capitalist economy, and commercial relations between the island and the United States, England and a few other countries expanded. This trade was stimulated by internal demand for a variety of goods (an internal demand that increased as the population increased) and in turn stimulated and was stimulated by the growth of commercial agriculture in the island. By the end of the century Spain supplied less than one-third of the total value of Puerto Rico's imports, the United States about one-fourth, and England and its possessions over one-fourth. These three countries alone accounted for close to 85 per cent of the island's total import trade. Germany, Cuba, and France were the remaining suppliers of importance.

At the end of the nineteenth century about 60 per cent of the goods imported into the island were manufactured commodities such as cotton fabrics, furniture, leather products, iron and steel goods, fabrics of hemp and jute, machinery and soap. The remaining 40 per cent were agricultural imports among which the most important were rice, wheat, flour and hog products. Most of the wheat came from the United States, as did the hog products. Cotton fabrics came primarily from the textiles factories of Catalonia in Spain.

To pay for these imports Puerto Rico at the end of the 19th century exported primarily coffee, sugar and tobacco (which together accounted for close to 90 per cent of the value of the island's exports). Puerto Rico's major markets at that time were Spain, which absorbed about 25 per cent of the island's exports; Cuba, which absorbed about 23 per cent—mostly coffee; and the U.S., France and Germany, each of which took about 10 per cent of Puerto Rico's exports. From Puerto Rico the United States imported primarily sugar. There is evidence that suggests that by the last quarter of the nineteenth century the Puerto Rican sugar industry was becoming increasingly dependent on the U.S. market. In the 1880s, for example, the United States was purchasing close to 80 per cent of the island's sugar exports. This growing dependency on the United States disturbed a few Puerto Ricans such as José Ramón Abad who, like José Martí in Cuba, was not only concerned about the growing economic dependency on the United States but also about the growing dependency of the island's economy on the production of the so-called after dinner crops: coffee, sugar, and tobacco.

The expansion of commercial agriculture in the course of the nineteenth century created a greater demand for labor to work on the sugar, coffee and tobacco establishments. As in the past, slaves continued to play a role in the economic life of Puerto Rico until the abolition of slavery in 1873. The demand for labor created by the agricultural expansion that got underway in the latter part of the eighteenth century brought about an increase in the number of slaves imported into the island. Between 1775 and 1865 the number of black slaves in Puerto Rico increased from 6,467 to slightly over 41,000.

In spite of official legislation (much of it dating back to the sixteenth and seventeenth centuries) designed to protect the slaves against excessive brutality from their masters, the slaves in the nineteenth century remained more or less at the mercy of their owners. This legislation was ordinarily ignored by Puerto Rican and Spanish slaveowners on the island and ordinarily by the Spanish authorities themselves. In fact, often Spanish governors issued laws that blatantly contradicted the spirit and the letter of previous legislation. In 1848, for example, as a consequence of a black slave rebellion in the neighboring island of Martinique and slave revolts near Vega Baja and Ponce in Puerto Rico, Governor Juan Prim issued the notorious *Bando Negro* designed to keep black slaves in Puerto Rico in line. By virtue of the new code, any act of resistance or insubordination on the part of a slave was punishable by death, any act of resistance against a white on the part of a free black was to be punished by cutting off the right hand of the black, a free black who insulted a white man was to be sent to jail for five years, and no blacks from Haiti, the United States, or the French Caribbean colonies (where slave resistance was on the increase) were to be allowed into Puerto Rico. In 1782, Abbad y Lasierra had written that in Puerto Rico the black slaves, "deprived of everything, are condemned to constant hard work, always exposed to the rigors of a brutal or greedy master." Almost 100 years later, Alejandro Tapia y Rivera wrote that "the slave is outside the law and subject to the self interest and arbitrariness of a man who calls himself his owner." Neither was being emotional; both were reflecting a social reality.

As in the past, black slaves in Puerto Rico did not accept their status passively. Individual acts of violence against slave owners were frequent; whenever possible, slaves ran away into the forests of the interior, and small slave rebellions and conspiracies were endemic during most of the nineteenth century. It was partially as an attempt to curb or put an end to slave resistance that Governor Prim issued his *Bando Negro*. Slave resistance continued, but it was a resistance with which the authorities easily coped. In Puerto Rico slave rebellions were quickly and easily repressed, not only because they often lacked effective organization and tended to be local in character, but also because the slave population of the island constituted a relatively small minority. As in Cuba and the sugar islands of the Lesser Antilles, slavery in Puerto Rico was linked to the sugar industry. Unlike in the other islands, however, the slave population in Puerto Rico during the nineteenth century constituted a relatively small proportion of the total population of the island. As Eric Williams has emphasized, the following table has no counterpart in Caribbean history:

Population	1827	1834	1860	1872
Total	323,838	357,086	583,181	618,150
Whites	162,311	188,869	300,430	328,806
Free non-whites	127,287	126,399	241,015	257,709
Slaves	32,240	41,818	41,736	31,635
Slaves as % of total	10%	12%	14%	5%

Source: Eric William, *From Columbus to Castro: The History of the Caribbean, 1492-1969* (New York, 1970), p. 290.

There are several factors that might explain why the proportion of slaves in the total population did not increase significantly in the course of the nineteenth century and eventually declined in the 1860s. Possibly, the slaves were not reproducing as fast as the non-slaves. It is also possible, but doubtful, that slaves were being manumitted in large numbers. Probably, however, the main explanation for the decline in the proportion of slaves in Puerto Rico is that there were several factors limiting the importation of slaves into the island. Slaves were expensive, and there were not many in Puerto Rico who had the capital necessary to import large numbers of them. Furthermore, in the first half of the nineteenth century Spain first limited and then abolished the slave trade in Puerto Rico. For reasons other than humanitarian, England abolished the slave trade in its colonies in 1807, then set out to pressure Spain into doing the same in hers. In 1817 Spain and England signed a treaty whereby Spain pledged itself to end the slave trade in Cuba and Puerto Rico in 1820. Under pressure from Cuban and Puerto Rican slave owners, however, Spain sought to avoid compliance with the treaty. But England continued to exert pressure on the Spanish government, and in 1835 another treaty was signed between the two governments. Not till 1845, however, did the Spanish authorities in Puerto Rico launch an effective campaign against the slave traffic. After that year the number of black slaves imported illegally into the island was insignificantly small.

Since slavery did not meet the labor needs of the expanding commercial agriculture of Puerto Rico in the nineteenth century, the landed elite turned to the free population of the island for labor. A large number of free blacks and mulattoes—who during the nineteenth century outnumbered the slaves—and a sizeable population of "poor whites" lived in the rural areas as subsistence farmers on lands to which they held no legal title. This impoverished population, which grew in the course of the nineteenth century, constituted at the beginning of the century a potential source of labor for both Spanish and Puerto Rican landowners in the island. The problem faced by these landowners was that the free poor population could not be readily persuaded to work as wage earners on the commercial establishments. Land was plentiful and it was easy for the free poor to eke out a simple existence by growing a variety of subsistence crops and raising a few domestic animals such as chickens and pigs. In 1830, for example, the total area under cultivation in Puerto Rico was about 6 per cent. In 1897, in spite of the expansion of commercial agriculture, the figure had risen only to about 14 per cent.

Since most of the free subsistence farmers could not be persuaded to work for wages in the commercial sector of agriculture, in the course of the nineteenth century a campaign was launched to force them to do so. Already in the late eighteenth century there had been complaints about the shortage of labor in the island and demands that something be done to make the independent subsistence farmers seek "useful" employment in the sugar, coffee and tobacco farms. By the end of that century there existed on the island *agregados*—"free" workers who lived as squatters on privately-owned lands and who worked periodically for the landowners in lieu of paying rent. It was in the nineteenth century, however, that significant efforts were made to turn subsistence farmers into workers in the commercial sector of agriculture. When he presented himself before the Cortes of Cádiz in 1809, Power y Giralt demanded the exclusion of squatters from Crown lands and control of these "landless" citizens. Because of the political turmoil in Spain between 1809 and 1823, little was done to meet the demands of the landowners. But once Ferdinand VII was once again secured on the throne of Spain after the chaotic liberal interlude of 1820-1823, these efforts were undertaken. After 1824 laws were promulgated that evicted those who lived as squatters on Crown lands or those who could not show legal title to the lands they cultivated. Island landowners also began to seize lands (actions which were "legalized" by sympathetic courts) worked by independent subsistence farmers. The goal of these acts was not primarily to bring new lands under commercial cultivation. In fact, by the second half of the century a lot of landowners owned large tracts of idle land. The goal was to create a landless peasantry who would be forced to seek employment or sharecropping agreements in the sugar, coffee and tobacco establishments in order to survive. In the 1820s the governmental and private campaign of evictions and land seizures began to pay off. Between 1824 and 1827 alone, the number of *agregados* increased from 14,327 to 38,906.

But the need for labor was such that greater measures were taken by the local authorities. In 1837, Governor Miguel López Baños issued a decree known as *Bando de Policía y Buen Gobierno*, which compelled all of the unemployed landless peasants to work on local plantations and farms. By virtue of this decree, workers were forced to register their names on municipal roles under penalty of fines. Several years later, in 1849, Governor Juan de la Pezuela extended the law so that workers were compelled to carry work books (*libretas reglamentarias*) similar to those still in use in South Africa today. These books recorded the workers' services and were maintained by the landowners who employed them. Workers could not change their places of employment if they had contracted debts with their employers. Loss of the work book was punished by forced labor without pay; repeated loss was punished by six months' imprisonment.

As a result of these laws, which were applauded by the majority of Puerto Rican and Spanish landowners in the island, the number of "free" workers in Puerto Rico increased rapidly in the course of the nineteenth century. According to David Turnbull, who visited Puerto Rico in 1840, there were in 1835 about 41,000 "free" workers, exceeding the slave population by several thousand. In subsequent decades the proportion of the population made up by "free" workers in the rural areas increased, while that of the slaves decreased. And whereas the slave population remained overwhelmingly black, the "free" workers included free blacks, mulattoes and whites. Turnbull wrote that in Puerto Rico "free" whites worked alongside slaves on the plantations.

The majority of the landless workers usually remained attached to a particular sugar plantation or coffee or tobacco farm. Usually they received a small plot of land to grow subsistence crops and raise a few animals. In the coffee and tobacco areas, the *agregados* usually entered into sharecropping agreements with the landowners on whose lands they lived. In the sugar plantations, they were usually required to work during the harvest season and at other times of the year in lieu of paying rent. The *agregados*, however, were not the only "free" workers in the island. Thousands of small farmers who managed to retain part of their land in spite of governmental and private efforts to evict them came to depend on the neighboring sugar, coffee and tobacco establishments for occasional employment. Since official currency was hard to come by (especially in the rural areas) the wages of these parttime workers usually took the form of vouchers (*vales*) that could be used to purchase commodities only in the stores set up by the employers for whom they worked.

There is evidence that suggests that like the black slaves, many of the subsistence farmers who were evicted from their small farms and forced (by law and necessity) to work in the commercial sector of agriculture resented and resisted the encroachment of agro-capitalism. It was this resistance, as well as the periodic slave rebellions and conspiracies, that in the early 1860s led local authorities in several parts of the island, especially in the sugar producing areas, to organize the *Guardia Rural*. The *Guardia Rural* was a rural police force that a few years later was joined by the Spanish *Guardia Civil* to enforce the labor codes and to protect the interests of Spanish and Puerto Rican landowners.

The laws regulating the activities of "free" workers in Puerto Rico were repealed in 1873—the same year that slavery was abolished in the island. Repeal of these laws, however, did not destroy their results. By 1873 there existed in Puerto Rico a large number of rural workers, harshly exploited and living an impoverished existence. The numbers of these rural laborers increased after 1873 and became even greater after the American occupation of Puerto Rico in 1898.

At the end of the nineteenth century about 85 per cent of the total population of Puerto Rico lived in the rural areas. Although there still existed throughout the island thousands of small independent subsistence farmers, rural society was essentially divided into two classes. At the top there was a relatively small elite of Puerto Rican and Spanish landowners who owned a large proportion of the land (almost all of the land devoted to sugar, coffee and tobacco production) and who enjoyed great power and social prestige. This elite could always count on the local Spanish authorities when faced with workers' resistance and insubordination. Below the landed elite, there were the *agregados* and the thousands of subsistence farmers who periodically worked on the sugar, coffee and tobacco establishments to supplement their incomes. Between the workers and their employers there often existed ties of *compadrazgo* (godparenthood) that allowed the landowners to camouflage the exploitative relationships under the guise of protecting "their" workers; in exchange for this protection, workers were expected to obey and respect their employers.

On the whole, the rural population remained poor, illiterate, isolated from the main urban centers, exploited and abused and often brutalized by the *Guardia Rural* and the *Guardia Civil*. But in spite of the harshness of life, the rural poor found time to amuse themselves. In the rural areas the most popular pastimes were dancing, horse raising and cockfighting—the latter being almost an addiction among many rural inhabitants. Periodically, the people of the rural areas would go to nearby towns to participate in religious festivals, to have their children baptized, to be married or just to gossip. Most of the towns of the interior were small and lacked many facilities, especially when compared with the coastal centers. The municipal governments of these towns were controlled by the landed elite and operated under the careful eye of the Spanish authorities. The permanent population of these towns was small, usually consisting of a few shopkeepers, local officials, artisans, household servants, a priest or two and, in the case of the larger towns, a few teachers and the families of some of the members of the landed elite. By the end of the nineteenth century these families ordinarily had properties and houses in the towns and resided there for part of the year while their lands were supervised by foremen usually related to them by kinship ties.

As a result of a growing population, expanding agriculture and growing commercial relations with the external world, the main urban centers in Puerto Rico in the course of the nineteenth century grew both in size and social complexity. In the nineteenth century the most important cities in Puerto Rico were coastal cities: San Juan, the political, ecclesiastical and commercial capital of the island; and Ponce and Mayagüez, both thriving commercial centers. In these cities the elite was composed of royal bureaucrats, military officers, higher clergy, merchants, some members of the landed elite and a relatively small group of professionals (lawyers, doctors and teachers). Below the elite were artisans, shop keepers and soldiers. And below these was an impoverished mass of household slaves, workers, street hawkers, beggars and the perennial thieves and prostitutes. Members of this lower social stratum ordinarily lived in shacks on the periphery of the cities. By the end of the nineteenth century the walled area of San Juan had a total population of nearly 32,000 and perhaps 15,000 more lived between the city and Rio Piedras.

The majority of the members of the urban elite were Spaniards. Almost all of the members of the bureaucracy (from the governor down), the military establishment and the higher clergy were Spaniards, born in Spain and loyal to the colonial metropolis. Although by the end of the nineteenth century there resided in the coastal ports an increasingly important community of Puerto Rican merchants, most of the members of the merchant community in these cities were Spaniards who, together with the few Puerto Rican merchants, controlled the import-export trade of the island. Between these merchants and the landed elite there were close economic relations. It was on these merchants that the sugar, coffee and many of the tobacco producers depended for the credit necessary to keep their operations going.

The growing affluence of the landed elite and the merchant communities and some improvements in the educational system made possible the growth in nineteenth century Puerto Rico of a group of Puerto Rican professionals and intellectuals who were usually related to members of the landed and urban elites. Occasionally an individual of lower class origins was able to get an education and (in a few cases) obtain a university degree; however, the majority of professionals and intellectuals in Puerto Rico in the nineteenth century were the sons of local merchants and landowners who had the status and money to provide them with an education. Since the island did not have a university, those who desired a university education had to go abroad. Most went to Europe, others to the United States and Latin American universities. It was out of this small group of Puerto Rican professionals and intellectuals—some of whom had studied in European universities and been deeply influenced by the nationalism that was rampant in Europe at the time—that the leadership for pro-independence and reformist movements came.

In attempting to explain the development of pro-independence and reformist activities in Puerto Rico in the course of the nineteenth century, it is important to take account of the growing sense of national identification that emerged during that century. Already in the latter part of the eighteenth century the historian Abbad y Lasierra had commented on the growing dislike toward Spaniards on the part of those born in

Puerto Rico, a dislike that manifested itself in a tendency among members of the creole elite on the island to think of themselves as different from Spaniards. This tendency became more marked and widespread (primarily among the professionals, intellectuals and members of the landed elite) in the nineteenth century. And it was the professionals and intellectuals who gave voice to this growing sense of national pride. In 1843, for example, a small group of young Puerto Rican writers in San Juan began the publication of the *Aguinaldo Puertorriqueño*, which included prose and poetry and which reflected the growing pride of young Puerto Rican writers in their land. The following year, another group of Puerto Ricans published in Barcelona, Spain, the *Album Puertorriqueño*, which was so nationalistic in sentiment that the Bishop of San Juan ordered the confiscation of copies of the book circulating in Puerto Rico. Among those involved in the publication of the *Album* was Manuel A. Alonso (1822-1889), a young Puerto Rican medical student who in 1849 published (in Barcelona) *El Gíbaro*, considered by many the first important piece of Puerto Rican literature. Using the language of Puerto Rican peasants to present vividly their mores and way of life, Alonso described faithfully and with pride the traditions and customs of his country.

National pride also was reflected in the growing interest of Puerto Rican intellectuals in the history of their island. By the middle of the nineteenth century there existed in Puerto Rico the *Sociedad Recolectora de Documentos Históricos de la Isla de San Juan Bautista*, and in the second half of the century a small group of Puerto Rican historians emerged on the island whose work reflected the growing interest among intellectuals in their past. There were, for example, Alejandro Tapia y Rivera, who published in 1854 the *Biblioteca Histórica y Geográfica de Puerto Rico*, and Salvador Brau, probably the most important Puerto Rican historian of the nineteenth century.

Pride in the land of their birth was so strong among Puerto Rican professionas and intellectuals that it brought with it an increasing bitterness towards the Spanish presence on Puerto Rico and the colonial status of the island. They resented the economic and "moral" backwardness of their land and identified Spanish rule as the source. They resented the arbitrariness of the Spanish colonial administration and the official policy of excluding those born on the island from administrative positions. Gradually some of the Puerto Rican professionals and intellectuals became more vocal in their demands for reforms, and as the years passed a few concluded that the only solution to the colonial problem and the humiliations that the colonial system imposed on them was total separation from Spain.

But a growing national pride alone does not explain the growing demands for reforms and eventually for independence that made themselves felt in the island in the nineteenth century. Economic factors must also be taken into accunt if one is to make sense of the way Puerto Rican politics developed in that century. There is an important and direct correlation between the various political movements that appeared in Puerto Rico in the nineteenth century and the emerging social classes on the island—a correlation that still needs to be studied in detail but whose outlines can be roughly described. As is to be expected, those whose jobs depended on the continuation of the colonial status quo vocally opposed any changes in the status of the island or reforms of a political nature. The Spanish officialdom and the Spanish military on the island were among these. So were the members of the higher clergy. In addition, those whose economic activities depended on the continuation of a close association with Spain were either totally against political reforms of any kind or opposed to reforms that might endanger that association. Spanish merchants (and a few Puerto Rican ones) involved in the trade between the island and Spain, generally supported the colonial authorities against those who demanded political changes. Many of the coffee growers (Puerto Rican and Spanish) who depended heavily on the Spanish and Cuban markets and whose product was protected in those markets against foreign competition (e.g. Brazil) tended to support either the colonial status quo or those groups who demanded some political reforms that would give them a greater voice in insular affairs but would keep Puerto Rico within the Spanish economic system. On the other hand, the handful of merchants who carried on the import-export trade between the island and the United States resented existing policies (tariffs, etc.) that hindered the further development of that trade and therefore tended to support changes that might bring freer commercial relations with the United States. Similarly, many sugar producers, whose main market was the United States, tended to support the demands for economic and political reforms voiced by the professionals and intellectuals. Economic interests, then, were a determinant factor in shaping Puerto Rican politics in the nineteenth century. However, national origins did play a role: Spaniards were more likely to favor closer relations with Spain than were Puerto Ricans.

Those who supported the colonial status quo and fought against any type of political reforms became known by the second half of the nineteenth century as *incondicionales* and later (when they organized themselves in a formal political party) as *conservadores* (conservatives). Perhaps the most important spokesman for this group was José Pérez-Moris editor of the *Boletín Mercantil*, the most important conservative newspaper in Puerto Rico. To Pérez-Moris, as to most conservatives, all demands for political reforms were treasonous and to be treated as such by the authorities. He was particularly infuriated by talk of "democracy" so often heard among reformist groups. Christ, after all, he once declared, had been executed by democratic acclamation.

Actively supported by the colonial administration, the Spanish military and the higher clergy, the conservatives enjoyed a powerful position in the island and did their best to use it against those who desired political reforms. Despite strong opposition, the reformist movement that emerged on the island during the first two decades of the nineteenth century not only survived but gained momentum in the course of the century.

The reformist movement in Puerto Rico not only faced formidable opposition within the island and among the metropolitan authorities, but also had to cope with important internal divisions. In the course of the nineteenth century the movement split into three groups, two of which sought reforms while keeping the island within the Spanish imperial system, and one of which concluded that the necessary reforms could only be achieved through independence. Of these groups the least important were the *asimilistas*, who enjoyed some support among Puerto Rican merchants and coffee planters tied to the Spanish metropolis, but who, nevertheless, remained a small and relatively impotent force throughout the nineteenth century. The goal of the assimilists was to end the colonial status of Puerto Rico and to have the island declared an integral part of Spain. Its inhabitants would then enjoy all the rights and privileges enjoyed by Spanish citizens. The assimilists, then, were in fact denying the separate identity of Puerto Rico.

Far more important than the assimilists were the *autonomistas* who were by the latter part of the nineteenth century the most important reformist movement on the island and who, as shall be shown below, accomplished some of their goals by the time of the U. S. occupation in 1898. Arguing that political authority is not legitimate unless it represents the members of the community over which that authority exercises power, the dream of the autonomists was to establish between Puerto Rico and Spain a relationship similar to that established between Canada and England. The autonomists, then, did not desire a complete break between Puerto Rico and Spain. Their major goal was to have Spain grant Puerto Rico (or grant the Puerto Rican elite) the right to play a central role in the administration of the island and in the shaping of economic policy for Puerto Rico. The autonomists not only desired full representation in the Spanish Cortes, but also municipal autonomy in the island and a greater role in the central administration of Puerto Rico. The autonomist movement drew its support primarily from the landed elite (especially the sugar producers) and merchants who were involved in the import-export trade with countries other than Spain. The leaders and chief spokesmen, however, were professionals and intellectuals. By the end of the nineteenth century the most important autonomist leaders on the island were Luis Muñoz Rivera (1859-1916), the son of an affluent merchant in the town of Barranquitas, a self-educated man, and founder of the newspaper *La Democracia* (1890); and José Celso Barboas, a black man born in Bayamón in 1857. The son of a bricklayer, Barbosa's intelligence caught the attention of his father's employer, who made it possible for him to study medicine at the University of Michigan. Of these two men, Muñoz Rivera became the more important and the more successful in realizing the goals he set for himself. And he was successful because he was the opportunistic politician par excellence. He once described himself as "eminently practical," and declared:

> We are not bent on fighting useless battles or pursuing the impossible. For those who cherish beautiful ideals, let us imagine whether the idea is possible and then make haste to follow its luminous path. If it cannot become a reality, let us limit our desire to the dictates of reason, rather than waste our energies in fruitless combat.

Within the autonomist movement in the latter part of the nineteenth century there were some men who went along with the opportunistic guidelines expounded by Muñoz Rivera and who became involved in the autonomist movement, not because they felt that autonomy was the real solution to the colonial problem but because they saw autonomy as one step (as a gateway) to full independence. Among these the most important were Román Baldorioty de Castro (1822-1889), a native of Guaynabo and a graduate of the University of Madrid; Rosendo Matienzo Cintrón (1855-1913), a native of Luquillo and also a graduate of the University of Madrid; and José de Diego (1866-1918), a native of

Aguadilla, educated in Spain and one of Puerto Rico's most important poets. After the U. S. occupation of 1989 both Matienzo Cintrón and José de Diego broke with the opportunistic politics of Muñoz Rivera and became outspoken advocates of complete independence for the island. The intransigency of the Spanish colonial authorities and the conservatives, the attitudes of the colonial metropolis towards Puerto Rico and the failure of the reformist groups to obtain any meaningful political reforms for the island led some of the more radical reformists to the conclusion that the only solution to the problems that afflicted Puerto Rico was independence from Spain. As was pointed out in the first part of this essay, pro-independence sentiment in Puerto Rico during the first two decades of the nineteenth century was almost nonexistent. That, however, is not to be interpreted as meaning that there were none in the island who advocated independence at that time. In fact, as early as 1809, when Power y Giralt was chosen as the Puerto Rican representative to the Spanish Cortes meeting in Cádiz, some members of the municipal council of San Germán urged that he petition the Cortes for independence, something that was anathema to him and that he totally ignored. Two years later, in 1811, a small pro-independence conspiracy was discovered and crushed by the Spanish authorities in San Germán. But these were small and isolated affairs that had no impact on island politics save to place the local Spanish authorities on their guard.

In spite of the repressive apparatus of the Spanish colonial administration in Puerto Rico, laws declaring treasonous pro-independence activities and the refusal of the Puerto Rican landed elite to back such activities, the pro-independence sentiment became more marked among the members of the professional and intellectual elite in the course of the nineteenth century. As already has been suggested, however, many of these saw independence as an impossible dream and decided to concentrate their efforts on the struggle for autonomy, which they saw as a step towards independence. A few, on the other hand, refused to follow this opportunistic path. In 1838 the Spanish authorities discovered in the island a conspiracy to declare Puerto Rico's independence. Of those involved in the conspiracy a few were exiled to Spain, others fled to Venezuela and a few were imprisoned in San Juan or executed. One of the nationalists, Buenaventura Quiñones, was found dead a few days after he was thrown into one of the cells of El Morro.

By the 1850s the chief spokesman of Puerto Rican independence on the island was Ramón Emeterio Betances. Born in Cabo Rojo in 1827 of an affluent family, he was educated in France, where he studied both in Paris and in Tolouse. He still was in Europe during the revolutions of 1848, events which influenced him deeply. After receiving a degree in medicine he returned to Puerto Rico in the 1850s and dedicated himself first to the abolition of slavery and then to the independence of his native land from Spain. While he carried on his medical practice in Mayagüez, he founded there a secret society. His activities were discovered by the authorities and he was forced to leave the island. After living in Paris for a few years, he once again returned to Puerto Rico and continued his struggle for independence. Early in 1867 the Spanish authorities once again discovered Betances' pro-independence activities and ordered him to report to the authorities in Madrid. Rather than do that, he secretly left Puerto Rico and went to New York City, where he established close contacts with Cuban revolutionary exiles. In a letter which was published in the *New York Herald*, Betances declared, "It is a waste of time, money, and energy to expect reforms from the Spanish government."

From New York and later from Santo Domingo, Betances set out to organize a rebellion in Puerto Rico. He tried to gain the support of autonomist spokesmen in Puerto Rico, such as Baldorioty de Castro, but these men refused his overtures. They remembered the failure of the conspiracy of 1838 and believed that because of the powerful military presence of Spain on the island a bid for independence was almost suicidal. Betances, however, refused to give up. In Santo Domingo he established the Puerto Rican Revolutionary Committee and continued his preparations for a revolt in Puerto Rico. Arms were gathered and men recruited. In the meantime, he established contacts with pro-independence elements in Puerto Rico. There his main contacts were Manuel Rojas, a native of Venezuela who owned a farm near the town of Lares; Mariana Bracetti, a native of Mayagüez and sister-in-law of Rojas; and Mathias Bruckman, a native of the United States who had lived in Puerto Rico for many years and who had become a close friend of Betances during the years Betances practiced medicine in Mayagüez.

By the beginning of 1868, Betances had moved to St. Thomas in the Virgin Islands. By this time a flag for the forthcoming republic had been designed and Betances had issued his famous Ten Commandments of Free Men. In these commandments he called for the abolition of slavery, the right to decide on taxes, religious freedom, freedom of the press, freedom of speech, freedom of commerce, freedom of assembly and the right to bear arms—a democratic political program that on the whole was unconcerned with socio-economic issues (there was no mention in the commandments, for example, of ending the expropriation of lands used by "squatters" or of ending the *agregado* system).

The revolt that Betances organized was scheduled for September 29, 1868. The Spanish officials in Puerto Rico were informed of the plans and pressured the authorities of St. Thomas into forbidding Betances and the troops he had gathered from leaving the island. His ship *El Telégrafo* was detained in St. Thomas and Betances was personally prevented from going to Puerto Rico. In spite of this setback, however, his collaborators in Puerto Rico decided to go ahead with the plan. On September 23, they marched from Rojas' farm and occupied the town of Lares. There they declared the independence of Puerto Rico, raised the flag of the new republic, and forced the parish priest to celebrate a *Te Deum* mass to honor the event.

How many men were involved in the Lares revolt still remains a subject of debate. The estimates run from a few hundred to several thousand. One thing is certain: The Lares revolt was a failure. It failed because the Spanish authorities had been informed of what was coming and had taken precautions. It failed because the rebels had acted in haste; it failed because the revolt received no support from the Puerto Rican elite, and, most important, it failed because the masses did not rally to it. Although Betances and some of his close collaborators had a genuine concern about some of the problems afflicting the Puerto Rican masses (they were, for example, outspoken advocates of abolition), his movement, like that of the autonomists, remained elitist in nature. There was no attempt to develop a socio-economic program that might have helped to mobilize the masses on behalf of the rebellion. Even the slaves, whose freedom was declared by the abortive republic did not rally to its support. But even if the rebels had gone to the masses, it is doubtful that they could have mobilized the masses in force. For one thing, the main concern of Betances and his followers was to establish independence. To the Puerto Rican peasantry that was an unimportant issue. They were concerned with socio-economic questions like land, not with forms of government. Years after the Lares revolt the Puerto Rican observer Francisco del Valle Atiles wrote that "as far as forms of government are concerned, the Puerto Rican peasant shows little concern." But even if the Puerto Rican peasantry had seen in independence the possibility of better lives for themselves, their mobilization would have been difficult. The presence of the *Guardia Civil*, the *Guardia Rural*, and regular Spanish troops in the rural areas, and the control exercised by the landed elite (which as a group opposed independence) over a large proportion of the peasantry would have made the mobilization of the rural masses on behalf of the revolt difficult.

The Lares revolt lasted for a few days. Within 24 hours the Spanish military had broken the backbone of the revolt, and although small bands of rebels continued to operate in the mountains for a few weeks thereafter, that resistance was easily crushed. Of those involved in the revolt several went into exile, a few were executed and hundreds of Puerto Ricans, many of whom were advocates of autonomy and had nothing to do with the revolt, were kept in the dungeons of El Morro for several weeks. Betances spent most of the rest of his life in Europe, and never again returned to Puerto Rico. But although it failed, the Lares revolt had its symbolic importance. It established a history of struggle and became a point of reference for all subsequent liberation fighters.

A few days after the Lares revolt, the military in Spain overthrew the monarchy of Queen Isabella II and political disorders spread throughout the country. Between 1868 and 1873, the new regime in Spain experimented with an imported monarch (Amadeo of Savoy) and prepared a new constitution for the country (1869) which provided for representation from the colonies. The monarchy of Amadeo did not last long. Those who supported the son of Isabella (the future Alfonso XII) and those who supported the Carlist pretender to the throne refused to back the new monarchy. Also, the new government had to cope with a destructive and violent revolt that broke out in Cuba in 1868 and lasted till 1878. Republican elements in Spain took advantage of the chaos and in 1873 took over the government and declared their country a republic. But the republican camp was divided between those who favored a centralized republic and those who favored a federal republic, and it had to face the opposition of monarchical groups, a Carlist revolt, a deteriorating economic situation and the spreading war in Cuba. In 1874 the Spanish military destroyed the republican government and restored the monarchy. In 1875, the son of Isabella II was crowned king of Spain.

If the failure of the Lares revolt strengthened the belief of many members of the professional and intellectual elite in Puerto Rico that independence was an impossible dream, the situation in Spain between 1868 and 1874 opened for them the vision of political reforms and greater participation on their part in the administration of Puerto Rico. Between 1868 and 1874 the Spanish government authorized the election of 15 deputies to represent Puerto Rico in the Cortes. It also permitted the election of municipal councils and of a Provincial Deputation, a sort of administrative council. Freedom of the press and freedom of petition were established, and political groups were allowed to organize on the island. Although the explanation for these concessions lies in part in the inherent "progressiveness" of the men who ruled Spain between 1868 and 1874, they are best explained in terms of an attempt by the new Spanish government to end the revolt in Cuba (concessions similar to those granted to Puerto Rico were also granted to Cuba) and keep the Puerto Rican elite from following the footsteps of its Cuban counterpart.

It was in the aftermath of the Spanish "revolution" of 1868 that the first formal political parties emerged in Puerto Rico. First to organize were the Puerto Rican reformists (most of them autonomists) who founded the Liberal Reformist Party in 1870. A few months later, the defenders of the colonial status quo established the Conservative Party. According to the rules set up by the Spanish metropolis, only adult males who could read and write were allowed to vote. Thus, in the early 1870s the two parties competed for an electorate of 20,000. Between 1869 (when the first elections for the Cortes were held) and 1874 (when the republican government was overthrown in Spain) the Liberal Reformist Party had the upper hand. It drew its support primarily from Puerto Rican professionals and intellectuals and from members of the landed elite. During that period Liberal Reformist deputies participated in parliamentary debates in Spain and voted. They also controlled most of the municipalities in Puerto Rico and the Provincial Deputation. But during this period they accomplished little in the way of bringing genuine political and economic reforms to the island. The only success, which can be attributed to a smaller sector of the Liberal Reformist Party, was the abolition of slavery in Puerto Rico.

In the first half of the nineteenth century some of those in the reformist movement became outspoken advocates of abolition. The abolitionist crusade—which developed in Puerto Rico parallel to the abolitionist crusade in Cuba—faced the opposition of both Spanish and Puerto Rican slave owners. In spite of this opposition, however, it grew and gained momentum after the abolition of slavery in the British West Indies in 1833 and in the French Antilles in 1848. Among those most active in the movement by mid century were Betances, José Julián Acosta, Baldorioty de Castro, Julio de Vizcarrondo and Eugenio María de Hostos (without question the intellectual giant of Puerto Rico in the nineteenth century). Some of these men not only freed their own slaves but also organized fund-raising activities to purchase the freedom of others. Within Puerto Rico, however, the abolitionist movement made little headway. Concluding that it was futile to carry on the struggle for abolition on the island itself, by the 1860s the most important leaders of the movement had settled in Spain to carry on their struggle there. Using the Spanish press to voice their arguments, they continuously attacked the institution of slavery as barbaric and behind the times. In Madrid, Puerto Rican and Cuban abolitionists joined and in 1865 founded the Sociedad Abolicionista Española. Among the founders of the Society were José Acosta and Julio Vizcarrondo. It was Vizcarrondo who founded in Madrid the paper *El Abolicionista Español.*

In spite of the efforts of Cuban and Puerto Rican abolitionists, the trend within the Spanish government was against abolition. The reason for this was not the belief of the heads of government in Spain that there was nothing evil or exploitative about slavery, but the argument of Cuban slave owners that the abolition of slavery would wreck the Cuban economy. This view carried a lot of weight in Madrid since Cuba was Spain's most valuable colony. Although in Puerto Rico (unlike in Cuba) the slaves constituted by the 1860s a small proportion of the population and were not crucial to the economy of the island, there were some Puerto Rican slaveholders who made the same argument. But because of the relative unimportance of slavery in Puerto Rico, the opposition of Spanish and Puerto Rican slaveholders was not as formidable as that of the Cubans. Also, as the years went by the argument of the abolitionists that slave labor was more inefficient and expensive than "free" labor began to strike a sympathetic chord among some of the slave owners themselves. "No really acceptable reason," said Puerto Rican abolitionists in a memorandum to the Spanish government in 1866, "can be given for the continuation of slavery in Puerto Rico. The general wealth of the island does not need it; its disappearance will not affect any productive element, and the self-interest of the owners must demand the overthrow of that institution." By the 1860s the main concern of Puerto Rican slave owners was not abolition per se, but that abolition be accompanied by compensation for the slaves they owned.

It was the situation in Spain after 1868 and the revolt that spread throughout Cuba in that year that gave the abolitionists the best opportunity to get their message across and to have slavery abolished in Puerto Rico. In the parliamentary debates the Liberal Reformist deputies from the island not only emphasized the inhumanity of slavery but also pointed out that Puerto Rico offered a suitable atmosphere for emancipation: The number of slaves was relatively small in proportion to the total population and the commercial sector of agriculture depended overwhelmingly on "free" labor. They were also careful to point out that by abolishing slavery in Puerto Rico and Cuba, Spain might be able to end the bloody rebellion that was going on in Cuba and that, they argued, had been precipitated by the intolerable situation in which Cuban slaves found themselves. They continually emphasized that almost all civilized nations had abolished slavery and that it was a blot on the Spanish nation to allow the institution to survive in its Caribbean possessions. Of the Puerto Rican deputies in the Spanish parliament, probably the most effective and eloquent speaker on behalf of abolition was Baldorioty de Castro. "I leave it to this Assembly," he once declared to the members of the Cortes, "to decide whether a Spanish province of 650,000 people should keep a handful of Negroes in bondage. . . . I leave it to them to decide whether a Spanish province can endure the enslavement of man by man, subjected to political servitude as well, with a tyrannical rule felt at home and in the public square."

The war in Cuba, the constant pressures brought upon the Spanish government by Puerto Rican abolitionists and sympathetic Spaniards in Madrid and the establishment of the Republic in Spain in 1873 finally brought the desired results. Among the leaders of the new republican government there were some who believed that slavery should be abolished immediately both in Cuba and in Puerto Rico. The opposition of Cuban slaveholders, however, and the possibility that such slaveholders might join the revolt then raging in Cuba made even the new republican government reluctant to abolish slavery on that island. Puerto Rico, on the other hand, presented a very different situation. Consequently, on March 22, 1873, slavery was abolished there. But it was an abolition with strings attached (strings designed to appease Puerto Rican slaveholders). By virtue of the law of 1873, the 31,635 slaves in the island at that time were required to enter into contracts with their owners for a period of not less than three years. If their owners refused to enter into such contracts, they were to enter into contracts with other persons or with the government. After five years the freedmen were to receive "political rights."

The abolition of slavery was about the only major success enjoyed by the Puerto Rican Liberal Reformist Party between 1870 and 1874. Aside from that, little changed in the island save the elite enjoyed greater control of municipal governments during that period and that formal political parties had been organized. After the overthrow of the republic in 1874, a reaction took hold in Spain that gave support to conservative and reactionary elements in Puerto Rico. The constitution of 1869 was abolished and a more conservative one drawn up. However, in an attempt to bring about some sort of conciliation between conservatives and liberals in Spain and to quiet down the increasingly vocal reformist minority in Puerto Rico, the conservative leadership of the restoration period in Spain (1874-1898) not only gave in to the demands of Spanish liberals for a role in the political system of the restoration, but also gave some concessions to reformists on the island. Political parties continued to be tolerated in Puerto Rico and so were municipal elections and the election of a few representatives to the Cortes. Electoral laws, however, were rewritten to limit the size of the electorate. By virtue of the electoral law of 1878, the vote was limited to males over 25 years of age who paid at least 125 pesetas a year in taxes or came within certain specified groups such as priests, retired officers, holders of academic or professional diplomas and public employees earning an annual salary of at least 2,000 pesetas. These categories enfranchised a large proportion of the Spaniards on the island, the small group of Puerto Rican professionals and intellectuals, and certain members of the Puerto Rican landed elite. In 1880, when the new electoral law was put into operation, only 2,004 out of an adult male population of 374,640 were eligible to vote.

Persecuted and discriminated against, the Liberal Reformist Party continued to exist but followed a policy of abstaining from elections after 1874. Furthermore, the Liberal Reformist Party became divided over the issue of the colonial status of the island. Originally, the party had included both assimilists and autonomists, and for a while the assimilists enjoyed great influence within the party. After the restoration of 1874 and the reaction that acompanied it, disappointed assimilists concluded that the autonomist solution was the best. In 1881 disgruntled assimilists left the Liberal Reformist Party and founded the Assimilist Party, whose aim was the complete assimilation of Puerto Rico with Spain. "Our position is not a mystery," one of the leaders of the new party wrote. "We desire that the future of Puerto Rico be forever united with that of Spain. We seek equality among all the members who form the great Spanish nation."

With the desertion of the assimilists, the Liberal reformist Party fell into the hands of outspoken autonomists. There were some, however, who questioned some party leaders' desire to openly espouse a formal platform for autonomy along Canadian lines. They were afraid that such an open espousal would invite reprisals on the part of the Spanish authorities. Under the able leadership of Baldorioty de Castro, who urged the members of the party to make a formal declaration on behalf of autonomy, the party changed its name to the Puerto Rican Autonomist Party in 1887.

The creation of the Autonomist Party brought the reprisals that some of the Liberal Reformers had feared. Urged and actively supported by the Conservative Party—which equated demands for autonomy with treason—Governor Romualdo Palacios launched a reign of terror against the members of the Autonomist Party, against those suspected of sympathizing with the goals of the party, and even against some of the assimilists as well. Assimilist and autonomist newspapers were closed down, and hundreds of suspects rounded up, thrown into jail, tortured and in some instances executed. The governor controlled communications to such a degree that for months no word could be sent to Spain about events on the island. Antonio S. Pedreira in his book *El Año Terrible del '87* wrote,

> In the jails innocent men and suspects were submitted to brutal tortures, tied with handcuffs, and tortured with little sticks in order to make them confess infamous lies. . . . There were mutilations, broken bones, stabbings, twisted testicles and assassinations, like that of the baker Juan Diaz, that of the director of the newspaper *EL Gato Flaco de Humacao* who was drowned in the excreta of a latrine and that of Corporal Ambrosio of Yauco, who was hung by his testicles.

It was not until the end of the year, when the authorities in Spain learned of what was happening in Puerto Rico and ordered Governor Palacios to end the campaign of persecution he had launched, that the terror subsided. Among those who suffered through the experience was Baldorioty de Castro. He emerged from prison emanciated and ill. Two years later he died in Ponce.

The terror of 1887 convinced many former autonomists that Betances had been right when he wrote in 1867 that "it is a waste of time, money and energy to expect reforms from the Spanish government." During the months the terror lasted, and in subsequent years many autonomists sought exile in neighboring Spanish-speaking islands and in New York City, where they established close relations with Cuban revolutionary groups, as Betances had done in the 1860s. By the early 1890s there existed in New York City a Puerto Rican Section of the Cuban Revolutionary Party, which had been organized by José Martí. In New York, in the Dominican Republic and in secret societies in Puerto Rico itself these men now prepared to struggle for independence.

In the meantime, the Autonomist Party continued to operate in Puerto Rico under the careful eye of the Spanish authorities. After the death of Baldorioty de Castro, the party fell under the control of Luis Muñoz Rivera and José Celso Barbosa. Between the two men there were quarrels. One source of the quarrel was personal in nature. Barbosa, for example, resented the elitist arrogance of Muñoz Rivera. More important, however, in explaining the conflict between the two men and the subsequent split within the party was the different tactics proposed by the two leaders to achieve autonomy for Puerto Rico. Both men realized that if autonomy was to be granted, the struggle on its behalf had to be carried to the Spanish political arena. It was agreed that the Autonomist Party should establish a working relationship with one of the Spanish political parties that might be sympathetic to the autonomists' goals. Barbosa, however, argued that the Autonomist Party should ally itself with the Spanish Republican Party. Muñoz Rivera, on the other hand, rejected an association with the Spanish republicans as foolish and unrealistic. With a clear conception of what Spanish politics were all about, Muñoz Rivera knew very well that the republicans in Spain were a small and impotent political force that had no chance of ever coming to power. Since he knew that the Spanish Conservative Party was adamant about refusing to give Puerto Rico any sort of autonomy, Muñoz Rivera concluded that the only option available to the Autonomist Party was to ally itself with the Spanish Liberal Party, then led by Práxedes Mateo Sagasta. Sagasta's party had been in power in the late 1880's and the chances were good that the party would enjoy power again. In spite of the outspoken opposition of Barbosa, the opportunistic tactics argued by Muñoz Rivera carried the day.

While Barbosa and Muñoz Rivera were arguing over tactics and pro-independence groups were organizing support within and outside Puerto Rico, the Cubans launched their second war for independence in 1895. The war (among whose first casualties was the poet and patriot José Martí) was bloody and destructive. Tens of thousands of Spanish troops were sent to the island to strengthen the already powerful garrisons there. The rebels, however, fought on. On the island, the Spanish commanders applied every savage technique in their effort to repress the liberation movement. Thousands of captives and suspects were tortured or executed. Tens of thousands of Cuban families were removed from rural areas and placed in camps that were described in the U. S. press at the time as concentration camps (decades later, during the Vietnam war, such camps were described as "strategic hamlets").

The war of independence in Cuba stimulated expansionist aspirations among U. S. policy makers, aspirations that dated back to the early part of the nineteenth century. In the United States business groups with interests in Cuba urged the government in Washington to intervene in the Cuban war to "protect American property and American lives." The "yellow press" emphasized day after day the brutal behavior of Spanish troops on the island and also urged intervention. With little reluctance, Washington decided to intervene. At first it tried to persuade Spain through diplomatic channels to give up Cuba. When those efforts failed, the United States used the sinking of the battleship *The Maine*—which had been sent to Havana harbor to protect American lives—as an excuse to declare war on Spain in early 1898.

In Puerto Rico, the outbreak of the war of independence in Cuba opened opportunities that Muñoz Rivera was quick to exploit. In 1896 he traveled to Spain and met with Sagasta. In his discussions with the Spanish Liberal leader, Muñoz Rivera emphasized that the Puerto Rican people were loyal to Spain but that they would no longer tolerate the blatant colonial status in which they found themselves. Sagasta was interested, but refused to make any commitments. Muñoz Rivera then returned to Puerto Rico. While on the island he learned of a pro-independence plot centered in the town of Yauco and through one of his subordinates in his newspaper *La Democracia* denounced the leaders of the conspiracy to Governor Savas Marín. Immediately thereafter the governor ordered the arrest of those involved in the plot while Muñoz Rivera hurried back to Spain to emphasize to Sagasta that the Yauco affair was but an indication of things to come should Spain continue to refuse to grant Puerto Rico some sort of autonomy. Sagasta was convinced, and in the spring of 1897 he and Muñoz Rivera signed a pact in which the former pledged himself to autonomy for Puerto Rico should he come to power in Spain. Soon thereafter, in August, the conservative head of the Spanish government was killed by an anarchist, and Sagasta was chosen to replace him and organize a new government. In November Sagasta kept the pact he had made with Muñoz Rivera and tried to end the war in Cuba by granting both Cuba and Puerto Rico autonomy. The Cuban rebels rejected anything short of independence. The Puerto Rican autonomists, however, received the offer with almost delirious delight. For decades they had opposed independence because many of them thought it was an unrealistic dream but primarily because they knew that in order for the island to get independence it would have to undertake as popular a war as that raging in Cuba. Eager to protect their economic interests and afraid and contemptuous of the masses, the majority of the autonomists were not about to follow a path that would have involved the mobilization of the masses for political struggle. The autonomy now granted to them by Spain would bring a minimum of social and economic dislocation to the island, would place them in a position of political power the Puerto Rican elite had never enjoyed before and would open avenues for further trade with countries such as the United States.

The Autonomous Charter that was granted by Spain to Puerto Rico in November 1897 conceded the island more autonomy (in matters of self government) than the government set up under U. S. domination after 1898. The Charter gave Puerto Rico the right to full representation in the Spanish Cortes, the right to participate in negotiations between Spain and other countries affecting the commerce of the island, the right to ratify or reject commercial treaties affecting Puerto Rico, and it specifically authorized the insular government to frame tariffs and fix customs duties on imports and exports. The Charter vested the power to legislate on internal affairs in a Parliament consisting of two houses: a partially elected Council of Administration of 15 members (7 of whom were to be named by the Governor-General), and an elected Chamber of Deputies of 32 members. To be a member of the Council or the Chamber, a man had to be a native of Puerto Rico or a citizen of Spain who had resided on the island for four consecutive years. The new Parliament could "pass upon all matters not specially and expressively reserved to the Cortes of the Kingdom or to the Central Government." The Charter itself could not be amended except on petition of the insular Parliament.

By virtue of the government created by the Charter, the official head of the government and the representative of the Spanish Crown in Puerto Rico was the Governor-General. He was appointed by the authorities in Spain and he exercised broad powers in matters relating to the Church (which still maintained its position as the only officially tolerated religious institution on the island), the armed forces, the maintenance of law and order and the enforcement of royal laws, decrees, treaties and other acts or measures of the home government that were applicable to

Puerto Rico. In other affairs, however, the Governor-General exercised executive authority on behalf of the cabinet (provisions for which were included in the Charter), which was responsible not to him but to the insular Parliament.

As a result of the first elections under the provisions of the new Charter, Luiz Muñoz Rivera and his followers won an impressive victory and he became the presiding officer of the insular cabinet. On July 17, 1898—the very day that Puerto Rico's first Parliament held its inaugural session—Spanish troops surrendered in Santiago de Cuba which signaled the end of Spanish resistance on that island. Eight days later, U.S. troops commanded by General Nelson A. Miles landed near Guánica in Puerto Rico and quickly proceeded to crush the little resistance they faced from Spanish troops on the island. On July 28, the insular Parliament disbanded, never to reconvene.

The U.S. occupation of Puerto Rico was not a mere side-effect, a peripheral military act, of the war between the United States and Spain. Nor was it the result of efforts by pro-independence Puerto Ricans in the United States who urged Washington to include the island in its plan of operations in order to "liberate" it from the Spanish yoke, as it had promised to "liberate" Cuba once the war with Spain got under way. The U.S. invasion was a deliberate, well-planned act, whose genesis antecedes the official declaration of war against Spain in 1898. By the end of the nineteenth century the United States had become a naval power of importance and was searching eagerly for coaling stations, provision centers and naval bases that would enable its ships to cross the seas with as few stops as possible. In 1891, for example, Secretary of State James Blaine wrote to President Harrison, "I believe that there are only three places of sufficient value to be taken: One is Hawaii and the others are Puerto Rico and Cuba."

But strategic considerations were not the sole (or primary) reason for the growing interest of the United States in Puerto Rico before 1898. In the last quarter of the nineteenth century the United States became an expansionist capitalist country in search of overseas markets for its products and of areas that would supply U.S. industries with raw materials and U.S. consumers with certain commodities that had to be imported. Puerto Rico was seen as an important potential market for U.S. goods (by 1898 the island's population was close to one million) and also as a place which could provide part of the sugar needs of the U.S. home market.

The beginning of the war between Spain and the United States and the realization among a few Puerto Ricans that the island would be occupied by the United States led some to urge the Puerto Ricans to take advantage of the war and declare their independence before the arrival of U.S. troops. That was the position taken by Eugenio María de Hostos and by Bentances. Bentances, who at the time of the war between Spain and the United States was dying in Paris, wrote:

> What are the Puerto Ricans doing? Why don't they take advantage of the blockade to rise up in a mass? It is essential that when the vanguards of the American army land they be réceived by Puerto Rican forces waving the flag of independence, and that it be the latter who give them their welcome.

But Betances' advice went unheard. Unconcerned about the issue of the political status of the island, the Puerto Rican masses either remained passive or welcomed the U.S. troops who were seen by many of the rural poor as liberators from the brutality of the *Guardia Civil*. Muñoz Rivera and other autonomist leaders refused to heed Betances' advice. They did not want a popular revolt. They were upset by the turn of events, but they did nothing to oppose the U.S. invasion, because they foolishly believed that the United States would give Puerto Rico outright independence or, at the very least, a system of autonomy like the one granted to the island by Spain in 1897. The North American troops invaded Puerto Rico, defeated the few Spanish troops who resisted, and established a colonial government. Under the peace treaty signed between Spain and the United States on December 1, 1898, Spain ceded Puerto Rico to the United States, providing that "the civil rights and political conditions of the territories ceded to the United States shall be determined by [the U.S.] Congress."

On September 13, 1898, a couple of months before the Treaty of Paris was signed, María de Hostos wrote in his diary while looking at Puerto Rico from the deck of the steamship *Philadelphia:*

> Yesterday I spent the whole day with my binoculars in my hands; from El Desecheo to El Ataud and from Borinquen Point to Point Ponce, I saw everything; I looked and looked again; I admired it, blessed it, and felt it. I felt it: I mean what the literary dialect expresses in that phrase, not what it says in itself. I felt for her and with her her beauty and her misfortune. I thought how noble it would have been to see her free by her own effort, and how sad and overwhelming and shameful it is to see her go from owner to owner without ever being her own master, and to see her pass from sovereignty to sovereignty without ever ruling herself.

NOTES

Most of the data and factual information in this essay was obtained from the following sources:

Abbad y Lasierra, Iñigo, *Historia geográfica, civil y natural de las Isla de San Juan Bautista de Puerto Rico* [1782] (San Juan, 1866).

Alonso, Manuel A., *El Gíbaro* [1849] (San Juan, 1949).

Atiles, Francisco del Valle, *El campesino puertorriqueño, sus condiciones físicas, intelectuales y morales* (San Juan, 1887).

Babín, María Teresa, *Panorama de la cultura puertorriqueña* (San Juan, 1958).

Babín, María Teresa, *The Puerto Ricans' Spirit: Their History, Life and Culture* (New York, 1971).

Berbusse, Edward J., *The United States in Puerto Rico, 1898-1900* (Chapel Hill, 1966).

Brau, Salvador, *Las clases jornaleras de Puerto Rico* (San Juan, 1882).

Carr, Raymond, *Spain, 1808-1939* (London, 1966).

Carroll, Henry K., *Report on the Island of Porto Rico* (Washington, D.C., 1899).

Cifre de Loubriel, Estela, "Los inmigrantes del siglo XIX—Su contribución a la formación del pueblo puertorriqueño," *Revista del Instituto de Cultura Puertorriqueña*, No. 7 (April-June, 1960).

Córdoba, Pedro Tomás de, *Memorias geográficas, económicas, y estadísticas de la Isla de Puerto Rico*, 6 vols. (San Juan, 1831-33).

Córdoba, Pedro Tomás de, *Memorias sobre todos los ramos de la administración de la Isla de Puerto Rico* (Madrid, 1838).

Cruz Monclova, Lidio, *Historia del año 1887* (Rio Piedras, 1958).

Cruz Monclova, Lidio, *Historia de Puerto Rico* (Siglo XIX), 3 vols. (Rio Piedras, 1952, 1957, 1962).

Cruz Monclova, Lidio, *Román Baldorioty de Castro, su vida y sus ideas* (San Juan, 1966).

De Diego, José, *Obras completas*, 2 vols. (San Juan, 1967).

Díaz Soler, Luis M., "The Abolition of Slavery in Puerto Rico, 1868-1873," *Caribbean Historical Review*, No. 1 (December, 1950).

Documents on the Constitutional History of Puerto Rico, 2nd. ed. (Washington, D.C., 1964).

Crónicas de Puerto Rico, 2 vols., edited by Eugenio Fernandez Menden (San Juan, 1957).

Flinter, George, *An Account of the Present State of the Island of Porto Rico* (London, 1834).

Foner, Philip S., *The Spanish-Cuban-American War and the Birth of American Imperialism*, 2 vols. (New York, 1972).

Fraga Iribarne, Manuel, *Las constituciones de Puerto Rico* (Madrid, 1953).

"Puerto Rico Through New England Eyes," 1831-1834, edited by Frank Otto Gatell, *Journal of Inter-American Studies*.

Gomez Acevedo, Labor, *Organización y reglamentación del trabajo en el Puerto Rico del siglo XIX* (San Juan, 1970).

Jimeno Angius, D.J., *Población y comercio de la Isla de Puerto Rico* (Madrid, 1885).

Maldonado-Denis, Manuel, *Puerto Rico: A Socio-Historic Interpretation* (New York, 1972).

Meléndez Muñoz, Miguel, "El Agrego: Patriarcalismo y feudalismo económicos," *Revista del Instituto de Cultura Puertorriquena*, No. 2 (January-March, 1959).

Memoria de los trabajos realizados por la Sección Puerto Rico del Partido Revolucionario Cubano, 1895-1898 (New York, 1898).

Mintz, Sidney W., "The Role of Forced Labor in Nineteenth Century Puerto Rico," *Caribbean Historical Review*, No. 2 (December, 1951).

Muñoz Rivera, Luis, *Obras completas*, 3 vols. (Madrid, 1920).

Osuna, Juan José, *A History of Education in Puerto Rico* (Rio Piedras, 1949).

Pagán, Bolivar, *Historia de los partidos puertorriqueños, 1898-1956*, 2 vols. (San Juan, 1959).

Pedreira, Antonio S., *El año terrible del 87* (San Juan, 1948).

Perloff, Harvey S., *Puerto Rico's Economic Future: A Study in Planned Development* (Chicago, 1950).

Ramírez de Arellano, R.W., *Instrucciones al Diputado don Ramón Power y Giralt* (Rio Piedras, 1936).

Rivero, Angel, *Crónica de la Guerra Hispanoamericana en Puerto Rico* (Rio Piedras, 1972).

Rosario, Pilar Barbosa de, *De Baldorioty a Barbosa: Historia del autonomismo puertorriqueño, 1887-1896* (San Juan, 1957).

Sendras y Burin, Antonio, *Como se gobierna en Puerto Rico* (Madrid, 1886).

Suarez Díaz, Ada, *El doctor Ramón Emeterio Betances, su vida y su obra* (San Juan, 1968).

Tapia y Rivera, Alejandro, *Mis memorias, 1826-1882* (New York, 1928).

Turnbull, David, *Cuba, with Notices on Porto Rico and the Slave Trade* (London, 1840).

Wells, Henry, *The Modernization of Puerto Rico: A Political Study in Changing Values and Institutions* (Cambridge, Mass., 1969).

Williams, Eric, *From Columbus to Castro: The History of the Caribbean, 1492-1969* (New York, 1970).

Williams, Eric, "The Negro Slave Trade in Anglo-Spanish Relations," *Caribbean Historical Review*, No. 1 (December 1950).

Background to the Emergence of Imperialist Capitalism in Puerto Rico

Angel G. Quintero Rivera

Fallacy of the Thesis of Colonial Capitalism in Spanish America

This article is the first chapter of a broad study on the class history of Puerto Rico. The analysis of the development of contemporary social classes and their conflicts requires an examination of the capitalist economy, on which these class relationships are based. The purpose of this article is to examine the background to the emergence of this type of economy in Puerto Rico.

Puerto Rican historical literature still includes no comprehensive analytical presentation of the pre-twentieth century Puerto Rican economy. All that exists is an extremely limited selection of studies on specific subjects. Interpretations of pre-twentieth century Puerto Rican economic history are to be found in works of a general nature and are, therefore, superficial and inadequate.[1] In these interpretations, the Puerto Rican economy in the nineteenth century is presented as a "rudimentary type of agrarian capitalism"—rudimentary in the technological sense. The great economic change at the beginning of the twentieth century is seen as basically one of degrees of technological

A. G. Quintero Rivera, "Background to the Emergence of Imperialist Capitalism in Puerto Rico", *Caribbean Studies* 13, No. 3 (October 1973): Reprinted by permission of the Author and the Institute of Caribbean Studies. Copyright 1973 by the Institute of Caribbean Studies, University of Puerto Rico.

development—the change from small to large sugar mills, from the *trapiche* to the *central*. In these analyses, capitalism emerges in Puerto Rico alongside Spanish colonialism, or at least as a result of the *Cédula de Gracias of 1815*, which did away with a number of institutional impediments to the expansion of commercial agriculture, and opened the way for commerce, which in turn opened a number of pathways for the development of this type of agriculture.

These interpretations fall within the same tradition as the theory popularized by Andre Gunder Frank[2] (though expounded earlier by Sergio Bagú[3]) in which the colonial economy of Hispanic-America is presented as a capitalist economy. The core of Gunder Frank's theory is that the colonial economy consists of a series of "links of exploitation" stretching from the worker on the land to the power of the metropolis. In each link (agricultural worker-farm owner, farm owner-city merchant, etc.) a ruling minority expropriates the fruits of the labor of a lower stratum (or part of what that lower stratum has in turn expropriated) for its own benefit. In this theory, capitalism is equated with exploitation, with the appropriation of the surplus through the expropriation of productive labor.

This equation is misleading since exploitation can be found in economies with very different systems of production: for example, in the slave economy, in the feudal economy and in the economy based on what Marx called "the Asiatic mode of production."[4] In fact, Sergio Bagú, following a similar line of argument, finds himself obliged to classify slavery as a capitalist institution.[5] But this could lead to the absurdity of speaking of capitalism in the economy of the pharoahs. Capitalism cannot be defined simply as a system of exploitation, but rather by the way in which this exploitation is structured and based. Capitalism is conformed by some relations of production structured in terms of, and resulting in, a specific mode of appropriation of the surplus, and only when this appropriation becomes the axis of the economy.

Another argument put forward in the theory of Gunder Frank and Bagú (an argument present also in many interpretations of nineteenth century Puerto Rican history) is that the Hispanic-American colonial economy was capitalistic because it resulted from capitalism, i.e., it was structured to complement international capitalism. But if our primary concern is the examination of certain social relationships that are structured on the basis of, and relative to, certain types of economy, then the latter must be classified not in terms of causes, but in terms of their nature or of what constitutes them. The Gunder Frank-Bagú thesis tends to emphasize the external relations of the economy, ignoring its internal relations. An analysis of the external relations is important (especially when one is dealing with a colonial economy where these relations are implicit in its very nature). Nevertheless, the significance of the external relations lies not in whether or not they are caused, but in how they influence or are fit into the dialectics of the internal relations.

The emphasis on external relations is linked to another important aspect of the thesis of "colonial capitalism": the identification of capitalism with commerce. This is the central point of the arguments presented in the interpretations of the Puerto Rican economy of the nineteenth century referred to above. According to these interpretations, proof that it was a capitalist economy lies in the considerable increase in commercial activity in Puerto Rico during that century. The equation of capitalism with commerce is also one of the pillars of the Gunder Frank-Bagú thesis. The root of this equation lies in some of the classics of the history of capitalism, and it still is the focal point of some of the most important academic debates on this economic system.

The equation of capitalism with commercial activity emerges primarily from the European experience, where the birth of capitalism was accompanied by an increase in commercial relations; even more so in contrast with the economic system which preceded it (feudalism) whose nature tended to limit commercial activity (which is not to say that commerce did not exist under feudalism, as Gunder Frank erroneously supposes).[6]

The historical identification of capitalism with commerce is not accidental. Commercial activity is structurally implicit in capitalism. The relations of production that shape the system are oriented toward the production of commodities, not so much for their use value, as for their exchange value. This does not imply, however, an identification between production of commodities and capitalist relations of production. In other words, although a certain type of productive relations would imply the production of comodities, the production of commodities does not necessarily imply a specific set of relations of production.[7] Those who adhere to the thesis that equates capitalism with commerce commit this fallacy. Although commercial activity is implicit in capitalism, it does not necessarily imply the existence of capitalism. There are an abundance of historical examples to testify to this.[8]

The thesis of "colonial capitalism," then, is based to a great extent on the fallacy of identifying capitalism with commerce. Both Manfred Kossok and Sergio Villalobos address themselves to this fallacy when they write that "the progressive integration of Latin America into the system of commercial relationships of the world market in the eighteenth century helped to reinforce and consolidate internal feudalism, since these commercial relationships were defined in terms of ownership of land . . ., of the exploitation of natural wealth by means of the exercise of rights over persons,"[9] that is to say, in terms of productive relations based on serfdom (the core of the feudal regime of production), and not on wage labor as capitalism would imply.

The identification of capitalism with commerce makes difficult an analysis of class relations, not only because of the confusion of terms it creates, but also because the only relationships taken into account by this thesis are those concerned with the distribution aspects of the economy, the relations among merchants, or, at the most, between the owners of the means of production and the merchants. If the production process is ignored, there is no basis for class analysis, which is directed basically at the conglomerate of relations arising from the structure of the productive process: the relations between producer and his product, the relationships between direct producers in a situation of social division of labor, the relations between them and the owners of the means of production and between both and the small independent producer.

The increase of commercial activity in Puerto Rico in the nineteenth century, then, cannot be used as evidence of a capitalist development in island or of the predominance of this type of economy.

Within class analysis the fundamental factor in the classification of economic systems is the organization or structuring of the relations of production (what Maurice Dobb has referred to as the regime of production, or the mode of production in the broad Marxist sense).[10] In capitalism these relations of production are encompassed by the concept of *wage labor*. This means that the direct producer has sold his labor power; that is, his productive capacity has become a commodity. The producer, as a man, then finds himself alienated from himself, because he is separated from one of his basic constituents: the capacity to produce. He is also separated from his product, as it does not belong to him, and separated also because his labor activity is not carried in terms of his product but by the wages he receives by selling this activity.[11]

The concept of wage labor implies the existence of people who are able to buy this labor power and convert it into productive capacity, supplying the worker with raw materials and instruments to work with.[12] The raw materials and the means of working them also are subject to the market. Thus, ownership of money is the source of a possible total control of the productive process. The process, as embodied in the social division of labor, will, moreover, tend toward the production of commodities that can be exchanged for money again, perpetuating control.[13] Through control of the productive process, the products can be valued higher than the cost of production, and by means of this surplus value the cycle of the accumulation of capital is initiated. In fact, wage labor already implies surplus value because if the worker has nothing to sell except his labor, the capitalist buying his labor power with wages buys the whole capacity of that labor power for reproducing itself in productive labor.[14]

The concept of wage labor implies a money economy. The direct producer sells his labor power to whoever controls the means of production. Nothing belongs to him except his wages. His life in society revolves around and through his wages, especially those aspects of his life directed towards the satisfaction of his material needs. He sells his labor power and buys what he needs with his wages. The expansion of an economy based on wage labor means that society will be organized around these money-relationships.

The existence of a money economy implies the development of a home market, an organization for the exchange of commodities and the buying and selling of labor. It is important to emphasize that it is not simply a question of the mere existence of trade or money in an economy, but of a *money economy* and a *home market;* a system in which money is the basis of economic relationships and in which the factors of production, as well as the products, are encompassed within a framework of exchange (also based on money).

The rise of the capitalist economy in Puerto Rico must be examined in terms of these elements. The basic questions are obvious: How was the economy progressively getting to be organized around wage labor? When can it be said that this is the center point of the structuring of the relations of production? It is also necessary to deal with matters implicitly linked to wage labor. For example, when can one speak of a money economy and a home market in Puerto Rico? In this article, I will try to trace the background of this process; the background of the rise of the capitalist economy in Puerto Rico, not only because it is necessary for understanding the emergence of this economic system, but because it helps us understand the particular nature of the capitalism that emerged on the island, and the political and social aspects of its subsequent development.

The Seignorial Hacienda

The economy of Puerto Rico developed very slowly during the first three centuries of Spanish colonization. Compared with the wealth of areas like Mexico and Peru, Puerto Rico—whose metal deposits were exhausted by the middle of the sixteenth century—was poor and consequently not a very attractive place for colonizers. The island was used mainly as a military bastion for the defense of Spanish vessels en route between Spain and its mainland American colonies, or as place where some of these ships could stock up with fresh water and supplies.

Apart from soldiers and Spanish officials in San Juan, the island was mainly settled by absconders, deserters, runaway slaves who had managed to escape from the plantations on neighboring islands and some soldiers who, having finished their military service on the island, decided to settle there.[15] Given a low rate of immigration and the rapid decline of the Indian population of the island in the course of the sixteenth century, the total population of Puerto Rico declined from about 50,000 Indians at the time of the Spanish occupation in 1508 to about 5,000 inhabitants at the beginning of the eighteenth century.

Puerto Rico thrived basically on a natural economy. Apart from a very insignificant and sporadic exportation of hides and a few other agricultural commodities, official trade was practically nil, though there is ample evidence of illicit trading or smuggling.[16] This, however, was more superfluous than fundamental to the economy. It took place mainly at the level of barter: ginger or hides for apparel (e.g. shoes, handkerchiefs, lace, jewelry) or for a good *machete* (Manchester blade).

Since local production was fundamentally for subsistence, the Spanish officialdom in San Juan had to depend on financial support from the rich colonial territories in other parts of the Spanish American empire (a system that became institutionalized in the *situado mexicano*). It was not until the end of the eighteenth century that Spain began serious efforts to turn Puerto Rico into a productive colony rather than a dependent one. This concern became a vital necessity when the Empire began to vanish at the beginning of the nineteenth century.

In the first two decades of the nineteenth century a large number of

Spanish families from the emancipated colonies on the Spanish American mainland arrived in Puerto Rico. So did French families from Louisiana and Haiti. Many of them brought their slaves and working tools (or some agricultural machinery) with them. The Spanish government gave them land and facilities to start cultivation. It did away with a whole set of impediments to trade that had been imposed on the island in favor of traders from Seville and, later, Cádiz. As a result, agricultural production for export increased rapidly. This was the situation that the interpreters of the economic history of Puerto Rico who are mentioned at the beginning of this article have erroneously seen as the origins or development of capitalism on the island.

As argued above, an increased activity in commerce is not a sufficient criterion for the classification of an economy. An analysis of the productive process, of the way production is organized socially, is needed. In this respect, the change accompanying the increase in agricultural production for export during the eighteenth and nineteenth centuries is essentially one from a subsistence agriculture of family production to what I have called a seignorial hacienda economy—both pre-capitalist systems of production.

Given the sparse population of Puerto Rico in the eighteenth century and first part of the nineteenth, the scarcest factor of the economy was labor, and the most readily available was land. There are no earlier figures available, but as late as 1830 only 5.8 per cent of the land was under cultivation. This proportion, although it increased, remained small throughout the nineteenth century. In 1897 it was only 14.3 per cent (see Graph 1). This low proportion of cultivated land was not the result of an unequal development of regions, as is common in Latin America, where the population is concentrated in certain areas while large areas remain completely outside the mainstream of the economic life of the country. The population of Puerto Rico in the eighteenth and nineteenth centuries was distributed fairly evenly throughout the island,[17] which meant that there was indeed a large amount of land available for cultivation.[18] In the eighteenth century, therefore, practically all the peasants (except the slaves) were independent producers. Given the choice, peasants prefer to work their own land rather than to work for others.

GRAPH 1. PERCENTAGE OF TOTAL LAND UNDER CULTIVATION (1830-1920)

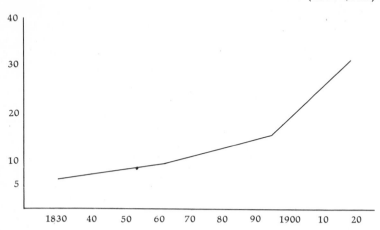

GRAPH 2. PERCENTAGE OF TOTAL LAND DEVOTED TO MAIN CROPS
(1827-1920)

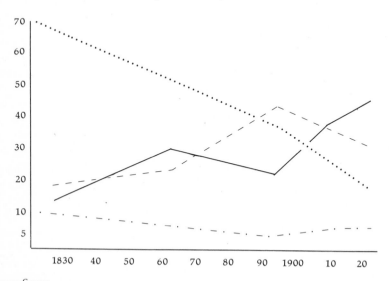

——— Sugar
------ Coffee
.... Minor Crops
. — . Tobacco

For the embryonic haciendas at the beginning of the nineteenth century, land was also a more readily available factor than liquid capital, which was indispensible for the importation of slaves (the slave trade, in any case, was then in its last years).[19] The labor problem facing the developing commercial sector of agriculture was, then, how to get the peasants—who were producing independently for their family subsistence—to work on the haciendas. This was progressively achieved in the nineteenth century, not by the hire and sale of labor (as the development of capitalism would imply) but through dominion of the land and of rights over persons—elements associated with the feudal regime of production.[22]

With the distribution of land to immigrants at the beginning of the nineteenth century (grants made to them by the Spanish government), many peasants found themselves in a situation where the land they had worked for years and had considered theirs was suddenly part of the dominion of some señor, and where the abundant land to which they usually shifted their crops or to which they could possibly move was now also privately owned. This development was accompanied by a series of "anti-vagrancy" laws promulgated by the colonial authoritiesand known as the *régimen de la libreta* (work-book regime) or white slavery. Anyone without trade or property had to carry a workbook signed by the proprietor under whom he was working. Nonpossession of such a book constituted a punishable offense.[23] In order to move from one part of the island to another, the workbook carrier needed the approval of the proprietor under whom he was working. It is impossible to conceive the development of a labor market under these conditions.[24]

Since land was the most abundant factor in the economy, this situation fostered a system where landowners 'graciously' allowed peasants the use of land under their dominion in exchange for work by the peasants in the hacienda or in the owner's demesne. The peasant was given the opportunity to cultivate land for his immediate subsistence needs while contributing to the commercial production of the hacendado. Since the urban population of Puerto Rico was small,[25] the commercial production of the hacienda was almost exclusively for export. Consequently, no home market of any consequence was generated and payment of labor with money made no sense.[26] Even at the end of the nineteenth century, the amount of money circulating on the island was very low and the monetary integration of the economy very weak.[27]

In a period of eight years (1824-1832) for which data is available, the proportion of *agregados* (as the resident farm laborers were called) rose by almost 300 per cent, while the total population of the island rose by 75 per cent.[28] By 1832 there were already clear tendencies of change from an agrarian structure based on small independent peasant producers to an hacienda economy. The estimate obtained for the social structure in that year is as follows:[29]

TABLE 1. PROPORTION OF PEOPLE OF THE TOTAL POPULATION BELONGING
TO FAMILIES OF:

Landowners	46.4%
hacienda owners	1.7%
small producers	44.7%
Agregados	32.5%
Slaves	10.5%
In trade	4.0%
(Not more than 1.8% in what is now generally referred to as merchants or businessmen)	
Artisans	2.4%
Soldiers	0.6%
Others	1.0%
Margin of error	2.6%
	100.0%

Towards the end of the century, the proportion of landowners had declined to 24.6 per cent. (7 per cent hacendados, 2.3 per cent small farmers and 21.6 per cent small independent producers on farms worked exclusively with family labor).[30] The haciendas came to cover almost half of the total land under cultivation (42.3 per cent), thus reducing the proportion of land worked by small farmers and independent family producers to 32.4 per cent. Jointly with the increase of commercial production the haciendas and the expansion of the *agregado* system, another type of tenancy developed: small farmers who worked the land with family labor (like the small producers) but whose holdings were such that they required some seasonal additional labor and whose production exceeded family subsistence needs. This type of farmer owned 25.3 per cent of the land under cultivation toward the end of the century.[31]

The hacienda, as a structure of production, progressively came to dominate the agrarian social structure. It did not attain, however, a position of control (though clearly a position of dominance). This hampered the emergence of situations of conflict among the various strata of proprietors. Moreover, the considerable proportion of medium-sized and small farmers, imprinted a character of continuum to the social stratification, thus hindering a situation of antagonism between the hacienda and the independent producer. In fact, the independent producer came to be linked with the hacienda structure through share-cropping agreements (*medianeros*), working part of the time on the hacienda in return for services or supplementary income, or through kinship ties with the *agregados*. Nor were these types of tenancy separated by different modes of production (in the limited sense): They shared what Marx described as the "petty mode of production." Apart from a few specific phases in the cultivation of coffee (the major commercial crop by the latter part of the nineteenth century) such as harvesting, where a primitive division of labor is found, productive labor in the haciendas was as individualized as on the farms of the small independent producers.

Life around the hacienda was communal. First, it went on almost entirely within the hacienda itself (it must not be forgotten that it was not until the last decade of the nineteenth century that the acreage devoted to commercial crops exceeded the acreage devoted to subsistence production—see Graph 2); and, second, it was shared by the various social strata. In contrast to the large estates in many areas of Latin America, the hacienda in Puerto Rico was generally administered by its owner, who also lived on it. He was an ever present element, as a person, in the life of the laborers and the small producers, just as they were, in turn, present in the life of the hacendado. To a large extent, they shared a common life, although with different roles and from a different social position. The position of the hacendado, whose basis was his control over the means of production, had developed precisely through the productive relations into a whole way of life, which in its dialectical relationship to his position of dominion came to form part of his class interests. Exploitation (expropriation of surplus) was necessary to satisfy the needs of consumption of his position of power and prestige. But just as important for his position—for his way of life—was that he should be respected, admired and even loved by the hacienda laborers and the small producers, with whom he shared his life. In this situation, to try to maximize profits—that is, to organize production in terms of exploitation—could have been harmful to his class interests. These class interests were more intimately linked to his position in his shared life than to profit maximization. The laborers, on the other hand, were tied to the hacienda work by factors other than purely economic rewards: by mutual services[32] and ritual ceremonies.[33] This agrarian structure, with its center or main spring in the hacienda, thus engendered a culture based on deference and paternalism, where the hacendado was (as Bloch says of the European feudal lord) "le premier habitant."

Gateways to Capitalism

The Puerto Rican economy in the nineteenth century was in the process of structuring itself around the hacienda. We cannot speak, therefore, of capitalism in the island, nor of a bourgeoisie or a proletariat. The socio-economic configuration and structural developments of that economy, however, opened some gateways to capitalism. Some of these arose internally within the hacienda economy itself; others from process related (though somewhat marginal) to it.

In the first place, the change from an economy of independent subsistence producers to an hacienda economy represented a structural step towards capitalism (in the sense of what Marx described as the "primitive accumulation of capital") that not only placed one class in a position of being able to purchase labor power, but which also separated the direct producer from the means of production. In this way the foundations for the development of a class needing to sell its labor power were laid.

Second, from the hacienda there emerged a superstructural gateway of some importance. The "outside" world of the Puerto Rican hacienda owners—the United States and Western Europe—was not by this time a feudal world, but one of developing capitalism. The *señores de hacienda* were beginning to identify with the bourgeoisie of these countries; they were reading its literature and philosophy and learning about its trade and wars. Many sons of hacienda owners were sent to study in these countries and the whole process affected them more directly. It is important to point out, nevertheless, that this influence was not simply the result of an intellectual fashion. It had its basis in the concrete life situation of the hacendados, in their situation as creoles faced with Spanish absolutism. "Bourgeois" liberalism provided the ideological tools for the self affirmation of a way of life that, considering a whole range of different circumstances, was becoming progressively differentiated from Spanish life and culture. Absolutism was faced with the principle of reason, and the freedom that rises from it. Faced with an authority of "government by privilege" which was oriented towards the defense of Spanish interests ,the creoles posed the principle of equality before the law.[34]

Thus, a class situated in the productive process in a position similar to that of lords in the feudal regime came to tinge its ideology with bourgeois values. This in turn had repercussions on productive relations. For example, by the last decades of the nineteenth century, when the population had increased considerably and the amount of land available had decreased, some hacendados, influenced by "the capitalist rationality of maximum exploitation of the factors of production," sought new ways of retaining the labor that would permit the maximum possible use of their land in commercial production. For this, the hacienda owner had to provide the workers with the prime necessities of life that previously had been grown by *agregados* on the individual subsistence plots made available to them by hacienda owners. Credit in what was called the hacienda shop (the counterpart of what was known in the United States as "the company store") gradually became a substitute for the plots. (The available documentation suggests that this was not a generalized phenomenon, but one to be found primarily in some large haciendas.) These shops sold on credit basic consumer goods to the laborers, who then had to pay back with labor on the hacienda for whatever they consumed. Some hacendados went a step further and instituted the system of vouchers (*vales*). They paid the workers with vouchers that could only be used in the hacienda shop. With this closed system of exchange, whether by vouchers or credit, the hacienda was assured a fixed minimum labor force in a situation of labor scarcity. At the same time, it ensured maximum profit from the land. Under these circumstances, one cannot speak of buying and selling of labor, nor of the integration of these workers into a money economy. The establishment of hacienda shops, however, was certainly a step in this direction. Nonetheless, social relations continued to be based on deference and paternalism. The hacendado increased or reduced credit arbitrarily for each laborer on the basis of personal relationships with him and according to what he paternalistically estimated the needs of each worker to be.

The superstructural "enbourgeoisement" of the hacendados was linked to a structural problem that was more far reaching: the marketing of the commercial production. The usual mechanics of trade were as follows: A class of merchants, mainly Spaniards, provided credit to the hacendados for their commercial production and were also in charge of marketing the produce.[35] In most cases this involved few monetary transactions. Under credit were included such items as seeds, agricultural machinery and fertilizers. In some cases the hacienda owner paid with part of the production that the merchant himself was in charge of exporting. As is to be expected, the merchants tried to make the most out of this situation of dependency in which the hacendados found themselves.[36] This structural situation was in itself a source of conflict.[37] The ideological opening of the hacendados to the bourgeois world reinforced their struggle to control the commercial aspects of their agricultural production. Puerto Rican politics was born, in fact, with this conflict between merchants (Unconditional Spanish Party or Conservative Party) and hacendados (Liberal Reformist Party, later Autonomist Party) in the last three decades of the nineteenth century. The hacendados fought for institutional credit facilities and access to international trade (trade with Spain and Cuba was controlled by the established merchants).[38]

This internal political struggle and the aspirations it carried were gradually separating the hacendados as a class from the hacienda laborers. The comprehensive common life described above, began to break down, and the shared ideological configuration gradually took two different roads. This became evident, for example, in the different conceptions of work of hacendados and laborers. While for the hacendado, who was turning progressively more towards commercial production in a situation of labor shortage (i.e. more work would have meant more production), work acquired the moral category of virtue; for the small producer or the *agregado*, whose concern was subsistence production, more work than was necessary made no sense. This situation slowly generated two distinct types of morality, which in turn meant a rupture in the "harmony" of hacienda life.[39] Its contradictions as a pre-capitalist mode of production turning towards the production of commodities emerged more clearly.

The credit relations between hacienda owners and merchants not only led the hacendados to get involved in trading activities, but also involved merchants in production.[40] If the hacendado had a bad harvest, he would have to pay off his credit in land. Thus, a considerable number of merchants were becoming landowners as well.[41] Apart from the different relations of production that arose on these farms (administered apparently by overseers—*mayordomos*), such incursions of the merchants into productivity brought about expositions, discussions and plans for the organization of agriculture exclusively on commercial lines, with relationships structured around the production of commodities. This is a process that during the nineteenth century begins to appear, primarily in the sugar cane industry.[42]

It was precisely in the sugar industry (which was losing importance in the second half of the nineteenth century when compared to the growing coffee sector of the' economy) where the emergence of gateways to capitalism was most evident. In contrast with the traditional patriarchal form of proprietorship, types close to corporative ownership were appearing in the sugar industry.[43] Technological specialization was becoming more marked at the manufacturing stage of sugar production,[44] and in both this stage and the agricultural one division of labor became more generalized. In addition, it was this industry that was most affected by slavery which in the Antilles moved more rapidly towards capitalism than the hacienda economy.[45]

It should be made clear that contrary to the experience of other Caribbean islands, the Puerto Rican economy was never predominantly a slave economy. The slave population never exceeded 11.5 per cent of the total population (1846). Furthermore, many of the slaves (the so-called domestic slaves, for example) were not directly involved in productive activities.[46] As on the other islands, however, in Puerto Rico slavery was intimately linked to the sugar industry (see Graph 3).[47] The sharp division in civil status implied by slavery, combined with a growing division in the productive process in the sugar industry,[48] resulted in a marked division between the life of the slaves and the life of the proprietors.[49] In contrast to the communal life shared by *agregados*, small producers, small farmers and hacienda owners, the sugar *ingenios* (mills) presented two distinct life styles,[50] that obviously were interlaced and affected by the paternalism and deference of the hegemonic structure of relations of society at large.[51] Thus, it is not strange that with the abolition of slavery in 1873 many sugar cane haciendas began to organize production on a wage basis (though because of the general organization of the economy and its hegemonic ideology, others tended to maintain the hacienda-*agregado* structure).

GRAPH 3. SLAVE POPULATION COMPARED TO SUGAR PRODUCTION
(1775-1875)

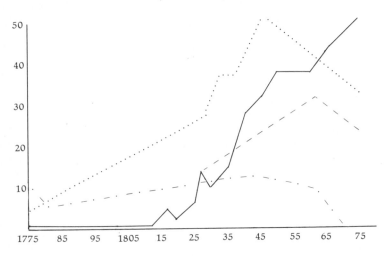

——— Sugar cane production, thousands of pounds
— — — Percentage of land in sugar cane out of total cultivated land
...... Number of slaves, in thousands
. — . Percentage of slaves out of total population

With the abolition of slavery and the decline of the sugar industry,[52] some of the slaves who had been employed in skilled jobs or crafts in the *ingenios* migrated to the large towns. The increase in the labor force of these towns provided by 1896 the basis for the creation and development of large-scale cigar factories based on wage labor.

It was precisely with the growth of the tobacco industry in the urban centers and the rebirth of the sugar industry in the countryside at the turn of the century that the Puerto Rican economy began a rapid transformation towards a capitalist economy. This transformation, rooted in the indigenous developments of the Puerto Rican economy in the nineteenth century, cannot be understood, however, without analysing the impact on the economy of the North American invasion of 1898, which gave capitalism in Puerto Rico a particular imperialist nature.

The Impact of the North American Invasion on the Structure of the Agrarian Economy

In 1898 Puerto Rico became a possession of the United States. The analysis of the impact of this change of sovereignty on the Puerto Rican economy is important since it meant, on the one hand, an acceleration (or precipitation) of processes toward capitalism already present in the latter part of the nineteenth century and, on the other, jointly with these processes a radical change in the nature of economic power.

Although in 1895 the sugar industry produced $4,400,000 in exports (29 per cent of the total value of the exports of the island), by 1920 it produced $74,000,000 and represented 66 per cent of the total value of exports.[53] In 1895 North American investment in the sugar industry was practically nonexistent, while toward the end of the decade of the 1920s almost half of the total production was in the hands of four companies from the metropolis.[54] Although of secondary importance, it is also interesting to note that in 1895 the value of tobacco exports was 4.4 per cent of the island's total and that 25 years later it had reached 19.3 per cent of the total. And while in 1895 there is no evidence of North American involvement in the Puerto Rican tobacco industry, by 1920 North American interests controlled practically all the manufacturing and marketing aspects of that industry.[55]

These changes have been interpreted by many analysts of Puerto Rican economic history as being basically the result of North American technical superiority.[56] Puerto Rico, according to these interpretations, came under North American rule by mere coincidence—as the result of a war between the United States and Spain, whose focal point was Cuba and with which Puerto Rico had nothing to do. Once under the United States, the modern technology of North American companies gained over a backward rudimentary economy. The process is thus conceived as inevitable and nonpolitical. This type of interpretation is erroneous, and its clarification is of fundamental importance for the analysis of the political conflicts in the decades following the North American takeover.

It is a mistake, in the first place, to argue that Puerto Rico and the Philippines became North American possessions simply as spoils of war, as a result of a military adventure. Though the center of the conflict was undoubtedly Cuba, both the Philippines and Puerto Rico were clearly within the North American expansionist interests at the end of the 19th century. There is ample documentary evidence attesting to the strategic-military interest of the U.S. in Puerto Rico before the war of 1898.[57] But economic reasons of a more profound character were also present. Regarding this point, J.A. Herrero has presented the following argument:

> Except in very specific products, the North American nation was conceived since its beginning as bound to purvey itself with the basic necessities of life (that is, within the mythology of self-sufficiency). Sugar was evidently one of the few products which the United States did not produce abundantly. It was necessary, then, to secure territories where sugar was produced or which could be turned into sugar producing areas.[58]

Thus, while towards the end of the nineteenth century 86 per cent of the sugar consumption of the United States was satisfied through imports, by 1932 only 0.4 per cent was imported. The territories acquired directly or indirectly—i.e. Hawaii, Puerto Rico, the Philippines and Cuba—contributed to 76 per cent of the sugar consumed in the United States (see Table 2).[59] It was no coincidence either, that these territories became fundamentally monoproducers of sugar.

TABLE 2. SUGAR CONTRIBUTED TO THE AMERICAN MARKET
SOURCES OF SUPPLY

	Average 1898-1901 Per Cent	1932 Per Cent
1) Louisiana (cane)	11.1	2.6
2) Western U.S. (beet)	3.2	21.1
3) Hawaii (cane)	12.0	16.4
4) Puerto Rico (cane)	2.1	14.7
5) The Philippines	.7	16.6
6) Cuba (cane)	16.6	28.2
7) Others	54.3	.4
TOTAL	100.0	100.0
(3 + 4 + 5 + 6)	31.4	75.9

Moreover, it should not be forgotten that the Spanish American War took place at a time of global imperialist territorial expansion. Describing that period, Paul Sweezy points out, for example, that "Africa, which had been less than 10 per cent under outside domination in 1875, was almost completely partitioned by the European nations during the next 25 years."[60] This was the period when the United States, France and

Germany emerged as competitors to England in industrial production. In these countries, manufacturing (originally oriented towards their own internal protected market) was reaching a level whereby it was being limited precisely by their own market. The expansion of these industrial economies not only created a need for new markets but also necessitated a broader influx of raw materials to be processed. Furthermore, given the capitalist nature of these economies, with a tremendous increase in manufacturing there followed accumulation of capital seeking investment. As the surplus of capital increased, interest rates declined and financiers were forced to seek low-wage labor markets for profitable investment.[61] That this process was taking place simultaneously in several formerly protected economies, and that these economics rivalled England in a relatively short time span generated a situation of competition for control of the nonindustrial countries of the world, preferably (given the protective pattern of the time) by the inclusion of these areas within the tariff and custom barriers of the industrial powers. This would insure a steady supply of raw materials, control of markets for manufactured products, and would provide a framework of security for their investments (i.e. capital exportation).[62]

The economic history of Puerto Rico in the years following the North American invasion fits perfectly into this pattern of imperialist development. Regarding the flow of capital from the U.S., it is of great significance that just after the war of 1898 ended, the Washington Bureau of Statistics reported large numbers of enquiries, "chiefly from the great producing and business centers," as to "the opportunities for American capital and skill to develop the resources of the island."[63] North American literature of Puerto Rico of the year 1899 also testifies to this interest in investment.[64] It is also of great significance that the first North American civil governor of Puerto Rico published an essay specifically on this matter as soon as he stepped down from office in 1901.[65] There are no total figures for investment during these years, but there are documents that indicate that during the four years following the North American occupation of the island, the Porto Rico American Tobacco Company purchased the main centers of tobacco processing and gained an early control of that industry.[66] There is also ample evidence showing that the sugar mills (*centrales*) that eventually controlled raw sugar production were established by North American companies during the first decade following the invasion of the island by North American troops.[67] These companies quickly displaced the French companies that had begun to invest in the sugar industry in the latter part of the nineteenth century.

Besides being oriented to supplying sugar for U.S. consumers, the development of the sugar industry after 1898 also was designed to serve as a source of raw material to be processed in the new colonial metropolis. No sugar refineries were permitted to be established in Puerto Rico (except for a few serving exclusively the Puerto Rican internal market, and established at a later date). Puerto Rico became, therefore, an exporter of raw sugar to be processed in the metropolitan economy.[68]

The emphasis on raw sugar production is intimately linked to an additional imperialist aspect of the North American takeover of Puerto Rico: the development of the island as a market for U.S. products. Interests from the metropolis eventually pushed Puerto Rico into a situation of a one-crop economy, of sugar mono-production and, by definition, an import-export economy. Mono-production developed jointly with metropolitan control of customs and tariffs and turned into the purest form of commercial imperialism. The North American military invasion paved the way for U.S. commercial interests. A North American eye-witness account noted, for example: "American commerce followed sharply upon the heels of the American Army."[69] And the development of that commerce was such that four decades later, during the climax of sugar mono-production, Puerto Rico was the greatest per capita purchaser of U.S. goods. With a population of two million, Puerto Rico was then the U.S.'s second largest customer in Latin America and the ninth largest in the world.[70]

It was not by mere coincidence, then, that Puerto Rico came to be under U.S. domination; the United States was indeed interested in Puerto Rico as a potential market for U.S. products and as a potential major source of sugar before the war of 1898. It is also erroneous to argue that the hegemony of U.S. companies in Puerto Rico was the result of technical superiority. There are two other factors of greater importance: first, a series of economic measures taken by the first North American governors, or directly by the metropolis, aimed at displacing insular producers and assuming control of the means of production; and second, a particular state in the development of the social classes and its conflicts that permitted this to happen.

The first of these economic measures that must be considered is the inclusion of Puerto Rico in the protective market of the United States, which formally took place in 1901 (though it had been envisioned at the time of the North American occupation of the island in 1898). This inclusion placed the cultivation of products required within this market in a favorable position. For Puerto Rico this meant sugar and tobacco. The coffee market in the United States was supplied by Brazil; Brazil produced the most inexpensive type of coffee and it was preferred by North American consumers. At the time of the U.S. occupation, the main markets for Puerto Rican coffee were in Europe.[71] The inclusion of Puerto Rico within the U.S. protective tariff system reduced the number of European ships that arrived in San Juan with European goods to be sold in the island (goods that under the new market structure being created by the United States would be imported from the North American metropolis) and that returned to Europe with Puerto Rican coffee to be sold in European markets. (Sending ships solely to transport coffee from the island to Europe would have been extremely expensive and would have made the price of Puerto Rican coffee in European markets forbiddingly high.) In addition, Puerto Rican coffee as a U.S. product faced after 1898 higher tariffs in its former European markets, especially in Spain.[72] These developments were immediately reflected in a rapid decline in the amount of coffee exported by Puerto Rico.[73]

In contrast to coffee production, sugar production had been decreasing during the last decades of the 19th century (see Graph 2) and had generated a situation by the time of the North American invasion whereby a large proportion of coastal land previously used for sugar production lay idle. The inclusion of Puerto Rico in the U.S. market created among many hacendados a desire to shift from coffee to sugar production[74] and among many landowners of idle sugar cane land a desire to put their lands under cultivation. (Tobacco was a crop requiring considerable attention and special care and was not adopted, as a general rule, by the big proprietors. In fact, tobacco in Puerto Rico became identified as "the small farmer's cash crop.")[75]

The second economic policy measure that must be considered is the change in currency decreed by President McKinley in January 1899. The Puerto Rican monetary unit, whose real value at the time of the invasion was estimated at .90 of a U.S. dollar,[76] was changed to dollars at a rate of exchange of .60, which in real terms constituted a forced devaluation. The main economic groups in Puerto Rico did not oppose the new law. The hacendados, whose commercial production was based on credit, had more debts than cash money, and even proposed a greater devaluation—a rate of exchange of .50 to the dollar. The merchants lost on the credit to the hacendados, but they had large stocks of merchandise purchased under the previous monetary system that they could now sell with higher profit levels.[77] They, in fact, proposed the .60 rate of exchange that was finally adopted. With opposition from only a few meagre and incipient banking interests, it was very easy for the metropolis to establish the new monetary system favorable to the dollar. The change, although apparently harmless, implied a reduction of approximately 33 per cent in the already scant liquid capital in the island.[78]

The two measures described above begin to make more sense when a third one is considered: the freezing of credit, also decreed in 1899 with the pretext that Puerto Rico was undergoing a period of monetary instability.[79] It already has been pointed out how the usual mechanics of commercial production functioned before 1898. The hacendados, through credit, grew commercial crops with which they would repay the loans, but withheld a surplus, which, given the pre-capitalist nature of the economy, was used for their own consumption needs.[80] The restraint on credit decreed in 1899 represented for the hacendados the elimination of the basis of their commerical production. In order to obtain necessary capital to continue production, they found themselves forced to sell some of their lands. The owners of idle sugar cane land also found themselves in a similar situation. The inclusion of Puerto Rico within the protected market of the United States had awakened their interest in cultivating idle lands, but the credit facilities that would have enabled them to do so had been frozen. In order to invest in production they were forced to sell part of their land holdings, or to sell it all to someone with capital to put it into production and move to the city with the cash thus obtained and enjoy a leisured and "refined" life.

This leads to a reconsideration of the two previously discussed economic measures. The inclusion of Puerto Rico in the U.S. market created among many coffee producers a desire to shift part of their lands to sugar growing. This required more capital than the continuation of coffee cultivation. Since a restraint had been placed on credit, these hacendados had only two alternatives: either sell even more land to start sugar cane production or stick to coffee production and open themselves to all the vicissitudes to which that crop would be subject within the new customs and tariff scheme.[81] But then who would be able to purchase the land that the coffee growers and the owners of idle sugar cane land needed to sell when the already scarce liquid capital in the island had been reduced by approximately 33 per cent with the introduction of the new currency system? These measures, therefore, encouraged the transfer of agricultural land to North American interests, who not only had dollars to invest but who were also willing to do so.

The situation of insular landowners was made worse by a fourth measure: the establishment of fixed prices for land, prices much below the estimated value in a free market. The rationale for this measure was control of land speculation, but its results were that those in need of selling part of their land holdings were forced to sell more than would have been necessary had the price of land not been fixed by the new colonial authorities.

The tax laws (approved in 1901) also aggravated the situation of Puerto Rican landowners. Taxes were imposed on the value of property, not on the earnings derived from it. The landowners who on account of the freezing of credit had no capital for commercial cultivation found themselves forced to pay proportionally the same taxes as the absentee companies that were expanding their sugar production. Having no capital for cultivation, many landowners were not able to pay such taxes and their properties were seized by the government and put up for sale at auctions.[82] Between 1901 and 1903 more than 600 cases of embargo were authorized by the colonial authorities.

A fifth, but somewhat different sort of measure, needs consideration: the so-called 500-Acre Law approved by the U.S. Congress in May of 1900, which limited to 500 acres the amount of land corporations could own in the island. It has been mentioned before that French interests had begun to invest in the sugar industry in the latter part of the nineteenth century. Also, groups of businessmen on the island had begun to organize on a corporate basis and were doing the same. These interests, which had been favored by the Spanish government, feared the new situation and tried to abide by the law at all times. The 500-Acre Law had the effect of limiting the opportunities of competitors to North American capital who sought to acquire land available for purchase as a result of the measures discussed above. Moreover, it has been argued that many of the non-U.S. corporations did sell part of their properties when they exceeded 500 acres. The North American companies, on the other hand, disregarded the new law and, in fact, the law remained a dead letter for over three decades. It served only as a Damocle's sword against the non-U.S. sugar interests in the crucial years immediately after the North American occupation of Puerto Rico. By 1910 North American companies controlled the most valuable sugar cane lands on the island.

The process of progressive control over the means of production by North American companies was reinforced by a combination of dominion of the new market, on one side, and the inherent weakness (or nonexistence) or a local bourgeoisie, on the other. The gateways to capitalism that had appeared in the nineteenth century generated certain processes through which a fistful of men came to be situated in the productive process in a position similar to that attributed to an industrial bourgeoisie: owners of means of production, oriented towards profit maximization, who organized the production of commodities on wage terms (for example, the owners of the large centers of tobacco processing, several owners of sugar mills or incipient sugar plantations). These "bourgeois" elements, however, had not yet matured as a bourgeoisie when the U.S. invasion of the island took place. In 1898 the numbers of this type of producer, or entrepreneur, were very small and the process of their formation very recent. It is not to be expected, therefore, that these producers would have configurated a conglomerate of shared and distinct interests, a "weltanschaunng" of their own, and a distinct common struggle. Many still responded ideologically to their class of origin: merchants or hacendados, which were classes in conflict. More frequently, each visualized its interests as a purely individual matter.

These "bourgeois" producers were unable to present a common front against the North American capitalist companies and they were inferior to these companies both in understanding and dominion of the new market situation that resulted from the U.S. takeover. Because of this, the "bourgeois" elements abdicated , and the North American companies soon reached an agreement with them. They purchased their establishments, and incorporated them as inferior co-owners (by giving them shares in the company) and as administrators and managers in the companies, which absorbed their holdings.[83] The North American companies allowed and took advantage of the desire of these "bourgeois" elements to preserve their position of local power. The Puerto Rican industrial bourgeoisie, then, died in its infancy. At the time it was beginning to emerge its members fell into intermediary or managerial positions.

To summarize, the acquisition of agricultural lands by North American corporations, the process of absorption of industrial establishments and the destruction of the small and incipient Puerto Rican bourgeoisie during the years immediately following the U.S. invasion of 1898 transformed Puerto Rico into an open field for the development of North American imperialist capitalism.

NOTES

1. See, for example, Julian Steward, et al., *The People of Puerto Rico* (Urbana, 1956), especially chapters 3 and 4; *Disquisiciones sociólogicas* [collection of essays by Salvador Brau].Edited by Eugenio Fernández Méndez, (San Juan, 1956), Introduction; Eugenio Fernández Méndez, *Historia de la cultura en Puerto Rico* (San Juan, 1964), chapter 3; and. Andrés Sánchez Tarniella, *La economia de Puerto Rico, etapas de su desarrollo* (Madrid, 1971), chapters 1 and 2.

2. Andre Gunder Frank, *Capitalism and Underdevelopment in Latin America* (New York: Monthly Review, 1967).

3. Sergio Bagú, *Economía de la sociedad colonial, ensayo de historia contemporanea de America Latina* (Buenos Aires, 1949).

4. Karl A. Wittfogel, *Oriental Despotism* (New Haven, 1967), examines the kind of society that formed around this "Asiatic mode of production" and presents in detail the differences between it and capitalist society.

5. Bagú, *Economía*, pp. 130-143. Eugene Genovese in *Political Economy of Slavery* and in *The World the Slaveholders Made* (New York, 1969) shows quite convincingly how an eonomy based on slavery produces a kind of society different from capitalist society, with different social classes and a different culture and social life.

6. Witold Kula, *Theorie economique du systeme feodal* (Paris, 1970). In this work, translated from the Polish, Kula examines broadly the nature and intensity of commerce under feudalism, breaking down the myth of feudalism as representing a completely closed system. On the other hand, he examines how the structure of production did tend to limit commerce.

7. This is in the short run, for although the production of commodities does not necessarily imply capitalist relations of production, it does tend to generate them. The relationship between commodity and capitalism is, therefore, historico-dialectical; it is not a relation of logical identity. (For example, "The market is a category of commodity economy, *which in the course of its development* is transformed into capitalist economy and only under the latter gains complete sway and universal prevalence." Opening words of V.I. Lenin's, *The Development of Capitalism in Russia* (Moscow, 1967).

8. ". . . merchant's capital belongs to the ante-diluvian forms of capital, which long precedes the capitalist mode of production and are to be found in the most diverse economic formations of society." Karl Marx, *Capital*, Vol. 3, Ch. X XXVI.

9. "Comercio y economía colonial de Hispano-América," in F. Braudel and E. Pereira Salas, eds., *Temas de historia económica hispanoamericana* (Paris, 1965).

10. "By mode of production Marx did not refer merely to the state of technique—to what he termed the state of the productive forces—but to the way in which the means of production were owned and to the social relations among men which resulted from their connections with the process of production." Maurice Dobb, *Studies in the Development of Capitalism* (London, 1946), p. 7. Therefore, *mode of production* is the basis of class relationships.

11. On these points see Karl Marx, "Alienated Labor," the first manuscript in his *Economic and Philosophical Manuscripts of 1844.*

12. This implies in turn a previous accumulation of capital (which Marx called "primitive") that gradually separates the direct producer from his means of production, thus making way for the control of these through accumulated surplus.

13. "... the division of labor manifests itself directly in the diversity of use-values which confront one another as particular commodities." Karl Marx, *A Contribution to the Critique of Political Economy* [1859] (London, 1971), p. 51.

14. Marx, *Capital*, Vol. 3, Chapter XLVIII, Part 3.

15. Alejandro O'Reilly, "Memoria sobre la isla de Puerto Rico," in Alejandro Tapia y Rivera, ed., *Biblioteca histórica de Puerto Rico,*" [1854] (San Juan, 1945).

16. Among several documents that testify to this state of affairs in commerce is the classic *Historia geográfica, civil y natural de la Isla de San Juan Bautista de Puerto Rico* by Fray Iñigo Abbad y Lassierra [1782] edited by José Julián Acosta y Calvo (San Juan, 1866), pp. 334-335. On the nature of illicit commerce see the work of Arturo Morales-Carrión, *Puerto Rico and the Non-Hispanic Caribbean* (San Juan, 1950).

17. See population figures by municipalities presented by O'Reilly, "Memoria"; Pedro Tomás de Córdoba, *Memorias geográficas, económicas y estadisticas de la Isla de Puerto Rico* (San Juan, 1831-1833), 6 Vols.; and *U.S. Census for the Island of Puerto Rico* (Washington, D.C., 1899), p. 43.

18. "Means of extending cultivation are within the reach of all persons, even the lowest class." George D. Flinter, *An Account of the Present State of the Island of Puerto Rico* (London, 1834), p. 17.

19. In 1817 Spain and England agreed to end the slave traffic within three years. Eric Williams, "The Negro Slave Trade in Anglo-Spanish Relations," *Caribbean Historical Review*, No. 1, Dec. 1950.

20. Graph 1 has been composed from figures presented by H.S. Perloff, *Puerto Rico's Economic Future* (Chicago, 1950), p. 14; Acosta, *Historia; Report of Governor Davis on the Industrial and Economic Conditions of Porto Rico* (Washington, 1899), pp. 18-19; and Arthur D. Gayer, et al., *The Sugar Economy of Puerto Rico* (New York, 1938), p. 21. (Perloff provides the figures for 1830, Acosta for 1862, Governor Davis for 1897, and Gayer, et. al., for 1910 and 1919).

21. Graph 2 has been composed from figures presented by Córdoba; *Memórias geográficas*; Acosta, *Historia; Report of Governor Davis*; and U.S. Governors' *Reports* (San Juan, 1910 and 1920). (Córdoba presents figures for 1827, Acosta for 1862, Davis for 1897, and the governors' *Reports* for 1909 and 1919.)

22. The economy of nineteenth century Puerto Rico corresponds perfectly to Dobb's description of feudalism: "a socio-economic system under economic status and authority were associated with land-tenure, and the direct producer was under obligation under law or customary right to devote certain quota of his labour or his produce to the benefit of his feudal superior." Maurice Dobb, *Papers on Capitalism*, p. 2.

23. Labor Gomez, *Organización y reglamentación del trabajo en el Puerto Rico del siglo XIX* (San Juan, 1970).

24. Sidney W. Mintz in "The Role of Forced Labor in Nineteenth Century Puerto Rico," *Caribbean Historical Review*, No. 2, Dec. 1951, presents these regulations as a road to capitalism in terms of the labor force that they created from previously independent producers. He overlooks the state of serfdom that these regulatons generated. Maurice Dobb has examined how in European history, situations of shortage of labor have made difficult the development of a free labor market. He argues that the emergence of capitalism was preceded by an abundance of labor, a product of the exodus of population to the cities in the later Middle Ages. Dobb, *Studies*, Chapters 2 and 6.

25. See Córdoba, *Memorias Geográficas,* (for 1832); Acosta, *Historia* (for 1866); Fernando López Tuero, *La reforma agrìcola,* (San Juan, 1891); and Adolfo de Hostos,

Ciudad murada (La Habana, 1948), p. 30.

26. Fernando López Tuero (in his *Estado moral de los factores de producción en Cuba y Puerto Rico* published in Madrid in 1896), describes the worker on a cash basis as follows: "when he has earned enought to satisfy his fancy, he quites the project and leaves." (Note that he uses the word fancy [*capricho*] and not necessities.) The Archivo General de Puerto Rico stocks an account book of the Hacienda Pietri (*Libro de cuentas de la Hacienda Pietri*, 1898) where most labor payment were in nonmonetary forms. Sidney Mintz also points to the scarce use of cash payments in the hacienda he analyses ("The Culture History of a Puerto Rican Sugar Cane Planation: 1876-1949," *Hispanic American Historical Review*, 1953).

27. Enrique Vijande, *La custión monetaria en Puerto Rico* (Madrid, 1889). The lack of national monetary integration is evidenced also by the amount of different currencies in circulation, including money coined in haciendas. This lack of integration is also reflected in the disparity of tax collections by municipalities. See, Abelardo de la Haba y Trujillo, *El impuesto de consumos en Puerto Rico* (San Juan, 1897).

28. Córdoba, *Memorias geográficas*, Vol. 6, Ch. IV.

29. Table I has been prepared from data presented in Córdoba, *Memorias geográficas*, and in his *Memoria sobre todas las ramas de las administración de la Isla de Puerto Rico* (Madrid, 1838).

30. Estimated from data presented in the 1899 Census.

31. Ibid.

32. Eric Wolf, in "San Jose: Subcultures of a Traditional Ciffee Municipality" (Steward, et al., *People*) presents various examples.

33. A good example of this type of ritual is co-parenthood. See Sidney Mintz and Eric Wolf, "An Analysis of Ritual Co-parenthood," *South Western Journal of Anthropology*, Vol. 6, No. 4 (1956).

34. On the liberalism of the Spanish American "criollo" (creole) see the illuminating work of Francisco López Cámara, *La génesis de la conciencia liberal en México* (México, 1954). The most important exponent of liberalism in Puerto Rico in the nineteenth century was Ramón E. Betances, author of "Los diez mandamientos del hombre libre", in Ada Suárez de Díaz, *El Doctor Ramón Emeterio Betances, su vida y su obra* (San Juan, 1968). Probably more representative of Puerto Rican liberalism in the nineteenth century was the thought of Román Baldorioty de Castro (one of the most important leaders of the Autonomist Party).

35. López Tuero, *Estado moral*, Ch. 2.

36. Adolfo Vendrell, *La caña de azúcar* (San Juan, 1892), p. 4. Vendrell uses terms such as usurers when referring to the merchants.

37. See, for example, Francisco Maymi Cruells, *¿Canje tenemos? Crisis segura* (San Juan, 1895).

38. See, Francisco Mariano Quiñnones, *Historia de los partidos Reformista y Conservador de Puerto Rico* (Mayagüez, 1889); Angel Acosta Quintero, *José Julián Acosta y su tiempo* (San Juan, 1965); and Pilar Barbosa Vda. de Rosario, *De Baldorioty a Barbosa* (San Juan, 1937), among others.

39. On the different conceptions of work, see, Salvador Brau, *Las clases journaleras de Puerto Rico* (San Juan, 1882); Francisco del Valle Atiles, *El campesino puertorriqueño* (San Juan, 1887); Federico Asenjo Arteaga, *Páginas para los jornaleros* (San Juan, 1879); and López Tuero, *Estado moral*, Ch. 2. On the effects of this on generating conflicts see the last two works.

40. These are in fact the two main roads to capitalism presented by Marx in the third

volume of *Capital,* in his discussion of the transition from feudalism to capitalism (Chapter 20).

41. Lidio Cruz Monclova, *Historia de Puerto Rico (Siglo XIX)* (San Juan, 1952), Vol. I, p. 696; and J.R. Abad, *Exposición agrícola e industrial de Tabaco* (Ponce, 1884), p. 92.

42. For example, Enrique Delgado, *Proyecto para la creación de una empresa de Factorías Centrales para la Isla de Puerto Rico* (San Juan, 1881). Among the nine persons said to be backing the project, eight are mentioned as "merchants and capitalists" and one is an engineer. Two of them are also said to be proprietors. No hacendado is mentioned.

43. For example, Central San Vicente, *Devolución de la central a su legítimo poseedor* (San Juan, 1889).

44. Central San Vicente is a good example. See, Santiago Mc Cormick, *Informe dado a la Excelentísima Diputación Provincial sobre el sistema de las Factorías Centrales para la elaboración del azúcar* (San Juan, 1880). More details are found in J. Ferreras Pagán, *Biografía de las riquezas de Puerto Rico* (San Juan, 1902), Vols. 1 and 2.

45. Eric Williams, *Capitalism and Slavery* (Chapel Hill, 1944); and Remy Bastien, "Plantation and Creole Culture," in OAS, *Plantation Systems in the New World* (Washington, D.C., 1959).

46. Luis M. Díaz Soler, *Historia de la esclavitud negra en Puerto Rico* (San Juan, 1965), Ch. VII.

47. Model of the graph suggested by Steward, et al., *People,* p. 46. Additional information was taken from D.J. Jimeno Angius, *Población y comercio de la islad de Puerto Rico* (Madrid, 1885), and the works cited in notes 17 and 21 above.

48. The slaves were not involved in a "petty mode of production" as the *agregados* and small producers were. They carried out collective tasks required by the sugar industry.

49. See, for example, the description of a former Cuban slave in Miguel Barnet, *Biografía de un Cimarrón* (Havana, 1966). (An English version of this work is available).

50. Fernández Méndez, *Historia,* pp. 14-26.

51. See description of social life in Díaz Soler, *Historia.*

52. A process that has not been considered essential to discuss and an analysis of which would imply the examination of several aspects of international trade and of internal production irrelevant to the arguments of this article.

53. Perloff, *Puerto Rico's Economic,* p. 136.

54. Brookings Institution, *Puerto Rico and its Problems* (Washington, D.C., 1930), p. 643.

55. Bailey and Justine Diffie, *Puerto Rico: A Broken Pledge* (New York, 1931), Ch. V.

56. Sánchez Tarniella, *La economia,* p. 69; Fernández Méndez, *Historia,* Ch. IV; and Steward, et al, *People,* Ch. V.

57. Correspondence of the Spanish-American War as cited by Charles Beard, "Territorial Expansion Connected with Commerce," in T.P. Green ed., *American Imperialism in 1898,* edited by T.P. Green (Boston, 1955), p. 25.

58. J.H. Herrero, *La mitología del azúcar,* p. 8. It is important to point out that many of the arguments in this section of this article have been developed from the work of Professor Herrero of the University of Puerto Rico and from the many discussions we have had on this matter.

59. U.S. Tariff Commission, *Report No. 73* (Washington, D.C., 1934), p. 159. as quoted by Herrero, *La mitologia,* p. 9.

60. Pual Sweezy, *The Theory of Capitalis Development* (London, 1962), p. 302. See also,

Peter Gang and Reimut Reiche, *Modelos de la revolución colonial* (México, 1970), p. 20.

61. H. U. Faulkner, *American Economic History*, 8th ed. (New York, 1959), pp. 554-555.

62. On U.S. imperialism see, Gareth Stedman Jones, "The History of U.S. Imperialism," in *Ideology in Social Science* edited by R. Blackburn,(London, 1972). In this article Stedman presents evidence that before the Spanish-American War the general consensus in the U.S. about the economic crises of the early years of the decade was that they were a consequence of "over production and lack of markets." (p. 225). See also, Chester Jones, *Caribbean Interests of the United States* (New York, 1916), pp. 23 and 28.

63. As quoted by Julius W. Pratt, "American Business and the Spanish American War," *Hispanic American Historical Review*, May 1934.

64. For example, A. G. Robinson, *The Porto Rico of Today* (New York, 1899), Ch. XI; W. Dinwiddie, *Puerto Rico: Its Conditions and Possibilities* (New York, 1899); and C. Morris, *Our Island Empire* (Philadelphia, 1899), p. 225.

65. Charles H. Allen, "Opportunities in Porto Rico" in Leonard Wood, et al., *Opportunities in the Colonies and Cuba* (New York, 1902).

66. Blanco Fernández, *España y Puerto Rico, 1826-1930* (San Juan, 1930), pp. 310-311. Robinson, *Porto Rico of Today*, is a witness to the fact that American capital was investing in tobacco processing just two weeks after the landing of the U.S. troops in the island.

67. Herrero, *La mitlologia*, adds that by 1910 North American companies controlled 62 per cent of total sugar cane land.

68. The North American interest in raw sugar for processing is confirmed by data presented in the U.S. Senate, 59th Congress, 1st Session, Doc. 250, *Production and Commercial Movement of Sugar, 1895-1905* (Washington, D. C., 1906). Figures for refined sugar imported by Puerto Rico from the United States are also found there (p. 95). The 1914 *Census of Manufactures* (U.S. Bureau of the Census), Washington, D.C., Vol. II, P. 428, mentions that the United States by this date was only buying raw sugar, and processing it not only for internal consumption but for export as well.

69. Robinson, *Porto Rico of Today*, p. 166. See also, William R. Corwine's *Report on Porto Rico*, which he prepared for the Merchants Association of New York in 1899.

70. Judd Polk, "Plight of Puerto Rico," *Political Science Quarterly*, Dec. 1942, p. 485.

71. An examination of data on exports from the island in the five years before the invasion by U.S. troops in 1898 is very illuminating. In 1895, for example, coffee exports were 62.9 per cent of the total value of exports, and the United States imported only 0.01 per cent of the total. At that time the U.S. was purchasing 35 per cent of the sugar exported by the island. (In other years before the invasion, sugar exports to the U.S. were even greater. In 1884, the U.S. purchased 88.3 per cent of all the sugar exported by Puerto Rico.) This data has been estimated on the basis of the figures presented in "Trade of Puerto Rico," by F.H. Hitchcock, chief, Section of Foreign Markets, U.S. Department of Agriculture, 1898, which appears as Appendix 1 in Dinwiddie, *Puerto Rico*.

72. U.S. Department of Commerce, *The West Indies as an Export Field* (Washington, D.C., 1917), p. 226; Porto Rico Official Economic Commission, *Porto Rico's Case and the Tariff Bill* (Washington, D.C., 1913), p. 7; Corwine, *Report*, p. 5; Jones, *Porto Rico*, p. 102.

73. U.S. War Department, Division of Customs and Insular Affairs, *Monthly Summary of Commerce of the Island of Porto Rico: July 1899-April 1900* (Washington, D.C., 1900). Raymond Crist in "Sugar Cane and Coffee in Puerto Rico. Part I, The Role of Privilege and Monopoly in the Expropriation of the Jibaro" (*The American Journal of Economics and Sociology*, Jan. 1948) presents another argument that is very convincing but that I have

not been able to corroborate. He says that since in the U.S. there were sugar and tobacco interests (and, one can add, North American interests engaged in production in Puerto Rico since the turn of the century) these pressured Congress to protect a fixed minimum price for their products. That coffee had no such interests, Crist says, resulted in a tremendous instability in prices. This, according to him, made the planning of production extremely difficult and led many hacendados out of production.

74. Within the ecological possibilities, since the best suited land for sugar cane cultivation—the coastal plains—is not the best for coffee production, which thrives best at the foot of the hills.

75. This identification runs from Abad, *Exposición* (p. 93) to the study of Steward, et al. in 1956 (chapter on Tabara).

76. Dinwiddie, *Puerto Rico*: p. 222.

77. As in fact occurred. See, U.S. War Department, *First Annual Report of the Governor of Puerto Rico* (Washington, D.C., 1901). pp. 65-66.

78. More details can be found in R.P. Porter, *The Currency Question of Porto Rico*, U.S. Department of the Treasury (Washington, D.C., 1899); and, again, in the illuminating analysis of Herrero, *La mitologia*, pp. 1-7.

79. U.S. War Department, *Report of the Porto Rican Military Governor* (Washington, D.C., 1900) as quoted by Herrero, *La mitologia*, p. 11.

80. I emphasize this usually, but not exclusively, since jointly with the gateways to capitalism that were opened in the nineteenth century the investment in production machinery increased. Moreover, in the hacienda economy the surplus was frequently used to acquire more land—the basis of power and status then—specially land where many *agregados* lived. Given the feudal nature of the production regime and the labor scarcity, this was the most valuable land and the one that represented the most prestige and power. This does not weaken in any way the point I want to stress: that the surplus of production did not generate an accumulation of liquid capital among the hacendados.

81. The situation of the hacendados became even more critical when the island was devastated by the San Ciriaco hurricane in 1899. The coffee crop of that year was practically lost. The ideology of the "establishment" has presented this hurricane as being *the* cause of the ruin and decline of the coffee hacendados (see, for example, Tarniella, *La economía*, p. 69). Puerto Rico had survived many hurricanes before; it was primarily the situation at the time of this hurricane—restraints on credit, lost of markets, currency devaluation—which made it such a disastrous event. Nevertheless, even without the hurricane the economic measures brought about by the "change of sovereignty" were dreary enough for a radical transformation of economic power in the island. More illuminating accounts of the situation of the coffee sector of the economy than these "natural disaster interpretations" are the annual reports of the first North American governors. See, for example, the report of 1905, p. 7.

82. Jose G. del Valle presents this situation in articles written for the publics press in 1901 and reprinted in *A través de 10 años* (Barcelona, 1907), pp. 116, 198. He points out that during the year "notices of auctions of farms seized by embargo overwhelmed the press every day." On the whole process see, José de Jesús Tizol, *El malestar económico de Puerto Rico* (San Juan, 1922), pp. 86-88.

83. Luis Toro, for example, owner of one of the two main centers of tobacco processing, sold his property to the Porto Rico American Tobacco Co. and was named manager of the enterprise. See, Blanco Fernández, *España y Puerto Rico*, pp. 310-311. This, and many

other cases, are presented in detail in Andrés Ramos Mattei's doctoral dissertation now in preparation.

84. In view of what I have presented in the first pages of this article the reader must be asking himself how and why the American companies established their production on a wage system basis, core of the capitalist mode of production. The analysis of this would take us from the backgrounds of the emergence of capitalism to the process of the emergence itself. I refer the interested reader to chapter 2 of my forthcoming book on the history of the Puerto Rican working class.

PART II

Puerto Rico in the Twentieth Century

Introduction

Puerto Rico is an extreme example of imperial domination. Unlike the rest of Latin America, where first the European colonialists and later U.S. investors were merely interested in extracting economic wealth, in the case of Puerto Rico, all facets of social and cultural life were penetrated and reshaped as instruments of control. The U.S. colonial officials, unlike the British, made little or no effort to maintain and manipulate traditional institutions as vehicles of indirect control. The U.S. imperialist experience in Puerto Rico was shaped by a totalitarian vision in the literal sense of the word. This was observed by none other than Theodore Roosevelt when he noted "the [U.S.] drive to remodel all Puerto Ricans so that they should become similar in language, habits and thoughts to continental Americans," The key features of Puerto Rican development under totalitarian imperialism include *dependency, exploitation, deracination,* as well as nationalist and popular resistence. As Morley and Vaughan document in their respective essays development through dependency misdevelops and distorts the economy, whether it be through foreign owned sugar plantations, manufactures or tourist plants: An agrarian society becomes an importer of food; an industrial society an exporter of labor; an island resort—a distant memory to hundreds of thousands enclosed in tenement jungles and mazes of dilapidated shacks. Dependency results in the misallocation of land, labor and public resources to meet foreign needs at the expense of the Puerto Rican people. Dependency means control of development decisions from the outside. And outside decision-makers, corporate executives, U.S. government officials and bankers calculate costs and benefits of investments and loans according to the criteria relevant to the larger needs of their firms—the profit margins. The "developmentalist" governments in Puerto Rico, unfortunately but not surprisingly apply the same criteria.

As Quintero brilliantly argues, the political class that rules for the U.S. corporations in Puerto Rico was recruited from the downwardly mobile agrarian elites and professional groups and has tied its social mobility and political success with the advance of U.S. business interests. Their imaginative and innovative thinking is applied to new ways of promoting business opportunities and avoiding the social problems which are subsequently created. Hence the recent history of official Puerto Rican politics is the story of a proliferation of schemes bound by a narrow vision.

Exploitation in all its manifestations has been the result of dependency: unemployment, migratory labor, low income for the laboring classes and wealth and luxury for the rich, especially the foreign rich and local *politicos*. Dependent development has sharpened class differences and heightened the heirarchical nature of Puerto Rican society, leaving little room for the free play of political and social forces, and fostering an authoritarian society well described by Eduardo Seda. Beyond exploitation, the totalitarian nature of U.S. imperialism in Puerto Rico has to some extent *deracinated* the society: primary and secondary group relationships have been attacked as well as affective relationships in an all-out effort to instrumentalize them for commercial and profitable use: families divide between island and mainland, English and Spanish, New Yorkian against Puerto Rican, statehood against independence, etc. As Quintero shows, the changes in the dependent economy lead to the break-up of class solidarity as well as kinship ties. Language and culture is eroded through commercialization and media manipulation from the outside. In contact with the racist U.S. Puerto Ricans become increasingly "color conscious"—dependency on a racist society exacerbates latent racist feelings.

Resistance and rebellion have been the responses of the Puerto Rican people to this inhuman condition. To the omnipresent imperialist, the Puerto Rican nationalist has affirmed the right of self-determination, Maldonado-Denis develops the consequences of total imperial domination to their logical anti-thesis: total liberation through socialist revolution. Quintero effectively refutes the notion of a passive or conservative working-class by documenting the militant history of class struggle in the 1930s and the conditions for its re-emergence in the present-time.

Puerto Rico in the Twentieth Century: A Historical Survey

Diana Christopulos

The United States entered Puerto Rico as an invading army on July 25, 1898. Puerto Rican civilians gave little aid to Spanish forces on the island, and a modern historian has described the 19-day invasion as "something of a triumphant procession."[1] Although American officials expressed shock at the extensive poverty and illiteracy on the island, they believed Puerto Ricans would quickly and willingly benefit from the North American presence. General Nelson A. Miles, the U.S. military commander, stressed the political advantages of his arrival when he announced, "The primary effect of this occupation will be the immediate transition from your former system of government, desiring [sic] that you accept with joy the system of the Government of the United States." Puerto Rican political leaders assumed the commander was pledging, at the very least, a continuation of the autonomy gained under Spain. In fact, General Miles was initiating a new colonial era in Puerto Rico.

Miles was only the first of four generals who governed Puerto Rico between July 25, 1898 and May 1, 1900 (see Edward J. Berbusse, S.J., *The United States in Puerto Rico, 1898-1900*, The University of North Carolina Press, 1966). Under their direction the U.S. army built roads, distributed food during emergencies, vaccinated the population against smallpox and practically eliminated yellow fever. However, the military governors made it clear that insular improvements did not require the direction, aid or consent of insular political representatives. They abolished both the provincial assembly and the insular cabinet set up under the Autonomous Charter of 1897 as "not compatible with American methods and progress."[2] Freedom of the press was sharply curtailed to forestall criticism of the martial order. During its tenure, the military government established a pattern of disregard for the Hispanic origins of Puerto Rican culture and institutions. The island's name was arbitrarily changed to "Porto Rico" to suit North American pronunciation and usage. The Roman Catholic Church's ancient ties with the Spanish state were broken, which left hundreds of clerics without salaries and ended Catholic domination of insular education. A peaceful invasion by Protestant missionaries and American school-teachers began filling the void left by the separation of church and state. In a private letter, one of the U.S. commanders revealed the tactless paternalism that frequently characterized the military government: "I am getting in touch with the people and trying to educate them to the idea that they must help themselves, giving them kindergarten instruction in controlling themselves without allowing them too much liberty."[3]

Puerto Rico's political elites found American dominance particularly galling. Forming a tiny portion of the population, insular political leaders were aristocratic, relatively wealthy and accustomed to sharing power in the local government. By 1900 these politicians were lashing out at the United States, protesting Puerto Rico's lack of political autonomy, uncertain trade conditions and continued subordination to the American military.

Although the U.S. Congress had little concern for Puerto Rican complaints, it did seek to clarify the political status of Puerto Rico, Cuba and the Philippine Islands, colonies seized by the United States during the Spanish-American War. Congressional debates over Puerto Rico reflected partisan and economic divisions. The Republicans, represented by Senator Joseph B. Foraker of Ohio, argued that Puerto Rico was a "nonincorporated" territory, belonging to the United States but not really part of it. According to Foraker, the island's people could be taxed and subjected to a tariff while being denied representation and other rights guaranteed by the Constitution. Foraker's description was a lengthy and euphemistic definition of a colony. Senators in the Democratic party, sickened by the U.S. military's bloody repression of a Philippine independence movement, introduced two resolutions opposing formal American colonies. The first stated that the United States had no constitutional power to acquire and govern territories permanently as colonies. The second stated that the United States would not govern any people without that people's consent. The resolutions had little effect. Many Democrats supported free trade between Puerto Rico and the United States, a position favored by certain American exporters. A Louisiana rice grower, for instance, happily noted that he could supply Puerto Rico with 10 million tons of rice if Congress would protect him from competition by bringing the island inside U.S. tariff walls.[4]

Republican expansionists wrote most of the Foraker Act of 1900, which Congress called "an act temporarily to provide revenues and civil government for Porto Rico." The law, also known as an organic act, defined the political and economic relationship between Puerto Rico and the United States. It differed significantly from the Autonomous Charter granted by Spain in 1897 and used by Puerto Rican elites as a model for *minimal* self government under the United States. A comparison of the two documents shows why politically vocal Puerto Ricans preferred the Autonomous Charter (see *Documents on the Constitutional History of Puerto Rico*, Office of the Commonwealth of Puerto Rico, 2d. ed., June 1964). First, Puerto Ricans had little voice in shaping the Foraker Act. Unlike the Autonomous Charter, the organic act owed almost nothing to the initiative of insular political leaders. Congressional committees heard testimony from Puerto Ricans, but the final bill neither reflected the desires of island politicians nor required the approval of the insular population. Second, the Foraker Act placed almost all political power in the hands of appointed rather than elected officials. Under both the Autonomous Charter and the Foraker Act, the colonial power appointed the governor and the local population elected the lower house of the legislature. However, the composition and powers of the upper house changed drastically with the passage of the Foraker Act. All 11 members of the new Executive Council were appointed by the U.S. President, and the act only required that five be Puerto Ricans. The Autonomous Charter's Council of Administration, with eight of its 15 members elected, had acted as both a law-making body and as the insular executive power except in times of emergency. The Executive Council, although serving as both a legislative house and a cabinet, was clearly subordinate to the presidentially-appointed governor. Third, the United States allowed Puerto Rico only token representation in Washington. At the time of the American invasion, the Spanish had apportioned the island 16 representatives and three senators in the Cortes, the Spanish equivalent of the U.S. Congress. The Foraker Act provided nothing more than a figurehead "resident commissioner," elected in Puerto Rico and allowed to speak but not vote in the House of Representatives. Fourth, the Foraker Act significantly reduced Puerto Rican control over local affairs. Although the insular legislature retained the power to draw up its own budget and approve certain appointments, it could no longer set its own tariffs or participate in the negotiation of commercial treaties with foreign countries. The Spanish governor-general had been able to recommend that the Cortes overrule insular legislation, but the American governor could veto bills directly. Two-thirds of both legislative houses could overrule the governor's veto, but the U.S. Congress expressly reserved the right to annul any bill passed in the Puerto Rican legislature.

In addition to its political sections, the new organic act included special provision for American businessmen interested in Puerto Rico. Goods from outside the United States would be subject to the same tariffs in Puerto Rico as on the mainland, but American products could enter the island duty-free after 1904. Insular products could also be shipped duty-free to the United States. Further, the Foraker Act extended the Coastwise Shipping Act to Puerto Rico, requiring the use of American ships for all insular-mainland trade. Congressional reformers scored a minor victory by including a provision that no corporation could own more than 500 acres of land in Puerto Rico. Unfortunately, the 500-Acre Act provided no penalties, and almost everyone ignored it for nearly 40 years.

With the passage of the Foraker Act, most insular political leaders became disillusioned with the U.S. government. The military government and the Foraker Act arrogantly disregarded the fact that Puerto Rico had ever approached governing itself and ignored the claims of some Puerto Ricans that Spain could not cede an autonomous state. With racist asides about childlike peoples, the United States presumed to teach Puerto Ricans the fundamentals of democracy. However, the United States did not permit an insular plebescite on political status until 1951.

One year after the passage of the Foraker Act, the Supreme Court dealt another humiliating blow to island politicians. In *Downes v. Bidwell*, the court upheld Senator Foraker's contention that Puerto Rico was a "nonincorporated" territory. Its citizens could be taxed, but they could not claim Constitutional rights such as trial by jury. To avoid simply calling the island a colony, the court cited numerous and ambiguous historical precedents. Finley Peter Dunne's "Mr. Dooley" offered his own summary of the court's findings:

First, that th' Disthrict iv Columbya is a state; second, that it is not; third, that New
York is a state; fourth, that that it is a crown colony; fifth, that all tates ar-re states
an all territories ar-re territories in th' eves iv other powers,'but Gawd knows what
they ar-re at home.

Puerto Rican political leaders had no doubts about the meaning of the
court's decision. Insular politicians of all persuasions angrily rejected
both *Downes v. Bidwell* and the Foraker Act as permanent definitions of
the island's civil order. Luis Muñoz Rivera, for example, had expected
the U.S. to improve on the Autonomous Charter of 1897. He
complained that instead, "we had the military government first and
afterwards . . . the Foraker Act, within which we see its autonomous and
petty kings arising."[5] Embittered by the loss of autonomy, he took to his
study and wrote a poem titled "Sisyphus" about the Greek king eternally
condemned to push a huge rock up a mountain, only to have it roll back
down just before reaching the top. In his opposition to the Foraker Act,
Muñoz Rivera manifested the elitism as well as the bitterness of his
generation. He argued for a voting age of 25 rather than 21 because, "the
Latin race "(i.e., the masses)" is excitable and undeliberative, and at the
age of 21 years a man . . . has not formed character."[6]

Unwilling to accept the colonialism of the Foraker Act, Puerto Rican
leaders organized new political parties based on alternative solutions to
the problem of colonial political status. The Republican Party campaigned for eventual statehood, while the Federalist Party proposed greater
autonomy and eventual independence. Although the Federalists probably had a numerical majority among voters, the Republicans won the
1900 elections. Federalists boycotted the polling places, charging that
American officials had gerrymandered insular election districts to assure
a Republican victory.

Strongly pro-American, the Puerto Rican Republican Party openly
identified itself with the United States party in power. Its strongest
supporters were urban business interests that had long dealt with trading
houses in New York, Philadelphia and Baltimore. Within a few years, the
party added the support of the powerful American sugar corporations
that rapidy entered the island after 1898. American tariff protection
allowed Puerto Rican sugar to compete for the mainland market against
the less expensive Cuban product, and sugar dominated the insular
economy by 1920. Although economic self-interest motivated most
Republicans, the party included a small group of American-educated

intellectuals whose commitment to statehood sprang from a genuine admiration for American political institutions. The party's leader, Dr. José Celso Barbosa, was one of these intellectuals. Celso Barbosa, a black man, expected both justice and economic progress from the party of Abraham Lincoln and William McKinley.

Unlike insular Republicans, Federalists were highly skeptical of the United States government. Groups that had supported autonomy during the latter half of the nineteenth century formed the backbone of the Federalist Party. Luis Muñoz Rivera, ex-president of the Autonomist Party, became the Federalist leader. His party gained additional and unexpected support from the island's coffee growers, who blamed their economic decline on United States trade policies. Their plight is discussed below.

In 1904, the Federalists merged with a small group of dissident Republicans and formed the Union Party. The Republican splinter group had concluded that the United States would never grant Puerto Rico statehood. As Unionists, they abandoned statehood and endorsed both independence and autonomy as acceptable alternatives. Unionists swept the 1904 elections and remained the majority party for 20 years. Despite its majority, the Union Party was seriously divided over the status issue. Muñoz Rivera emphasized independence until 1912, when he prompted and won a party fight to make autonomy the preferred status. Convinced that United States economic and military requirements would prevent a voluntary American departure, Muñoz Rivera shifted his efforts to obtaining greater self government under United States rule. A large, independence-minded minority (*independentistas*) led by José de Diego, remained in the party to challenge Muñoz Rivera. A smaller group existed with Rosendo Matienzo Cintrón and formed the Independence Party (*Partido Independentista*) in 1912. The new party died with its leader in 1913.

Although every Puerto Rican political party wanted major changes in the Foraker Act, the "temporary" law remained in effect for 17 years. In 1909 the insular legislature used one of its few powers, control of the budget, to force Congressional discussion of its complaints. The legislature refused to pass a new budget for 1910. Congress did discuss the matter, and it agreed with President Taft that Puerto Ricans were ungrateful to the United States government. It quickly amended the Foraker Act with the Olmsted Act, providing that the previous year's budget would remain in effect any time the insular legislature failed to pass a new one. In 1912, Congress reacted to continued pressure from Puerto Rican politicians and began hearings on a new organic act. The final bill, known as the Jones Act, did not pass until February 1917. The Jones Act made several formal changes without decisively altering arrangements provided for in the Foraker Act. A 19-member elected senate replaced the Executive Council as the legislature's upper house. However, the council continued as a cabinet appointed by United States officials, and almost all power remained in the executive branch. In addition to the governor's veto and the Congress's annulment power, the Jones Act gave the American president an unconditional veto over insular legislation. Finally, the second organic act granted Puerto Ricans American citizenship and a special version of the Bill of Rights. Islanders ruefully noted that the honors of citizenship included eligibility for the military draft just three months before war was declared on Germany. However, the Supreme Court ruled in 1922 (*Balzac v. the People of Puerto Rico*) that the Jones Act did not make Puerto Rico an "incorporated" part of the United States and did not extend the full protection of the Constitution to Puerto Ricans.

Although Puerto Rican political status remained unsettled and largely unchanged in the first 30 years of American hegemony, insular social and economic conditions changed rapidly. The government built new roads, cut the death rate by almost one third, and strung telephone and telegraph lines across the island. Heavy educational expenditures brought the percentage of school-age children in classrooms from an abysmal eight per cent in 1898 to about 50 per cent in 1930 and lowered the illiteracy rate from 82 per cent to just over 50 per cent.[7] Of course, these publicly-funded material improvements also facilitated penetration of the island by American capital. Better transportation and communication opened new areas for massive sugar plantations. Healthy workers who had been educated to be on time and perhaps speak a little English were much more useful than undisciplined laborers.

In taking over the island economy, the Americans accelerated several trends initiated during the last decades of Spanish rule. Like the Spanish, they increased the amount of land under cultiation. Similarly, they devoted a larger share of the land to cash crops, with a proportionate decrease in the area used for subsistence crops. In 1898 food crops accounted for 32 per cent of the cultivated acreage. By 1930 they representd only 14 per cent. As a result of these changes, Puerto Rico became increasingly dependent on the export of a few agricultural goods.

The Americans also initiated several new developments in the insular export economy. Tobacco and a variety of tropical fruits that were almost never exported during the Spanish period became important cash crops. Manufacturing remained a minor category, never accounting for more than a quarter of all exports, but both the textile and cigar industries grew rapidly after the American takeover.[8] Most importantly, sugar replaced coffee as Puerto Rico's leading export. Between 1898 and 1930, sugar acreage climbed from 15 percent to 44 per cent of all cultivated land. Coffee dropped from 41 per cent to 33 per cent in the same period. The value of exports rose quickly from $8.5 million in 1901 to $103.5 million in 1928, and sugar consistently accounted for about half the total.

A series of policy measures and natural events combined to destroy the insular coffee industry after 1898. The United States failed to duplicate Spain's protective tariff on coffee. Sugar, tobacco, and textiles received protection from foreign competition, but coffee did not. The high-quality Puerto Rican bean cost nearly twice as much as its Brazilian and Colombian rivals, and Congress would not consider doubling the price of coffee merely to insure that Americans would wake up to a better taste in the morning. In 1899, the hurricane San Ciriaco compounded the problem by destroying 80 per cent of the coffee crop. World War I blockades took a heavy toll of European continental markets. Coffee growers who survived the war had lost almost all their trees in 1929 to San Felipe, the most powerful hurricane ever recorded in Puerto Rico. Those who continued to grow coffee found few buyers during the Great Depression. Between 1900 and 1930, coffee production plummeted from over 20 million pounds to less than 5 million pounds. Not surprisingly, the coffee growing regions of the interior became strongholds of independence sentiment. By 1930, thousands of coffee workers had become migrants to the cane-fields and the urban slums.

American tariffs did more than close the mainland market to insular coffee producers. They also forced Puerto Ricans to pay the same prices as American consumers for "foreign" goods. If American beef producers persuaded Congress to pass a high tariff against Argentine beef, Puerto Ricans had to pay the same high meat prices as American consumers. Of course, Puerto Ricans ate more rice than beef. Since Louisiana rice growers had some influence in Congress, islanders had to pay two to three dollars more for 100 pounds of rice than the Japanese price on the international market. Under the Smoot-Hawley tariff of 1930, the highest in American history, Puerto Ricans had to pay mainland prices for virtually all their products at a time when their per capita income was less than one-tenth of the American level.

Puerto Rican consumers suffered further from the Coastwise Shipping Act, which stipulated that the island must use the American merchant marine for all trade with the mainland. The law effectively limited 80 per cent of Puerto Rico's imports and over 90 per cent of its exports to four American steamship lines. Islanders actually subsidized the American shippers, who would not have been competitive in a free market, to bring them expensive food and consumer goods.

Although some Puerto Ricans benefited from the American presence, mainlanders controlled most of the new agricultural wealth. Four American companies, the South Porto Rico Sugar Company, the Fajardo Sugar Company of Porto Rico, Central Aguirre Associates and the United Porto Rico Sugar Company, controlled 50 per cent of the 1930 sugar crop. Similar conditions prevailed in tobacco and fruit growing. Mainlanders often did not own the land, but they exported 80 per cent of the tobacco and 60 per cent of the fruit crop.[9]

As the export figures suggest, some Puerto Rican planters prospered under United States domination. A few local managers of American corporations echoed their approval of the political and economic status quo. Along with most insular professionals, the planters and managers formed a Puerto Rican middle class that was dependent on American markets, commercial treaties, and good will for its continued existence and comfort.

Owners of small and medium-sized plantations became reliant on larger producers. In sugar, for instance, the smaller planters *(colonos)* no longer ground their own cane. In 1910, there had been 500 sugar mills, many of them very small. In 1930 only 46 large corporate mills *(centrales)* remained. *Colonos* complained that the centrales undervalued their cane and took a disproportionate share of the profits, but they had no alternative grinding facilities. Tobacco farmers had to deal with American buyers, who controlled both the credit market and the local price of tobacco.

Puerto Rico's class of landless workers, both urban and rural, grew in size and in economic vulnerability after the American arrival. Between 1898 and 1930, the island's population grew by almost 60 per cent. At the same time, adult male unemployment rose from 17 per cent to over 30 per cent. The cane worker of the 1930s exemplified the problems of landless labor. During most of the year *(el tiempo muerto)*, he had little or no work. Puerto Rican wages had improved, but they still averaged less than one-half the average for other tropical countries producing the same goods.[10] The sugar worker could buy more rice with one hour's labor in 1930 than in 1897, but he bought rather than grew much more of his food by 1930. According to one study, he had to work 104 days to pay for his family's food in 1930, a task that had required only 70 days of work in 1897. At the end of the 1920s, the Puerto Rican sugar worker spent *94 per cent* of his income for food, a proportion matched only in Asia.[11]

Thirty years of United States domination of the insular economy even nullified important American medical contributions to the island. The cause and cure for hookworm, a debilitating and often fatal parasite, were discovered in Puerto Rico in 1901. A U.S. military doctor found that the parasites enter the body through cracks and scratches on the soles of the feet. Until adequate sewage lines could be provided for the island, the wearing of shoes offered the best protection against hookworm. However, neither the U.S. corporations nor the federal government had any interest in providing the people with shoes. In addition, the American tariff raised the price of shoes so that only one fourth of the 1930 population had ever worn a pair. Ninety per cent of the rural population continued to be infected to some degree with hookworm. Diseases such as hookworm, enteritis and malaria made the Puerto Rican death rate the western hemisphere's highest.

The high prices of shoes and staple foods, the predominance of sugar and large corporations and the growing numbers of landless workers could all be related to Puerto Rico's political and economic ties with the U.S. The tariff and the Coastwise Shipping Act were the most obvious bonds, and their benefits corresponded neatly with the requirements of mainland economic interests. Yet the Puerto Rican legislature could do nothing about high prices or the sugar economy. Only the U.S. Congress could change the tariff.

In addition to political and economic domination, the U.S. presented a new menace to Puerto Rico. The island's Hispanic language, religion, and social heritage were constantly challenged by the well-heeled North American culture. Intellectuals and professionals were most attuned to the new threat, and they feared that economic dependency would mean the end of Puerto Rican culture. Muñoz Rivera spoke for the intellectuals and the professionals when he predicted:

In the future there will be abundance, physical well-being, a richness of fruits and metals; but there will be no country. And if there is, it will belong to Americans and their sons and grandsons. In half a century it will be a stain to wear a name of Spanish culture.[12]

Cultural battle lines were drawn over the insular education system and the impractical U.S. policy of teaching all classes in English. Elitist Puerto Ricans opposed both the education of the masses and the introduction of English in the schools. They argued that the United States was trying to destroy essential social distinctions and obliterate Hispanic culture while creating a better investment climate for American corporations.

American officials did little to dispell the image of cultural imperialism. They clearly considered education and Americanization synonymous cures for all of Puerto Rico's ills. Within a few years, the island was flooded with American teachers drilling students in the English language, assigning them work from American textbooks, and instructing them in the values of American business society. The educators undoubtedly believed schools were a panacea for the island's social problems, but the United States also expected to reap commercial benefits. As the U.S. commissioner of education on the island wrote to a friend,

Technical and industrial education here will give us a corps of young Puerto Ricans, trained in both the English and Spanish language and in our industrial and commercial methods who will be valuable pioneers in extending our trade in South America . . . they ought to accomplish much in extending our commerce and in creating new markets for our manufacturers.[13]

While the Puerto Rican elites argued over education and status, the masses continued in their poverty. They remained relatively indifferent to politics because they saw no connection between their own problems and abstract discussions of their political relationship with the United States. Many of the poor who had expected better conditions when the U.S. army replaced the brutal Spanish Guardia Civil were acutely disappointed by the actual result. In many cases, working conditions probably deteriorated. Cane workers lost the local *hacendado*, who was occasionally benevolent, and gained the American sugar corporation, which was run for profit only. As the cane workers became disillusioned with the Americans, they took the initiative and tried to unionize the cane fields. Their strikes were quickly repressed. Using the muscle of the insular police, management simply locked the tenants (*agregados*) inside the plantation, locked the day laborers out, and continued to work the cane fields.

In the first four decades of U.S. rule, only one insular political party dealt seriously with the problems of the workers. The Socialist Party, which concentrated on material improvements for the laboring classes, was the only political organization that attracted genuine mass support. Republicans and Unionists often bought votes to provide a facade of popular legitimacy, but they scorned and feared the lower classes. Even a radical *independentista* such as José de Diego contended that the Puerto Rican laborer needed more education before exposure to the "subversive" ideas of labor unionism.[14]

The Socialist leader, Santiago Iglesias, introduced unionism in Puerto Rico. Born in Spain, he arrived in the island as an exiled trade unionist in 1896. Three years later he formed a political party (*Partido Obrero Socialista*) and required its members to join his labor union (*Federación Libre de Trabajadores de Puerto Rico*). Iglesias did not advocate revolutionary socialism, nor did he recognize the role of U.S. imperialism in perpetuating insular poverty. He favored eventual statehood and an American standard of living for the Puerto Rican worker. He became a good friend of Samuel Gompers, conservative leader of the American Federation of Labor. His party discussed the problems of labor—wages, prices, working conditions, hours—and ignored the status issue.

After reorganizing as the Socialist Party (*Partido Socialista*) in 1915, the party quickly gained support. It elected a senator and a representative in 1917 and garnered 60,000 votes in 1920. In 1924, Iglesias unwittingly began a process of political suicide when he led the Socialists into the *Coalición* with the Republicans. The party of the workers joined the party of the property-owners and exporters to pursue statehood and the spoils of political victory. Although Iglesias may have felt he acted in the laborers' best interests, he effectively moved his party into junior partnership with the Republicans. Socialist voting strength peaked in 1928, when the party won almost half of the seats in both houses of the legislature. By 1932, workers realized that the party was failing to keep its promises of more jobs and better working conditions. Socialist totals declined steadily, and no party had broad mass support again until 1940.

The Republican-Socialist *Coalición* typified the willingness of Puerto Rican politicans to ignore insular problems during the 1920s and concentrate on the profitable aspects of U.S. domination. By 1922, the deaths of Muñoz Rivera, De Diego, and Celso Barbosa had muted even the status issue. Antonio Barceló, who succeeded Muñoz Rivera as the Unionist leader, engineered the removal of independence as a status alternative in the party platform. Unionists joined dissident Republicans under Josè Tous Soto in a pro-statehood Alliance (*Alianza*) in 1924. Alianza leaders offered a solid political base for the corporate sugar economy. Barceló's brother-in-law managed the Fajardo Sugar Company, and Tous Soto doubled as Speaker of the House and attorney for the South Porto Rico Sugar Company.[15] Superior organization, almost the only important difference between the *Alianza* and the *Coalición*, brought *Alianza* majorities until 1932.

Insular politicians often benefited financially from their relationship with the United States, but they also resented the arrogance of its domination. American officials proved to be paternalistic racists, proudly ignorant of the island's political history and naively sure of their own civilization. Uninterested in any Puerto Rican responses except gratitude and subservience, the U.S. government displayed a classical imperial attitude towards the island. It usually ignored Puerto Rican demands, but it insisted on controlling everything on the island. Representative forms of government existed, but they were emptied of political content. American officials used the democratic facade to indict Puerto Ricans for their own political and economic failures. Whatever their problems, islanders were supposed to be grateful for American rule, as presidents Taft and Coolidge pointed out when Puerto Ricans talked too loudly about substantive democracy.

American indifference towards the Puerto Ricans may well have been related to the American attitude towards formal colonies. The U.S. Constitution makes no provision for colonies—nor, in a sense, for Puerto Ricans. Informal expressions of colonialism such as economic and cultural penetration were perfectly acceptable and required no reference to the Constitution. However, the U.S. had developed no governmental patterns in the early twentieth century for possessions not destined for statehood. The result was to deny Puerto Ricans both the paternalism sometimes available from openly colonialist powers and the freedom to govern themselves.

Conditions did not improve in the 1930s. The 1929 Wall Street stock market crash resounded in economically-dependent Puerto Rico, and added to the island's burden of impoverishment. By 1933 only 35 per cent of the working population was gainfully employed.[16] The 1932 hurricane, San Cipriano, compounded the misery with 225 deaths, over 100,000 left homeless, more than $30 million in property damage, and devastation of small fruit farmers' orchards.

Finally reversing its laissez faire attitude towards Puerto Rico, the Roosevelt Administration tried to extend the New Deal to the island. (see Thomas G. Mathews, *Puerto Rican Politics and the New Deal*, University of Florida Press, 1960) Two successive agencies, the Puerto Rican Emergency Relief Administration (PRERA) and the Puerto Rico Reconstruction Administration (PRRA), made superficial attempts to deal with the island's massive problems. PRRA spent almost $60 million on resettlement programs. Over a million people were on PRRA relief in 1938, but tens of thousands remained unemployed and unaided.

Puerto Rican planners knew that the island's problems went deeper than the American stock.market. They devised an extensive program, known as the Chardón Plan, to curtail insular dependence on sugar cane, absentee owners and imported foods. Despite initial approval from President Franklin Roosevelt, the Chardón Plan was not enacted. Bickering American administrators and obstructive economic interests reduced it to nothing more than a useful model for future island governments.

While the governments in San Juan and Washington debated, the island population began actively demonstrating its frustration. To protest high prices, residents of San Juan boycotted gasoline retailers and demonstrated against bread and flour dealers. University students and longshoremen staged strikes and counterstrikes against the U.S. governor's plan for greater Americanization of island schools. In the upland coffee regions, popular insurgents drove out agents of the Land Bank of Baltimore because the bank threatened to foreclose mortgages on bankrupt middle class coffee growers.[17]

The most dramatic examples of popular militancy occurred in the sugar industry, which controlled half of the cultivated land and over one-third of the agricultural work force. Cane workers at the South Porto Rico Sugar Company went on strike late in 1933. In early 1934, they were joined by employees of the Fajardo Sugar Company and Central Aguirre Associates, so that the entire eastern section of the industry came to a standstill. The continuing prosperity of the sugar corporations made them a natural target for hungry workers. Fajardo's parent corporation, the American Sugar Company, actually tripled its profits between 1931 and 1932, at a time when only seven corporations on the New York Stock Exchange could declare comfortable profits.[18] The sugar corporations, fearing the growing radicalization of the workers' demands, granted moderate wage increases.

Small sugar planters (*colonos*) also found reason to protest. To help American corporations in Cuba, the U.S. government had increased the massive Cuban sugar quota at the expense of the Puerto Rican quota. The unexpected cut left Puerto Rico with a 200,000 pound sugar surplus in 1933. The major *centrales* protected themselves by grinding only their own cane and refusing that of the colonos. In response, small growers formed the *Asociación de Colonos*, with Jesús T. Piñero as president. Piñero appealed to the Roosevelt Administration for relief, and *colonos* eventually received sole rights to a fixed proportion of the sugar quota.

Intellectuals voiced their dissatisfaction through renewed endorsement of cultural nationalism, which reached its twentieth century peak during the 1930s. Its most articulate expression, Antonio S. Pedreira's *Insularismo*, appeared in 1934. *Insularismo* was the major effort to define and defend Puerto Rican national identity, and the work influenced a whole generation of insular leaders. Pedreira concluded that the United States had increased economic output at the expense of intellectual, political and social excellence. He argued that only a vigorous reaffirmation of insular character and traditions could overcome the greed and mediocrity that typified the new order. Anti-American in nature, *Insularismo* was also perhaps more aristocratic than nationalistic:

> The customary values Pedreira wanted to preserve are those—dancing, horse riding, acting, witty conversation—of a leisure-class stamp and not obviously identifying a Puerto Rican 'national character.'

A mild racism also flawed Pedreira's work, as when he attributed insular confusion over identity to the mixing of races. However, certain radical politicians of the 1970s have echoed his emphasis on the cultural effects of domination by the United States, placing it within a more democratic view of social development.

Among political parties, the nationalist renewal was signaled by polarization over the status issue. By 1928, both the Union-Republican Alianza and the Republican-Socialist *Coalición* had endorsed statehood as the preferable alternative. Sensing the underlyng discontent of urban and rural workers, the *Alianza* reorganized in 1932 as the Puerto Rican Liberal Party. Its aging and wily leader, Antonio Barceló, dramatically inserted a call for independence in the party platform.

Barceló's supporters included a vigoorous new generation of intellectuals, one of whom was Luis Muñoz Marín. Muñoz Marín was the son of autonomist leader Luis Muñoz Rivera, and he represented a new type of insular politician. Born in Puerto Rico in 1897, familiar with island politics and politicians, he also was fluent in English and had spent half of his youth on the mainland. While in the United States, he cultivated political friendships and published poetry and political essays in two languages. His work appeared in the *American Mercury*, the *Nation* and other periodicals. In 1926 he became the editor of *La Democracia*, a Unionist newspaper founded by Muñoz Rivera. Muñoz Marín's early political writings expressed concern for the welfare of the people, blamed the United States for their plight and insisted on eventual independence. He lashed out at the United States, charging, "The American flag found Puerto Rico penniless and content. It now flies over a prosperous factory worked by slaves who have lost their land and may soon lose their guitars and their songs."[20] In Muñoz Marín's view, the root of insular problems could be easily expressed:

> One cannot observe Puerto Rican life close up without reaching the conclusion that every form of tutelage is morally degrading . . . This is the political illness of Puerto Rico and its only cure is a dose of unadulterated sovereignty.[21]

However, he modified his criticism of the United States after Franklin Roosevelt's election in 1932. Muñoz Marín explained his goals as a Puerto Rican Liberal in a letter to a friend:

> We are for independence, but we don't bait the United States unless driven to it. We have a special tenderness for the Democratic party . . . because of its traditional liberal attitude towards Puerto Rico and the Philippines. We are opposed to begging money from the American taxpayers and instead claim the right to have our own tariff, to get rid of the coastwise shipping laws, and to be empowered to regulate absentee ownership.[22]

The Liberals were not the only party supporting independence in 1932. They had a vocal competitor in the Puerto Rican Nationalist Party. Founded by José Coll Cuchi in 1922, the Nationalist Party finally acquired enough signatures for the island-wide ballot in 1932. By then it had a new leader, one of the most controversial figures in Puerto Rican history. Pedro Albizu Campos, like Muñoz Marín, had an American education. While earning a law degree at Harvard University, he developed friendships with Irish and Indian students who were radically committed to overthrowing the British Empire. His wife, a Radcliffe student, was a Peruvian leftist. After Harvard and World War I service in the American army, Albizu Campos had no ambiguous feelings about the United States as a colonial and racist power. He attacked the United States for Puerto Rico's spiritual enslavement and condemned its influence throughout Latin America. As the Nationalist leader, he exhibited great pride in Hispanic culture, unwillingness to compromise with existing powers and readiness to sacrifice himself for Puerto Rican independence. He greatly admired the Cuban martyr, José Martí, and he established contacts with radical Latin Americans of his own time. A two-year trip in the 1920s acquainted him with hopeful revolutionaries in Haiti, Cuba, Peru and the Dominican Republic and with successful revolutionaries in Mexico.

Although Albizu Campos cared about his people's material welfare, he made their cultural heritage and political independence his primary concerns. On an island where thousands suffered extreme poverty, he concentrated on political ideals. Manuel Maldonado-Denis has pointed out that Albizu Campos was most successful in raising the national consciousness of Puerto Ricans (see *Puerto Rico: A Socio-Historical Interpretation*, Random House, 4th ed., 1972). However his active support was drawn primarily from intellectuals, students, and coffee planters. The masses, while perhaps sympathetic, did not join Albizu Campos' movement, because he failed to demonstrate the link between independence and economic improvement.

In 1932 the Nationalists formed a loose coalition with the Liberals. For the first time since 1924, voters had a clear choice on the status issue, Liberals and Nationalists representing independence and Republicans and Socialists promoting statehood. Although the Liberals received more votes than any single party, the Republican-Socialist *Coalición* won its first majority. Albizu Campos drew less than three per cent of the votes in his race for resident commissioner, and he ran far ahead of other Nationalist candidates.

After the 1932 elections the Nationalist party turned to extra-electoral tactics. Albizu Campos correctly noted that the elections were dishonest, but he grossly overestimated his own mass support. The insular police reacted by suppressing the Nationalists, and many of them retaliated violently against both insular and federal governments. As early as 1932, a Nationalist leader was killed—and avenged—in the coffee-growing region around Utuado.[23] In October 1935 Albizu Campos spoke out against student apathy at the University of Puerto Rico. His suggestion that the men were effiminate and the women drunkards provoked a student demonstration, and brought together an explosive mixture of anti-Nationalist students, Nationalists and insular police. The police killed three Nationalists, and an additional Nationalist and policeman were wounded. At the Nationalist funeral, Albizu Campos vowed that a mainland American would die for every Nationalist killed.

Four months later, in February 1936, two young Nationalists killed Insular Police Chief Francis Riggs, an American. The Nationalists were not allowed to make their trial a public forum. Puerto Rico had no death penalty, so police killed the youths as they "tried to escape." The death of Riggs shook the island's entire political system. The immediate results were Albizu Campos' political martydom and Senator Millard Tydings' introduction of a bill for Puerto Rican independence. Within two years, the events following from Riggs' murder would initiate a new era in insular political history.

The federal government used the pretext of Riggs' death to suppress the whole Nationalist party. As one Liberal congressman explained, "The regime wishes to guarantee vengeance for the death of the American."[24] The government blamed Albizu Campos, and he was soon indicted along with seven of his followers. The prosecution was a mockery of justice. The federal government decided that a Puerto Rican court could not be trusted to return a guilty verdict. For Albizu Campos to be tried in a federal court, he had to be indicted for the political crimes of sedition and conspiring to overthrow the government rather than for the criminal charges of incitement to violence and complicity in murder. For the most part, his "sedition" and "conspiracy" consisted of advocating independence in public places. A federal requirement that jurors speak English meant that few Puerto Ricans were empaneled, but the first trial resulted in a hung jury. Undeterred, the government selected a more pliable jury within two weeks and won a guilty verdict. Albizu Campos was sentenced to nine years in the federal penitentiary in Atlanta, Georgia.

The prosecution of Albizu Campos for advocating independence was especially absurd in light of the fact that a U.S. senator had introduced a bill for Puerto Rican independence shortly before the Nationalists came to trial. Ironically, Senator Millard Tydings of Maryland had been a close friend of Francis Riggs and had nominated him for the position of insular police chief. As chairman of the Senate Territorial and Insular Affairs

Committee, Tydings was more familiar than most Americans with Puerto Rico. During a 1933 visit he had written President Roosevelt, "It would certainly be better for us if we were out of this place, and conversely, much worse for Puerto Rico."[25] Like many observers, both mainlanders and Puerto Ricans, he believed that independence would mean economic disaster. The Tydings Bill, introduced in April 1936, was a vindictive move on the senator's part. He undoubtedly thought he was punishing the island for his friends' death or at least forcing Puerto Ricans to face th implications of independence. Tydings had the covert support of President Roosevelt and his cabinet. In a political miscalculation unmatched in Puerto Rican history, Secretary of the Interior Harold Ickes urged the bill's introduction "because of the quieting effect that [I] anticipated it might have on Puerto Rican public opinion."[26]

The Tydings Bill scrambled all existing political alignments in Puerto Rico. At one point in the hectic spring of 1936, Liberals, pro-independence Republicans and Nationalists formed a United Front in favor of the bill. Liberal leader Antonio Barceló vowed to support independence "even though we die from hunger." Albizu Campos argued that President Roosevelt's support of the Tydings Bill made further legal formalities unnecessary and proposed immediate independence. However, the front soon crumbled. Prison walls silenced Albizu Campos. Most insular Republicans, actively backed by American corporations, vocally rejected the bill. The most puzzling opposition came from Muñoz Marín, a major figure in the Liberal Party's independence faction.

In rejecting the Tydings Bill Muñoz Marín joined the distinct minority of insular politicians who treated political status as something more than an easily-changed slogan. He understood that independence was a real possibility and that the highly dependent insular economy would be dangerously strained by a sudden American withdrawal. Puerto Rican agronomist Pedro Chardón reported that independence under the Tydings provisions would "double and treble the island's prevailing starvation and could result in nothing short of chaos."[27] Muñoz Marín insisted that the United States owed Puerto Rico more than a fond farewell after dominating insular development for forty years. Instead of accepting the Tydings Bill, he urged the Liberal Party to lobby for better terms and a new independence bill.

With Muñoz Marín counseling against immediate independence and Barceló in favor, the Liberal Party became hopelessly divided. The party's support came from two major groups. The urban middle class faction of lawyers, writers, professors, teachers and shopkeepers favored independence. The professionals of this group felt a strong commitment to Hispanic culture and saw little danger in an independent economy. Urban shopkeepers thought independence would allow them to regain the customers they were rapidly losing to North American chain stores. The smaller sugar growers (*colonos*) formed the party's second major faction. They were benefiting from New Deal provisions which protected their American markets, and they opposed immediate independence. Neither Barceló nor Muñoz Marín could unite the party. Barceló alienated the *colonos* with his lack of concern for the economic consequences of independence. Muñoz Marín confused urbanites by opposing immediate independence. He tried to get party support for a more generous independence bill, but he lost an executive committee power struggle and was ousted from the party.

In the end, the controversy surrounding the Tydings Bill demonstrated the irony and impotence of Puerto Rico's political dependence on the United States. A senator's anger and a cabinet officer's ignorance thoroughly rearranged the insular political system. The bill itself died innocuously in committee, smothered by American corporations that had business in Puerto Rico. The Liberal Party was the major casualty. Because of the split in their ranks, the Liberals lost the 1936 elections. They registered 48 per cent of the popular vote, but lost the vast majority of individual election districts. The Republican-Socialist *Coalición* remained in power.

While the Liberals and the *Coalición* fought for voters, the remnants of the Nationalist Party continued demonstrating in the streets. The American governor, ex-admiral Blanton Winship, saw the Nationalist marches as a test of his own will, and he began denying permission for the parades. In early 1937 he relented and said he would allow a Nationalist march on Palm Sunday in Ponce, the island's second-largest city. Winship reversed himself and withdrew permission only 24 hours before the scheduled parade. His arbitrary action encouraged Nationalist defiance. On Sunday morning, 80 young Nationalist cadets and 12 girls walked into a police force of 150 well-armed men. When the shooting ended, 17 marchers and 2 policemen were dead, and over 100 people were wounded. Photographs and testimony of attending doctors confirmed that the event deserved its popular name, "The Ponce Massacre." The vast majority were shot from behind, and not one civilian could be shown to have had a gun. An American Civil Liberties Union investigation called this police riot a "gross violation of civil rights and incredible police brutality."[28] The United States government decided not to investigate the event.

Although the Ponce Massacre outraged Puerto Ricans, most of them continued to be more concerned about hunger, jobs and material welfare than about the political issue of independence. Luis Muñoz Marín used his understanding of popular desires to restructure his crumbling poliitical base. In 1938 he organized the Popular Democratic Party (*Partido Popular Democratico*, PPD) with the pledge that "status is not an issue." Many insular intellectuals and professionals believed Muñoz Marín was only dropping that status issue temporarily. They felt sure he would seek independence after the Popular Party won an election, and many of them followed him into the new party.

Between 1938 and 1940 Muñoz and his *Populares* took their campaign to the countryside. They adopted the broad-brimmed hat (*la pava*) of the solitary mountain peasant (*jíbaro*) as their symbol on the ballot. Their slogan was "Bread, Land and Liberty" (*Pan, Tierra, y Libertad*). In their platform, they made no mention of independence and stressed enforcement of the 500-acre law. The *populares* made a host of specific promises, including agricultural cooperatives, minimum wage legislation and homes for sharecroppers. Traveling from town to town in an old car, Muñoz Marín talked to people about their problems and tried to break down the well-established tradition of vote-selling. He compared the vote to a weapon for the protection of one's family. Rather than selling it for a pair of shoes, the people should *lend* it to Muñoz Marín so that he could fight for their economic betterment. He urged them to pit virtue against money (*verguenza contra dinero*). If they felt short-changed after four years, the people could throw him out of office. For the first time since the early days of the Socialists, a Puerto Rican political party won popular support without paying for it. A cane worker described his reaction to the new party:

Before, at political meetings the leaders would hold forth, and it was truly eloquent oratory, truly lovely. But what we heard we did not understand—orations about the mists, the seas, the fishes, and great things. Then, when Muñoz Marín came, he didn't come speaking that way. He came speaking of the rural workers, of the cane, and of things that were easier to understand. And the people could go along with him . . . And so they learned to trade the mists and the sea for the plantain trees and for the land they were going to get if they gave the Popular party their votes.[29]

In November of 1940, the Popular Party won its first victory. The Populares were not in a clear majority, but the votes of three splinter party members gave them control of the insular legislature. Muñoz Marín became president of the Puerto Rican Senate. The PPD consolidated its position in 1944 by winning undisputed control of the legislature.

The results of the 1940 elections reflected major changes in island politics. The most obvious was mass support for the Popular Democratic Party, with strength concentrated in rural areas. The Popular victory also demonstrated the disarray of all the other parties. The Republican-Socialist Coalición was torn by internal divisions and demoralized by the death of Santiago Iglesias in 1939. Liberal chief Antonio Barceló died in 1938. When his sucessor adopted a pro-statehood position, Liberal *independentistas* flocked to the Popular Party. They had no other choice, since Nationalist leader Albizu Campos remained in federal prison.

Finally, the 1940 elections marked a turning point in Puerto Rican history. The next 30 years would bring a moderate increase in political autonomy and dramatic changes in the local economy. The great sugar corporations would be replaced in importance by textile corporations, Hilton hotels, Union Carbide, Phillips Petroleum, Kennecott Copper and other mainland giants. In 1940 Puerto Rico was predominantly agricultural and had virtually no industry. By 1970 it was among the world's 20 most industrialized areas.

When the Popular Party took power in 1941, it had promised a specific list of social and economic reforms. However, such reforms required a sympathetic American governor, one who would aid rather than obstruct new programs. Luis Muñoz Marín appealed to President Roosevelt to appoint a governor who was more than a disciplinarian or an unemployed political retainer. Roosevelt responded by naming Guy Rexford Tugwell in the fall of 1941. Tugwell had moved easily between the Columbia University faculty and various government positions. A leading theorist of the New Deal, he had considerable experience with the problems of both farmers in general and Puerto Ricans in particular. Beween 1935 and 1937 he had directed the controversial Resettlement Administration, a bureau that distributed land and arranged low-interest loans for impoverished tenants in the United States. Many farm interests considered his activities socialistic. Tugwell had visited Puerto Rico twice before becoming governor. In 1940, he headed a group researching means for enforcement of the island's 500-Acre Act. As governor, Tugwell sought to forge a partnership between government and business, with government the senior partner. Although he distrusted bankers and corporate leaders, he never suggested an end to private enterprise. His goal was to create an efficient, powerful and reasonably honest bureaucracy to spread the benefits of capitalist society.

Like Tugwell, Muñoz Marín was interested in working with private enterprise rather than dismantling it. His party initiated expropriation of the great sugar estates, but the 500-Acre Act was never fully enforced, and large cane fields remained in private hands. Muñoz Marín's Popular Democratic Party strongly resembled Roosevelt's Democratic Party in its celebration of "pragmatism" and a "middle way" between fascism on the right and socialism on the left.

Although its final achievements were limited, the PPD originally pleased its rural supporters by quickly moving to enforce the 500-Acre Act and improve the lives of agricultural workers. The Land Act of 1941 served as the main reform vehicle. Its most innovative feature was the creation of proportional profit farms that were owned by the government, run as large-scale plantations, and worked by landless laborers (*agregados*). At the end of each year, the *agregados* divided the farm's profits among themselves. The government mandated a Land Authority to buy land, establish farms, hire qualified managers, and supervise profit distribution. By 1950 the government had acquired nearly half the holdings in excess of 500 acres and was operating 48 proportional-profit farms. Another feature of the Land Act, provided for in Title V, was the establishment of new rural communities for *agregados*. The Land Authority bought acreage unfit for large-scale agriculture and gave *agregados* plots of three acres or less to use as they pleased. To prevent loss of the lands because of indebtedness, the Land Authority retained the titles. Over 13,000 tiny plots had been distributed by 1945. In addition to implementing the Land Act, the government regulated agricultural wages and broke the sugar corporations' control over AGREGADO labor. Many cane workers felt that the PPD had improved their lives (see Sidney W. Mintz, *Worker in the Cane: a Puerto Rican Life Story*, Yale University Press, 1960).

However, the shortcomings of the Popular Party's agricultural program became obvious within a decade. By 1950 the party had lost interest in total enforcement of the 500-Acre Act. The government continued to distribute land and placed 400,000 people in Title V communities by 1964, but it concentrated on extremely marginal acreage and ignored remaining larger holdings. Many of the tiny farms were isolated and infertile, and all of them were too small for subsistence farming. Several of the 48 proportional-profit farms were losing money because of poor management and worker discontent. Private sugar corporations no longer controlled the insular economy, but the government had failed to provide sufficient jobs and land for the rapidly growing rural population.[30]

Rather than diversify agriculture, the PPD decided to undertake the industrialization of Puerto Rico. Tugwell and Muñoz Marín agreed that agriculture had reached the saturation point, since all arable land was in use. They thought that industry alone could provide new employment opportunities and a solid base for economic development. Tugwell wanted to postpone creation of new industries until World War II supply shortages ended, but Muñoz Marín insisted on an early start. Excise receipts from insular rum helped Muñoz Marín win the argument. A wartime liquor shortage greatly whetted mainland thirst for the Caribbean beverage, and the excise revenues financed new island industries.

Between 1942 and 1947 the government emphasized public ownership of new industries. The Industrial Development Company, popularly known as *Fomento*, organized companies to produce rum bottles, cardboard boxes, structured tile, bricks, sewer pipes and other goods. It took over the Puerto Rican Cement Corporation from the PRRA. In an effort to promote tourism, Fomento built the island's first large hotel, the present Caribe Hilton. After five years, the government decided its program had been a failure. *Fomento* had opened 2,000 new jobs, but 200,000 were needed. Its investments generated $4 million annually, but the island needed another billion dollars.[31]

In 1947 the PPD government began opening Puerto Rico to mainland investors, offering them a cheap labor supply, well-controlled labor unions and liberal tax incentives. Muñoz Marín announced that the program would promote private investment without subjecting Puerto Rico to uncontrolled exploitation by American corporations, but the only serious controls were those on wage levels and worker organizations. Minimum wages were controlled by the government and maintained well below mainland levels. The closed shop was banned except in local commerce and selected interstate industries. The *Confederación General de Trabajadores* (CGT), which received PPD support for its militant organization of the sugar workers during the early 1940s, had become an arm of the Popular Party by 1950. It expelled *independentistas* and affiliated itself with the mainland CIO. During the 1950s competing AFL-CIO internationals eroded CGT organization in urban areas. AFL-CIO successes led to the complete removal of some wage disputes from the island, because absentee owners and mainland union representatives arranged the settlements. Only one-third of the island's workers were organized by 1969, and they went on strike only one-third as often as their mainland counterparts. At that time, Puerto Rican workers averaged an hourly wage of $1.82 compared with $3.10 for the same groups in the United States. Yet the island's high unemployment rate, which never sank below ten per cent even in official figures, prompted most Puerto Ricans to accept low wages.[32]

The Industrial Incentives Act of 1947 outlined the benefits available to private investors in Puerto Rico. The most important provision was a 10-year exemption from insular taxes for any corporation that built a plant in a new industry, expanded in an approved existing industry, or constructed a new hotel. Since the Jones Act already exempted Puerto Rico from federal income taxes, corporations could virtually escape taxation for 10 years. The government later extended the period to 17 years in some industries. U.S. investors, who estimated they could quadruple their mainland profit levels, poured into the island during the 1950s.[33] By suspending corporate taxation, the government deprived itself of income necessary to finance badly needed social reforms and an independent economic base. It excercised minimal control over the use of capital after a plant was constructed. Investors from the United States could freely remove their profits from the island instead of funneling them back into the Puerto Rican economy.

To provide further encouragement to investors, *Fomento* sold its own industries to private businessmen and became the major agency of a development program known as Operation Bootstrap. Bootstrap's extensive mainland advertising campaign alerted Americans to the advantages of doing business in Puerto Rico, vacationing in San Juan's Condado district and drinking Puerto Rican rum. In addition, Bootstrap administered the program of Aid to Industrial Development, which helped mainland investors by recruiting and training workers, building factories to rent and sell on liberal terms and providing free technical advice.

A recent publication for American investors abroad summarized

Puerto Rico's advantages for the foreign capitalist. It explained the incentives program, noted the ease with which profits may be repatriated, and concluded:

"Relatively little can be said about government regulation, as the Puerto Rican economy is rapidly becoming a showpiece of free enterprise . . . the Puerto Rican economy is largely integrated into that of the U.S. . . .

Consequently, the government's role is . . . largely indirect. The government does not subject management to any special requirements, and labor need not be given a voice on the board of directors or in the management of the corporation. Non-Puerto Rican investment or ownership is allowed in all areas. Puerto Rico does not enforce any special code covering investment in oil or mining, local-content requirements . . or controls on new investment or expansion of existing investment.[34]

As the government changed its economic policies, it also reorganized the bureacracy that administered them. *Fomento* gathered most of its complex and wide-ranging activities under a single office, the Economic Development Administration (EDA), in 1950. The EDA gained jurisdiction over numerous semi-independent boards and commissions that had appeared during Tugwell's administration. These included the Government Development Bank, which provided economic aid to investors, and the Land Authority, which supervised agrarian reforms. Overall responsibility for developmental planning lay with the newly-created Economic Division of the Planning Board.[35]

An experienced group of local administrators, Tugwell-Muñoz Marín appointees, headed the new insular bureaucracy. Born in Puerto Rico and educated in the United States, they remained major political figures for over 20 years. Teodoro Moscoso, first director of *Fomento*, eventually presided over President John F. Kennedy's Alliance for Progress. Rafael Picó began as chairman of the Planning Board and went on to serve as Treasurer of Puerto Rico and president of the Government Development Bank. A former *independentista*, Sol Luis Descartes, had a 20-year career as director of the Land Authority's Planning Division, head of the Office of Statistics, Treasurer of Puerto Rico and director of the insular power authority. Jaime Benítez, another former *independentista*, was rector of the University of Puerto Rico for 25 years. Roberto Sánchez Vilella, an unobtrusive but efficient worker, was both a legislative aid and a high-ranking administrator for Muñoz Marín.[36]

By the time Muñoz Marín retired in 1964, the PPD could cite an impressive list of material improvements. The island's standard of living appeared to be luxurious compared with other parts of Latin America. However, Puerto Rico was part of the United States economy, and Puerto Ricans paid American prices for their goods. Insular incomes never approached those of the poorest states, and many statistics merely reflected the success of mainland corporations in the island.

Insular social reform programs offered improvements, but failed to meet the population's needs. The government built miles of new roads and 34,000 units of low-cost urban housing. Water and sewage systems were extended to every urban center on the island. After the PPD instituted free medical care, life expectancy reached 70 years and the death rate was lower than in the United States. For the first time, Puerto Ricans could apply for welfare benefits. However, 40 per cent of all dwellings were still inadequate in 1960. Urban renewal efforts stopped the growth of San Juan's slums without reducing their area or population. Urban slums and many rural areas lacked adequate water and sewage facilities. Jobless Puerto Ricans could expect *less than $12 a month* from the Welfare Department, a pathetic sum at American price levels.

The government continued to expand educational facilities, but the school system still exhibited serious shortcomings. Despite rapid population growth, insular schools accommodated 90 per cent of the children aged six to 12 years. Literacy improved from 69 per cent in 1940 to 83 per cent in 1960. High school classes grew more rapidly than any other group, and enrollment at the University of Puerto Rico nearly tripled between 1950 and 1964. University teaching standards were substantially revised and improved. Nevertheless, problems remained at every level of the school system. Dropout rates were high, and the average adult had only four and a half years of education. Those who stayed in school suffered from overcrowding, half-day sessions, and a continued overemphasis on the English language. At the University of Puerto Rico, Rector Jaime Benítez confined young scholars to a *"casa de estudios"*—roughly, "ivory tower"—form of education. Pro-independence student strikes in 1948 provoked repressive action by the administration. Benítez engineered the passage of regulations banning "partisan" political activities and speakers on the campus, giving the PPD a monopoly over student forums. As one scholar has noted, "to assume the emergence of 'political activities' that are not 'partisan' is rather like requesting a system of marriage without sex."[37]

Operation Bootstrap attracted hundreds of new industrial plants, but

American corporations enjoyed most of the financial benefits while Puerto Ricans had to cope with new problems created by industralization. One billion dollars in new investments entered Puerto Rico between 1950 and 1960, and dramatically shifted the island's economic emphasis from sugar to industry. In 1940 sugar accounted for almost 40 per cent of all income and almost 70 per cent of all exports. By 1964, industry earned four times as much as agriculture. Heavy industry, such as petrochemicals and copper, had begun replacing the light, consumer-goods industries of the 1950s. The move to heavy industry created two new problems. First, factories tended to become capital-intensive, using very expensive, sophisticated machinery and only a few, highly-sklled workers. Heavy industry thus threatened to produce higher unemployment rates. Second, the new petrochemical and mineral industries multiplied insular problems with air and water pollution.

Unemployment remained a chronic Puerto Rican dilemma. World War II and the end of the Depression helped drop official levels from 18 per cent in 1940 to 13 per cent in 1950, but the government was unable to make significant improvements under Operation Bootstrap. The actual numbers of unemployed and underemployed probably averaged over one-third of the working population. Although the number of jobs grew by 28 per cent between 1940 and 1964, the population increased more than 34 per cent. As agricultural jobs disappeared, workers left to fill new positions in the cities, refill the urban slums, or try their luck in the United States.

Figures on average income grossly distorted actual conditions, because income was very unevenly distributed. Per capita income rose from about $100 annually in 1940 to over $1,000 annually in 1964. However, the poorest 20 per cent of the people lived on only five per cent of Puerto Rico's personal income while the richest 20 per cent monopolized over half of that total. Eighty per cent of all families earned less than $3,000 dollars a year, placing them below the official United States poverty level. The average family income of $3,818 compared very poorly with the mainland average of $7,430. In 1962, 300,000 of the island's 2.6 million people were on relief, and 650,000 were receiving surplus food from the United States. [38]

As a result of *Fomento's* activities and World War II, mainland contacts with Puerto Rico multiplied geometrically. The hegemony of American sugar interests was broken, but its replacement was a much greater military, industrial and cultural mainland presence. During

World War II, the United States established military bases throughout the island. They covered over 10 per cent of the total land area by 1964. The Strategic Air Command's Ramey Air Force Base and extensive naval gunnery ranges on offshore islands made Puerto Rico a key element in United States Caribbean defenses. A recent publication of the Council on Foreign Relations has concluded:

> denial or curtailment of American national interest in the Caribbean would in practice be difficult to reconcile with the maintainance of an American world role and with any attempt to use American influence, even in a restrained manner, in support of a world order consistent with American institutions and aspirations.[39]

New American industries made Puerto Rico dependent on the United States in two ways, both of them long familiar to the island. First, the firms were usually subsidiaries of absentee corporations. Their directors extracted huge salaries and profit remittances, distorting Puerto Rican development. Second, the American corporations themselves were subject to national business cycles and federal tariffs and trade laws. Like any American state, Puerto Rico could be harmed by a recession or a change in external trade policies. In the early 1960's, for example, the United States renegotiated textile agreements with the European Common Market to the detriment of Puerto Rican mills and workers. The island eventually suffered from Spanish and Italian competition. Unlike the states, it had no voting representatives to oppose the changes.

Finally, their higher incomes and improved transportation-communication system exposed Puerto Ricans to a widening flood of American consumer goods and services. The cars, telephones, and televisions came from the United States, as did most of the television programs. Increasing numbers of Puerto Ricans sent their sons and daughters to American colleges and universities. As one insular scholar remarked, "If Puerto Rico is a bridge between two cultures it is a bridge with three lanes going in one direction and only one in the other."[40]

Through the efforts of the Popular Party, the material well-being of the masses joined political status as a major insular political issue. Muñoz Marín and his followers linked the two issues by arguing that special political ties with the United States were essential to insular economic development. By rejecting the statehood alternative, they maintained an image of cultural nationalism and avoided an embarrassing failure in the U.S. Congress. Their insistence on ties with the United States had a self-fulfilling character, since Operation Bootstrap made Puerto Rico increasingly dependent on the United States and multiplied American interests on the island. The PPD development strategy effectively closed off alternative solutions to the problems of low wages and high unemployment. Political subordination to the United States prevented the island from changing its external trade policies to allow the importation of cheaper goods or the protection of local industries. Economic reliance on mainland corporations made cheap labor an integral part of the industrial incentives program.

Puerto Rico's labor surplus spilled over into the mainland after World War II, when large numbers of Puerto Ricans began migrating to the continent. About 70 per cent of the migrants were between the ages of 15 and 39, peak years of economic productivity. Many of them left San Juan slums such as *"El Fanguito"* (*"*Little Mud Hole)*"* and *"La Perla"* (*"*The Pearl*"*) to live in New York's *"El Barrio"* (East Harlem) or "Little Korea," a section of the South Bronx famous for its gang wars during the 1950s. Before 1940, migration to the United States averaged fewer than 2,000 persons annually. The number reached 46,000 in 1946, averaged 41,200 during the 1950s, and peaked at 69,000 in 1953. The Puerto Rican population on the mainland rose from 70,000 in 1940 to 900,00 in 1960. By 1970, there were more Puerto Ricans in New York City than in San Juan.

Several factors explain the migration. American corporations in Puerto Rico easily filled their needs for inexpensive, unskilled labor, but mainland factories, restaurants and farms faced a shortage of immigrants and rural Americans willing to accept low wages after World War II. The colonial relations between Puerto Rico and the United States greatly facilitated migration. Puerto Ricans needed no passports or special papers to work on the mainland. Furthermore, the Federal Aviation Administration allowed very low air fares between San Juan and the United States. The most important factor may have been the formal policies of the insular government. Unable to provide jobs for its population, the government shifted the responsibility for employment to the poor by urging them to leave the island. It treated American cities as a frontier, a population "safety valve." Through the migration division of its Department of Labor, the Puerto Rican government encouraged immigration and aided immigrants in the United States. The head of the migration division served as an unofficial ambassador in New York City.[41]

Whatever, the failures of the Popular Party, its political successes continued. The PPD consistently won over 60 per cent of the popular vote after 1944 and rarely lost an election district. The familiar bossism and pre-election voter intimidations of its predecessors soon replaced the party's early idealism. Its strong organization and reliable support among rural workers allowed it to survive challenges on both sides of the status issue, first from *independentistas*, then from the Statehood Republican Party *(Partido Estadista Republicano,* PER.)

Although Muñoz Marín had declared "status is not an issue," many of his liberal-*Independentista* followers doubted that he would abandon independence after supporting it for two decades. They were wrong. When they realized their mistake, many of them joined Concepción de Gracia in leaving the PPD and forming the Puerto Rican Independence Party *(Partido Independentista Puertorriqueño,* PIP). Founded in 1945, the PIP was the major opposition party until the 1956 elections. The Nationalist Party also revived after Pedro Albizu Campos returned from the Atlanta penitentiary in December 1947. When Rector Jaime Benítez refused to allow an Albizu Campos speech at the university in 1949, students responded with a nearly-unanimous strike. However, the rule against "political" speakers remained in effect.

Under pressure from independence supporters both inside and outside his party, Muñoz Marín lobbied in Washignton for greater political autonomy. Both Tugwell and President Harry S. Truman favored an elected governorship by the end of World War II. When Tugwell left in 1947, Truman made Jesús T. Piñero the island's first Puerto Rican governor. A year later, Muñoz Marín became the first beneficiary of the Elective Governor Act of 1947. Recognizing status as the major issue of the 1948 campaign, he revived a 1920s proposal for a Commonwealth or *Estado Libre Asociado* (Associated Free State). Puerto Rico would have its own constitution but continue in a special relationship with the United States. Muñoz Marín called his 1948 gubernatorial victory a mandate for commonwealth status, but it was really a vote of confidence in his leadership. Under his leadership, unemployment had dipped, the poor received a slightly larger share of the national income, and labor unions could count on government support against the sugar planters. Rural workers in particular, did not object if he wanted a commonwealth.

However, the commonwealth proposal roused fears of permanent subordination to the United States within the Puerto Rican Nationalist Party. The insular government was harrassing Nationalists with Law 53, an anti-free speech bill passed in 1947. A Puerto Rican version of the anti-subversive Smith Act, the "Law of the Muzzle" made it a felony to:

> Promote, advocate, advise, or preach voluntarily and knowingly the *necessity*, *desireability*, or *suitability* of overthrowing, paralyzing, or subverting the insular government or any of its political divisions, by means of force or violence.[42]

During and after the 1948 student strikes, scores of Nationalists and PIP members were detained for vaguely defined "seditious" activities. Embittered Nationalists took violent action in 1950 when the U.S. Congress passed Pubic Law 600, authorizing a special referendum on the drawing of a commonwealth constitution by insular delegates. Puerto Ricans could vote only "yes" or "no" since neither statehood nor independence appeared on the ballot. The Nationalists responded with a series of attacks on insular and federal authorities. On October 28, 1950, a Nationalist-led mutiny at the Rio Piedras prison resulted in 100 escapes and the death of two guards. Two days later four Nationalists attacked the governor's mansion in San Juan, killed a policeman and lost their lives. During October Nationalist uprisings also occurred in Jayuya, Utuado, Arecibo, Ponce and Mayagüez. Clashes with the police and National Guardsmen produced 29 dead and 51 wounded.[43]

On November 1 two Nationalists attacked the Blair House in Washington, temporary home of President Truman. One Nationalist and one Secret Serviceman were killed. The other Nationalist received a death sentence, which Truman commuted to life imprisonment. The attempt on Truman's life also brought swift repression in Puerto Rico. On November 2 the insular government arrested the entire Nationalist leadership and many members of the PIP. Albizu Campos was given a 79-year sentence under Law 53, but Muñoz Marín pardoned him in 1953. The Nationalists struck again in March 1954. Three men and a woman entered the U.S. House of Representatives, opened fire, and wounded five congressmen. As a result, 13 Puerto Ricans were convicted of conspiracy, and Albizu Campos' pardon was revoked.

The United States had designed the United Nations as, in part, a tool for dismembering the formal British and French colonial systems. Prodded by Puerto Rican *independentistas*, the U.N. soon turned to the issue of *American* colonies. According to U.N. rules, the United States had to supply details of social, economic and educational conditions in all territories that were not self-governing. The United States considered Puerto Rico an internal affair and did not welcome international scrutiny except on guided tours. The paradoxical status issue provided a solution. The United States could keep Puerto Rico to itself by making it appear to be self-governing. Congress joined Muñoz Marín in supporting commonwealth status. On June 4, 1951, almost 70 per cent of those voting endorsed the commonweath in the first status plebescite under United States rule. Less than a year later the people voted to accept the constitution drafted by PPD representatives and approved by the U.S. Congress. As a young man, Muñoz Marín had scoffed at autonomy as "freedom with a long chain." On June 25, 1952, he inaugurated the Commonwealth Constitution by raising the Puerto Rican flag beside the American flag. This was the anniversary of the American invasion in 1898.

Compared to the earlier Autonomous Charter and the Jones Act, the Commonwealth Constitution does provide for broader individual liberties and a more completely Puerto Rican executive branch. However, the constitution avoids a clear definition of the political relationship between Puerto Rico and the United States, merely noting that the insular government exercises its powers "within the terms of a compact agreed upon between the people of Puerto Rico and the United States of America." Public Law 600, which authorized the plebescite and constitutional convention, introduced the idea of "compact" as follows:

> fully recognizing the principle of government by consent, this act is now adopted *in the nature of a compact* so that the people of Puerto Rico may organize a government pursuant to a constitution of their own adoption. (emphasis added)

The legal idea of a compact stems from the times of the *Mayflower* in the United States and has tended to imply an equality of rights and obligations among those who agree to it. However, not even the Popular Party has consistently advanced one definition of the term as it applies to Puerto Rico and the United States. Before the passage of Public Law 600, Resident Commissioner Fernós Isern told a House committee that the bill "would not change the status of . . . Puerto Rico . . . It would not alter the powers of sovereignty acquired by the United States . . .under the the terms of the Treaty of Paris."[44] By 1952, Muñoz Marín was arguing that the compact worked a major change in Puerto Rican status, that the island was no longer an American colony, and that any future changes could only occur with the consent of the Puerto Rican people.

Unfortunately for Puerto Rico and the PPD, the United States government has rarely agreed with Popular Party rhetoric on the commonwealth. The Senate committee that reported Public Law 600 stated, "The measure would not change Puerto Rico's fundamental political, social, and economic relationship to the United States."[45] Public Law 600 provided that the Commonwealth Constitution had to be approved by the U.S. Congress, a requirement that forced Puerto Rico to strike several particularly liberal welfare measures from its constitutional draft. Many sections of the Jones Act remained in force through the Puerto Rican Federal Relations Act, passed in 1950. Tax and tariff rules, borrowing restrictions on the insular government and other portions of the old act were copied verbatim.

Perhaps the clearest explanation of the compact is found in Resolution 22 of the Puerto Rican constitutional convention, which defined the commonwealth as:

> . . . a state which is free of superior authority in the management of its own local affairs but which is linked to the United States of America and hence is part of its political system *in a manner compatible with its federal structure.* (emphasis added)

The major shortcoming of the commonwealth lies in the fact that virtually no aspect of local life is free of the superior federal authority. Federal control of foreign policy does not necessarily interfere with local autonomy. However, the United States also decides who may enter Puerto Rico, where Puerto Ricans may go, and whether Puerto Ricans will fight in foreign wars. Banking, currency and the mails are under federal jurisdiction, as are all laws concerning bankruptcy, naturalization and citizenship. The United States controls the media by licensing radio and television stations and by censoring books and works of art through the customs system. Puerto Ricans still have no voice in their tariffs and trade arrangements, and they must still transport their goods in American ships. The United States retains unlimited power to expropriate Puerto Rican lands and property. The drastic limits on insular autonomy have led many Puerto Ricans to ridicule the "compact" as nothing more than a cosmetic device to hide American sovereignty on the island.

In foreign relations the United States has capitalized on the ambiguity of commonwealth status. The United States notified the United Nations in 1952 that Puerto Rico had become a "territory with self-government" and therefore did not require annual reports on its social, economic and educational conditions. In 1966, however, the United States officially proclaimed its control over the island for military reasons and refused to join 14 Latin American nations in signing a treaty to ban the testing, use, production and storage of nuclear weapons in Latin America. The United States objected to the Treaty of Tlaltelolco because it specifically included Puerto Rico and the Virgin Islands in the nuclear-free zone.[46]

Although the PPD insisted that the Commonwealth Constitution settled the status question, neither the voters nor the other political parties agreed. Four months after the formal ratification of the commonwealth, in November 1952, the Puerto Rican Independence Party made the strongest showing in its history, and won almost 20 per cent of the popular vote. Police repression, public apathy towards independence and continued econommic growth under Muñoz Marín seem to have demoralized the PIP after 1952. Its popular support shrank to 22,000 votes, less than two per cent of the total, by 1964. As the PIP declined, the Statehood Republican Party (PER) steadily crept up on Muñoz Marín in the gubernatorial elections. The PER won over 13 per cent of the vote in 1952, about 25 per cent in 1956, and over 30 per cent in 1960. The PPD totals barely changed from 1952 to 1960, growing from 429,000 to 457,800. In the same period, the PER's vote rose from 88,100 to 252,300.

Statehood found support among the middle and lower classes of Puerto Rico's rapidly growing urban areas. Many urbanites felt that the rurally-based PPD was insensitive to housing shortages, welfare needs, public service inadequacies and utter misery in some of the slums. The newly-arrived middle class that bought General Electric appliances, drove Chevrolets and watched *Bonanza* embraced a rabid, 100 per cent Americanism. To the middle class, statehood would mean full citizenship and a final break with the traditions of rural poverty. As one PER legislator put it:

> . . . we're tired of having our leaders go up to Washington with tin cups, asking for handouts. If the United States won't give us statehood, why the hell did they give us U.S. citizenship in 1917? We want *complete* equality, not just some halfway measure.[47]

Even though it claimed that the commonwealth was an ideal solution, the PPD made a series of attempts at further improving Puerto Rican status. In 1957, an American congressman joined the insular resident commissioner in sponsoring the Fernós-Murray Bill, an abortive attempt to win greater autonomy in the fixing of tariffs. Five years later the insular assembly passed Joint Resolution No. 1, which asked that the United States resolve the status question by recognizing the island's local autonomy. Muñoz Marín and President John F. Kennedy exchanged several letters on the same topic. Finally, in 1963 Congress established the Joint Commission of the United States and Puerto Rico for the Study of Status (STACOM) to investigate the status question and make recommendations. Congress appointed seven Americans and six Puerto Ricans to the commission. After months of testimony and the withdrawal of the insular representative for independence, STACOM reached the anticlimactic conclusion that statehood, commonwealth and independence were all honorable and possible alternatives. STACOM also recommended a second plebescite on the status issue.

In July 1967 Puerto Ricans dutifully went to the polls. They could vote for independence, statehood or continued commonwealth status, but the results were not binding on the U.S. Congress. Both the PIP and the PER labelled the arrangement a phony plebescite. The PIP boycotted the election, but the PER could not keep its members in line. Most of them followed Luis A. Ferré into a second statehood party, the New Progressive Party (*Partido Nuevo Progresista*, PNP). With the motto "Statehood is Security," they won 38.9 per cent of the vote. Commonwealth remained a heavy favorite, winning 60.5 per cent. Less than one per cent of those voting chose independence. However, the status issue remained lively and unresolved.

In addition to the Progressives, several new political parties appeared in the 1960's. In 1960, the bishops of the Catholic church misinterpreted a PPD platform statement on criminal legislation that "only those acts which the general concensus of Puerto Ricans consider immoral . . . can be prohibited with punishment." They organized the Christian Action Party (Partido Acción Cristiana, PAC) to counteract what they called "the modern heresy that the popular will decides what is moral and immoral." The PAC also opposed government birth control clinics and supported religious instruction in public schools. Its two American-born bishops issued pastoral letters declaring a vote for a PPD a mortal sin, a position Cardinal Cushing and other high Catholic officials quickly attacked. The party won only 6.6 per cent of the gubernatorial vote in 1960 and 3.3 per cent in 1964.[48] On the left, the most prominent new group was the Pro-Independence Movement (*Movimiento Pro-Independencia*, MPI). Founded in 1961, the extra-electoral MPI led draft resistance and anti-election activities throughout the decade. Finally, the

People's Party (*Partido del Pueblo*) became the island's third statehood party in 1967.

By 1964 Muñoz Marín was 66 years old. He wanted the Popular Democratic Party to outlive him, and he decided to challenge the rules of Puerto Rican politics by retiring before dying. At an emotional nominating convention,he named longtime aide, Roberto Sánchez Vilella, to succeed him as candidate for governor. PPD politicians accepted Muñoz Marín's choice, mustered the usual 60 per cent majority, and prepared to go on as before. However, Sánchez Vilella soon alienated old *politicos* by appointing members of the New Progressive Party to executive positions. His influence plummeted because he did not have an independent base within the party, and he lacked charismatic appeal among the voters. By 1968 even Muñoz Marín had abandoned him. The party rejected Sánchez Vilella's bid for renomination and settled on an unattractive, little-known candidate. However, the governor convinced the one-year-old People's Party to jettison its statehood platform and make him its standard bearer. Sánchez Vilella's divorce and remarriage to a young secretary brought the voters out to hear him—and to see his new wife. He ran a poor third in the election, but he effectively split the PPD vote.

The beneficiary of the PPD infighting was Luis A. Ferré, candidate of the New Progressive Party, who won the 1968 election with 45 per cent of the popular vote. The Popular Party had suffered its first defeat after 28 years of political hegemony. Many Puerto Ricans assumed that the PPD's day had ended and that the island would be approaching statehood by 1980. Under Ferré, Puerto Rico appeared to continue developing at an impressive rate. The gross national product increased over ten per cent annually, and the government planned rapid expansion in tourism and heavy industry. As an heir to the Puerto Rican Republican Party, Governor Ferré hoped to forge special bonds with the Nixon Administration as Muñoz Marín had done with the Democrats. When opponents identified him with "Americanization", Ferré tried to downplay cultural issues and status by simply aligning himself with progress in Puerto Rico. Polls predicted an overwhelming victory for Ferré in November 1972. Instead, he suffered a defeat by the Popular Party. Ferré garnered 561,000 votes to his opponent's 603,000. The PDP also won both houses of the legislature, capturing 72 of the island's 78 election districts. The PIP earned four per cent of the vote, a slight improvement over its 1968 totals.

Puzzled journalists and politicians interpreted the election as a new mandate for the commonwealth and a rejection of independence, but the issue was far more complicated. The PPD victory resulted from two major elements. First, the electorate responded to economic hardships and international tensions by moving to the left. Second, the PPD found that it, too, could move rhetorically left and reconstitute its majority around a young, charismatic leader.

Figures on economic growth hid serious problems in Puerto Rico's economy. Heavy investments by copper and petrochemical firms raised the gross national product but provided few jobs and masked declines in other parts of the economy. A mainland recession eliminated job opportunities for young Puerto Ricans and contributed to a general decline of tourism in the Caribbean. The Ferré government, which favored private enterprise, was forced to buy luxury hotels to prevent them from closing. Low tariff walls and improving wages rendered the island's large textile industry incapable of competing with Italian and Spanish imports. About 62,000 textile workers lost their jobs in 1970 alone. To attract new mainland firms, Fomento advertised an official unemployment-underemployment rate of 34.4 per cent.[49]

The local effects of United States hot and cold wars encouraged negative feelings towards statehood among the populace. Puerto Ricans watched their sons being drafted to fight in Vietnam while well-educated Cuban refugees moved in to compete for the few highly-paid jobs with American corporations. When residents of the off-shore island of Culebra insisted that the U.S. Navy stop using their beach as a gunnery range, Ferré sided with the Navy. The Navy made the political mistake of supporting Ferré's reelection, a move which alienated many Puerto Ricans.

Finally, certain elements in Ferré's style of government eroded his electoral base. The Federation of Pro-Independence Students (*Federación de Universitarios Pro-Independentista*, FUPI), a university affiliate of the MPI, had been actively protesting the Vietnam war for several years. In 1970 antiwar students insisted that ROTC programs be ended on campus. The Ferré government replied that "only a strident minority of radicals oppose the ROTC" and sent police to end the agitation. Police fired into a group of rock-throwing students and killed a girl who was watching from a nearby balcony. The girl's death prompted a university referendum which disproved the government's "strident minority" theory. About 80 per cent of the students voted, and over half favored the abolition of ROTC. Ferré did not confine his government's repressive activities to the university campus. When the PIP helped organize squatter takeovers of public lands, Ferré authorized island police to raze the communities. On 14 different occasions, police and bulldozers moved in at 5 a.m. to destroy squatter shacks. The expulsions drew fire from the Puerto Rican Bar Association, which criticized Ferré for failing to secure warrants. The Bar Association also pointed out that Ferré was ignoring middle class "squatters" including a high-ranking member of his government, who had built beachfront homes on public lands owned by the Navy.

Anti-Ferré groups found an alternative in the reinvigorated Popular Democratic Party. The PPD had always maintained control of the insular senate. Its president, Rafael Hernández Colón, managed to reunite both the voters and the PPD politicians. At first, 36-year-old Hernández Colón seemed to offer nothing more than a handsome face and a strong commitment to commonwealth status. However, he quickly capitalized on Ferré's weaknesses. He stressed economics and sounded a note of cultural renewal, if not cultural nationalism. On election day, the PPD offered a candidate for those opposed to statehood in general and Ferré in particular. Colón lost San Juan and Ponce, but carried Bayamón, a large suburb of the capital. The suburban middle classes offered a strong replacement for the PPD's shrinking rural base.

After 75 years of rule by the United States, Puerto Rico has become an economic, political and cultural colony of the mainland. The Popular Democratic Party ended the abuses of the sugar economy during the 1940s, but Operation Bootstrap increased insular economic dependence on the United States. American investments in Puerto Rico now total $2.5 billion. The island is the United States' largest per capita export partner and fourth largest customer overall. Lobbyists for the major corporations would undoubtedly oppose radical changes in Operation Bootstrap. With their huge investments, American interests have a decisive influence on insular economic policy. Private industry finds high unemployment rates attractive rather than reprehensible, so the government promotes migration instead of economic reorganization. Corporations can finance a limited middle class, but most of the population remains expendable. The insular government cannot fund effective aid programs for the unemployed and unemployable because it allows corporations to escape taxation. Federal aid is limited, because American congressmen have little interest in promoting unpopular welfare measures for a voteless population.

Any move towards greater political independence would threaten United States military and diplomatic interests in Puerto Rico. The island is a key position in the Caribbean defense system and a jumping off point for enforcement of the Monroe Doctrine, which has largely been a Caribbean affair. Furthermore, the United States has a strong prestige commitment to Puerto Rico as a Third World showcase. Rejection of commonwealth status could easily be seen as an American failure.

In the past, Puerto Rico's economic weakness has been used as the major argument against both statehood and independence. Federal taxes, the PPD constantly warned, would make statehood expensive, while lack of free trade with the United States would make independence an economic disaster. Insular nationalists have frequently avoided economic discussions and have insisted that independence was necessary for reasons of dignity and cultural affirmation, regardless of the financial consequences. However, the continuing poverty of Puerto Rico's masses has made it clear that only an independent government would be free to end the island's lopsided development. Independence would be a very difficult proposition, but many of Puerto Rico's people already are living very difficult lives.

NOTES

1. Edward J. Berbusse, *The United States in Puerto Rico, 1898-1900* (University of North Carolina Press, 1966), p. 65.

2. Ibid., p. 82.

3. Ibid., pp. 82, 88.

4. Ibid., p. 155.

5. Ibid., p.230.

6. Ibid., p. 119.

7. *Politics and Education in Puerto Rico: A Documentary Survey of the Language Issue,* edited by Erwin H. Epstein, (Scarecrow Press, 1970), p. 52.

8. Victor S. Clark, et al., *Porto Rico and Its Problems* (The Brookings Institution, 1930), p. 404.

9. Bailey W. and Justine W. Diffie, *Porto Rico: A Broken Pledge* (Vanguard Press, 1931).

10. Ibid.

11. Clark, *Puerto Rico*, pp. 31-31.

12. Adalberto López, *Puerto Rican Nationalism: A Survey* (mimeographed, State University of New York at Binghamton, 1971), p.23.

13. Berbusse, *United States*, p. 214.

14. Gordon K. Lewis, *Puerto Rico: Freedom and Power in the Caribbean* (Harper and Row, 1963), p. 61.

15. Henry Wells, *The Modernization of Puerto Rico: A Political Study of Changing Values and Institutions* (Harvard University Press, 1969), p. 101.

16. Thomas G. Mathews, *Puerto Rican Politics and the New Deal* (University of Florida Press, 1960), p. 130.

17. Juan Antonio Corretjer, *Albizu Campos y las huelgas en los años '30* (Liga Socialista Puertorriqueña, 1969).

18. Mathews, *Puerto Rican Politics*, pp. 131-132.

19. Lewis, *Puerto Rico: Freedom*, p. 239.

20. Luis Muñoz Marín, "The Sad Case of Puerto Rico," *American Mercury*, Vol. 16, No. 52 (February 1929), p. 136.

21. Quoted in Manuel Maldonado-Denis, *Puerto Rico: A Socio-Historical Interpretation* (Random House, 4th ed., 1972), p. 83.

22. Mathews, *Puerto Rican Politics*, p. 30.

23. Corretjer, *Albizu Campos*, passim.

24. Mathews, *Puerto Rican Politics*, p. 251.

25. Ibid., p. 107.

26. *The Secret Diary of Harold Ickes. Volume 1. The First Thousand Days* (Simon and Schuster, 1953), pp. 547-48.

27. Mathews, *op. cit., Puerto Rican Politics*, p. 258.

28. Ibid., p. 313.

29. Sidney W. Mintz, *Worker in the Cane: A Puerto Rican Life History* (Yale Univeristy Press, 1960), p. 187.

30. Wells, *Modernization*, pp. 137, 148.

31. Ibid., p. 149.

32. Karl Wagenheim, *Puerto Rico: A Profile* (Praeger, 1970) pp. 128-131; "Puerto Rico: A National Profile," *International Business Series Publications*, Ernst and Ernst, 1971, p. 13

33. Charles T. Goodsell, *Administration of a Revolution: Executive Reform in Puerto Rico Under Governor Tugwell, 1941-1946* (New American Library, 1964), p. 179.

34. Wagenheim, "Puerto Rico: A National Profile," pp. 15-27.

35. William H. Stead, *Fomento: The Economic Development of Puerto Rico* (National Planning Association, 1958), p. 11.

36. Goodsell, *Administration*, passim.

37. Lewis, *Puerto Rico: Freedom*, p. 395.

38. Oscar Lewis, *La Vida* (Random House, 1965), p. xi.

39. Robert D. Crassweller, *The Caribbean Community: Changing Societies and U.S. Policy* (Praeger, 1972), p. 59.

40. Maldonado-Denis, *Puerto Rico*, p. 214.

41. For a brief survey of the Puerto Rican migration to the U.S. mainland see, Adalberto López, "The Literature of the Puerto Rican Diaspora," *Caribbean Review*, Vol. V, No. 2 (Spring, 1973), pp. 5-11.

42. Quoted in Maldonado-Denis, *Puerto Rico*, p. 197 (emphasis added).

43. Byron Williams, *Puerto Rico: Commonwealth, State or Nation?* (Parents Magazine Press, 1972), pp. 170-71.

44. Wells, *Modernization*, pp. 230-231.

45. Ibid., P. 391.

46. *New York Times*, February 13, 1967.

47. Salvatore Adonio, "What Happened in Puerto Rico?", *Hispanic American Report*; Wells, *Modernization*, pp. 272-273.

49. Stan Steiner, "The Poor in Puerto Rico," *New Republic*, 165 (December 11, 1971), pp. 8-9.

Colonial Policies of the United States*

Theodore Roosevelt

In October 1898 the American flag was raised over the island and Major General John R. Brooke became military governor. The local cabinet in Puerto Rico was retained, and the work of remaking Puerto Rico into a possession of the United States commenced. Brooke was succeeded almost immediately by General Guy B. Henry, who dissolved the insular cabinet and established government departments.

Meanwhile, our currency replaced that of Spain, our stamps the Spanish stamps. We took at once certain actions that are very characteristic of our people. We established a Board of Health and a Department of Education, we did away with such punishments as chains and stocks, and we organized an insular police force; then, as a tribute to our underlying Puritanism, we abolished the government lottery and outlawed cockfighting.

In Puerto Rico itself the feelings of the people were divided. Some of them had thought that we were going merely to push the Spaniards out and then turn over the conduct of their affairs to them. When they found this was not the case they voiced their protests. The feeling went no deeper, however. Relationships were amicable and genuine friendships grew up between the Americans who were working in the island and the Puerto Ricans.

The Americans who served there, in the by and large, were conscientious and sometimes able as well. Great strides were made along a number of lines. The first of these was health. Bailey K. Ashford, a

*Excerpts from Colonial Policies of the United States, by Theodore Roosevelt. Copyright 1937 by Doubleday & Company, Inc. Reprinted by permission of the publisher.

doctor in the American army, did remarkable work. Not only was he a good organizer but, in addition, a distinguished scientist, and he made notable discoveries in the field of tropical parasites. With him his work was not a means of earning a livelihood but literally a passion.

Before the arrival of the Americans, sanitary and health conditions in Puerto Rico had been exceedingly bad. After the organization of the department of health they steadily improved. The mortality rate both for adults and infants has declined sharply, but they never have been nor are they today really good.

Another division of government that made extraordinary progress also was the Department of Education. At the time of the occupation the number of students in schools was 25,000. By 1917 this had risen to 152,000. Public works were greatly developed. A fine road system was begun. Waterworks, etc., were undertaken. Meanwhile, trade had expanded. Imports in 1901 were $8,918,000; in 1917 they had jumped to $53,545,000. Exports had shown an even more remarkable increase. In 1901 they were $8,583,000; in 1917 they were $80,970,000. To phrase it in different fashion, the total trade had increased over those years approximately 800 per cent. Much of the increment in export can be traced to sugar, in which during these seventeen years exports had gone from $4,700,000 to $54,000,000. Sugar had thus become, by all odds, the most important cash crop of the island. Tobacco, like sugar, went mostly to the United States. The Puerto Rican coffee never has done so. It is costly to grow and cannot compete, therefore, on a price level with the product of the other great coffee-raising centers of South America. It depends for its sale mainly on those who appreciate a special flavor and goes to various European centers. At times in the United States I have had some hostess tell me her coffee was exceptional, always imported from Vienna, and I have recognized Puerto Rican coffee that has made the round trip. Besides the three products named above, the citrus-fruit industry was started, and needlework placed on a commercial footing.

The above is a rough sketch of the progress registered under our original scheme of government. The method of approach, however, is really more significant, because through the method of approach one can see at least what the governors of the island and the bureau in Washington with which they dealt were developing as a general policy. In brief, that policy was to Americanize Puerto Rico and thereby confer on her the greatest blessing, in our opinion, within our gift.

To begin with, as I have said, practically all important executives during this period were American, with the exception that toward the end of the period three Puerto Ricans were named as department heads.

The theory of the American administrators was not merely to give a good administration but to set an example and lay down lines for those who should follow in their footsteps. It always was our idea that these posts should eventually be held by Puerto Ricans, but it was our belief that they should not go to Puerto Ricans until the road was grooved so deeply that the carriage of state could not slide out of it into the ditch.

At this time and in consonance with this policy of Americanization, a commission considered the entire law of Puerto Rico and proposed codes which we approved for its modification and change. Puerto Rico, of course, before our occupation had been under a civil code derived from the Roman law, which we superseded in general with our adaptation of the English common law.

Perhaps more significant of the line we were following than any of the above was our attitude on education. When we arrived in Puerto Rico practically no one spoke English. Spanish was the language of the island and had been since its foundation. Even with the cultivated classes their knowledge of foreign tongues was generally confined to French. We set out deliberately to change this and to make Puerto Rico English speaking. We brought down American teachers for the schools and made it the basic language for the curriculum.

We had no colonial service and we did not develop one. Most of the men who filled executive positions in Puerto Rico went there from the United States with no previous experience whatsoever, speaking not a word of Spanish. Most of them had no conception either of Spanish culture or temperament. Most of them never learned to speak Spanish fluently, and many of them never spoke it at all.

Incidentally, I heard many amusing stories when I was in Puerto Rico of contretemps along this line. Once an American judge, who understood not a word of Spanish, was making an address on the Fourth of July. He spoke in English of George Washington, of liberty, etc., in sonorous periods and was much gratified by the thunderous applause which greeted the translation of his speech made by his interpreter. As a matter of fact, the interpreter had availed himself of this opportunity to deliver in the name of the judge a scathing diatribe against one of the local political parties.

When I went there as governor, I had had no experience worthy of the name and spoke only a halting Spanish. I did, however, start to learn the language at once and was reasonably fluent in it before long. Up to that time I was the only governor who had been able to make his speeches in Spanish and to dispense with an interpreter when dealing with local leaders. Indeed you might say it was our policy not to speak Spanish. A number of people who had served there before told me before I took over that it was better to force the Puerto Ricans to speak to me in English or to use an interpreter than to speak Spanish. I am inclined to think that in the majority of cases this policy represented mere laziness on the part of the individuals.

This Americanization was much more than a large group of Puerto Ricans had anticipated. The community had felt vaguely at the time of the Spanish-American War that the United States was merely taking them over from Spain to give them their freedom, or at least to give them complete control over their internal affairs. Their first disappointment was the Organic Act, which pre-empted, practically all the government powers to presidential appointees who were Americans. Their next was the resolute attempt to stamp out local customs and culture and to substitute English for Spanish. At once a party of opposition developed which took as its plank independence for Puerto Rico. The party was rather vague as to when and how this independence should come, but that was good politics, for it enabled the leaders to unite varying factions beneath their banner. In one of the early elections this party refused to go to the polls at all. Politics being politics, it accused the United States and its representatives in Puerto Rico of every conceivable crime. Flowery speeches were made, in which the Puerto Ricans were represented as downtrodden slaves and the United States as a tyrant. One orator, a plump little pouter pigeon, in a frenzy of excitement during his speeches used to tear down the American flag and dance a hornpipe on it.

Of course the statements were ridiculous, as the United States was doing its level best, at considerable sacrifice and expense, to aid the Puerto Ricans and was accomplishing notable results along many lines. On the other hand, the Puerto Rican point of view was inevitable. The people, particularly the upper classes, who were predominantly Spanish in blood, considered themselves as lineal heirs in America to Spanish culture and tradition. Equally with the Americans, they were lazy in learning a foreign language. What is more, they felt that in substituting English for Spanish they were abandoning their ancestral tongue. Over and above all, it was gall and wormwood to them to feel that they were not competent to administer their own affairs and that they, so to speak, had to be kept in leading strings. It was an admission of inferiority that they were unwilling to accept. Other conditions contributed also to the friction between the races. American capital had gone into the development of industry. This was particularly true in the sugar industry. Because of business efficiency and sufficient capital the American sugar companies had grown and prospered out of all proportion with those owned by Puerto Ricans. Human nature asserted itself and the Puerto Ricans maintained that the Americans had robbed them and were exploiting the island for their benefit at the expense of the natives. Again there were two sides to the question. Undoubtedly the American corporations had gathered into their hands the best tracts of land and made handsome earnings thereby. Undoubtedly certain of the companies did treat the Puerto Ricans in rather summary fashion, and probably as a result of these operations many Puerto Ricans found themselves without property. On the other hand, the American companies brought wealth into the island, gave more employment and created better living conditions than would have been the case had the development been limited entirely to Puerto Ricans. Of course there was an absolutely fair break as far as competition was concerned. The Americans had no advantage other than what came to them through their abilities.

I arrived as governor of Puerto Rico in 1929 and found the following situation. Economically the island was in bad case. The population under the American administration had grown so extraordinarily rapidly that the people living on the island numbered about one million six hundred thousand. It was one of the most densely populated areas per arable square mile in the world. The people still depended upon agriculture as their main means of livelihood. The rich coastal plain was largely in the hands of big sugar companies. The small farmer had been forced back into the rugged and comparatively barren hills. Poverty was widespread and hunger, almost to the verge of starvation, common. As the rich coastal lands were most valuable for sugar production, the growing of vegetables, etc., was greatly circumscribed. The main diet of the people consisted of salt codfish, rice and beans, all three imported, the beans and rice coming mainly from the Orient. Every city or large town had its slum, where the squalor and filth were almost unbelievable.

As a logical result of this the island was disease ridden. Tuberculosis had reached an astonishingly high rate. In the lowlands there was much malaria. There was sickness from hookworm and from intestinal parasites, besides, of course, pernicious anemia. Suffering had been greatly augmented by a recent, very severe cyclone.

Financially conditions were in bad shape also. In spite of the financial aid extended by the United States the general poverty was such that revenues were scant. Not only were they scant but they had been wasted, in many instances, on projects of doubtful value. The government had had recourse also to the age-old practice of communities that find themselves in financial difficulties. They had borrowed and floated bonds to meet deficits. Not only this, but large bond issues had been sold for projects that were entirely out of keeping with a community as poor as Puerto Rico. For example, a hospital for the insane had been constructed on a scale as lavish as that of the wealthiest community in the continental United States, and operating costs were beyond the capacity of the insular government. A sanitarium for tubercular patients had been built with the same lavishness, but its capacity was only 247, whereas those suffering in the island were estimated at some forty thousand. A new leper colony had been undertaken. A superb and rather ornate administration building had been completed but the money had run out before adequate housing for the lepers had been constructed. There had been an Unemployment Commission. Outside of drawing its compensation, it had done little. A voluminous report was printed, at government expense, which consisted mainly of copies of Australian labor reports. One original suggestion was that canaries should be obtained and given to the poor, who could teach them to whisle "The Star-Spangled Banner" and then sell them to the American tourists. A great deal of money had been spent, to no point, on partly constructing a superb marble capitol. A penitentiary of most modern design was also practically complete. It had mosaic doors imported from Spain and running water in the cells.

Incidentally, thereby hangs a tale. It was being finished through convict labor. The cells in it were commodious as compared to the average Puerto Rican house. It is said that one day some of the convicts who were working outside ran away to the nearest village and got very drunk. The warden punished them. When they returned in the small hours of the morning he refused to let them back into the jail.

Most of the municipalities were either bankrupt or close to it. Only a few of them made any pretense to balancing their budgets. The insular government itself had not actually balanced its budget for seventeen years.

The drive to Americanize the island had gradually slowed down. The use of English was less general than it had been six or eight years previously. The leaders of two of the larger parties spoke only Spanish. Politically, the country was going through a realignment. As with most Latin peoples, party allegiance was more personal than in the Anglo-Saxon countries. One of the major parties had split into smaller groups, and in the legislature a combination was necessary to achieve control. The largest single party had as one of its planks Puerto Rican independence; the minority opposition wished statehood.

Very evidently the first problem at hand was economic. Accordingly, in my inaugural address I told the people that, even though it might be perfectly right and understandable that they should be concerned over what their future political status might be, the pressing need of the moment was economic rehabilitation. With conditions such as I have outlined the next question to decide was wherein lay the root of the trouble. This, too, unfortunately, was easy to determine. Though many causes contributed, the chief factor was the great overpopulation in an agricultural community, and this could only be alleviated, not remedied. We immediately undertook a series of endeavors. First, we made a frank statement of just what conditions were and released it to the newspapers in the United States. At the same time we organized a society to feed destitute Puerto Rican children, provide milk stations, etc. Second, we made a survey of what existing businesses could be built up and what new ones established. To aid us in this we organized a Bureau of Commerce and Industry. We tried to build up truck gardening among the people by such methods as appealing to the sugar companies to give their workmen ground on which to grow vegetables. We established better methods of distribution. We organized markets. We also developed a Homestead Commission which financed and put back on the soil Puerto Rican families capable of farming. Finally, we cut out all unnecessary expense possible. In this the executive office was greatly aided by the fact that the law gave the governor the power to blue-pencil any specific item in the budget presented to him by the legislature without vetoing the entire measure.

While this was being done, a political struggle was in process. It seemed to me that there were three ultimate goals toward which policy could be shaped. The first of these was statehood; the second, some kind of dominion status; and the third, absolute independence, such as is enjoyed by the Dominican Republic, Haiti and Cuba.

All involved great difficulties. Statehood, I think, though I was able to find no statement to that effect, had been the unconscious aim of previous administrations, particularly those during the early days. I believe that those administrators unconsciously, in hammering at the Americanization program, were thinking of Puerto Rico as a territory that would eventually be taken into the Union as the western states had been. Undoubtedly this solution would have been best had conditions been different. There were, however, too many great obstacles in the way. The first of these was that, in order to achieve results, an entire people had to be made over in their language and their methods of approach on life—an almost impossible task. It is one thing for a Spaniard to come to the United States to live and through his everyday contacts attune himself to our method of thought. It is another matter to try, with a handful of officials, to change an entire people in the land where they have been born. Fundamentally we are different from the Spanish Americans, and by saying this I am not saying that we are either better or worse. Nonidentity does not imply either superiority or inferiority. The difference of which I have spoken is evident in everyday life, the ordinary small amenities. For example, we would say on meeting a man merely, "How do you do?" A Spanish-speaking Puerto Rican, with far greater courtesy, would, in addition, ask, "¿Cómo está su estimada esposa y su distinguida familia [How is your estimable wife and your distinguished family]?" If he is of the old school he will close a personal letter with q.b.s.m.—*quien besa su mano* [who kisses your hand]. Puerto Rican girls are brought up in the Spanish tradition. The sex relationship is entirely different. Small personal habits are dissimilar. A Puerto Rican orator turns phrases in his ordinary address which our people would consider flowery.

Next in point of difficulty on the road to statehood was the poverty of the island. Not only was Puerto Rico entirely unable to assume the burdens that all states carry with reference to sustaining the federal government, but, in addition, she needed desperately contributions from the federal government to sustain her. What is more, with the terrific population density, the small extent of the fertile land and the limited natural resources, it was practically impossible to envisage any period in the future when she would be able to take up these federal burdens. Finally, in assuming this as our goal, we gambled on the political attitude of mind of the continental United States. Would it be willing to place two Puerto Rican senators in the Senate and the corresponding congressman in the lower house? After balancing all of these in my mind I decided that statehood was not a possibility and that it would be base to hold it up as such.

Next there came the question of independence. From the strictly material point of view this would be the best solution as far as the United States is concerned. However, independence at this time would be tantamount to condemning to death some five hundred thousand or more Puerto Ricans, for with the ties once cut between the island and our country, the economic condition of the island would be so infinitely bad that tens of thousands would die of disease and starvation.

There remained the possibility of a dominion status, and this is that toward which I directed my work. I felt that such a goal, if attainable, would be best both for the United States and for Puerto Rico, and that furthermore, if unattainable, it did not preclude independence, as would statehood if achieved.

To begin with, to gain such an end there would be no reason to continue the hopeless drive to remodel all Puerto Ricans so that they should become similar in language, habits and thoughts to continental Americans. Second, a financial status which contemplated an economic condition only sufficiently good to maintain her own internal government was far more imaginable than one where the island would have to contribute toward the maintenance of the federal government. A dominion status also could carry the same advantages as statehood as far as trade relations are concerned. The tariff barriers would not be raised against Puerto Rican products, and, therefore, her major industries, which are now entirely dependent on markets within the United States, would not be destroyed. Lastly, the pride of her people would be satisfied on realizing self-government within their own borders.

Of course I knew that this goal would be far in the future. Much had to be done before it was a possibility. It was, however, to my way of thinking the best plan.

So far I have spoken only of my plans from the standpoint of Puerto Rico. From the standpoint of the United States I could readily see advantages also. We as a nation must look in all probability on the countries of our hemisphere as our closest associates in the future. Of these, all below the Rio Grande have Latin traditions and a greater or lesser amount of Latin blood. Puerto Rico might well be our connecting link. She might be, so to speak, our show window looking south. Her educated people, though primarily Latin in culture, blood and tradition, would speak English and be acquainted with America and America's method of thought. Under these circumstances they would be ideally suited for representatives of American banking or industry in the Latin-American countries. Some special arrangement might be consummated whereby they would be available for consular or diplomatic work. Accordingly, I shaped my policies to this end. I told the people that they should be proud of their Spanish language and traditions and preserve both, but that they should learn English and acquaint themselves with America's method of thought. I explained to them that one did not eliminate the other, and that by adding the second to the first they were enriched, not impoverished.

In order to give a warrant of my good faith in this, I worked particularly hard on my Spanish. Deciding that the only way to learn to swim was to jump into water that was over my head, I made my speeches in Spanish. Languages do not come to me easily, and I made many comic mistakes. Once, when addressing a group of parents on school problems and desiring to impress them with my knowledge of the subject, I used a direct translation from English into Spanish of "I have four children myself." Unfortunately, the meaning is not the same. I found out I had informed the startled audience that I had given birth to four children! When I told the president of the Puerto Rican Senate, who was lunching with me immediately afterwards, what had happened, he merely lifted his eyebrow and said, "Pero, Señor Gobernador, todo es posible en los trópicos [But, Mr. Governor, everything is possible in the tropics]." At another time when introducing a distinguished general, and wishing to say he was a bachelor, I made a slight slip and announced him as a "tapeworm."

On the economic end we made good gains. We publicized and broadened the market for Puerto Rican needlework, both my wife and I at times acting as salesmen. We built up the production of vegetables. We spread agricultural knowledge among the small farmers by using demonstration trucks which went from community to community. Our fiscal policy was successful also. We obtained a grant of money from the federal government which we employed for road construction in such fashion as to make existing roads better and cheaper to maintain and at the same time give work to many who would otherwise have been unemployed. We pared down the island government budget, discontinued all operations which were not strictly necessary, and eventually succeeded in balancing it. Some of the slums we were able to clean up through the construction by the government of small houses, and we placed a certain number of families on farms of their own through the Homestead Commission. Neither of the last two policies, however, worked as well as I had hoped, the former because it got into politics, the latter because the land obtainable was either too costly or too barren to be of much value.

I was really sorry to leave the island when my term had finished, and I felt I had left friends there and an interesting problem by no stretch of the imagination solved.

Origins of the Puerto Rican University Student Movement Under U.S. Domination (1903-1930)

Isabel Picó

During the first 30 years of U.S. domination in Puerto Rico, significant changes occurred in the educational superstructure that altered the formative process of university youth, successor, although in a different way, to that created during the nineteenth century by the relative economic prosperity of the island's landowning bourgeoisie. With the change from a semifeudal hacienda-type agriculture to a system of capitalist plantations that accompanied the U.S. occupation, college education continued to serve the descendants of landowners and some businessmen. However, new economic and political conditions brought about the development of new college institutions and of an educational culture in accord with the socio-economic formation of agrarian capitalism.

Under U.S. domination, Puerto Rico became a sugar cane plantation colony that produced raw materials for exportation to the markets of the colonial metropolis. Gradually a new social structure came into being, controlled by powerful North American corporations and their administrators and technicians. The metropolis maintained its power to direct, coordinate and change the productive process. Imperialist control over employment had repercussions over the college education established by the colonial authorities. Higher education under North American rule became an instrument for the socialization of a native leadership to serve the interests of the metropolis and its representatives in Puerto Rico.

From its very beginning, the colonial government showed interest in establishing a state university that would train professionals to be middlemen between that government and the Puerto Rican people to consolidate political and economic control. In 1903 Commissioner Samuel McCune Lindsay, one of the most influential ideologists of the educational system envisioned by the colonial regime, proposed the creation of the University of Puerto Rico along the following lines:

> The educational problem of Porto Rico is twofold. The masses must be taught to read and write, and to know something of the elementary branches of study, and to understand the simpler institutions of American rule. . . . Quite a different sort of education is also necessary: the training of leaders, of men and women who shall not only possess culture, but whose culture shall not be alien and incidental as that too often is which comes from abroad, but which shall be indisserverably bound up with the progress of the island, and united with our national ideals. The makers of public opinion, and those who shall hold responsible positions in government, in professional life, in business, and in society must have in their own island an opportunity for higher training. [1]

Legally founded in 1903 as a Norman School with a Department of Agriculture, the University of Puerto Rico operated for 30 years almost exclusively as a training ground for teachers for the new system of public education created by the colonial authorities.[2] During this period new departments and faculties were added to the university. In 1910 the Arts and Science Faculty was established. In the following year the School of Agriculture and Mechanical Arts was set up in Mayagüez. In 1912 the already existing Pharmacy and Law Schools were added to the university system. The School of Medicine was established in 1924, the School of Commercial Administration in 1926, and the Department of Hispanic Studies in 1926.[3] With the gradual expansion of these programs and an increase in the number of university students from 173 in 1903 to 4,524 in 1938,[4] the foundation was secured for a bourgeois educational culture for the training of Puerto Ricans as teachers, bureaucrats in government and commercial enterprises, agricultural experts, doctors, lawyers and other professionals.[5]

The bourgeois tendency of university education in Puerto Rico during the first decades of North American rule, should also be seen as a result of changes occurring in the traditional landowning class. During this period landowners not only lost the little political power they had acquired through the Autonomic Charter of 1897, but economic power as well.[6] As their role as a class declined, these groups searched for methods to adapt themselves to maintain their social prestige. In their struggle to preserve their social position and the way of life characteristic of the local upper class, they found security in those professions that were not dominated by the foreigners in the new productive structure and in the growing commercial activity of towns and cities.[7] Likewise, money and influence were used to enable their sons and daughters to obtain college degrees to compensate for their declining access to capital and lands that were becoming scarcer every day. In this context, higher education became a very important factor in easing the decline of this class and opening access to new leadership positions and sources of economic power. As a consequence of these developments, college students became the social agents in the transition from Spanish to U.S. colonial domination.

Besides pressures brought about by this class transformation, the first generation of students that attended the University of Puerto Rico felt the imposition of a foreign culture that tried to mold Puerto Ricans into loyal subjects of the new colonial power through cultural assimilation. In her study of the Puerto Rican public school system between 1900 and 1930, Aida Negrón de Montilla amply documents the most obvious attempts at cultural domination and political subordination through the educational system: the imposition of the English language, the use of books in English and North American teachers, the importation of curriculum material from North American schools, the celebration of North American holidays and compulsory patriotic exercises and military training.[8] All these elements of political culturalization were extended to higher education. Also, during these years the Normal School of the University was subject to the pedagogic principles of mainland teachers colleges. Knowledge of English was made a legal requirement in granting teachers their certificates. Most of the faculty at the Normal School was composed of North American professors and study trips to the mainland were encouraged to acquaint future Puerto Rican teachers with the ways of life and customs of the new colonial power.

It was precisely because of these new circumstances that the development of a national consciousness among Puerto Rican university students during the period from 1903 to 1930 was slow and accidental and accompanied by apparently contradictory trends. On the one hand, one finds acceptance, adjustment and adaptation to the new way of life and study conditions; on the other hand, one finds a reaction to the new colonialism—with political and cultural expressions following closely the prevailing currents of society in general. As a result of the conflicts that were affecting the island under the impact of the new economic, political and cultural imperialism, a small sector of the university student body developed a critical conscience and a dissident political position.

The great trauma of the first 20 years of U.S. colonial rule in Puerto Rico left its scars in a disoriented and submissive student body. The authorities of the expanding university structure found little resistance to their efforts to apply their educational ideology. Centuries of political servitude had generated among Puerto Ricans an intense desire for education. Thus, among the members of the small student population there was a firm determination to sacrifice whatever was necessary to obtain that education.

At this early stage in the development of the university, the educational innovations of the new colonial authorities were well received, particularly among women for whom educational opportunities offered more personal independence and the opportunity to participate in a profession such as teaching.[9] But also among men who grew up under the new university educational system, there was ready acceptance. In 1914, for example, a student publication pointed out that the system of instruction "except for a few errors, is as good as that of other more developed countries in pedagogy."[10] The overwhelming superiority of the United States seemed evident not only to men but also to women. It created in them a sense of inferiority and dependence, and its natural correlation: the belief that by absorbing knowledge of the metropolis they could be equal to the ruling class. This attitude became stronger as the new government insisted that Puerto Rico, being an ignorant country, could not govern itself. In 1904, the head of the Normal School described University students as a group of eager and industrious youth coveting an education not only for its commercial value but also as a means of obtaining power.[11] Indeed, university training for many students offered an opportunity for personal development, economic privilege and relative closeness to political power. However, it also engendered acquiescence and submissiveness in student behavior.

In 1918 Antonio Pedreira, then a student at the university, criticized university youths because of their neglect of and sense of impotency for collective action. "Aside from our studies," he said, "the only thing we can organize earnestly is a society dedicated to collecting funds for graduation. . . . And this society, like literary societies and other groups with very narrow views, can only provoke more or less vain arguments and speeches."[12] The portrait of the passive and dependent childish student that emerges from Pedreira's criticism is not only a stereotype but represents the real immaturity of adult students encouraged by an institution that discouraged effective organization of students and promoted social and athletic activities. In his annual report for 1905-1906 the director of the Normal School mentioned the good discipline of the students. He also discussed the widespread acceptance of oratory contests in English, athletic tournaments, the monthly newspaper *The Puerto Rican Student* (published in English and Spanish), the Campos Choral Society, and other similar activities sponsored by the administration.[13]

The Student Faculty Council organized in February 1916 was during these early years of North American domination the only organization backed by the university administration to channel student participation in university affairs. Composed of members of the faculty, five students and the dean, the Student Faculty Council had as its fundamental objectives: to promote harmony and a common interest among students and teachers, and to encourage among members of the university a general interest and responsibility in the orderly conduct of the institution.[14] Many decades elapsed before university students subject to this form of educational colonialism recovered from the traumatic experience of the conquest by the superior power of the North American metropolis and began to act for themselves.

The rejection of the colonial situation started moderately, not as a rebellious movement against colonialism or against the university, but as a movement of cultural affirmation directed toward creating a new image of the civilized Puerto Rican. The cultural societies established during this stage of student activism, from 1912 to 1918, expressed the Puerto Rican student's defense against the North American position of superiority and acted as a shield for the feeling of Puerto Rican inferiority. By 1919 eight cultural societies had been founded. These societies served as centers of discussion and debate in the small student community and dedicated their efforts to popularizing the works of illustrious Puerto Rican patriots whose names the societies carried. Among them, the Salvador Brau Society and the Eugenio María de Hostos Society succeeded in establishing a beach head in the movement of cultural affirmation.[15]

The first student publication we have knowledge of, *Alma Mater: Revista Quincenal de Arte y Ciencias*, was also a manifestation of the growing movement towards cultural affirmation. Published in 1913-1914 by students of the Normal School of the University of Puerto Rico, it included nine small books and expressed the efforts of young Puerto Ricans to prove to themselves and their new rulers the worth of their land as a civilized country. This anxiety is clearly expressed in a letter from Justo Pastor Rivera to teachers and students regarding the need for a Puerto Rican library to stimulate recognition of national values, of what was genuinely Puerto Rican. "I believe," he wrote, "that in order for our country to be considered educated and worthy by the great North American colossus, we must prove with mathematically convincing facts that we have our Spanish writers, our poets inspired by beautiful odes and patriotic ballads dedicated to our homeland."[16] The student press and cultural societies expressed nationalist trends in an obscure form, praising cultural and linguistic values of the hispanic tradition and the Puerto Rican past. "Being such the importance of the press and societies of literary character," wrote Luis Muñiz Souffront in his message, *A la Juventud Puertorriqueña*, "it is necessary that we become interested young Puerto Ricans, in both activities, paving the way that will bring us to the peak of our aspirations: to form a great nation, free and useful to itself and to humanity in general."[17]

In November 1919 university students united the efforts of the various cultural societies and founded the Student Association of the University of Puerto Rico.[18] The Association tried to publish a periodical, but it was not until 1923 that the first newspaper of university students was founded with Antonio S. Pedreira as its first editor. The idea of establishing the *Porto Rican Collegian* emerged among a group of students and teachers in the Student Faculty Council. Published in the official language of the university at that time (English) and emphasizing cultural and educational activities, the newspaper sometimes included some student contributions in Spanish, usually fiction and poetry. Because of its nature as the "official" periodical, the *Porto Rican Collegian* was usually limited to describing academic, social and athletic activities on campus and avoided controversial and political issues. In the editorial of the first issue of the newspaper the editors expressed the needs and limited aspirations of university students at that time:

> The University of Porto Rico has long recognized the need for a representative student periodical. Insulated as we are, we cannot have a constant medium of publicity unless such a journal is established and permanently supported by the student body. But publicity has not been our sole or even main purpose for

establishing the first college paper in the history of our university. Our highest aim is to give expression to the ideals of truth and culture that we have long cherished. We hope to bring the university into closer touch with the outside world, not only with the island but with other lands. On our pages names and achievements that shall constitute our university heritage will be recorded and perpetuated. It will be our goal to impress upon the people of Porto Rico the fact that we are alive, that we labor for the fulfillment of our most sacred ideals, that we recognize as our greatest need a broad liberal education.[19]

The *Porto Rican Collegian*, like other student publications of that period, reveals the romantic and messianic views that university students had of themselves as a privileged group. At the same time, these first attempts to organize student associations and express ideas through publications demonstrate the low level of organization and student power of that period. However, one can trace back to them the first attempts to use cultural traditions as a defense mechanism in the struggle for survival. These efforts revealed the concerns not only of students but also of a small number of bourgeois intellectuals and the landowning class.

The period from 1914 to 1929 is one of great importance in university life and in the development of the student body in Puerto Rico. It corresponds to the awakening of a group of students to the problems of the country and the students' identification with national reform forces. During this period the national political opposition presented a timid defense against the colonial power that culminated in the pro-independence plank of the platform of the Union Party and an antagonistic attitude toward the growing militancy of the sugar cane plantation proletariat and the newly created Socialist Party. During this period the base for student struggle, which reached its maximum development in the decade of the 1930s, was secured. Already in the 1920s certain patterns of student political activity, of its allies and detractors were clearly established. From their inception, student politics reflected the battle of the small Puerto Rican bourgeoisie and the landowners' class, the battle was being conducted at two different levels: first, against the colonial power and, second, against the Puerto Rican working class.[20]

The awakening of students to political life must be framed within the context of events outside of the university and particularly within the context of the metropolis-colony conflict. This conflict was becoming more intense due to the educational policy of progressive deculturalization, the imposition of North American citizenship in 1917, and the repercussions of World War I. The protest movement against the use of

English as the official language in the schools gained considerable support.[21] The Teachers Association founded in 1911 assumed the defense of the Spanish language with tenacity. In 1913 and 1915 the Chamber of Delegates introduced several resolutions making compulsory the use of Spanish in the schools and in judicial processes. The first student demonstrations under North American rule occurred at the time of the Chamber of Delegates' historic debate supporting the project of José de Diego, who favored teaching in Spanish.[22] These acts of protest seem to have concentrated in the capital's high schools. In Santurce's Central High a serious incident ended with the expulsion of Francisco Grovas, a student who collected signatures favoring the project. The student body went on strike and was ordered expelled by the Commissioner of Public Education. *La Democracia,* organ of the Union Party, asked the Chamber of Delegates to intervene in order to prevent political persecution, but *El Tiempo,* organ of the pro-statehood annexation movement, favored the sanctions imposed on the students.[23] Consequently, the parents of expelled students founded the José de Diego Institute and made Spanish the teaching medium. After these incidents, the language issue became one of the most important in the student struggle in Puerto Rico. It was also one of the issues that united national reform forces in the metropolis-colony conflict and separated them from the labor movement. The language issue received little support among workers, who were remote from the educational structure and concerned for more and better schools of vocational and technical training for the working class.

With the approval of the Jones Act, which gave Puerto Ricans North American citizenship (notwithstanding strong opposition within the Chamber of Delegates), political unrest in the country continued within the educational institutions. While referring to the more active students, an observer called them "young Turks" and explained their reaction as follows:

> Many of these young people were children during the Spanish American War. They were the product of a new atmosphere and were born in a political climate in which political status was the sole and most important issue. It is not strange that they were more radical, less flexible and less conciliatory than the previous generation. For these men, the Jones Act was not enough. The permanent status of Puerto Rico still had to be solved.[24]

At the end of 1918 and as a consequence of World War I, a civic movement developed to claim for the island the right to self determination in accordance with the arguments made in Europe by President Woodrow Wilson. The students of the University of Puerto Rico, together with representative groups from various high schools, responded to this movement. In January of the same year the students petitioned the Chamber of Delegates for the approval of a resolution requesting "independence for Puerto Rico since this is the only solution compatible with the ideals and interests of the Puerto Rican people."[25]

As was to be expected, the university authorities resorted to repression in face of the growing student activism. Dean Charles St. John received from the Commissioner of Education a letter that was published in the island's press, demanding a list of all members of the graduating class of the Normal School that had signed the petition submitted to the Chamber of Delegates. In his letter, the Commissioner ordered that all those students be excluded from teaching positions since their "loyalty to the United States is in doubt."[26] The students of the Normal School, whose leadership had prompted the petition, were not intimidated, however. In that same year they petitioned the Chamber of Delegates twice, demanding approval of a law for a plebescite to define the political aspirations of the majority of the Puerto Rican people and demanding the right of women to vote. In this petition they advocated such a right "because we understand that a country is not for men only, it belongs to everyone equally and they have a perfect right to decide with their votes the future of their country." In a third petition signed by 20 students, the right was requested to hear José Coll y Cuchi, a pro-independence attorney who had been denied permission to speak on the university campus. The students also protested at this time against Dean St. John's arbitrariness and the "Kaiseristic" attitude of the Commissioner of Education.[27] These protests were important for the emerging student movement since they went beyond the previous pre-political stage and entered into a period in which students themselves recognized the need for a transformation:

We students are the offspring of an old and glorious race which left its helm and feudal sword a long time ago to dedicate itself to new and more fruitful and useful conquests for humanity. We are a generation of Puerto Ricans who have been educated in North American methods under the American flag. It is true that we have studied the lives of its great men and learned the value of its free institutions.

And those great men and those great institutions have given us admirable lessons of the most pure patriotism and the most sublime desire for the independence of our country.[28]

With all the limitations in organization and ideology this generation (nurtured on José de Diego's defense of the ideal of independence) gave the student struggle its first liberal nationalist orientation. Student protest was to a great extent intimately related to the problem of political status, the right of free speech on campus, and the arbitrariness of disciplinary measures. Without strong organization, student activism was a kind of flashing light, a repetition of separated incidents without organized or programmatic continuity.

A great part of the decade of the 1920s was characterized by severe repression. Students with "radical" propensities were summarily expelled or suspended. In 1921, for example, when Governor Reiley went by the university on his way to the interior of the island, a group of students stood at the gates of the university crying for a free Puerto Rico.[29] A few days later the following letter appeared in the island's press signed by student Cristobal Fernández Sosa, who apparently had not participated in the demonstration but who expressed solidarity with the protest:

The attitude of the students of the University of Puerto Rico has only been a cry to protest against the governor who has abused and underestimated the flag of the future Republic of Puerto Rico.[30]

Immediately after the publication of this letter, Sosa was summarily suspended from the university for violating Rules 17 and 18 of the University. Similar repressive measures also were adopted against a group of professors who participated in these acts of defiance. Such professors were given two alternatives: renounce their membership in political organizations or renounce their positions in the University.

The authoritarian attitude of university authorities explains to a certain extent the usual apolitical nature of student publications and organizations as well as the neutrality of most faculty members in university conflicts. When the protest could not be expressed directly or when it failed in lessening the evils of colonialism, the students disguised their rejection in a cultural garb. The strict controls established over the student body and the faculty lessened the intensity of activity during the great part of the 1920s. However, some small, and not so small, groups of students continued participating sporadically in acts of protest. The most notable and only strike movement during that decade occurred in March 1924 when a jury disqualified members of the university's team during an athletic tournament. A strike was called and the firing of Dean St. John was demanded. As a result 200 students were suspended. The protest involving the athletic tournament became an avenue of political protest. One of the slogans during the protest, for example, accused the university administration of being "an imperialist ungovernment."[31]

These first expressions of student unrest at the university of Puerto Rico after World War I and the decade of the 1920s show an antagonism between two of the elements that intervened in the students' life and that with the passing of time became more intense. The administration and the student body clashed while the faculty generally maintained neutrality in the conflict. In 1948 Marique Cabrera related this antagonism to the "intimate contradiction of the primary organism." Cabrera referred to the university as an instrument of political socialization within the colonial regime of the administration and to students as the only element of change within the organism.[32]

By the end of the 1920s students started to gain a clearer awareness of their political role. This process of acquiring consciousness, which culminated in the mass protests of the 1930s, was made possible by the modifications introduced in the limited reorganization of the university system in 1925 and by certain academic changes that occurred during Thomas Benner's administration.

The administration of Benner had a decisive impact on university life. In 1925 the University of Puerto Rico was separated from the Department of Public Education. Up to that time its principal function was to supply teachers for the public education system established by the colonial government at the beginning of the century. This program was at the same time a powerful force of indoctrination through which Puerto Ricans were exposed to the basic elements of U.S. values in a massive form and were drawn away from their hispanic heritage.[33] With the founding of the Department of Hispanic Studies in the summer of 1927 the new chancellor started to develop a specific field of knowledge following the tradition of the best North American universities. To achieve this new goal a policy was adopted inviting prominent individuals to reinforce the local faculty. Tomás Navarro Tomás, Américo Castro, Angel Valvuena Prat, Fernando de los Ríos, Gabriela Mistral, and others left a deep impression on the students with whom they came into contact at the university during their stays there. There can be no doubt that these professors, most of whom sympathized with Spanish republicanism and some of whom were of socialist orientation, were a decisive influence in university life.[34] The awakening of students to the political message of Pedro Albizu Campos (a man who would figure prominently in the political scene during the decade of the 1930s), for example, was caused in part by the presence of José Vasconcelos at the University in 1926. Vasconcelos had met Albizu Campos and had been impressed by his uncompromising commitment to Puerto Rican independence. Vasconcelos' lectures and his book *Indología* contributed to making students and faculty aware of Albizu's personality and nationalist message. In an act of homage to Vasconcelos, the emerging nationalist sentiment was expressed in a speech by student Samuel Quiñones:

> The yanquis are here—without ever consulting the feelings of Puerto Ricans; the yanquis, through the trust, take over our lands; they corrupt our politicians with bribery; in schools they take away our Spanish language which is the last refuge of our fighting patriotism.

According to Vasconcelos, "In all my life and after having been in all kinds of revolutionary meetings, I had never witnessed such conscious and resolved revolt."[35] This student assembly was a warning of the crisis that would grow during the 1930s in the island and in the university.

The decade of the 1920s ended with the firing of Chancellor Benner for political reasons. In 1929 Antonio Barceló, President of the Puerto Rican Senate, was forced to vote in favor of a budgetary measure presented by House Speaker José Tous Soto that seriously affected the university. Although both men were members of the Board of Trustees of the University, Tous Soto announced he would resign if the measure was not approved and in this way threatened the power of the Alliance of Barceló's Unionists and Tous Soto's Republicans. Concerned about this possibility, Barceló went along with the measure. In the next budgetary session student pressure favored the University against the wishes of Speaker Tous Soto and a new budgetary measure was approved. Weeks later the Republican leader had his revenge when Benner was ousted by the Board of Trustees without charges in a vote of 4 to 3.[36] His firing was a prelude to the decade in which social and political fragmentation became more intense and visible.

Notwithstanding the reorganization of 1925, the University of Puerto Rico continued to be an institution subject to the political orders of the Board of Trustees, upon which the colonial government and local political parties imposed their criteria. Benner's ouster affected the growth of the student movement, because it showed the existence of political intervention at the university and the impotence of the university in preserving its autonomy without an adequate student organization. For the first time in the history of the university both students and faculty united to defend university autonomy. The students spontaneously reacted in numerous letters published by the press, in a meeting called to protest the dismissal of Chancellor Benner and in the hostile reception to Governor Roosevelt a few months later. When the governor visited the university, students distributed leaflets with the slogan "Politicians off our University."[37] In spite of these activities, however, it was not till the mid-1930s that students developed a full awareness that without autonomy it was impossible for the university to develop into a serious institution of higher learning.

To fully understand the period of the 1920s in which the student movement sprouted, one must analyze the content, character and ideological orientation of the first student political expression. This will allow us to understand how cultural nationalism acquired expression as militant political nationalism and an ideology interested in change. The collective experience of the new colonialism did not generate immediately a nationalist ideology. The first student associations and student publications also were far from being socially radical. The students were a privileged group, coming principally from the traditionally landowning class and the small urban bourgeoisie. Thus, U.S. colonial domination was questioned on the basis of traditional values.

The only data relevant to the political attitudes of students during the 1920s is found in a poll taken by *La Democracia* in 1927. The poll dealt with the preference of students for Puerto Rican political leaders of the immediate past.[38] Of the 300 students who answered the questionnaire, 60 per cent favored Luis Muñoz Rivera, while 21 per cent favored Eugenio María de Hostos and 19 per cent, José de Diego. The latter two leaders represented the pro-independence ideology, while Muñoz Rivera represented the autonomist view. It is important to notice that none of the students showed preference for any pro-statehood leaders. This may indicate that at the time of the poll autonomist and independence tendencies prevailed above assimilation among the students. Since its origins a division has existed in the study body along the former two currents, a division that changed form and aspect but continued to be more or less the same in essence from 1922 to the last years of the 1940s. However, this division was not clear at the time, because there were no student political organizations to represent those positions.

There also was an ambiguous relationship between the students and the political parties of the period, particularly between students and the Union Party. This party at the same time changed from one ideology to another. Evidently, deep social roots existed—class roots that caused this ambiguity among Unionists who even adopted statehood as a possible programmatic alternative.[39] Although during the first two decades of North American colonial rule only a few students were militant members of political parties, many sympathized with the Unionist Party, with the Independence Party founded in 1912, or with the Nationalist Party founded by dissidents of the Union Party in 1922 when the latter eliminated independence from its platform.[40] Between 1919 and 1924 students had a particularly good relationship with the Unionists who dominated the Chamber of Delegates, forwarding petitions to them, endorsing some of their projects, and receiving the backing of the party's leaders directly or through *La Democracia.* In 1924 when the first university strike occurred the Chamber of Delegates ordered an investigation of Dean St. John, whom the students accused of exercising imperialist authority when he suspended 200 students. The legislative commission discredited the university authorities. Part of the explanation for the close ties that existed between the students and the Union Party was family ties: Antonio Barceló, Jr., the leader of the student movement, was also the son of Antonio Barceló, President of the Union Party.[40]

As a result of the ties between the Unionists and the students, the first youth political organization was created in which high school and university students participated. In 1919 the Nationalist Association of Puerto Rico was founded within the Unionist Party to maintain the independence issue at a time when an internal struggle between independence advocates and autonomists was taking place.[41] The Nationalist Youth formed within the new organization was the first student organization of a political character. Among its most active members were Samuel Quiñones, Vicente Geigel Polanco, Antonio Colorado, Guillermo Silva and others who later figured prominently in the autonomist and independence movements of the island.[42] In 1922 when the Union Party eliminated independence from its platform and replaced it with an autonomist formula, the Nationalist Youth backed the defense made by Walter McJones at the party assembly of keeping the ideal of independence as part of the party's platform.[43] When the Nationalist Party was created in that year, the Nationalist Youth participated in the Constituent Assembly and backed the Declaration of Principles of the Nationalist Party and its principal leaders, José Coll y Cuchi and José S. Alegria.[44] Samuel Quiñones and José Paniagua, President and Vice-President of the Nationalist Youth, were elected as secretaries of the Assembly.[45]

The Nationalist Youth, in allegiance with the Nationalist Party, limited itself to denouncing the colonial regime and to sporadic acts of protest and propaganda against the government and the university administration. The activities of this group set the political pace for an academic community that basically was indifferent to political issues and it influenced a group of students that later held positions of leadership in other political organizations and in the most prestigious intellectual circles. However, militants in this organization were limited to a small group within the student body, and, although at times verbally aggressive, they were only moderately effective. Frequently the legitimate complaints of the students were lost in small talk.

Notwithstanding the limited scope of action of the Nationalist Youth, its impact was significant upon the organizations that succeeded it. The Nationalist Youth was a transitional organization between the cultural associations of the early part of the century and the more militant groups of the 1930s. Combining debate with civic activities, it furnished a means of political experience without generating strong opposition from government and university authorities.[46] Like cultural societies and the student press, the Nationalist Youth was further proof of the development of a national consciousness among certain students and their timid challenge to the colonial regime.

However, the students' nationalist attitudes during the first two decades of North American colonial rule were not always accompanied by progressive attitudes on socio-economic issues. Neither the student population, nor even the vanguard groups during this period seems to have identified with the emerging radicalism of the working class. The family ties of the majority of students with traditional agricultural interests and colonial capitalism directed the energies of the students toward traditional values that characterized landowners and the literary intelligentsia opposed to assimilation. This traditionalism extended to the most varied aspects of social and cultural life.

A poll conducted by F.R. Morse in 1926-1927 showed the presence of conventional attitudes among university students, particularly among males who were most active in politics. Three-fourths of the men canvassed and one-fourth of the women were opposed to women's right to vote, an issue that was widely discussed during those years. The great majority of the men chose more traditional professions such as medicine, law and engineering. Women favored those professions but chose engineering in second place. Both groups considered parents' dislike for the future partner as a serious obstacle to marriage. Only one-fourth of both groups expressed themselves in favor of divorce in cases of infidelity, cruelty, alcoholism or little love for the children. Three-fourths of the men and two-thirds of the women rejected the idea of marriage to a person of a different race. Ninety-six per cent of the males answered that they would require their wives to be virgins but only 41 per cent of the women agreed. Two-thirds of the men said women should stop working when married; less than one-third of the women agreed.[47]

The university students' ideological framework of the 1920s was basically conservative on social issues with a strong tie to family and patriarchy. They were more liberal in religious matters, but a traditional racial prejudice is shown in matrimony. There seems to be no generation gap between them and their parents concerning these attitudes. Unfortunately, the data available does not include information on political attitudes that would allow for broad generalization. The general impression is that only a small minority of the student body showed progressive tendencies on socio-economic matters. It is interesting to observe that women—maybe because of the nature of the issues involved—showed a greater degree of liberalism on social matters.

The traditional attitudes among Puerto Rican university students in the 1920s were derived from an economic structure that had been gradually losing ground within the U.S. colonial system but that persisted during this transitional period and served to resist the new forces that directly or indirectly undermined widely accepted social values. It is not strange that the class ties among the majority of students with the traditional agricultural sector and the small urban bourgeoisie left deep roots in student ideology, in its demands and in the selection of its allies.

The student struggle during the 1920s was totally separated from the struggle of the working class. There are no signs whatever that the students established any ties with labor unions, or that they participated in the labor demonstrations, strikes and pickets that characterized that decade. Neither is there any evidence that suggests that students became interested in the problems of the working class. Their identification with the Union Party and its principal leaders who represented to a great extent the traditional enemies of the Puerto Rican working class (at least from the workers' point of view) also militated against any sort of joint action between students and workers.

In the university the class conflict between the sons of the landowners, the urban bourgeoisie and the Puerto Rican proletariat manifested itself in the attitudes of students to the demands of workers' organizations for the type of education they saw as relevant to their members. The *Federación Libre de Trabajo* (FLT) and later the Socialist Party expressed themselves in favor of mass education, particularly in favor of technical and vocational training for the workers, and rejected the landowners because they were against rural education.[48] The socialists saw the university as a center for the bourgeoisie and higher education as a luxury that should not receive priority given the need for educational facilities for the great majority of the population. The Union Party, especially its leader Antonio Barceló, on the other hand, had always been a defender of the university and had used his political muscle to channel public funds towards its development and improvement. In 1929 a series of articles were published in the island's press, which criticized the university's expenses and those of the administration. Socialist Senator Santiago Iglesias referred to the university as "a house of luxury" and suggested a reduction in legislative appropriations for the university so that other more important activities could be financed.[49] This resulted in a major legislative battle regarding the university's budget. A committee presided by Antonio Colorado received the backing of students in public and private high schools who expressed themselves against any legislation that would transfer or reduce funds for the university.[50] This was one of the many occasions in which students defended themselves as a group against the demands of an increasingly militant Puerto Rican proletariat.

The cultural nationalism and timid political nationalism that emerged among Puerto Rican students during the first two decades of North American colonial rule picked up momentum in the decade of the 1930s as Puerto Rico was overwhelmed by the economic crisis of the depression and the island entered a period of unprecedented political activism on behalf of independence. During that decade Puerto Rican university students became more militant and more politically involved, as evidenced by the many strikes that took place during that period. In 1932 the *Federacion Nacional de Estudiantes Puertorriqueños* (FNEP) was created by militant students, who set about establishing contacts with student organizations in other parts of Latin America and who became increasingly outspoken against the university structure and the colonial regime. Many university students became involved in the struggle for Puerto Rican independence and although no meaningful alliances were set up between the students and the working class, student publications of the decade indicate that the students were developing a consciousness of the socio-economic problems afflicting the Puerto Rican people on behalf of social change. It was a time during which some students went out on the streets to battle with the forces of colonial oppression; a time when the university was described as "totalitarian and fascistic". Yet, in spite of this growing activism among Puerto Rican university students, the majority of them continued to hold elitist views and to be concerned primarily with issues directly relevant to university life such as the language issue, university autonomy and political freedom within the university. At the end of the decade of the 1930s the Puerto Rican student movement still was weak and enjoyed little political influence. Nevertheless, it was a student movement that had broken the psychological chains that had held it back in the past. The movement now was more aware than ever that the evils that continued to characterize the university system could not be separated from the colonial status in which the island found itself.

NOTES

1. Samuel McCune Lindsay, "The Public School System of Porto Rico," *Register of Porto Rico* (San Juan, 1903), p. 78.

2. According to official records the University of Puerto Rico graduated 2,791 students from 1903 to 1923. Of these 29 received a Liberal Arts degree, 100 received degrees in pharmacy, 15 received degrees in education, 1,095 received certificates to teach in primary schools, and the rest sub-collegiate training for the magistrate. *Register of Graduates of the Rio Piedras Departments, 1903-1923* (Rio Piedras, 1924).

3. Gildo Masso, "Universidad de Puerto Rico: Compendio de una historia de 30 años," *The Puerto Rican School Review*, Vol. XVI, No. 9 (May 1932), p. 10.

4. "Matrícula en la Universidad de Puerto Rico, desde sus origenes hasta el presente (1900-1948)," mimeographed, General Archives of the University of Puerto Rico.

5. During this period most students in the primary schools were from the working class but they left school at an early age to take jobs or to become just another number among the unemployed. See, Isabel Picó de Hernández, "Americanización?: Comentarios en torno al libro de la doctora Aida Negrón de Montilla," *La Escalera*, Vol. V, Nos. 5-6 (November, 1971), pp. 33-36.

6. During the first ten years of North American rule in Puerto Rico, 2,582 agrarian owners lost their lands. Between 1910 and 1920, the figure was 17,293. Some of these former landowners joined the ranks of the rural proletariat. Others became settlers on sugar cane or tobacco plantations or dedicated themselves to planting minor fruits, the processing of which was controlled by North American corporations. Most of the displaced landowners, however, moved to the urban centers. See, José A. Herrero, *En torno a la mitología del azúcar: Un ensayo en historia económica de Puerto Rico, 1900-1970*, mimemographed (Rio Piedras, 1970), p. 14.

7. Angel Quintero Rivera, "El desarrollo de las clases sociales y los conflictos políticos en Puerto Rico," in *Problemas de desigualdad social en Puerto Rico*, edited by Ramírez, Buitrago Ortíz and Levine (Rio Piedras, 1972).

8. Aida Negrón de Montilla, *Americanization in Puerto Rico and the Public School System, 190-1930* (Rio Piedras, 1970).

9. From its beginnings the University of Puerto Rico had a large group of women in its registry. The graduating class of 1907, for example, included nine women and four men. Throughout the history of the University the proportion of women has almost always been higher than that of men.

10. Luis Muñiz Souffront, "A la Juventud Puertorriqueña," *Alma Mater*, Year I, No. 6 (January 15, 1914), p. 2.

11. *Report of the Commissioner of Education for Porto Rico to the Secretary of the Interior for the Fiscal Year Ended June 30, 1904* (Washington, D.C., 1094), p. 297.

12. Antonio Pedreira, *El Diluvio*, 1918, p. 159.

13. Carmen Gómez Tejera and David Cruz López, *La escuela puertorriqueña* (Connecticut, 1970), p. 160.

14. *Catálogo Anual y Prospecto de la Universidad de Puerto Rico*, 1919-1920, p. 26.

15. For a description of the activities of the cultural societies see *Anuario El Cordero*, published by the class of 1915 of the Normal School of the University of Puerto Rico.

16. Justo Pastor Rivera, "Por nuestra literatura," *Alma Mater*, Year I, No. 1 (November 1913), p. 9.

17. Muñiz Souffront, A La juventud," p. iii.

18. Assur Bani Pal, "La Asociación de Estudiantes de la Universidad de Puerto Rico," *El Mundo*, November 28, 1919, p.8; "Desde la Universidad," *El Mundo*, December 11, 1919; "La Universidad contribuye para una caseta de tuberculosos," *El Mundo*, December 2, 1919.

19. *Porto Rican Collegian*, Year 1 (1923), p. 1.

20. See, Gordon K. Lewis, *Puerto Rico: Libertad y poder en el Caribe* (Rio Piedras, 1969), p. 157.

21. For an analysis of the language issue in Puerto Rico and the efforts of the Teachers Association to resolve it, see, Luis Muñiz Souffront, *El Problema del idioma en Puerto Rico* (San Juan, 1950).

22. Negrón de Montilla, *Americanization*, p. 140.

23. *La Democracia*, January 2, 1915, p. 2.

24. Robert Hunter, "Historical Survey of the Puerto Rico Status Question, 1898-1965," in *United States-Puerto Rico Commission on the Status of Puerto Rico. Selected Background Studies* (Washington, D.C., 1966), p. 77.

25. *La Democracia,* March 1, 1919, p. 5.

26. *Porto Rican Progress,* January 1, 1919.

27. *El Mundo,* March 4, 1919, p. 3.

28. *La Democracia,* January 22, 1919.

29. "La Universidad de Puerto Rico y el Gobernador Reiley," *El Tiempo,* October 26, 1921, p. 3; "Los estudiantes de la Universidad," *El Tiempo,* October 27, 1921.

30. Carlos Pietri, "Voz de Alerta," *El Tiempo,* October 27, 1921.

31. For details of this incident see, Thomas Benner, *Five Years of Founding: The University of Puerto Rico, 1924-1929.*

32. "*Manrique Cabrera believes that students are less at fault,*" El Mundo, *June 2, 1948, pp. 10, 12.*

33. Negrón de Montilla, *Americanization.*

Francisco Manrique Cabrera, *Historia de la Literatura Puertorriqueña* (Rio Piedras, 1969), p. 283.

35. José Vasconcelos, *Indología,* pp. xxi-xxii.

36. Benner, *Five Years of Founding.*

37. Interview with Manuel Negrón Nogueras, one of the leaders of the protest against Barceló. See also, letter from Antonio Colorado, Manuel Negrón, Jr., and Filiberto Vázquez in *El Tiempo,* May 8, 9, and 11, 1929.

38. *La Democracia,* May 27, 1927, p. 1.

39. Gervasio García interprets the contradictory political platform approved by the Unionist Party in 1904 in terms of the social composition of that party, the contradictory interests of sugar and coffee growers, and the position of the professional sector before the new government. Gervasio García, "Apuntes sobre una interpretacion de la realidad puertorriqueña", *La Escalera,* Vol. IV, No. 1 (June, 1970), p. 30.

40. Bolivar Pagán, *Historia de los partidos políticos puertorriqueños* (San Juan, 1959), pp. 146-149.

41. Ibid., p. 202.

42. José Coll y Cuchi, *El Nacionalismo en Puerto Rico* (San Juan, 1923), pp. 156-158.

43. "La Juventud Nacionalista y el gesto de McJones," *El Mundo,* November 8, 1922, p. 1.

44. "Acuerdo de la Juventud Nacionalista sobre la fundación del Partido," in Coll y Cuchi, *El Nacionalismo,* p. 157.

45. *El Mundo,* September 18, 1922.

46. An example of this type of civic activity is mentioned in the press regarding the collection of funds for the victims of a hurricane in Santo Domingo. "El Comité De Estudiantes Universitarios envían por conducta del Partido Nacionalista la suma de $498.50 para las víctimas de Santo Domingo," *La Democracia,* September 29, 1930, p. 2.

47. Benner, *Five Years of Founding,* pp. 67-70.

48. See, "The Tyranny of the House of Delegates of Puerto Rico," in Angel Quintero Rivera (ed.), *Lucha Obrera en Puerto Rico* (Rio Piedras, 1972), pp. 47-55.

49. Benner, *Five Years of Founding,* pp. 120-127.

50. Ibid., p. 123.

The Development of Social Classes and Political Conflicts in Puerto Rico*

Angel G. Quintero Rivera

The political history of Puerto Rico generally has been interpreted either in terms of great political leaders or in terms of the internal ideological conflict over the colonal status of the island—that is, the conflict among those favoring assimilation to the metropolis, those in favor of "autonomy," and those for independence. These approaches often are intermingled, since the great political leaders are seen in terms of their positions regarding the status issue, and the conflict over status is personalized in the maximum leaders. This essay aims to show the limitations of these approaches[1] and the importance of analyzing (jointly with the colonial problem) the development of class conflicts in Puerto Rico's colonial situation.[2]

The concept of class is used in this essay as a historical formation, not as a statistical occupational category; not as a thing that is, but as a phenomenon that happens. As the English social historian E. P. Thompson has stated:

*This article has been abridged by the author from the original published in Ramírez, Buitrago, and Levine, eds., *Problemas de desigualdad social en Puerto Rico* (San Juan: Libreria Internacional, 1972). This book is being translated into English and will appear with the title *Problems of Social Inequality in Puerto Rico*. The version of the article which appears here was translated from the Spanish by Adalberto López and has been abridged slightly in the text and greatly in the footnotes. The article appears here with the permission of the author.

Class happens when some men, as a result of common experiences (inherited or shared) feel and articulate the identity of their interests as between themselves, and against other men whose interests are different from (and usually opposed to) theirs. The class experience is largely determined by the productive relations . . . Class consciousness is the way in which these experiences are handled in cultural terms: embodied in traditions, value-systems, ideas, and institutional forms.[3]

Therefore, in our view, a social class cannot be analyzed except within the context of the socio-economic structure that serves as the foundation of its experiences and in terms of its relation or conflict with the other classes, where its reactions, makings and creations become manifest.

The Plantation Economy

The study of the history of social classes in Puerto Rico in the twentieth century has to begin with an analysis of the process of change from a semi-feudal hacienda economy to an economy dominated by capitalist plantation agriculture. This transformation began in the latter part of the nineteenth century, but really gathered impetus with the North American occupation of the island in 1898. The economic policies of the first North American governors were geared to facilitate the creation and growth of large North American sugar and tobacco companies. Already by the end of the second decade of this century, these companies (specially those involved in sugar production) had become masters of the Puerto Rican economy.[4]

The sugar plantations, although in a rural setting, developed basically the same relationships that are identified with the capitalist system; which has been usually analyzed as an urban phenomenon.[5] First, the relations between employer and employee were of a purely economic character.[6] The former considered the employee an economic good and strived to get the maximum profit out of his work. Second, man no longer sold his produce but his labor power. The sale of his labor power came to constitute his main economic activity; he became a wage earner. Third, since the sale of his labor power bcame the principal economic activity of the worker, his economic life came to be centered on money. The agricultural worker no longer produced for himself; once he sold his labor power he was left with nothing but his wages, which he needed to meet his needs. In this context, economic betterment meant higher wages that would allow him to increase his purchasing power. Fourth (and closely related to what has been said above), man was separated from his product. Separated, because he did not own it, and because the division of labor that was introduced by the plantation-mill complex did not allow him to produce something in its totality (the worker went to cut the sugar cane, not to produce sugar). The worker was also separated from his product, because the technological changes introduced into the plantation-mill production process did not allow him to understand the productive process as a whole.

Finally, the plantation system generated a trend toward homogeneity among the workers. This trend is found in the settlement patterns that the system generated: primarily, housing clusters or small villages (*aldeas*) exclusively inhabited by plantation workers.[7] The pattern was more homogenizing when these villages were created by the sugar companies themselves.[8] The trend towards homogenization is also found in the relations between capital and labor. If the relations between owner and worker were purely economic in character, and the difference among the workers' wages minimal, the relations between owner and worker were therefore, fundamentally the same for all. All workers were subject to the same form of exploitation. In addition, the tasks performed on the plantation were of such a nature that they limited the possibility for the development of special skills. Thus, social distinctions among the workers were hindered.

The breakdown of the social relations that had characterized life in the hacienda—dominant economic structure prior to the establishment of the plantation system—had two very important results. First, the elimination of the affective bonds and shared life between owner and worker allowed interstrata struggle, and, second, the weakening of these vertical social relationships strengthened the horizontal ones.[9] The life of the worker went on almost exclusively within his own class, and a more clear-cut class culture developed.

Furthermore, the commercial character of plantation agriculture—the concentration on the production of a cash crop oriented towards an external market—made the plantation dependent on a favorable wider social system, on what Edgar Thompson has called "the social system of plantations."[10] Similarly, as has already been suggested, the plantation system generated a money economy and a home market. These developments helped to broaden the vision of the workers. They did not find themselves solely under one administrator or owner, but in the lowest scale of an entire social organization on which the plantations depended: they were not the "long-suffering ones" *(los sufridos)* of the hacienda, but the poor *(los pobres)* of Puerto Rico.

As the plantation economy spread through Puerto Rico, a rural proletariat began to emerge. The myths of hacienda life crumbled for this group which, given its position in the new system of production, began to develop an image of an ideal new social order at the same time that it struggled to establish it.[11] This class found (and formed) organizational expression in the Free Federation of Laborers (*Federación Libre de Trabajadores*—FLT) whose genesis dates back to the organizational activities of artisan groups at the end of the nineteenth century, but which materialized in the large sugar cane plantations and tobacco processing factories. From the FLT emerged the Socialist Party, which was basically its political arm. Aiming towards the creation of a new order of social relations, the political expression of the working class turned against the social order which then prevailed: against the hegemonic culture of hacienda life. Its antagonic class was, therefore, the Puerto Rican hacienda owners.

It is worthwhile, at this point, to make a brief conceptual digression to the ways in which Puerto Rican history has been interpreted, an issue raised at the beginning of this article. The emergence of the FLT and the Socialist Party have been usually interpreted from the perspective of the great-leader conception of history: as the creation of labor leader Santiago Iglesias Pantín. I have attempted to present a new perspective in analyzing this phenomenon; to explain the emergence of the FLT and the Socialist Party in terms of the change from a semi-feudal hacienda economy to a capitalist plantation agriculture, analyzing the development of a new class situation and the conflicts it generated.[12]

Bearing in mind the class nature of the Socialist Party and the socioeconomic structuring of the society at the moment, one can better understand the makings and actions that led to the formation of this class-struggle organization. Only in this way can one understand and explain the strikes, the burning of sugar fields, the fiery speeches of anarchists such as Eduardo Conde, the large number of workers' papers that appeared in the early years of this century (*El Porvenir Social, Yo Acuso, La Miseria, Alba Roja, El Pan del Pobre . . .*), the participation of Santiago Iglesias in the conventions of the American Federation of Labor, the workers' study groups (where workers met to discuss the great socialist writings), the creation of the Red Circle of Proletarian Theater and other similar developments.

The Triangular Conflict of the First Decades Under North American Domination

The emergence of capitalist agriculture in the island also had a tremendous impact on the Puerto Rican *hacendados* and subsistence farmers. Some of these subsistence farmers became workers in the sugar plantations.[13] Others began to plant sugar cane to be processed in the North American sugar mills (the small *colonos*) or to plant tobacco whose processing and marketing was controlled by North American companies. These formerly independent farmers became then dependent on the North American companies and on the commercial system.

The *hacendados,* which constituted the hegemonic class in terms of its dominance in the way of life, could not be considered the dominant segment within the ruling class during the period following the North American invasion of 1898. The government imposed by the invaders destroyed the political power the hacienda owners had enjoyed before,[14] with the implications this had on the loss of control over economic policies. Gradually, they also lost their dominant position in the economy to the North American sugar and tobacco companies, which followed upon the heels of the North American troops. This undermined their hegemonic position.[15] By the first decade of North American domination the *hacendados* had begun to present (though timidly) an opposition, which culminated with the pro-independence declaration of the political party that represented their class (the Unionist Party) in 1913.[16]

Thus, in these first decades of North American colonial rule in Puerto Rico, a triangular political conflict was evident: on the one hand, there was the recently developed plantation proletariat; on the other, the *hacendado* class (with the backing of hacienda laborers and peasants); and above both, the colonial power (with its Puerto Rican intermediaries). This triangular conflict combined the phenomena of internal class struggle and class-based conflicts with the colonial metropolis.

The party that represented Puerto Rican hacendados, the Unionist Party, had also the largest political support. It won the election of 1904 and was not defeated at the polls until 1932. The political organization of the plantation proletariat constituted during this period a minority force when compared to the Unionist Party. Many areas of the island still were under the economy of haciendas and peasants, and in the plantations the process of transforming a total vision of world and social life, rooted in the agrarian situation that previously existed, was a process that required time. Given these political realities, the plantation proletariat had to resort on occasions to the power of the metropolis (to organizations like the American Fedration of Labor—AFL—or directly to the government of the United States) in its struggle against its antagonic class, the hacendados.[17] This had a tremendous impact on its ideology.

The practice of appealing to the power of the metropolis has led those who have interpreted the politics and history of Puerto Rico in terms of the status issue to place the Socialist Party and the FLT during those first decades of North American colonial rule among the groups favoring assimilation to the metropolis.[18] Yet, the issue of the island's status was not a frequent theme in working-class writings of that time; the status issue was of secondary importance, not the center of their concern and activities. Also, there was no unanimity within the workers' movement on the status issue. On the contrary, there were great differences that often generated bitter arguments in the Party's conventions.[19] In addition, the available documents show that taking a position on the status issue in those first decades meant a difficult and painful process for many working class leaders.[20] Some of these leaders, for example, saw an independent republic as a prerequisite for socialism, for the creation of the new social system to which they aspired. At the same time, however, they realized that independence at that time would have brought about the absolute political preeminence of the *hacendados*. Independence would have turned the triangular political conflict into a dual conflict, in which the hacendados would have been in a more advantageous position. The apparent assimilist character of some of the actions of the FLT was really a weapon or shield in their class struggle against the Puerto Rican *hacendados*. It was the class struggle which led the workers into taking a position on the status issue, not vice-versa.

It is important to keep this point clearly in mind, because in order to analyze the nature of the political conflicts in these decades it is necessary to identify the social groups who represented or supported the colonial metropolitan power in the island's internal politics, and it is erroneous to include the plantation proletariat and their organizations among these groups. The social groups that represented the interests of the metropolis in Puerto Rican politics were mainly the groups that formed the core of support of the pro-statehood Republican Party (Republican, because of its ties with the American Republican Party). Within this party one can distinguish three principal social groups.[21]

First, there were the Puerto Rican middlemen at the service of North American corporations: specifically, managers, corporation lawyers, and so on down the corporation bureaucratic hierarchy to foremen. Some of these managers and lawyers gradually became shareholders in the companies, and by the late twenties and thirties were among the wealthiest families on the island.

In a similar social situation were a small group of Puerto Rican landowners who were able to reorganize their holdings and productive system along the lines of the North American companies. A narrow conception of class interests might lead some to conclude that there was a situation of potential antagonism between these local landowners and the absentee-owned companies, their competitors in the capitalist economic game. The foundations of their economic power were based, however, on the capitalist mode of production, on the entire socio-economic organization that the plantation system created. Since this socio-economic organization was being threatened both by the socialists of the FLT and the *hacendados* of the Unionist Party, the class interests of Puerto Rican plantation owners came to be centered on the defense of the system, which was the basis of their position in the means of production.

Plantation agriculture, with its concentration on a single export cash crop, reduced greatly the availability of certain goods previously produced locally. This explains the rapid growth of a merchant class in Puerto Rico that became tied to the U.S. market. Since the island was now under the tariff system of the United States, the merchants who flourished during the first decades of the century were those dealing with trading houses in New York, Baltimore and Philadelphia, and not the old merchant group that had controlled the trade between the island and Spain.[22] The success and *raison d'etre* of the new merchant class (and the Puerto Rican middlemen alike) was the integration of the Puerto Rican economy into that of the United States. For the merchants, as for the middlemen, statehood represented the perpetuation of this integration.

The third social group that formed the core of support of the Republican Party—and that to a great extent gave the Party its ideology, in the way of life it proposed—were the professionals of the beginning of the century: doctors, engineers, federal employees and a small group of white-collar workers. Their interests as a social group were centered around the development of a modern, professionalized and bureaucratized way of life in which they would play a central role. To these professionals as a group the North American preeminence in the island meant a possible gateway for "modernization."

The Revival of the "Bourgeoisie"

The decade of the thirties in Puerto Rico was a period of hopelessness and uncertainty. The three main political groups had lost their significance in terms of the way of life they represented. The social structure of the hacienda, which the Unionist Party supported, was in bankrupcy. The hope of a new "modern" social order that the North Americans had been expected to bring and that had been advocated by the Republican Party in its early years was destroyed by the blatant colonial policies of the United States itself.[23] (The governors of the island, for example, were usually appointed to pay for political debts or political favors, and the island became a sunny spot where North American military officers and politicians could retire with an honorable position.)[24] Finally, the Socialist Party—the party of the workers—had fallen into a simple trade-unionist position, striving only for higher wages and better living conditions, and thus burying the aspirations of the working class for a new and radically different social order.

The thirties were also years of crisis for international capitalism, the years of the world depression. The depression made the contradictions within the capitalist system more evident. The plantation economy, with its emphasis on the production of one cash crop, had placed the island's economy in a position of total dependency on the commercial system. The great crisis in international commerce had, therefore, disastrous consequences on the Puerto Rican people. The depression accounted for a tremendous rate of unemployment in the island: 60 per cent of the labor force. (The FLT did not organize this mass of unemployed workers, which was then, definitively, one of the most important sectors of the working class. It lost, thus, its relevance as *the* working class struggle organization in this situation.[25]) Faced with these developments, hopelessness became general among the various sectors of Puerto Rican society.

The only political group that in the thirties represented an alternative of hope for a different way of life was the Nationalist Party. Some of the elements in this alternative, however, were unacceptable to the culture and ideology of the Puerto Rican proletariat.[26] Nevertheless, the Nationalist Party, though a small group, was at the center of the major political events of the thirties.

The breakdown of the hacienda social organization and the growing importance of the professions in a socio-economic system of greater macro-integration (and specifically the importance of public school teaching with the expansion of the educational system) led many *hacendados* and owners of medium-sized farms to sell their lands in order to assure a professional education for their children. Many moved to the large urban centers to facilitate their children's education. Thus, this second generation of the *hacendado* class became more linked to the liberal professions than to agriculture. This generation—born when the social structure of the hacienda was beginning to crumble and when its class had lost its political and economic hegemony—found itself in a secondary position in the social hierarchy. This fostered the development among its members of a more radical ideology oriented to change. The image of modernity which the Republicans of the beginnings of the century had presented, was transferred to this new social group.[27] With strong roots in the traditions and culture of the hacienda system, this new petty-bourgeoisiemaintained the support of the hacienda laborers and of the small *colonos*, while at the same time its new and more radical ideology and its lower social position made possible an alliance with an important sector of the proletariat that had become discontented with the decaying political organizations that in the past had represented it.[28]

Since the *hacendados* had lost their class hegemony and also to a very great extent the control over the means of production, the Puerto Rican plantation proletariat came to realize that the *hacendados* were no longer their antagonic class. By the Thirties it had become clear to the island's proletariat that its real class enemies were the great absentee North American corporations which controlled the sugar industry.[29] These corporations had also been, for many years, the enemies of the *hacendados* and small *colonos*. These corporations were the image of colonial capitalism in Puerto Rico; a system whose contradictions and weaknesses had been made clear by the crisis of the world depression. Thus, an alliance of workers, small *colonos*, a few remaining *hacendados*, and the new ''*hacendado* bourgeoisie'' emerged in the form of the Popular Democratic Party (PPD), whose program was basically one of opposition to the evils and injustices of the economic and political colonialism represented on the island by the power of the great North American sugar corporations. The PPD won control of the insular senate in the elections of 1940 and an ample majority in both the senate and the house of representatives in all the elections from 1944 to 1964.

These victories were accompanied by the granting of greater self-government to the island, to the point where it could be said, for the first time in the history of Puerto Rico under U.S. colonial rule, that the PPD was not only the majority party but the governing party as well. The PPD government initiated a series of radical programs. Among these was the nationalization of certain privately-owned utilities (electrical service, for example) and attempts at agrarian reform. Although initially in favor of independence,[30] the *Populares* decided to let the status issue rest during the years of World War II[31] and concentrated their efforts on their economic program.

The key posts in the insular government in the decade of the forties went mostly to members of the new generation of radical professionals (mostly sons of the old *hacendados*).[32] The social structure of the hacienda being destroyed, this group, as a class, needed to find a new economic basis to establish its social hegemony. Following the example of Roosevelt's New Deal and always hoping for the support from New Deal administrators in the US, this class found in government planning of the economy a new base for economic power: They emerged as technocrats in a new industrial welfare state. After an initial attempt to develop state-owned enterprises, the new technocrats concluded that the easiest way to bring about the industrialization to which they were committed was to attract (in a planned manner) private North American capital to the island. Realizing that independence and radical socio-economic programs were an obstacle to this, the leadership of the PPD adopted autonomy as its political goal, took a more moderate stand and moved progressively to the right on socio-economic issues.[33]

Industrialization was brought about primarily by attracting subsidiaries of North American firms. The new industrialization policy of the PPD government (i.e. the policy of facilitating North American investment) depended greatly on maintaining a low wage level that would be attractive to North American investors. In 1950, for example, the average hourly wage in Puerto Rico industries was 27 per cent of the average hourly wage in the United States.[34] To maintain such a wage level, government control of labor unions (or, at the very least, deliberate efforts to weaken them) became a necessity.

Thus, the decade of the forties was one of conflict between two groups that had allied themselves at the beginning of the decade: a conflict between the emerging class of technocrats (sons of the old *hacendados*) and the working class. It was not difficut for these technocrats to establish control or to weaken the labor movement in Puerto Rico, for during the decade of the forties Puerto Rican society experienced a series of social processes that gradually fragmented the working class as a class; destroyed a whole "culture" in which the plantation proletariat was forged.

This occurrence, which can be labeled the "unmaking of the plantation proletariat" has to be seen in terms of the transformation which the Puerto Rican economy experienced in the forties; a transformation from plantation to industrial economy. Although this process got under way in the early Forties, it became particularly intense at the end of that decade and thereafter. (See Graph 1) This transformation of the economy changed the structure of production. It changed what had served as a base for shared experiences, around which there had been developing an identity of interests; interests of a purely economic nature, and interests that implied a whole way of life.

GRAPH 1. RATE OF GROWTH OF THE SUGAR INDUSTRY AND OF
MANUFACTURING (AVERAGE PERCENTAGE EVERY FIVE YEARS).

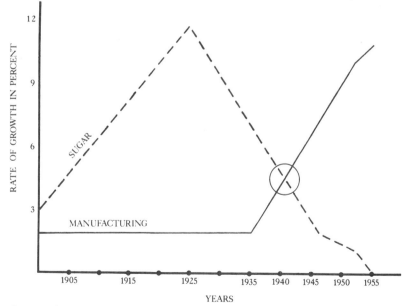

(Source: This graph is taken from José Herrero, *La mitología del azúcar, un ensayo en historia económica de Puerto Rico* [manuscript of a book in preparation],though we are merely reproducing the general tendencies of the curves not the exact relationships between coordinates.)

During the forties other processes reinforced this "unmaking" which, as has been explained, had as its basis the economic transformation that the island was undergoing. Among these changes one can point to the following: First, the emergence of a new social type in Puerto Rico, the veteran, who was a result of World War II and the Korean War. Many veterans were of plantation-proletariat origin, but making use of the facilities made available to them by the Veteran's Administration (facilities for study, loans for small businesses or to buy cars and become taxi or *públicos* drivers and credit facilities to purchase homes in new middle class housing development) gradually separated them from their class of origin.[35] Whereas in the first three decades of North American rule, the only means available to the plantation proletariat to improve its economic condition was collective trade union action (strikes, collective bargaining), the Veteran's Administration introduced a channel for individual economic improvement. This opened cleaveges in the culture of combativeness of the proletariat.

In the same way, the massive emigration of Puerto Ricans to New York and other industrial centers in the US mainland, an emigration that was encouraged and facilitated by the PPD government,[36] gave working-class families on the island a channel for individual economic improvement without class struggle.

As has been pointed out above, the Puerto Rican program for industrialization relied greatly on the establishment on the island of subsidiaries of North American firms. The unions that represented the workers in the home firms in the United States set out to unionize the Puerto Rican workers employed by the subsidiaries on the Island. U.S. trade unions (the so-called 'internationals') invaded the island and created a climate of competition among the unions to represent the workers. This also contributed to the growing cleaveges in working-class solidarity, which had emerged among the plantation proletariat and historically had been channeled through a single labor union, the FLT.

The third factor that reinforced the "unmaking" of the plantation proletariat was the change in the legal structure concerning labor relation brought about by the Taft-Hartley Law. The illegalization of solidarity strikes (of fundamental importance in the history of the FLT), the measures that implied abolition of wildcat strikes (which had been a characteristic tactic of the Puerto Rican proletariat in its struggle), and the complicated procedures that placed the rich North American unions in an advantageous position in the conflict with local labor unions to represent Puerto Rican workers, brought about the disintegration of the type of struggle which the plantation proletariat had been developing.

Since industry offered better wages than agriculture, the new class of "sons of old *hacendados*" made use of the drive towards industrialization (Operation Bootstrap) as *mystique* to control the class struggle, to bring passivity to the working class and its organization.[37] Luis Muñoz Marín—main leader of this new class and governor of Puerto Rico from 1948 to 1964—For example, stated in a speech he delivered to a congress of workers, that the function of the labor movement in Puerto Rico was to *cooperate* with the "economic development" of the island; a development being carried out or guided by the government. He implied that to "cooperate with economic development" meant not to disrupt government policies or frighten or alienate foreign investment (which, as has been explained above, formed the base for the industrialization of the island) by any sort of militant struggle.[38]

Since better wages were associated with industry, and since industry was brought about through government efforts, economic well-being was seen as being dependent on government. Whereas in the plantation economy economic improvement was linked to the collective trade-unionist struggle, in the new situation of industrialization it became associated with submission to government programs. In this way, the class of "sons of old *hacendados*" revived (with the differences in new socio-economic structure) the paternalism of the old hacienda system.[39]

During the entire decade of the fifties, industrialization was seen as being brought by or linked to the programs of the Economic Development Administration (*Fomento*). Yet, by the late sixties (industrial capitalism being firmly established in the island) industrialization begins to be seen as an autonomous phenomenom. And faced with this new pattern of relations of production the working class began a process of remaking.

At the end of the forties, as a result of the process of industrialization, the social structure of the island began to change in its middle strata. A small group of Puerto Ricans who were able to become industrialists and merchants along North American lines and style emerged; a group whose class interests were linked to the type of socio-economic organization of the United States.[40]

The old guard of the Republican Party—the middlemen of the plantation economy—maintained control of the party in spite of the fact that the party was progressively becoming a party of new middlemen.[41]

The potential conflict that this development implied came to a climax in 1966 when a group of new middlemen took over and created a new party: the New Progressive Party (PNP). Taking advantage of the internal conflicts that were raging within the PPD and the growing disenchantment with that party the PNP won the elections of 1968.

The electoral triumph of the PNP represented the victory of those in Puerto Rican society whose interests are intimately linked to the colonial relationship between the United States and Puerto Rico, and who, by advocating statehood, seek to make that relationship permanent. It was a victory made possible, nevertheless, by an urban working class protest vote against the PPD.[42] In this sense, its electoral support had a very weak basis: the residents of *caserios* and *arrabales*, for example, were not committed to the PNP's politics; they supported this party as a protest against a government which they had begun to realize was not for their benefit. The weak base of '68 PNP's electoral support was demonstrated by their defeat in the following elections, when working-class people cast again their protest vote. The phenomenon of the protest vote, jointly with a recent intensification in labor militancy and other forms of working-class defiance, is an indication of the beginning of the remaking of a working class consciousness; a consciousness that will eventually lead to the formation of a working-class political force that will again seek the transformation of society in terms of the proletariat's culture of solidarity

NOTES

1. Some of these limitations are analyzed in Gervasio García in "Apuntes sobre una interpretación de la realidad puertorriqueña," *La Escalera*, Vol. 4, No. 1 (1970.)

2. I have presented in more detail elsewhere the problem of the conceptions of history in interpretations of our national reality. See *Lucha obrera en Puerto Rico*, edited by Angel Quintero Rivera (Rí o Piedras, 1971), Preface. See also, Angel Quintero Rivera, *El liderato local de los partidos y el estudio de la política puertorriqueña* (Río Piedras, 1970). In the latter work I specifically criticize the "great leader" conception of our political conflicts (or "theory of the grandee").

3. E. P. Thompson, *The Making of the English Working Class* (London, 1968), pp. 9-10.

4. For details see, Raymond Christ, "Sugar Cane and Coffee in Puerto Rico," Part I; "The Role of the Priviledge and Monopoly in the Expropriation of the Jibaro," Part II; and "The Pauperization of the Jibaro—Land Monopoly and Monoculture," in *American Journal of Economics and Sociology*, Vol. 7, nos. 2-3 (1948). For facts on the domination of North American sugar corporations see B. W. and J. W. Diffie, *Porto Rico: A Broken Pledge* (New York, 1931) and Victor S. Clark, et al., *Porto Rico and its Problems* (Washington, D.C., 1930), especially the appendices.

5. Sidney Mintz makes a good presentation of this issue in "The Folk-Urban Continuum

and the Rural Proletariat Community," *The American Journal of Sociology*, Vol. LIX, No. 2 (1953).

6. Sidney Mintz, "The Plantation as a Socio-Cultural Type," in OAS, *Plantation Systems in the New World* Washington, D.C., (1959). See also, Julian Steward, "Perspectives on Plantation," Ibid.

7. *Symposium on the Geography of Puerto Rico*, Edited by Clarence F. Jones and Rafael Picó (Río Piedras, 1955), pp. 343-361, presents maps that illustrate the patterns of settlement in rural areas given the type of cultivation to which these areas are devoted. The pattern of settlement in small villages (*aldeas*) in areas devoted to the cultivation of sugar cane are in clear contrast to the patterns of total dispersion which appear in areas devoted to the cultivation of tobacco and minor crops, crops generally identified with small independent landholders. The maps showing areas under coffee cultivation, generally identified with the hacienda pattern of land tenure, show certain population clusters. But in these areas, the isolated household predominates (and the degree of isolation of these households is greater than in the areas devoted to the cultivation of tobacco and minor crops).

8. The Roig Company, in the region of Yabucoa and Humacao, and the Aguirre Company in municipalities such as Santa Isabel, for example. Photographs and descriptions of some of these settlements created by the companies themselves are found in *The People of Puerto Rico, A Study in Social Anthropology*, edited by Julian Steward, (Urbana, 1956) and in Sidney Mintz, *Worker in the Cane, a Puerto Rican Life History* (New Haven, 1960).

9. This manifests itself, for example, in the patterns of *compadrazgo* (co-parenthood). Among the plantation proletariat, the *compadres* were generally friends, co-workers; in areas of Puerto Rico where small or medium-sized peasants predominated, the ties of *compadrazgo* were usually established principally among relatives; and in *hacienda* situations, the workers tended to establish such ties with those above them (e.g. the *hacendado*) in the social ladder. See, Sidney Mintz and Eric Wolf, "An Analysis of Ritual Co-Parenthood," *Southwestern Journal of Anthropology* Vol. 6, No. 4 (1950).

10. Edgar Thompson, "The Plantation as a Social System," in OAS.

11. In my work, *Lucha obrera en Puerto Rico*, I present an extensive bibliography that includes references to these centers as well as to the development of the image of and aspirations for, a new society. Also, one of the documents presented in this anthology, "Páginas rojas" by Juan S. Marcano (a shoemaker of Caguas), is in itself an example of the ideal social order to which the Puerto Rican working class aspired in the second decade of this century.

12. This approach does not imply that the specific actions of leaders or militants lack importance. My argument is that these actions—obviously indispensible for a comrehensive analysis—have to be placed in the context of economic history and the dialectics of class conflicts.

13. See, Miguel Melé Muñoz, "La pequeña propriedad en el desarrollo de Puerto Rico," in *El libro de Puerto Rico*, edited by E. Fernández García, San Juan, (1923). See also, José Enamorado Cuesta, "Porto Rico after 24 years of American Rule" *Current History* (April 1923). A sociological analysis subsequent to these studies is found in Crist, "The Pauperization of the Jibaro."

14. A few months before the North American occupation of Puerto Rico in 1898, the island had acquired from Spain an Autonomic Charter. This document practically conceded political power in the island to the class of *hacendados*.

15. This helps us understand the position of Mariano Abril, ideological spokesman of the *hacendados* and Muñoz Rivera's right-hand in the newspaper *La Democracia,* towards working-class organizations. His position may be summarized as follows: The *hacendados* have been losing their power, so there does not exist in Puerto Rico the basis for a class struggle. All segments of society are equally oppressed by colonial capitalism, which constitutes the real enemy. (Mariano Abril, *El socialismo moderno,* San Juan 1911). With respect to this issue see also the attacks which José de Diego launched against the FLT in his "Cuestiones obreras," a speech he delivered as President of the House of Delegates and which appears in his Nuevas campañas *(Barcelona 1916).*

The transformation of economic structures which Puerto Rico experienced during these first years under North American colonial rule, not only placed the class of *hacendados* in a different social position, but also transformed their very nature. The tremendous growth of commercial activity—even at the level of everyday life—and the importance which the professions began to assume in a system of greater macro-integration, gradually pushed the class of *hacendados* into a process of "bourgeoisification." This class maintained its roots, however, in the hacienda life (at least until the decade of the 1930s) and the economic relations which that implies. For this reason, the most correct term to be used when referring to this class in the second and third decade of this century may be perhaps a combination of terms or a combined term, for example, "the hacendado bourgeoisie."

16. Bolívar Pagán, *Historia de los partidos políticos puertorriqueños* San Juan, (1959), Vol. I, p. 156.

17. A very clear example of this can be seen in the *Memorial* which the FLT sends to the U.S. Congress in 1913 under the title *The Tyranny of the House of Delegates of Porto Rico* which has been reprinted in Quintero Rivera, *Lucha obrera.*

18. Interpretations within the "theory of the grandee" add that it was due to the fact the Santiago Iglesias, being a Spaniard by birth, did not feel *"el llamado de la nacionalidad"* ("the call of nationality").

19. In the Assembly of the Socialist Party in 1919, a group of the most important leaders of the Party (Manuel F. Rojas, Secretary General; Alfonso Torres, who later on was chosen Secretary General; and Julio Aybar, Vice President of the Assembly and editor of the most important workers' newspaper at that time —*Unión Obrera*— among others) defended the "Socialist Industrial Republic" as a goal. Discussion on this issue was lengthy and heated, but no vote was taken on it. (Partido Socialista Puertorriqueño, *Programa, Constitución Territorial y Actuaciones,* 1919, which also appears in Quintero Rivera, *Lucha obrera.* Bolívar Pagán in his *Historia de los partidos,* presents a somewhat tergiversated account of the incident).

20. For example, Manuel F. Rojas, who in the assembly of the Socialist Party in 1919, was the one who led the offensive in favor of the adoption of a resolution supporting a Socialist Republic, in 1914 had written the book *Cuatro siglos de ignorancia y servidumbre en Puerto Rico* in which he expounds, with obvious pain, his objections to independence, objections which he explains in terms of the class situation at that time.

21. An analysis of social groups in the Republican Party is difficult for three main reasons: First, from 1904 (when the Unionist Party won the elections) to 1917 (when the Socialist Party participated in elections for the first time), the Republican Party was the opposition party. Even after the creation of the Socialist Party, a clearly proletarian party, the Republican Party continued to be an opposition party to those sectors of society that could not identify themselves with the working class. In this sense it brought into its fold

members of groups similar to those in the Unionist Party who were disgusted or in competition with them. (In almost all small Puerto Rican towns there were Puerto Rican *hacendados* in the Unionist Party and rival *hacendados* in the Republican Party. Already in 1914, a foreign observer, A. H. Verrill, indicated that there was a lot of "sporting" in these parties, something pointed out twenty years later by the Puerto Rican essayist Antonio S. Pedreira in his *Insularismo* published in 1934).

Second, in spite of being an *opposition party* in terms of the internal political struggle, the colonial situation of the island and the triangular nature of political conflict which has already been pointed out, permitted the Republican Party to be to a certain extent the *government party*, given its identification with the most powerful element in the "triangle": the metropolis. Thus, the governmental patronage received by the party attracted to the party a number of people who wanted a share in that patronage. This development was pointed out as early as 1899 by W. Dinwiddie, has been repeated in various subsequent documents, and was even elevated to the level of being used to categorize the party by the political scientist Robert W. Anderson in *Party Politics in Puerto Rico* (Standard, 1965). To categorize the party essentially in terms of patronage, however, is to lose sight of the more fundamental issue of what were the class interests which the party represented. But, nevertheless, the fact that the element of patronage was present in such a significant way obviously makes difficult an analysis of internal social groups.

Third, the leader of the Republican Party, Dr. José Celso Barbosa, was a Negro and his leadership introduced the racial element in support for the party. This type of support was found primarily among negroes in the middle sectors of urban society (school teachers, musicians, minor bureaucrats, a few artisans). This racial base of support, however, is not found among black members of the proletariat who refused to identify themselves with Barbosa who, in spite of being black, carried on the life style and had the world vision of the bourgeoisie. (In his writings on the racial issue one can detect a tremendous unconsciousness regarding the problem of social classes. See, José C. Barbosa, *Problema de razas,* (San Juan, 1937).

These are three elements of great importane in the Republican Party which make difficult a class analysis of the political movement this party represented, since they represent interests and sources of support which are interlaced with class interests. Nevertheless, I sustain that in spite of the fact that these elements are important, an analysis of social groups in the Republican Party is far more illuminating and helps one understand in a more profound way the positions which the party assumed.

22. Thomas Mathews, *Puerto Rican Politics and the New Deal* (Gainsville, 1960) and A. Hyatt Verrill, *Porto Rico, Past and Present* (New York, 1914), also identify small merchants with the Republican Party.

23. See, for example, Luis Muñoz Marín, "Porto Rico: An American Colony," *The National* (April 1925), Diffie, *Porto Rico;* and Lepoldo Cuban, "A Porto Rican View of American Control," *Current History* (March 1930).

24. This is described in detail by Roberto H. Todd in his *Desfile de governadores de Puerto Rico, 1898-1943* (San Juan, 1943). It is interesting to point out that Todd was not anti-American. On the contrary, he was pro-American, and one of the leading spokesmen of the Republican Party. He presents these details with some bitterness and disillusionment.

The North American, A.H. Verrill (*Porto Rico,* p. 134) pointed out as early as 1914 this tendency to use the governorship of Puerto Rico as a reward for political favors in the U.S.

25. Data for unemployment in, Porto Rico, *Report of the Governor* (Washington, D.C., 1930). The unemployed organized themselves independently to struggle for a transformation of the system. In 1940,the unemployed were a major source of support for the Popular Democratic Party. See Juan Sáez Corales, "El movimiento organizado de los desempleados y la industrialización de Puerto Rico," in CGT, Asociación de Chóferes, *Album* (1941).

26. For example, its solemnity, its Catholicism, its defense of the Hispanic tradition.

27. This is tied to the relations which this group gradually established with the leaders of the New Deal in the United States. See, Mathews, *Puerto Rican Politics*, 257. See also the memoirs of the New Deal North American governor, Rexford G. Tugwell, *The Stricken Land* (New York, 1947).

28. This was principally the group which months before the elections of 1940 had abandned the FLT and had created a new syndicalist organization, the General Confederation of Workers (CGT).

29. Already in 1936, a member of the Socialist Party, José L. Novas ("Política puertorriqueña," *Ambito*, 1936) proposed the creation of "a united anti-imperialist front on behalf of independence and social justice."

30. See, the political platform of the PPD of 1940 in PPD, *Compilación de programas* (San Juan, 1956).

31. This appears to have been the policy of leftist groups: it was necessary to liquidate facism first; to enter into conflicts with the United States at that time would have been to weaken the power of the Allies. See, for example, the political report presented before the second national assembly of the Communist Party by its president Juan Santos Rivera, *¡Contra Hitler en el mundo! ¡Contra el hambre en Puerto Rico!* (San Juan, 1942).

On the importance for the United States of holding on to Puerto Rico during the war years see, Judd Polk, "Plight of Puerto Rico" *Political Science Quarterly* (December 1942) and, better yet; Tugwell, *Stricken Land*. Tugwell relates how he tried to convince Puerto Rican politicians to let the status issue rest until the war was over.

32. See, Tugwell, *Stricken Land*; Thomas Aitken, *Poet in the Fortress* (New York, 1964); and Clarence Senior, "Research and Administration in Economic Reconstruction," *Journal of Social Issues* (1947), as examples.

33. This process is presented in critical terms by Gordon K. Lewis, "Puerto Rico: A Case Study of Change in an Underdeveloped Area," *Journal of Politics*, XVII (1955), pp. 614-50, and in favorable terms by E. P. Hanson, *Transformation, The Story fo Modern Puerto Rico* (New York, 1955), On that issue see also, Luis Nieves Falcón, "El Futuro ideológico del PPD," in *Diagnóstico de Puerto Rico* (Río Piedras, 1971).

34. Lloyd G. Reynolds and Peter Gregory, *Wages, Productivity and Industrialization in Puerto Rico* (New Haven, 1965), p. 20.

35. John P. Augelli in "San Lorenzo: A Case Study of Recent Migrations in Interior Puerto Rico," *American Journal of Economics and Sociology* (January 1952), describes this situation in a town in the interior of the island. Other descriptions can be found in Steward, *People of Puerto Rico*.

36. This has been inferred from the following document: Puerto Rico, Department of Labor, *Trade Unions and the Puerto Rican Workers* (Rio Piedras, 1952) and from the "clarification" of Teodoro Moscoso in *Un discurso y una aclaración* (San Juan, 1950).

37. A concrete example can be found in the attacks which the PPD launched against the organization of a labor union in one of the state enterprises. The leader of that union at the

time, Félix Morales, reacted with a magnificent reply. See, Félix Morales, *Tres Maquinarias y lucha con fantasmas* (San Juan, 1945).

Another example is constituted by the speech of Teodoro Moscoso, one of the most important architects of the industrialization policies of the PPD, entitled *El progreso técnico y los trabajadores* (San Juan, 1958).

38. Luis Muñoz Marín, *Función del movimiento obrero en la democracia puertorriqueña* (San Juan, 1957). Moscoso, in his *Un discurso*, clearly pointed out that the solution to the economic problem of Puerto Rico laid in industrialization through foreign capital investment and that "the great task of the labor movement" was to help create "the favorable conditions" necessary to attract that capital: "any demand that is so excessive that it forces to close one single industry is an attempt against the welfare and the future of the entire Puerto Rican people."

Ralph Hancock, *Puerto Rico, A Success Story* (Princeton, 1960), chapter 8 (Manpower) explains how in face of this situation, the struggle of the labor movement was carried at the governmental administrative level (specifically within the Minimum Salary Board) rather than at the level of the industry.

39. Muñoz Marín in *Función del movimiento obrero* openly tells the workers that improvements in their standard of living have been brought about by the government rather than by the efforts of the labor unions.

40. The Ferré family is probably the best example of this group of Puerto Ricans.

41. Robert W. Anderson, *Party Politics*, points this out in general terms.

42. Marcia Quintero, *La elecciones de 1968 en Puerto Rico, análisis estadístico por grupos socio-económicos* (San Juan, 1972); and Rafael Ramírez," Marginalidad, dependencia y participación política en el arrabal" in Rafael L. Ramírez, Carlos Buitrago Ortiz, and Barry B. Levine (eds.), *Problemas de desigualdad social en Puerto Rico* (San Juan, 1972) or his *Politics of the Urban Poor* (in press).

Dependence and Development in Puerto Rico

Morris Morley

Initial assertions of an identity of interest between the United States and Latin America developed in the 1820s with the enunciation of the Monroe Doctrine and the more mystical doctrine of manifest destiny—both of which operated to justify United States interventionary activity in terms of its advantages to the intervened country. The United States used the Monroe Doctrine, with its non (European) colonization principle and its notion of a uniquely American system, to lay the foundations for its eventual hegemony in Latin America. It unilaterally intervened in various countries throughout most of the nineteenth century in order to establish or maintain acceptable political elites, policies and institutions, to develop and expand favorable trade and business relationships, and occasionally to annex territory. Toward the end of the nineteenth century, the problems associated with a new industrialization functioned to encourage a concerted United States policy of economic expansion on a global scale. In respect of this policy, Latin America—especially Central America and the Caribbean area—was of primary importance.

The changeover from a basically agrarian, commercial, nonindustrial society to a world industrial power was manifested in the development of the large corporation, which in turn became a crucial factor in the evolution of United States expansionist ambitions in the 1890's. Possessing an "overwhelming economic power which made it possible to bypass traditional imperialism,"[1] the large corporation also possessed a particular view of the world that it effectively propagated among the highest echelons of government. This view argued that economic expansion overseas was a way of solving the pressing domestic economic problems of the time and of simultaneously defusing the possibilities of internal social revolution. The need for external markets to absorb the industrial surplus, for raw materials and for miltiary bases to support the development of a global economic empire was to characterize United States industrial-capitalist expansion.

The decision to intervene militarily in Cuba and Puerto Rico in 1898 initiated this new foreign policy designed to protect and expand existing United States economic interests in Latin America. What John Quincy Adams in 1823 had called "natural appendages to the North American continent,"[2] became, in 1898, formal colonies under U.S. military rule.

Roots of Economic Dependence 1898-1940

United States economic penetration of Puerto Rico necessitated a political environment conducive to the flow of capital into the island and to the subsequent activities of U.S. investor interests. Consequently, U.S. policy during the early period was primarily directed toward creation of a political and administrative infrastructure that facilitated such penetration.

The military and strategic aspects of this policy, rooted in the Monroe Doctrine and manifest destiny, were based on the notion of the Caribbean area as a closed U.S. domain. Strategic and commercial imperatives were closely linked throughout the nineteenth century, and the United States continued to underwrite Spanish rule in the Caribbean as long as the area remained politically stable and economically accessible to U.S. commercial interests. By the 1890s, Spanish control was being seriously threatened by indigenous nationalist movements that U.S. policy makers perceived as detrimental to stability and order, and to existing and future U.S. economic interests. The result was a series of U.S. military interventions, and the replacement of Spain by the United States as the hegemonic power in the Caribbean. U.S. military control of Puerto Rico, observed an historian of the period, brought with it "the establishment of order and, most important, the willingness of capital to enter the country...."[3]

Any ideas that Puerto Ricans may have harbored about the institution of a democratic political process were promptly rejected by U.S. policy makers. The notion of mass political participation would result, if at all, from a sustained period of elite rule and tutelary government.

"The people generally," declared General George W. Davis, U.S. military governor from 1898 to 1900, "have no conception of political rights combined with political responsibilities. Privileges they all desire, but they seem to have very little conception of political responsibility and the obligation of all to bow to the will of the majority."[4]

The withdrawal of U.S. military forces in 1900 was accompanied by the imposition of the First Organic (Foraker) Act which outlined the structure of the new civilian government. The island governor would be a U.S. presidential appointee, and the U.S. Congress retained the power of veto over any laws passed by the island's Legislative assembly. The Puerto Rican government also was denied any role in the negotiation of U.S. trade treaties that might adversely affect the Puerto Rican economy. This dependency underwent little change as a result of the Second Organic (Jones) Act of 1917. United States citizenship was extended to the island population, but the power of the appointed U.S. governor and the U.S. Congress (in which Puerto Rico had no vote) remained unchanged. Both Acts encouraged the formation of an 'Americanized' political structure based on strong executive control and the separation of power principle. The goal of U.S. policy makers was to develop politically elite clients who were responsive, not to the indigenous population, but to U.S. economic elites penetrating the country.

Independence for Puerto Rico never was seriously considered by the U.S. government during the pre-1940 period. Congressional rejection of the Tydings Bill (1936) supporting independence for the island was one of the more visible examples of this attitude. Puerto Rico continued to be "an unincorporated territory of the United States,"[5] and the potential for extensive local political and social organization was severely limited by the actions of the U.S. government.

The educational system was a major target of those "Americans in the insular bureaucracy who had been sent to Puerto Rico for the specific purpose of implementing a federal policy of Americanization."[6] Religious education was banned, public education for girls and coeducational classrooms were instituted, and the study of 'the American way of life' and U.S. history was given a prominent place in the educational syllabus. But more important, the study of English was made compulsory, and between 1904 and 1915 was substituted for Spanish as the language of instruction in public schools. These factors contributed to the emergence of an educational system that, in part, identified the belief system of the Puerto Ricans with the values and goals of the U.S. capitalist-entrepreneur. They encouraged psychological dependence on the United States through indigenous groups who came to support cultural and political assimilation with the U.S. Cultural imperialism was viewed by U.S. policy makers as an important determinant in the development of an internal class structure that would support external economic penetration and dependency.

Between 1898 and 1930, the movement of United States capital into the Puerto Rican economy destroyed the traditional pattern of individual land ownership and consolidated the dominance of the large external corporation. Of 107 foreign corporations operating in Puerto Rico in 1922, 103 were U.S.-owned.[7] Prior to 1898, coffee and sugar accounted for 41 per cent and 15 per cent respectively of the total cultivated land. By 1930,as a result of large-scale American investment ($10 million alone between 1900 and 1910), sugar had assumed a dominant position in the economy. It accounted for 44 per cent of all the land under cultivation. Four U.S. corporations produced 50 per cent of the total sugar crop in 1930 and together controlled almost 40 per cent of the agricultural wealth of the island.[8] In 1936, Puerto Rico was a sugar monoculture economy in which 2 per cent of sugar farms owned or controlled 65 per cent of all land growing sugar cane.[9]

U.S. penetration and control of the sugar industry gave impetus to the entry of U.S. capital into other areas of the Puerto Rican economy. U.S. corporations played a prominent role in the tobacco and fruit industries, were the major source of investments in public utilities (telephone, gas, light and power) and, together with Canadian interests, owned over half of all Puerto Rican bank resources in 1929. Increased U.S. demand for Puerto Rican needlework products encouraged U.S. entrepreneurs to import the necessary raw materials and establish a low quality, low cost operation carried on mainly in private homes. By the late 1920s, this industry was employing approximately 50,000 women and children under the most exploitative 'sweatshop' conditions. The great majority of these workers received wages of from 15 to 25 cents a day.[10] In the process, a long tradition of high quality needlework was practically destroyed.

A major effect of U.S. investor policies was a change in the pattern of land tenure. Whereas the coffee industry was labor-intensive, small scale, easy to market and required a minimal capital outlay, the cultivation of sugar normally required large tracts of land and substantial capital investment. The transformation of the Puerto Rican economy wrought by U.S. investors resulted in the virtual proletarianization of the agricultural labor force. Landless, they sought employment in a sugar industry where the vast majority of workers held jobs only during the months of the sugar harvest and earned wages as low as 62 cents a day.[11]

U.S. corporate interests, supported by the political power of the appointed governor, established and maintained links with indigenous political elites to protect their economic activities in Puerto Rico. Political parties, dependent on financial contributions from the sugar industry and allied interests, refused to enforce the 500 acre provision of the First Organic Act. Furthermore, the repatriation of corporate profits to the U.S. and the resultant decapitalization of the economy were not subject to any local control.

The policies of the U.S. government also facilitated the entry of the American investor into the Puerto Rican economy and the economic dependence of Puerto Rico on the United States. The increasing transfer of U.S. government funds, in particular, complimented the actions of the capitalist—entrepreneur and helped finance economic penetration.

The application of the U.S. tariff laws to Puerto Rico after 1898 meant that in return for the duty free entry of local products into the U.S. market, all Puerto Rican purchases from other countries would be subject to the exceedingly high U.S. tariff duties. Thus, the development of substantial trading relationships outside of the U.S. market was difficult, if not impossible. In 1930-1931, the United States accounted for over 95 per cent of Puerto Rico's exports and approximately 90 per cent of the country's imports.[12] Puerto Rico's inclusion in the Coastwise Shipping Act of the United States also gave U.S. shipping companies a monopoly over the island's commercial trade. These companies were able to raise arbitrarily freight charges when they deemed it necessary, without regard for any negative effects these actions might have on the Puerto Rican economy.

The complimentary relationship between the U.S. government and U.S. economic interests was most fully evident in respect of sugar. The principal reason for the expansion of the sugar industry was the U.S. government's decision to extend it complete tariff protection against all non-Cuban sugar and 80 per cent of Cuban sugar.[13] However, in 1934, the new Reciprocal Trade Agreements Act reduced Puerto Rico's tariff advantage in order to give priority to Cuban and U.S. sugar interests.

This decision all but eliminated the small cane farmer and ensured the dominance of the large sugar corporations.

Finally, significant amounts of U.S. federal funds entered the Puerto Rican economy, especially after the 1929-1933 depression, for public works, agricultural subsidies and other activities. U.S. government funds appropriated for Puerto Rico during the period 1933 to 1946—in direct aid and loans—amounted to almost $230 million.[14] These funds played a vital role in opening up the country to American exports, manufactures and investments.

Consequences for Puerto Rican Development

The Puerto Rican economy at the end of the first four decades of American rule was misdeveloped and stagnant. An extreme dependence on sugar, chronic unemployment and underemployment, absentee monopoly land ownership and a steady decapitalization in the form of external profit remittances were features of the society. ". . . Aside from sugar, private interests on the mainland made no significant effort to exploit the resources of the Island through capital investment."[15] The economy remained geared to a stagnating industry subject to political decisions taken outside of the country. Within this industry, four U.S. corporations held sway over 40 per cent of sugar output and more than 50 per cent of total sugar acreage.[16] The U.S. government's support for the maintenance of the economic status quo was evidenced by its summary rejection of the Puerto Rican Policy Commission's "Chardón Plan." Prepared under the auspices of the U.S. Department of Agriculture, "Chardón Plan" represented a detailed study of the most serious problems plaguing the Puerto Rican economy. The U.S. government was highly critical of its major recommendations—particularly those pertaining to the need for agrarian reform—and preferred, instead, to engage in marginal reforms while the basic economic arrangements remained intact. Continuous and almost total U.S. control over Puerto Rico's foreign trade paralledled these developments. Between 1930 and 1940 this dependence actually increased. Almost 97 per cent of Puerto Rico's total trade was with the United States in 1940, compared with just under 93 per cent in 1930.[17]

The growth of a sugar monoculture and the concentration of land ownership in the hands of some large U.S. corporations and a few wealthy Puerto Rican families—such as the Serralles family—drastically affected the emerging internal class structure. Puerto Rico did not experience the development of a national bourgeoisie along the lines of those groups that emerged in ninetheenth century England and the United States; that is, a dynamic, anti-aristocratic bourgeois class conscious of its common interests as a class and of its common interests as against those of other classes. The Puerto Rican colonial elite, lacking the ability and/or capacity to engage in capital accumulation became "intermediaries between the hegemony of the colonial power and Puerto Rican society."[18] They were administrators for the absentee owners of large corporations, committee to economic self-aggrandizement and limiting the social demands of the masses.

The situation of the urban and rural proletariat changed minimally between 1898 and 1940. Governments during this time were criticized for being "of the insolent rich, of the corporations, of the oppressors, of the miserable judicial, political and religious bosses. . . ."[19] The majority of wage laborers in 1928 received from 60 to 80 cents a day. A study of the Puerto Rican economy by the Brookings Institution in 1930 called the life situation of the masses "deplorable." The per capita income of Puerto Ricans declined from $126 in 1930 to $120 in 1940.[20]

Unemployment and exploitation of labor were accompanied by another factor which further exacerbated the situation of the Puerto Rican worker. The sugar and, to a lesser extent, tobacco industries had expanded on land previously engaged in food production for local consumption. Consequently, a precipitous decline in food production occurred, necessitating increased purchases of foodstuffs (because of the tariff laws) from the expensive U.S. market. This had a substantial effect on the cost of living, as illustrated by the fact that 33 per cent of the cost of food imports from the U.S. in 1928 stemmed directly from the tariff.[21]

Luis Muñoz Marín aptly described the stark reality of the four decades of Puerto Rican development after the U.S. military intervention in 1898:

> . . . the development of large absentee-owned sugar estates, the rapid curtailment in the planting of coffee—the natural crop of the independent farmer—and the concentration of cigar manufacture into the hands of the American trust, have combined to make Puerto Rico a land of begars and millionaires, of flattering statistics and distressing realities. More and more it becomes a factory worked by peons, fought over by lawyers, bossed by absent industrialists, and clerked by politicians. It is now Uncle Sam's second largest sweatshop.[22]

Dependent Industrialization: The New Economic Development Strategy, 1940-1973

The decision to identify economic development with a policy of industrialization and the later promotion of the tourist industry represented sharp breaks with the pre-1940 dependence on agriculture. These strategies were designed to attract foreign capital to the island, and they led to a form of dependent industrialization as opposed to the dependent agriculture of the earlier period. Foreign capital controlled industrial enterprises while employing a group of landless, middle sector functionaries serving the needs of this capital. The pattern of dependent industrialization expressed itself in a marked dependence on U.S. capital (both private and government) and U.S. economic aid (both direct and indirect). A stable political climate, little or no threat of expropriation, no restrictions on external profit remittances, and the ability to maximize profits through tax exemptions and labor exploitation were encouraging signs to the U.S. investor. Of the 1,406 firms promoted under the industrialization program between 1948 and 1967, nearly 70 per cent were set up by foreign capital and almost 90 per cent of these were owned by U.S. intersts.[23]

By 1940 the agricultural sector had entered a period of increasing stagnation. The crucial sugar sector was unable to compete on the international market, partly because of the U.S. relationship and partly because of the lack of technology and a highly mechanized productive process. The tobacco industry also was in decline. Nevertheless, over 60 per cent of the employed population were engaged in activities related to agriculture, which was also the major preoccupation of the banking, commercial and financial sectors. In addition, almost half of the urban labor force were employed in the home needlework industry financed by U.S. capital and managed by local entrepreneurs. "The hazardous dependency upon agricultural production was graphically illustrated . . . in the statistics of the insular export trade (for 1946), with sugar contributing just over 7 per cent, and needlework products nearly 16 per cent. Puerto Rico was clearly in the general category of primary-producing countries exporting for a world market and subject to international price fluctuations and political arrangements beyond their power to infuence."[24]

With the overwhelming support of the rural masses, the Popular Democratic Party (hereafter P.D.P.), under the leadership of Luis

Muñoz Marín, was swept into political power in the 1940 national elections. Muñoz Marín had campaigned on a platform of:

Definitive enforcement of the 500 acre law, to distribute thousands of acres among workers and farmers, with the necessary facilities for their life on the land and for its cultivation.[25]

According to the 1940 Census of Agriculture, 342 farms covered or were in excess of 500 acres of land. These farms included 31 per cent of all the agricultural land and 44 per cent of the total value of land, buildings and equipment.[26]

U.S. government concern for the popular nationalism of the new government was soon allayed by its actions. An authority on the land reform program observed that Muñoz Marín was "not preaching revolution against Washington . . . He actually hoped for aid from the Federal government which, he suggested, could limit sugar quotas for the corporations to the amount of sugar that could be produced on 500 acres, and withold subsidies from the violators."[27] The 1941 Land Law, which established the Land Authority to enforce the 500 acre restriction, specified that land would be acquired in one of three ways—through expropriation with adequate compensation, by public sale, or through mutual agreement between the Land Authority and the corporation(s) concerned. The policy, as implemented, did not deviate from these methods. In the meantime, government aid to the agricultural sector was being directed toward the landowner rather than toward the landless agricultural laborer.

By the late 1940's, it was clear that the abolition of the corporate latifundio had not taken place, and was not about to occur. Only 12 of the 33 corporations holding land in excess of 500 acres had been drastically affected by the 1941 Land Law. Of the four U.S. corporations that dominated the sugar industry, two continued to retain control of all of their land.[28] The Puerto Rican goernment's commitment to redistributive policies gave way to an emphasis on increasing productivity as a means whereby the country might solve its chronic economic problems. Productivity was equated with industrialization which, in turn, was bound to result in a "dependence on mainland capital, as the government had attempted to build industrial plants during the war and discovered more capital was needed than it had. Politically, this dependence prohibited any radical break with the United States."[29]

The continued political hegemony of the United States government over Puerto Rico and the refusal of client political elites to support any major changes in the island's political status have been important factors favoring U.S. economic penetration. The electoral success of the P.D.P. in the 1948 national elections, for example, was based in part on its support for a Puerto Rican constitution. However, the P.D.P.—supported legislation introduced into the U.S. Congress to this end was not intended to alter the island's client status. The U.S. House Committee on Public Lands in reporting on the proposed legislation observed that it "would not change Puerto Rico's fundamental political, social and economic relationships to the United States."[30] Only the Nationalist Party opposed the legislation, calling it "a colonial measure intended to keep the island permanently 'enslaved' to the U.S. . . ."[31] But Muñoz Marín had long since discarded his earlier support of independence in favor of a 'permanent union' with the United States.

In March 1952, a referendum was held in Puerto Rico on the proposed constitution. Although the vote in favor of ratification was decisive, over 20 per cent of the electorate opposed it. U.S. Congressional approval of this decision was accompanied by the following statement by the Chairman of the U.S. House Committee on Public Lands:

> I think it may be stated as fundamental that the Constitution of the United States gives Congress complete control and nothing in the Puerto Rican constitution could affect or amend or alter that right . . . .[32]

The United States government was not prepared to abrogate its determinant role in the affairs of Puerto Rico under any circumstances.

The P.D.P. has continued to support a dependent political status for Puerto Rico *vis a vis* the United States and—with the exception of the 1968 elections won by the pro-statehood New Progressive Party—has remained the majority party on the island since 1940. The present P.D.P. Governor, Rafael Hernández Colón, elected in 1972, has stressed the need for "maximum self-government" only within the context of the Commonwealth or "permanent union" framework.[33] This framework has facilitated the entry of foreign capital into the island and the resultant external control over the economy.

The new industrialization strategy began in 1942 with the establishment, by the Puerto Rican government, of an Industrial Development Company, a Development Bank and a Planning Board. In 1950, the various government agencies involved in the new program were placed under the authority of the Economic Development Administration (FOMENTO). The promotion of Puerto Rico as an ideal location for external investment in industrial enterprise was largely initiated with the Industrial Incentives Acts of 1947 and 1948. These Acts offered a series of tax exemptions as inducements to foreign investment. At the same time, the government continued to emphasize the advantage of lower wage scales in Puerto Rico as compared with the United States. This "Operation Bootstrap" program also was prepared to support the new capitalist entrepreneur in a number of other ways: through technical assistance, the training of personnel for the new factories, loans and other financial subsidies.

The tax exemption law of 1947-1948 was described by Milton C. Taylor, in his detailed study of the subject, as follows:

> Even under the least favorable circumstances, the tax exemption program assures eligible mainland investors tax savings which appear to be financially appealing; while under the most advantageous circumstances, virtually complete tax avoidance is possible both during the process of earning income and when profits are avoided.[34]

It therefore came as no surprise when the Economic Development Administration reported in 1956 that subsidiaries of U.S. enterprises operating in Puerto Rico under the tax exemption program were averaging up to 10 times the profits obtained by the parent company in the United States.[35] By 1960, over 600 U.S. business-industrial concerns had entered the island economy.

Table 1 sharply illustrates the ability of the U.S. investor to maximize profits as a result of tax exemptions.

The Industrial Incentives Act as revised in 1963 continued to provide for complete tax exemption for qualifying firms, as well as exemption from property taxes, license fees and excise and other municipal taxes. Furthermore, depending on the industrial sector in which the foreign enterprise decided to locate its operation, complete tax exemption could now be enjoyed for a period of up to 17 years (as compared with a maximum of 10 years under the previous Acts). For firms locating in areas away from metropolitan San Juan in particular, other government incentives included payment of "the costs of training supervisory personnel, salaries of supervisory personnel while training production workers, payment of building rent, payment of mortgages on building purchases, payment of freight on machinery and equipment from point

TABLE 1

If your net profit after U.S. corporate income tax is—	Your net profit in Puerto Rico would be—	Your gain from tax exemption	
		Amount	Percent
$17,500	$25,000	$7,500	43
$29,500	$50,000	$20,500	69
$53,500	$100,000	$46,500	87
$245,500	$500,000	$254,500	104
$485,500	$1,000,000	$514,000	106

Source: U.S. Congress, Senate, Hearings before the Select Committee on Small Business, *Tax Treatment of U.S. Concerns with Puerto Rican Affiliates*, 88th Congress, 2nd Session, April 16 and 17, 1964 (Washington, D.C.: U.S. Government Printing Office, 1964), p.326.

of origin to plant site, and costs of certain additional facilities needed to carry on the operation—such as power stations, transformers, electrical installations, machinery and equipment installation and other relevant costs."[36] The Economic Development Administration, through its "Operation Bootstrap," has assisted nearly 2,000 foreign enterprises, through a total investment of over $2 billion, to set up operations in Puerto Rico since 1940.[37] The inducements to foreign investors have been substantial: a stable political climate with no threats of expropriation, excessive tax exemptions, low production costs, a plentiful supply of cheap labor, a lack of controls over the repatriation of capital, government subsidies and loans and other incentives contributing to profit maximization. The industrialization program also has generated an increasing dependence on U.S. capital. At least 100 of the 500 largest U.S. corporations have located in Puerto Rico under the auspices of the Economic Development Administration. U.S. investments have been channelled into chemicals, petroleum refining, petrochemicals, textiles, footwear, surgical products, metal products and machinery, electrical products, electronics, pharmaceuticals and motor vehicles. These investments have been made by U.S. corporations asuch as General Electric, Ford Motor Company, Kayser-Roth, Phelps Dodge, R.C.A.—Westinghouse, Commonwealth Oil Refining, Gulf Oil, Union Carbide, Sun Oil, Phillips Petroleum Company, PPG Industries, Hooker Chemical Corporation, American Cyanamid and Reichhold Chemicals.

The bulk of foreign investment during the 1950's went into chemicals and the consumer goods industry. The majority of these operations were U.S.-owned and most of their machinery and raw materials were imported. The profit differential between the Puerto Rican subsidiaries and equivalent U%S%-located subsidiaries was considerable. In 1957, the average manufacturing profit in Puerto Rico before taxes was 34 per cent on investment and 16 per cent on sales, compared with U.S. figures of 20 per cent and 8 per cent.[38] However, the latter figures were subject to U.S. federal tax assessments while the profits made in Puerto Rico were tax exempt.

The number of new factories in operation as a result of "Operation Bootstrap" grew from 548 in 1957-1958 to 1,003 in 1964-1965, and then jumped dramatically to 1,674 in 1967-1968 when heavy capital investments were beginning to establish a foothold in the Puerto Rican economy.[39] By 1973, total investments in the petrochemical sector alone were almost $1.3 billion.[40]

There were two important features of this heavy industry expansion process. First, it was characterized by the introduction of capital-intensive technology that increased production and profitability but generated few jobs and even exacerbated the unemployment problem. Between 1962 and 1967, for example, the average number of Puerto Rican workers employed in the factories set up under the industrialization program declined from 80 to 55 per factory.[41] Existing petrochemical plants, on the other hand, have only been able to create the meager total of 7,700 new jobs.[42] This type of expansion made labor costs a small proportion of the overall expenditure of foreign corporations and allowed for the payment of relatively high wages to the semi-skilled labor force employed in these plants and factories. Such a policy minimized the possibilities of labor unrest in a situation where stability of the labor force was essential, and maximized profits for the external investor.

The second feature of this process was its marginal contribution to the overall socioeconomic development of Puerto Rico. These subsidiaries of foreign corporations were linked to the corporations as part of vertically integrated structures. They were "enclaves" in the penetrated society, engaged in "assembly plant" industrialization— via the importation of large quantities of capital equipment and raw and semi-processed goods. When Phillips Petroleum Company decided to invest $45 million to develop a petrochemicals complex in Puerto Rico in 1967, *Business Week* observed:

Actually, petrochemicals are only one reason why Phillips and other oil companies want to set up shop in Puerto Rico. After petroleum imported onto the island has been refined, a large amount becomes motor fuel, which can be shipped to markets on the U.S. East Coast.[43]

More recently, the Puerto Rican government announced plans for a new $560 million petrochemicals complex "to handle about two million (barrels per day) of crude oil, half to be transhipped in small tankers to the United States East Coast and the other million to be refined locally."[44] By 1969-1970, 40 per cent of Puerto Rico's imports were in the form of raw materials to be processed and refined on the island, and then reshipped to the United States for sale and consumption.[45]

Some other tendencies regarding the industrialization process should be noted. Since 1960, there has been an increasing trend on the part of existing foreign investment to make future investments, not in the expansion of existing operations, but in the acquisition of indigenous enterprises. Between 1960 and 1966, U.S. entrepreneurs outlayed $55 million in pursuit of this activity.[46] This increasing denationalization of the Puerto Rican economy has been accompanied by the displacement of small and medium sized local retail and wholesale businessmen by U.S.-owned supermarkets and department store chains such as Grand Union, Sears and J.C. Penny. U.S. consumer goods industries, however, have shifted their Puerto Rican subsidiaries to locations away from the island—emphasizing the power of external corporations to make decisions independently of the particular economies in which they have investment interests. "In the case of Bacardi's insistence on locating a new bottling and labelling plant in Jacksonville, Florida, the most the government could extract from the company was the undertaking that all the rum bottled in the new plant would be of Puerto Rican origin, thus protecting revenue from excise taxes—$54 million last year—and an important source of income for the island's fast-failing sugar industry."[47]

There has been some attempt on the part of the present Puerto Rican government to diversify its sources of investment for industrialization away from an almost total dependence on U.S. capital. But no effort has been made to alter the terms of dependence. The giant Japanese multinational corporations, Nippon Zeon and Mitsubishi, in collaboration with Commonwealth Oil Refining, have agreed to invest $15 to $20 million in a petrochemicals project for the production of components used in the manufacture of synthetic rubber and other chemicals, most of which will be exported.[48]

Infastructural economic assistance by the U.S. government has been a key ingredient in Puerto Rico's economic development program. Direct U.S. government expenditures on the island for military operations and numerous subsidies, grants, credits, guarantees and services have played a central role in the ability of Puerto Rican governments to finance programs of education, housing, health and welfare—and to cushion the consequences of a large and continuing balance of payments deficit that has been a fact of life for all island governments since 1940. The remission of U.S. federal taxes ($50 million in 1959 to about $261 million in 1970) and customs duties, for example, "have been the major source of finance for the social security system."[49]

Table 2 indicates the singular importance of direct and indirect U.S. government aid to the development effort.

TABLE 2. U.S. FEDERAL GOVERNMENT EXPENDITURES AND LOANS MADE BY FEDERAL CREDIT AGENCIES IN PUERTO RICO, 1945-1966. SELECTED YEARS ($ MILLION)

Year	Total Federal Government Expenditures	Loans made by Federal Agencies
1945	104.8	2.4
1950	119.6	3.4
1955	189.3	5.6
1960	189.8	31.1
1965	264.7	16.7
1966	326.2	95.6

Sources: Rita M. Maldonado, *The Role of the Financial Sector in the Economic Development of Puerto Rico* (New York: Federal Deposit Insurance Corporation, 1970), p.32.

Net government expenditures averaged in the vicinity of 11 per cent of the island's gross national product during the 1945-1966 period.[50] U.S. government aid in the form of customs duties, excise duties and grants-in-aid amounted to $390,741,000 in 1972.[50]

External economic assistance promoting U.S. penetration has, at the same time, prevented or incapacitated indigenous sources from engaging in capital accumulation for investment in industrial activities. A steady increase in the per capita annual income has not effected the level of savings, which has remained extremely low or even negative over the last three decades. Puerto Rican governments and U.S. investors have fostered this consumptionist orientation, largely benefiting the U.S. exporter. It also has resulted in the establishment of a number of sophisticated advertising agencies and market consultant firms, such as U.S. subsidiaries of McCann-Erickson and Young & Rubicon. Between 1953 and 1963 consumer spending of the average Puerto Rican family increased by 84 per cent, according to a study by the Puerto Rican Department of Labor.[51]The greatest increases in expenditure were on personal items, houses, household goods, motor vehicles and overseas travel. Total spending on food and basic needs, as a proportion of overall consumption spending, actually declined. A feature of this development has been the increasing purchase of imported goods. In 1967, imported consumer items represented 25.2 per cent of total consumption in Puerto Rico as compared to only 4 per cent in the case of the United States.[52] This has been a contributing factor to the island's balance of payments difficulties.

Thus, U.S. government assistance has acted as a device for facilitating the export of U.S. goods to Puerto Rico. In the process it has undercut efforts by indigenous industrialists to develop local industries. Aid has functioned as a political tool to facilitate economic exploitation and, indirectly, capital drainage.

Industrialization and the Socioeconomic Situation of the Masses

1. Income

The rapid growth in personal incomes in Puerto Rico since 1940 has not resulted in a more equitable distribution of income, nor in any substantial lessening of the income disparities between urban and rural areas. In 1972, per capita income stood at $1,713.[53] After more than three decades, Muñoz Marín's initial policy of an annual per capita income of at least $2,000 still is to be achieved.

After the first six years of P.D.P. rule, the resident commissioner of distribution remained virtually unchanged despite economic expansion, of wage earners on the island had incomes not exceeding $500 a year.[54] During the period 1940-1950, 70 per cent of all families received 30 per cent of the insular income, and the majority of wage earner's families did not include anyone who was fully employed. Two-thirds of rural wage earning families were in this situation as compared to two-fifths of urban families.[55] Even though annual per capita climbed from $120 in 1940 to $764 in 1963, the distribution of income became increasingly skewed. Between 1953 and 1963 the total money incomes received by the poorest one-fifth of the population declined from 5 per cent to 4 per cent, while the share of the one-fifth of the population with the highest incomes increased from 50.5 per cent to 51 per cent. The major beneficiaries of this trend were the burgeoning middle sectors, whose share of money incomes rose from 46.8 per cent to 49.5 per cent.[56] In other words, income distribution remained virtually unchanged despite ecnomic expansion, while the position of the lower income groups relatively worsened. Furthermore, in respect of urban-rural differences, we find that the per capita income of San Juan residents in 1963 averaged $1,062 compared to $484 for the rest of the island.[57]

The Division of Public Welfare of the Puerto Rican Health Department estimated that $2,000 was the minimum annual income needed to satisfy a family's basic living requirements in 1964. But, acording to Puerto Rican Planning Board data for that year, 25 per cent of families earned less than $500 annually, almost 43 per cent earned less than $1,000 annually and nearly 70 per cent of families earned incomes below $2,000.[58] No significant upward trend is observable in subsequent years. Over 100,00 families still receive incomes of less than $500 a year, and in 1968-1969 emergency food supplies had to be distributed to 20 per cent of the island's families.[59]   Income distribution has continued to be a persistent problem for successive Puerto Rican governments. No serious attempts have been made to implement policies designed to redistribute income nationally and to close the gap between urban and rural income levels.

2. Wages

The puerto Rican wage scale structure has been employed by island governments as an inducement, second only to tax exemptions, to attract foreign capital. A recent full page advertisement in the *New York Times* by the Economic Development Administration exemplified this policy:

Puerto Rican workers are eager, skilled and dependable. Real wages are closer to the minimum than on the mainland. There are no federal taxes on corporate or personal income in Puerto Rico. And Puerto Rico can offer you up to 100 per cent tax exemption from Commonwealth and local taxes on income and property.[60]

By the end of the 1940s, wage levels for workers in industry and agriculture remained abysmally low, both in absolute terms and in comparison with equivalent wage levels in the United States. The average weekly earnings of the Puerto Rican agricultural worker in 1945 was $5, while his counterpart in industry received $12 a week. By comparison, the average weekly wage of the U.S. worker employed in industry in 1945 was $47.50.[61] Average hourly wages in the Puerto Rican industrial sector were almost three and a half times lower than the U.S. average.[62] In some Puerto Rican industries, the exploitation of labor—for U.S. benefit—was even worse than these figures suggest. The average hourly wage in the 'sweatshop' needlework industry was less than 35 cents—at a time when the U.S. Department of Commerce concluded that a reasonable standard of living for a fully employed worker in this industry would require at least 81 cents an hour.[63]

For over two decades, Puerto Rican governments have opposed application of the U.S. minimum wage standards to Puerto Rico on the grounds that it would be "fatal to industrialization."[64] It would not only seriously affect Puerto Rico's ability to compete on the international market, but it would increase unemployment and endanger the continued existence of many local enterprises. The U.S. Congress has, by and large, supported this position, and allowed the application of a lower (than U.S.) minimum wage on an industry-by-industry basis. Whereas the U.S. minimum wage tends to be the base wage, the minimum wage in Puerto Rico approximates the average wage. The present P.D.P. government has vigorously pursued this wage exemption policy.* The puerto Rican working class, as a consequence of this policy, has been forced to pay U.S. prices for imported foodstuffs and other commodities with wages well below the U.S. minimum level.

Employees making less than $1.40 per hour under the most recent wage order be increased 12 , an hour annually from the effective date until they reach $1.40. Thereafter their wages are increased by 15 , per hour each year until parity is achieved with the mainland minimum. Employees earning $1.40 or more an hour be increased 15 , per hour each year after enactment until parity is achieved. See *Congressional Record*, Vol. 119, No. 125, August 2, 1973, p.S15503.

---

*Although subjected to a Presidential veto, minimum wage legislation authorizing a raise in the U.S. minimum wage from $1.60 to $2.20 passed the Congress in August 1973. This legislation included the following provision regarding employees in Puerto Rico and the Virgin Islands:

As revealed in Table 3, the ability of Puerto Rico to achieve wage parity with the United States is seriously open to doubt. Not only has the wage differential between the two countries remained substantial over time, but it has increased in recent years.

TABLE 3. AVERAGE HOURLY EARNINGS OF PRODUCTION WORKERS IN MANUFACTURING INDUSTRIES, PUERTO RICAN AND UNITED STATES, 1959-1972

Year	Puerto Rico	United States	Differential
1959	.87	2.19	1.32
1960	.92	2.26	1.34
1961	.99	2.32	1.33
1962	1.06	2.39	1.33
1963	1.13	2.46	1.33
1964	1.18	2.54	1.36
1965	1.24	2.61	1.37
1966	1.30	2.72	1.42
1967	1.39	2.83	1.44
1968	1.55	3.01	1.46
1969	1.65	3.19	1.54
1970	1.76	3.36	1.60
1971	1.88	3.56	1.68
1972	1.99	3.81	1.82

Sources: International Labour Office, Geneva, *Yearbook of Labour Statistics*, 1968 (pp. 525, 526) and 1972 (p. 547); U.S. Department of Labor, Bureau of Labor Statistics, *Monthly Labor Review*, August 1973, p. 114; U. S. Department of Labor, Workplace Standards Administration, *Minimum Wage & Maximum Hours Standards under the Fair Labor Standards Act*, submitted to Congress, 1971, p. 37; U. S. Department of Commerce, Social and Economic Statistics Administration, Bureau of the Census, *Statistical Abstract of the United States, 1972*, p. 235

In the six year period 1959-1956, the differential in average hourly earnings increased by 5 cents from $1.32 to $1.37. In the following six year period 1966-1972, the differential increased by 45 cents. A similiar trend is evident with regard to the average weekly earnings of production workers in manufacturing industries in Puerto Rico and the United States.[65] The ability of Puerto Rican governments to hold down wages for the benefit of the external investor has been one of the 'social costs' of the country's industrial growth.

3. Employment

Stagnation in the agricultural sector and the increasing tendency toward the growth of capital-intensive industrial enterprises has resulted in the persistence of a serious unemployment problem in Puerto Rico. This situation would have been far worse had not 621,000 persons of employment age migrated to the United States between 1950 and 1972.[66]

In 1940, almost 50 per cent of the employed labor force was engaged in agricultural production, which accounted for 31.2 per cent of the country's national income. By 1972, only 4.4 per cent of the labor force were employed in agriculture, compared to 19.2 per cent in manufacturing, 18.4 per cent in trade, 17.8 per cent in government and 17.1 per cent in services.[67] Total employment declined between 1950 and 1960, primarily because new technologically sophisticated industrial plants were unable to absorb a rapidly expanding labor force. The labor force was expanding partly because unemployed agricultural laborers were drifting into the urban areas. In 1962-1963 enterprises assisted by the Economic Development Administration created 21,300 new jobs, while the natural increase in the working population alone exceeded this figure nearly threefold.[68] Unemployment during the 1950s and early 1960s hovered at between 12 and 14 per cent of the labor force, although such figures didn't reflect under-employment and ignored the factor of external migration. The average annual unemployment rate for males during the period 1950 to 1958, for example, was approximately 25 per cent in the 14 to 24 age group.[69]

Nearly half the population continued to depend for its livelihood on agriculture in 1967, even though government assistance to agriculture remained inadequate. High levels of under employment and unemployment and the movement of untrained rural workers to the cities were features of island life; and farm production continued its rapid decline. Sugar production dropped every year after 1963, and the 1966-1967 crop was 463,000 tons below the U.S. quota for Puerto Rican sugar. Tobacco production also fell substantially during these years.[70] Meanwhile, the majority of employment opportunities being created by the new industrialization were for skilled technical personnel.

In 1971 the Puerto Rican Planning Board issued a study on the employment situation in which it tacitly agreed with the contention of a number of authorities that unemployment on the island was close to 30 per cent of the labor force, and that it would have been much higher "were it not for large scale migration to the United States mainland and an expanding number of job-seekers who have simply dropped out of the labor force and are uncounted."[31] Nevertheless, the government has continued to support the development of capital-intensive industry that requires skilled labor that is in short supply on the island. The Economic Development Administration continues to ignore the unemployment situation and to emphasize that "heavy industry is our answer."[72]

4. Tourism

The decision by the Puerto Rican government in 1949 to invest over $7 million in the construction of the island's first tourist hotel (the U.S.-owned Caribe Hilton) was followed by a number of other inducements designed to encourage the growth of a tourist industry. Under the Industrial Incentives Acts, tourist hotels owned or operated by foreign corporations or individuals were entitled to the full benefits of the tax exemption program. This government subsidized industry, perceived as crucial to the industrialization effort, functioned to generate minimal consequences in terms of internal economic development.

The expansion of the tourist sector resulted in increased economic activity in the construction trades industry. Both these developments extended U.S. control of the economy and increased Puerto Rican dependence. The building boom was centered in the urban areas, and contributed little to the country's productive resources or to the living conditions of the Puerto Rican working class. On the contrary, these new (predominantly U.S.-owned) tourist hotels, gambling casinos and apartment buildings further decapitalized the economy through an increase in external profit remitances. A characeristic of this development was the growth of luxury hotels at the expense of low or moderate cost accomodations. The Puerto Rican Industrial Development Company and the Government Development Bank made fifty-two loans to hotels and guest houses between 1949 and 1964, totalling $11,875,000. However over 60 per cent of these funds were intended for the building of eight luxury hotels.[73] The accompanying rise in tourist costs "all but eliminated the lower income visitors, while those with incomes in excess of $10,000 have increased 41 per cent to an average of nearly 60 per cent of the annual total number of visitors to Puerto Rico."[74]

The phenomenal growth of the tourist industry during the last decade is evidenced by the following figures. Numbers of tourists to Puerto Rico rose from 350,000 in 1960 to over 1,000,000 in 1970. Tourist expenditures increased from $60 million in 1960 to more than $200 million in 1971. By the end of 1971, the number of first class hotel rooms had risen to almost 10,000.[75] Paralleling this growth has been the creation of a variety of nonproductive service sector employment opportunities characterized by low wages and the growth of a lumpen proletariat that attached itself to the industry.

Gordon Lewis, in a study of the satellite character of the tourist-based Virgin Islands economy, describes a situation that might usefuly be applied to Puerto Rico:

(The Virgin Islands is) a tropical extension, frequently artificial and always vulnerable, of the American capitalist economy. Its extraordinary dependence on imports . . . has intensified . . . as the tourist industry, through the dispersion of income into the local structure . . . has generated new demands for imported food and clothing, consumer durables and materials and equipment required by trade and industry. The tourist industry itself is derivative, while a sizeable proportion of its receipts are returned to the United States mainland for the purchase of supplies and services and to those foreign sources from which the gift shops obtain much of their merchandise.[76]

Consequences of the New Economic Development Strategy

In voicing his support for the dependent industrialization policy and the maintenance of the existing political and economic relationships between the United States and Puerto Rico Muñoz Marín has referred to Puerto Rico as "a political mutation . . . a Latin American country compoased of good citizens of the United States."[77] This position has been reiterated, with small variation, by all Puerto Rican governments since 1940.

This development strategy—based on external penetration and control—has had serious negative consequences for Puerto Rican society. Dependent ruling groups, rooted in urban and foreign elites, have proved incapable of integrating internal skills (manpower) and resources for autonomous and rational economic development. The use of tax exemptions to encourage foreign corporate investment, for example, has depleted government resources and undercut the government's ability to finance indigenous industrial expansion and development of the public service sector.

The United States has played a determinant role in the Puerto Rican economy and polity since 1940. Politically, there has been no major challenge to the unilateral power of the U.S. government over the island. Limited political autonomy has remained a constant—with the acquiescence of client political elites. Economically, the integration of the domestic elites into the enterprises of the U.S. corporation has allowed the latter to influence the behavior of the indigenous political elites and, over time, to wield increasing power and control over the society. The investment decisions of the U.S. corporation has, furthermore, resulted in the island's uneven and distorted economic development. *

U. S. domination of the Puerto Rican economy has undermined the country's claim to be a sovereign entity. Total U.S. investments in the economy amount to over $1.3 billion.[78] U.S. investors continue to control over three-quarters of all assets in the industrial-manufacturing sector. The First City National Bank of New York and the Chase Manhattan Bank alone hold in the vicinity of one-third of the total assets of all banks chartered on the island. U.S. capital also controls other important sectors of the economy: the retail industry, housing construction, insurance, communications, domestic and foreign transportation, tourism and associated service sector operations. "Indeed, the old type of sugar absenteeism has merely been succeeded by a new type of industrial absenteeism. The absentee landlord of the old days has been replaced by the absentee shareholder of the new."[79]

The U.S. Federal Regulatory Agencies, responsible for overseeing the actions of U.S. corporations, have tended to support their unhindered operations in Puerto Rico. These corporations employ only a small minority of Puerto Ricans in important managerial positions, and their decisions regarding production, location and employment are made by the Central Offices in the United States—based on needs and perceptions as part of a global network—with little regard for the social and economic consequences such decisions might have for Puerto Rico. "The surplus is in reality tied to the needs and strategy of the corporation as a whole."[80]

Economic dependence has made Puerto Rico highly vulnerable to

---

*Imperialism, in its overall features, is both developmental and exploitative. Foreign corporate investment initially creates new productive facilities and extracts wealth. In the long-term, however, it usually results in lopsided development (the creation of 'enclaves' of high production), and reinforces the class divisions and regional differences in the society. This has been the Puerto Rican experience.

changes and fluctuations in U.S. economic activity. The U.S. economic recession of 1953-1954 almost halted migration from Puerto Rico to the United States and drastically reduced the level of U.S. investment in the island. The number of U.S. subsidiaries established under 'Operation Bootstrap' averaged three a month during the period July-December 1954, as compared to 10 a month during the first six months of 1953.[81] A second U.S. recession in 1957-1958 also had serious consequences for the Puerto Rican economy. Production for export among established firms declined and the newly established enterprises were unable to absorb the additional unemployed workers who resulted. The decline in migration to the U.S. also was accompanied by the return of Puerto Rican workers in the U.S. "whose low seniority in their U.S. jobs made them among the first to be layed off."[82]

Werner Baer has argued cogently that Puerto Rico did not experience the full impact of these recessions because of their short duration and the "substantial backlog of investment commitments" that had accumulated during the preceeding period. The fact that the U.S. recessions did not persist over a much longer time period meant that new capital investments in Puerto Rico were not significantly curtailed. Since the relative impact of the growth trend was unlikely to continue indefinitely, future U.S. economic recessions conceivably could be more damaging to the Puerto Rican economy. Baer calculated that without the "growth trend factor" of the 1950s, exports and labor earnings would have declined far more than they actually did during the years 1953-1954 and 1957-1958.[83]

The effect of the 1970-1971 U.S. recession on the Puerto Rican economy offers some evidence in support of Baer's contention. More than 100 factories closed down, and the number of new plants and expansions promoted by the Economic Development Administration fell by 23 per cent in 1970 and 21 per cent in 1971.[84] The U.S. Small Business Administration made 7,402 disaster loans to Puerto Rican enterprises affected by the recession, amounting to over $18 million. By comparison, only 10 loans, totalling $160,000, were made during the entire period 1963 to 1969.[85] Manuel Casiano, administrator of the Economic Development Administration, blamed these developments on "the prolonged economic recession in the U. S."[86] Inflation, declining exports, the inability to diversify trading relationships and the downward trend in previously bouyant growth sectors such as tourism and manufacturing all were consequences of the impact of the U.S. recession on the Puerto Rican economy. Not surprisingly, the "traditional safety valve" of out-migration to the U.S. fell from 44,082 in 1969-1970 to 1,811 in 1970-1971.[87]

The Class Structure

The changeover from dependent agriculture to dependent industrialization has had a fundamental impact on the Puerto Rican class structure. The traditional agricultural elites were displaced by the urban entrepreneur, the government bureaucrat and the capitalist rancher. The new upper class is in commerce (such as the Ferré family), finance, government, real-estate, construction and the high-paying professions. Dependent industrialization also has generated an expanded middle sector "strongly committed to the attainment of possessions, comfort and convenience, economic and physical security, quality education, and other modern values."[88] The consumptionist orientation of this group spawned enterprises based on the importation of U.S. goods to satisfy its needs. Salesmen, clerks, managers and advertisers—acting as 'middle men' for the U.S. producer—promoted and encouraged this tendency. The marked hostility of this middle sector group toward the working class has been paralleled, in the political arena, by its support of the pro-statehood New Progressive Party. This support was a crucial factor in the victory of Luis Ferré and the New Progressive Party in the 1968 national elections.

Dependent industrialization has failed to reduce the level of stratification (inequality), class differentiation and the low level of mobility that previously existed. It has resulted, however, in the emergence of a class of dependent indigenous capitalists "who have taken adantage of the process of industrialization to make a profit in the construction industry, in real estate speculation, in mortgage and loan businesses, and as intermediaries and agents for the great North American companies."[89] It has also created a disorganized and exploited working class lacking stable sources of income and employment. Within this class three groups can be delineated: a small segment of semi-skilled, relatively highly-paid workers in the new capital-intensive industries; a traditional industrial proletariat of low paid labor, and a burgeoning subproletariat that has no prospects for absorption into the industrial labor force.

This subproletariat strata is composed largely of individuals attempting to escape the poverty, exploitation and lack of opportunities in the rural areas. They move to urban slums or to the outskirts of the cities, and their conditions of life are characterized by intense social and economic deprivation—by a subsistence urbanism. Their impact on the national allocation of resources and on the productive system is negligible. Employed mainly in the service sector in occupations linked to the tourist industry—petty vendors, street peddlers, clerks, promoters, entertainers, caterers, prostitutes, drug sellers, shoe-shine boys, messengers, gardners, car watchers, doormen and porters—their life situation is one of unstable work opportunities, low pay and continual insecurity. The quasi-service occupations, in particular, require no capital and are marginal to the economy as a whole. This subproletariat group has been aptly referred to as "supporting characters."[90] They are "a loose group of social 'floaters' sustained by very little sense of group consciousness,"[91] a fact well illustrated by their apparent support of the pro-middle sector, pro-statehood New Progressive Party in the 1968 national elections. By 1970, employment in the service sector had risen to 16.7 per cent of the total employed labor force, and was surpassed only by manufacturing with 19.3 per cent and the wholesale-retail trade with 18.7 per cent.[92]

The disintegration of corporate agriculture initially weakened the basis for the organization of a cohesive working class that could have provided the foundation for a political movement. The social basis for a working class movement was increasingly fragmented by the subsequent industrialization process that led a large sector of the working class (especially the subproletariat) to perceive the problem of poverty in individual terms, susceptible to individual solutions, leading to individual mobility. The result has been a stable and controlled working class rather than a class-conscious one.

The U.S. government and U.S. corporate investors have contributed heavily to the proletarianization and marginalization of a large segment of the Puerto Rico population, and to the denationalization of the island's economy. These developments, in turn, have generated a number of social and economic inequalities which have persisted over time. The most important of these have revolved around the questions of income and employment.

Puerto Rico's annual per capita income growth since 1940 has been quite remarkable when compared with those of other Latin American countries. However, such comparisons provide a misleading yardstick with which to measure the island's performance, because of the incorporation of the Puerto Rican economy within the U.S. economic structure. The valid comparison is with the United States.

We can see from Graph 1 that the absolute differential between Puerto Rico and the United States has increased substantially since 1951, and that the gap has been widening at an increasing rate since the mid-1960's. In 1972, the average per capita income for the U.S. was $4,492 (Mississippi $3,137), while that of Puerto Rico stood at only $1,713. Furthermore, inflation has had a more serious effect on wages in Puerto Rico. The compound rate of inflation from 1950 to 1967 averaged 3 percent per year in Puerto Rico, but only 1.9 per cent in the U.S.[93] In 1972 the cost-of-living index for Puerto Rico rose 3.8 per cent.[94]

FIGURE 1. PER CAPITA PERSONALL INCOME, PUERTO RICO AND UNITED STATES. 1951-1972 (SELECTED YEARS)

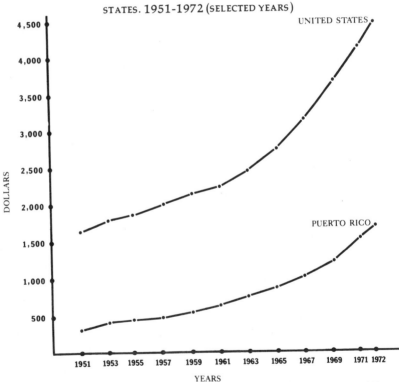

Sources: U.S. Department of Commerce, Office of Business Economics, *Survey of Current Business*, Vol. 51, No. 8, August 1971, p. 31 & Vol. 53, No. 8, August 1973, p. 43; Rita M. Maldonado, op. cit., p. 44; Economist Intelligence Unit, *Quarterly Economic Review of Puerto Rico*, No. 4, 1969, p. 10 & No. 4, November 1971, p. 14; Government Development Bank for Puerto Rico, *Puerto Rico: Financial Facts, 1972*, November 1972.

Unemployment figures for Puerto Rico and the United States also present a sharp contrast (Table 4).

TABLE 4. RATE OF UNEMPLOYMENT, PUERTO RICO AND UNITED STATES, 1950-1972. SELECTED YEARS (%)

Year	Puerto Rico	United States	Differential
1950	13.7	5.3	8.4
1955	14.3	4.4	9.9
1960	12.1	5.6	6.5
1961	12.6	6.7	5.9
1962	12.6	5.5	7.1
1963	11.8	5.7	6.1
1964	11.1	5.2	5.9
1965	12.0	4.5	7.5
1966	12.3	3.8	8.4
1967	12.2	3.8	8.3
1968	11.6	3.6	8.0
1969	10.4	3.5	6.9
1970	11.2	4.4	6.8
1971	11.9	5.9	6.0
1972	12.3	6.2	6.1

Sources: International Labour Office, *Yearbook of Labour Statistics*, 1957 (pp. 151, 152) and 1968 (p. 387) and 1972 (p. 427); U. S. Department of Commerce, Social and Economic Statistics Administration, Bureau of the Census, *1970 Census on Population. General Social and Economic Characteristics. United States Summary*. June 1972, p. 1-350; Commonwealth of Puerto Rico, Department of Labor, Bureau of Labor Statistics, *Employment and Unemployment in Puerto Rico*, Fiscal Years 1971-72 and 1971-72. Special Labor Force Report. Number 71-1E, p. 3; U. S. Department of Labor, Manpower Administration, *Area Trends in Employment and Unemployment*, July 1973, p. 37.

Puerto Rico has experienced an unemployment rate of over 12 per cent for the years 1950 to 1972, while the U.S. yearly rate has averaged just under 5 per cent. The unemployment differential has remained relatively unchanged over this period. A slight lessening of the gap in recent years has been a function, not of an improved situation in Puerto Rico, but of an increase in unemployment in the United States. The kinds of U.S. enterprises attracted to Puerto Rico under the industrialization program have been designed to exploit labor and take advantage of relative wage scales, rather than to expand employment opportunities. The incapacity of this type of industrialization to absorb the laboring class has been instrumental in shoving migrants into the U.S. urban slums.

In 1972, the situation in agriculture was critical. Almost 15 per cent of the agricultural labor force were unemployed and there was a continued migration to the urban areas, particularly among sugar and coffee workers.[95] In the recent period, government investment in agriculture has been negligible, notwithstanding the fact that the island's agricultural trade deficit has continued to grow. This deficit has been largely responsible for the overall balance of trade deficit, which has increased Puerto Rico's foreign debt service requirements to approximately 20 per cent of its annual export earnings.[96] Yet agricultural development remains neglected and the increasing poverty of the masses is ascribed to a rapid population growth, medical advancements and the effects of U.S. economic recessions on out-migration, rather than to structural defects in a development program based on dependent industrialization. A study of the economy in the late 1960's, commissioned by the Puerto Rican Department of Agriculture, concluded on the following note:

> The danger signals for Puerto Rico are clear. In an economy with few raw materials and a growing labor force, agriculture must be developed to provide food, to eliminate agricultural-import requirements, to establish home demand for industrial output, and to provide jobs in rural areas.[97]

Proletarianization and marginalization have had their greatest impact on the internal migrant driven to the urban areas because of the stagnation in agriculture and the possibilities offered by urban industrialization.* These migrants formed the bulk of the subproletariat strata. They have enjoyed marginal improvements in their life situation—such as increased schooling and medical care—as a consequence of their changed locale. However, many social scientists have attempted to magnify these relative improvements, to maximize these marginal changes outside of the relevant framework within which they should be analyzed, viz, in terms of urban society. Rather than emphasize relative improvements over previous circumstances, it is more accurate to focus on the absolute exploitation in present circumstances. The class structure thus becomes the most relevant unit of comparison. 'Improvements' in the situation of the subproletariat must be evaluated in terms of the position of the classes in the same urban milieu. From this perspective, as we have seen, the subproletariat is the most excluded class in society in receiving government services, and in its capacity to make any significant impact on national politics.

In assessing the consequences of the growth of the tourist industry on Puerto Rico's development process a number of questions present themselves. Who benefits from tourist development? Have specific classes taken advantage of this process? Has the tourist industry contributed to an improvement in the socioeconomic situation of the masses, or has it been merely another way of concentrating wealth? The major beneficiaries of tourism in Puerto Rico have been foreign (primarily U.S.) investors. The tourist industry has not generated new sources of income for reinvestment in productive activities on the island. Rather, it has absorbed government capital in the form of tax exemptions, subsidies and loans. In 1971, for example, the Puerto Rican government loaned the "financially troubled" Dorado Hilton up to $500,000 and announced that four or five other hotels in similar circumstances would receive loans of from $50,000 to $1 million.[98] U.S. capital in the form of hotel and other accomodation investment, U.S. manufacturers with an increased market for U.S. goods, U.S. transportation industries (especially airlines) and U.S. tourists have benefited most from the tourist development. The incentives offered the U.S. investor have been geared to profit maximization.

The expenditures made by Puerto Rican governments have created the basis for tourism on one hand and the degradation of the mass of the population on the other. The 'spillover' from the benefits accruing to

---

*Since 1940, urban-rural migration has been continuous and pronounced. The urban population increased by 58 per cent between 1940 and 1950, while the rural population increased by only 1 per cent. In the following decade, the population of San Juan and the adjoining municipalities increased by 27.4 per cent. Between 1960 and 1970, the urban population increased from 44.2 per cent to 58.1 per cent. See Commonwealth of Puerto Rico, Puerto Rico Planning Board, Bureau of Economics and Statistics, *Puerto Rico, Statistical Yearbook 1951-1952*, p. 1; Henry Wells, *The Modernization of Puerto Rico* (Cambridge, Mass.: Harvard University Press, 1969), p. 186; U.S. Department of Commerce, Social and Economic Statistics Administration, Bureau of the Census, *1970 Census of Population, Vol. 1*, 'Characteristics of the Population.' May 1972. p. 53-9. In contrast, the development strategy of the Castro government in Cuba has been in the direction of stabilizing, if not increasing, the agricultural population. By concentrating productive investments in expanding the agricultural sector and in building up the agricultural population [via the provision of schools, medical facilities, etc.]—to keep people gainfully employed in the rural areas—the growth of urban shantytown/slum settlements and a sub/lumpen proletariat has been prevented. In 1967, for example, the migration of persons from Havana to the rural province of Oriente [28,203] exceeded by over three thousand the movement of persons from Oriente to Havana [24,989]. See James Petras, "Socialism on One Island: A Decade of Cuban Revolutionary Government," *Politics and Society*, Vol. 1, No. 2, February 1971, p. 211.

U.S. capital and the U.S. tourist has been the creation of a lumpenproletariat. The social and political overhead costs of tourism have included prostitution, organized crime, gambling (which the *Hispanic American Report* called, in 1958, "one of the government's main sources of revenue"[99]) and drug addiction. According to local government authorities, approximately 100,000 of the island's 2,700,000 people are addicted to drugs.[100] The "social physiognomy" of San Juan has been transformed into a replica of pre-1959 Havana.[101]

Tourism also has contributed to the deterioration of the physical environment through car rental agencies, sandwich stands, souvenir shops and restaurants. Client political elites have facilitated the penetration of U.S. oil and petroleum interests into the economy without attempting, until very recently, to control the massive water pollution aspects of their activities. In human terms, tourism has led to the emergence of a dependent proletariat strata clustered in low-paying occupations. This represents the industry's "pay-off" to the indigenous population. In return for the rights to acquire natural resources to construct hotels and gambling casinos, and repatriate profits abroad, the U.S. investor offers degrading and unstable job opportunities to a segment of the population.

Tourist development also has resulted in the virtual expropriation of areas of public domain by U.S. and Puerto Rican investors. Luxury hotels have been built along the finest beach fronts, which are then declared off-limits to all but hotel guests. Puerto Rican government attempts to reverse this trend have been unsuccessful, partly due to the lack of a comprehensive long-range plan applied to land resources. A government decision to refuse permits for the construction of luxury hotels in the Condado section of San Juan is instructive in this respect. The aim of government policy was "to stop the development of a tourist 'wall' between Puerto Ricans and their sea. At the same time, permission to construct high rise condominium apartments on the same choice real estate produced the tourist 'wall' everyone was trying to prevent."[102]

The Ferré government (1968-1972) accelerated the construction of tourist facilities. During the final legislative session before the 1972

---

* Owen Jefferson has convincingly argued, in a study of the Jamaican tourist industry, that "the impact of tourist expenditure tends to be associated with an almost intolerable rise in the cost of living in the areas concerned." Owen Jefferson, "Some Aspects of the Post-War Economic Development of Jamaica," in *Readings in the Political Economy of the Caribbean*, eds., Norman Girvan and Owen Jefferson (Kingston, Jamaica: New World Group Ltd., 1972), p. 117.

elections, the Puerto Rican Congress "approved various bills giving this industry a strong boost, including tax exemption to real estate investment trusts that are created on the island, exemption of condominium financing and a 50 per cent tax exemption to guest house opertors."[103] Total tourist expenditure in 1972 was $259 million, an increase of $25 million over the previous year.[104]*

Conclusion: Dependence and Puerto Rican Industrialization

The old dependency of classical imperialism created export-oriented societies with structures of production geared to the needs and demands of the metropolitan capitalist economies. These penetrated societies were characterized by metropolitan capital investments in extractive raw material industries and agriculture. They also represented markets for the export of manufactured goods from the metropolitan centers. The new dependency of the post-1945 period "is basically technological-industrial dependence,"[105] made possible through the support given it by strategic economic classes within the penetrated society. It is "a condition in which the growth or expansion of a firm or country is contingent upon the need to import capital products or techniques over which it has little or no control; because the society lacks the ability to substitute other products, sources or funds or techniques, and because it lacks the internal capacity or drive to innovate or create."[106] Dependence, in this view, is not a function of the decision to import technology, but of the type of technology imported and its relationship to the development process. In a dependent capitalist society such as Puerto Rico, imported technology has a negative impact on the socioeconomic situation of the masses and it is not viewed by local elites as leading to autonomous development based on indigenous sources. On the contrary, it is a means whereby external forces institutionalize their control over the development process through the creation of dependent domestic elites.*

---

*An autonomous country "depends primarily on the mobilization of internal resources and has the capacity to choose the source of its external inputs." James Petras & Thomas Cook, "Dependency and the Industrial Bourgeoisie: Attitudes of Argentine Executives Toward Foreign Economic Investment and U. S. Policy," in *Latin America: From Dependence to Revolution*, ed., James Petras (New York: John Wiley & Sons, 1973), p. 144. Both autonomy and dependence are relative notions. Cuba, for example, has a skewed trade pattern *vis a vis* the Soviet Union, but it has retained its ability to make choices and explore different options regarding the allocation of internal resources. The Soviet Union neither owns Cuban economic resources nor maintains a direct leverage over internal economic development.

One form of this dependence is evident in present-day Argentina, where external penetration and the resulting dependence are supported by both foreign and national groups in the industrial sector. The fact of dependence is not in dispute; only the terms under which it takes place are matters for discussion. Argentine industrial executives in national firms support dependency that does not result in their total displacement by foreign capital. As Petras and Cook have observed:

> External dependence is not an external phenomenon: it has its roots in the attitude: and behavior of almost all Argentine industrial executives. The Argentine executive seems to perceive foreign entrepreneurship as necessary to Argentine development.
> .. National capital is integrated into a dependent relationship with foreign capital. This interconnection of interests makes the industrial executives a major conduit for external penetration.[107]

Another contemporary example of dependent industrialization in Latin America is the case of Brazil. Like Puerto Rico, Brazilian economic growth since 1964 has been characterized by a distorted industrial development based on capital-intensive heavy industry and the creation of a consumption-oriented middle class. While the growth rate reached 11.3 per cent in 1971, inflation—averaging around 20 per cent annually—has been a continuing problem.[108] The industrialization program has developed on the basis of a wide range of financial inducements to foreign capital to invest in the country. The expansion of the productive base has been accompanied by regional imbalance, structural unemployment and increasing marginality, labor exploitation, and social and political repression of the Brazilian lower classes. The agricultural sector in Brazil has been stagnating and between 1967-1971 for each dollar increase in foreign reserves the Brazilian foreign debt grew by $1.80.[109] In Brazil, the integration of the state and foreign capital in the economic expansion has been an important factor in the dependent capitalist development: "... both are the principal participants in the key dynamic investment and productive sectors, and there is no important contradiction between them as far as the decision making process is concerned."[110]

Although there is no one dependency model, some development theorists have argued that dependency characterized by capital drainage leads to underdevelopment and permanent stagnation.[111] Yet, both the Brazilian and Puerto Rican experiences suggest that growth can occur through dependency. Brazil, with an enormous market and a government able to depress wages and engage in widespread repression, has created high rates of growth over a short period of time through a massive influx of foreign capital. However, any theory of dependent capitalist development must distinguish between growth (GNP) and development (social justice, the distribution of power, etc.).[112] Societies can exhibit development without growth. Post-1959 Cuba's economic expansion and capital investment in diversified productive activities has been paralleled by a low overall rate of growth. This is a function of the transition toward future economic autonomy. Brazil, by comparison, has exhibited growth without development. So, it would appear, has Puerto Rico. Specifications of the conditions under which one or the other takes place involve an analysis of the class structure of the society, of the social framework within which development takes place.

The impact of external forces on Puerto Rico's development process has been twofold. In the short-term, foreign investment created new productive facilities and contributed toward a substantial growth rate. * In the long-term, these investments have distorted the pattern of economic development that has occurred. Furthermore, the conditions for the entrance of foreign investment into the economy have been incompatible with the growth of strong, autonomous social and political organizations of the lower classes. One of the social and political costs of dependence on external capital for development has been the emergence of a controlled labor force rather than militant, politically conscious working class movement. Where countries project a strong sense of national cohesiveness and have a strong, centralized and disciplined political organization, external penetration is made more difficult.

---

*Maurice Halperin has perceptively noted that the concept of gross national product (GNP) is a misleading concept to apply to underdeveloped or developing societies, because it invariably includes both goods and services. But, for an economy like Puerto Rico's, "only the production of material goods can have any relevance to growth." Services, on the other hand, "absorb capital and other resources desperately needed for production and hence retard economic growth." Evaluation of the meaning of GNP also depends on the kind of production that is taking place. ". . . an increase in output that reflects the expansion of monoculture or foreign exploitation of natural resources or the manufacture of luxury goods for domestic consumption would invariably be counted as a contribution to economic growth in the statistical compilations. However, in terms of the only kind of growth that makes sense for an underdeveloped country, the principle connotations of such an increase would very likely be unfavorable." Maurice Halperin, "Growth and Crises in the Latin American Economy," in *Latin America: Reform or Revolution?*, eds., James Petras and Maurice Zeitlin (Greenwich, Conn.: Fawcett World Library, 1968), pp. 60-62.

Puerto Rican governments rationalized a policy of industrialization based on foreign investment by reference to the notion of capital scarcity. Only an influx of capital, it was argued, could trigger development in a capital scarce society. However, the problem has been the lack of controls over the use of earnings within the country (conspicuous consumption, external profit remittances, etc.). The crux of the issue has been the misuse of resources and the utilization of the surplus created by the capital-intensive technology. The nature of the State determines the nature of surplus disposal, whether it will favor national or sectoral development. Imported technology has not bee organized for overall societal development, as the continuing unemployment and poverty amply demonstrates. The capital intensive pattern of industrial enterprise has absorbed a minimum of laborers in a labor surplus society. The Puerto Rican political elites have ascribed this problem to rapid population increases, and emphasized the imortance of migration to the U.S. But the critical factor is not the population per se, but the relationship of the population to the productive forces. Where the latter continues to develop new job opportunities, the unemployment-population problem no longer exists. In rapidly developing countries based on egalitarian patterns of development—such as revolutionary Cuba—there are actual labor shortages. Conversely, a growing population can also be an asset in attempts to get out of underdevelopment. In the context of a revolutionary socialist political leadership—Communist China is a case in point—manpower can be substituted for the lack of machinery and external economic assistance.*

The industrialization process has had a negative impact on political consciousness in Puerto Rico. Massive movements of capital and ideas from the United States has affected a whole series of related services such as education, culture and the mass media. This development has undercut the basis for radical political appeals and has created a dependent strata of subproletarians and lumpen-proletarians. The external manipulation of consciousness has created formidable obstacles for revolutionaries seeking a social basis for fundamental socioeconomic and political change.

---

*The ability to motivate people to work and sacrifice implies a capacity on the part of the political elites to gain belief and trust, and the moral authority to impose discipline where necessary. This is impossible in a rigidly stratified society such as Puerto Rico where sacrifices would result in differential impacts on different classes.

NOTES

1. William A. Williams, "The Large Corporation and American Foreign Policy," in *Corporations and the Cold War*, ed., David Horowitz (New York: Monthly Review Press, 1969), p. 78.

2. *John Quincy Adams and American Continental Empire: Letters, Papers, Speeches*, edited by Walter LaFeber (Chicago: Quadrangle Books, 1965), p. 129.

3. Chester Lloyd Jones, *Caribbean Interests of the United States* (New York: D. Appleton & Company, 1916), p. 100.

4. Quoted in Robert J. Hunter, "Historical Survey of the Puerto Rico Status Question, 1898-1965," in *Status of Puerto Rico*. United States-Puerto Rico Commission on the Status of Puerto Rico, 1966 (Washington, D.C.: U.S. Government Printing Office. 1966), p. 56.

5. Ibid., p. 76.

6. Henry Wells, *The Modernization of Puerto Rico* (Cambridge, Mass.: Harvard University Press, 1969), p. 87.

7. Thomas C. Cochran, *The Puerto Rican Businessman* (Philadelphia: University of Pennsylvania Press, 1959), p. 23. Although there was a high proportion of individual land ownership at the time of the U.S. military intervention, 2.18 percent of the farms accounted for over 72 per cent of the agricultural land. "A high percentage of farmers were owners, but the bulk of the land belonged to a chosen few." Bailey W. and Justine Whitfield Diffie, *Porto Rico: A Broken Pledge* (New York: The Vanguard Press, 1931), p. 22.

8. Ibid., pp. 140-141, 53.

9. Rita M. Maldonado, *The Role of the Financial Sector in the Economic Development of Puerto Rico* (New York: Federal Deposit Insurance Corporation, December 1970), p. 23.

10. Diffie and Diffie, *Porto Rico*, p. 181.

11. Matthew O. Edel, "Land Reform in Puerto Rico, 1940-1959," Part One, *Caribbean Studies*, Vol. 2, No. 3, October 1962, p. 27; Also see Diffie and Diffie, *Porto Rico*, pp. 85-86.

12. Puerto Rico Planning Board, Bureau of Economics and Statistics, *Puerto Rico, Statistical Yearbook, 1951-1952* (Commonwealth of Puerto Rico), p. 221.

13. Diffie and Diffie, *Porto Rico*, p. 141.

14. Rita M. Maldonado, *The Role*, p. 24.

15. Thomas C. Cochran, *Puerto Rican Businessman*, p. 41.

16. Rita M. Maldonado, *The Role*, p. 23.

17. Puerto Rico Planning Board, Bureau of Economics and Statistics, *Statistical Yearbook*, p. 221.

18. Manuel Maldonado-Denis, *Puerto Rico: A Socio-Historic Interpretation* (New York: Vintage Books, 1972), p. 80.

19. Santiago Iglesias discussing the period of U.S. Governor Yager (1913-1921), as quoted in *The United States in Puerto Rico 1898-1900* by Edward J. Berbusse (Chapel Hill:

University of North Carolina Press, 1966, p. 228.
    20. Victor S. Clark, et al., *Porto Rico and its Problems* (Washington, D.C.: The Brookings Institution, 1930), p. xx; Rita M. Maldonado, *op. cit.*, p. 24.
    21. Diffie and Diffie, p. 155.
    22. Luis Muñoz Marín, "The Sad Case of Porto Rico," *The American Mercury*, Vol. XV1, No. 62, February 1929, pp. 138-139.
    23. Rita M. Maldonado, *The Role*, p. 27. For some earlier studies of the program see Teodoro Moscoso, "Industrial Development in Puerto Rico," *The Annals*, Vol. 285, January 1953, pp. 60-69; W. Arthur Lewis, "Industrial Development in Puerto Rico," *The Caribbean Economic Review*, Vol. 1, No. 1 & 2, pp. 153-176; William H. Snead, *Fomento: The Economic Development of Puerto Rico* (Washington, D.C.: National Planning Association Pamphlet, No. 103, March 1958).
    24. Gordon K. Lewis, *Puerto Rico: Freedom and Power in the Caribbean* (New York: Harper and Row, 1968), p. 115.
    25. Edel, "Land Reform," Part One, p. 30.
    26. Harvey S. Perloff, *Puerto Rico's Economic Future: A Study in Planned Development* (Chicago, Illinis: University of Chicago Press, 1950), p. 34.
    27. Edel, "Land Reform," Part One, p. 31.
    28. Edel, "Land Reform," Part Two, *Caribbean Studies*, Vol. 2, No. 4, January 1963, p. 48. In 1961, one of the four largest U.S. corporations, Central Aguirre, was still remitting profits of almost $1 million a year. Ibid.
    29. Edel, "Land Reform," Part One, p. 56.
    30. Quoted in U.S. Congress, House, Committee on Interior and Insular Affairs, *Puerto Rico, A Survey of Historical, Economic, and Political Affairs, 1959* (by Robert J. Hunter). 89th Congress, 1st Session, Committee Print, November 25, 1959 (Washington, D.C.: U.S. Government Printing Office, 1959), p. 16.
    31. *Hispanic American Report*, Vol. 111, No. 11, November 1950, p. 22.
    32. Quoted in U.S. Congress, House, Committee on Interior and Insular Affairs, *Puerto Rico: A Survey*, p.19.
    33. Quoted in Carl T. Rowan, "Critical Puerto Rican Challenge," *Washington Star*, August 3, 1973, p. A11.
    34. Milton C. Taylor, *Industrial Tax-Exemption in Puerto Rico* (Madison: University of Wisconsin Press, 1957), p. 28.
    35. *Hispanic American Report*, Vol. IX, No. 11, December 1956, p. 534.
    36. Ernst & Ernst, *Puerto Rico: A National Profile* (International Business Series Publications, March 1971), pp. 24-25.
    37. Ibid., p. 19; "Puerto Rican Economy Moving Ahead Rapidly," *Journal of Commerce*, August 16, 1971 (Section 2), p. 19.
    38. Economist Intelligence Unit, *Quarterly Economic Review of Cuba, Dominican Republic, Haiti and Puerto Rico*, No. 30, May 1960, p. 9.
    39. Commonwealth of Puerto Rico, *Puerto Rico, U.S.A.* (Washington, D.C., September 1971), p. 61.
    40. "Puerto Rico's Vast Petrochemical Plans Raise Both Economic Hope and Questions," *Business Latin America*, May 24, 1973, p. 168.
    41. Miguel Soler, "The Proletarization of the Puerto Rican," *NACLA Newsletter*, Vol. 1, No. 5, July 1967, p. 3.
    42. "Puerto Rico's Vast Petrochemical Plans," p. 168.

43. "A Boost For Puerto Rico Boom," *Business Week*, July 29, 1967. p. 69.

44. "Puerto Rico's Vast Petrochemical Plans," p. 167.

45. Ernst & Ernst, *Puerto Rico*, p. 9.

46. Economist Intelligence Unit, No. 4, October 1966, p. 12.

47. Ibid., No. 3, August 1971, p. 13.

48. "Puerto Rico Lands Large Japanese Venture For Its Growing Petrochemical Sector," *Business Latin America*, July 19, 1973, p. 226.

49. Sir Harold Mitchell, *Caribbean Patterns: A Political and Economic Study of the Contemporary Caribbean* (New York: John Wiley and Sons, 1972), p. 118; "Puerto Rico: Commonwealth for ever?," *Latin America*, Vol. 1, No. 14, July 28, 1967, p. 106.

50. Rita M. Maldonado, *The Role*, p. 32.

50A. commonwealth of Puerto Rico, Department of the Treasury, Office of Economic and Financial Research, *Economy and Finances, Puerto Rico 1972*, p. 26.

51. "Puerto Rican Family Spending Survey Probes Changing Consumer Habits," *Business Latin America*, February 8, 1968, p. 46.

52. Rita M. Maldonado, *The Role*, p. 39.

53. Commonwealth of Puerto Rico, Government Development Bank, *Puerto Rico: Financial Facts, 1972* (November 1972).

54. "Aid Planned Here For Puerto Ricans," *New York Times*, January 1, 1947, p. 25.

55. Sol Luis Descartes, "Financing Economic Development in Puerto Rico," *The Caribbean Economic Review*, Vol. 11, No. 1, May 1950, p. 85; "Puerto Rico Finds Income Increase," *New York Times*, August 1, 1954, p. 25.

56. Rita M. Maldonado, *The Role*, pp. 24, 44; Henry Wells, *Modernization*, p. 156.

57. "Puerto Rican Family Spending Survey," p. 48.

58. Isal Abstracts, *Puerto Rico*, Vol. 4, No. 34 (Year 4), p. 13.

59. *NACLA'S Latin American & Empire Report*, Vol. V1, No. 6, July-August, 1972, p. 4.

60. *New York Times*, March 21, 1971, p. 58.

61. Harvey S. Perloff, *Puerto Rico's Economic Future*, p. 149.

62. *Facts on File*, Vol. X, No. 524, November 10-16, 1950, p. 369.

63. *Hispanic American Report*, Vol. V1, No. 7, August 1953, p. 21.

64. Luis Muñoz-Marín, as quoted in *Hispanic American Report*, Vol. VIII, No. 10, November 1955, p. 470.

65. AVERAGE WEEKLY EARNINGS OF PRODUCTION WORKERS IN MANUFACTURING INDUSTRIES, UNITED STATES AND PUERTO RICO, 1959-1972 ($)

Year	Puerto Rico	United States	Differential
1959	31.78	88.26	56.48
1960	33.56	89.72	56.16
1961	36.56	92.34	55.78
1962	39.33	96.56	57.23
1963	40.99	99.63	58.64
1964	44.09	102.97	58.88
1965	45.57	107.53	61.96
1966	48.30	112.34	64.04
1967	52.00	114.90	62.90
1968	57.74	122.51	64.77
1969	61.20	129.51	68.31
1970	64.59	133.73	69.14
1971	69.94	142.04	72.10
1972	74.23	154.69	80.46

Sources: International Labour Office, Geneva, *Yearbook of Labour Statistics*, 1968 (pp. 525, 526) and 1972 (p. 571); U. S. Department of Labor, Bureau of Labor Statistics, *Monthly Labor Review*, August 1973, p. 114: U. S. Department of Commerce, Social and Economic Statistics Administration, Bureau of the Census, *Statistical Abstract of the United States, 1972*, p. 235.

66. Economist Intelligence Unit, *Quarterly Economic Review*, Annual Supplement 1972, p. 31. During the 1948-1952 period, the labor situation was further eased by the absorption of some 40,000 men into the U.S. armed forces as a result of the Korean War. Most of these men would otherwise have been part of the civilian labor force looking for employment. See A.J. Jaffe, *People, Jobs and Economic Development* (Illinois: Free Press of Glencoe, 1959), p. 46.

67. Rita M. Maldonado, *The Role*, pp. 29-30; Commonwealth of Puerto Rico, Department of the Treasury, op. cit., p. 7.

68. U.S. Congress, Senate, Hearings before the Select Committee on Small Business, *Tax Treatment of U.S. Concerns with Puerto Rico Affiliates*. 88th Congress, 2nd Session, April 16 and 17, 1964, (Washington, D.C.: U.S. Government Printing Office, 1964), p. 74.

69. See Table 4 in text; Everett W. Reimer, *Social Planning: Collected Papers 1957-68*. CIDOC Cuaderno No. 22 (Cuernavaca, Mexico: Centro Intercultural de Documentacion, 1968), pp. 67-68.

70. Tobacco production declined from 37,900 lbs. in 1965 to 9,920 lbs. in 1969. Economist Intelligence Unit, op. cit., No. 3, July 1967, p. 12 and No. 1, January 1968, p. 2.

71. "Companies to Feel Puerto Rican Labor Pinch," *Business Latin America*, July 8, 1971, p. 214.

72. Manuel Casiano, administrator of the Economic Development Administration, as quoted in Ibid.

73. Robert C. Mings, "Puerto Rico and Tourism," *Caribbean Quarterly*, Vol. 14, No. 3, September 1968, p. 16.

74. Ibid., p. 18.

75. Commonwealth of Puerto Rico, Department of the Treasury, Office of Economic and Financial Research, *Economy and Finances, Puerto Rico 1968*, pp. 9-10.

76. Gordon Lewis, "The U.S. Virgin Islands: Prototype of the Caribbean Tourist Economy," in *Politics and Economics in the Caribbean*, eds., T.G. Matthews and F.M. Andic. Special Study No. 8 (University of Puerto Rico, Rio Piedras, Puerto Rico: Institute of Caribbean Studies, 1971), p. 237.

77. Luis Muñoz Marín, "Puerto Rico and the U.S., Their Future Together," *Foreign Affairs*, Vol. 32, No. 4, July 1954, p. 541.

78. Economist Intelligence Unit, *Quarterly Economic Review*, No. 1, January 1969, p. 11.

79. Gordon K. Lewis, *Puerto Rico: Freedom and Power* p. 143. The U.S. Pentagon also owns 13% of Puerto Rico's land area, testifying to the island's strategic importance as a base from which the U.S. can exercise its control over unstable political situations in the Caribbean. See *NACLA'S Latin America & Empire Report, op. cit.*, p. 4.

80. Norman Girvan, "Multinational Corporations and Dependent Underdevelopment in Mineral-Export Economies," *Social and Economic Studies*, Vol. 19, No. 4, December 1970, p. 516.

81. U.S. Congress, Senate, Hearings before the Select Committee on Small Business, p. 252.

82. Economist Intelligence Unit, *Quarterly Economic Review*, No. 22, June 1958, p. 10.

83. Werner Baer, *The Puerto Rican Economy and United States Economic Fluctuations* (University of Puerto, Rio Piedras, Puerto Rico: Social Science Research Center, 1962), pp. 146-147.

84. "Industrial Growth in Puerto Rico Slowed Sharply in Fiscal 1971," *Wall Street Journal*, August 23, 1971, p. 23.

85. *Congressional Record*, Vol. 119, No. 124, 93rd Congress, 1st Session, p. E5335.

86. Quoted in "Industrial Growth in Puerto Rico," p. 23.

87. Economist Intelligence Unit, *Quarterly Economic Review*, No. 1, February 1972, p. 15. The position of the U.S. as the island's only significant trading partner has weakned only marginally in recent years. In 1969-1970, the U.S. received approximately 89 per cent of Puerto Rico's exports and supplied just under 80 per cent of its imports. In 1971, the figures were 76 per cent and 92 per cent respectively. See Puerto Rican Planning Board, Bureau of Economics and Statistics, *External Trade Statistics, 1970* (June 1972), pp. 399, 552; U.S. Department of Commerce, Social and Economic Statistics Administration, Bureau of the Census, *Statistical Abstract of the United States, 1972*, p. 798. For the impact of the recession on the tourist industry, see Banco Popular de Puerto Rico, *Progress in Puerto Rico: Basic Facts*, Vol. VII, No. 2, Second Quarter 1971.

88. Henry Wells, *Modernization*, p. 333.

Manuel Maldonado-Denis, *Puerto Rico*, p. 176. In pre-1959 Cuba, U.S. economic penetration had also transformed the Cuban bourgeoisie into "a dependent comprador stratum of foreign business interests." James O'Connor, *The Origins of Socialism in Cuba* (Ithaca: Cornell University Press, 1970), p. 22.

90. Eduardo Seda-Bonilla, "Dependence as an Obstacle to Development: Puerto Rico," in *Readings in the Political Economy of the Caribbean*, eds., Norman Girvan and Owen Jefferson (Kingston, Jamaica: New World Group Ltd., 1972), p. 104.

91. Gordon K. Lewis, *Puerto Rico: Freedom and Power*, p. 189.

92. Economist Intelligence Unit, *Quarterly Economic Review*, Annual Supplement 1972, p. 32; Commonwealth of Puerto Rico, Department of the Treasury, Office of Economic and Financial Research, *Economy and Finances, Puerto Rico 1972* (November 1972), p. 7.

93. Rita M. Maldonado, *The Role*, p. 43.

94. Economist Intelligence Unit, *Quarterly Economic Review*, No. 2, May 1973, p. 16.

95. Ibid., No. 3, August 1972, p. 11 and No. 1, February 1973, p. 13. Sugar production declined from 625,000 tons in 1967 to 325,000 in 1971. Tobacco production in the same period declined from 12,184,000 lbs. to 4,821 lbs. Ibid., Annual Supplement, 1972, p. 34. The number of active sugar mills dropped from 41 in 1934 to 15 in 1971. See Puerto Rican Department of Agriculture, Office of Agricultural Statistics, *Facts & Figures on Puerto Rico's Agriculture 1969-70* (Santurce, Puerto Rico, June 1970), p. 34.

96. H. Erich Heinemann, "Puerto Rico: The Word is Growth," *New York Times*, June 17, 1968, p. 58. Puerto Rico's balance of payments deficit has grown from over $40 million in 1940-1941 to in excess of $520 million in 1967-1968. See Puerto Rico Planning Boad, Bureau of Economics and Statistics, *Puerto Rico, Statistical Yearbook, 1951-1952*, p. 221 and Puerto Rico Planning Board, Bureau of Economic and Social Analysis, *Statistical Yearbook, Puerto Rico 1968*, p. 169. Another factor contributing to this state of affairs related to the U.S. statutory requirements giving U.S. shipowners a monopoly of shipping lanes between the two countries. U.S. shipowners, with at least the passive support of the U.S. Maritime Board, have acted arbitarily to increase freight and other costs on a number

of occasions. Between 1946 and 1958, for example, freight charges were increased on five separate occasions. See Earl Parker Hanson, *Puerto Rico: Ally for Progress* (Princeton, New Jersey: D. Van Nostrand Company, 1962), p. 77. In no instance was the Puerto Rican government as much as consulted. These actions have often meant the demise of indigenous enterprises operating on low profit margins.

97. H. Erich Heinemann, "Puerto Rico: Growth," p. 58.

98. "Puerto Rico Steps Up Tourism Rescue Effort, Plans Loans to Hotels," *Wall Street Journal*, April 19, 1971, p. 10.

99. *Hispanic American Report*, Vol. XI, No. 11, December 1958, p. 613.

100. "Puerto Rico Takes Action on Problem of Drug Addiction," *New York Times*, July 29, 1973, p. 51.

101. Quoted from 'Declaration of Puerto Rican Socialist Party' in *NACLA'S Latin America & Empire Report*, Vol. V, No. 8, December 1971, p. 13.

102. Robert C. Mings, "Puerto Rico and Tourism," p. 14.

103. "Puerto Rico's Legislative Session Not as Hard on Business as Expected," *Business Latin America*, July 20, 1972, p. 230.

104. Commonwealth of Puerto Rico, Government Development Bank, *op. cit.*

105. Theotonio Dos Santos, "The Structure of Dependence," in *Readings in U.S. Imperialism*, eds., K.T. Fann and Donald C. Hodges (Boston, Mass.: Porter Sargent, 1971), p. 228.

106. James Petras & Thomas Cook, "Dependency and the Industrial Bourgeoisie: Attitudes of Argentine Executives Toward Foreign Economic Investment and U.S. Policy," in *Latin America: From Dependence to Revolution*, ed., James Petras (New York: John Wiley & Sons, 1973), p. 144.

107. Ibid., p. 162.

108. J. Serra, "The Brazilian 'Economic Miracle'," in *Latin America: From Dependence to Revolution*, p. 133.

109. Ibid., pp. 108-109.

110. M.C. Tavares & J. Serra, "Beyond Stagnation: A Discussion on the Nature of Recent Developments in Brazil," in *Latin America: From Dependence to Revolution*, p. 77.

111. See, for example, Andre Gunder Frank, *Capitalism and Underdevelopment in Latin America* (New York: Monthly Review Press, 1969) and Susanne Bodenheimer, "Dependency and Imperialism: The Roots of Latin American Underdevelopment," in *Readings in U.S. Imperialism*, op. cit., pp. 155-181.

112. Fernándo Henrique Cardoso fails to make this distinction in an otherwise interesting essay, "Dependency and Development in Latin America," *New Left Review*, No. 74, July-August 1972, pp. 83-95.

The Socializing Functions of Power in Puerto Rican Society

Eduardo Seda

In its annual meeting of 1955, the United Nation's General Assembly approved a resolution to encourage the study of civil rights in all nations of the world by offering technical assistance for such studies. The government of Puerto Rico, at that time headed by Luis Muñoz Marín, was one of the few nations to take advantage of this opportunity. To that effect, the assistance of Roger N. Baldwin, consultant to the Secretary of the United Nations and former President of the American Civil Rights Union, was obtained. A Civil Rights committee was organized in 1956 whose recommendations led to the derogation of the repressive Law 51 of 1948 and to the release of 13 persons jailed for political "crimes" based on that law. In 1958, a research branch with a budget assigned by our legislative assembly was added to the Civil Rights Committee for the purpose of studying the institutional viability of civil rights in the electoral process, in the courts of justice, in the hiring and firing practices of the administrative branch of government, in the educational system and in the political culture. I was selected to direct the study on the political culture. The following data constitute a brief summary of the results of a study conducted in 1957-58 and of a follow-up study conducted in 1967-68.[1]

The results of these studies indicate that the basic principles of democracy, beginning with the notion that the authority of the state in a democratic regime emanates from the consent of the governed, are not known by most people in Puerto Rico. Furthermore, anti-democratic patterns of thought and belief prevail over democratic ones. Substantial sectors of our population are totally ignorant of the ideas and principles of civil liberties and popular sovereignty, the indispensable condition for dissent and effective participation in a democratic community.

The principles stated in the Puerto Rican Constitution making consent of the governed a precondition of the authority of government, the principle that limits the authority of the state and guarantees an opportunity to all sectors of opinion to express their views as a precondition for free choice among the electorate, and the principle that delegated authority makes government officials representatives and not patrons with unlimited personel power: All these basic assumptions lack any profound support among Puerto Ricans.[2] Civil rights are ignored by very substantial proportions of the Puerto Rican population that assume government authority to be limitless in time and scope. The following tables highlight the findings of the 1957 and 1967 studies and show that many of the results found in the first study have been replicated in the latter study.

TABLE 1. NUMBER OF CIVIL RIGHTS KNOWN

Number of Rights	% that know	
	1957	1967
None	47.2	42.3
1-2	28.3	24.9
3-5	20.0	22.3
6-8	3.2	7.2
9-12	0.9	1.7
12 or more	0.1	1.6

A considerable number of people in Puerto Rico perceive themselves as dependent upon the absolute authority of the government. Since they conceive the state as limitless in its authority, they consider themselves helpless and dependent. In other words, a great segment of the Puerto Rican society ignores the principles of how to organize the social processes that lead to a government by consent of the governed, to freedom to express and communicate one's positions in the political community, to tolerance of dissent, and to limitation of the authority of the state by Civil Rights.

TABLE 2. SUMMARY OF ATTITUDES TOWARD A CIVIL RIGHTS IN THE PUERTO RICAN CULTURE

Response of the population to various situations	% of the population	
	1957	1967
Would deny permission to offer a public lecture to a group belonging to a different religion...	42.6	41
Would deny permission to pass out leaflets to the political opposition..	50.7	40
Would deny permission to pass out leaflets favoring the Popular Democratic Party................................	5.9	6
Would deny permission to pass out leaflets favoring communism...	71.7	67
Would deny permission to communists to give a public lecture..	64.4	78
Would deny permission to an atheist to give a public lecture..	62.6	59
Would dismiss a communist from his employment..	40.7	28.9
Would dismiss an atheist teacher from his employment..	76.8	61.7
Would dismiss a teacher favoring the nationalization of industries from his employment.........................	18	17
Would eliminate a book favoring the nationalization of industries from all libraries..	28	41
Would eliminate a book written by an atheist from all libraries..............................	72.2	63
Would eliminate a book contrary to one's own religion from all libraries...	49.3	45

Response of the population to various situations	% of the population	
Could not mention even one civil right...	47.2	42.3
Indifferent to the arrest of a person for distributing leaflets favoring the Popular Democratic Party...............................	66.3	64.5
Would not do anything if he found the mayor stealing public funds...	37.1	41.8
Never has attempted to avail himself of the freedom of the press...	97.2	95.85
Would not do anything if persons belonging to a different religion were arrested for distributing leaflets.............................	81.9	84
Would not do anything if communists were arrested for distributing leaflets..	83.6	93.9
Indifferent to the arrest of nationalists for distributing leaflets..	86.8	89
Would not do anything if persons distributing leaflets against one's political preference were arrested....................................	76.3	67.4
Would deny permission to nationalists to give a public lecture..	60.9	*
Would dismiss someone in favor of nationalizing industries from his employment.......................	11	*
Would dismiss a communist teacher from his employment.......................	58.7	*
Would jail all communists.................................	32.5	*
Would eliminate a book written by a communist from all libraries...........................	64.5	*

*Not asked in 1967.

If we could translate this statistical summary into an image of the web of interpersonal relationships in the political community, we would find significant segments of the population passively opposing and passively resisting the rights of dissenting political groups to express their views in the general debate which must prevail about relevant issues in a democratic community. I say "passively" because they would not exercise their right to dissent and exchange their opposing point of view in a democratically responsible way. Even the sectors of society that know some civil rights do not seem to relate these rights to the principle of electoral consent made viable by alternative choices (dissent), guaranteed by civil rights. For example, they do not relate freedom of speech, freedom of association, and the prohibition against discrimination for political belief as instrumental to the goal of diversifying and strengthening the point of view of the electorate.

We find a repressive attitude directed against dissident political points of view. This repressive attitude is often called vigilance against those who want to undermine law and order. These segments of the population that feign a vigilante position for "law and order" in depriving segments of the public opinion of their right to express themselves, become very servile and docile when a monopoly of power is assumed by the state. In so doing, they abolish democratic principles. For example, 70 per cent of the population sample in 1957 would be unmoved by the arrest of a person for distributing leaflets in which their religion was criticized. Another 14 per cent would help the arrest, and only 16 per cent would believe the arrest to be unwarranted. In the 1957 study the proportion of "apathetic non-civic minded" goes up to 76.3 per cent when persons distributing leaflets against one's political ideas are arrested by the police. In 1967 the proportion, although a bit diminished, still is high at 67.4% of the population sample. Even when members of the Popular Democratic Party are arrested by the police, 66.3 per cent of the sample in 1957 would be unconcerned. That proportion was almost replicated in the 1967 study when 64.5 per cent stated they would show a similar passivity before such an arrest.

In our 1957 study, in response to questions designed for an authoritarian scale by Adorno and Frenkle in California,[3] 73.1 per cent answered that there are only two kinds of people—the weak and the strong. It was agreed by 90 per cent that "every leader should be strong." In the 1967 study, affirmative answers to these two points were shown by 61.54 per cent and 60.35 per cent respectively. In Puerto Rico we hear constantly about the "need" for leadership whenever a group or movement lacks a "charismatic" chief.

These embarrassing findings raise questions that are very difficult to answer. At the time of our first study, Puerto Rico had acquired an international reputation as a sort of "showcase of democracy". In both studies, our findings did not support that optimistic conclusion. To disentangle the contradiction between the image and the reality, we had two avenues of research and casuality. The diachronic approach to causality leads us toward an historical account of our colonial experience. The synchronic or contemporary functional analysis leads us into a study of the socializing functions of power.

The Historical Approach

The historical approach deals with the question in terms of residues or survivals of collective habits derived from the historical experience of the society. If we follow the historical explanation, we would find in the brutality of the Spanish colonial regime in Puerto Rico, evidence of constant reinforcements of authoritarian patterns of thought and behavior. This starts with the genocide of the aboriginal Taino population, and continues with the enslavement of a population kidnapped from the African continent to satisfy the greediness of the Spanish invaders. We can see an obsession with unlimited power among governors like Salvador Meléndez Brauna: at the beginning of the nineteenth century he dismissed councilmen and ordered the arrest of the mayor of Aguada, who was attempting zealously to place under justice the royal tax collector of the port of Aguadilla, a protegée of the governor. For the purposes of covering up his infringement of rights, this governor attempted to accuse of conspiracy Ramón Power, the Puerto Rican delegate to the Cortes of Cádiz, and Alejo Arizmendi, the Puerto Rican bishop. We also can mention Governor Juan de Pezuela and his notorious pass system, which introduced a virtual state of peonage among thousands of agrarian workers on the island. We are reminded of Governor Romualdo Palacios, who in 1887 launched a campaign of terror against those politically-active groups who were demanding political and other reforms for the island. This was a time in which the members of the Civil Guard patrolling the country roads would amuse themselves by terrorizing the peasantry. According to Antonio S. Pedreira, the civil guard patrol upon meeting a jíbaro would ask him,

"Are you wet or dry?" Ignoring what was meant by "wet or dry," the terrified jíbaro would select either choice under pressure from his questioners. If he picked "wet", he was beaten, "so that you get dry." If he picked "dry," he was beaten "so that you get wet."[4] Fear of the Civil Guard remains among our country folk who even in our times lower their voices upon referring to these incidents.

The advent of the American occupation was a set-back to our emerging democratic evolution since it toppled our autonomic government conceded by Spain two years before the invasion. This autonomic charter guaranteed internal sovereignty within a provincial status with representation in the central government. Our political representatives welcomed the American troops in the hopes that they came to liberate us completely and not to remain as the new masters. With the American invasion our situation became democratic in form, colonial in content. Muñoz Marín describes this formal democracy corrupted by patronage:

> Although a community can be ruled by a few men willing to rule it in a nice way, some kind of supporting majority is demanded by the democratic yen. So a majority was found. To be a member of this majority all you had to do was to proclaim yourself an ardent American in bad English or in no English at all. If you were a member of the majority, you could become a streetcleaner of a health inspector, or you could recommend some poor henchmen for either jobs.

With the American occupation, our prosperous coffee market in Europe was eliminated and substituted by the produce of large scale sugar plantations. Land concentration or *latifundia* destroyed our peasantry and turn it into a landless rural proletariat. According to Diffie and Diffie, 60 per cent of our productive land went into the hands of four big American sugar corporations.[6] Poverty and discontent led us to the point of revolution in the 1930s and was placated by welfare placed in the hands of Muñoz Marín who since 1936 has used it as patronage.

In 1940 the coming into power of the Popular Party opened up a new phase in our history and brought an enthusiasm known in other places as revolutionary euphoria. In his inaugural speech, Muñoz Marín said, "The sun rising over our mountains has melted our chains of misery and colonialism." Independence was then considered "just around the corner". Our people were confident of the future. Very soon, however, independence, freedom and nationalism became taboo words. Populism led to a multitude of "changes not to change," to a trivialization of the political spectacle. Thus, electoral campaigns became a game of patronage in which public funds were spent to reinforce political loyalties to the party in power, and not to enact the political program for which the party in question was elected.[7] While political status was alleged to be "not in issue," welfare state giveaways were used as power reinforcement to imprint dependency, social irresponsibility, and the image of opulence. All government programs were conducted with the aim of corrupting democratic processes by means of patronage. Development programs with incentives of tax exemption and cheap labor were soon to be handed over to American corporations. Government enterprises were then shortly given on credit to private investors. The "surplus" members of the popualtion were sent to the United States where they invariably were forced to live in the worst slums under conditions of prejudice and inhumanity. Meanwhile, 80 per cent of our national wealth went into the hands of foreign investors, who soon took over our press,[8] our radio and all our mass media and used them to foster a waste economy to fit a welfare commonwealth structure.

The Socializing Functions of Power

The publication of our first study, in 1963, provoked a great deal of concern among those in Puerto Rico who had been encouraged to believe that Puerto Rico was a showcase for democracy. Legislation was approved to control racial discrimination in hotels,[9] schools and other public places. Programs for democratic education were begun in the mass media. University students were required to read parts of my report and other reports written by the Governor's Committee on Civil Liberties about abuses of power among the police, the courts of justice, and in legislative and administrative spheres of the society.

In 1967 we were given the opportunity to take a second measurement of the civic culture of Puerto Ricans. Results showed that the picture had not improved in any significant way. Again we were forced to face very intriguing questions,[10] the answers to which we believe must be found in the socializing functions of power. If there is any validity to the hypothesis that our regime has power to socialize the members of the society to the political culture that best fits its purposes, then this question must follow: "Why haven't our presumably democratic regimes achieved this exhalted goal?"

In a synchronic search for determinants for the failure of the Puerto Rican democratic body politic to socialize Puerto Ricans in a democratic ethic, we must look among those oligarchic groups invested with the capacity for socializing functions (that is, with power to reinforce an anti-democratic tradition stemming from a colonial situation and perpetuated at present in a neo-colonial situation).

The reason for the failure of Puerto Rico's Civic Rights educational program must be sought according to the model of a non-democratic power structure that reinforces behavior contradictory to democratic principles. In the political behavior of governmental representatives in Puerto Rico, we found a pattern of action that contradicts everything the mass media might say about democracy. Within a *prebenda* pattern, political administrative officials allocate the resources of their agencies as patronage to accrue personal obligation as political capital. A great deal of the resources of public agencies are spent in image building for incumbents, thus limiting the resources available for the legitimate functions of the agency. Followers are sought to fulfill the function of *confianza* (trustee) or private agent of the incumbent, and not to act as agent for a public commitment.

Rewards are obtained upon becoming a *confianza* man to a higher up, and rewards are given to those willing to ingratiate themselves and play the *prebenda* game, so renouncing all impersonal principles such as political rights becomes a prerequisite for success and continuity in office. Patronage allocated as personal favor in exchange for ingratiation is tightly interwoven into the power structure, from the highest to the lowest level. The highest sources of power in Puerto Rico reside in the government and in North American business enterprises that control 80 per cent of all Puerto Rican annual investments. To a large extent, government resources are derived from transaction and exaction from the Federal government. Given the *probenda* patterns, ingratiation with American clients becomes a prerequisite for success in Puerto Rico.

At the same time, almost the totality of our external trade is monopolized by American markets. An island the size of Puerto Rico thus occupies sixth place in the United States market of the Americas. Incomes in Puerto Rico are derived almost completely from North American enterprises, from Puerto Rican immigrants in New York sending money to relatives in Puerto Rico, from migrant agricultural laborers and from American tourists. Under these circumstances, colonization is inevitable unless power can be generated in another sector. Given the waste of resources invested in narcissistic image building, the possibilities of developing an indigenous bourgeoisie are limited.

Neocolonialism implies the placing of an external colony in the position of an internal colony. Puerto Rico has been placed as a Welfare Commonwealth in American welfare capitalism. Funds from the Office of Economic Opportunities, Food Surplus programs, unemployment benefits, social security, veteran pensions, matched funds for health, public works, educational programs such as Head Start, drug addiction control, foundation funds for university professors and administrators which lead the university into the prevailing corruption), are placed in the hands of politicians for and as patronage. To these areas of direct American influence we must add American control of the means of production and the almost total American control of advertisements. As the owners of the means of production, American enterprises are in a position to offer to the opulent society the means of satisfying the whims of consumerism created by the mass media. These enterprises thus acquire the power to fabricate self-images favorable to their continuity.

Concomitant to this ideological control of the Puerto Rican society, cheap labor demands in the metropolis make available to Puerto Rico one of the worlds' most desired labor markets. From 1945 to 1960, 500,000 Puerto Ricans left their homeland to live in the worst slums of the United States. An average of 30,000 Puerto Ricans yearly have abandoned the island to become marginal cheap labor in the American labor market.

The economic power structure in the hands of North Americans is paralleled by the political structure controlled from Washington. According to ex-President of the Puerto Rican Bar Associations, Noel Colón Martinez, there are many areas in which the theory of consent of the governed does not apply. The Congress of the United States controls our external trade, our tariff system, our aviation, navigation, international treaties of trade, our currency, our banks, naturalization, external migration, our port regulations and our licensing of radio and television stations. It has power to overrule decisions made by Puerto Rican courts, power to impose minimum wages, power to expropriate land forceably. According to Colòn Martinez,[11] these are areas in which the Law 600 could not interfere; then remain closed even after the pompous 1967 plebiscite in which the appearance of consent was given to the Puerto Rican Constitution.

Since all power is in the hands of those who ingratiate themselves with Americans, intolerance for ideas of independence is prerequisite for success within the *prebenda* system. Those who support independence are the fools and villains, the "separatists" and "subversives" within the social drama where political rights are practically ignored by the members of the society. Although political rights are heard about in the educational campaigns we have mentioned above, political praxis is a constant reinforcement of the undemocratic attitudes that always have been the rule in the political life of this society.

In Puerto Rico, constitutional guarantees against discrimination for political beliefs are violated under the slightest pretext by the police. Those employees in American enterprises suspected of being for independence are harrassed constantly by the F.B.I. and C.I.A. In the company offices and on company time, these employees are submitted to questioning, the purpose of which is to intimidate them and make life difficult for them among co-workers and bosses. According to the Civil Rights Commission, the police maintain a blacklist that includes often names of people who were independentistas as far back as 1936. Once a person's name is placed on the blacklist, all agencies of the government, as well as private agencies that maintain business with the United States, will be very reluctant to offer him employment. We often hear of people on the blacklist seeking jobs in government agencies with former friends who tell them that they would give them a job only under the condition that they keep their mouths shut.

It is a known fact that punishment or negative reinforcement[12] is not as effective as reward in the forming of habits. With unlimited resources for *prebenda* bribery, our government can afford a liberal facade and actually control social behavior through *prebenda* or corrupt bribery for conditioning the political community.

A regime based on political bribery taps the multimillion-dollar funds of the welfare state of the United States by making itself deserving of all the purposes of these programs. At present there are government agencies dedicated to discovering where funds can be made available in different federal spending programs.[13]

The fountains of federal spending in Puerto Rico are opened or closed on the basis of "deserving" behavior by the Puerto Rican. Those unwilling to play along will soon be out of the game, marginalized, ignored and, in a few cases, exposed to political persecution. A Puerto Rican poet has dramatically described the shameless collective bribery that prevails in our island:

> I have met so many people who in approaching me look away that I have forgotten the face of people. In the theatre, in the street—everywhere—I meet rows and rows of backs as if by a strange coincidence people had to look always somewhere else.

A faithful description of the petty manipulations people become involved in to make themselves available to the good will of the dollar machinery would gain a prize in the theatre of the absurd. In our study on civil rights we met this spider web of manipulation very early. In the 1967 study, we were restrained by the director of the Social Science Research Center, Luis Nieves Falcón, from hiring candidates with excellent academic records and great interest in research, because they were "politically untrustworthy" (meaning by that, supporters of independence). However, I was able to smuggle in one such candidate. During a student disturbance, I sent him out as an observer. Since he was on the police blacklist, he immediately was taken in by the police, beaten, jailed and then fired from his job by the University. The constitutional principle that a person is considered innocent until proven guilty was ignored even by the university chancellor who was a former member of the civil rights commission. Subsequently, a court of law declared him innocent.[14]

People in the spider web of power purposefully violate the principle of civil rights and make their behavior unpredictable; they condition their subordinates to respond to them on a particularistic frame of reference. This personalistio scheme necessarily creates instability in the relation. Sycophants, tail lifters and yes-men abound, but when they get a better paying offer turn against their masters and become subservient to someone else.

People in a position of power develop a *prima donna* type of sensitivity to any sign of personal "disloyalty." The cult to their personality is their main concern, while the objectives of the agency for which they work remain ignored. Followers are brought in to create the inner core of *confianza* people who make themselves deserving by being obsequious and adulatory. The resources of public agencies are diverted to a point of exhaustion by their channelization into prebendarian functions rather than into social objectives. Public funds thus devoted to patronage eventually destroy the possibility of the agency's success. We have shown in our study of agrarian reform how this use of an agency's funds for patronage destroys the purpose for which that agency was created, namely that of human amelioration.[15]

Image builders, no matter how incompetent otherwise, are the order of the day for any position. Politicians to manipulate public opinion: that's the thing. Those whose political sense of smell (*olfato político*) is highly developed can anticipate changes in the prebendarian oligarchy and immediately begin to cultivate the favor of those deemed to rise in a veritable Kafkian absurdity. Human relations are manipulated according to the cash potential of the person in the power structure. Human relations thus have the quality of merchandise that Marx predicted under capitalism.

Within this context that we have described, genuine friendships and authentic relatedness are always suspect, given the prevailing opportunism that makes for exploitative friendships. In the same way that human aggregates are producd on the basis of *confianza*, conflicts are conceived as disloyalty on a personal level. Thus aggregates based on this trivialized agenda of *confianza* are constantly rocked by questions of jealousy, envy and competitiveness. This is more so in those areas where the top dog has no other form of reward than his own personal charisma. As a result, there is a constant fragmentation, a high level of suspiciousness, and a chronic condition of disorder and hopelessness.

The personalistic regime that emerges as a result of the prebendic structure imposes bribery as a reinforcement for interpersonal relations backed by *confianza*. By using public funds or prebendic bribery, followers are recruited as supporters of "public figures," and are conditioned to offer praise and respect to the "leader" while ignoring principles.[16] Loyalty in the confianza context is to the person as an individual, and not the generic idea of the human being, and thus is in contraposition to the norms that should rule in institutional contexts. In the personalistic context, the public resources assigned for the operation of public programs (with public funds) are used as bribery for the purpose of gaining followers and for building up the political image of oligarchs. In ignoring the social objectives of the agencies and in marking public funds by means of bribery for image building, the economical resources of the society are pilfered.

The radical individualistic syndrome that results from this condition would seem to be shared with our neo-colonial brothers of Latin America. A recent novel by Gabriel Garcia Marquez portrays the futility and the hopelessness inherent to this individualistic hypertrophy.[17] Even Simón Bolívar expresses his despair when confronted with the trivialized society rocked by hypertrophied individualism:

Latin Americans are ungovernable. Those who have served the revolution have been tilling in the sea. In Latin America treaties are pieces of paper, constitutions are books, elections are combats, freedom is anarchy, and life is a torment.[18]

Mario Monteforte Toledo writes that in Mexico the radical movements are cannibalistic.[19] In Puerto Rico, independentist groups constantly are dividing and subdividing for reasons of jealousy, envy and quarrelsomeness.

Postscript

An Argentinian friend of mine, upon seeing the trivializations that begin to prevail in the United States, said, "In this we are masters. They can be our pupils." Dependency fostered by populistic solutions of "change not to change" creates in the United States the same "culture" we have described for Puerto Rico. In other words, the structural requirements are socializing Americans to the extreme opposite value of their Protestant Ethic. Populism has taken hold in the United States with its concommitant trivialization of the historical spectacle.[20] Poverty pimping in the United States follows the exact same pattern as the *prebenda* politics we have described for Puerto Rico. Structurally speaking, trivialization means "change in order not to change."

NOTES

1. The results of of the 1957-58 study were published in *Los Derechos Civiles en La Cultural Puertorriqueña* (Rio Piedras, 1963), an award winning book from the Instituto de Literatura Puertorriqueña.

2. The argument that there are "ideals" against which one is comparing "reality" is usually made by those for whom the social "reality" is comforting. All social reality is idea; it is constituted by cultural patterns, social roles, status, mores, folkways, sacred laws, all of which are constituted by normative (ideal) expectancies derived from socially delimited cognitive maps and supported by evaluative standards and ideas of the power-holding cliques.

3. T. W. Adorno, et al., *The Authoritarian Personality* (New York, 1967).

4. Antonio S. Pedreira, *El año terrible del '87* (San Juan, 1948).

5. Luis Muñoz Marín, "The Sad Case of Puerto Rico," *American Mercury*, XVI, No. 62 (February, 1929).

6. B. W. and J. W. Diffie, *Porto Rico, A Broken Pledge* (New York, 1931).

7. See Eduardo Seda, *Social Change and Personality in an Agrarian Reform Community* (Evanston, 1972), for a description of the corruption of the land reform turned into *prebenda*.

8. Upon taking over the Puerto Rican daily newspaper *El Mundo*, a former editor of the *Miami Herald* fired first rate Puerto Rican journalists such as Nilita Vientos Gastón, Dr. José Arsenio Torres, and others. Under similar conditions, *El Imparcial* fired novelist César

Andreu Iglesias whose column "Cosas de Aquí" was one of the most outstanding pieces of journalism on the island.

9. See, "Social Structure and Race Relations", *Social Forces*, XL, No. 2 (December 1961) and "Entre dos formas de prejucio racial", in Eduardo Seda, *Réquiem por una cultura* (Rio Piedras, 1971).

10. This situation is paralleled by one described by Joseph D. Lohman. A teacher very persuasively portrays cultural differences during her lesson hour. The students seem impressed. Yet when it comes to dealing in an actual life situation with a student from a different subculture, she fails the test of ethnocentrism and destroys the effectiveness of her verbal lesson. (Joseph D. Lohman, *Cultural Patterns in Urban Schools* [Berkeley, 1967]).

11. Noel Colón Martinez, "Los partidos políticos en Puerto Rico," a paper delivered on June 3, 1968 in the Ateneo Puertorriqueño.

12. "Thorndike's original position was to the effect that learning is a reversible process, reward strengthening and punishment weakening it. However, as a result of a long series of experiments on verbal learning in human subjects carried out later in his professional life, Thorndike (1931, 1932) came to the conclusion that his original position was in error and while reward does indeed facilitate learning, punishment does not weaken it." (O. Hobart Mowrer, Learning Theory and Behavior [New York, 1960]).

13. According to José L. Vázquez Calzada, ". . . the net national income between 1950 and 1960 increased by 27 per cent while the foreign debt of the government sector increased by more than 1000 per cent. In 1950, the public debt was 14 per cent of the net income, whereas in 1965 it had risen to 41 per cent of the net income. . . . The problem that our external debt creates is that payments to meet that debt plus the interest are growing at a faster rate than the growth of foreign investment." (José L. Vázquez Calzada, *El desbalance entre recursos y población en Puerto Rico* [San Juan, 1966]).

14. I am referring to the case of Rafael Rodriguez Santiago, fired ironically enough, by the chancellor of the University of Puerto Rico, Abraham Díaz Gonzalez, a former member of the Civil Rights Commission.

15. See Seda, *Social Change*.

16. "First, if a political system is not characterized by a value system allowing the peaceful 'play' of power, democracy becomes chaotic. This has been the problem faced by many Latin American states." (S. M. Lipset, *Political Man, The Social Bases of Politics* [Garden City, 1963]).

17. Gabriel Garcia Marquez, *Cien años de soledad* (Buenos Aires, 1968).

18. L. Langras and G. Massa, *Historia de la civilización Latino Americana* (New York, 1965).

19. Mario Monteforte Toledo, *Una manera de morir*.

20. See, Seda, *Réquiem*.

Tourism in Puerto Rico*

Mary K. Vaughan

Along the San Juan oceanfront stretches a line of luxury hotels, which until recently were the tallest buildings in Puerto Rico. In the midst of them stands the Caribe Hilton, the "Grand Dame" of Puerto Rican hotels and the only one making money in 1973. Twenty million dollars worth of pleasure and idle time, the Caribe sprawls over acres of lush garden and sandy beach—a world unto itself of pools and tennis courts, bars and night clubs, dining rooms and gaming tables, and plushly furnished rooms. Its air-conditioned lobby looks like Grand Central Station crowded with North Americans—complaining, flirting, whining, hussling, playing bingo and bridge, drinking *piña coladas*, nursing sunburns, nagging at the blond social hostess and snapping fingers and tongues at the Puerto Ricans—bellboys, bartenders and desk clerks. Behind metal doors, the Hilton is not as glamorous: In the kitchen young men toss cans of Libby's pineapple from shelf to counter and scrub grease off ovens and grills, while down the corridor in the hot, unventilated laundry room, men and women guide Cannon sheets through giant Perma-Press machines. Outside guests stroll through gardens of palm trees where flamingos pose near flowerbeds and carefully tended pools. A fence of

*The writer would like to express her appreciation to the following people for their assistance and information: Ernesto Díaz and Raul Meléndez of the Unión Gastronómica de Puerto Rico, Cesar Andreu Iglesias, Pedro Díaz of the Helio San Gerónimo Hotel, Carlos Gallisá, Miles Galvín, Carlos Diago and Edgardo Iglesias of the Department of Tourism and Polly Radick and Chris Mootz of Northwestern University.

corrugated iron runs around the garden and north to the ocean. There, at its locked gate, Puerto Rican youths try unsuccessfully to gain entrance to the beach. Although the beach is public property in front of a government-owned hotel, Hilton International claims it as a private "Tennis and Beach Club." In front of the Caribe stands a U.S. military compound likewise fenced off with the warning: "Federal Property—No Trespassing." To the west of the hotel—behind MacDonald's—stands the Puerto Rican-owned Normandy Hotel, an empty shell of concrete and corroding window frames, a crumbling testimony to the vicissitudes of "free enterprise."

To understand the nature of the tourist industry in Puerto Rico one must understand the tourist industry in the United States, for it is the latter which has determined the direction and fate of tourism in Puerto Rico. In 1962 the U.S. hotel industry was in trouble. Average return on investment dropped to two per cent as jets cut the stays of businessmen in downtown areas, the elite's migration to the suburbs reduced catering and banquet services, and motels sprang up on highways and near airports.[1] One means of escaping the depression and saturation at home was to move into the international market, which became more attractive as jets shortened the distances between parts of the globe. Further stimulated by rising incomes of the North American upper and middle classes and the need to supply the increasingly mobile U.S. businessman with American-style hotels, the lodging chains moved abroad. Primarily because of overseas expansion, Hilton increased its revenues from $37.2 million in 1957 to $80.3 million in 1964. In 1965, Hilton's 31 hotels on five continents accounted for 40 per cent of its profits.[2]

When airlines and travel agencies introduced charter flights and package tours, tourism became the largest item in world trade and generated $14.1 billion in 1968. Of this amount U.S. tourists spent $5 billion overseas to claim a near monopoly on the luxury tourist supply.[3] As a service infrastructure expanded in the U.S. to facilitate North American travel abroad, the ultimate beneficiaries of international tourism were U.S. travel and advertising agencies, credit card and car rental companies, airlines and aircraft manufacturers, oil companies, shipping lines, and makers of luggage, cosmetics, pharmaceuticals, apparel and camera equipment.[4]

The exapnsion of tourism led to concentration of ownership. In 1966, when U.S. airlines invested millions of dollars in jumbo jets, they moved to insure their investment by increasing their hold on the tourist market.

To secure passengers, they began to build luxury hotels and to buy up hotel chains. By 1971, two thirds of the largest airlines had acquired hotels.[5] As early as 1945, Juan Terry Trippe, president of Pan American Airlines, had set up Intercontinental Hotel Corporation to build hotels on Pan Am's routes; by 1971 Intercontinental operated 80 hotels in 47 countries. In 1968, TWA bought Hilton International, spun off of Hilton Hotel Corporation in 1964.[6] In 1970, United Airlines bought Western International, then the third largest hotel chain with 43 hotels abroad. American Airlines' subsidiary, Sky Chef, the world's largest airline caterer, operated eleven hotels in 1971 under the mark of Flagship. In 1971, Eastern Airlines had two hotels in Puerto Rico, one in Hawaii, and several in the Virgin Islands, managed by Laurence Rockefeller's Rockresorts, in which Eastern had a 40 per cent interest. Laurence Rockefeller himself owned 100 per cent of Eastern Airlines preferred stock.[7]

ITT's purchase of Avis-Rent-A-Car and the Sheraton hotel chain in 1967 marked the advent of the hospitality conglommerate—the vertically integrated corporation controlling every facet of the international tourist trade from travel agencies and computerized reservations systems to airlines, cruise ships, car rental companies, hotels, restaurants and credit card services.[8] With access to international financing, the global corporation offered the cost-cutting advantages of world management, purchasing and marketing. Holdings were large enough to support lower occupancy rates, overbuilding, and market downturns, while such organization ensured the corporation "revenues and profits that would otherwise go elsewhere."[9] Holiday Inn, the world's largest and fastest growing lodging chain, owns the second largest inter-city busline in the United States, steamship lines, a construction company, furniture and food processors and distributors and printing and insurance companies. It assures itself business through a $124 million computerized reservations system interconnecting regional offices and inns by 50,000 miles of leased wires and communications satellites.[10] Where companies are not thoroughly integrated, they are intertwined through interlocking directorates, joint ventures and marketing agreements. Hotel Corporation of America and Western International share a reservations, promotion and credit card service. American Airlines Flagship Hotels operate Americana hotels owned by Loews, one of the largest chains and a diversified hotel-cinema-tobacco corporation, which derives 60 per cent of its revenues from Lorillard Tobacco Company.[11] Loews in turn manages Howard Johnson Motor Lodges. American Airlines offers package tours with accomodations at "rival" hotels abroad. Western International and Laurence Rockefeller belong to a consortium that owns 30 per cent interest in the fast-growing Travelodge motel chain, in which Trust Houses, Ltd. of Britain also has shares. The latter and Western International share a referral system for travelers seeking rooms. Although Western International is a subsidiary of United Airlines, it has entered a joint venture with Braniff to spend $150 million developing tourism in Latin America in the 1970's.

While this integration clearly favors U.S. transportation lines, hotels and other facilities over national and non-chain interests abroad, the corporations have expanded primarily by absorbing capital from the country of operation. Throughout the world, tourism promoters have sought to persuade governments and national entrepreneurs to put up the vast sums necessary for hotel plant and tourist infrastructure. In general, U.S. chains lease and manage properties abroad for a set fee and/or a percentage of gross operating profits.[12] While Intercontinental and Western International will invest up to 10 per cent in the construction of hotels, as a rule the onus of investment falls upon local governments and entrepreneurs many of whom must borrow abroad to finance hotels. Conrad Hilton became highly skilled in persuading countries to provide the land, building, furniture, decorations and operating equipment for his hotels. "We like the investors to supply even the egg cups," says Curt Strand of Hilton International.[13] Although hotel workers' union dues built the Havana Hilton, Hilton usually manages hotels for "governments, wealthy orientals and Texas millionaires."[14] Typical owners tend to be local magnates tied in with various transnational corporations. Harold Lee, chairman of the real estate development company that owns the Intercontinental Mandarin in Hong Kong, is also director of local operations for British American Tobacco, Schweppes, and Coca Cola.[15] Management on the other hand is made up of a cadre of "trained internationals available for reassignment anywhere in the world", with loyalties only to the headquarters of the hotel chains.[16]

U.S. chains practice minimum investment with maximum return. In 1965, Hilton claimed a market value of $150 to $200 million on an initial investment of $12.3 million, $3 million of which it had invested overseas. On this $3 million (a large slice of which had been raised in the country of operation), Hilton earned an exorbitant 20 per cent return in 1964, 10 per cent more than hotel accountants assume to be profitable.[17] "No hotel company could make in the U.S. what we make overseas," boasts Conrad Hilton.[18] The capital amassed from individual hotels gave the chains global power and mobility; it enabled them to milk one area and promote another, moving swiftly from beach to mountain top to make the fastest dollar. As Hilton International says, it chooses sites purely because they are "bouyant markets."[19]

With the growth of tourism came academic promoters connected with national and international lending institutions, U.S. universities, research institutes, and management consultant firms;—spokesmen who tried to persuade capital-scarce and poverty-stricken countries that tourism could make a positive contribution to national development. In feasibility reports for the World Bank and U.S. Agency for International Development, H. Zinder and Associates, Inc. (a Washington consulting firm), argued, for example, that tourism generated foreign exchange and helped solve the balance of payments problems of Third World countries. They claimed that it raised incomes and generated jobs while increasing tax revenues. To these contributions, David H. Davis of the World Bank added that tourism generated demand for local products and took profitable advantage of existing resources in land, natural scenery, and labor. Writing in the *Bank of London and South America Review*, Doreen Crompton de Calvo suggested that unlike some industries, tourism did not deplete natural resources.[20] In a $200,000 report for the Puerto Rican Commonwealth in 1967, the Stanford Research Institute argued that tourism fostered human understanding and cultural appreciaton.[21] Terrence Cullinan, a member of the Stanford Team and an employee of U.S. Natural Resources, a California-based international corporation with interests in oil, timber, land, and recreational development, stretched this argument to claim that tourism established a national identity for the recipient country and preserved national culture by utilizing folk culture and establishing museums.[22] In articulating tourism's positive contribution to development, David H. Davis advised that for it to succeed, foreign private investors needed local credit and capital, a package of tax incentives including tax holidays and liberalization of import quotas and tariffs, freedom to remit profits, assurance of quick returns, and a commitment from local government to finance an infrastructure of public utilities, transportation and entertainment for visitors.[23]

Although Operation Bootstrap bureaucrats have extended such guarantees to foreign capital and although they insist that tourism has brought benefits to Puerto Rico, the overwhelming amount of evidence thus far collected indicates this type of private enterprise has not contributed positively to national development. Puerto Rico's investment in tourism began in 1945 when the government leased the Condado Beach Hotel, built by Cornelius Vanderbilt in 1919, to Executive House, Inc., of Chicago. In 1949, Governor Muñoz Marín decided that Puerto Rico needed a second first-class hotel to attract U.S. businessmen. Investing $7.4 million in the construction of the Caribe, Muñoz Marín wrote to leading U.S. hotelmen asking if they wanted to manage it. When the burly Texan Conrad Hilton replied in his broken Spanish, "Muy distinguido señor," he got the contract that launched Hilton abroad. Although the Caribe Hilton became one of the most profitable luxury hotels in the world, Hilton was better known in the 1950's for his operation in Havana, which stood at the center of a tourist vortex of gambling, prostitution and drugs known in the United States as Gay Havana. In this period, the luxury hotels of Puerto Rico served an exclusive North American clientele who were somewhat less ostentatious in their use of Puerto Rico's beaches and casinos. The hotels became status symbols of the Puerto Rican and the Caribe Hilton soda fountain a favorite place for the children of the island elite. The subsequent "Miamization" of San Juan occurred in the 1960's with the explosion of the U.S. tourist industry. Between 1963 and 1969, large U.S.-styled "water-front palaces," interspersed with night clubs, New York fashion shops, and neon-lit discotheques, loomed up in Isla Verde and on Ashford Avenue along what came to be known as the Condado "strip." Built largely with Puerto Rican capital and managed by U.S. chains, the hotels extended their occupation of Puerto Rico's beaches and expanded their gambling facilities to attract wealthy U.S. tourists, many of whom had vacationed in Havana before the Cuban Revolution.

While the majority of Puerto Rican hotels were Puerto Rican-built, five of the largest were built or bought by U.S. entrepreneurs. Woolworth owned El Convento. Louis Puro, president of New York-based Purofied Downs (the world's largest pillow-maker), bought the El San Juan from Pan Am in 1960 to turn it into a Las Vegas-style casino establishment. American Airlines acquired the lease on the Americana from Loews. Together the El San Juan and the Americana reaped 41.7 per cent of casino income in Puerto Rico in 1967.[24] With profits from the El San Juan, Puro bought a hill overlooking the Caribbean and Atlantic to build the $32 million El Conquistador. A self-contained tourist complex complete with a private landing field, a dock for cruise ships, convention halls, a $2.5 million spa for "corporate fatties," and a casino referred to as "a sort of hushed temple to money," the El Conquistador is to its owner "the greatest hotel in the world."[25] With loans from the Puerto Rican government, Eastern Airlines fenced off 1,575 acres of Puerto Rican land on the shoreline road to Arecibo to build a tourist enclave of golf courses, hotels, condominiums, night clubs and restaurants, run by Laurence Rockefeller's Rockresorts.

On the other hand, Puerto Rican capital built the Sheraton, four hotels leased to Hilton, the Holiday Inn, Howard Johnson's, the Ponce Intercontinental, and non-chain hotels like the Darlington (now the Borinquen), Miramar and Racquet Club. One of the largest investors was the Commonwealth government. Of $128.5 million invested in hotels in 1970, the Commonwealth had over $52 million invested in tourist properties and loans to hotel builders.[26] As the public investment corporation that has built factories and extended funds to U.S. firms such as General Electric, Westinghouse and Ford, the Puerto Rico Industrial Development Company (PRIDCO) in 1969 had $20.2 million of its $52.5 million in total commitments invested in tourist projects including loans to Rockefeller, Louis Puro, and Holiday Inn.[27] PRIDCO received one-third of its annual rental income from four hotels it owned (Caribe Hilton, Mayaguez Hilton, La Concha and Barranquitas). At the height of the tourist industry's prosperity, this income was just adequate enough to cover debt service on PRIDCO bond issues from New York banks.[28]

American-owned and managed hotels showed the greatest profits between 1965 and 1969. Dominating the Puerto Rican tourist industry in size, income and numbers employed, the U.S. hotels set the tone for the industry. Most had gambling casinos. Because the Puerto Rican-owned Darlington had no casino it was on the verge of bankruptcy when Luis Ferré bought it in 1970 and used his influence as governor to obtain a casino license. The U.S. hotels occupied Puerto Rico's beaches. Without a beach-front, no hotel succeeded. Thus the Miramar closed in 1970 and stands today a concrete ghost of empty rooms and broken windows overlooking the Condado Lagoon. Furthermore, to prosper the hotels had to be widely advertised in the U.S. and American-styled in service and architecture. El Convento in a colonial convent in Old San Juan consistently lost money for both reasons.

According to one Puerto Rican hotel administrator, in this period the chains milked Puerto Rico. To increase profits, they raised room rates to exorbitant prices so that a night at the Americana cost $63.[29] To cut costs, they let machinery and equipment run down.[30] There is no way of calculating the profits they took out of Puerto Rico because transnational corporations' accounting procedures allowed for extensive manipulation. For instance, according to Carlos Gallisá, *independentista* leader and former tourism administrator, a fork lost in Miami was written off in San Juan when San Juan was making money. The bulk of profits were made in casinos, but because casinos were taxable and hotel operations were not profits often were transferred to hotels. More lucrative still was heavy gambling done on credit with losses collected in New York.[31] If profits themselves are not precisely calculable, it is probably safe to say that as a rule they were not reinvested in Puerto Rico.

While the managing chains drew money from the hotels, they left local owners to pay heavy mortgages and high interest rates not deducted from the gross operating profits on which management's cut was based. At the same time, the owners were at the mercy of management in terms of how efficiently and profitably their hotels were run. For instance, Hilton leased the San Gerónimo to prevent it from competing with the Caribe next door. Hilton made profits from using the San Gerónimo to house the spill-over of guests from the Caribe, but the hotel was allowed to run down while nothing was done to promote it. Owner René Aponte Caratini was unable to meet his mortgage and interest payments. In April 1971 when Hilton dropped its lease in the midst of the general crisis affecting the Puerto Rican tourist industry, Aponte faced foreclosure from the Chase Manhattan Bank. Hilton, on the other hand, was thriving because of its earnings at the Caribe and in other parts of the Caribbean.[32]

In this period disaster hit the Puerto Rican tourist industry. Dependence on the U.S. market resulted in a tumble of visitors during the business recession. Other factors revealed Puerto Rico's vulnerability to the United States. Puerto Rico was outcompeted by tourism elsewhere sponsored by the same airlines and hotel companies that had made money in Puerto Rico. Cheap package tours to Europe, the winter ski trade in the U.S., promotion of other Caribbean resorts, and the trend of airlines to open new routes led tourists elsewhere. The airlines also encouraged a new form of Caribbean vacationing known as the fly-cruise. The cruise liners were known as "floatels" and offered room and board for tourists; they simply bypassed the island. As the tourist market attracted the U.S. middle class consumer with package tours and as the wealthy tourist could now choose from many vacation spots, people turned away from the expensive luxury hotels on the Condado "strip."[33]

In March 1971 workers at the Condado Beach were abruptly fired when Executive House declared bankruptcy and cancelled its lease. Guests arriving at breakfast were forced to leave immediately carrying their own luggage. Hilton dropped its contracts at the Dorado Hilton and the San Gerónimo, where workers quickly perceived the implications of the crisis and solidified as a militant body of *independentistas*. At the Racquet Club, the staff applied to the government for a loan to run its sinking hotel as a cooperative. They were turned down by the Department of Tourism, which not as perceptively as these workers engaged in a costly "face-saving" operation granting emergency loans and buying up failing hotels like the Condado Beach, San Gerónimo, and Racquet Club. Woolworth simply gave El Convento to the government and saddled it with a $4 million debt. According to Roberto Bouret, then head of the Puerto Rican Hotel Association and now director of the Department of Tourism, the hotel lobbies looked like "undertakers' parlors between funerals."[34] In 1971, 12 out of 14 casino hotels claimed a loss of $4,628,757.[35]

Meanwhile the Department of Tourism argued that the industry continued to generate national income—$223 million of $823,041,000 in 1970, according to their statistics.[36] A study of 11 casino hotels done by Economic Associates of Puerto Rico has accused both Fomento and the Tourism Development Company of producing "misleading statistics" to create a favorable investment climate.[37] At the very least, their means of calculation are unreliable. They claim to base the number of visitors on hotel registrations, but tourist expenditures are based on occasional spot-checks at the San Juan airport.

In 1970 the government claimed that it derived $40 million in taxes from tourism. The only discernible tax returns from tourism were the five per cent room tax, a one per cent gambling chip tax, and casino income taxes. The five per cent room tax yielded $2.4 million in 1970-71 and paid the principal and interest on bonds of the Compañia de Fomento Recreativo, which financed historical monuments primarily for the benefit of tourists.[38] The chip tax equalled $3,002,774 in 1972 and went into a government scholarship fund.[39] The non-exempt casinos' share of taxes dropped from a peak of $1,109,686 in 1968 to $144,473 in 1971.[40] This revenue in total amounted to under $5 million. It would not have been substantially increased by hotel income taxes, because for most hotels there are none. The Puerto Rican tax incentive program developed by Arthur D. Little, management consultants, exempts tourist hotels from income, real estate, personal property, municipal and commonwealth taxes and taxes on consumption articles and imports for periods from 10 to 17 years. In 1967, of 29 hotels investigated by the Stanford Research Institute, 24 were totally or partially tax exempt. When the original tax privileges run out hotels expand their property to obtain further tax concessions: Income is switched to the new wings of buildings in accounting procedures. If the tourist industry yields substantial government tax returns, a large slice must come from the income taxes paid by hotel workers, over five per cent of the average hourly income.

Nor can it be argued that rents from government-owned hotels have substantially assisted Puerto Rican development. With $67,945,000 invested in tourism in August 1973, PRIDCO had $7 million in outstanding loans it was doubtful of retrieving. In 1972, PRIDCO derived $1.3 million from hotel rents—less than any year since 1956. In the opinion of PRIDCO director, Esteban Dávila Díaz, hotel rents did not justify the substantial investments PRIDCO had made.

Large investments of the Commonwealth government in tourist infrastructure that is of limited use to the Puerto Rican people must be weighed against declining revenues from tourism. Operation Bootstrap managers provided foreign entrepreneurs with the expensive infrastructure which World Bank spokesman David H. Davis advised. While it is difficult to distinguish between infrastructure built for manufacturing and infrastructure for tourism, a few costly projects directly related to tourism exemplify the abuse of public funds. The Puerto Rico Ports Authority has spent well over $20 million in the last three years expanding airport facilities to accommodate jumbo jets.[41] According to Doreen Crompton de Calvo, such an expenditure is exorbitant for a small country, especially in view of the return in income and the jobs generated.[42] Despite the investment in jumbo jet landing facilities, the number of tourists has declined and the number of jobs has not increased. Related to the jumbo jets is the Ports Authority's investment of several million dollars in a tourist pier for cruiseliners. The rise of cruise-packages has severely hurt the Puerto Rican tourist industry. According to an official of the Chicago Branch of the Tourist Development Company, seven out of eight arrivals at the San Juan airport proceed from the airport to the cruise pier and spend neither time nor money in Puerto Rico.[43] One of the sponsors of cruise packages is Eastern Airlines. In competition for passengers on a world-wide basis, Eastern prejudices the hotel industry in Puerto Rico in which it has interests. It does not see itself prejudicing the profits of its own Puerto Rican hotels, as they are luxury and convention hotels and are unaffected by the fly-cruise packages directed at the middle class U.S. tourist.

According to a study of tourism by Puerto Rico's Management Aid Center, tourism is the country's second largest export after textiles and clothing. As the International Union of Official Travel Organizations notes, because "existing knowledge of tourism is very imperfect," the item "tourism" in the balance of payments should be weighed against other items not apparently linked with it. These would include on the debit side expenditures of national tourists abroad, goods imported for the tourist industry, interest payments and profit repatriation of foreign capital, remittances of non-nationals employed in the tourist trade, publicity and advertising.[44]

For Puerto Rico the most astounding figure on this account would be the over $280 million spent by Puerto Rican tourists abroad in 1971-72, more than Puerto Rico's tourist income.[45] This item does not include the expenditures of Puerto Rican workers who have gone to the United States because they could not find jobs in Puerto Rico. It refers to the affluent Puerto Ricans who have bitten the bait of the tourist agencies, airlines, and hotels that bring U.S. tourists to Puerto Rico. According to one *turismo* administrator, every man, woman and child in his neighborhood has visited Walt Disney World at least once. Increasing the debit side would be government and hotel expenditures on advertising and promotion. In 1966-67 hotels spent $3.3 million on advertising and the government over one million.[46] Ogilvy and Mather has the total Puerto Rican government account, which in 1966 was $2,083,336, the largest government promotion account in the world.[47] Further capital outflow occurs in unrestricted profit remittance, while the government spends its tourist rents servicing its debt to New York banks.

Also uncalculated in the tourism account is the income of non-Puerto Ricans employed in the tourist industry. North Americans manage the large hotels and own and manage many of the smaller hotels and guest houses; they also own many of the retail shops and occupy skilled positions as hotel social directors and sporting experts. Although these people may not always remit their income to the United States, in assessing income generated by tourism, a distinction should be made between national income and income of "nationals" on the grounds that tourism as it is currently constituted gives a substantial advantage to expatriates who speak the same language and know the customs of the tourists.[48]

The most crucial factor in the tourist account would be the import of supplies and equipment used by the tourist industry, Doreen Crompton de Calvo points out that although tourism may be a strong foreign exchange earner, when the industry is foreign-controlled and dependent upon imports, this purpose may be undermined.[49] The argument that tourism stimulates secondary industries does not hold for Puerto Rico. Even the goods purchased by tourists in Puerto Rico are not Puerto Rican-made, for contrary to prescription, a solid Puerto Rican crafts industry has not been encouraged. Most of the crafts in gift shops have been imported from Haiti, Mexico, Hong Kong and Thailand.

Because Puerto Rico's industries are runaway plants that assemble parts and products shipped back to the U.S. or petrochemical plants that use the island as a base for international shipments, Puerto Rican industry provides hotels and restaurants with very little. U.S. hotel and restaurant suppliers have in any case followed the chains in their expansion. Although *Business Week* in 1963 stated the over half the air-conditioning, electrical equipment, kitchen and laundry facilities and plumbing came from the United States, the figures for Puerto Rico would appear to be larger.[50] Institutional glass, silverware, porcelain, chemical concentrates, laundry and dry-cleaning equipment, carpeting, floors, furniture and silent ceilings come from the United States. A quick trip through the stuffy Hilton laundry room reveals Cissell washers, Spencer Dry-Cleaning and Chicago Dryer Company equipment, Perma-Press ironing machines and Canon sheets. Hotel rooms are U.S.-equipped from mattresses to Kleenex-dispensers to Kohler waterfaucets.

Most crucial to Puerto Rican development, food and liquor are imported from the United States. According to Senator Justo Mendez, Puerto Rico imports 90 per cent of her food. Even the oranges petty traders sell in the streets are Sunkist from Florida.[51] According to veteran journalist Cesar Andreu Iglesias, the only Puerto Rican foods served in hotels and restaurants are roots and plantains. The vegetables on the table at the Puerto Rico Sheraton have been picked in New Jersey by Puerto Rican migrant workers whose fathers once worked the now uncultivated land of Puerto Rico. The rice on the tables at the Caribe

Hilton has been processed by Mexican and Chicano workers in California. El Piruli Continental Gourmet Restaurant at the Flamboyan features "steaks and chops flown in fresh from Gourmet Packers of New York." La Reina Restaurant imports seafood from Spain and advertises the "Best U.S. Prime Steak in town."

Further, the tourist industry actually has contributed to the decline of Puerto Rican agriculture through its impact on land values and land use. Operation Bootstrap systematically ignored agriculture while it sent land values soaring for potential industrial and tourist use. Land prices shot too high to sustain small and medium-size farmers while the large U.S. and Puerto Rican sugar growers held onto their land for speculative purposes and/or sold it to local and U.S. developers for hotels, factories and housing projects.[52] Given foreign control of Puerto Rican development through unrestricted import of capital and technology and monopolies in marketing and transportation, it should not be surprising that construction and real estate speculation were among the remaining lucrative slots open to local profiteers. The Ferré family's Puerto Rico Cement Company supplied 93 per cent of Puerto Rican cement in 1971.[53] Eduardo Fossas, a director of Puerto Rico Cement, is also president of Metropolitan Builders, Inc., one of the largest construction firms in San Juan. The Rexach family has the biggest building company in Puerto Rico which, like other builders such as ITT (Levitt Town) and the Rockefellers (IBEC), is a heavy investor in middle income housing projects, luxury condominiums, and hotels.[54] In recent years investment has passed from hotels to luxury condominiums exemplifying a way in which the particular form of Puerto Rican tourism "undevelops" the country. Built for quick profits, sold to wealthy New Yorkers, then rented to tourists by development companies, the condominiums have taken tourists away from hotels while they employ very few workers. A serious source of competition for the hotels, according to Roberto Bouret, the condominiums in 1971 absorbed $282 million of investment capital versus $220 million in hotels.[55] According to Ernesto Díaz, head of the hotel workers' union, "This business is for the banks, the construction companies, and the wealthy tourists"—not for the Puerto Rican workers whose jobs it eliminates.[56]

The trend of unemployment contradicts the argument that tourism in itself generates employment. Capital pursues profit, not human welfare. Despite the claims of Puerto Rican and North American entrepreneurs that they have invested in Puerto Rico to provide jobs, when hotel workers through their unions increased their wage from $1.25 in 1966 to $2.20 in 1971 both investors and the Stanford Research Institute cited "excessive" wages as cause for investing in condominiums and cheaper labor areas. Despite the fact that hotel workers' wages have not kept pace with inflation, hotel management has blamed the failure of the industry on "high" wages and fringe benefits. In fact, it is the particular circumstance of dependent development that caused that failure: the rising costs of imported goods from the United States, deliberate mismanagement by U.S. chains and competition within the U.S.-based tourist industry.[57] Contrary to the claims of tourism's employment generating capacities is the fact that within recent years jobs have not expanded and that they probably will decline in the future.

According to the International Union of Official Travel Organizations, the jobs that tourism directly creates are relatively few.[58] Of a labor force of 926,000, 8,931 are employed in hotels in Puerto Rico.[59] The government argues that tourism provides 30,000 jobs indirectly, although no breakdown of these jobs is given.[60] As there are few secondary industries, the indirect jobs would probably be in transportation (airport employees, 4,500 in 1967, taxidrivers, 1,247 in 1967) and in restaurants (1,060 workers covered by the minimum wage in 1970).[61] Export-import houses, local distributors for hotels and restaurants supplies and retail stores employ relatively few people.

In assessing the employment generation of tourism, little attention is paid to the kinds of jobs that tourism creates for Puerto Ricans—at best, menial jobs in hotels and, at worst, employment such as prostitution. Nor do promoters examine the unemployment tourism engenders—especially in agriculture because of land speculation, land "developments," and use of the U.S. as a source of supply. A small but interesting example of the unemployment that tourism creates was a campaign to rid the streets of small vendors, including kiosks of sweets and fruits and magazine stands, because, according to the mayor of San Juan, they "make the city ugly and are not well seen by the tourists who visit us."[62]

This attitude, obsequious toward North Americans and discriminatory against Puerto Ricans, typifies the Tourist Development Company and Operation Bootstrap personnel who have believed that only U.S. capital and management know-how could "save" the island varyingly referred to as "culturally deprived," "hopeless, starving, sick" and an "underdeveloped agrarian society."[63] As one pro-Commonwealth spokesman answered an *independentista*, "Industries from the States did not come to the island as colonial exploiters. We begged and beseeched and cajoled industry to come. Sure, we offered them high tax advantages and high profits and lower minimum wages than they would pay in the States. So what? They rescued the island. Does life-saving have a price?"[64] This grovelling eagerness to let the United States "develop" Puerto Rico has led to the "un-development" of tourism. So anxious to serve the U.S. chains has the government been that it established no ground rules to regulate hotel mismanagement, profit remittance, physical and cultural pollution, land use or imports. Typical of the government's eagerness to please the foreigner at the expense of the Puerto Rican is the lavish use of scarce water and electricity by air-conditioned hotels—some with TV's in every room—while contaminated water is pumped into slums and towns. Hotels' use of these resources has pushed utility prices beyond the reach of the poor, while schoolchildren's meals are often cut because the faucets have been turned off and water is not available for cooking.

Tourism has required vast expenditures of capital with less and less visible return. In order to continue within the present framework, the Department of Tourism will have to spend greater sums. Roberto Bouret projects increased spending on promotion in the United States which the Puerto Rican Hotel Association has urged "even at the expense of public education."[65] To attract convention business, the Department of Tourism is investing $50 million in a center they have leased to Hyatt, one of the fastest growing U.S. hotel chains.[66] In keeping with the wishes of the Puerto Rico Hotel Association, Bouret has suggested the abolition of the casino chip tax and the introduction of slot machines—thus reducing government revenue while expanding gambling. Bouret anticipates decentralizing tourism in such a way that it would invade the lives of more and more Puerto Ricans. In a continued abuse of valuable land, he plans to turn coffee and sugar plantations into resorts. All the while, the Department of Tourism pounds its fists because giant corporations like Eastern Airlines will not cooperate with its expansion plans. Eastern's decisions have never been made on the basis of what is good for Puerto Rico.

The least tenable of the arguments put forward by Operation Bootstrap and tourism promoters is tourism's contribution to cultural understanding. While Conrad Hilton claims that his hotels foster international brotherhood, it would be difficult to convince the Puerto

Rican youths outside the gate blocking entrance to the Caribe Hilton beach. All over the world, Hilton and other chains provide "American style hotels for Americans."[67] "The day is not far distant," predicts *Business Week*, "when weary Americans will be able to sip a dry martini and look across the bazaars, souks, and thatched roofs of far-off cities, to see the familiar signatures of Howard Johnson, Holiday Inn, Ramada, Marriott, Sheraton, Sonesta, Travelodge, Western International, Intercontinental, and a host of others."[68] Hilton's cultural understanding rarely extends beyond the concrete flying carpet over the entrance to the Istanbul Hilton. So obtuse is the chain that one observer at the Tehran Hilton noted, "Except for a few oriental rugs and Persian chandeliers, the place could just as easily have been in Phoenix."[69] This cultural offensive has not been without opposition. For 10 years the Rome City Council blocked a building permit for the Hilton Cavalieri. "I guess they didn't want to see free enterprise in action there," comments a Hilton executive, "The Commies said the hotel was being built for billionaires."[70]

Promting tourism within the "free" enterprise framework involves selling a country as a product. As a Latin American businessman put it, "We have to do as good a selling job on our countries as Hawaii has done. I think we have more to offer."[71] Selling North Americans on travel has also been a project for promoters. As Somerset R. Waters, president of the Travel Research Association, said, "We have through advertising convinced the American public of the necessity of owning a home, having an automobile, and washing machine." Now the agencies have had to sell them on "the benefits of a vacation, the need to get away, to relax."[72] Today the biggest market for U.S. ad agencies after automobiles and liquor is travel, sold to North Americans through playing off the lowest common denominators of ignorance, impulse and fantasy. Travelling became an escape from the pressures, the isolation and dullness of American society. By means of "teaser" and "dream" advertising, the Caribbean became "The Great Escape Route."[73] For example, Americans learned that Puerto Rico was a tropical paradise of white beaches, rainforest, gentle breezes and romance—a virgin paradise without people, or, as ex-Governor Ferré optimistically called his country, "the sunporch of the United States."[74]

Otherwise, tourists learned Puerto Rico was a place to indulge. Typical of ads was one for the El San Juan. "For nights of fun and days of sun," it read, "the new exciting El San Juan Hotel." The ad pictured couples dancing around a pool. There was no sign of Puerto Rico or the Puerto

Ricans.[75] This omission was no accident. When the Virgin Islands Government Information Center tried picturing the people of the islands in an ad, *Advertising Age* promptly panned it:

> The reasons for visiting the Virgin Island—we are confident—are many, and most of them have to do with the pleasure, diversion, the relaxation, the comfort the visitor finds, rather than the background of the island people. If this ad really reflects the Virgin Islands we see little reason for going. We can find people such as those pictured on Staten Island and the fare is less.[76]

As a New York lawyer wrote:

> The important thing for New Yorkers on a winter vacation in Puerto Rico is to get out of San Juan in a hurry. We do not leave the bustle and dirt of New York, where 725,000 Puerto Ricans live in tall buildings, to see the bustle and dirt of San Juan, where 500,000 Puerto Ricans live in tall buildings; and the sight of expensive concrete hotels bristling side by side at a muddy beach is neither soothing nor exotic. The beauty and strangeness of the island lie outside the city.[77]

If tourism encourages a sense of national identity and promotes "cultural appreciation," as Terrence Cullinan says, in Puerto Rico it promotes a false sense of culture. To Puerto Rican and North American tourism promoters, Puerto Rican culture appears to be synonymous with selected elements of Spanish "culture." According to Victor M. Rivera, former director of tourism, tourism flourishes because of Puerto Rico's "old world Spanish flavor."[78] *Que Pasa*, the government-published tourist guide, boasts of the Spanish architecture, cuisine and entertainment in San Juan. As the high-class call girl Xaviera Hollander explains it, "That night he took me to romantic Old San Juan, where we ate a delicious Spanish meal, walked through the narrow cobblestone streets, and stopped in a quaint little bar to listen to flamenco guitar music."[79] Remodeled, set off by neon lights, and billed as Puerto Rican culture are the ancient fortresses built by African slaves, conscripted Spanish soldiers, Indians and mulattos at the command of the Spanish. With restored churches and convents, the forts form part of an artificial history unpeopled by Puerto Ricans. In their use of uninformed Spanish stereotypes, U.S. hotels and restaurants adopt names symbolic of Spanish exploitation such as El Conquistador Hotel, the restaurants La Reina, El Cabildo, El Cid, El Alhambra, and the gourmet dining room at the San Gerónimo, the Mesa Imperial. Decorator Jonathon Lannigan flew to Peru to find pieces of Pizarro's armor to deck the El Conquistador where the Sovereign Court dining room contains portraits of princes, kings, queens and pretenders in an aesthetic style dubbed "instant Prado."

To the extent that Puerto Rican culture is promoted it is either the "haute culture" of the metropolitan elite captured in the endless promotion of cellist Pablo Casals, or the bizarre quaintness of "local color" in "native" religious fiestas. At Costa Mermejo, a new resort in the southwest, local investors have broken ground to build a hotel and condominium cottage complex that will resemble the pre-Colombian villages of the Taino Indians. Scrupulously avoided or referred to in tourist guides as "eyesores" are slums like La Perla, the real evidence of North American impact on the island. Crouched between the sea and the walls of the Old City, La Perla absorbs those expelled from the land and the jobless of San Juan into make-shift shacks that regularly are washed away by Atlantic storms.

Beyond the image of Spanish and "primitive" quaintness, promoters try to give Puerto Rico the image of an international center offering Cuban, Argentinian and European cuisine along with "Lindy's Kosher," "Scotch and Sirloin," and "Beef, Bird, and Brew," at the Holiday Inn. One travel writer comments of Puerto Rican food, "You will not taste it in the hotels . . . Very rarely does a Puerto Rican dish appear on their menus and when it does, it is almost certain to be a modified version of the real thing."[80] Retail stores offer more of Mexican glass and Oriental silks than they do of Puerto Rican crafts. Anthropologist Eduardo Seda noted the bastardization of the Puerto Rican language to which this form of "internationalism" has contributed.[81] The Cocolobo Discotheque, Cecilia's Place, Tropimar and Bohio Bars, Fuente de Soda el Nilo, El Patio de Sam and El Gaucho Steak House are only a few of the linguistic deteriorations tourism has promoted.

Caribbean economists Karl Levitt and Iqubal Gulati have commented on the "type of tourist development which creates enclaves of privilege within which American and Canadian visitors by their mere presence demonstrate the social and economic advantages which accrue to wealth and color."[82] The Puerto Rican government believes that one of tourism's positive contributions is its attraction of "successful people from every part of the mainland."[83] These symbols of human success, which Puerto Ricans are evidently encouraged to imitate, are by and large white North Americans who earn over $25,000 a year.[84] To Puerto Rico they export the pleasures of self-indulgence away from productive work and social responsibility. Gambling, sex, overeating and overdrinking are their contributions to Puerto Rican development. "San Juan swings a lot more than any town from Miami south to Panama City," writes *Business Week*, "Have you sampled the casino at El Conquistador . . . big enough to house a 747? Or a lobster at Ladi's. . . . The deservedly big names are Americana and El San Juan, both with Las Vegas style entertainment."[85] Describing the "razzmatazz" vacations at El Conquistador, one promoter exclaimed, "It's Hedonism. It's opulence. It's the end of Western civilization."[86] Little wonder the Stanford Research Institute team should comment on "the growing impression that large numbers of visitors are affecting the culture and life of Puerto Rico unfavorably."[87]

Raul Vecenty Labiosa writes in *Claridad*, that sooner or later the United States dumps all its garbage on Puerto Rico.[88] With the surrender of Batista's Havana to the Cuban revolutionaires, Puerto Rico assumed from Cuba a $200 million drug trade in which large island dealers are linked with the New York and Florida mafia. Dealers have encouraged the use of drugs among the unemployed Puerto Rican youth so that on the streets of slums such as La Cantera young people inject themselves in broad daylight. With the proliferation of head and unisex shops, the Old City has become the center of a freak scene dominated by an ostentatious and mercenary form of North American homosexuality. North Americans also export a mercenary form of heterosexuality so well described by the "Happy Hooker" Xaviera Hollander, who spent the winter months of 1970 in Puerto Rico in a round of sex and drug orgies. Tourism's pretension to creating cultural understanding should be set against the real possibility that thousands of North Americans may never know anything more about Puerto Rico than what Xaviera Hollander depicts in her best-seller—its uses as a center for hussling.

Advertising has encouraged escapades like Ms. Hollander's. Every travel brochure pictures women on beaches, by pools, in bars and on stage in keeping with the maxim of American advertising that ads should picture "a particular type of woman, perhaps best described as the cocktail dinner date potential." Most of these women are blond North Americans. Puerto Rican women are expected to entertain North American men from less egalitarian positions—i.e. as secretaries, waitresses and night club performers. *Claridad* caught the "girlie show" at Louis Ferré's Hotel Borinquen in the spring of 1972:

Master of Ceremonies (In English): Let's see Evelyn . . . Let's see. . . . Are you wearing panties today? Come here, let me see. Ah! Evelyn is a good girl. Come, show these gentlemen. Come. Evelyn isn't wearing panties. Evelyn is from Bayamon—this is pure Puerto Rican meat.

Master of Ceremonies: Sandra. Again without panties? Good. Good. Sandra likes to walk about without panties. It's lots of fun. Right, Sandra?

After nearly an hour of watching the women, sometimes with panties and without bras, the master of ceremonies announces that the first part of the show is over.

Master of Ceremonies: Perhaps this part of the spectacle has seemed a little boring. But don't go away. Now comes the dirtiest part of the show.

Nude women then come out ambling among the tables where the wealthy executive clientele is eating, seductively displaying among other things, what ex-Governor Ferré has called 'the most Poetic part of the woman.'[89]

Prostitution in Puerto Rico has been encouraged by gambling. "The principal economic factor maintaining the financial stability of the tourist industry," gambling constitutes one-quarter to one-half the income of major hotels.[90] Casinos have brought organized crime to Puerto Rico. According to a former croupier, as early as 1962 the Americana sponsored junkets offering heavy gamblers room, board, drink and women. In the 1970-71 recession, the Americana, El Conquistador and El San Juan aggressively promoted gambling and junkets to increase profits.[91] In 1966, the Stanford Research Institute team noted the growing presence of organized crime in Puerto Rico:

Known syndicate associates have come to Puerto Rico in a way that suggests (to law officers acquainted with their operations) infiltration into management of some casinos. Some questionable business associations of at least one hotel owner have been reported to government officials.[92]

The report notes that leaders of organized crime made regular trips to Puerto Rico and suggests infiltration into ownership and management of a casino hotel and close associations with higher government officials who are stockowners in hotels.[93] Ex-Governor Ferré, for instance, is a close associate of Max Orovitz, a Florida operator linked with the syndicate abroad and the establishment of casinos in the Bahamas. Orovitz, who was indicted for stock fraud by U.S. attorney Robert Morgenthau, is a director of Maule Corporation, a Florida cement company in which the Ferré family holds large interests.[94]

The cultural offensive tourism has launched against Puerto Ricans has provoked a mounting counter-offensive. In 1970, *independentistas* invaded the Condado beaches to protest the hotels' pre-emption of public property. Pouring through the lobby of the Caribe Hilton and out on the beach, they were arrested and removed by order of Roberto Lugo, general manager of the hotel. When Dora Pasarel, Administrator of Parks and Public Recreation, supported "the beaches belong to the people" campaign, Lugo, who built his career in pre-revolutionary Cuba, told her that the Caribe's beach was a private "club," despite the fact the hotel is subsidized by Puerto Ricans' tax dollars. Backing the protest were the armed actions of the Comandos of Armed Liberation (CAL) who exploded 21 bombs one night near the Condado strip. In the spring of 1972, they bombed the Rockefeller's Cerromar hotel during a Miss Universe contest. Governor Ferré increased police and security expenditures from $63 million in 1968 to $138 million in 1971 flooded the Condado strip with many regular and undercover policemen. To make the Puerto Rican hotel workers more "responsive" to tourists' orders the government is spending increasing sums of scarce capital. In 1970, the Department of Tourism introduced Operation Bienvenido "to show citizens and workers how important a sincere welcome is to a tired, arriving visitor; how important it is to have a friendly atmosphere surround them during their stay. We try to promote once more the Golden Rule: 'Do unto others what you would like the others to do unto you!'[95] In 1972 the Tourist Development Company spent $155,000 trying to get Puerto Ricans to smile in its "Su Sonrisa Vale un Millón" campaign, only to see it cancelled—in their opinion—by the "disastrous image" projected in the United States by the strikes of water, light and garbage workers of the summer of 1973.[96]

NOTES

1. "As Good as Polaroid?" *Forbes*, March 15, 1967, p. 61; "New Life in the Hotel Field," *Financial World*, October 17, 1962, p. 10.

2. "Worldwide Boom in Jet-age Hotels," *Business Week*, August 8, 1970, p. 23; "Global Surge in Tourism Aids Hilton International," *Barron's*, August 9, 1965, p. 21.

3. Doreen E. Crompton de Calvo, "Tourism in Latin America," *Bank of London and South America Review*, April 1969, p. 206; "Tourism: A Durable Boom," *Financial World*, May 14, 1969, p. 6.

4. "Tourism: A Durable Boom," p. 6.

5. Harold E. Lane, "Innkeeping: A New Role for the Airlines," *Columbia Journal of World Business*, July-August, 1967, p. 44.

6. In 1964, the Hilton Hotel Corporation's Board of Directors voted to "spin off" international holdings as a separate company under the same management. Shareholders in the Hilton Hotel Corporation received one share of Hilton International for every two shares they held in the Hilton Hotel Corporation.

7. Lane, "Innkeeping," p. 2.

8. "There are too Many Rooms at the Inn," *Business Week*, June 12, 1971, p. 62.

9. "Reveille for Hoteliers," *Fortune*, September 1969, pp. 112, 146.

10. Ibid., p. 111.

11. "Fly American: Stay Americana," *Business Week*, August 12, 1972, p. 116.

12. "Will There be Tourists to Keep Them all Full," *Business Week*, November 2, 1963, p. 108.

13. "Reveille," p. 114.

14. "Hilton's Fortunes Ride the Jets," *Business Week*, July 1, 1967, p. 53.

15. "Royal Debut for Hotel," *Business Week*, November 2, 1963, p. 104.

16. "Hilton's Fortunes," p. 56.

17. "Will There be Tourists," p. 108.

18. "Reveille," p. 114.

19. "Conrad Hilton's International Shoestring," *Dun's Review and Modern Industry*, April, 1965, p. 50.

20. Crompton de Calvo, "Tourism," p. 203.

21. Stanford Research Institute, *Report on Tourism in Puerto Rico*, 1967, 11-13.

22. Terrence Cullinan, "Tourism Beyond the Rio Grande," *Texas Business Review*, August, 1969, pp. 221, 224.

23. David H. Davis, "Investing in Tourism," *Finance and Development*, March 1967, pp. 4-6; David H. Davis, "Potential for Tourism in Developing Countries," *Finance and Development*, December, 1968, p. 38.

24. *New York Times*, April 1, 1969, p. 16.

25. Robert H. Boyle, "Paradise Purified," *Sports Illustrated*, January 13, 1969, p. 22.

26. Eliezar Curet Cuevas, *Estudio económico de la industria del turismo en Puerto Rico* (Management Aid Center, Santurce, February 1971), pp. 2, 32.

27. PRIDCO, *Annual Report*, 1969; Estevan Dávila Díaz, "Ponencia ante la Honorable Comisión de Industria y Comercio de la Cámara de Representantes de Puerto Rico sobre la industria del turismo," August 13, 1973, p. 6.

28. Stanford, *Report on Tourism*, II-133.

29. Ibid., II-7, II-133.

30. Ibid., VI-98-99.

31. Ibid., VII-51.

32. "Chill Wind Nips Island Hotels," *Business Week*, April 3, 1971, p. 17.

33. Roberto E. Bouret, "Comentarios del Sr. Roberto E. Bouret, Director Ejecutivo de la Compañia de Fomento de Turismo ante la Comisión de Industria y Comercio de la Cámara de Representantes en Torno a la Resolución de la Cámara 137", August 14, 1973, pp. 2-4; "The Boom Heard Round the World," *Business Week*, June 28, 1969, p. 53; "Winter is Less Than a Wonderland," *Business Week*, March 7, 1970, p. 21; "Winter Vacations Shiver a Little," *Business Week*, December 13, 1969, p. 36.

34. "Clouds Over Puerto Rico," *Time*, May 24, 1971, p. 87.

35. Junta del Salario Minimo, *La Industria Hotelera* (San Juan, 1972), p. 59.

36. Curet Cuevas, "Estudio económico," p. 13.

37. Economic Associates of Puerto Rico, *An Analysis of the Trend of Operations in Eleven Casino Hotels in Puerto Rico During the Period 1965-1970* (San Juan, 1973), p. 1.

38. Junta dél Salario Minimo, *La Industria Hotelera*, p. 13.

39. Economic Associates, *An Analysis*, p. 25.

40. Ibid., p. 36.

41. "Air and Port Facilities Being Greatly Expanded," *Commercial and Financial Chronicle*, October 29, 1970, p. 10.

42. Crompton de Calvo, "Tourism," pp. 211-212.

43. See also, Bouret, "Comentarios," Economic Associates, *An Analysis*, p. 34.

44. Travel Research Journal, *Study on the Economic Impact of Tourism on National Economies and International Trade* (Geneva, 1966), p. 39.

45. Interview with Carlos Diago, Tourism and Development Company, San Juan, August 31, 1973.

46. Stanford, *Report on Tourism*, I-II-57.

47. "Other Governments Outspend States for Tourism," *Advertising Age*, July 18, 1966, p. 48.

This point is briefly made in John Dryden and Mike Faber, "Multiplying the Tourist Multiplier," *Social and Economic Studies*, March 1971, p. 68.

49. Crompton de Calvo, "Tourism", p. 203.

50. "Will There be Tourists," p. 108.

51. Mary Greenbaum de Zuleta, "More of the Same Won't Do," *The Nation*, October 23, 1972, p. 361.

52. Ibid.

53. "Ferré y su hijo, Una alianza para el progreso familiar," *Claridad*, June 25, 1972, p. 6.

54. "Land Boom in Puerto Rico Offers Many Opportunities," *Commercial and Financial Chronicle*, September 17, 1964, p. 8.

55. Bouret, *Comentarios*, p. 11; "Roberto Bouret discute el futuro del turismo en Puerto Rico," *El Mundo*, September 24, 1973, p. 16; "Tourism Facing a Bleak Future," *San Juan*

Star, August 15, 1973, p. 3; Young and Rubicon Inc., *Commonwealth of Puerto Rico. Tourism Development Comany. Special Advertising and Promotional Program, May-November 1971* (San Juan, 1973), p. 5.

56. Ernesto Díaz, "Los trabajadores, la industria de turismo y sus perspectivas," Ponencia presentada a la Comisión de la Cámara de Representantes que estudia las condiciones de la industria del turismo, August 8, 1973, p. 11.

57. For employers' arguments see, Stanford, *Report on Tourism*, VI-106, 110, II-100-1; Economic Associates of Puerto Rico, *An Analysis*, pp. 2, 5, 31; Ernesto Díaz, "Los trabajadores," p. 12; Young and Rubicon, *Commonwealth of Puerto Rico*, p. 5.

58. International Union of Official Travel Organizations, *Study* . . . , p. 43,

59. Ernesto Díaz, "Los trabajadores," p. 12; Curet Cuevas, *Estudio Económico*, p. 15.

60. Ernesto Díaz, "Los trabajadores," p. 12.

61. Stanford, *Report on Tourism*, II-14, VIII-45; U.S. Department of Labor, *An Economic Report of the Restaurant and Food Service Industry in Puerto Rico. August 1970* (Washington, D.C., 1970), p. 23.

62. *Claridad*, September 6, 1970, p. 7.

63. Evelyn Marvel, *Guide to Puerto Rico and the Virgin Islands* (New York, 1963), p. 18; "Bootstrap's Financial Arm Accelerates Industrialization," *Commercial and Financial Chronicle*, September 19, 1963, p. 60.

64. Ruth Gruber, "There are Few *Independentistas* in Puerto Rico, But . . .", *New York Times Magazine*, May 21, 1972, p. 44.

65. Bouret, *Comentarios*, p. 15; "Clouds Over Puerto Rico," p. 87.

66. Bouret, *Comentarios*, p. 19.

67. "Hilton's Fortunes Ride the Jets," p. 50.

68. "Worldwide Boom," p. 33.

69. "Hilton's Fortunes Ride the Jets," p. 54.

70. "Conrad Hilton's International Shoestring," p. 33.

71. "Selling South America to Tourists," *Printer's Ink*, June 12, 1964, p. 46.

72. "U.S. Tourism: A Big Job for Marketing," *Printer's Ink*, April 27, 1972, p. 23.

73. "Caribbean: A Travel Boom," *Printer's Ink*, July 10, 1964, p. 53; "In the Travel Field, What Makes Your Ads Memorable," *Advertising Age*, February 1, 1965, p. 77.

74. "Optimistic View of Commonwealth's Economy is Soundly Based," *Commercial and Financial Chronicle*, October 21, 1971, p. 2.

75. "San Juan Resort to Resort to Understatement in Ads," *Editor and Publisher*, June 8, 1963, p. 17.

76. "Dwelling in an Unreal World. The Virgin Islands," *Advertising Age*, January 18, 1965, p. 84.

77. Meredith M. Brown, *Saturday Review*, January 27, 1968, p. 44.

78. *Commercial and Financial Chronicle*, October 5, 1967, p. 2.

79. Xaviera Hollander, *The Happy Hooker* (New York, 1972), p. 126.

80. Marvel, *Guide*, p. 59.

81. Eduardo Seda, *Réquiem por una cultura* (Rio Piedras, 1971), pp. 53-54.

82. Karl Levitt and Iqubal Gulati, "Income Effect of Tourist Spending: Mystification Multiplied. A Critical Comment on the Zinder Report," *Social and Economic Studies*, September 1970, p. 326.

83. *Puerto Rico USA*. Office of the Commonwealth of Puerto Rico (Washington, D.C., 1969), p. 26.

84. Stanford, *Report on Tourism*, II-30.
85. "What's on in Puerto Rico," *Business Week*, January 2, 1971, pp. 49-50.
86. "Paradise Purified," p. 22.
87. Stanford, *Report on Tourism*, II-1.
88. *Claridad*, June 25, 1972, p. 6.
89. Translated by NACLA, "The Ferré Family," from *Claridad*, June 2, 1972, p. 6.
90. Curet Cuevas, "Estudio económico," p. 26; *New York Times*, April 1, 1969.
91. Ibid.; "Clouds Over Puerto Rico."
92. Stanford, *Report on Tourism*, II-19.
93. Ibid., VII-52.
94. NACLA, "The Ferré Family," p. 13.
95. "Fully Trained Employees to Greet Puerto Rico's Tourists," *Commercial and Financial Chronicle*, October 29, 1970, p. 10.
96. "Roberto Bouret Discute el Futuro del Turismo en Puerto Rico," p. 16.

Puerto Rico: The National and Social Struggle During the Twentieth Century*

Manuel Maldonado-Denis

The goals of this essay are to examine: (1) the problems and prospects of the Puerto Rican movement for national liberation beginning in the decade of the 1970s; (2) the problems and prospects for the Puerto Rican pro-independence struggle in the context of the electoral victory of the Popular Democratic Party during the elections of 1972, and (3) the changing international situation and its implications for the movement of national liberation in Puerto Rico. Although these three themes are obviously interrelated, they will be treated separately here for purposes of analysis.

Problems and Prospects of the Puerto Rican Movement for National Liberation Beginning in the Decade of the 1970s

Writing on the process of the conquest of Latin America by U.S. imperialism, Octavio Ianni points out that it was in the context of such a conquest that the victory of socialism in Cuba emerged. And it is in this context also that Puerto Rico slowly is being incorporated into the United States. "Perhaps," writes Ianni, "the destiny of those two islands symbolizes the limits of the historical possibilities reserved for the peoples of Latin America."[1]

Without any desire to enter into a polemic with the distinguished colleague on the issue of the degree of "incorporation" of Puerto Rico

---

*Translated from the Spanish by Adalberto López.

into the United States—an issue which in no way can be considered as a consummated fact—I believe that his perception of the problem is correct. U.S. imperialism does see in Puerto Rico the model, the archetype, of what should constitute "the strategy for development" of those countries denominated with the euphemism of underdeveloped. The triumphant Socialist revolution in Cuba is seen as the antithesis, the anti-model of dependent countries. This is so because the problem of the *dependency of Puerto Rico* and the obvious colonial status of the island makes us particularly susceptible to U.S. imperialist penetration. The origins of this dependency, as Ianni and other Latin American sociologists have correctly pointed out, have to be sought in the structures that have given birth and accentuated dependency and not in psychological interpretations of the national character, or "the docility of the Puerto Rican."

In contrast to the rest of Latin America, the Puerto Rican people have not yet been able to break with colonial structures—at least in their classical form. Based on U.S. imperialism's direct control of all forms of Puerto Rico's collective life, this reality takes on the character of a qualitative difference, not merely quantitative, when it is compared with such dependent countries as, for example, the Dominican Republic. This fact gives the anti-imperialist struggle in Puerto Rico its peculiar character, even if we could consider that, given the common enemy, dependency, in the case of Puerto Rico it is a question of degree and not a difference in species.

What I wish to emphasize is that the very nature of colonialism in Puerto Rico has profound consequences. It is not a question of a phenomenon purely at the superstructural level, but a global question that reaches the most remote levels of our collective life. Colonialism as a system has its own logic and legality. Thus, it reinforces and in turn is reinforced by the attitudes, orientations, ideas and beliefs that contribute to produce and to reproduce it.

It is not that colonialism had been tolerated passively by all of the Puerto Rican people. The continuous struggle of several sectors of the Puerto Rican people for their independence demonstrates the contrary. Nevertheless, the problem of that struggle was—both in the case of Puerto Rico and Cuba—that it had to evolve under socio-historical conditions that retarded independence until the end of the nineteenth century.

The independence of Latin America was achieved by internal and external conditions that were propitious. The internal social forces sought to put an end to colonial structures that were in irreconcilable conflict with the interests of the colonial creole elite. In this respect, Celso Furtado writes: "During the struggle for independence, one can perceive two movements which were present in the subsequent evolution of Latin America: on the one hand, there emerges a Europeanizing bourgeoisie which attempted to liquidate the pre-Columbian and colonial past; and on the other hand, there appeared forces which tended to break with the structures of domination imposed by the colonial regime and which sought to integrate the native masses in the socio-political structures and to define an autonomous cultural personality."[2] These internal forces were able to prevail in part because the international situation was favorable. Spanish imperialism was suffering the tremendous losses caused by her struggle to oust the French invaders from her territory. Also, England—which already visualized its role as the hegemonic power in the western hemisphere—aided the liberation movement in Latin America. Nevertheless, the restoration of Ferdinand VII in 1814 signified the elaboration of a Spanish policy determined to maintain, under all circumstances, control over Cuba and Puerto Rico; on the other hand, Spanish imperialism was determined to realize the reforms it had refused to undertake in those territories that won their independence. At the same time, the independence of Latin America was accepted by the newly emerging power, the U.S. as a consumated fact;   but with the clear reservation that the "status quo" was to be maintained in Cuba and Puerto Rico. The policy of the United States—expressed quite clearly in the Congress of Panama in 1826—was clearly against the independence of Cuba and Puerto Rico. Thus, the internal reinforcement of the colonial regime together with external circumstances (U.S. opposition to independence) retarded the liberation of the two islands.

When the struggle for independence matured in Cuba and Puerto Rico in the decade of the 1860s, the forces of world imperialism had taken the offensive and already were reaching the summit of their power. Sergio Benvenuto was right when he wrote recently that the Cuban movement for national liberation of 1868—as well as that of Puerto Rico in that same year—was made "against the universal tendency," since "three-fifths of the world—without counting Europe itself—and half of its population, fell under direct European control during the process of the Cuban struggle for independence (1869-1898)."[3] A North American historian, dealing with the same issue, states that "In the years from 1820 to 1900

Great Britain alone had added 4.75 million square miles to its territory, an area considerably larger than the total area of the United States. During the same period, the French acquired 3.5 million square miles and the Germans one million."[4] This historical circumstance—made worse by the development of U.S. imperialism that culminated in the war against Spain in 1898—affected the revolutionary process both in Cuba and Puerto Rico at the end of the nineteenth century. When Puerto Rico and Cuba fell under the direct control of U.S. imperialism, the latter decided to govern Puerto Rico directly, while reserving for Cuba a neo-colonial regime. It was the beginning of imperialist penetration into Puerto Rico under the North American aegis.

Under these circumstances, the anti-imperialist struggle in Puerto Rico had to face an expanding empire guided by a messianic ethic (in the sense that the U.S. considered its "destiny" bringing "civilization" to its recently-acquired colonies).

The military, economic, cultural and political penetration of Puerto Rico immediately after 1898 had as a goal from the very beginning strengthening dependency of its people in order to incorporate it. The Puerto Rican experience thus has great importance for all countries on the continent, since it illustrates how imperialism has proceeded in its goal of conquering the peoples of Latin America. In our case one has the most advanced case of the attempt to reduce a society to collective impotence.

If the Puerto Rican people have not yet achieved their formal independence, it has been because the class that could have achieved it never went beyond being what Gunder Frank has called a "lumpen-bourgeoisie." The Puerto Rican bourgeoisie of the nineteenth century never achieved the level of maturity and development achieved by the Cuban bourgeoisie of that period. As is pointed out below, the development of productive forces in Puerto Rico did not reach the development of those in Cuban society.

The process that led to giving over the national patrimony, which took place in Cuba and Puerto Rico beginning in 1898, caused Puerto Rico to follow the path of alienating the patrimony that we witness during the first four decades of North American domination, but with one important difference in comparison to Cuba: In becoming converted to a country with an export economy during this period Puerto Rico follows a road Cuba had taken already not without attaining in the core of society a bourgeoisie similar to that of Cuba. Puerto Rico's bourgeoisie is extremely weak and in a dependent position when it undertakes its reform projects—like other Latin American countries—under the slogan of "developmentalism" characteristic of the post-World War II period. But developmentalism within a colonial framework reinforced new forms of economic dependency and promoted the emergence of a parasitical class that identified totally with the hegemonic class of the colonial metropolis. As Ianni acutely observed: "The truth is that imperialist relations create parasitical social groups. It is obvious that structural dependency provokes distortions (deformaciones) in the productive structure of the subordinate country (by the proliferation of some sectors and the atrophy of others). In the same sense, it is evident that the relations of dependency create parasitical social groups; or, better, transform the dominant "native" class and also some groups in other social classes into beneficiaries of that dependency."[5]

The Puerto Rican bourgeoisie never reached a stage of development that placed its interests in contradiction to those of the metropolis. The nationalist sector of that bourgeoisie has been a sector of some numerical importance, but of little economic and political power. The "lumpen" bourgeoisie was formed as a class with ties to the metropolis and thus was unable and unwilling to think of and support Puerto Rican independence. Only the nationalist sectors less "integrated" to the metropolis can—by way of an alliance with the working class which has emerged at the height of "developmentalism"—constitute a force capable of breaking with the principle structural cause of dependence: colonialism.

It is the recognition that today only the working class can constitute the backbone of a movement of national liberation that has led pro-independence parties to realize that there can be no independence without socialism and no socialism without independence. In its origins, the Puerto Rican working class was composed primarily of agrarian workers such as sugar cane workers and tobacco workers (tabaqueros). It was a working class that lacked the necessary force to undertake the twofold struggle on behalf of social justice and independence. Moreover, its struggle was on the whole directed against the weak national bourgeoisie that emerged during the first three decades of North American rule. During the crisis of the colonial system that took place in the decade of the 1930s, the Puerto Rican labor movement was able to create an efficient instrument of struggle against imperialism through the founding of the General Confederation of Workers (CGT). But this organization succumbed before the divisive tactics and political clout of the Popular Democratic Party and its developmental project. The very same developmentalism, however, has contributed to the emergence and development of a large urban working class. It is this urban proletariat—properly organized and with an efficient instrument to channel its struggle—that constitutes the main hope for Puerto Rico's struggle to end the imperialist penetration that is like an incubus over its political, economic and cultural development.

When the urban proletariat emerged as a class *in itself* it was faced with becoming politically conscious and converting itself into a political class *for itself*, a force best suited to serve as the principal agent of revolutionary social change in Puerto Rico. Given these circumstances, the Puerto Rican proletariat has before it the only ideology that historically has represented the interests of the working class: Marxism-Leninism. The old ideology of North American "trade unionism" that directed the labor movements in Puerto Rico during the first decades of this century has shown its total bankruptcy faced with the situation of the Puerto Rican worker under a colonial-capitalist regime. Because of its understanding of the new historic conjuncture that our people are experiencing, the Puerto Rican independence movement has transcended the old schemes based on romantic and apocalyptic notions of the revolutionary process and has gravitated towards a Marxist interpretation of that process.

At the same time, the parasitical, ultra-dependent character of the Puerto Rican bourgeoisie is becoming more apparent every day. It is obvious that those social strata of the weak Puerto Rican bourgeoisie that embraced nationalism, when faced with the systematic process of expropriation to which they were victims under the wave of North American capital that fell upon our people during the first four decades of this century, were never in a condition to successfully realize an anti-colonial revolution in Puerto Rico. The very contradiction between its immediate interest as a class and the interests of the working class that dominate this period of our history impede an alliance of classes, a union of anti-colonialist forces against U.S. imperialist domination in Puerto Rico. Without the support of the working masses it was extremely difficult, not to say impossible, for the small national bourgeoisie to break with the colonialist yoke. That was made clear by the nationalist ideology itself, which was against the thesis of class struggle and favored the idea that the nation was a phenomenon "beyond classes." The working class itself failed to recognize its true enemy—imperialism—and disintegrated in internal struggles with the small national bourgeoisie. In the ideological hodgepodge spun from a mixture of Spanish anarcho-syndicalism, North American trade unionism and pseudo-revolutionary rhetoric extracted from the French bourgeois revolution of 1789, Santiago Iglesias and his supporters in the leadership of the Free Federation of Workers ended by creating ideological confusion in the Puerto Rican workers movement.

But if the Puerto Rican bourgeoisie of the first 40 years of North American domination in Puerto Rico was weak and parasitical, the present-day bourgeoisie, composed of import-exporters and inter-mediaries of the great industrial, commercial and financial firms of the United States, is more so. During the last 30 years the process of consolidating the dependency of the Puerto Rican bourgeoisie has increased by giant steps. Only a few sectors among small bourgeois-professionals, small industrialists, small merchants, etc.—see nationalism as a possible political and economic solution to the problem of depend-ency of Puerto Rico. But no one should deceive himself: the Puerto Rican bourgeoisie long ago exhausted its historical possibilities as an agent of social change in Puerto Rico. The only alternative open to the nationalist sectors of the Puerto Rican bourgeoisie at this historical moment is, therefore, to negate itself as a class and to incorporate itself into the struggle of the popular masses in favor of independence and socialism. That incorporation implies the adoption by the nationalist sectors of the bourgeoisie of socialist ideology.

Karl Marx and Lenin understood, in their time, the great importance of movements of national liberation in the struggle against imperialism at the global level even if one cannot deny that the former succumbed on occasion to the distorting prism, product of his own European formation. Nationalism is a reactionary ideology when it serves to create among the exploited masses a false consciousness regarding the character of their true enemy and to obfuscate the fundamentally internationalist per-spective of all revolutionary struggles. The typical case of this type of reactionary nationalism is found in highly industrialized capitalist countries such as the United States where the bourgeoisie very ably manipulates chauvinism and ethnic differences to derail working class struggles. But nationalism can be a progressive force when it takes the character of an anti-imperialist and anti-colonialist ideology. This proposition is singularly valid in the case of colonies such as Puerto Rico.

It is the case, however, of a progressive force which is so only when it participates in the process of national liberation conscious that once that liberation is achieved it has achieved its historical mission. It is here that a turning point confronts every nationalist movement in Puerto Rico, since once national liberation is achieved, there will be the tendency—so ably described by Franz Fanon—for the nationalist bourgeoisie to put on the shoes of the old dominant classes.

In light of the Puerto Rican experience, nationalism—as a catalyst of the anti-imperialist and anti-colonialist conscience of our people—has played a central role in Puerto Rico's political development during this century. It is this facet that has to be incorporated in Puerto Rico's struggle for independence and socialism to achieve a higher synthesis in which are combined the indivisible struggles, the self-determination of Puerto Rico and the socio-economic demands of the popular masses.

It is within this context that one must understand the conversion of the Pro-Independence Movement (MPI) into a Marxist-Leninist Party, the Puerto Rican Socialist Party (*Partido Socialista Puertorriqueño*), a conversion which was formalized on November 26, 1971, as well as the increasing radicalization of the *Partido Independentista Puertorriqueño* (PIP). The historical reason for the leftward shift of the national liberation movement in Puerto Rico has to be understood as part of a growing radicalization among broad sectors within the Puerto Rican independence movement with respect to the problem of the class struggle and the revolutionary changes that today are manifest on a world scale. In Puerto Rico the event of major relevance and influence in the new orientation of the movement for national liberation has been without doubt the Cuban Revolution. Revolutionary Cuba, as the vanguard of the Latin American Revolution, has provided pro-independence Puerto Ricans with the valuable example of combining theory and practice in the process towards national liberation and the construction of socialism.

The Return to Power of the Popular Democratic Party

The defeat at the polls suffered by the Popular Democratic Party in the elections of 1968* after a period in power of 28 days—led many to believe that the political hegemony of the *populares* had come to an end and that

---

*During the elections of 1968 875,000 people voted. The New Progressive Party led by Luis A. Ferré received 44% of the votes, the Popular Democratic Party 42%, The People's Party of Sánchez-Vilella, a former member of the PPD, received 81,000 votes.

a new era was about to begin during which the forces supporting annexation (i.e., statehood) who found themselves in power would bring about an inevitable and increasing polarization of Puerto Rican society between annexationists and anti-annexationists. One of the major results would be the shift of more sectors of the population to the cause of independence. This thesis of "polarization" was fed by the whole process of "revolt against institutions" that was evident on a world scale during the 1960s and that in the specific case of the   U.S. was summarized in the struggle against the war in Vietnam.

The elections of 1972 shattered the hopes of those who saw the expected process of "polarization" as a positive step towards independence and made us realize that in many cases we inserted our desires between theory and reality. We had misjudged the timing of the debacle of the Popular Democratic Party. Moreover—perhaps I should say worst yet—we overestimated the electoral force of a rejuvenated *Partido Independentista Puertorriqueño* which showed signs—at least in appearance—of becoming a viable alternative before the eyes of the Puerto Rican electorate on the eve of the elections of 1972. Neither of these things happened. The PPD won an overwhelming victory against its rival the New Progressive Party (PNP) (pro-statehood) led by Luis A. Ferré The PIP received barely enough votes to maintain its electoral standing and elected one senator and two representatives to the insular congress.*

In explaining the defeat of the PPD in 1968 two major factors must be taken into consideration: (1) the split within the party that led to the creation of the Partido del Pueblo by Robert Sánchez Vilella, a former staunch supporter of Luis Muñoz Marín and the successful gubernatorial PPD candidate in 1964; and (2) a growing and widespread discontent in the face of the long-term control of the PPD, which manifested itself in a vote of protest in favor of the *Partido Nuevo Progresista.* During its four years in the colonial government, the PNP undermined the basis of its 1968 electoral victory and became the victim of three parallel—though interrelated—developments: Widespread administrative corruption, and

---

*In spite of an elaborate media campaign in which he spent close to $3 million, Luis A. Ferré lost the governorship to Rafael Hernández Colón by close to 100,000 votes. The smashing victory of the PPD included control of both the insular Senate and the House of Representatives and 72 of the island's 79 municipalities. The only major urban centers lost to the PPD were San Juan and Ponce.

nepotism, which characterized the party's four years in power; stubborn efforts to push Puerto Rico towards statehood, which the majority of the Puerto Rican people clearly opposed, and the regroupment of the divided Popular factions in the old party and the channeling of popular discontent toward the ends designed by the PPD.

All of these factors led to the overwhelming defeat of the PNP in 1972 and the return to power of the most powerful political party that has existed in Puerto Rico up to the present. The PPD is an illustration of those Populist social movements so characteristic of many Latin American countries. Neither can one ignore the enormous influence Luis Muñoz Marín still enjoys among the masses of his party. Given the resurgence and recent victory of Peronism in Argentina one must admit the very important role played by populist movements in the Latin American context. The return to power of the PPD in 1972 has to be seen from that perspective.

However, in Puerto Rico, populism was skillfuly used to gain the support of large sectors of the Puerto Rican population without promoting the genuine and active participation of the masses in the making of decisions that vitally affect them. On the contrary, major decisions vitally affecting Puerto Rico's collective life—such as the project of Teodoro Moscoso to establish a Superport in Puerto Rico—are made by imperialist power circles looking after their immediate interests, and the Puerto Rican people have neither the first nor last word in the matter.

On the other hand, the crisis of the colonial economy that began to manifest itself in the end of the past decade has given no sign of lessening. On the contrary, it threatens to become even more acute. The best example of this is the high rate of unemployment and underemployment on the island. It is a case of structural problems inherent in the role that today Puerto Rico is assigned to play within the global economic strategy of imperialism. One can note in that context how the Puerto Rican economy has evolved during this century: from an economy dedicated to the monocultivation of sugar cane (1898-1940) to an economy geared to promoting medium and light industry proceeding from the U.S. through tax exemptions (1940-1959) and, finally, the establishment on Puerto Rican soil of great petrochemical companies. All this has brought about serious dislocations in the Puerto Rican economy, dislocations that have increased unemployment and have brought about an enormous rural-urban exodus and a great migratory movement.

It is obvious that the so-called "Operation Labor Force" that served as the focal point of the campaign of the Economic Development Administration had a relative success at a time when U.S. capitalism was riding the crest of the wave of prosperity that followed World War II. In the decade of the 1970s the situation is quite different. The United States no longer can dictate unilaterally the conditions for international relations. Both its economic and military might have suffered heavy blows during the decades of the 1960s and 1970s. The establishment of petrochemical companies in Puerto Rico and the project for a superport in Aguadilla must be seen in terms of the energy crisis the United States is experiencing, and within the framework of the new role that has been assigned to Puerto Rico within the global economic strategy of capitalism. In every case the government economists themselves have been forced to admit that the problem of unemployment is not being resolved, but it is becoming worse as a result of the programs launched by the Economic Development Administration.

The Changing International Scene and its Implications for the Movement of National Liberation in Puerto Rico

At the end of World War II the United States emerged not only victorious in war but also with an industrial apparatus practically intact and a monopoly over the atomic bomb. The Soviet Union, on the other hand, found itself decimated and destroyed after experiencing the barbarous invasion by the Nazis. All this was followed by the Marshall Plan, the Truman Doctrine, the Act of Bogotá. In the meantime, the dollar became enthroned as the dominant currency.

But at the advent of North American hegemony itself were born the forces which in the following period altered the correlation of forces on the international scene. In Asia the Chinese Revolution emerged triumphant, thus dealing a devastating blow to the pretensions of the U.S. to world domination. The Korean War demonstrated that the imperialist military apparatus was not invincible and that the people could triumph over their aggressors. Similarly, Soviet parity in the realm of thermonuclear armament re-established the equilibrium of a divided Europe threatened by the revanchism of John Foster Dulles. The Vietnamese victory at Dienbienfu signaled the end of imperialist hegemony in South-east Asia. And in the Americas, the triumph of the Cuban Revolution made it absolutely clear that a new historical period had begun in which progressive and revolutionary forces have altered the correlation of forces that existed at the beginning of the Cold War. Puerto Rico has not remained on the periphery of these developments. On the contrary, the movement for national liberation in Puerto Rico has been enriched as a consequence. Fidel Castro noted that "the correlation of forces has changed extraordinarily, in favor of peace, in favor of the progressive people." The colonial case of Puerto Rico had repercussions at the UN when its Committee on Decolonization declared that Resolution 1514 (XV) of the U.N. was applicable to Puerto Rico and that it was up to a special committee to decide how that resolution was to be applied.

Similarly, the PSP (formerly MPI) has established fraternal relations with socialist and anti-imperialist countries who have supported the Puerto Rican movement for national liberation. Among those countries that have stood out in this sense is Government and People of Revolutionary Cuba who have expressed a profound solidarity with the Puerto Rican people.

The end of U.S. hegemony and the ascendancy of progressive and revolutionary forces throughout the world have had, then, a beneficial impact on the cause of national liberation in Puerto Rico, especially when one observes that the crisis which the colonial metropolis is undergoing (Watergate, the fall of the dollar, rivalries with its capitalist allies) has broken the myths most jealously cultivated by the mass media servicing the sysem. Nevertheless, it is important to keep in mind that imperialism is not going to collapse tomorrow nor is it going to go down voluntarily. It is quite possible that the very decline of the metropolis that is being witnessed might lead to a hardening of its policies towards Puerto Rico, a prelude to a fascism produced by circumstances in the U.S. For that all Puerto Ricans should be prepared.

NOTES

1. Octavio Ianni, *Imperialismo y Cultura de la Violencia en la América Latina* (México: Siglo XXI, 1970), p. 18. (The emphasis is mine). See also, Andre Gunder Frank, *Lumpenburguesia y Lumpendesarrollo* (México: Era, 1971).

2. Celso Furtado, *La Economía Latinoamericana desde la Conquista Ibérica hasta la Revolución Cubana* (México: Siglo XXI, 1969), p. 37.

3. Sergio Benvenuto, "Una imagen del mundo en 1868," *Casa de las Américas* (La Habana), No. 50, 1968.

4. David Healy, *U.S. Expansionism: The Imperialist Urge in the 1890s* (Madison: University of Wisconsin Press, 1970).

5. Ianni, *Imperialismo y Cultura*, p. 42.
History PR, pages 427-430, G. 71

PART III

Puerto Ricans on the Mainland

Introduction

Every phase of U.S. capitalist expansion, past and present, external and internal, has served to disrupt and disintegrate Puerto Rican society. On the island corporate farming undermined the world of the small farmer and turned him into a plantation worker. Through the mechanization of agriculture and with the decline of the sugar industry the plantation workers were driven off the land and forced to seek alternative employment. In the city foreign owned industries and hotels used few workers but many resources and forced ex-rural workers into the slums or out of the country. Under the aegis of U.S. capitalism Puerto Rico exported its own people to the U.S. as cheap labor and imported affluent North Americans to consume local resources. The U.S. had the best of all possible worlds: cheap labor for the garment industry sweatshops, farms and restaurants and a de-populated island as a pleasure haven and military base at bargain basement prices.

Puerto Rican 'migration,' a subject studied by social scientists at the level of individual motivations, is best understood in terms of the larger socio-economic forces that transform societies (and "allocate labor") and dictate the terms and place of individual existence. While Puerto Rican farmers struggled to improve the cultivation of their crops, giant U.S. corporations bought their land. Sugar workers and their unions fought to improve wages, and the plantation-owners shifted production to other areas—leaving many without work or future. While hotel workers strove to improve salaries, the corporations filed bankruptcy papers. In demand as a source of labor in jobs that U.S. white workers refused, Puerto

Ricans became the reserve army of unemployed, underemployed, 'subemployed' who filled the seasonal needs of the agricultural interests and the low paying positions in industry and services. Most Puerto Ricans on welfare are employed: Their wages are below the subsistence level, and the state, subsidizing the profits of businessmen, must provide the difference. U.S. capital has pursued Puerto Ricans for almost a century, leaving them few economic and political resources to resist the vicious mechanisms that transfer their work into the wealth of others. The study by ther U.S. Department of Labor, *The New York Puerto Rican: Patterns of Work Experience*, amply documents the *conditions* created by U.S. capital expansion and its *impact* on the Puerto Rican people: disintegration of island society and reintegration as a reserve army of cheap labor on the mainland. Puerto Ricans are imported to provide essential services at low wages on demand, and institutions and officials perpetuate their oppressed position to serve the needs of the economy. López points to the "divisive" political and social consequences of the effects of the disintegration/re-integration phenomena in his essay, *The Puerto Rican Diaspora: A Survey*. The process of integration through subordination, while essentially a product of capitalist expansion (and serving its needs), is maintained and reinforced by social and political institutions. As Herbert Hill conclusively documents, trade union organizations far from serving as liberating movements, have functioned to confine Puerto Ricans in positions of low-paid unskilled laborers, reserving leadership and skilled work for white "ethnics." Puerto Ricans are prevented by the combined economic and social forces of the larger society from finding effective institutional channels for substantial change, and their discontent has found expression in individual and political forms of rebellion: The poet of the sidewalk, the social rebels and the revolutionary militants defy the dehumanizing conditions of existence. Alienated beyond alienation, the militant struggles to find a way back to his roots, to his people, to himself; to return again whole and face the multi-faced oppressors who torment his people — in the name of freedom.

Unlike the militants, the intellectuals seek explanations, or, better said, provide them; the bold provide answers, the prudent ask questions; the skeptics question the questions. Among the latter, Bonilla surveys what he prudently describes as the 'options' open to Puerto Ricans today. The problem he poses is not one of survival but of defining a need for what he describes as a "future vision of a state of the world satisfactory to us." In Cuba that need was met through a profound social revolution. In the U.S., resistant to any meaningful changes, public and private life deteriorates to the point where not only oppressed minorities but all those who are not solidly entrenched within the system will soon be forced to search for answers "beyond survival" in order to survive.

The Puerto Rican Diaspora:
A Survey

Adalberto López

1. The Migration

It is doubtful that historians will ever discover who was the first Puerto Rican to migrate from the island to the United States; it is certain that not many were doing so before the United States took Puerto Rico from Spain in 1898. In the second half of the nineteenth century a few affluent Puerto Rican students studied in North American universities, and a handful of Puerto Rican revolutionaries periodically spent time in New York City plotting against Spain, usually working hand in hand with Cuban revolutionary organizations in that city. Numerically more important and certainly less fortunate were the several hundred Puerto Ricans who migrated to New York in search of work or who traveled to California by way of Panama, usually after spending some time in the cane fields of Hawaii.[1] In any event, in the nineteenth century the Puerto Rican migration to the United States was insignificant; by 1910, 12 years after the occupation of Puerto Rico by U.S. troops, the number of Puerto Ricans living on the mainland did not exceed 1,600.[2]

In the first 40 years after Puerto Rico became a colonial possession of the United States, the island underwent a dramatic, often painful, transformation. On the wake of the military occupation by North American troops in 1898, the government in Washington and its insular representatives drafted and implemented a series of policies shrouded in the rhetoric of benevolent paternalism but designed primarily to facili-

316

tate the penetration of the island by North American capital and the operations of the dozens of U.S. companies that established themselves on the island in the early part of this century.[3] To facilitate the movement of people and the transportation of commodities, roads and bridges were built; to indoctrinate Puerto Rican children with the value system of the colonial metropolis—i.e. to "Americanize" them—schools were opened all over the island; to train a class of intermediaries and managers, Puerto Rico's first university was established; and to create a better living environment for metropolitan investors and the colonial officialdom, and, possibly, to create a healthier and therefore more productive labor pool, improvements were made in health and sanitation facilities. In 1917, Washington imposed U.S. citizenship upon Puerto Rico and thousands of young Puerto Ricans found themselves in the U.S. armed forces fighting and dying in Europe. Commercial relations between the United States and Puerto Rico grew rapidly, and the island quickly became one of the metropolis' most important overseas markets.[4] Simultaneously, there was a growing concentration of agricultural property in the hands of a few families and absentee North American corporations and the creation of a cash-crop, monoculture, plantation type of economy whose lifeblood was sugar and which led to the emergence of a large rural proletariat whose wages were low and who ordinarily spent part of the year unemployed.[5]

The full consequences of these developments on Puerto Rican society and their effects on migration to the United States remain to be studied and analyzed. One can observe, however, that between 1899 and 1940 the island's population grew from 953,243 to 1,869,255 (primarily the consequence of a rapidly declining annual death rate and a more or less stable birth rate)[6] and that during the 1920s and 1930s there was a growing migration from the rural areas toward the cities and from the island to the United States. With citizenship, Puerto Ricans were free to travel between the colony and the metropolis without the delays and restrictions imposed on other immigrant groups by the U.S. Immigration Service. By 1920 the Puerto Rican population on the United States mainland had risen to almost 12,000, with Puerto Ricans living and working in 44 of the 48 states. Ten years later there were some 53,000 Puerto Ricans on the mainland; by 1940 the figure was close to 70,000 (See Table I).

TABLE 1.* THE PUERTO RICAN MIGRATION TO THE CONTINENTAL UNITED

Year	Puerto Rican Birth	Puerto Rican Parentage	Total
1898	a	a	a
1910	a	a	1,513
1920	a	a	11,811
1930	a	a	52,774
1940	a	a	69,967
1950	226,110	75,265	301,375
1960	596,280	259,444	855,724
1970	811,000	618,664b	1,429,664b

a Data not available.

b These figures do not include third-generation Puerto Ricans. Estimates on the number of third-generation Puerto Ricans on the mainland range from 50,000 to 300,000.

*Sources: Laurence Chenault, *The Puerto Rican Migrant in New York City* (New York, 1938); U.S. Census data, 1940-1970; The New York Times, March 5, 1973.

TABLE 2.* THE PUERTO RICAN MIGRATION TO THE CONTINENTAL UNITED
STATES (1946-1971)

Year	Number of Migrants	Year	Number of Migrants
1946	39,911	1959	29,989
1947	24,551	1960	16,298
1948	32,775	1961	-1,754a
1949	25,698	1962	10,800
1950	34,703	1963	-5,479a
1951	52,899	1964	1,370
1952	59,103	1965	10,000
1953	69,124	1966	30,000
1954	21,531	1967	34,000
1955	45,464	1968	18,500
1956	52,315	1969	-7,000a
1957	37,704	1970	44,000
1958	27,690	1971	1,800

a Minus figures indicate that during that year more Puerto Ricans returned to Puerto Rico than Puerto Ricans migrated to the mainland.

NOTE: Keeping an exact record of how many Puerto Ricans leave the island every year to live on the mainland is impossible. Thus, all the figures above are rough estimates. In fact, the figures given for the last few years have been questioned by Puerto Rican militants on the mainland who feel that they are too low and the result of a deliberate effort by the Puerto Rican government to minimize the size of the number of people leaving the island. See, *New York Times*, September 7, 1971.

*Sources: For the period 1946-1964, Migration Division, Puerto Rico Department of Labor, Facts and Figures, 1964-65 edition; for the period 1964-1971, New York Times, September 7, 1971.

Although the causes for the massive exodus of Puerto Ricans from the island to the United States in the post-World War II period remain to be studied and analyzed in detail, the explanation for that exodus lies in a combination of rapid population growth in an island 3,435 square square miles in size, high rates of unemployment in Puerto Rico, the prospects of greener pastures on the mainland, efforts by the insular colonial government to channel "surplus" population out of Puerto Rico. The demand of U.S. corporate interests on the mainland for cheap labor, especially in the so-called "services" sector, agriculture, and highly competitive industries such as the garment industry also was an important factor.

It was in the years immediately following the end of World War II, however, that the Puerto Rican migration to the United States reached massive proportions. Between 1940 and 1950 an average of 18,700 Puerto Ricans migrated to the United States annually. In the decade of the 1950s the average rose to 41,200 per year, and in the 1960s it declined to an average of about 14,5000 annually (see Table II and Graph II). In 1953 alone, when the migration reached its peak, about 69,000 Puerto Ricans left the island to settle on the United States mainland. In 1960 the number of Puerto Ricans living in the states was almost 900,000 and in 1970 the number had increased to between 1.5 and 2 million, the figure varying with the inclusion or exclusion of third-generation Puerto Ricans (See Table I).

Between 1899 and the 1940s the rate of population natural increase in Puerto Rico rose rapidly from 14.3 to 20.1 per 1,000 of population.* In 1940 the population of the island was about 1,800,000; by the early

---

*This was due primarily to a sharp drop in the annual death rate (31.4 per 1000 in 1899 to 15.8 per 1000 in the 1940s) without a parallel drop in the annual birth rate (45.7 per 1000 in 1899; 40.6 per 1000 in the 1940s). *Facts and Figures*, p.3.

1960s it was over 2,500,00.[7] (It has been estimated that given the present rate of natural increase, by the year 2000 Puerto Rico will have a population of at least 5,000,000 persons).[8] Puerto Rico not only entered the decade of the 1940s with a large population per square mile, but also with a high rate of unemployment and underemployment that was not relieved significantly by the developmental program of the Popular Democratic Party of Luis Muñoz Marín. In spite of the construction of hundreds of factories by U.S. companies (attracted to the island by a variety of incentives such as tax exemptions) the economy was not able to absorb a growing labor pool. In fact, statistical evidence suggests that by the early 1950s the developmental program of PPD, with its emphasis on capital-intensive industrialization, aggravated the unemployment problem, especially in the agricultural sector, which became less and less important after 1940. In 1950, in spite of the massive exodus of Puerto Ricans which got under way in the 1940s, the rate of unemployment in the island was 13.7 per cent. In 1972 it was 12.3 per cent, while on the U.S. mainland it was 6.1 per cent. These rates, of course, do not include the tens of thousands of underemployed persons on the island. Whatever the claims of the Popular Democratic regime to having performed an "economic miracle" in Puerto Rico, it was abundantly clear to the vast majority of Puerto Ricans and to those visitors to the island who ventured beyond the self-enclosed world of the great hotels that poverty was widespread and that for tens of thousands of the island's population channels for economic improvement did not exist.

It was the chronic lack of employment on the island on one hand and the demand on the mainland for cheap unskilled or semi-skilled labor in competitive industries (such as the garment industry) and in the "service" sector (janitors, dishwashers, hotel maids, bus-boys, etc.) on the other that accounted primarily for the beginning of a massive migration of Puerto Ricans to the continental United States in the 1940s. The illusory hope of material improvement, of making it in the American dreamland, led tens of thousands of Puerto Ricans to migrate to the mainland. The migration was facilitated by low rates of air transportation between the island and the mainland that were permitted by the Federal Aviation Administration at the request of the PPD government. The latter facilitated and encouraged outward migration as an "escape valve" which it considered beneficial to the island's development and without which, given the patterns of economic growth established by that government, the rate of unemployment in the island would have been unmanageably high. In a study published in 1966, Dorothy and James Bourne estimated that given the rate of population growth and the patterns of economic growth in Puerto Rico in the post-World War II period, without outward migration the rate of unemployment in the island in 1970 would have been 24.7 per cent.[9]

From a demographic point of view the "escape valve" has indeed been successful since, as José Hernández Alvarez has pointed out, "the migration to the United States not only removed one-third of the island's population, but also meant that the children of the Puerto Rican migrants were not added to the population."[10] Alvarez also is quite perceptive when he points to the "escape valve" as an important factor in social control. Had it not been for the withdrawal of one-third of Puerto Rico's population, the social forces for change, which had been generated as a result of the revolution of rising expectations brought about by the PPD developmental program, probably would have propelled the island's population into much more severe situations of unrest and conflict.[11] It also is quite possible that the desire to maintain the population "escape valve" may in part explain why the PPD leadership gave up its earlier commitment to Puerto Rican independence and opted for closer relations with the United States.

GRAPH 1. PUERTO RICO'S POPULATION GROWTH (1930-1965)

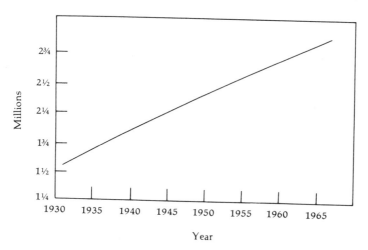

Year

GRAPH 2.   NET MIGRATION FROM PUERTO RICO TO MAINLAND (1946-1971)

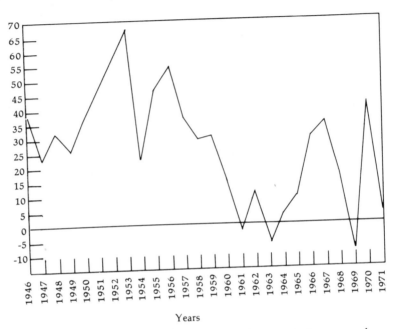

Years

Puerto Ricans, then, migrated to the United States in large numbers not because they hoped for more exciting lives in the big cities of the colonial metropolis or because they had any particular attachment to the U.S. way of life, but primarily because their economic situation had become intolerable on the island and the industrial cities of the mainland appeared to offer them jobs and a better material life. The vast majority of those who migrated were rural, poor, unskilled, relatively young, and seldom with more than a few years of elementary school education. That these Puerto Ricans were attracted to the mainland by the hope of material improvement is illustrated by the fact that at times of economic recession on the mainland the rate of migration declined, and many Puerto Ricans already on the mainland—who were often the first to be fired during such recession—returned to the island. During the mainland recession of 1953-1954, 1957-1958, and the early and late 1960s, the rate of migration from Puerto Rican to the mainland dropped, and the number of Puerto Ricans returning to the island from the mainland Increased.[12] (See Graph 2)

2. Puerto Ricans on the Mainland

Although by the late 1940s there were Puerto Ricans living in all states of the union, the vast majority of Puerto Rican migrants settled in the New York City metropolitan area. In 1950, 80 per cent of Puerto Ricans living on the mainland lived in New York City. By 1960 that proportion had declined to 60 per cent as more Puerto Ricans migrated from New York City, or from the island directly to industrial centers such as Chicago, Philadelphia and Jersey City. This trend led some observers to predict an internal "diaspora" in which the second and third generation of mainland Puerto Ricans would spread throughout the nation. In absolute terms, there is still a net migration of Puerto Ricans from New York City and from the island to other industrial centers in the United States (as evidenced by the results of the 1970 census). Nevertheless, the proportion of mainland Puerto Ricans living in New York City has remained stable at around 60 per cent. Also, the majority of Puerto Ricans who have migrated from New York City to other parts of the country have done so to areas on the eastern seaboard, often quite close to New York City (see Table 3).

TABLE 3 : THE TEN U.S. CITIES WITH THE LARGEST NUMBERS OF PUERTO RICANS ACCORDING TO THE 1970 CENSUS

City	Number of Puerto Ricans
New York City	887,119
Chicago	86,277
Philadelphia	40,930
Jersey City	38,033
Newark (New Jersey)	37,009
Los Angeles-Long Beach	31,210
Paterson (New Jersey)	24,113
Miami	18,918
San Francisco-Oakland	15,231
Boston	11,565

Total: 1,190,405

NOTE: None of the figures above includes third-generation Puerto Ricans.

In the 1930s and 1940s the majority of Puerto Ricans arriving in New York City were settling in Manhattan. And within Manhattan a large proportion moved into East Harlem in the Upper East Side of Manhattan, an area that became known among Puerto Ricans as *El Barrio*. Today *El Barrio* cuts deep into Manhattan, "on two square miles of the highest priced rock in the world," from the East River to Central Park and roughly from 96th to 130th streets on Manhattan's east side.[13] At the end of the nineteenth century East Harlem was mainly German and Irish. Italians began to settle there in the early 1900s, and by 1910 the Italian migration was so vast that Italians had become the second largest group in the area. Jewish immigrants were moving in at the same time as the Italians. By the 1920s East Harlem had become economically depressed and the Germans and Irish had virtually disappeared from the area. Italians and Jews also were moving out, and Puerto Ricans (and blacks from Central Harlem) were beginning to move in. Already in 1930, an Italian doctoral student was writing of an "invasion" of East Harlem by Puerto Ricans. "These people speak their native language, which is Spanish," he wrote, "and they are commonly called 'spics.'"[14] To describe the movement of Puerto Ricans into East Harlem as an invasion is misleading. The growth of the Puerto Rican population in the area was slow and in the late 1930s Italians still constituted the most important ethnic group in the area.[15] But by then it also was the home of the largest Puerto Rican community in the United States. It was during the decades of the 1940s and 1950s, when the exodus from Puerto Rico reached massive proportions, that the Puerto Ricans came to outnumber the Italians (the majority of whom moved out) and East Harlem became increasingly known as Spanish Harlem.

But East Harlem was not the only area of Manhattan being occupied by Puerto Ricans. In the 1950s large numbers of them were settling on the Lower East Side, the West Side and Upper Manhattan. Thousands of them were also moving into the other boroughs of New York City, especially Brooklyn and the Bronx. By 1960 there were more Puerto Ricans living in the Bronx and Brooklyn than in Manhattan. And in the course of the decade of the 1960s the trend among Puerto Ricans was to settle in the Bronx and Brooklyn. In fact, during the 1960s the Puerto Rican population of Manhattan actually declined, from about 225,500 in 1960 to about 185,000 in 1970.[16] The Puerto Rican population of the Bronx and Brooklyn, on the other hand, rose rapidly during the same period. Brooklyn, which experienced the largest increase of all five boroughs, had by 1960 a Puerto Rican population of 180,000; by 1970 that figure had increased to close to 400,000.[17] Richmond and Queens, refuges of an increasingly racist white middle and working class, did not experience such sharp growth in their Puerto Rican populations during that decade. In 1960, for example, Richmond had about 2,500 Puerto Ricans. Ten years later the figure had risen to about 5,000.[18] Within the Bronx the major areas of Puerto Rican concentration in 1970 were the South Bronx, Hunts Point, and Morrisania; within Brooklyn, Puerto Ricans generally were found in Williamsburg, Greenpoint and South Brooklyn (see maps of Manhattan, the Bronx and Brooklyn below).

MAJOR AREAS OF BLACK AND PUERTO RICAN POPULATION IN MANHATTAN, BROOKLYN, AND THE BRONX (1970)

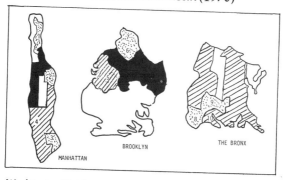

1. Washington Heights
2. East Harlem
3. Lower East Side
4. Lower West Side
5. South Brooklyn
6. Williamsburg
7. Greenpoint
8. South Bronx
9. Morrisania
10. Hunts Point

▦ Majority of Population Puerto Rican
▨ Majority of Population Puerto Rican and Black
■ Majority of Population Black

(*Sources:* 1970 Census data; *The New York Times*, March 6, 1972 and May 29, 1973).

Up to now, the type of Puerto Rican migrant we have been discussing is the migrant who moves to the mainland with the idea of staying for at least a few years. But there is another type of migrant who up to recently has been ignored by sociologists, government officials and Puerto Rican community leaders on the mainland: the Puerto Rican seasonal migrant.

The story of the Puerto Rican seasonal migrant remains to be told.*
What is known now is that by 1970, approximately 50,000 Puerto
Ricans—most of whom are young (21-30), married and have had less
than 5 years of schooling—migrated from Puerto Rico to the United
States to work on mainland farms (mainly in Connecticut, Delaware,
Massachusetts, New Jersey, New York, Ohio and Pennsylvania) for
periods of six to nine months before returning to the island. Just as the
migration of other Puerto Rican migrants has been encouraged and
facilitated by the government of Puerto Rico, U.S. business and the U.S.
government, the migration of Puerto Rican seasonal migrants has been
encouraged by Puerto Rican and U.S. labor contractors as well as agro-
businessmen in need of cheap seasonal labor.

3. Spicks, Spiks, or Spics? The "Puerto Rican-Americans"

The tens of thousands of Puerto Ricans who migrated to the U.S.
mainland with hopes of somehow "making it" in the American dreamland, did not find the green pastures they had expected. Wherever they
settled, the vast majority of them found themselves sharing with blacks
and, in California, with the Chicanos the poverty and degradation of
ghetto life. The women were overworked and underpaid in bleak
garment factories, the men usually got the dirtiest and least rewarding
jobs (those white workers refused to take), and they were all usually the
proverbial "last to be hired and first to be fired." During the 1950s there
appeared to be some marginal improvements, but Puerto Ricans still
remained at the bottom of U.S. society. Ghetto life in *El Barrio*, one of the
worst slums in the country, the Lower East Side, the South Bronx, and in
sections of Chicago, Philadelphia and other industrial centers continued
to be for Puerto Ricans a nightmare of cold winters in unheated and
roach-infested apartments, of decaying and overcrowded buildings
owned by unconcerned and rapacious landlords. It was a world of
unsympathetic and bigoted social workers and teachers, brutal policemen, broken families, small children bitten by rats and young men and
women driven by their surroundings and hopelessness to crime and drug
addiction.[20] In these circumstances and usually in years when the job
market on the mainland was tight, thousands of Puerto Ricans returned

---

*Ricardo Puerta, a young Puerto Rican scholar, has made a beginning and his study should
be coming out within a year or so.

to the island.[21] But the majority of Puerto Ricans in the United States, who felt that they could not hope for a better life in their homeland, remained in the ghettos of the mainland cities and returned periodically to the island for brief visits. The seasonal migrants, overworked, underpaid and crowded into unsanitary living conditions, were exploited by corporate farmers for the harvest of fruits and vegetables destined for the tables of an America oblivious to their plight. Here and there a Puerto Rican would make it up the economic ladder into a white collar job or profession. A rare few made use of their successes to attempt to do something about the conditions under which their compatriots lived, worked and died. The majority of these upwardly mobile individuals either returned to the island or disappeared into the suburbs or "respectable" neighborhoods, sometimes anglicizing their names or passing themselves off as Spaniards to avoid being labelled "spics" by their racist suburban neighbors.

Perhaps most tragically of all, as the years passed thousands of Puerto Ricans internalized the prejudices of the very society that was exploiting and humiliating them. White Puerto Ricans who on the island had lived next to black Puerto Ricans, now avoided black Americans and often referred to them as "niggers"; black Puerto Ricans often did their best to emphasize their Puerto Rican-ness so as not to be confused with American blacks. And there were a few Puerto Ricans who believed that other Puerto Ricans on the mainland were what they were said to be by the racist society to which they had migrated: drifters, thieves, criminals, loud-mouth dirty people who had moved to the mainland solely to get on welfare roles. This process of internalization of anti-Puerto Rican prejudice among many Puerto Ricans was strengthened by a variety of factors. In the schools Puerto Rican children who often knew only a few words of English were given I.Q. tests in English designed for middle-class whites. They did poorly and were then told, often quite bluntly by unsympathetic teachers, that they were just plain stupid. Guidance counsellors in schools did their best to channel Puerto Rican junior high school graduates into trade schools. Working on the premise that Puerto Rican students were not college material, they often told those students and their parents that it was not in the students' best interest to go to high schools designed to prepare students for college. In the Lower East Side of Manhattan in the mid-1950s young bright Puerto Ricans were pushed by unconcerned and bigoted school officials into schools where they were taught to chop meat, fix cars, clean airplanes, or cook in the city's restaurants, while less intelligent white students went to the more academic high schools and from there on to college. During the late 1950s the number of Puerto Rican students in "prestigious" New York City public high schools (Stuyvesant, Bronx High School of Science, and Brooklyn Technical High School) was infinitesimal. In 1962, in a graduating class of almost 700 students in Stuyvesant High School in Manhattan, there were only three Puerto Ricans.

The biased nature of the mass media in cities such as New York strengthened the tendency of some Puerto Ricans to turn against other Puerto Ricans. English language (e.g. *The Daily News*) and Spanish language newspapers (all owned and controlled by non-Puerto Ricans) invariably sensationalized the crimes of Puerto Ricans and gave Puerto Rican readers an image of their people as criminals.

Given the institutional constraints and prejudices of the society in which they lived, the nature of the mass media, and the attitudes of teachers and those in charge of shaping educational policy in the educational system of the cities, it is not surprising that many Puerto Ricans came to feel ashamed of being Puerto Ricans.*

In spite of the discrimination and humiliations to which they were subjected, the Puerto Ricans in industrial cities such as Chicago and New York remained politically passive in the decades of the 1940s and 1950s. It was not that they were not interested in politics; it was simply that the gateways to political participation were closed to them. In New York City Puerto Ricans were kept from political participation first by a literacy test that was conducted in English; then, as the Board of Elections became "enlightened," by an equivalent sixth grade educational requirement that most first generation Puerto Ricans did not meet. Also, the vast majority of politically inclined Puerto Ricans (who within the Puerto Rican community constituted a minority) were kept, directly

---

*I grew up in the Lower East Side of Manhattan in the 1950s and I was among those who were ashamed of being Puerto Rican. In the junior high school I attended the guidance counsellors wanted me to go to a school for meatpackers. I had to sell my soul to go to one of the prestigious high schools in the city. In high school, to the surprise of my teachers, I did superbly well. And I actually believed what I was constantly being told by the teachers and white students: that I was "different" from other Puerto Ricans; that I was an "exception." What little was left of my soul I sold to go to college. It was only after I left the nightmare of the ghetto that I realized what New York City had done to me and to thousands of other Puerto Ricans. True, I "made it" in the American dreamland, but the price I've paid has been exceedingly high.

or indirectly, from joining political clubs that were dominated by old-line Italians and Irish.

Within the Puerto Rican ghettos community organizations appeared to try to cope with some of the social and economic problems of Puerto Ricans, but these organizations rarely drew national attention or funds and ordinarily limited themselves to asking for small and inadequate funds from urban government. Occasionally, an enterprising and clever Puerto Rican with political ambitions would learn the intricacies of urban politics, creep into the urban political power structure, and by delivering periodically some Puerto Rican votes for non-Puerto Rican politicians, would often end up with minor positions in the administrations and staffs of those whom they had helped to elect. But these individuals were few, and the Puerto Rican who was himself elected to office was rare. In 1937 a Puerto Rican was elected to the New York State assembly, a feat that was not repeated till 1953. Compared with the modest achievements of black and Chicano *politicos*, those of the Puerto Ricans were insignificant. There was not among them even a counterpart of the black NAACP or the Chicano LULAC (League of United Latin American Citizens), save the somewhat ineffectual Council of Puerto Rican and Spanish Organizations of Greater New York founded in 1952 by Puerto Rican *politicos* to "get out the vote." Throughout the 1950s more and more Puerto Rican workers joined labor unions, but within these unions they were discriminated against and rarely enjoyed any power or influence. Among labor union leaders anti-Puerto Rican sentiment was as rampant as it was among the white workers whom those leaders represented.

Then came the chaotic—to some, the glorious—decade of the 1960s. The black civil rights movement became more aggressive. Riots exploded in the black ghettos of several cities. In 1966 Stokely Carmichael made popular the phrase "black power." Soon other young black militants like H. Rap Brown were breaking with the pacifist and legalistic approach of their elders in the civil rights movements and calling for black self-assertion, black pride, and black independence. It was around this same time that the Black Panther Party came into being.

The Chicanos in California and the Southwest took a page from the book of the spreading Black Power movement and they, too, became more militant in their struggle to put an end to the exploitation and degradation to which they had been subjected and were being subjected. Militant Chicano organizations came into being and Chicano marches and demonstrations became common. In California, Cesar Chavez organized Chicano agricultural workers and in 1965 launched the by-now historic strike against the grape growers of the southern part of that state. In New Mexico the glory-shouting Assembly of God evangelist, Reis López Tijerina, first challenged the validity of the state's claims to certain public lands. He then made his much-publicized courthouse raid in Tierra Amarilla, which instantly turned him into a hero of the left in the United States. While Chavez and Tijerina were drawing national attention, Chicano street gangs in East Los Angeles were outfitting themselves as Brown Berets, and Chicano students in universities throughout California and the Southwest were forming aggressive associations that demanded more emphasis on the history and culture of their people.

With blacks and Chicanos attracting federal attention, federal funds, and liberal sympathy and admiration, the American Indians, one of the most ignored and brutalized minorities in the United States, launched their own militant movement with an ideology and approach similar to that of the blacks and Chicanos. The Puerto Ricans, too, were stirred by the developments of the 1960s and they came to the attention of the nation. Riots exploded in Puerto Rican ghettos in the east. New York *políticos* of Puerto Rican background who in the past had operated under the shadows of Democratic politicians suddenly rediscovered themselves as Puerto Ricans. They set out to mobilize the Puerto Rican communities in the same way as Black and Chicano *políticos*, and their job was facilitated by the abolition in New York City of previous requirements which had disenfranchised the vast majority of Puerto Ricans in that city. In 1965 Herman Badillo, who when speaking to Puerto Rican audiences presented himself as 100 per cent Puerto Rican but who in front of non-Puerto Rican groups de-emphasized his Puerto Rican-ness, became the first Puerto Rican to be elected a New York City borough (the Bronx) president. In 1971, he became the first Puerto Rican ever to hold voting membership in the U.S. House of Representatives and in the following year was one of the main contenders for the Democratic nomination for mayor of New York City. By 1965, New York office holders included a Puerto Rican city councilman, a justice of the civil court, a State Senator and three State Assemblymen.

Just as Puerto Rican *políticos* were becoming more active in Puerto Rican communities, many young Puerto Ricans—many of them second and third generation—became more militant on behalf of those communities. Black militants had founded Black Panthers and Chicano militants the Brown Berets; in the late 1960s young Puerto Rican militants set out to imitate that pattern. In 1967 a Chicago Puerto Rican street gang, the Young Lords, turned political and quickly became the most militant organization of Puerto Rican youth in the United States. In the fall of 1968 the group took over Armitage Street Methodist Church, renamed it the People's Church, and turned it into its headquarters, a day care center and a health clinic. While busy working for their communities in Chicago, the Puerto Rican militants of the Young Lords Organization were also busy building coalitions with other community organizations and with militant Puerto Rican groups in other cities. Close contacts were established with young militants in New York City who became affiliated with the Chicago-based group. In 1969, however, the New York group split with the Chicago group over the issue of tactics and the importance of ideology in their movement and founded the Young Lords Party.[22]

Like the Black Panthers, the Young Lords Party was organized into ministerial divisions with specified lines of authority and levels of responsibility. Based in the Bronx and led by young Puerto Ricans like Pablo "Yoruba" Guzmán, Juan "Fi" Ortíz, and Felipe Luciano, the Young Lords Party set out to do in the Puerto Rican ghettos of New York what the Black Panthers and Brown Berets were trying to do in black and Chicano ghettos: to end the exploitation and humiliation to which Puerto Ricans were being subjected and to create in them a sense of pride. "We will not allow the brutalization of our community to go without any response," Felipe Luciano declared. "For every Puerto Rican who is brutalized, there will be a retaliation."[23]

In December 1969 the First Spanish Methodist Church in *El Barrio* was occupied by armed members of the Young Lords Party for 11 days. During the occupation the Young Lords organized a program of free breakfasts for Puerto Rican children, a day care center, and a program for the distribution of clothing to people in the community. They founded a newspaper, *Palante* ("Forward"). And in July 1970 they led a group of almost 200 Puerto Ricans in an occupation of Lincoln Hospital, a squalid 346-bed institution that was created as a nursing home for runaway slaves in 1839. The hospital had been universally deplored as inadequate and obsolete but served 400,000 residents in the South Bronx.[24] The goal of the occupation of the hospital, commonly known among the residents of the South Bronx as "the butcher shop," was to dramatize conditions in the hospital and to make it more responsive to the health needs of the Puerto Ricans and blacks of the South Bronx. After a 12-hour occupation of the hospital, the Associated Press quoted Dr. Antero Lacot, the hospital's chief administrator, as saying that the Lords did a service to the community by dramatizing conditions at Lincoln.[25]

There can be no doubt that the riots that occurred in Puerto Rican ghettos, the activism of Puerto Rican *politicos* and the growing militancy of Puerto Rican youth in the decade of the 1960s had some important and beneficial results. Perhaps most important of all, in the course of the late 1960s Puerto Ricans developed a sense of pride in being Puerto Rican that had been absent among many Puerto Ricans in the past. Being Puerto Rican was no longer a source of shame, but a source of pride, and the phrase "Puerto Rican is beautiful" became as common within Puerto Rican ghettos as the phrase "black is beautiful" was within black ghettos. But the activism of the late 1960s had other positive results. The plight of a people that in the past had been ignored, suddenly came to the attention of the federal as well as city and state governments and institutions of higher learning. Reluctantly the government set out to pacify the increasingly restless Puerto Rican communities by meeting some of their demands. Federal and municipal funds were provided to support community projects and finance housing developments. State and city administrations increased the number of Puerto Ricans working for them. Pressures were brought upon labor unions to open up more opportunities for Puerto Rican workers. Programs were introduced to try to curb police brutality. At Lincoln Hospital more Puerto Ricans were added to the staff. Dr. Julio Cesar Galarce, a Puerto Rican, replaced Dr. Antero Lacot as head administrator of the hospital and Dr. Helen Rodriguez, also Puerto Rican, was named to replace Dr. Arnold Einhorn as chief of pediatrics.[26] In the public educational system programs were launched to meet the needs of Puerto Rican students. More Puerto Rican teachers were hired, bi-lingual programs were introduced, and in many schools (even at the elementary level) courses on Puerto Rican history and culture were created.

Changes occurred at the college and university level also. To meet the demands of young Puerto Rican militants in the South Bronx, Hostos Community College was founded there in 1969. Its president, Candido de León, became the first Puerto Rican in the United States to hold the post of college president. Throughout the state of New York, where the vast majority of Puerto Ricans on the mainland reside, the State

University system launched a program designed to bring more Puerto Rican students to its campuses. In the City University of New York (CUNY) a program of open admissions was instituted that quickly brought about a rapid increase in the number of Puerto Rican students in CUNY units. Even private institutions set about recruiting Puerto Rican students and setting aside scholarship funds to finance their education.

The Puerto Rican students who entered the universities (especially those in New York State) in the late 1960s and early 1970s were on the whole the children of the ghetto, and they carried with them the militancy of ghetto youth. In many campuses of New York State they pressured university, college and community college administrations to establish Puerto Rican studies programs or departments. By the beginning of the decade of the 1970s such programs or departments existed in Brooklyn College, Manhattan Community College, Bronx Community College, Queens College, the State University of New York at Buffalo, and several other CUNY and SUNY units in the state.[27] In addition, by the early 1970s there existed Puerto Rican research centers at SUNY-Buffalo, Queens College, Brooklyn and CUNY. The demands of Puerto Rican students for the creation of Puerto Rican studies programs and research centers were accompanied by demands for courses on Puerto Rican history and culture and the problems of Puerto Ricans in the United States, and for Puerto Rican faculty members to teach them.

But in spite of the sound and fury of the 1960s, governmental and institutional efforts to cope with some of the problems faced by Puerto Ricans on the mainland were feeble when seen in terms of the magnitude of the problems of Puerto Rican communities. Furthermore, these meager efforts to cope with community problems became less and less visible during the 1970s. Many militant organizations were victimized by police repression, infiltration and frame-up trials; others lost their initial vigor. Community leaders were coopted into government jobs, and riots in the ghettos came to an end. A feeling that the "crisis" that had overwhelmed the nation in the 1960s had ended became increasingly pervasive. The sense of urgency to do something about the plight of Puerto Rican communities became less marked; and federal funds to support community projects were rapidly cut down. A subtle reaction against the demands of Puerto Rican and other minority groups for social jutice set in, a reaction that picked up momentum after the re-election of Richard Nixon in 1972. Formal compliance with the legal requirements of "affirmative action" led to the drafting of reports, the gathering of statistics and the preparation of goals for the future. These were substitutes in most instances for implementation of those goals.

Thus, in the early 1970s the vast majority of Puerto Ricans living on the mainland remained concentrated in bleak ghettos where life continued to be as nightmarish as it had been in the past. The descriptions published in the 1950s and 1960s of the poverty and squalor of life in *El Barrio* were still applicable in the early 1970s. By then the South Bronx, where tens of thousands of Puerto Ricans lived, was still one of the most terrifying slums in the United States. In January 1973, Martin Tolchin of *The New York Times* described the South Bronx as "violent, drugged, burned out, graffiti-splattered and abandoned. Forty per cent of the 400,000 residents are on welfare, and 30 per cent of the employable are unemployed."[28] "Rage is a condition of life in the South Bronx," wrote Tolchin, "it permeates the rubble-strewn streets and the unheated tenements. It blazes in the eyes of youth gang members and smolders in the brooding faces of mothers huddled on predawn lines at welfare centers and stacked in rows of benches in hospital emergency rooms and clinics, where many wait an entire day to see a physician."[29] The South Bronx, said Dr. Harold Wise, founder of the Martin Luther King Jr. Health center, "is a necropolis—a city of death."[30] Even for a native New Yorker, the voyage across the Willis Avenue Bridge is a journey to a foreign country; rage and fear are the overriding emotions in a landscape of despair, a world of youth gangs (over 130 of them), dilapidated schools and burned out buildings. The South Bronx is the most devastated area in New York City and probably in the nation. Perhaps not as terrifying, but still nightmarish are the Puerto Rican ghettos of the Lower East Side of Manhattan, South Brooklyn, Williamsburg and Greenpoint.

In spite of some progress made in the educational system in the 1960s, during the 1970s it was still relatively unresponsive to the needs of Puerto Rican students. The assumption that Puerto Rican children were stupid remained widespread among many teachers who were charged with educating those children. Criteria to evaluate "intelligence" and potential educational attainment remained essentially white middle-class. Thus, it was not surprising that the dropout rate of Puerto Ricans in public schools remained exceedingly high. In the public high school school system of New York City, for example, the dropout rate of Puerto Ricans between their junior year in December 1969, and what would have been senior graduation in 1970 was 58.2 per cent. The figure for black students was 51.4 per cent, and 27.2 per cent for whites and others.[31] At the college and university level, the situation was no better during the early 1970s. Whereas in 1971 almost 23 per cent of children in public schools in New York City were Puerto Rican, only 4 per cent of the student body of CUNY and less than 1 per cent of the student body in the State University system was Puerto Rican. In that year only 1.5 per cent of the Puerto Rican population of New York City had received a college education.[32] In colleges and universities Puerto Rican studies programs and departments were coming under increasing criticism by increasingly hostile faculties and administrations. "What will majors in Puerto Rican studies find to do?" they ask, while cheerfully passing out undergraduate degrees in eighteenth century French drama and medieval history.[33]

In the early 1970s the rate of unemployment among employable Puerto Ricans in New York City was over 10 per cent (a figure that does not include under-employment). Of those employed only 2 per cent were professionals while 70 per cent were concentrated in the unskilled, semi-skilled and service jobs that are the most low paid.[34] According to a report published by the U.S. Department of Labor in 1971, "Puerto Rican workers were the most deprived of all workers residing in New York City's major poverty neighborhoods. They were far more likely than others to be unemployed or to hold lower paying jobs."[35] In labor unions the numbers of Puerto Rican workers in the early 1970s were higher than they had been in the past, but policies to keep them out of the high-paying trades and union training programs were still widespread. In the higher echelons of labor union organizations the few token Puerto Ricans enjoyed little if any influence at all.

As in the past, in the 1970s the plight of Puerto Rican seasonal migrants still was ignored, although there were some attempts to bring the migrants' situation to the attention of the nation. Most of these migrants were from the poorest municipalities in Pueto Rico such as Las Marias where the per capita income is $413 a year, and Comerio where it is $418. In the states these workers continued to work from dawn to dusk and to live in dilapidated row houses without adequate sanitary facilities. They did not have the federal protection allowed to non-migrant workers. Irate over the living conditions of Puerto Rican migrant workers in the states, a group of churchmen and others in Puerto Rico established in 1970 the Permanent Committee of Support and Solidarity with Puerto Rican Migrant Farm Workers. One of the goals of the new group was to solicit funds for an orientation campaign to alert Puerto Rican farm workers to the problems they will face on the mainland and to tell them where to go to voice their grievances. The group also hoped to bring Cesar Chavez to the island "to impress on him the importance of extending his drive to unionize migrant farm workers to the East Coast as he did with grape pickers in California"[36] At the time of the creation of the Permanent Committee, the Puerto Rican Lawyers Association petitioned Luis A. Ferré, governor of Puerto Rico at the time, to stop sending migrant workers to farms in New Jersey after the Association conducted its own investigation of those farms.[37] But these efforts were not particularly successful. Cesar Chavez showed very little interest in the plight of Puerto Rican migrant workers, the Permanent Committee found it difficult to get funds, and the Puerto Rican government continued to facilitate the movement of seasonal migrant workers from the island and back. Even after the defeat of Ferré in 1972, all that was done by the government of Puerto Rico was to set up a special director within Puerto Rico's migration division to look into the working and living conditions of Puerto Rican migrant workers in the states.[38]

Given the harsh conditions under which Puerto Ricans continued to work and live in the United States during the 1970s, it is not surprising that the rate of return migration to the island increased during that period. Part of the explanation for that return migration has been the increasing difficulty faced by first generation Puerto Ricans on the mainland in finding jobs in an economy where there is a declining demand for unskilled labor in urban industries. But another factor is involved: urban living conditions in the U.S. have deteriorated to the point that Puerto Ricans on the mainland do not think that the availability of better paying jobs on the mainland is worth the price they have to pay in living conditions. Many of those who returned to Puerto Rico in the early 1970s were from the higher social and economic levels of the mainland community who sought to spend their last years in the homeland they had left decades before. But among those who were returning to the island, there were thousands of impoverished and disenchanted individuals who no longer could tolerate life in the ghettos of New York City and other U.S. industrial centers. Many of them were concerned with the growing rate of drug addiction among their children, about crime in the streets, and about the type of education their children were receiving in the U.S. The attitude among of these returning migrants was that if things were bad in Puerto Rico (which in 1972 had an unemployment rate of 12.4 per cent) they were worse on the mainland. It is important to keep in mind, however, that the vast majority of those who were returning to the island for good in the early 1970s were first generation Puerto Ricans. Those who have been born and raised on the mainland are staying on the mainland and continue to face the problems and degradation of ghetto life. It is with these second and third generation Puerto Ricans on the mainland that the solution to the problems of Puerto Rican communities in the states can be found.

4. A Nation Divided: Puerto Ricans and Neo-Ricans

Aside from the exploitation and degradation that migration has meant for hundreds of thousands of Puerto Ricans, the next most important consequence has been the division created in the Puerto Rican nation. Today the Puerto Rican nation is divided (irrevocably so) into two communities: the inner community (i.e. Puerto Ricans who are born, live, and work in Puerto Rico) and the outer community (Puerto Ricans who live and work on the mainland). The two communities share some problems and there still exists between them psychological ties that are being strengthened. Nevertheless, their differences exceed their similarities. Painful as it may be, it must be recognized by Puerto Ricans, both on the mainland and on the island, that the problems of the Puerto Rican communities on the United States have become American problems and that the struggle on behalf of those communities must be fought on the mainland and within the context of American society and American politics.

During the 1960s (and even today) among militant Puerto Rican organizations and militant Puerto Ricans the notion was widespread that the solution to the problems afflicting the Puerto Rican people on the mainland was tied to the resolution of the colonial status of Puerto Rico and that, somehow, once Puerto Rico achieves its independence those problems would be resolved. In the early 1950s the Puerto Rican Affairs Committee of the U.S. Communist Party adhered to this notion. Yet, in 1954 that Committee issued the *Handbook of Puerto Rican Work*, in which it admitted how erroneous the premise was and concluded that the problems of Puerto Ricans on the mainland were not an island problem, but a mainland one. The conclusion went unnoticed, and today there are thousands of Puerto Rican intellectuals and students on the mainland who still adhere to the erroneous belief that once Puerto Rico becomes independent the problems of Puerto Rican communities on the mainland will be resolved. That error led the Young Lords Party to shift their emphasis from militant action in the mainland ghettos to an emphasis on behalf of the struggle for Puerto Rican independence. Fortunately, the leaders of the Young Lords Party, who were rejected by pro-independence groups in Puerto Rico, eventually realized the error they had made, changed the name of their organization to Puerto Rican Revolutionary Workers Organization, and once again shifted their emphasis to the struggle for the Puerto Rican communities on the mainland.

The realization that the struggle on behalf of the Puerto Rican outer community (the "Neo-ricans," as they are becoming increasingly known) must be fought on the mainland, and not in Puerto Rico, is becoming more widespread, especially among second and third generation Puerto Rican students. In search of their cultural roots they go to Puerto Rico to study and discover, sometimes quite painfully, that the homeland of their parents or grandparents, no longer is theirs. Most of these students like Puerto Rico and find their experiences there valuable, but they are often made to realize that they are not "real Puerto Ricans." They return to the mainland with a new awareness of the direction to which they must direct their efforts. Several months ago one of my students who went to the island to study for a semester wrote to me:

> Well, Puerto Rico is fabulous. The good always out-weighs the bad. By "bad" I mean things I never knew existed, and more closer to home—the fact that I am a 'New Yorican'. In New York I am a 'spic'; here I am a 'New Yorican'. It is a terrible feeling. To be called a 'New Yorican' is very derogatory and I don't like it. True, I was born and raised on the mainland, but that's not my fault. Due to economic conditions my parents migrated—why do I have to be condemned for it?"

In spite of the growing awareness of the direction to which the Puerto Ricans of the outer community must direct their efforts, there still are many (both on the island and on the mainland) who stubbornly refuse to recognize the division in the Puerto Rican nation that has been created by the diaspora. Some claim that the division does not exist, since Puerto Ricans travel back and forth between the island and the mainland. But such back-and-forth travel applies primarily to the first generation of Puerto Ricans, a generation which still looks back to Puerto Rico with nostalgia (the nostalgia so beautifully and movingly presented in the song *En mi viejo San Juan*) and part of which still hopes to return to the island for good someday. But even among the first generation of mainland Puerto Ricans, a sizeable proportion of it has made the mainland its permanent home. And among second and third generation Puerto Ricans, back-and-forth travel between the island and the mainland is not common. The vast majority of second and third generation Puerto Ricans are on the mainland to stay.

There are many parallels between the outer community of Puerto Ricans and the communities of Algerian workers in France and of Chicanos in the Southwest and in California. Years ago there was a common assumption among fighters for Algerian independence that once Algeria became independent Algerians in France would return to their homeland. Algeria became independent and today there still are tens of thousands of Algerians working and living in ugly slums in Paris and other French industrial centers. Mexico is an independent country. Yet, there still are millions of Chicanos living in ghettos in the United States. There are some, of course, who argue that it is not national independence in itself that is important, but the *type* of regime that is established once independence is accomplished. In other words, the argument is that what is essential is independence *with* socialism. But anyone who has any inkling of what Chicanos are all about is aware that if tomorrow Mexico were to become a socialist republic liberated from dependency on the United States, the vast majority of Chicanos would remain in this country, just as if Puerto Rico were to become a socialist republic tomorrow the majority of Puerto Ricans on the mainland would remain on the mainland.

The notion that independence and socialism in Puerto Rico will resolve the problems faced by Puerto Rican communities on the mainland is unrealistic. In what way will the creation of a Puerto Rican socialist republic end the nightmare of life in the South Bronx? In what sense will it heat unheated apartments, drive rats and roaches from the tenements into which so many Puerto Ricans are crowded, put an end to police brutality in the ghettos, and discrimination against Puerto Rican workers in the labor unions? In what sense will such a socialist republic make the school systems of the mainland more responsive to the needs of Puerto Rican students?

None of the above should be interpreted as an implication that Puerto Ricans on the mainland should turn their backs on the land of their parents and grandparents or that they should cease to be concerned about the colonial status of the island and involved in the struggle for the independence of Puerto Rico. On the contrary, I firmly believe that it is important for the outer community to maintain contacts with the inner community. It is important that Puerto Rican students on the mainland study the history and culture of Puerto Rico, just as it is equally important that they keep abreast of contemporary developments in the island. I am not trying to imply that the establishment of an independent socialist Puerto Rican republic will have no impact whatever on Puerto Ricans on the mainland. The establishment of such a socialist republic undoubtedly will strengthen the sense of identity and pride in being Puerto Rican that is becoming increasingly widespread among members of the outer community. Also, an independent Puerto Rican socialist republic will be instrumental in bringing to the attention of the international community the plight of Puerto Ricans on the mainland. Nevertheless, the notion that the establishment of a socialist republic in Puerto Rico will resolve major problems faced by Puerto Ricans of the outer community must be destroyed, for only when that notion is given up by Puerto Rican militants on the mainland will a truly meaningful struggle on behalf of the Puerto Rican people on the mainland take place.

Many of the Puerto Rican intellectuals and young militants on the mainland (such as those in the Puerto Rican Revolutionary Workers Organization) have become or are becoming aware that Puerto Ricans are a divided nation and that the struggle for the solution to the problems afflicting Puerto Rican communities on the mainland must be fought within the context of mainland society and politics. But among them there is a tendency that, although important, can weaken that struggle if it is allowed to go to extremes: This is the tendency to concentrate on theory and ideology rather than on practice. Militant Puerto Ricans are becoming increasingly aware (just as black and Chicano militants are) that the problems of their communities are the result of the system under which those communities are humiliated and exploited. No sensitive observer can fail to see the contradictions of capitalism in the United States: It is a society in which millions suffer deprivations of all sorts, but which has the productive apparatus to feed most of the world and to provide its citizens with a decent standard of living. It is one in which millions of hens are killed to bring up the price of eggs, in which people go hungry and yet millions of dollars are spent on hotels and beauty shops for cats and dogs. It is a society in which a vice president steals and gets away with it but a poor man steals and ends up in Attica prison.

The capitalist system in the United States is becoming increasingly bankrupt. It is a system that does not meet basic human needs. Thus, the conclusion is certainly sound that only when that system is destroyed and replaced by socialism, which is truly concerned about human needs, will the causes of the problems afflicting blacks, Indians, Chicanos, Puerto Ricans and other groups disappear.

But to sit back and claim that nothing meaningful can be done until the entire system is destroyed is dangerous and can be easily turned into an escape for those who just do not have the strength and the commitment to become involved in militant action on behalf of the Puerto Ricans of the outer community. American society is inherently a conserative society; the capitalist system is well entrenched and well-defended even by those who are hurt by it:—the U.S. working class. U.S. labor bureaucrats are part of the establishment that oppresses Puerto Ricans and other minorities in this country. Racist attitudes are widespread not only among the leaders of the U.S. labor movement, but also among a large sector of the white American working class, which ought to be looked upon as an enemy rather than as an ally in the struggle for social justice in this country. Given the conservative and, in many cases, the reactionary nature of U.S. trade unionism, large sectors of the white American working class, and American society as a whole, those who struggle against the system face tremendous obstacles. The chances that capitalism will be overthrown in this country in the immediate future are small. Thus, the struggle for socialism must be seen as part of a long term struggle that includes a transitional program based on issues that directly affect the lives of the Puerto Rican people on the mainland today.

To summarize, a successful struggle on behalf of the Puerto Rican communities in the United States must be based on a foundation whose cornerstones are the realizations that the independence of Puerto Rico is not the key to the solution of the problems faced by those communities and that the inherent source of those problems, the U.S. capitalist system, will be around for a long long time to come. Equally important must be the realization that the leaders of the struggle on behalf of the Puerto Ricans of the outer community will come from second and third generation Puerto Ricans on the mainland. They are generations that are increasing numerically, that have been the product of the ghettos, and that are free of the nostalgia for the island that still characterizes the first generation of mainland Puerto Ricans. In sum, the children must lead their fathers as well as themselves.

Even after this foundation has been built, the problems faced by those who are leading or will lead the struggle on behalf of the Puerto Ricans of the outer community will be great and the results often disappointing. The struggle must be carried on at every level in every institution of mainland society. It must be carried on within the educational system (both at the pre-college and college level), within health and welfare organizations in the cities, within the legal structure of urban society, within the federal programs that still exist at the community level, within the context of urban, state and federal politics, and, most important of all, within the factories where the majority of Puerto Ricans on the mainland work. Puerto Rican students coming out of law schools should return to their ghetto communities to provide free legal system while at the same time working in institutions from which they can further assist their people. Puerto Rican students coming out of medical schools should return to the ghettos to work in ghetto hospitals and establish health clinics for their people. Puerto Rican students coming out of schools of education should move into urban educational systems and ghetto schools. In sum, young Puerto Rican militants must develop ties with their people even if it means working within institutions that oppress their communities. And all the time they must be making efforts to establish linkages with Puerto Rican factory workers. But before establishing those linkages Puerto Rican militants and intellectuals must free themselves of elitist attitudes. They should not go among the workers as leaders to tell the workers what to do and how to do it, but as allies in a common struggle. Admittedly, all that has been proposed is a piecemeal approach blocked everywhere by tremendous obstacles. But given the direction American society has taken in the 1970s, it is the only viable and productive approach available to Puerto Rican militants.

The young Puerto Rican lawyers, doctors, teachers, social workers and political activists must be militant, and in order to be militant must reach a level of consciousness about the problems afflicting Puerto Rican communities. They must have a commitment to those communities—a commitment and level of consciousness that will prevent them from being coopted into high-paying jobs in firms, institutions and governmental units, which would remove them from physical proximity to Puerto Rican communities and would lead them to put their own material well-being above the needs of their people. In part it is at the college and university level that the needed commitment and level of consciousness has to be created. It is at this level that the Puerto Rican intellectual can play a central role—assuming that he has not already been coopted into the university establishment. If he is seriously concerned about the plight of his people on the mainland, he must use his position within the university to increase the number of Puerto Rican students both at the undergraduate and graduate level, to see that the needs of those students are met through the creation of Puerto Rican studies programs whose emphasis should be on the study and analysis of the problems of mainland Puerto Ricans, to defend those programs in face of increasing criticism from conservative and often reactionary faculties and administrations, and to work together with those students through study groups and other activities. The Puerto Rican intellectual, however, should not limit his role to the confines of the university. He must venture beyond the halls of the ivory tower and establish relations with community groups, with factory workers. And he must do this free of the elitist thinking that still characterizes so many Puerto Rican intellectuals.

The Puerto Ricans who achieve the level of commitment, consciousness and militancy needed for the struggle on behalf of their communities must look out for the pitfalls that will be all around them. They must not fall into the pitfalls of emphasizing theory to the point that it becomes more important than practice. Neither should they fall into the pitfall of condemning what has been described by some as "mindless activism" (i.e. practice without theory), which is more productive than a lot of theory and no activism at all. They should be wary of Puerto Rican intellectuals who preach that Puerto Rican ghetto communities should not be concerned primarily with mundane bread-and-butter issues while they themselves live in comfortable homes and apartments in the suburbs or within the womb-like comfort of a university campus. They should shy away from Puerto Rican *politicos* who are in most cases more concerned about advancing their political careers than about the problems of the people they claim to represent. Finally, Puerto Rican militants must be careful not to step into the pitfall fo believing that all Puerto Ricans on the mainland are "sisters" and "brothers". Just as in Puerto Rico there are tens of thousands of Puerto Ricans who have profited from and supported the colonial status in which the island finds itself, so are there on the mainland Puerto Rican parasites who bleed Puerto Rican communities like leeches. There are those (like some of the *politicos*) who under the guise of serving the Puerto Rican communities, exploit them for their own ends. There are the racketeers, the businessmen, the doctors, the lawyers, who use their Puerto-ricanness to prey on other Puerto Ricans. There are the Puerto Rican intellectuals who use Puerto Rican students to advance their own careers, who use the college lecture tour circuit to fill their pockets with cash that could be used by Puerto Rican student groups for more productive purposes. These individuals must be identified, and, when possible, weeded out from our midst.

The partial solution to the problems afflicting Puerto Rican mainland communities—and I say partial because given the nature of American society those problems will never be totally resolved until the entire socio-economic system is overhauled—lies primarily in the emergence of a militant leadership of the type I have described above. That leadership, free of elitist attitudes and romantic notions about the immediate overhaul of the American socio-economic system, must work together with the masses of Puerto Ricans in the ghettos and in the factories. That leadership must come together in a national network. Once the necessary linkages among militant Puerto Rican organizations have been established, the next essential step is to establish linkages with other oppressed minorities such as blacks, Chicanos, and American Indians; for the problems of those minorities are almost identical to the problems of Puerto Ricans. In the past Puerto Ricans, blacks, Chicanos and Indians have been divided, each carrying its struggle more or less independent of the others. Part of the explanation for that has been the rivalry—often encouraged by the federal government—among black, Chicano, Puerto Rican and, to a much lesser extent, Indian *politicos* and community leaders for political spoils and federal grants. Also part of the explanation has been the racism and ethnic hostility that are institutionalized in American life and that have served to pit the oppressed minorities of this country against each other. It is up to the young black, Chicano, Indian and Puerto Rican militants to break the chains of racism and ethnic hostility, to end the rivalries among their communities, and to come together in a united front. Establishing such a front will be difficult, but it must be attempted, for only through such a united front will the struggle of oppressed minorities in the United States for social justice make a major leap forward.

NOTES

1. Harold J. Alford, *The Proud Peoples: The Heritage and Culture of Spanish-Speaking Peoples in the United States* (New York, 1972), p. 124.
2. Laurence Chenault, *The Puerto Rican Migrant in New York City* (New York, 1938), p. 53.

3. For a sophisticated analysis of this process see, Angel Quintero Rivera, "Background to the Emergence of Imperialist Capitalism in Puerto Rico," Chapter I of his forthcoming book, *The Making and Unmaking of a Proletariat in a Colonial Society: A Sociological History of the Puerto Rican Working Class.*

4. By 1940, with a population of almost two million, Puerto Rico was the greatest per capita purchaser of U.S. goods. At that time the island was the U.S.'s second largest customer in Latin America and the ninth largest in the world. Quintero Rivera, *Making and Unmaking.*

5. Manuel Maldonado-Denis, *Puerto Rico: A Socio-Historic Interpretation*, (New York, 1972), pp. 306-307.

6. Migration Division, Puerto Rico Department of Labor, *A Summary in Facts and Figures*, 1964-1965 edition, pp. 2-3.

7. Ibid., p. 2.

8. Joseph Monserrat, "Symposium on Puerto Rico in the Year 2000," *Howard Law Journal*, Fall 1968, p. 12.

9. Dorothy and James Bourne, *Thirty Years of Change in Puerto Rico* (New York, 1966), p. 45.

10. José Hernández Alvarez, "The Post-Development Crossroads of Puerto Rican Migration," in *A New Look at the Puerto Ricans and Their Society* (Brooklyn College, 1971), p. 75.

11. Ibid., p. 75.

12. Werner Baer, *The Puerto Rican Economy and United States Economic Fluctuations* (Rio Piedras, n. d.), pp. 33-59; *The New York Times*, February 22, 1970 and September 7, 1971.

13. Patricia Cayo Sexton, *Spanish Harlem: Anatomy of Poverty* (New York, 1966), p. 7.

14. Salvatore Cimilluca, *The Natural History of East Harlem from 1880 to the Present* (unpublished M.A. thesis, New York University, 1931), p. 30.

15. Francesco Cordasco and Rocco Galatioto, "Ethnic Displacement in the Interstitial Community: The East Harlem Experience," *Phylon*, Fall 1970, p. 11.

16. Migration Division, *Facts and Figures*, p. 17; *The New York Times*, March 6, 1972.

17. Migration Division, *Facts and Figures*, p. 17; *The New York Times*, March 6, 1972.

18. Migration Division, *Facts and Figures*, p. 17; *The New York Times*, March 6, 1972.

19. Ricardo Puerta, "El puertorriqueño invisible," *La Escalera*, May 1972, pp. 22-31.

20. For a vivid and literary account of life in *El Barrio* in the 1940s and 1950s see, Piri Thomas, *Down These Mean Streets* (New York, 1967). For other accounts of life in *El Barrio* in the 1950s see, Dan Wakefield, *Island in the City: The World of Spanish Harlem* (Boston, 1959) and Christopher Rand, *The Puerto Ricans* (Fair Lawn, New Jersey, 1958).

21. For an account of return migration to Puerto Rico see, José Hernández Alvarez, *Return Migration to Puerto Rico* (Berkley, 1967).

22. Frank Browning, "From Rumble to Revolution: The Young Lords," *Ramparts*, October 1970.

23. For accounts of the Young Lords Party see, Browning, From Rumble to Revolution; and Michael Abramson (ed.), *Palante: The Young Lords Party* (New York, 1971).

24. *The New York Times*, January 17, 1973.

25. *The New York Times*, November 30, 1969.

26. *The New York Times*, November 17, 1970.

27. For a listing and description of several of the Puerto Rican studies programs and

departments in New York State see, University of the State of New York, State Education Department, *Puerto Rican Studies Programs and Related Courses* (Albany, 1973).

28. *The New York Times*, January 15, 1973.

29. *The New York Times*, January 17, 1973.

30. *The New York Times*, January 15, 1973.

31. María Canino, "The New York Public School System and the Puerto Rican," in *A New Look at the Puerto Ricans and Their Society*, p. 102.

32. Josephine Nieves, "The Metropolis and the Puerto Rican Community," in *A New Look*, p. 108.

33. Frank Bonilla, "Beyond Survival: Por que seguiremos siendo puertorriqueños," in *A New Look*, p.96.

34. Nieves, "The Metropolis," p. 108.

35. U.S. Department of Labor, *The New York Puerto Rican: Patterns of Work Experience* (Washington, D. C., 1971), p. 1. The expectation voiced in the first edition of *Beyond the Melting Pot* by Daniel P. Moynihan and Nathan Glazer that the Puerto Ricans would leap frog from their Black neighbors did not occur. "To the contrary, Puerto Ricans emerged from the decade [of the 1960s] as the group with the highest incidence and poverty and the lowest number of men of public position who bargain and broker the arrangements of the city." (Daniel P. Moynihan and Nathan Glazer, *Beyond the Melting Pot*, 2nd ed., p. 1 xix).

36. *The New York Times*, September 20, 1970.

37. Ibid.

38. *The New York Times*, May 6, 1973.

The New York Puerto Rican:
Patterns of Work Experience*

U.S. Department of Labor

This report presents findings from the Urban Employment Survey on the labor market experience, economic status and social characteristics of Puerto Ricans of working age who resided in Central and East Harlem, the South Bronx and Bedford-Stuyvesant between July 1968 and June 1969. The Urban Employment Survey provides the first detailed body of socio-economic data on persons of Puerto Rican birth or parentage residing in major New York City poverty areas since the 1960 Census.

Puerto Rican workers were the most deprived of all workers residing in the city's major poverty neighborhoods. They were far more likely than others to be unemployed or to hold lower paying jobs. Typically, they held blue-collar or service jobs requiring relatively little skill. They were greatly handicapped in the competition for employment by poor educational background: On average, Puerto Ricans 25 and over had not gone beyond the eighth grade, while the majority of the area's residents 25 and over had completed high school or gone beyond. Lower educational attainment, unfavorable occupational attachments and concentration in industries with relatively large seasonal fluctuations in employment combined to make for high unemployment among Puerto Rican workers: nearly 10 per cent of them were jobless during the survey period, almost three times the rate for the City's white workers in 1969,

* Edited version of U.S. Department of Labor, *The New York Puerto Rican: Patterns of Work Experience* (Poverty Area Profiles, No. 19, Washington, D.C., May 1971).

and twice the rate for the City's Negro workers.

Poor education and low-skill, low-status jobs made for relatively low earnings: More than half of the 19,000 Puerto Rican men 20-64 years old who were at work at full-time jobs earned less than $100 a week during the survey period; the great majority of these men were married household heads and family breadwinners.

Partly as a consequence of the lower earnings position of family breadwinners, Puerto Rican family income in poverty areas ran far below the citywide (as well as below the overall poverty-area) average. Fifty per cent of all Puerto Rican families had annual incomes of less than $5,000—twice the proportion for the city's families generally. Two-thirds of all Puerto Rican families had less than $6,000 in income—again twice the proportion for the city. Moreover, Puerto Rican families were two to three times more likely to live in poverty than all of the city's families. Nearly one out of every three Puerto Rican families in the city's poverty areas had incomes below the national poverty threshold for nonfarm families for 1968. For all families in New York City, the comparable proportion was 11 per cent.

Other key findings from the study of Puerto Ricans in New York City's major poverty areas follow:

1. The Puerto Rican working age population residing in these areas—86,000 persons during the survey period—was younger than the City's population as a whole. Nearly three out of every four Puerto Ricans 16 and over were less than 45 years old, compared with one out of every two persons in the city generally. One out of every four Puerto Ricans was 16-24 years old, as against less than one out of every five of all the City's inhabitants.

2. One out of every three Puerto Rican families was headed by a woman. This was three times the corresponding proportion of households nationally, but lower than for Negro families in the City's poverty areas, 41 per cent of which were headed by women.

3. The average size of Puerto Rican families was considerably larger than that of all the City's families or of Negro families dwelling in poverty areas. Thus, one-third of all Puerto Rican families had five or more members, compared with less than a fourth of all Negro families, and one-sixth for the City.

4. The labor force participation rate of men 25-54 (93 per cent) was in line with the corresponding citywide rate, and higher than the rate for Negro men 25-54 in poverty areas (85 per cent).

5. The labor force participation rate for women 25-54 (28 per cent) was far below the citywide rate (50 per cent). It represented only about half of the rate for Negro women in this age group in poverty areas (57 per cent).

6. Fewer than one-fifth of employed Puerto Rican men held professional, technical, managerial or craft positions. By comparison, well over two-fifths of all of the City's male workers held such jobs in 1969. Only one-fourth of all employed Puerto Rican women performed clerical or sales work, while one-half of the City's women work force did.

7. Puerto Ricans were heavily employed in manufacturing industries, a declining sector in New York City. Two-fifths of all Puerto Rican workers had factory jobs. Payroll data suggest that only a little over one-fifth of all of New York's workers are employed in manufacturing.

8. The Puerto Rican unemployment rate averaged 9.6 per cent during the survey period. The rate for men 25-54 years old was 7.9 per cent. Higher-than-average unemployment among Puerto Rican workers may in part be related to seasonal fluctuations in nondurable industries in which a large proportion of them are employed. In the apparel industry in New York City, for example, employment figures during the year 1969, fluctuated by 8 per cent between the peak month and trough month, compared with 3 per cent for all of the city's industries.

9. Measured against what many employers today regard as a minimal standard of job qualification—graduation from high school—Puerto Rican workers were seriously disadvantaged. Four out of every five male Puerto Rican workers reported less than a high school education. Younger Puerto Rican workers (18-34) generally were better educated than older ones, but the educational-attainment gap between them and their age mates nationally remained wide: only 25 per cent of the men and 52 per cent of the women had four years of high school or more, compared with 70 per cent and 79 per cent of the labor force 18-34 years old nationally.

Growth of New York City's Puerto Rican Population

The population of Puerto Rican birth or parentage is one of the fastest growing ethnic groups in New York City. According to estimates from the Population Health Survey conducted by the Center for Social Research of City University, the number of Puerto Ricans in the five boroughs averaged about 800,000 in the years 1964-66, nearly one-third again as high as the 602,000 counted by the Census of 1960.[1] The City's Puerto Rican population numbered around 925,000 in 1968 if the rates of growth of the first half of the sixties persisted—a not unreasonable assumption considering that net migration from Puerto Rico accelerated in 1965-68 from the levels earlier in the decade, and that a large proportion of the migrants are likely to have settled in the city.[2] In 1968, the Puerto Rican population represented about 12 per cent of the city's total population, compared with 8 per cent in 1960.

The growth of the City's Puerto Rican population during the sixties, though rapid, was slower than it had been during the fifties. The migration component of the increase, two-thirds during the earlier decade, was probably considerably less in the sixties, judging by the net migration figures. Between 1950 and 1960, the number of persons of Puerto Rican birth of New York City rose by 242,000; the number of Puerto Rican parentage increased by 124,000. Between 1961 and 1968 net migration from the Island to the mainland amounted to 101,000 persons, many of whom did not settle in New York, although past trends suggest that the majority did. The excess of births over deaths has thus clearly become the more important component of growth in the City's Puerto Rican population. This means that the third generation—born of parents themselves of Puerto Rican parentage and born here—is rapidly gaining in numbers—but is also being "lost" as an identifiable ethnic group to surveys (such as the Urban Employment Survey or the Census) which are limited to persons of Puerto Rican birth or parentage.[3] Therefore, intergenerational changes in the social and economic status of Puerto Ricans would not be ascertainable beyond the second generation.

By definition, then, Puerto Rican residents of the City's major poverty neighborhoods were of the first or second generation. The statistical importance of third-generation Puerto Ricans in New York City at any rate still lies mainly in the future. Women residents of Puerto Rican parentage who were born here and were of childbearing age in 1960 (15-44) represented only one-tenth of *all* Puerto Rican women residents in this age group; female residents of Puerto Rican parentage who were 5-34 years old in 1960 constituted one-quarter of all Puerto Rican females in this age group in 1960. The great majority of Puerto Ricans in New York City will thus be of the first and second generation for some time to come.

FEMALES OF PUERTO RICAN ORIGIN, BY SELECTED AGE GROUPS, IN
NEW YORK CITY, 1960

	5-34	15-44
Total	194,300	163,300
Of Puerto Rican birth	143,300	147,500
Of Puerto Rican Parentage	50,900	15,800
Per cent of total	26	10

Source: U.S. Census of Population: 1960, final Report PC(2)-10. Subject Reports, *Puerto Ricans in the United States*, page 92.

The growth of the City's Puerto Rican population seems likely to continue to be sustained in good part by continued immigration, since the migration potential of persons of working age residing in Puerto Rico remains substantial, considering the Island's continued large supply of underutilized manpower. This supply was estimated at more than 300,000 in 1967, nearly twice as high as in 1950.[4] More than half of all persons in this group were 16-24 years old, and it is from this group that migrants most likely recruit themselves: According to a sample survey covering the fiscal year 1966, almost two-thirds of all migrants from Puerto Rico were 14-24 years old.[5] The large underutilized supply of manpower partially reflects high unemployment rates: In 1969, 11 per cent of the labor force in Puerto Rico was unemployed; 21 per cent of young men 16-24 years old, and 16 per cent of young women in this age group were jobless.

Ethnic Definition and Color

Whether a respondent to the Urban Employment Survey was of Puerto Rican origin was determined on the basis of answers to questions as to his place of birth, or that of either of his parents. A person was of Puerto Rican origin if (1) he was born in Puerto Rico, or (2) either or both of his parents had been born there. Although all Puerto Ricans were regarded as Spanish-Americans, not all Spanish-Americans encountered in the City's poverty areas were Puerto Ricans. If a respondent was not of Puerto Rican origin but indicated that Spanish was spoken in his parents' home when he was a child, he too was classified as Spanish-American. During the survey period, about 97,000 Spanish-Americans of working age (16 and over) resided in the City's major poverty neighborhoods, of whom close to 86,000 or nearly nine-tenths were of Puerto Rican birth or parentage.

	Total	White	Negro and other races
All Spanish-Americans	96,800	75,300	21,500
Puerto Ricans	85,700	68,900	16,800
Per cent of total	89	92	78

Nearly 17,000 or 20 per cent of all Puerto Ricans were of Negro or other races. The proportion of Negroes in the Puerto Rican population residing in poverty areas was far higher than that indicated by the Census of 1960 ·for all of New York City (4 per cent). The high proportion of black Puerto Ricans in 1968-69 may well have been related to .the generally high concentration of blacks who reside in these neighborhoods, but may also have been due to differences in classification methods.

Demographic Characteristics

The analyses and data presented in this report refer to only a segment of the Puerto Rican population living in New York City. The total number of persons represented by this segment, including children under 16, is estimated at 150,000, between one sixth and one seventh of the City's estimated total Puerto Rican population.

The working-age population of Puerto Ricans residing in the City's poverty areas covered by the Urban Employment Survey during the July 1968-June 1969 period averaged 86,000, including 38,000 men and 48,000 women 16 and over. It tended to be considerably younger than the City's population generally. Nearly three quarters of all Puerto Ricans 16 and over were less than 45 years old, compared with only about one half for the City. (Their distribution was, however, closely in line with that of the City's total Puerto Rican population of 14 and over in 1960.)

These and similar differences in age structure reflect to some extent the heavy influx of young migrants from Puerto Rico over the past two decades, and possibly also some outmovement of older Puerto Ricans, who either returned to the Island or moved to other, perhaps better neighborhoods.

	Puerto Ricans in poverty areas 1968-69	New York City 1969
Civilian population, 16 and over.....	85,700	5,708,000
percent distribution......	100	100
16-24............................	25	19
16-19	13	8
25-54............................	59	49
25-44	46	33
55 and over..................	15	32

Analysis of the marital status of Puerto Ricans residing in poverty areas suggests a significantly lower incidence of broken families than among Negroes in these areas, although the incidence was higher than among the American population as a whole. One out of every four married Puerto Rican women 20-64 lived without her husband, a ratio which compares with nearly two out of every five married Negro women and with one out of every 18 for the United States.

The 1960 Census for the New York metropolitan area shows that, then, the husband of one in every seven married Puerto Rican woman 20-64 was absent. (See also Table 1).

	New York City poverty areas, 1968-69		United States March 1969
	Puerto Rican	Negro	
Married women, 20-64.....	29,000	72,900	42,341,000
Per cent with husband absent....	26	38	6

One third of all Puerto Rican family heads were women, a proportion that was lower than that for Negroes (two fifths), yet the severity of social and economic problems may have been greater for Puerto Rican than for Negro women in this group. This probability is suggested by the substantial differences in the size of families, as well as in labor force participation rates and family income, discussed in subsequent sections.

Puerto Rican families tended to be larger than families in the City generally or Negro families residing in poverty neighborhoods. One third of all Puerto Rican families counted five or more members, as against less than a fourth of all Negro families, and one sixth of all of the City's families. Only about one fifth of all Puerto Rican families had two members—half the proportion for Negroes or for the City at large (see Table 2). Data on the age of family members are not available, but it is not unlikely that low labor force participation rates among Puerto Rican women partially stem from greater family responsibilities involving small children.

The number of unrelated Puerto Rican individuals—persons unattached to families and either living in households of their own or with nonrelatives—constituted 13 per cent of the Puerto Rican population 16 and over in poverty areas—a level about in line with the national figure. This relatively small proportion strikingly contrasted with that for Negroes, among whom unrelated individuals made up more than one fourth of the working-age population.

Unrelated individuals as per cent of population

Major New York City poverty areas	Per cent
Puerto Rican	13
Negro	26
United States	7

TABLE 1. MARITAL STATUS OF PUERTO RICANS AND NEGROES, 20-64 MAJOR NEW YORK CITY POVERTY AREAS, JULY 1968-JUNE 1969, AND UNITED STATES, 1969

Marital status	Poverty areas		United States
	Puerto Rican	Negro	
Men			
Total, all persons	30,400	75,700	49,533,000
Per cent distribution	100	100	100
Single (never married)	19	23	15
Married, spouse present	69	56	78
Married, spouse absent	7	16	3
Widowed or divorced	4	5	4
Women			
Total, all persons	39,200	116,700	53,666,000
Per cent distribution	100	100	100
Single (never married)	13	19	11
Married, spouse present	55	39	74
Married, spouse absent	19	24	5
Widowed or divorced	13	18	10

	New York City poverty areas, 1968-69		United States March 1969
	Puerto Rican	Negro	
All heads of families with 2 or more persons	34,400	85,600	50,416,000
Female	10,900	35,300	5,381,000
Per cent of total	32	41	11

TABLE 2. SIZE OF FAMILIES, MAJOR NEW YORK CITY POVERTY AREAS,
JULY 1968-JUNE 1969, AND NEW YORK CITY, 1968

Size of family	Poverty areas Puerto Rican	Negro	New York City
All families...................34,600		86,000	2,121,000
Per cent distribution......... 100		100	100
2 persons.......................... 22		41	41
3 persons.......................... 25		21	23
4 persons.......................... 20		16	18
5 persons.......................... 17		10	9
6 or more persons.............. 17		12	8

Source: Center for New York City Affairs of the New School for Social Research, *City Almanac,* February 1970. Based on special tabulations from the March 1969 Current Population Survey obtained from the U.S. Department of Commerce, Bureau of the Census.

Labor Force

The labor force of Puerto Rican persons residing in the City's major poverty areas totaled approximately 44,000 men and women, or 51 per cent of the Puerto Rican population 16 and over. About 39,000 men and women were employed, and more than 4,000, or nearly 10 per cent of the labor force, were unemployed. The jobless rate was almost three times as high as that for New York City as a whole during the survey period (see Table 3).

The age structure of the Puerto Rican labor force was weighted towards the younger age groups even more than that of the total Puerto Rican population 16 and over. Three quarters of all Puerto Rican workers were under 45, reflected in part in the higher participation rates for Puerto Rican men.

TABLE 3. EMPLOYMENT STATUS OF PERSONS, 16 AND OVER, BY SEX, PUERTO
RICANS, MAJOR NEW YORK CITY POVERTY AREAS, JULY 1968-JUNE 1969,
AND NEW YORK CITY, 1969

Employment status	Poverty area Puerto Rican	New York City
Both Sexes, 16 and over		
Civilian noninstitutional population	85,700	5,708,000
Labor force	43,600	3,255,000
Participation rate	50.9	57.0
Employed	39,400	3,139,000
Unemployed	4,200	117,000
Unemployment rate	9.6	3.6
Not in the labor force	42,100	2,453,000
Men		
Civilian noninstitutional population	38,000	2,579,000
Labor force	29,800	1,935,000
Participation rate	78.4	75.0
Employed	27,100	1,867,000
Unemployed	2,700	68,000
Unemployment rate	9.1	3.5
Not in the labor force	8,200	645,000
Women		
Civilian noninstitutional population	47,700	3,129,000
Labor force	13,800	1,321,000
Participation rate	28.9	42.2
Employed	12,300	1,272,000
Unemployed	1,500	49,000
Unemployment rate	10.9	3.7
Not in the labor force	33.900	1,808,000

Note: Sampling variability may be relatively large in cases where the numbers are
small, particularly for estimates under 5,000 for the major New York City
poverty areas (and 50,000 for New York City). Small differences between
estimates as well as small estimates should be interpreted with caution.
Figures may not add up because of rounding.

TABLE 4. CIVILIAN LABOR FORCE, BY AGE AND SEX, PUERTO RICANS, MAJOR NEW YORK CITY POVERTY AREAS, JULY 1968-JUNE 1969, AND NEW YORK CITY, 1969

Age and sex	Poverty Area Puerto Rican	New York City
Total, all persons......................................	43,600	3,255,000
Men		
Total, all persons.....................................	29,800	1,935,000
Per cent distribution...............................	100	100
16-24..	20	14
16-19..	9	4
25-54..	72	63
25-44..	57	43
55 and over..	7	23
55-64..	6	17
65 and over..	1	6
Women		
Total, all persons.....................................	13,800	1,321,000
Per cent distribution...............................	100	100
16-24..	32	22
16-19..	14	7
25-54..	58	57
25-44..	41	36
55 and over..	11	21
55-64..	10	17
65 and over..	1	4

The labor force participation of Puerto Rican men was roughly in line with local levels; it tended to run above that of Negro men residing in poverty areas. Male Puerto Rican youths 16-19 were somewhat more likely than their age mates in the City generally to be working or looking for work. The rate for adult men 25-44, 96 per cent, was virtually the same as for all of the City's men in this age group. Older Puerto Rican men, however, had significantly lower labor force participation rates than their age mates citywide (see Table 5).

TABLE 5. LABOR FORCE PARTICIPATION RATES* PUERTO RICANS, MAJOR NEW
YORK CITY POVERTY AREAS, JULY 1968-JUNE 1969, AND NEW YORK CITY,
1969

Age and Sex	Poverty area Puerto Rican	New York City
Total, all persons..................................... 51		57
Men		
Total, all persons..................................... 78		75
16-19..47		36
20-24..**		75
25-44..96		94
45-54..83		92
55 and over... 40		55
Women		
Total, all persons.................................... 29		42
16-29..36		38
20-24..38		60
25-44..26		48
45-54..39		55
55 and over... 20		26

*Per cent of civilian noninstitutional population, 16 and over, in the labor force.
**Rate not shown where base is less than 5,000.

It is noteworthy that the 1960 Census for New York City shows a
participation rate of 38 per cent for Puerto Rican women 14 and over; the
higher rate may have reflected greater job opportunities at the time in
nondurable manufacturing for semiskilled women workers with a poor
educational background. These opportunities have tended to contract
and this may to some extent have accounted for the low rates in the City's
poverty areas in 1968-69.

Occupational Patterns

Most Puerto Rican workers dwelling in the City's poverty neighborhoods held low-status, low-skill jobs. Two-thirds of the men did
semiskilled or unskilled blue-collar and service work, nearly twice the
proportion of all of the City's male jobholders. Those employed in jobs
requiring professional, technical, managerial or craft skills accounted for

CHART I. LABOR FORCE PARTICIPATION RATE OF WOMEN, BY MARITAL STATUS

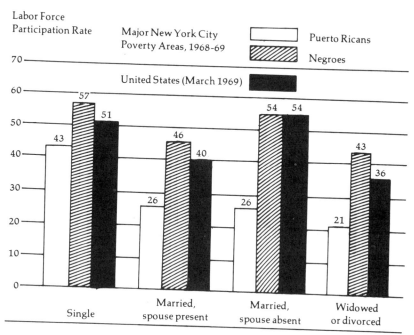

Labor Force Participation Rate

Major New York City Poverty Areas, 1968-69

☐ Puerto Ricans

▨ Negroes

United States (March 1969) ■

fewer than one-fifth of the total—less than half the corresponding proportion for all of the City's employed men (see Table 6).

Differences in the occupational distribution between Puerto Rican women and women in the City generally were similarly sharp. Half of all of the City's women workers performed clerical or sales work, but only one-fourth of all Puerto Rican women did. Only one-third of the City's women workers held semiskilled or unskilled blue-collar or service jobs, as against two-thirds of the Puerto Rican women.

The occupational distribution of Puerto Rican men residing in the City's poverty areas in 1968-69 was not markedly different from that of all of the City's Puerto Rican men in 1960. The proportions of professional, technical, managerial, and craft workers were virtually the same. The proportion of semiskilled blue-collar workers was somewhat lower, while that of clerical and service workers was a little higher.

Among employed Puerto Rican women who lived in poverty areas in 1968-69, white-collar jobs were of greater relative importance than they had been for all of the City's employed Puerto Rican women in 1960. Nevertheless, the general shift to white-collar work may have made it more difficult for Puerto Rican women to obtain jobs, considering their poor education background—and may have contributed to lowering their labor force participating rate.

TABLE 6. OCCUPATIONAL DISTRIBUTION OF EMPLOYED WORKERS, BY LEVEL OF SKILL AND KNOWLEDGE, PUERTO RICANS, MAJOR NEW YORK CITY POVERTY AREAS JULY 1968-JUNE 1969, AND NEW YORK CITY, 1969

Occupation by sex	Poverty area Puerto Rican	New York City
Number of workers, 16 and over	39,400	3,139,000
Men		
Number of workers	27,100	1,867,000
Per cent distribution	100	100
Professional and technical workers	2	15
Managers, proprietors, officials	4	14
Skilled blue-collar workers	13	17
Subtotal	19	46
Clerical and sales workers	16	21
Semiskilled blue-collar workers and laborers	42	23
Service workers	22	11
Subtotal	80	55
Women		
Number of workers	12,300	1,272,000
Per cent distribution	100	100
Professional and technical workers	5	14
Managers, proprietors, and officials	3	5
Skilled blue-collar workers	3	1
Subtotal	11	20
Clerical and sales workers	28	50
Semiskilled blue-collar workers and laborers	50	17
Service workers	11	15
Subtotal	89	82

TABLE 7. OCCUPATIONAL DISTRIBUTION OF WORKERS BORN IN PUERTO RICO, AND OF PUERTO RICAN PARENTAGE, BY LEVEL OF SKILL AND KNOWLEDGE, NEW YORK CITY, 1960

Occupation by sex	Born in Puerto Rico	Puerto Rican parentage
Number of workers, 14 and over	179,513	14,989
Men		
Number of workers	118,288	9,096
Per cent distribution	100	100
Professional and technical workers	2	7
Managers, proprietors, officials	4	4
Skilled blue-collar workers	11	16
Subtotal	17	27
Clerical and sales workers	11	24
Semiskilled blue-collar workers and laborers	51	35
Service workers	21	13
Subtotal	83	72
Women		
Number of workers	61,225	5,893
Per cent distribution	100	100
Professional and technical workers	3	6
Managers, proprietors, officials	1	2
Skilled blue-collar workers	2	2
Subtotal	6	10
Clerical and sales workers	12	56
Semiskilled blue-collar workers and laborers	75	25
Service workers	8	9
Subtotal	95	90

It is likely that the occupational distribution among workers of Puerto Rican parentage and born here is more favorable than among workers of Puerto Rican birth (data on this subject were not collected in the Urban Employment Survey). This is suggested by the 1960 Census, which shoed that persons of Puerto Rican parentage were more likely than those born in Puerto Rico to hold jobs requiring higher levels of education or skill. But this more favorable occupational distribution was limited to only about 8 per cent of *all* Puerto Rican workers in New York City in 1960—i.e., those who were born in the continental United States (see Table 7). (The proportion of Puerto Ricans of working age residing in poverty areas in 1968-69 who had been born here was 14 per cent during the survey period).

Employment by Industry

An outstanding characteristic of the industry distribution of Puerto Rican workers from the City's poverty neighborhoods was their concentration in manufacturing: two out of every five of these workers held a factory job. No strictly comparable figures on the industry distribution of all of the City's workers are available, but payroll data on wage and salary employees may serve as a yardstick.[6] These data show that manufacturing employment in New York City declined 13 per cent between 1959 and 1969, and that in the latter year, little more than one in every five of the City's wage and salary employees worked in manufacturing. By this yardstick, then, a disproportionately large number of Puerto Ricans held jobs in a declining sector of the City's economy.

Industry	Percent distribution Puerto Ricans poverty areas, 1968-69	All workers New York City, 1969
Manufacturing.................	42	22
Services..........................	19	20
Trade.............................	18	20
Government.....................	9	14
Finance, insurance, real estate....	6	12
Transportation and public utilities....	5	9
Contract construction and mining....	1	4

These workers were somewhat less concentrated in manufacturing than were all of the City's Puerto Rican workers in 1960, when nearly three-fifths held factory jobs. Even by the end of the sixties Puerto Ricans did not share fully in jobs in the City's growing white-collar industries.

One such industry has been government where payrolls rose 35 per cent over the 1959-69 decade. One out of every seven of the City's wage and salary employees held a government job in 1969, but only one out of every eleven Puerto Ricans from poverty areas did so during the survey period. Only 6 per cent of Puerto Rican workers from poverty areas were employed in finance, insurance, and real estate, which account for about 12 per cent of the City's payroll jobs.

Unemployment

The unemployment rate of the Puerto Rican labor force residing in major New York City poverty neighborhoods, at 9.6 percent during the survey year, was more than 2½ times higher than for the City's workers generally in 1969 (3.6 percent), and half again as high as for Negroes in these neighborhoods (6.5 percent) (see Chart II).

CHART II. UNEMPLOYMENT RATES BY AGE

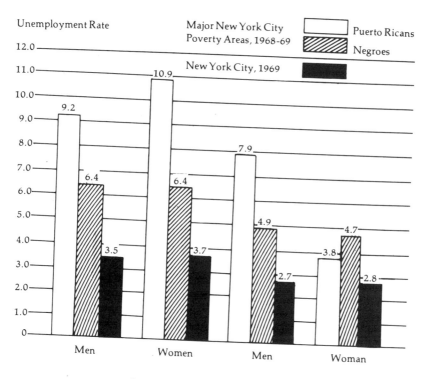

Whereas normally the jobless rate for women is higher than for men, among Puerto Rican workers the pattern was reversed. Adult men 25-54 had a rate of nearly 8 per cent, compared with less than 4 per cent for women in this age group.

*See Appendix I for a discussion of under-employment, an issue not discussed in this study.

TABLE 8. UNEMPLOYMENT RATES BY OCCUPATION OF LAST JOB, PUERTO RICANS, MAJOR NEW YORK CITY POVERTY AREAS, JULY 1968-JUNE 1969, AND NEW YORK CITY, 1969

Occupation	Poverty area Puerto Rican	New York City
Total	9.6	3.6
White-collar workers	6.2	2.2
Professional and technical workers	*	2.5
Managers, proprietors, officials	*	2.3
Clerical workers	6.1	2.4
Sales workers	*	2.3
Blue-collar workers	10.5	4.9
Craftsmen and foremen	*	2.6
Semiskilled workers	12.3	5.7
Unskilled workers	*	7.8
Service workers	6.8	3.8

*Rate not shown where labor force is less than 5,000.

Puerto Rican workers were heavily represented in occupations such as semiskilled and service work where unemployment rates tend to run above average (see Table 8). For example, the unemployment for semiskilled workers in New York City in 1969, 5.7 per cent, was more than half again as high as the overall rate.

Furthermore, Puerto Ricans were frequently attached to industries with pronounced seasonal fluctuations in employment. Thus, in the apparel industry in New York City, employment moved by 8 per cent between the months of high and low employment in 1968, and in miscellaneous manufactures by 19 per cent. In the City's industries as a whole, seasonal movements barely exceeded 3 per cent during 1968.

SELECTED NEW YORK CITY INDUSTRIES, 1969

	Per cent change in employment between high and low month
All industries	3.1
Nondurables	6.4
Apparel	7.7
Miscellaneous manufactures	19.4

Seasonality of employment in nondurable industries would thus be a factor in the high unemployment among Puerto Rican workers from poverty areas, a large proportion of whom were attached in these industries (see also Table 9).

TABLE 9. SEASONAL FACTORS FOR EMPLOYMENT IN SELECTED NONFARM INDUSTRIES, NEW YORK CITY, 1969

Month	All nonfarm industries	Nondurables	Apparel *	Miscellaneous manufactures**
January	.983 L	.963 L	.956	.907 L
February	.984	.992	1.016	.934
March	.994	1.004	1.026	.952
April	.998	.987	.986	.969
May	1.001	.995	.994	.996
June	1.010	1.005	.999	1.016
July	.999	.970	.949 L	.967
August	1.001	1.018	1.020	1.042
September	1.001	1.025 H	1.030 H	1.063
October	1.007	1.025	1.028	1.083 H
November	1.010	1.023	1.019	1.076
December	1.013 H	.990	.975	.996

*SIC group No. 23. Includes other finished textiles.
**SIC group No. 39. Includes jewelry and silverware, musical instruments, toys and sporting goods, pens, pencils and other office and artists' materials, notions, and other miscellaneous manufactures.
L-low month; H-high month.

Work Experience and Extent of Unemployment

The disadvantaged economic status of Puerto Ricans residing in the City's poverty areas was closely related to the following work-experience characteristics:

(1) The proportion of the working-age population with work experience during the year preceding the interview was lower than that of Negroes in these areas or in the United States generally.

(2) The number of voluntary part-time workers among women and teenagers (who frequently make an important contribution to family income) was comparatively small.

(3) The proportion of persons who experienced unemployment at some time during the year tended to run above average.

About 46,000 Puerto Ricans 16 and over residing in the City's poverty areas held a job at some time during the year prior to the interview. That number represented 53 per cent of the Puerto Rican population in these areas—a proportion which was markedly lower than that for all persons 16 and over in the United States who reported work experience in 1968 (68 per cent). It was also lower than that of Negroes from the City's proverty areas (64 per cent) (see Table 10).

TABLE 10. PERSONS WITH WORK EXPERIENCE AS PER CENT OF CIVILIAN POPULATION, BY SELECTED AGE GROUPS, PUERTO RICANS AND NEGROES, MAJOR NEW YORK CITY POVERTY AREAS, JULY 1968-JUNE 1969, AND UNITED STATES, 1968*

Age and sex	Poverty areas		United States
	Puerto Rican	Negro	
Total, 16 and over............................	53	64	68
Both sexes, 16-19............................	53	60	67
Men, 20 and over............................	83	80	87
25-54..	91	88	97
55 and over.......................................	42	60	63
Women, 20 and over........................	31	54	51
25-54..	31	62	58
55 and over.......................................	21	38	22

*Persons who were employed at some time during the year preceding the interview in major New York City poverty areas, and during 1968 for the United States.

The smaller relative number of Puerto Ricans with work experience mainly reflected the low proportion of adult women (20 and over) who had worked at some time in the course of the pre-interview year. Less than a third of these women had done so, compared with more than one half of all adult women nationally or of Negro women in the City's poverty areas. Puerto Rican youths 16-19 also were less likely than their counterparts nationally to have been exposed to the world of work.

Among Puerto Rican men, there was a tendency for the proportion with work experience to decline rapidly after age 45. Only about four-fifths of all Puerto Rican men 45-54 had work experience during the pre-interview year, and only two-fifths of those 55 and over. These proportions compared quite unfavorably with those for men in these age groups nationally, and were also out of line with those for Negro men in the City's poverty areas.

Like the majority of the Nation's work force, the majority of Puerto Ricans who reported work experience had held full-time, year-round jobs during the 12 months preceding the interview. In contrast, only a small proportion of Puerto Ricans worked at part-time jobs. Only one out of every 12 Puerto Rican women with work experience had worked part-time, less than one-third the comparable proportion of women nationally. Insofar as Puerto Rican youths 16-29 had work experience, they were less likely to have held part-time jobs than their age mates nationally, and a womewhat larger proportion of them were employed part of the year at full-time jobs (see Table 11).

Unemployment was experienced at some time during the 12 months preceding the interview by nearly one out of every five of all Puerto Ricans who had been working or looking for work, compared with one in eight of all workers nationally during 1968. As might be expected, the proportion of Puerto Rican women and teenagers who had experienced unemployment was higher than that of men, but it ran considerably above the corresponding national averages as well. Moreover, the unemployment experience of Puerto Rican women tended to be worse than that of Negro women residing in the City's poverty areas.

Educational Attainment

Inadequate education handicapped Puerto Rican workers in the competition for jobs, and was prominently associated with their unfavorable occupational distribution and high unemployment.

Measured against what many employers regard as the minimal

TABLE 11. WORK EXPERIENCE, PUERTO RICANS, MAJOR NEW YORK CITY
POVERTY AREAS, JULY 1968-JUNE 1969, AND UNITED STATES, 1968

Work experience	Total, 16 and over	Both sexes, 16-19	Men, 20 and over	Women, 20 and over
Poverty area—Puerto Rican				
Total, working or looking*	47,300	6,300	27,200	13,800
Per cent distribution	100	100	100	100
Usually worked full time	89	63	96	87
50-52 weeks	63	17	79	52
Less than 50 weeks	26	46	17	35
Usually worked part time	8	30	3	8
Did not find job	4	6	2	2
United States				
Total, working or looking*	91,480,000	9,826,000	48,268,000	33,386,000
Per cent distribution	100	100	100	100
Usually worked full time	80	42	93	72
50-52 weeks	57	8	74	45
Less than 50 weeks	23	34	19	27
Usually worked part time	19	53	6	26
Did not find job	1	4	**	2

*Employed or unemployed at some time during the year preceding the interview for
Puerto Ricans, and in calendar-year 1968 for the United States.
**Less than 0.5 per cent.

UNEMPLOYMENT EXPERIENCE

Per cent of total who Worked or looked	Major New York City poverty areas, 1968-69		United States 1968
	Puerto Rican	Negro	
Total, 16 and over	18	15	12
Both sexes, 16-29	33	36	24
Men, 20 and over	13	13	10
Women, 20 and over	21	13	12

standard of job qualification—graduation from high school—Puerto
Rican workers were seriously underqualified: Four out of every five
Puerto Rican men in the labor force 18 and over residing in the City's

poverty areas, and three out of every four Puerto Rican women, reported less than a full high school education. While the younger generation of Puerto Ricans—workers under 35—had more schooling than the older, the level of education which it had in fact attained was below that of its age mates generally (see chart III). Workers of Puerto Rican parentage born in the continental United States probably received more schooling than workers born on the Island, judging by 1960 Census patterns (the Urban Employment Survey did not differentiate between the two groups). But, as already noted, only a small minority of Puerto Ricans of working age who live in poverty areas were born on the mainland.

Puerto Rican workers must compete in a labor market dominated by men and women who are more than three times as likely to have completed high school or to have gone beyond. Data on education attainment of New York City area residents 25 and over (when the formal process of education has usually been completed) demonstrate that a wide educational gap prevails in the local labor market (see Table 12).

CHART III. PERCENT OF LABOR FORCE WITH 4 YEARS OF HIGH SCHOOL OR MORE

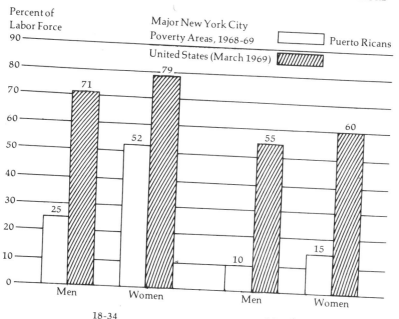

TABLE 12. EDUCATIONAL ATTAINMENT OF THE POPULATION 25 AND OVER, PUERTO RICANS, MAJOR NEW YORK CITY POVERTY AREAS, JULY 1968-JUNE 1969, AND NEW YORK METROPOLITAN AREA, 1967

Education attainment	Poverty area Puerto Rican		New York metropolitan area
	Men	Women	Total
Total, all persons, 25 and over	28,400	35,800	6,600,000
Per cent distribution	100	100	100
No school	6	11	*
Elementary school, 8 years or less	55	53	29
High School, 1-3 years	26	20	17
4 years	11	14	32
College, 1-3 years	2	1	9
4 years or more	**	1	12
Median years of school completed	8.5	8.2	12.1

*Persons with no schooling are included in totals for elementary schooling.
**Less than 0.5 per cent.

According to these data, over one-half of the New York area's residents 25 and over had completed high school and one-fifth had gone to college or graduate school. In contrast, only about one-seventh of all poverty-area Puerto Ricans 25 and over had finished high school; an insignificant number had attended college. On average, New York area residents had completed 12.1 years of schooling, as against 8.3 years for Puerto Ricans—a level of schooling last recorded for Americans 25 and over some 30 years ago, when the educational requirements of the occupational structure were considerably more modest than they are today.

As already noted, younger Puerto Rican workers (18-34) were more likely than older ones to have graduated from high school or to have gone on to college, but the more pertinent comparison is with their age mates generally, with whom they compete directly for jobs. Between these two younger groups, the education gap remained wide, as indicated by years of school completed, which averaged 10.6 for 18-34 year old Puerto Rican workers, and 12.6 for workers in this age group nationally.

Some indication of the chances for advancement of employed Puerto Rican workers is given when median years of school completed are grouped by occupation and compared with national averages. For many occupational groups, the number of Puerto Rican workers was too small to yield significant comparisons, but the statistically significant data are suggestive. Puerto Ricans employed as semiskilled workers, for example, had on average less than 9 years of schooling, compared with about 11 years for such workers nationally. Puerto Rican men who held jobs as service workers had little more than 8 years of schooling, as against 11.6 years for service workers generally. Lack of adequate education—when "adequate" is defined in terms of the prevailing national norm—probably inhibits occupational mobility among Puerto Rican workers, confining them to low-status jobs with little promise of upward mobility.

MEDIAN YEARS OF SCHOOL COMPLETED, BY SELECTED OCCUPATION

	Puerto Ricans New York City poverty areas, 1968-69		United States March 1968	
	Men	Women	Men	Women
All employed workers.......	10.8	9.9	12.3	12.4
White-collar workers.......	10.8	*	n.a.	n.a.
Clerical workers...............	*	*	12.6	12.6
Sales workers..................	*	*	12.8	12.3
Blue-collar workers..........	8.8	8.6	n.a.	n.a.
Semiskilled workers.........	8.7	8.6	11.1	10.6
Service workers...............	8.3	8.7	11.6	11.6

*Median not shown where base is less than 5,000.
n.a.—Not available.

Low educational attainment (sic) also increased the probability of Puerto Rican workers being unemployed. In gerneral, unemployment rates of workers 18 and over are inversely related to their educational attainment. However, even at each given level of educational attainment, Puerto Rican workers had a higher jobless rate than workers nationally. Their rate also tended to be higher than that of Negro workers in the City's poverty areas. Thus, while nationally 3.5 per cent of the male labor force 18 and over with 8 years of elementary school or less was unemployed in 1969, 8.9 per cent of the comparable group of Puerto Rican workers was jobless during the survey period (see Table 13).

TABLE 13. UNEMPLOYMENT RATES BY EDUCATIONAL ATTAINMENT OF THE CIVILIAN LABOR FORCE, 18 YEARS AND OVER, PUERTO RICANS, MAJOR NEW YORK CITY POVERTY AREAS, JULY 1968-JUNE 1969, AND UNITED STATES, MARCH 1969

Educational attainment	Poverty area Puerto Rican		United States	
	Men	Women	Men	Women
Total...	8.0	7.8	2.6	4.0
Elementary school*.................................	8.9	5.6	3.5	4.8
1-7 years..	8.8	**	3.5	4.3
8 years..	8.5	**	3.3	4.6
High school, 1-4 years...........................	7.6	8.6	2.8	4.5
1-3 years.......................................10.0		**	4.2	3.0
4 years or more.................................	3.8	**	1.8	3.3

* Includes persons with no schooling.
** Rate not shown where labor force is less than 5,000.

The difference in unemployment rate at each level of educational attainment reflects in part the less favorable occupational and industry distribution of Puerto Rican workers. It probably also stems from language barriers, and from discrimination which these workers encounter in the labor market.

Migration Status

The great majority of Puerto Ricans of working age residing in the City's poverty areas were immigrants. Only about one seventh was born in the City—a small proportion, but still about twice as large as that indicated by the 1960 Census for New York City's total Puerto Rican population 14 and over. Most Puerto Ricans had lived here at least five years at the time of the interview—but fewer than two out of every five had lived here at age 16 (see Table 14).

Younger men and women were more likely than older ones to have lived in the City at age 16. Three out of every four persons 16-24 years old had resided here at age 16, but only a minority of men and women 25 and over—one-fifth—had lived here at age 16, with the proportion declining with advancing age.

The migration data imply that a large number of Puerto Ricans had been reared, and received part or all of their education on the Island. Yet, they evidently shared certain social characteristics with Island resident generally to only a limited extent. For example, years of schooling completed by men 25 and over who lived in Puerto Rico in 1960 averaged 4.8; for Puerto Rican men 35 and over who resided in the City's poverty areas 8-9 years later, they averaged 8.1. The proportion of younger Puerto Ricans in poverty areas able to speak English is not reported by the Urban Employment Survey, but was probably considerably larger than that reported for persons 10 years old and over who resided in Puerto Rico in 1960—38 per cent. That proportion was twice as high as in 1930, denoting a clear uptrend in the number and proportion of persons in Puerto Rico with a knowledge of English: For younger migrants, then, language would appear to be a less formidable barrier to employment than for the older ones.

TABLE 14. PUERTO RICANS BY WHERE THEY LIVED AT AGE 16, MAJOR NEW YORK CITY POVERTY AREAS, JULY 1968-JUNE 1969

Residence at age 16	Total	16-24	25-44	45 and over
Total, all persons....................................	85,700	21,400	39,700	24,500
Men				
Total, all persons....................................	38,000	9,500	17,700	10,700
Per cent distribution...............................	100	100	100	100
In New York City.....................................	35	75	27	8
In large or medium urban area*.................	26	8	29	39
In small city**...	30	16	32	42
In rural area***...	9	1	13	12
Women				
Total, all persons....................................	47,700	11,900	22,000	13,800
Per cent distribution...............................	100	100	100	100
In New York City.....................................	37	77	32	9
In large or medium urban area*.................	22	5	24	34
In small city**...	33	17	35	46
In rural area***...	8	1	9	10

*Cities with 50,000 or more inhabitants or large-city suburbs. Excludes New York City.

**Cities with less than 50,000 inhabitants.   ***Open country or farm.

TABLE 15. PUERTO RICANS BY WHERE THEY WERE BORN, MAJOR NEW YORK
CITY POVERTY AREAS, JULY 1968-JUNE 1969

Residence when born	Total	16-24	25-44	45 and over
Total, all persons...............................	85,700	21,400	39,700	24,500
Men				
Total, all persons..................................	38,000	9,500	17,700	10,700
Per cent distribution.............................	100	100	100	100
In New York City.................................	16	43	9	5
In large or medium urban area*................	31	43	35	36
In small city**......................................	40	32	42	49
In rural area**......................................	11	2	14	11
Women				
Total, all persons..................................	47,700	11,900	22,000	13,800
Per cent distribution.............................	100	100	100	100
In New York City.................................	12	30	8	3
In large or medium urban area*................	32	21	35	36
In small city**......................................	47	45	45	50
In rural area***....................................	9	4	11	10

*Cities with 50,000 or more inhabitants or large-city suburbs. Excludes New York
City.
**Cities with less than 50,000 inhabitants.
***Open country or farm.

Nearly half of all Puerto Ricans of working age residing in the City's
poverty areas were born in urban centers with populations of 50,000 or
more. In addition to those who were born in New York, about one third
were born in larger urban areas outside the continental United States.
Most of the rest were born in cities or places with less than 50,000
inhabitants; only a small proportion were born in the open country or on
farms (see Table 15).

Employment status	Proportion who did not live in New York City at age 16
Total population......................................	65
Civilian labor force.................................	64
Employed..	67
Unemployed..	47
Not in labor force....................................	66

The labor force status of Puerto Ricans did not vary as between those who had resided in the City at age 16 and those who had not. However, the unemployment rate was sharply higher among those who had lived here at age 16, probably reflecting the greater youthfulness of this group.

Earnings

A large majority of Puerto Rican workers residing in the City's poverty neighborhoods earned less than $100 a week during the survey period. Three-fifths of the adult men 20-64 and nearly all of the adult women had gross pay below that amount. Among Negroes residing in these neighborhoods, a somewhat lesser—albeit still large—proportion of adults earned under $100 per week—about two-fifths of the men and three-fourths of the women (see Table 17). Both Puerto Rican and Negro workers were disadvantaged, however, by comparison with all of the City's workers, two-thirds of whom earned more than $100 as of October 1969.

TABLE 17. WORKERS EARNING LESS THAN $100 PER WEEK, BY SELECTED AGE GROUPS, PUERTO RICANS AND NEGROES, MAJOR NEW YORK CITY POVERTY AREAS, JULY 1968-JUNE 1969

Age and sex	Total *	Number earning less than $100	Per cent of total
Puerto Rican			
Total, all persons	32,400	22,900	71
Men, 16 and over	22,300	13,900	62
20-64	20,400	12,300	60
Women, 16 and over	10,200	6,600	86
20-64	9,000	7,300	61
Negro			
Total, all persons	102,500	63,600	61
Men, 16 and over	50,800	23,800	47
20-64	45,300	19,500	43
Women, 16 and over	51,500	39,600	77
20-64	46,100	33,700	73

*Total refers to persons at work who reported earnings; it excludes persons who did not report their earnings. Thirteen per cent of the 37,800 Puerto Ricans at work during the week preceding the interview did not report their earnings, and neither did 18 per cent of the 126,100 Negroes at work during that week.

Particular concern attaches to the relatively large number of male Puerto Rican household heads 20-64 years old, who worked fulltime—35 hours or more—and grosse less than $100 in weekly pay. Most of these men were breadwinners and many headed families whose relatively large size may have prevented their wives from working and thus from contributing to family income. Nearly three-fifths of these men reported earnings below $100; two-fifths earned between $75 and $99; and one-fifth had earnings of less than $75. (Among Negroes, about two-fifths of all male household heads working full time had weekly earnings of less than $100).

TABLE 18. ANNUAL EARNINGS OF YEAR ROUND FULLTIME WORKER HOUSEHOLD HEADS, 20-64, MAJOR NEW YORK CITY POVERTY AREAS, JULY 1968-JUNE 1969

| | Puerto Rican | | Negro | |
Earnings	Men	Women	Men	Women
Total..	18,600	2,600	42,400	20,700
Per cent distribution....................	100	*	100	100
$0-2,999......................................	7	-	4	13
$3,000-3,999...............................	16	-	10	29
$4,000-4,999...............................	28	-	23	25
$5,000-5,999...............................	23	-	23	18
$6,000 and over...........................	26	-	40	15
Median annual earnings..............	$4,965	-	$5,570	$4,261

*Per cent and median not shown where base is less than 5,000.

Median annual earnings of Puerto Rican men heading households and working the year round at full-time jobs fell just under $5,000 during the survey period (that of similarly situated Negro men was just under $5,600). Nearly one fourth of these Puerto Rican men had gross annual earnings of less than $4,000; another 28 per cent had earnings between $4,000 and $5,000 (see Table 18).

Puerto Rican workers' low earnings reflect their low levels of skill and education, as well as their being employed in relatively low-paying industries or establishments. Hourly pay of Puerto Rican men averaged $2.23 during the survey period, and $1.85 for Puerto Rican women. The comparable figures for Negro men and women were $2.55 and $1.92. No strictly comparable wage data for all of the City's workers are available. The $3.17 average hourly earnings of the City's manufacturing production workers in 1969 gives a rough indication of the pay lag of poverty-area residents.

Men, 16 and over at work during week preceding interview	Puerto Ricans	Negroes
Median weekly hours worked..	40.3	40.4
Median weekly earnings..	$ 90	$ 103
Pay per hour..	$2.23	$2.55
Women, 16 and over, at work during week preceding interview		
Median weekly hours worked..	40.0	40.1
Median weekly earnings..	$ 74	$ 77
Pay per hour..	$1.85	$1.92

Income

The generally low earnings of Puerto Rican workers residing in the City's poverty neighborhoods were reflected in low incomes for their families. Of the more than 34,000 families with two or more members—and of the close to 7,000 families with four members—half reported annual incomes of less than about $5,000. Furthermore, the great majority of the 11,000 Puerto Ricans who were unattached to families, living either by themselves or with others to whom they were not related, had less than $5,000 in income; two thirds had less than $4,000 (see Chart IV).

The incidence of low income was roughly twice as high among Puerto Rican families in these neighborhoods as among the City's families generally, of whom less than one fourth had under $5,000 a year in 1968, roughly the same as the proportion of families nationally. Among Negro families, too, incomes tended generally to run higher than among Puerto Ricans, although they still lagged behind the City's families in general. As might be expected, families whose head had worked at some time during the year preceding the interview, as well as unrelated individuals with work experience, were likely to have higher incomes than those without work experience. Even so, more than one-fourth of all Puerto Rican family heads who had worked the year round at full-time jobs reported less than $5,000 in annual family income (see Table 19).

CHART IV. ANNUAL INCOME OF FAMILIES AND UNRELATED INDIVIDUALS

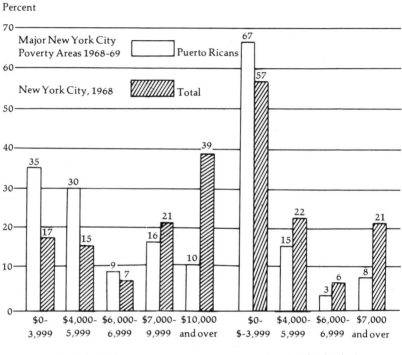

Familes with 2 or more persons   Unrelated individuals

The median income of Puerto Rican families, $5,054 during the year preceding the survey period, represented less than three-fifths of the median income of American families generally, and nine-tenths of that of Negro families nationally. It compared with $5,806 for Negro families residing in the City's poverty areas.

The median income of unrelated individuals of Puerto Rican birth or parentage, $3,176, was higher than the corresponding national median, but taking account of the younger age structure of the Puerto Rican population, it probably ran below the national medians standardized for age. Thus, 25-34 year old unrelated individuals in the United States at large had a median income of $5,852 in 1968, and those 35-44 years old, one of $5,275.

TABLE 19. FAMILY INCOME UNDER $5,000 BY WORK EXPERIENCE OF
PUERTO RICAN FAMILY HEADS AND UNRELATED INDIVIDUALS, MAJOR NEW
YORK CITY POVERTY AREAS, JULY 1968-JUNE 1969

Work experience	Total	Income under $5,000	
		Number	Percent of total
Heads of families*			
With work experience..............................	22,400	7,200	32
Full time...	21,800	7,000	32
Year round...	17,800	5,000	28
No work experience................................	12,000	9,700	81
Unrelated individuals**			
With work experience..............................	6,800	5,100	75
Full time...	6,700	4,800	72
Year round...	4,900	3,400	***
No work experience................................	4,500	4,100	***

*Families with 2 or more persons.
**Unrelated individuals are persons living alone or with nonrelatives.
***Per cent not shown where base is less than 5,000.

	Major New York City poverty areas 1968-69		United States March 1969
	Puerto Rican	Negro	
Working wives:			
All husbands, wife present......................	19,100	40,200	44,400,000
All working wives, husband present........	5,900	22,600	17,600,000
Per cent, working wives..........................	31	56	40

Poverty

The facts presented in the section on income suggest that widespread poverty and deprivation exist among Puerto Ricans residing in the City's Urban Employment Survey areas. Added dimension is lent these facts when family income is examined in terms of the cutoffs designated by the Social Security Administration as the poverty threshold. These cutoffs are for nonfarm residents in the United States, and reflect size of family. For 1968, they read as follows:

Size of Family	Poverty threshold
1 member	$1,748
2 members	2,262
3 members	2,774
4 members	3,553
5 members	4,188
6 or more members	5,496*

*Represents average for families with 6-11 members.

Close to one third of all Puerto Rican families lived in poverty by the stringent definitions of the Social Security Administration. More than one-fifth of all 2-person families, one-fourth of all 4-person families, and close to one-half of all families with six or more members had incomes below the poverty threshold. Puerto Rican families were almost three times as likely to live in poverty as all of the City's families (see Table 20).

A particularly serious aspect of poverty is that it affects large numbers of children. Two-thirds of the 10,600 Puerto Rican families with incomes below the poverty line had four or more members; close to one-fifth had three members. While age breakdowns of family members are not available, most members of famiies with three or more persons were children under 16. Many Puerto Rican children are thus growing up in disadvantaged conditions.

A manifest reason for poverty was the fact that about one out of every three Puerto Rican household heads had not worked during the year preceding the interview. Thirteen per cent of all male household heads, 20-64, (probably mostly men over 45), and 68 per cent of all female household heads 20-64—all of whom headed families with 2 or more persons—reported no work experience for the pre-interview year. The majority of all Puerto Rican household heads (about three-fifths) who had no work experience had incomes below $3,000. Only about one-eighth of household heads *with* work experience had such low incomes.

TABLE 20. INCIDENCE OF POVERTY AMONG FAMILIES AND UNRELATED
INDIVIDUALS, PUERTO RICANS, MAJOR NEW YORK CITY POVERTY AREAS,
JULY 1968-JUNE 1969, AND NEW YORK CITY, 1968

Size of family	Total	In poverty Number	Percent of total
Puerto Rican			
All families...................................	34,400	10,600	31
2 persons....................................	7,400	1,600	22
3 persons....................................	8,500	2,000	24
4 persons....................................	6,900	1,800	26
5 persons....................................	5,800	2,300	40
6 or more persons.........................	5,800	2,800	48
Unrelated individuals....................	11,300	3,800	34
New York City[1]			
All familes..................................	2,121,000	224,000	11
2 persons....................................	874,000	85,000	10
3 persons....................................	492,000	37,000	7
4 persons....................................	380,000	41,000	11
5 persons....................................	199,000	24,000	12
6 or more persons.........................	176,000	38,000	21
Unrelated individuals....................	964,000	272,000	28

[1] For source, see footnote to Table 2.

Puerto Rican household heads, 20-64

	Total	Men	Women
Total.......................................	39,400	26,100	13,300
No work experience...........................	12,300	3,300	9,000
Per cent of total.............................	31	13	68

APPENDIX I

(From: *Labor Force Experience of the Puerto Rican Worker*, United States Department of
Labor, Bureau of Labor Statistics, Regional Reports, Number 9, June 1968, pp. 25-26)

Increasingly it is clear that the unemployment rate which counts those
unemployed in the sense that they are actively looking for work and
unable to find it, gives only a relatively superficial index of the degree of

labor market maladjustment that exists in a community. The subemployment rate also includes those working only part-time when they are trying to get full-time work; those heads of households under 65 years of age who earn less than $60 per week working full-time and those individuals under 65 who are not heads of households and earn less than $56 per week in a full-time job; half the number of "nonparticipants" in the male 20-64 age group; and an estimate of the male "undercount" group which is of very real concern in ghetto areas.

UNEMPLOYMENT AND SUBEMPLOYMENT RATES IN THREE NEW YORK CITY
POVERTY AREAS* NOVEMBER 1966

	Unemployment rates		Subemployment rates	
	Total	Puerto Rican	Total	Puerto Rican
Total.................................	7.5	9.8	29.1	33.3
Harlem.........................	8.1	11.8	18.6	28.1
East Harlem..................	9.0	9.7	33.1	36.9
Bedford-Stuyvesant.....	6.2	7.8	27.6	29.7

*Harlem, East Harlem, and Bedford-Stuyvesant

When these four components are added to the traditional unemployment rate, the dimensions of the problem begin to take shape. We find that the sub-employment rate for Puerto Ricans in slum areas in New York is 33.1 per cent in contrast with the 10 per cent unemployment rate. Indeed, in the area of major Puerto Rican concentration—East Harlem—it rises to 37 per cent. In other words, for every officially counted unemployed Puerto Rican worker, there are at least two others who have a very real problem in terms of labor force maladjustment.

NOTES

1. *Estimates of Population Characteristics*, New York City, 1964-1965-1966, by Leonard S. Kogan and M.J. Wantman, Population Health Survey, Center for Social Research, Graduate Center, The City University of New York, June 1968, Table IV.

2. The following net migration figures were furnished by the Migration Division of the Commonwealth of Puerto Rico, based on data from the San Juan office of the Immigration and Naturalization Service, U.S. Department of Justice and Puerto Rican Planning Board

(the minus sign indicates net outflow from the continental United States to Puerto Rico):

1961	-1,754
1962	10,800
1963	-5,479
1964	1,370
1965	16,678
1966	28,753
1967	26,553
1968	23,853

3. Persons of Puerto Rican origin comprise "migrants from Puerto Rico and their children. No census data are available on third and later generations of Puerto Rican origin." U.s. Bureau of the Census, U.S. Census of Population: 1960, Subject Reports, Puerto Ricans in the United States, Final Report PC (2)-1D, pages VIII.

4. "The Employment Situation in Puerto Rico and Migratory Movements between Puerto Rico and the United States," by H.C. Barton, Jr., Special Adviser for Economic Affairs, Legislature of Puerto Rico, in *Summary of Proceedings: Workshop on "Employment Problems of Puerto Ricans,"* Center for Study of the Unemployed, Graduate School of Social Work, New York University, May 20-21, 1967, New York, New York, page 39.

5. *Estimates of Population Characteristics*, p. 41.

6. Payroll data include multiple jobholders, as well as nonresident jobholders (i.e., commuters). These and other differences in coverage limit the comparability of payroll data and household data. For a detailed discussion of these differences, see "Comparing employment estimates from household and payroll surveys," by Gloria P. Green, *Monthly Labor Review*, December 1969.

Guardians of the Sweatshops: The Trade Unions, Racism, and the Garment Industry*

Herbert Hill

If the racial practices of building trades unions are representative of the conservative "old-line" craft unions in the AFL-CIO, an examination of the operations of the International Ladies Garment Workers Union will reveal the social consequences of the policies and practices of a union that has a "progressive and liberal" reputation.

With some important exceptions, such as District 65 of the Retail, Wholesale and Department Store Workers Union, the American Federation of State, County and Municipal Employees, and Local 1199 of the Hospital Workers Union, no significant large-scale efforts have been made by AFL-CIO affiliates to organize the tens of thousands of Negro and Puerto Rican workers who have entered the New York labor market in the past decade. (In 1965 District 65 of the Retail, Wholesale and Department Store Workers Union conducted a successful strike involving over two thousand employees in the New York textile converting industry for the specific purpose of opening new job opportunities for Negro and Puerto Rican workers. No other union in the New York City area has resorted to strike action for the same objective.) Instead, as the unskilled labor force in New York City rapidly becomes Negro and Puerto Rican, there is a corresponding expansion in the membership and number of local unions operated by independent, corrupt labor organizations. These gangster-ridden independent unions in league with greedy employers with whom they sign "sweetheart"

*Excerpted from *New Politics*. Reprinted here with the permission of the author.

agreements are victimizing many thousands of workers in a variety of marginal shops in cheap-production industries.[1] In 1957, as a result of several indictments by the New York County District Attorney and other law-enforcement agencies, together with public exposure by the Association of Catholic Trade Unionists of the widespread operations of racket unions, the major New York City labor unions established the AFL-CIO Committee on Puerto Rican Affairs. In 1958 the Mayor's Committee on Exploitation was established with representation from the AFL-CIO Central Labor Council, the ILGWU, and other powerful labor organizations. These committees, whose leaders publicly pledged to drive labor racketeers out of New York almost a decade ago, have had little or no effect. A clue to the reason for this failure has been provided by Morris Iushewitz, Secretary of the New York AFL-CIO Central Labor Council. When Iushewitz was asked if the AFL-CIO Committee on Puerto Rican Affairs would ever initiate unfair labor practice charges with the NLRB against an employer or independent racket union jointly engaged in exploiting Puerto Rican workers, he stated that it would not do so.[2] The conclusion is warranted that expansion of these gangster-controlled unions is in large measure due to the conservative policies and practices of such major AFL-CIO affiliates in New York City as the ILGWU. Rather than engage in expensive and troublesome organizing campaigns, these unions prefer to enjoy the wealth, power, and prestige they achieved many years ago. In response, workers who are the victims of racket unions grow increasingly distrustful of all labor unions—including the International Ladies Garment workers union.*

The ILGWU is one of the richest and most powerful unions in the American labor movement and is unique in many respects. It operates in the basic manufacturing industry of New York City, and by virtue of its control of the New York State Liberal Party and its large financial contributions to the national Democratic Party, it is a force in New York municipal, state, and national political affairs.

It is also one of the most bureaucratically controlled unions, and there is a direct connection between the lack of internal union democracy and

---

*The 1964 New York State Labor Relations Board Report indicates that of its thirteen hundred cases approximately four hundred were brought by "independents." Not all of these are racket unions but the evidence suggests that disreputable independent unions are successfully expanding their jurisdiction. See also the New York State Labor Relations Board press release, December 22, 1959.

the depressed status of Negro workers within the union and the industry. Members of the ILGWU are not permitted to engage in internal political activity and are prevented from participating in the formulation of union policy on matters vital to their interests. They are specifically denied the right to have clubs, groups, or caucuses within the union except for a designated period of three months before the conventions held every two years, or with the formal approval and permission of the General Executive Board of the International union. How can workers gain support for choices contrary to those of the union administration unless they are permitted to organize to discuss their own interests and press for the election of candidates responsive to their needs? The answer is that without permission in writing from the General Executive Board they are specifically forbidden to do so by the ILGWU constitution, which prohibits all internal union caucuses, groups, and clubs,[3] an incredible denial of the democratic rights of the workers.

Although the membership of the ILGWU is denied the same right to internal political activity that is accepted as commonplace in the United Automobile Workers, the Typographical Workers and other major labor organizations, the union leadership functions every day, using the dues money of all of its members to maintain itself in power. To be eligible to run for President or Secretary-Treasurer, a member must be a delegate to the national convention, a condition that immediately limits the number eligible to approximately a thousand of the union's 442,318 members. Eligibility rules further require that a candidate for these offices must have been a member for ten years and a paid officer for at least five. In order to be a candidate for the General Executive Board, a member must be a delegate to the convention, a member of five years' standing, and a paid officer of three.[4]

An analysis of the composition of the delegates to the last three ILGWU conventions indicates that out of the 442,318 union members,

---

*The Bureau of Labor Management Reports of the U.S. Department of Labor during 1963 investigated a complaint from the ILGWU member in New Bedford, Mass. The Bureau found improper election practices by the ILGWU and ordered a new election. Unfortunately the federal agency has not acted in regard to the election practices of the international union. In another but related case the U.S. Department of Labor moved in a federal district court to set aside the 1966 election within the National Maritime Union because the international union eligibility requirements for union office violated, it was charged, federal labor laws stipulating that any member in good standing can run for office in a union. See George Home, "Curran Attacks Lawsuit by U.S.," *The New York Times,* January 3, 1967.

the number eligible to run for the General Executive Board is less than three hundred. Those eligible for the post of President or Secretary-Treasurer number less than two hundred. Thus, of the membership of the ILGWU less than one fifth of 1 per cent are eligible to run for the General Executive Board and less than one twentieth of 1 per cent for the presidency or the secretary-treasurership.*

For the more than 145 thousand Negro and Puerto Rican members of the ILGWU the situation is even worse. As a result of the restrictive requirements, *no more than four or five nonwhite persons are eligible for the General Executive Board, and virtually none at all for the top leadership positions.* This explains why there is not a single Negro Vice-President or member of the General Executive Board of the union and why the local managers, who are usually hand picked by the union leadership, include no Negroes or Puerto Ricans.**

The ILGWU constitution makes possible a rigid bureaucratic control of the entire union organization. Rank-and-file members have no chance to organize opposition caucuses or participate in policy decisions. For all practical purposes ILGWU elections are simply plebiscites to ratify appointments already made by the leadership. (A further indication of the bureaucratic control of the ILGWU is found in the fact that union officials have been forced to deposit signed, but undated, resignations with the president of the union. Brief for Petitioner, 5, ILGWU, 131 NLRB 111, 1961. See also Charles Halpern, "Recognition of a Staff Union of Business Agents Under the National Labor Relations Act," *Yale Law Journal*, Vol. 72, No. 5, April 1963, 1076-87.)

In New York City, where the largest part of the garment industry is still concentrated, the ILGWU has introduced a form of rationalized control over the relationship among the manufacturers, jobbers, and contractors, which comprises the foundation upon which this otherwise chaotic industry operates. Thus it has established an unusual form of labor union power. Dr. Kenneth Clark, Director of the Social Dynamics Research Institute of the City College of New York, has written:

> The ILGWU is probably the most decisive force in the ladies' garment industry in New York City because it has rationalized and established industry practices and

---

**After public criticism of the ILGWU's racial practices, a Puerto Rican representative was appointed to the union's General Executive Board in March 1964. However, there is still not a single Negro who is a General Executive Board member or an officer of the international union.

established union control over a scattered multiplicity of small, highly competitive shops. Both employers and workers regard the union as the major power in the industry.[5]

Dr. Clark has also cited the plight of the nonwhite worker in the International Ladies Garment Workers Union in New York City as "a significant example of the powerlessness of the Negro worker in a major trade union with a 'liberal' reputation . . ."[6]

It is the ILGWU's position that it attempts to keep the garment industry from moving out of New York, in order to maintain the jobs held by its members in the city. In reality the union has used its extensive power to regulate the industry in solving the problems of the employers rather than in advancing the interests of the great mass of workers, who continue to exist in a condition of poverty. This is especially true for the thousands of Negro and Puerto Rican workers who are concentrated in the low-wage sectors of the industry in New York City. A dynamic union with the ILGWU's financial and other resources could engage in vigorous organizing efforts outside New York City. However, the ILGWU has adopted a different course. It becomes increasingly clear from an examination of ILGWU contracts that the union attempts to keep the garment industry in New York City by maintaining low wages and minimal standards for the majority of workers, who do not have an opportunity to vote upon this matter and are not consulted on this and related policy decisions directly affecting their immediate welfare, but form the large dues-paying membership that constitutes the base of the union's extensive political and financial operations.

Soon after the Second World War the ILGWU adopted a policy of wage restraint, that contrasted sharply with its earlier wage policy. This approach coincided with the rapid increase of nonwhites in the garment industry labor force. Thus in January 1967, when the Dressmakers Joint Council of the ILGWU began negotiations with employers the union reported that the minimum weekly wage was $52.50 and the average weekly wage $77. The Dressmakers Joint Council has a large concentration of Negro and Puerto Rican workers in its membership.[7]

Early in 1963 the important research study known as the HARYOU Report was released and further confirmed this analysis of the status of Negroes within the ILGWU. This research project, jointly financed by U.S. government and New York City funds, was conducted for over eighteen months and published under the subtitle "A Study of the

Consequences of Powerlessness and A Blueprint for Change." The report states:

> The status of Negroes in the power councils of organized labor in New York City is most tenuous if not nonexistent. The persistent pattern of racial discrimination in various unions, including some which still enjoy the reputation of being liberal, reflects the essential powerlessness of Negroes to affect the conditions of their livelihood. HARYOU's difficulty in finding a suitable representative of labor for its Board of Directors highlighted the fact that there is no Negro who occupies a primary power position in organized labor in New York City. There are a few Negroes who are constantly referred to as representatives of labor, but upon careful examination it is found that these Negroes, for the most part, hold their positions at the pleasure of more powerful white bosses or leaders. Even in those unions where the bulk, or all, of the workers are Negroes, and Puerto Ricans, the top overt or covert leadership is almost always white. There is evidence that under these circumstances the union leaders are not always above entering into sweetheart contracts, or other types of conspiracies with the bosses, to the disadvantage of the Negro and Puerto Rican workers.

The ILGWU, as the largest and most influential union in the city, is certainly a major factor in perpetuating this condition.

The record of the ILGWU in the fight for a $1.50 minimum wage revealed its interest in keeping New York City a low-wage community. The proposal for a $1.50 city minimum wage was first made in 1959 by several civic groups, including various Negro and Puerto Rican organizations. When it was initially discussed by the AFL-CIO Central Labor Council of New York City, the ILGWU representative, Charles Zimmerman, (a Vice-President of the ILGWU) informed the Council that the ILGWU opposed the plan and that it would withdraw from the Central Labor Council if that organization supported it. Harry Van Arsdale, President of the New York Central Labor Council, in an effort to avoid an open conflict with Zimmerman, would not permit the question to be voted upon. Subsequently, after public pressure had been brought to bear, the Central Labor Council voted to approve the proposal, but Zimmerman was absent from those later meetings.

In 1961 Mayor Robert F. Wagner refused to support the Isaacs bill for a $1.50 minimum wage. Again, in January 1962, six Democrats and two Republicans on the City Council sponsored a bill that would have instituted a $1.50 minimum wage with no exemption by January, 1963. The bill was referred to a committee. Wagner made no comment but his spokesmen in the Council opposed the bill on the grounds that it was unconstitutional, dealing with matters pre-empted by the state and federal government, and that it would have an adverse effect on business.

A Citizens' Committee for a $1.50 Minimum Hourly Wage was formed in February 1962, including A. Philip Randolph; Roy Wilkins; James Farmer; Juan Mae, President of the Federation of Spanish Societies; David Livingston, President of District 65 of the Retail, Wholesale and Department Store Workers; and several influential clergymen and representatives of other trade union groups.

In April the Mayor announced plans to establish a Citizens' Commission on the City Economy. He named as its Chairman Louis Broido, City Commerce Commissioner and Co-Chairman of the Liberal Party Committee-at-Large. The business members were John Snyder, President of U.S. Industries; Lloyd Dalzell, Chairman of Dalzell Towing Company; and, as alternate, Ralph Gross, Executive Vice-President of the Commerce and Industry Association. The labor members were David Livingston of District 65, Retail, Wholesale and Department Store Workers Union and Luigi Antonini, first Vice-President of the ILGWU, with Howard Molisani, Manager-Secretary of ILGWU Local 98, and Sol Barkin, Research Director for the Textile Workers as alternates. The public members were Edward Lewis, Director of the New York Urban League, and Hector Bunker of the Banco Popular de Puerto Rico, with alternates Douglas Pugh of the Brooklyn Urban League and Dr. Francisco Trilla, President of the Puerto Rican Hispanic leadership Forum.

It might be assumed that the business representatives would be opposed to raising the minimum wage and the labor spokesmen for it and that the public members and the Chairman would therefore decide. However, with Broido, a well-known Liberal Party leader, and ILGWU Vice-President Antonini both against the $1.50 minimum wage, the chances for an affirmative report were not good, even if both members supported a higher wage. (In May representatives of the New York Teamsters Union Joint Council 16 accused the ILGWU of adopting "a conscious policy of artificial restraint of wage increases." A letter from the Teamsters to the Democratic majority on the City Council was made public, asking for the removal of Antonini and Moslisani from the Commission, and declaring, "Surely you must or should know that the ILGWU has a vested interest in the perpetuation of exploitation, low-wage pockets, and poverty in New York City.")

The Commission began by studying the desirability of a $1.25 city minimum wage, although the bill before the Council called for $1.50. In June, Wagner declared that he was giving top priority to drafting a law to establish "a $1.25 minimum wage for all employment in New York City, authorizing necessary exemption." The exemptions included workers employed by firms in interstate commerce (garment workers), domestics, and employees of voluntary agencies, including nonprofit hospitals.

Arnold Witte, General Manager of the Commerce and Industry Association of New York City, writing in the October 5, 1962 New York *World-Telegram & Sun*, cited the ILGWU's opposition to the city minimum-wage bill. He noted that "the garment workers, the largest union of the largest industry in the city, has refused to endorse this legislation." A. Philip Randolph charged that Wagner was "perpetuating a hoax," declaring this was further proof that the Commission "was set up merely as a public relations device to forestall action on the bill for $1.50 minimum which has been pending before the City Council since January 9."

Finally, after long delay, Commission Chairman Broido drafted a report which did not even mention the $1.50 minimum, and submitted it for approval to David Dubinsky, President of the ILGWU, and Alex Rose, President of the Hatters Union, before other committee members had received it. It recommended a $1.25 minimum effective October 1963, a month after the federal $1.25 minimum was set to go into effect. However, Livingston of District 65 persuaded Snyder to vote against the report and it was rejected by Livingston, Snyder, and the two public members. The majority drafted a new report in favor of the $1.50 minimum wage and covering workers in inter-and intra-state commerce, as well as domestics and employees of voluntary agencies. It was reported unofficially that the ILGWU's Molisani was against it, but the record listed him as abstaining.

Murray Kempton commented:

The Liberal Party . . . is a despotism of David Dubinsky sometimes tempered by Alex Rose. Louis Broido, an organizer of the Liberal Party, was chairman of the Mayor's Committee to investigate the minimum wage; he was dubious about $1.25 and absolutely against $1.50. Howard Molisani, the ILGWU's deputy on the committee, abstained from voting at all. How marvelous is the ILGWU. It has a position on Vietnam and Algeria; but it has no position on wages in its hometown.[8]

The City Council passed the bill; the Board of Estimate passed the bill;

and the Mayor signed it. But when the New York State Court of Appeals voted four to three to confirm a lower-court ruling declaring the law invalid, Wagner announced that he would not carry the case to the U.S. Supreme Court.

On February 13, 1963 a mass demonstration was held at the state capitol in Albany in support of legislation establishing a $1.50 minimum wage law. Several major trade unions participated, as did the NAACP, the Negro American Labor Council, and many other groups. The ILGWU was conspicuous by its absence. (In 1965 Governor Nelson Rockefeller vetoed a $1.50 statewide minimum wage law enacted by the legislature.)[9]

Periodically, workers' discontent with the union's practices erupts and receives public attention. In 1957 four hundred Negro and Puerto Rican members of the ILGWU employed at a plant in the Bronx picketed the offices of the union in protest against the ILGWU's failure to represent them adequately as the collective-bargaining agent. These workers later filed a petition with the National Labor Relations Board seeking the de-certification of the International Ladies Garment Workers Union as their representative. In their request to the NLRB the workers documented a series of charges against the union. Although the ILGWU succeeded in voiding the de-certification procedure, the case is significant, as it represented a spontaneous effort of Negro and Puerto Rican workers to secure a measure of democratic rights within the union and to stop collusive practices with the employer.

Demonstrations also occurred in 1958 when Puerto Rican members of ILGWU Local 62 (third largest in the international) employed at the Q-T Knitwear Company in Brooklyn marched around the factory with placards reading, "We're Tired of Industrial Peace. We Want Industrial Justice." A *New York Herald Tribune* reporter noted after interviewing the strikers that the wildcat strike was a protest against their boss and "more important, against the workers' own union."[10]

Workers have publicly protested on other occasions against the union's practices, as did the employees of Plastic Wear, Inc., located in the Bronx. In this 1958 case two hundred members of ILGWU Local 132 demonstrated in front of the international union headquarters with signs reading: "80% of our members speak Spanish. A meeting conducted in English is a farce." Demonstrators shouted, "Mr. Dubinsky, we don't want your contract!" Other demonstrations have occurred when union members protested against "back-door deals" which they describe as "helping the bosses more than the workers."[11]

The degeneration of this union is all the more significant because of its early pioneering radicalism. This spirit was expressed in the preamble to the 1918 constitution, which reads:

> Resolved that the way to acquire our rights as producers and citizens and to bring about a system of society whereby the workers shall get the full value of their products, is to organize industrially into a class conscious union represented on the various legislative bodies by representatives of a political party whose aim is the abolition of the capitalist system.

In the early history of the ILGWU the preamble was more than a ritualistic concession to a politically conscious rank and file. The union, as an institution, encouraged the development of a progressive social consciousness among its members and was committed to social causes beyond the immediate economic concerns of garment workers. The contrast between the ILGWU's radicalism in the past and its present political conservatism and bureaucratic manipulation of workers dramatically illustrates the moral and social decline of the American labor movement.

Nevertheless, tradition and heritage are not easily extirpated. The ILGWU leadership is still obliged to pay homage to the spirit of its militant origins and to project the image of an enlightened, socially conscious union. Its sensitivity to attacks by civil rights leaders on the union's discriminatory practices is evidenced by the vast sums it has spent in recent years in advertising campaigns that attempt to create the impression that the ILGWU continues as a militant, equalitarian organization. It is this continuing verbal commitment—even if inconsistent with its actual practices—which provides some hope that the criticisms leveled against the union by workers and civil rights activists may have a positive effect.

The conservative transformation of the ILGWU is most significantly evidenced by the status of nonwhite workers within the industry and the union in New York City. The nonwhite proportion of the population in New York increased from 13 per cent in 1950 to 22 per cent in 1960. By 1970, based on projections of the Department of City Planning, Puerto Ricans and Negroes will account for at least 30 per cent of the city's population. In the past two decades the number of Negro and Puerto Rican workers in the garment industry has been rapidly growing, and they now constitute a significant part of the work force. Many ILGWU locals have a majority of nonwhite members, but with some rare exceptions these workers remain concentrated in the lowest-paid unskilled and semiskilled job classifications with virtually no opportunity for promotion to other categories. A study of wages in New York City released by the Bureau of Labor Statistics of the U.S. Department of Labor on June 27, 1962 indicates that the city had become a low-wage area, and that between 1950 and 1960 wages for apparel workers there fell from second place among sixteen industry categories to eleventh place and dropped below the national average for all manufacturing. The wage rates of unskilled and semiskilled garment workers, most of whom are nonwhite, were found to be below subsistence levels as indicated by the 1960 Interim City Workers Family Budget for New York City ($5048) established by the Bureau of Labor Statistics.[12]

In 1960 the average wage of all unionized garment workers in New York City was $2.40 an hour. In March 1963 the average was $2.39, a decline in hourly wages of a penny an hour and a decline in real wages of nine cents an hour at 1959 price levels, according to data from the Bureau of Labor Statistics. It should be noted that the statistical data, significant as they are, are deceptive since the median income figure includes the wages of highly paid cutters and pressers who earned over $4 an hour and are almost exclusively white. (In March 1966, according to the Bureau of Labor Statistics, the wage-spread in the New York garment industry was between $1.25 an hour and $8 an hour.)[13] In 1963 between 15 and 20 per cent of the ILGWU membership in New York City was earning less than $1.50 an hour.*All the available data indicate that this group consisted almost entirely of Negro and Puerto Rican workers. Thus, a significant percentage of Negro and Puerto Rican ILGWU members in the period between 1960 and 1965 not only experienced a drop in real earnings but also received an income that was below the figure which the Bureau of Labor Statistics rates as the poverty level for an average family in New York City. Commenting on this development

---

*It is significant to note the shift in the rank of average hourly earnings among industrial workers in Birmingham, Alabama and New York City during the ten year period between 1950 and 1960. In 1950 New York ranked tenth and Birmingham thirty-third among forty-six cities in relation to average hourly earnings of production workers. In 1960, New York City had fallen to thirtieth place and Birmingham was tenth. See "Employment, Earnings, and Wages in New York City, 1950-1960," Bureau of Labor Statistics, Middle Atlantic Regional office, New York, June 1962, Table 6, 24.

within the ILGWU, Murray Kempton in the *World-Telegram & Sun,*
July 27, 1965, wrote:

> It is a source of sadness and not of mockery that after 60 years of labor
> statesmanship, the real wages of their members could be declining a little year by
> year and that one out of every seven could well be an element in the city's poverty
> statistics.

It was perhaps also a source of sadness for David Dubinsky, who was
obliged to admit the reality of "many" low-paid organized garment
workers. Thus, in an interview with A.H. Raskin, Dubinsky stated:
"Here is our union, a pioneer in pensions, welfare, paid vacations. We led
everyone else in factory wages only a few years ago; now we are being
criticized because our wages are too low. And it is true, many of them are
low; that has affected me deeply. Where did we go wrong?[14] (In June
1966 Dubinsky at the age of seventy-four, after thirty-four years as
President of the ILGWU, resigned and was succeeded by Louis Stulberg,
the union's Secretary-Treasurer.)

The powerful opposition of the ILGWU to training programs in the
garment industry under the auspices of the federal anti-poverty program
indicates the harmful social consequences of this union's restrictive
practices.

As a result of demands by the International Ladies Garment Workers
Union and the Amalgamated Clothing Workers of America (both AFL-
CIO affiliates), federal agencies refused to provide funds for manpower
training programs in the apparel industry operating within the New
York metropolitan area. A typical example of this development is the fate
of the training program proposed by the United Community Corporation, the anti-poverty community action agency for Newark, New
Jersey. This group operated under Title II, the Community Action
Program of the Economic Opportunity Act of 1964. When representatives of the Newark agency requested an explanation for the refusal of
the Office of Economic Opportunity to provide funds for an apparel
trades job training program for 545 workers (200 of whom were welfare
recipients), they were told by officials of the Department of Labor that
the basis for the rejection was the refusal of the two unions to approve
the job training program.

On August 22, 1963 the Department of Labor, which administers the
Manpower Development and Training Act, received a fourteen-page

statement of the "position of the International Ladies Garment Workers Union and the Amalgamated Clothing Workers of America, on the question of subsidized training programs in the apparel industry of the United States." In this document, signed by Lazare Teper, Research Director of the ILGWU, and Milton Fried, Research Director of the ACWA, the union argued that,

> It is our considered judgment that the subsidized training of apparel workers under the Manpower Development and Training Act is unnecessary . . . on the basis of our many years of experience in the apparel industry we are convinced that such training of apparel workers is not only a waste of federal funds but sets in motion forces detrimental to the health and stability of our industry." [Union document, p. 2]

They also stated that,

> the hiring of inexperienced workers by the industry is central to its functioning.
>
> . . . training and the possession of a specific apparel skill is not an essential requirement for employment in the apparel industry and . . . the training of inexperienced workers by the employer is a normal phase of the apparel business.
>
> Since skill has never been and is not now a precondition of employment in the apparel industry, government subsidization of the training of apparel workers is not required to provide employment in the apparel industry.
>
> . . . finally government subsidies for training apparel workers encourages increased instability in a highly unstable industry.

The report concludes:

> These considerations apply to government financed training programs under the Area Redevelopment Act, as well as the Manpower Development and Training Act. We, therefore, respectfully urge that the Department of Labor as a matter of policy not sponsor or approve any training program for apparel workers under the Manpower Development Act.

Both the ILGWU and the ACWA have used their considerable political power to prevent in Newark and elsewhere the same sort of training programs that are operating with public funds in many other industries.

The union argument, that there is no need for training skilled workers, is directly contradicted by statements made by officials of the ILGWU including Gus Tyler, the Assistant President of the union. Mr. Tyler has written:

> There is a shortage of skilled sewing machine operators. Nobody knows this better than the ILGWU. Some employers have either closed shop in New York or threatened to fold up for lack of skilled operators.[15]

In the same article he also referred to the "advanced skills" required by the ladies' garment industry. In addition it should be noted that some ILGWU contracts provide for a "learners" status of ten months and several union agreements require that a year shall pass before a new employee is entitled to the full rate of pay. The statement of the apparel labor unions is also contradicted by recent manpower data on the industry. According to the "Occupational Training Needs Survey," Research Series No. 18, September 1964, prepared and compiled by the State of New Jersey, Department of Labor and Industry, Division of Employment Security:

> By 1965 there will be a shortage in three of the six semiskilled occupations surveyed. These occupations are: machine presser in the garment, laundry, and cleaning and dyeing industries. By 1968 [in addition to those occupations expected to be in short supply in 1965] there will be shortage of sewing machine operators and hand pressers in the garment, laundry, cleaning and dyeing industries.

These data are extremely significant as they directly relate to the proposal submitted to the Office of Economic Opportunity for funding by the Newark anti-poverty council. Furthermore, Newark has been officially declared a depressed area with extremely high unemployment among Negroes. Recognizing the acute needs of the Negro community, the federal agency was attempting to provide training for two hundred welfare recipients. Such job training programs, which will enable the long-term unemployed to leave the relief rolls by obtaining jobs as a result of newly acquired skills, is the essence of any real war against poverty.

The insistence of the two apparel unions that there is no necessity for training workers in the garment industry and their ability to prevent new training opportunities under the anti-poverty program have a special implication for Negro workers. Negro applicants for jobs in the garment industry are often asked if they have had previous experience. Because they have been denied the opportunity to obtain such experience, they are either denied work or employed only in menial and unskilled jobs. How often have Negroes plaintively expressed it thus: "If they don't give me a job so I can learn, I will never get experience, and without experience nobody will hire me." The ILGWU's restrictive practices are to a large degree responsible for the acute lack of job mobility among Negro garment workers.

In its presentation to the federal government, the ILGWU repeatedly insisted that manufacturing plants are small and that the industry does not require skilled workers. But at the September 1965 meeting of the ILGWU's General Executive Board, President Dubinsky announced the establishment of a new Master Agreement Department. According to *The New York Times* of September 8, 1965, this new department will "deal with the giant apparel companies that have burgeoned in the women's garment industry in recent years." *The Times* report observes that

> While the average garment concern is still a small one, union officials say that in less than a decade the big companies have grown to a point where they now produce a fifth of all women's apparel. They operate across product lines, link plants in many states, regions, markets and union divisions, and often employ thousands of workers under a single management, the board said.

The development of many large companies with modern production methods that require new skills has been evident for some time. But even though nonwhites constitute a potentially large source of skilled-labor recruitment for this industry, they have been effectively denied such opportunities mainly as a result of restrictive labor union practices. Secretary of Labor Willard Wirtz stated on March 1, 1966 at a meeting of the National Board of the Coat and Suit Industry: "Industry reports show that companies were having difficulty finding people with skills. In terms of fully prepared people there is a shortage." He also noted that the impending shortage called for preparations to take care of the expanding needs in industry and asked for support of the on-the-job training program.[16] David Dubinsky, according to *Women's Wear Daily* of March 2, 1966, in response to the Secretary's statement "scored the Administration's assistance programs for on the job training as they applied to the coat and suit industry."

In the Harvard University study, *Made in New York: Case Studies in*

Metropolitan Manufacturing (Harvard University Press, 1959) it is noted that Negroes and Latin Americans

> were largely to be found in the less skilled lower paid crafts and in shops making the lower price lines and in this industry their advancement to higher skills was not proceeding very rapidly. In the higher skilled coat and suit industry the new ethnic groups have hardly made an appearance.

> In short, Negro and Puerto Rican women, who are on the lower rungs of the city's economic ladder, have become important in the New York garment industry, but they work mainly in the more standardized branches, and with few exceptions, unlike the Jewish and Italian men of earlier days, they do not become highly skilled tailor system workers on dresses or "cloaks." As a result, a shortage of skilled sewing machine operators is developing.

The New York Times of June 7, 1967 reported that "15 girls in a Lower West Side branch of the neighborhood Youth Corps armed themselves with cherry cream pies and soft drinks yesterday to retain the sewing machines they love." This was another instance where the ILGWU attempted to abruptly terminate an apparel trades training program in New York City operated at several locations by the Neighborhood Youth Corps with federal funds provided by the Office of Economic Opportunity. The programs involved groups of teen-age girls mainly Negro and Puerto Rican high school "dropouts" who bitterly defended their sewing machines and their right to learn a craft.[17]

This apparel training program was finally saved only by private donations which made possible the delivery of new machines and bolts of fabric to the community training centers after the federal funds were withdrawn. On June 13, 1967 the *New York Post* quoted Jerry Kolker, project director of the local Youth Corps training program, who said that "Neither the government nor the union will cooperate with us. But now we have enough machines and money to keep going, even if they come to collect them again." Kolker added: "We have asked them [the unions] for their help in developing training programs and working out a solution to this problem but the ILGWU won't answer." Ironically, those labor unions which in the past were important vehicles for improving the economic condition of workers now use their power to prevent the entry of certain groups of workers into the labor market or to lock these groups permanently in unrewarding menial and unskilled job categories.

The New York Times of August 18, 1962, reporting on the testimony of Moe Falikman, Business Manager of Cutters Local 10, before a hearing of the Subcommittee of the House Committee on Education and Labor stated, "Mr. Falikman explained that Local 10 had no formal training program for cutters and no apprentice system." That led Congressman James Roosevelt to observe that "with the changing pattern of population in New York it seems to me you would have gone to some lengths" to provide training and jobs for members of racial minorities.

"We are not an employment agency," Mr. Falikman replied.

"But you are," Mr. Roosevelt declared. "I'd have greater faith in you if you would face this situation honestly and say, yes, this needs looking into."

After consulting with a union attorney, Falikman did agree that he would look into it.

The New York Times of August 25, 1962, in reporting Mr. Dubinsky's appearance before the House Subcommittee stated that he denied that it was the union's responsibility to upgrade Negroes and Puerto Ricans, "as much as we would like to see them go to higher brackets. The union," he said, "is not an employment agency." Other ILGWU officials appearing before the Subcommittee insisted that upgrading and promotion was not the union's responsibility. "We are not an employment agency," they all said.

But in the testimony reprinted in the October 1, 1962 issue of the ILGWU newspaper *Justice*, in reply to a question as to why Negroes and Puerto Ricans do not advance in the union or in the industry, Dubinsky is quoted as saying, "We are doing everything under the sun on this score."

Either the ILGWU is "doing everything under the sun" or "we are not an employment agency, it's not our responsibility." The union cannot have it both ways.

After many complaints from Negro workers against the ILGWU, and the filing of charges of racial discrimination against the union with the New York State Commission for Human Rights,[18] an investigation of the status of non-white workers within the garment industry and within the ILGWU was made by the Committee on Education and Labor of the U.S. House of Representatives during 1962. As part of the Congressional investigation a series of public hearings were held in New York City and Washington, D.C. At the request of the House Committee on Education and Labor, the author, the NAACP's Labor Secretary, functioned as a special consultant to the Congressional Committee.

An additional factor prompting the Congressional investigation was that the National Labor Relations Board in 1962 had found the ILGWU guilty of unfair labor practices in relation to a union of its own employees.[19] The ILGWU unsuccessfully opposed an NLRB order for a certification election among its employees and then refused to recognize and bargain with the Federation of Union Representatives (FOUR) after that union won the election and was certified as the collective-bargaining representative. The ILGWU was found guilty of coercing members of FOUR and was ordered on several occasions by the NLRB to cease reprisals against employees who support the Federation of Union Representatives, but the ILGWU for years has conducted a campaign of harassment and dismissal against FOUR supporters and has spent vast sums in litigation appealing NLRB orders. It is interesting to note that other important international unions have recognized unions of their own employees but the ILGWU remains adamant in its refusal to recognize FOUR.*[20]

One of the revealing consequences of the public exposure of racial practices within the ILGWU was the action taken by the union's General Executive Board to cancel an agreement with the Workmen's Circle Home for the Aged in New York City because of the discriminatory admission practices of that organization. After the union with much fanfare announced the project (see June 1, 1961, issue of *Justice* with headline over masthead reading "ILG Wing of 'Circle' Home Opening June 11"), Negro union members protested the use of union funds to build a facility not available to them. After the congressional investigation the Dubinsky leadership became more sensitive to public criticism and canceled the discriminatory agreement.

According to the Report of the General Executive Board to the Thirty-second Convention of the ILGWU, Miami Beach, Florida, May 12,

---

*It is not only union representatives who had legitimate grievances against the Dubinsky leadership. The 650 office employees, organized in their own union (Local 153 Office and Professional Employees) went on a one-day strike on December 16, 1965. The immediate issue over which the long-dissatisfied office workers struck concerned a notice by the ILGWU, which had heretofore paid all the Social Security payments of these workers, that it would pay only 50 per cent after January 1, 1966. Employers normally pay only 50 per cent, but since in this case the union's payment of the whole amount was built into the office workers' wage levels, the workers interpreted the notice as a wage cut. After bargaining and achieving little satisfaction, they walked off their jobs. To our knowledge, the only serious account in the daily press appeared in the trade paper of the garment industry, *Women's Wear*, December 17, 1965.

1965,[21] the union in 1959 began the construction of an ILGWU wing at the Workmen's Circle Home in the Bronx for retired union members at a cost of $1,300,000. After the ILGWU wing was dedicated on June 11, 1961, ". . . the Workmen's Circle Home refused to process several applications of non-Jewish ILGWU members,"[22] even though the wing was built with the dues money of all union members. Anticipating public exposure, the ILGWU leadership canceled the discriminatory agreement with the Workmen's Circle.[23]

Among the several examples of discriminatory practices cited at the hearings is that of the status of the "push boys" auxiliary unit known as 60-A. Local 60, the Pressers' local, controls jobs that on an hourly rated basis are the highest-paying jobs in the garment industry in New York, the average wage in 1962 being almost five dollars an hour. According to testimony, Local 60 had an all-white membership. Sixty-A was and is simply an appendage to Local 60. Its members are almost entirely Negro and Puerto Rican, and work as shipping clerks, push boys, and delivery men, earning in the vicinity of fifty dollars per week. Yet 60-A, with twice the membership of Local 60, has never been chartered by the international as a separate local, and the manager of 60, who is a presser, also functions as the manager of 60-A. In the annual reports filed with the Bureau of Labor-Management Reports of the U.S. Department of Labor, a joint report is filed for 60 and 60-A, although every ILGWU local union files individually. In addition, one must note that all the business agents for Local 60 are elected by the local's members, but the three Negroes who perform similar functions in 60-A are appointed and designated as "delegates" rather than business agents.[24]

Also cited in the hearings was the case of a Negro worker, Ernest Holmes, against Local 10 of the ILGWU, then pending before the New York State Commission for Human Rights. On April 4, 1961 a complaint was filed against Local 10 of the International Ladies Garment Workers Union with the New York State Commission for Human Rights. On May 18, 1963, twenty-five months later, in the case of *Holmes vs. Falikman*,[25] the ILGWU entered into a stipulation agreement upon which the complaint was finally withdrawn. In the settlement obtained by the Commission the union agreed to admit Holmes into the Cutters local of the ILGWU, to assist him in seeking employment and in gaining training experience as an apprentice cutter. This is precisely what the State Commission had ordered the ILGWU to do a year before when a finding of "probable cause" was issued by the investigating commissioner. *The*

New York Times of July 2, 1962, in a report headlined "Union Told to Get Job for a Negro," stated:

> A garment cutters' union has been ordered by the State Commission for Human Rights to arrange for employment of a Negro at union rates commensurate with his skill and to admit the Negro into union membership if his work is satisfactory.

The Times story also stated: "With regard to the union, the decision found that 'the evidence raises serious doubt as to its good faith to comply with the State Law Against Discrimination in the matter of this complaint; and that there was "probable cause" to credit the allegations of the complaint.' "On September 14, 1962 Rupert Ruiz, Investigating Commissioner of the New State Commission for Human Rights, in a letter to Emil Schlesinger, Attorney for Local 10, stated that the Commission had "repeatedly requested and for a period of eight months tried to obtain data pertinent to a resolution of the charges of discrimination against Amalgamated Ladies Garment Cutters Union—Local 10. These efforts were unsuccessful. The failure of representatives of that local to cooperate in the investigation, despite their promises to do so, left me no alternative but to find probable cause to credit the allegations of the complaint.' "

The ILGWU was involved in a previous case before the State Commission brought by a Negro union member on the issue of separate nationality locals. Nationality locals have been illegal since 1945 in New York under the State Anti-Discrimination Law. Title VII, the Equal Employment Section of the Civil Rights Act of 1964 further requires the elimination of such locals and some unions have moved to disband them. On May 18, 1966, at a tempestuous meeting of the New York Furriers Union Joint Council (affiliated with the Amalgamated Meat Cutters and Butcher Workmen, AFL-CIO) the forty-year-old Greek Fur Workers' local was dissolved. The fifteen-hundred member local union went out of existence and its members transferred to other locals affiliated with the Furriers Joint Council, as a result of action by the international union to comply with Title VII. According to *The New York Times* of May 19, 1966:

> After lengthy hearings and an impartial finding by Professor Samuel Bader of the Brooklyn Law School, the council's parent union, the Amalgamated Meat Cutters and Butcher Workmen, decided that the continued existence of the local violated at least the spirit of the Federal Fair Employment Act.

Although the Furriers Union and other labor organizations have moved to disband nationality locals because of the requirements of Title VII, the International Ladies Garment Workers Union continues to maintain two Italian language locals in New York City: Local 89 designated as the Italian Dressmakers Union and Local 48 designated as the Italian Cloakmakers Union. According to the Report of the General Executive Board of the ILGWU dated May 13, 1965, Local 89, the largest local in the international union, has a membership of 20,898 and Local 48 has a membership of 8047.

In 1946 a formal complaint was filed with the State Commission by a Negro member of Local 22 who was barred from higher-paying jobs controlled by Local 89.[26] After the Commission had notified the ILGWU that the existence of nationality locals was a violation of state law, a conference was held on January 22, 1947, at which the ILGWU entered into an agreement with the Commission that it would not bar Negroes, Spanish-speaking or other persons from membership in the Italian locals. Twenty years later not a single Negro or Spanish-speaking person holds membership in the two Italian locals which have control of some of the highest-paying jobs in the industry and the ILGWU has taken no action to comply with the state law.

A major factor to be understood about the status of Negro workers in the ILGWU is the relationship between Negro powerlessness within the union and economic exploitation. In 1956 the average weekly wage for garment workers in New York City was $55.60. The average over-all manufacturing wage for the city was $74.76. Extensive interviewing of Negro and Puerto Rican workers by the author and other investigators indicates that these workers were and remain concentrated in the lowest-paid categories of employment, with very little, if any, job mobility. During 1956 (a boom year in the garment industry) Negro and Puerto Rican workers took home as little as $2500, but for the highly skilled cutters and pressers, virtually all of whom were white, $8000 was not unusual.

For many locals in New York City in which the overwhelming membership is Negro and Puerto Rican, the wage schedules provided in the collective bargaining are a disgrace to the American labor movement. In these agreements the so-called "minimum wages" are in fact most frequently the maximum wages. In this category are floor girls, shipping clerks, trimmers, and sewing-machine operators in the low-priced dress field and in the so-called "miscellaneous locals" with their large concentrations of Negro and Puerto Rican workers.

The basic contract between Local 98 and the Manufacturers Association in effect until August 14, 1963, provided the following minimum wages—p. 7, Article 4(a):

Floor girls	$1.15 an hour
Operators	1.20
Shipping Clerks	1.20
Cutters	1.20*

Wage scales of other ILGWU contracts in force until 1963 in those locals with a high concentration of nonwhite workers were as follows:

Local 32: Pressers, operators, cleaners, examiners	$1.15
Local 40: Operators, shippers, floor girls	1.15
Local 62: Operators, ironers, examiners, finishers	1.15
Local 91: Operators, ironers, cleaners, finishers	1.20
Local 98: Operators, shipping clerks, cutters, floor girls	1.15

Several new contracts were negotiated at the expiration of those cited above. As a result of the increase in the federal minimum wage to $1.25 an hour there was a small upward adjustment of wage scales. However, the pattern described above remains intact. (On February 20, 1967 a new three-year agreement covering eighty thousand dressmakers employed in ILGWU shops became effective. According to the AFL-CIO *News* the new contract provided for the following weekly wages, ". . . $68 for examiners, $75 for drapers, $65 for cleaners and others, $67 and $72 for shipping clerks,"[27]

The *Baltimore Sun* and other major newspapers across the country carried a North American Newspaper Alliance report datelined New York, June 4, 1964, under the headline "Most Garment Worker Paychecks Are Below Johnson Poverty Level." The report began:

---

*These are cutters of plastic material who are not under the jurisdiction of the Cutters Local 10.

A majority of the 800,000 members of two garment unions, usually ranked among the "most aggressive" in the country, average less than the $3000 yearly in take-home pay that the Johnson Administration has declared is the poverty level.

The unions are the Amalgamated Clothing Workers and the International Ladies Garment Workers Union.

After describing the low average wages earned by members of the Amalgamated Clothing Workers, the report went on:

Most ILGWU members fared worse. The ILGWU's 1964 contract with women's apparel manufacturers for floor workers (common laborers in other industries) provides for an average of $1.50 an hour with skilled machine operators drawing $1.90 an hour. These two categories account for close to 90 per cent of the ILGWU membership of more than 400,000. . . .

A huge majority of ACW and ILGWU members are Negroes and Puerto Ricans which are the principal groups singled out for help in the "war on poverty" in the cities.

On April 16, 1967 the New York Congress of Racial Equality (CORE) held a press conference to protest the 1967 agreements signed by the ILGWU and stated that the "ILGWU has for years permitted conditions to exist which keep the vast majority of black workers in the lowest-paying jobs and has denied black workers a policy-making voice in the union through restrictive constitutional provisions."[28]

In announcing that CORE was engaged in the "formation of a black caucus to fight bias and powerlessness in the ILGWU" Roy Innis, Chairman of Harlem CORE, stated:

The growing number of black workers coming to Harlem CORE to lodge complaints against the ILGWU and the disgraceful contracts signed in 1967 make it imperative that immediate action be taken. CORE is now assisting black garment workers of New York City in organizing for the right of black people to participate in basic policymaking for their own protection. With the help of CORE a black caucus is now being organized to fight for the basic democratic rights of all nonwhite workers and eliminate racial discrimination in one of the richest and most powerful unions in the world.[29]

In reality there are two categories of workers in the ILGWU: a relatively small number of highly skilled white workers with seniority and stability of employment who earn high wages and for whom the union performs a variety of protective functions, and the great mass of unskilled low-paid workers, mostly Negro and Puerto Rican, who exist in a permanent condition of semipoverty and are the base of the industry's work force as well as of the union's membership in New York City. As a result, the city must subsidize the low-wage garment industry. The extent of the public subsidy which the substandard garment industry in New York requires is indicated in part by unemployment compensation payments. In 1956, unemployment compensation payments in New York City totaled $127,686,000. It is significant that in that highly profitable year for the industry over thirty million dollars, or 24 per cent, went to workers in the ladies' garment industry who as a group accounted for only 3½ per cent of the city's total work force. The garment industry, as well as other low-paying industries, is subsidized by federal, state, and municipal agencies in a variety of other ways. But in each case, as the city's largest low-wage manufacturing industry, it receives a highly disproportionate share of these subsidies.

Perhaps it is axiomatic that any serious exposure of the anti-social practices of an entrenched bureaucracy, such as that of the ILGWU leadership, would be met with anger and resentment. Yet the ILGWU response has been so extreme that it reveals much about the union leadership and its allies in the liberal community. Instead of making an honest effort to deal with criticisms both before and after they were made public, the ILGWU attempted to smear its critics. Union spokesmen charged the critics with being "Communist agents," "racist slanderers," and anti-Semites.[30]

The Jewish Labor Committee, which consists largely of ILGWU officials, distributed a memorandum by Emmanuel Muravchik, National Field Director, dated November 16, 1962 which repeated the union's charge that the NAACP's criticism of the racial practices of the ILGWU "contributes to anti-Semitic feelings" but makes no attempt to deal substantively with the real issue of racial discrimination and the denial of democratic membership rights within the ILGWU.

To Muravchik's charges, Roy Wilkins responded in a letter dated October 31, 1962 as follows:

We assert with the greatest emphasis that nothing, absolutely nothing, in Mr. Hill's recent or more remote statements can be construed as anti-Semitic. This is a grave charge to make. It requires more substantiation than your flip reference in a part of a sentence. The charge is not only against Mr. Hill, but against the NAACP itself. We do not deign to defend ourselves against such a baseless allegation. Its inclusion in the resolution, as well as in the statements to the press . . . is unworthy of an organization like the Jewish Labor Committee which, in the very nature of things, must be concerned with the seriousness of such a charge and with the evidence required to give it substance. No such evidence has been submitted in this case beyond the citation of the use by Mr. Hill of one word, "ethnic," out of a total of 4500 words in his testimony before the House subcommittee. The relevance of his comparison of the ethnic composition of the membership of the ILGWU can hardly be questioned in this context. . . .

We reject the proposition that any segment of the labor movement is sacrosanct in the matter of practices and/or policies which restrict employment opportunities on racial or religious or nationality grounds. We reject the contention that bringing such charges constitutes a move to destroy "unity" among civil rights groups unless it be admitted that this unity is a precarious thing, perched upon unilateral definition of discrimination by each member group. In such a situation the "unity" is of no basic value and its destruction may be regarded as not a calamity, but a blessed clearing of the air.

In this connection, it is well to reiterate a facet of this discussion which appears to have escaped the attention of the various reviewers and resolution writers. It is that Herbert Hill, our Labor Secretary, has one duty and that is to serve the interests of the Negro workers through the NAACP. Other groups, including trade unions, have powerful machinery to protect their principal interests. Mr. Hill is employed to maintain anti-discrimination work in the employment field as his top and only priority. He is not for trade unions first and Negro workers second. He has no divided loyalites.

Wilkins indicates that the whole concept of a Negro labor coalition is worthless to Negroes, if such a coalition means a gentlemen's agreement to refrain from attacking racial discrimination within labor unions.

In his letter Wilkins also pointed out that many copies of the Muravchik memo had been sent to unions with the request that they adopt resolutions condemning the NAACP, all based upon their own "bare statement and interpretation" of the NAACP's charges, ignoring the factual accuracy of the assertions. Therefore the Jewish Labor Committee was spreading "a climate of hostility to the Naacp."

When you declare in 1962 that the NAACP's continued attack upon discrimination against Negro workers by trade union bodies and leaders places "in jeopardy" continued progress toward civil rights goals or endangers the "unity" among civil rights forces, or renders a "disservice" to the Negro workers, or raises the question "whether it is any longer possible to work with the NAACP" you are, in fact, seeking by threats to force us to conform to what the Jewish Labor Committee is pleased to classify as proper behavior in the circumstances.

Wilkins cited the NAACP's awareness "that the trade union movement can be a strength to the Negro population of our country whose employed portion is largely in the working class," but noted that for too long and "almost too faithfully" the NAACP followed "the procedure of waiting and working in every possible way to resolve union-race situations without open breaks." But care and respect born of concern for the long-run welfare of Negro workers, as well as concern for the unions as protection for all workers, "should not be regarded as foreclosing a frontal attack, irrespective of the opponent of the Negro worker." Wilkins noted that in 1959 the NAACP had offered to meet with officials of the ILGWU to discuss complaints from Negro garment workers who were also NAACP members, but that the offer was dismissed in a summary fashion by the union leadership.

The NAACP's fundamental attitude toward organized labor was further delineated in a letter from Wilkins to George Meany on December 7, 1962. Wilkins wrote that "there is no difference of opinion between the NAACP and the AFL-CIO upon the desirability of a harmonious relationship among all those who are sincere in their desire to serve the cause of human rights. . . ." However, he stated that while Meany had assured the NAACP that the AFL-CIO did not hold that unions are beyond the legitimate range of criticism, a scanning of NAACP reports from the 1930s on revealed that organized labor had repeatedly rejected and "denounced thoroughly legitimate and soundly based criticism of discriminatory policies and practices of unions in the organized labor movement." Moreover, the evidence showed that opposition to the AFL-CIO policy of nondiscrimination was not centered in only "a few local unions and their members," as Meany claimed. Mr. Wilkins added:

> We do not believe these charges of discrimination are untrue. We do not believe an enumeration and a substantiation of them constitutes an "attack" upon organized labor. In our view, the conditions covered by these charges constitute a formidable barrier to the enjoyment by millions of Negro workers of employment opportunity and of greater security in our economy.

Going on to cite the discriminatory practices of affiliated AFL-CIO unions and stressing that they constituted a national pattern that had the approval of various international unions, he continued:

> It remains our view that no collective bargaining agreement which provides for separate racial seniority lines can be said to be nondiscriminatory. It is our further

view that where this type of agreement is kept in effect over a period of years, despite repeated protests and requests for alteration, the union has forfeited its right to bargain collectively for all the workers and that the proper agency, the NLRB, may fairly be petitioned to revoke the certification.

But Wilkins noted that invoking decertification procedures and court action in the campaign to eliminate discriminatory practices was a last resort, since the destruction of unions is *not* the NAACP's objective, "despite accusations to the contrary." It is only "the precarious situation of the Negro worker," Wilkins emphasized, which "spurs our impatience." He ended:

> The conclusion is inescapable that desegregation in the labor movement has proceeded at no more rapid a rate than the disgraceful crawl of public school desegration in the South. When it is considered that unions are declared opponents of segregation through numerous resolutions and policy statements, whereas the Southern states are declared proponents of segregation, the matching snail's pace understandably raises eyebrows in the Negro community.

The exposure of the status of nonwhite workers in the ILGWU, together with the revelations about the monolithic control of the union, provoked a debate that had widespread repercussions in the "liberal-labor community." Typical of the comments from those who had accepted the image of the ILGWU as a progressive and democratic union were: "Why does the NAACP single out the ILGWU?" "Aren't there unions with far worse records than this one?" These questions are usually asked by those who will candidly acknowledge that the charges are justified in large measure, but bridle at concentrating so much fire on an allegedly progressive union which passes fine resolutions on civil rights and contributes to worthy causes. This approach is unwarranted for the following reasons:

> 1. The ILGWU, the largest union in the largest manufacturing industry in the nation's largest city, directly affects the economic welfare and dignity of hundreds of thousands of Negro and Puerto Rican men, women, and children in New York.

> 2. The "go soft on Dubinsky[or Stulberg]"line has the disagreeable connotations of "Uncle Tomism": it suggests that the liberal and Negro community should be appreciative of small favors and not attack "benefactors" even if those friends aren't perfect. The documentation reveals that in reality the ILGWU has bestowed no "favors" on the Negro and has acted in a discriminatory manner—hidden under the rhetoric of its liberal past.

3. The question "Hill is really right but why make such a fuss over a progressive union?" is asked by those who substitute sentimentality for thought, and wish fulfillment for reality. The progressive label is only a nostalgic hangover from a dead past. The word suggests militancy, internal democracy, and social vision. On none of these counts does the ILGWU qualify.

4. The ILGWU leadership is greatly concerned with presenting a progressive and liberal public image, without a critical examination of the social consequences of its policies and practices. Perhaps the most dismal factor in the entire situation is its inability to admit that anything at all is wrong. But, as I have already pointed out, since the ILGWU leadership does care greatly about its public image, it is possible that vigorous public pressure might have salutary effects.

There are indications that as a result of exposure and criticism of the ILGWU some Negroes and Puerto Ricans have obtained better-paying jobs and that the operational bar against their entering leadership positions will eventually be breached. After the NAACP's activity a Puerto Rican for the first time was appointed to the union's General Executive Board, Negroes have been employed in hitherto "lily-white" staff positions within the union, and ILGWU officials are less arrogant in their daily treatment of the Negro membership. Eventually the ILGWU may feel obliged to do something about the substandard wage levels in the industry which victimize primarily the Negro and Puerto Rican workers.

Ten years after the merger the pattern of racial discrimination by labor unions in many important jurisdictions, especially in the skilled craft occupations, remains intact. Some instances of isolated progress have occurred as a result of actions before the National Labor Relations Board, the filing of complaints with federal and state anti-discrimination agencies, the securing of court orders and organized public pressure from the Negro protest movement. But this "progress" does not represent a basic elimination of the patterns of racial discrimination practiced by major sections of organized labor.

There has recently occurred a fundamental change in the immediacy of the goals and in the level of aspiration that Negroes hold in relation to all the institutions of American society, including labor unions. Virtually all the concessions made by "liberal" whites, including union leaders, are forthcoming only as a reaction to Negro protest, to Negro anger, and each concession quite properly creates the realistic basis for the next demand. Labor union leaders, in common with many others, are tragically incapable of understanding the dynamics of contemporary

Negro protest. Thus, they express petulance and bitter resentment at increasing Negro demands and frequently are most indignant because "Negroes don't appreciate what we are doing for them."

Across the country many powerful labor unions are an important part of the "liberal labor" coalitions that are in control of municipal governments. The fundamental failure of this coalition, nationally and locally, is expressed most sharply in the deteriorating condition of the Negro in the cities, and the vast expansion of racial ghettos and urban rot. Furthermore, labor unions with vast treasuries that control banks and real estate, purchase high-yield securities on the stock market, and engage in a variety of enterprises are not using union funds for socially desirable purposes.

Organized labor has not used its political influence and financial power to eliminate segregated slums and to alter the dehumanizing status of Negroes locked in the racial ghettos of the urban North. When the building trades unions directly prevent Negroes from working on highly visible public construction projects or when unions such as the International Ladies Garment Workers Union prevent training opportunities for unemployed Negro workers in their jurisdictions, they are directly contributing to the growing racial crisis of the cities.

In a period of racial unheaval and vast dislocation in the urban centers, labor unions whose base is in the cities have become part of that political coalition attempting to maintain the status quo, a status quo that can no longer be tolerated by the urban Negro. Data released by the U.S. Department of Labor on September 5, 1967, indicate that more white workers were employed than at any previous time in the nation's history, but that during the same period more Negroes were unemployed than ever before. At the same time that white workers are earning the highest wages in the nation's history, the economic status of Negro wage earners is deteriorating and the differential between the income of white and Negro workers continues to increase.

As the polarization between the white working class, which shares in the affluence of American society, and the black sub-proletariat, which is kept outside of the labor force and is fundamentally alienated from the social order, increases, organized labor as a social institution becomes more conservative.

A most hopeful development is the significant rise in Negro caucuses inside certain labor organizations and the growth of independent "black unions." These include the Independent Alliance of Skilled Crafts in

Ohio, the Maryland Freedom Labor Union, and the Allied Workers International Union in Gary, Indiana, among others. The public attack made by Walter Reuther, President of the United Automobile Workers Union, against the conservative leadership of the AFL-CIO may also become important. In resigning from the Federation's Executive Council, Mr. Reuther denounced the Meany leadership as "the complaisant custodians of the status quo," and prominent among Reuther's criticisms of the Federation's policies and practices was the failure to develop a meaningful commitment to the cause of civil rights and job equality. Emil Mazey, Secretary-Treasurer of the United Automobile Workers Union, resigned from the Civil Rights Committee of the AFL-CIO and denounced its failure to eliminate racist practices in organized labor.

As the racial situation does not change for the overwhelming majority of Negroes and as the economic status of colored workers continues to deteriorate, the entire Negro community becomes increasingly aware of the profound disparity between promise and performance. Thus, there is a new impatience and a rejection of token adjustment and of the "Uncle Tom" who represents racial shame and white paternalism. The dramatic events of recent years in the North as in the South clearly indicate that only the sharpest confrontations with discriminatory institutions can bring change and progress for colored workers, that the white man listens only after the Negro has created a crisis. This is as true for organized labor as for most other institutions in American society.

A consequence of this development is the steady deterioration of relations between the Negro protest movement in its diverse forms and the vague arrangement of groups assembled under the worn banner of "liberalism," a liberalism that has been in retreat and decline for over a generation. White "liberals" in the North can no longer deflect the Negro attack away from their own discriminatory practices, from their own neighborhoods and institutions, by expressing outrage at Southern racism. The white groups traditionally identified with "liberalism" in the North are facing a crisis over their own racial practices, and the so-called "Negro-liberal-labor coalition" is repeatedly subjected to stresses and tensions.

Today, more so than at any time in the past, the order of priority on social issues is vastly different for whites and Negroes. As very real differences and conflicts over programs and tactics develop between the Negro movement and the white liberals, the coalition is increasingly weakened and loses operational meaning. It is hoped that after the debris of the past and present is swept aside, a new constellation of forces may develop in which the Negro can share responsibility and leadership, a new movement in which the interests of colored people are not subordinated to "other considerations" and where there is a genuine appreciation of the unique social experience of the Negro in American life. But such an alliance can develop only when organized labor sheds its bureaucratic conservatism and becomes a dynamic force, capable of organizing millions of unorganized workers in the South and elsewhere, and prepared to challenge the status quo. Thus, the struggle for racial equality and internal democracy within labor unions is a struggle for the regeneration of organized labor as a significant social movement within the United States.

NOTES

1. See speech of Sam Zagoria, member of NLRB, to the Twelfth Annual Institute on Labor Law, The Southwestern Legal Foundation, Dallas, Oct. 28, 1965, NLRB_ Washington, D.C.

2. *Spanish Speaking Workers and the Labor Movement,* A Report of the Association of Catholic Trade Unionists (New York, 1957), 2.

3. P. 52, Article 8, Section 16 of the ILGWU Constitution (1959 ed.).

4. P. 14, Article 13, Section 6 of the ILGWU Constitution. For an analysis of union constitutions, see "Union Constitutions and the Election of Local Union Officers," Labor Management Services Administration, U.S. Department of Labor, April 1965, Washington, D.C.; also "Union Constitution Provisions: Election and Tenure of National and International Union Officers," Bulletin No. 1239, U.S. Department of Labor, 1958.

5. Kenneth B. Clark, *Dark Ghetto: Dilemmas of Social Power* (Harper & Row, New York, 1965), 43.

6. Ibid., 43.

7. Damon Stetson, "Stulberg Doubts a Garment Strike," *The New York Times,* Jan. 26, 1967.

8. Murray Kempton, "The Wage Fight," *New York Post,* Aug. 21, 1962.

9. Murray Seeger, "Governor Vetoes $1.50 Minimum Pay: New Bill Is Likely," *The New York Times,* April 17, 1965.

10. Peter Braestrup, New York *Herald Tribune,* Oct. 8, 1958.

11. Ibid., Oct. 7, 1958.

12. For a documentation of the status of nonwhite workers in the ladies garment industry in New York City and in the ILGWU, see Congressional Record—House (Testimony of Herbert Hill on Racial Practices of ILGWU), Jan. 31, 1963, 1596-1599. See also Herbert Hill, "The ILGWU—Fact and Fiction," *New Politics,* 1962, No. 2, 7-27.

13. U.S. Department of Labor, Bureau of Labor Statistics, "Occupational Earnings—Women's and Misses' Dresses," Aug. 1966, 1 (No. 66-176).

14. A.H. Raskin, "DD and the American Dream," *The New Leader*, April 11, 1966.

15. Gus Tyler, "The Truth About the ILGWU," *New Politics* II, 1, 12.

16. *The New York Times*, March 2, 1966.

17. See Herbert Hill, "Sewing Machines and Union Machines," *The Nation*, July 3, 1967.

18. Holmes v. Falikman, C-7580-61 (N.Y. State Commission for Human Rights, 1963); see Herbert Hill, "Twenty Years of State Fair Employment Practice Laws: A Critical Analysis," *Buffalo Law Review*, XIII (Autumn 1964), 34-35.

19. *The New York Times*, Aug. 14, 1962, "Garment Union Is Found Guilty of Coercion by NLRB Aide." The news report stated that "A National Labor Relations Board trial examiner found the International Ladies Garment Workers Union guilty of unfair labor practices today" and noted that the trial examiner urged, ". . . that the garment union leaders be ordered to stop 'interfering with . . . restraining and coercing' staff employees who are also members of the Federation of Union Representatives. The Associated Press report appearing in the New York *Post*, Aug. 13, 1962, stated, "The International Ladies Garment Workers Union was judged guilty today of unfair labor practices in trying to prevent its employees from forming their own labor organization." See Murray Kempton, "The Bitter Joke," New York *Post*, March 10, 1961, and "A Primer For Bosses," New York *Post*, May 9, 1961; also Peter Braestrup, "Union Within Union Set For ILGWU," *The New York Times*, April 15, 1961.

20. *Decision and Order*, April 29, 1965. Case No. 2-CA-8849. National Labor Relations Board, International Ladies Garment Workers Union, and Federation of Union Representatives.

21. Report of the General Executive Board to the Thirty-third Convention, ILGWU, Miami Beach, May 12, 1965, 57.

22. Ibid., 58.

23. Ibid.

24. See *Congressional Record*—House, Jan. 31, 1963, 1496-99. (Testimony of Herbert Hill on the Racial Practices of the ILGWU). See also Hill, "The ILGWU Today—The Decay of a Labor Union," *New Politics*, Summer 1962, and Hill, "The ILGWU—Fact and Fiction," *New Politics*, Winter 1963.

25. *Holmes v. Falikman C-7580-61* (N.Y. State Commission for Human Rights, 1963).

26. *Hunter v. Sullivan Dress Shop, C-1439-46* (N%Y% State Commission Against Discrimination, 1947).

27. AFL-CIO News, "80,000 Win 15% Hike in Dress Pact," Feb. 4, 1967, 1.

28. CORE_ Press Release, April 16, 1967.

29. Ibid. See also *The New York Times*, May 3, 1967, "CORE to Organize within ILGWU."

30. Many articles, letters, and memoranda were involved in this debate. Among the most important are the following: Herbert Hill, "The ILGWU Today: The Decay of a Labor Union," *New Politics*, Summer 1962; Gus Tyler, "The Truth about the ILGWU," *New Politics*, Fall 1962, Herbert Hill, "The ILGWU—Fact and Fiction," *New Politics*, Winter 1963, (reply to Tyler); American Jewish Committee, National Labor Service, "Is the ILGWU Biassed?," document dated Nov. 5, 1962; Jewish Labor Committee, Memorandum dated Nov. 16, 1962 by Emanuel Muravchik, National Field Director (covering much the same material as the AJC document); Paul Jacobs, "David Dubinsky: Why his Throne is Wobbling," *Harper's*, Dec. 1962; J. Fogel, article in the *Jewish Daily Forward* (in Yiddish),

Dec. 10, 1962, (reply to Jacobs); Henry Lee Moon, Director of Public Relations, NAACP, "NAACP and Labor" Letter, 31, *New Leader*, Jan. 7, 1963; Daniel Bell, "Reflections on the Negro and Labor," *New Leader*, Jan. 21, 1963.

Voices of Anger and Protest *

Puerto Rican Obituary
by Pedro Pietri

They worked
They were always on time
They were never late
They never spoke back
When they were insulted
They worked
They never went on strike
Without permission
They never took days off
That were on the calendar
They worked
Ten days a week
And were only paid for five
They worked
They worked
They worked
And they died

They died broke
They died owing
They died never knowing
What the front entrance
Of the first national bank
looks like

Juan
Miguel
Milagros
Olga
Manuel
All died yesterday today
And will die tomorrow
Passing their bill collectors
On to the next of kin
All died

* The poem by Pedro Pietri and the essays by Iris Morales and Felipe Luciano are from *Palante!* by Michael Abramson and the Young Lords Party. Copyright (c) 1971 by Michael Abramson and the Young Lords Party. The poem and essays are used here with the permission of McGraw-Hill Book Company. The short story *Bayaminiña* by Pedro Juan Soto appeared originally in his book *Spiks*. It has been translated from the Spanish by Julio Rodríguez-Luis and appears here with the permission of the author.

Waiting for the Garden
of Eden
To open up again
Under a new management
All died
Dreaming about america
Waking them up in the middle
of the night
Screaming: Mira! Mira!
Your name is on the winning
lottery ticket
For one hundred thousand
dollars
All died
Hating the grocery stores
That sold them make-believe
. steak
And bullet-proof rice and
beans
All died waiting dreaming
and hating
Dead Puerto Ricans
Who never knew they were
Puerto Ricans
Who never took a coffee break
From the ten commandments
To **KILL KILL KILL**
The landlords of their cracked
. skulls
And communicate with their
Latin Souls

Juan
Miguel
Milagros
Olga
Manuel
From the nervous breakdown
streets

Where the mice live like
millionaires
And the people do not live
at all
Are dead and were never alive

Juan
Died waiting for his number
to hit
Miguel
Died waiting for the welfare
check
To come and go and come
again
Milagros
Died waiting for her ten
children
To grow up and work
So she could quit working
Olga
Died waiting for a five
dollar raise
Manuel
Died waiting for his
supervisor to drop dead
So that he could get a
promotion

Is a long ride
From Spanish Harlem
To long island cemetery
Where they were buried
First the train
And then the bus
And the cold cuts for lunch
And the flowers
That will be stolen
When visiting hours are over
Is very expensive

Is very expensive
But they understand
Their parents understood
Is a long non-profit ride
From Spanish Harlem
To long island cemetery
Juan
Miguel
Milagros
Olga
Manuel
All died yesterday today
And will die again tomorrow
Dreaming
Dreaming about Queens
Clean cut lily white
    neighborhood
Puerto Ricanless scene
Thirty thousand dollar home
The first spics on the block
Proud to belong to a
    community
Of gringos who want them
    lynched
Proud to be a long distance
    away
From the sacred phrase:
    Qué Pasa?

These dreams
These empty dreams
From the make believe
    bedrooms
Their parents left them
Are the after effects
Of television programs
About the ideal
white american family
With Black maids

And Latin janitors
Who are well trained
To make everyone
And their bill collectors
Laugh at them
And the people they represent

Juan
Died dreaming about a new
    car
Miguel
Died dreaming about new
    anti-poverty programs
Milagros
Died dreaming about a trip to
    Puerto Rico
Olga
Died dreaming about real
    jewelry
Manuel
Died dreaming about the irish
    sweepstakes

They all died
Like a hero sandwich dies
In the garment district
At twelve o'clock in the
    afternoon
Social security numbers to
    ashes
Union dues to dust
They knew
They were born to weep
And keep the morticians
    employed
As long as the pledge
Allegiance
To the flag that wants them
    destroyed

They saw their names listed
In the telephone directory of
    destruction
They were trained to turn
The other cheek by
    newspapers
That misspelled who
    mispronounced
And misunderstood their
    names
And celebrated when death
    came
And stole their final laundry
    ticket

They were born dead
And they died dead

Is time
To visit Sister Lopez again
The number one healer
And fortune card dealer
In Spanish Harlem
She can communicate
With your late relatives
For a reasonable fee
Good news is guaranteed

Rise Table Rise Table
Death is not dumb and disable
Those who love you want to
    know
The correct number to play
Let them know this right
    away
Rise Table Rise Table
Death is not dumb and disable
Now that your problems are
    over

And the world is off your
    shoulders
Help those who you left
    behind
Find financial peace of mind
Rise Table Rise Table
Death is not dumb and disable
If the right number we hit
All our problems will split
And we will visit your graves
On every legal holiday
Those who love you want to
    know
The correct number to play
Let them know this right
    away
We know your spirit is able
Death is not dumb and disable
RISE TABLE RISE TABLE

Juan
Miguel
Milagros
Olga
Manuel
All died yesterday today
And will die again tomorrow
Hating fighting and stealing
Broken windows from each
    other
Practicing a religion without
    a roof
The old testament
The new testament
According to the gospel
Of the internal revenue
The judge and jury and
    executioner
Protector and eternal bill
    collector

Secondhand shit for sale
Learn how to say Cómo Está
    Usted
And you will make a fortune

They are dead
They are dead
And will not return from the
    dead
Until they stop neglecting
The art of their dialogue
For broken english lessons
To impress the mister bosses
Who keep them employed
As dishwashers porters
    messenger boys
Factory workers maids stock
    clerks
Shipping clerks assistant
    mailroom
Assistant, assistant, assistant,
    assistant
To the assistant, assistant
    dishwasher
And automatic smiling
    doorman
For the lowest wages of the
    ages
And rages when you demand
    a raise
Because it's against the
    company policy
To promote **S PIC S   S PIC S
S PIC S**

Juan
Died hating Miguel because
    Miguel's
Used car was in better
    condition
Than his used car

Miguel
Died hating Milagros because
    Milagros
Had a color television set
And he could not afford one
    yet
Milagros
Died hating Olga because
    Olga
Made five dollars more on the
    same job

Olga
Died hating Manuel because
    Manuel
Had hit the numbers more
    times
Than she had hit the numbers
Manuel
Died hating all of them
Juan
Miguel
Milagros
Olga
Because they all spoke broken
    english
More fluently than he did

And now they are together
In the main lobby of the void
Addicted to silence
Under the grass of oblivion
Off limits to the wind
Confined to worm supremacy
In long island cemetery
This is the groovy hereafter
The protestant collection box
Was talking so loud and proud
    about

Here lies Juan

Here lies Miguel
Here lies Milagros
Here lies Olga
Here lies Manuel
Who died yesterday today
And will die again tomorrow
Always broke
Always owing
Never knowing
That they are beautiful
    people
Never knowing
The geography of their
    complexion

PUERTO RICO IS A BEAUTIFUL
PLACE
PUERTORRIQUEÑOS   ARE   A
BEAUTIFUL RACE

If only they
Had turned off the television
And tuned into their own
    imaginations
If only they
Had used the white
    supremacy bibles
For toilet paper purpose
And made their Latin Souls
The only religion of their race
If only they
Had returned to the
    definition of the sun
After the first mental
    snowstorm
On the summer of their senses
If only they
Had kept their eyes open
At the funeral of their fellow
    employees

Who came to this country to
    make a fortune
And were buried without
    underwears

Juan
Miguel
Milagros
Olga
Manuel
Will right now be doing their
    own thing
Where beautiful people sing
And dance and work together
Where the wind is a stranger
To miserable weather
    conditions
Where you do not need a
    dictionary
to communicate with your
    hermanos y hermanas
Aquí se habla español all the
time
Aquí you salute your flag
    first
Aquí there are no dial soap
    commercials
Aquí everybody smells good
Aquí TV dinners do not have
    a future
Aquí wigs are not necessary
Aquí we admire desire
And never get tired of each
    other
Aquí qué pasa Power is
    what's happening
Aquí to be called negrito y
    negrita
Means to be called **LOVE**

"I became the one that translated... the go-between."
by Iris Morales

My family can not be called typical, because it excludes a lot of things that other people experience. But there are a lot of threads in the family structure which are typical of all Puerto Rican families. My family just happens to be a very straight type of Puerto Rican working-class family. We weren't affected by drugs. We weren't affected by daughters going out and getting pregnant. Instead, we were affected by daughters going out and doing organizing, becoming political.

Both my mother and father came to New York in 1947. They met here at a dance, got married, and in 1948 I was born. In Puerto Rico my father was a cane cutter. He was the oldest son of about nine children, so when things got rough, he came over here to make some money to be able to send back to the family. My mother was the oldest of nine children also (an older sister had been killed by a lover). After her parents died she became the one who took care of all the other children, so she never knew any kind of childhood. My father worked in a hotel when he first came here, as a dishwasher. Then I guess he graduated to elevator operator—and he's been there ever since. My mother at first didn't work, she just devoted herself to having a family and taking care of the house—the traditional role of women. But, financial things got kind of tight and she was forced to go out and get a job, and that's when problems between them started, because my father, in very strong Latin tradition, felt that was threatening—that a woman should go out and work and have her own money and gain her own independence.

My mother didn't speak any English—she still doesn't—so I became the one that translated. It meant that she was ashamed to go to school because she couldn't speak English and talk to the teachers, and she didn't look as good as the other Americans, the other mothers. It meant that she always had to play a behind-the-scenes role, and she could never assert herself in dealing with any kind of institution.

I was the one that was the go-between. This happens to a lot of older children in Puerto Rican families—they become the link between the Puerto Rican culture and the American culture and the Puerto Rican way of life and the American institutions. They become, in a sense, the ones that come up against oppression the most. For example, when the landlord comes to the house to pick up the rent, it's the oldest one who speaks English who has to translate for the mother. When they go down to the unemployment office, it's the oldest one who goes as a translator, or when they go to the hospital. . . . So the oldest child usually comes in contact with these institutions, and feels, you know, the way that Puerto Rican people are treated.

We first lived on 124th Street, but it was torn down to build a project. So after that we lived on 106th Street, and they're still living there. The apartment has about five little rooms, and I always had to share a room with my younger sister because we always had to have boarders to help pay the rent, although at that time the rent wasn't very high.

My mother worked in the factories and my father worked two jobs in the hotel. He would leave the house about five-thirty in the morning, and he wouldn't come home till four or five. I don't really know what wages he was making because that's one thing that was kept from us. You know, this is something that happens in Puerto Rican families, where the parents have all the authority and the children don't question. There's even a saying in Spanish to the effect that children should speak only when spoken to.

The mother's just one step above the children—she doesn't question anything that the father does—and that's the way it was in my family. If I ever wanted any money, my mother would tell me to go to my father and ask for it. If I ever wanted to go anywhere, I would have to ask my father. If I ever wanted to have anyone over to the house, I would have to ask my father. And my father was not very close to us—he was very distant. He was maintaining his role as an authority figure, and an authority figure doesn't get involved with children or with the wife.

And then, of course, you also have the thing, *machismo*, which is very strong, so that the man feels he has to go out with other women. My father always did that—there was always another woman—and all I remember is my mother sitting and crying. So I developed very negative attitudes toward Puerto Rican men.

My mother's not that old, she's in her middle forties, but she looks like she's in her fifties or sixties—completely destroyed, constantly sick. They say she has a nervous condition. Actually, it's just a reaction to oppression. She's worked in a factory for twenty-three years.

There was one thing that was always very big in the family, that there were no brothers, that my father didn't have any sons. He himself was the oldest son of the oldest son of the oldest son. I was supposed to be a son but I wasn't, and then there were no other sons to carry on the family name. That really got to my pops, so I guess that's one of the reasons he started running around, trying to develop a son somewhere else.

My father can be sick or whatever, but he's never missed a day of work—not even a day—because you've got to support, you've gotta do it. It's a strong thing, you know: "In Puerto Rico I worked and got my money, and here I'm working and getting my money. But I can't make ends meet. I can't pay the rent, my wife went out to work. . . ." He's completely crushed. His whole conception of manhood, which is fucked up anyway, is destroyed.

One time he was dealing in running numbers so that he could supplement, but he got caught, so he stopped that. What happened was that he just kind of gave up trying to deal with things and tried to pretend that everything was okay by developing something else on the outside. He would have nice clothes that he would buy for himself and for his other woman, and in that way pretend that things were okay. Or he goes to Puerto Rico and gives out money to relatives, like he's rich.

In the beginning I remember they used to talk a lot about going back to Puerto Rico. When I was four we went, and then after six years we went again. My mother would always tell me how, although it was hard for her there, it was much nicer—she didn't have to deal with the cold and people who spoke English and people who were in the factories. That at least she would be among her own. My father was coming from a more mercenary kind of thing where he wanted to go back and show that he had made good here, and buy a house and maybe some land and stuff like that. But as we got a little older we started seeing that it was kind of a fantasy, so that now my mother just talks about going back to visit, because she knows she doesn't have any hope of going back there to live. She doesn't have any hope of ever leaving that apartment—and she's been wanting to move for the last ten years. She filed an application with the projects because, you know, when you live in a tenement, the projects are always better. They're cleaner, they don't have rats and roaches, or it doesn't appear that they do. So that's what she aspires to now.

When I went to school I was placed in a class where I was the only Puerto Rican. That helped me a lot in one sense, and it fucked me up in another. The way that it helped me was that I began to see contradictions. Like, we lived on the West Side, a liberal white community, and all the white kids would go home one way, and I would go home another. All the white kids dressed a certain way, too. Like, the girls' skirts didn't get wrinkled, and mine did. They talked about going away to camp, and I would talk about going to *El Barrio* for the summer. I got to see these contradictions very young, but as a result I became timid and felt inferior. I became very ashamed of my family, because they weren't what it was to be American.

You know, we lived in a typical kind of ghetto apartment—no hot water. Sometimes we would go for days without taking a bath, and I would see myself next to the other kids and feel that I was dirty, because I was not white. Or, you know, there'd be rats, and I'd stay up sometimes hoping that the rats wouldn't get into the baby's crib. I'd keep the light on all night and take turns watching with my other sister. My sister and I slept in one room that was divided by a curtain into two. The baby slept on the other side of the curtain, and my sister and I slept in the same bed. It'd get so ridiculous, you'd fight over blankets, you'd fight over . . . I mean, everything is always very antagonistic in that kind of setting. You don't have any privacy, so that if you feel upset or you want to cry, you can't slam the door to your room and go upstairs—you just lock yourself in the bathroom. You could even hear the neighbors next door, there were always people out on the street. . . . I remember when I got into a really big school thing, the guys in the summertime would be playing the congas and it'd get really noisy out on the block, and I'd get pissed at them because I couldn't do my schoolwork, you know.

I started blaming my parents for not giving me anything better. I started hating them—feeling that it was their fault and that they were stupid and that if they'd really worked hard they could have gotten something better, rather than realizing that they were just being victimized and that there was no place for them to go, there was nothing for them to do.

In our family it has always been us two older sisters who have played the pioneer roles. You go to school, coming from a very strict, patriarchal type of family, and you have a conception of things that you can do and things that you can't, and these conceptions start to be broken down. For example, you find that other kids stay over at each other's houses, which is something that you would never be allowed to do as a female. And I wasn't allowed to go to the library until I was in junior high school, when the teachers forced me to go, 'cause my mother and father, coming from a rural thing, didn't know what that was all about.

I was supposed to always come home right from school. I could never visit anyone and no one could visit me—you didn't have strangers in the house because of the fear of strangers, the feelings of inferiority. And I developed these feelings too. I wouldn't have people over to my house—especially the kids that I went to school with, the white kids—because I felt that my house didn't live up to their standards. So I was in a kind of limbo situation. I hung out with the kids on the block, but I went to school with other kids who didn't really consider me part of them because they considered me part of the Puerto Ricans, whom they didn't exactly like.

When I was in seventh grade, I was very friendly with this girl named Susie whom I'd known since kindergarten. She knew that her parents didn't like Puerto Ricans, but she was gonna show them that I was okay—so she took me to her house for lunch. I went and I was very uncomfortable, because I didn't know all this table etiquette and shit. At home we usually ate on the bed or on the floor or in front of the TV or wherever we could eat, 'cause the kitchen wasn't big enough to hold the whole family. I had tried to dress right and speak correctly and not let my accent show, and I thought everything went okay. But that afternoon at school, her father came in and told me that he had a pair of gloves lying on the kitchen table when I was there and when I left they weren't there anymore, and did I know where they were. So I got very indignant and said, "Yeah, that's all we Puerto Ricans do is steal." I just told him off. I refused, I refused to degrade myself and deny that I had taken them—I just said, "Fuck it." You know, you wanna think that, I can't change your ways. Eventually the gloves were found and he wrote me a letter apologizing for this, but I just couldn't accept it.

When I was in eighth grade I got involved in a thing with the kids from the neighborhood where we stole a hundred dollars. I got caught. The truant officer—his name was Big John—caught me counting the money out on the street, 'cause I was *stupid*. They took me to my father's job, and he was humiliated because I had put him through such shame, and they took me to my mother's job and she cried. We came home and my father gave the hundred dollars to the truant officer, plus fifty dollars so that he wouldn't take me in and give me a JD card. And after that I wasn't in with that group of kids. When I went back to them, they said, "Where's the money?" And I said, "Well, you know, I don't have it 'cause my father gave it as a bribe." And they said, "Oh, man, you fucked up, and you're full of shit!" I said, "Fuck it, man. You know, it was either me getting a record or giving the money." But they didn't understand.

My sister—the one two years younger than me—would go to school, but she wasn't part of it either, and she never got into being with people on the block. She was quieter and more timid.

Since the two of us older kids had not turned out so hot because we had gone to public school—which my mother thought accounted for it—she put my other sister into a Catholic school so she could turn out better. The Catholic school had a lot of Irish kids, and the nuns were coming from a thing very oriented toward *them* and not at all toward Puerto Ricans—so that my sister wouldn't even admit that she was Puerto Rican. Finally she turned into a whole street thing. She just decided that she was gonna deal with the people on the block and fuck everything else. She didn't deal with school at all, although she's very bright. She became very rebellious.

And the youngest one—well, you know, all of us got scared because the public school didn't work, my mother said, and the Catholic school didn't work, so we found a way of putting her in private school. *She's* fucked up because she knows she doesn't belong there. She gets into fights with the kids all the time. They organize gangs and they fight each other, and there's a lot of racism going on.

All of us, you see, went through different kinds of things, and yet there's that common thing where we didn't fit for some reason or another, because we were labeled from the beginning, we were made tokens. You know, when you're a kid and being oppressed, you don't understand that it's a whole system, capitalism. All you see is that your pops comes home, when he comes home, and that there ain't enough bread there for the family, or that your mother works at a factory and why can't she work someplace else, why doesn't she learn how to speak English. Like, I used to get on my mother about that all the time. As a matter of fact, the teachers in school used to tell me, "Make her speak English, so that you can speak bettter English."

The rest of the family—aunts, uncles, cousins, and everybody else—considered us kind of odd because we wanted to go on, get more education, and we were kind of rebellious. I started doing organizing when I was young, I started out with the people in my building, trying to organize them into a tenants' group. I was about fifteen, and they thought I was crazy, 'cause what kind of woman goes around knocking on doors and telling people all this kind of stuff? They just saw that I didn't have any respect, 'cause that's a big thing in Puerto Rican families to have respect—and especially in my age group, you have to have respect for your family, and you have to learn how to cook and take care of children, because that's what your role is going to be. When I or my other sister would go out, my mother would say, "Well, you think you're a man—you think you're a man." I got a beating one time for coming home at three-thirty, because I was always supposed to be home at three. I used to stand on the corner and talk to the guys and girls from school, and when I came home one time at three-thirty, for the third or fourth time in a row, I got a really bad beating. For weeks I couldn't walk well. And that's how you teach respect—very physically. You know, very authoritarian.

The Catholic Church was another thing too. What happens is you have to go through all the rituals—baptism, communion, confirmation—even if your family is not into a deeply religious bag. There's that whole thing about having to confess your sins—*everything* is a sin in the Catholic Church—you get that on top of the strictness and the patriarchy. And since the Catholic Church is kind of elitist, that whole cultural thing of inferiority is reinforced. The Catholic Church says you have to dress well to come into the House of God, that boys and girls can't mingle together. The Church also reinforces that authoritarian thing with the father and with the mother, and the kind of controls they have over you, 'cause, you know, God is looking out. It's just taken for granted that there is God and there is the Church, and that you have to respect it—and that goes hand in hand with the whole respect that you must have for elders, the whole respect you must have for your parents, the whole respect for your teachers, the whole respect for authority.

You know, sometimes I sit and I wonder how all my development came, politically. And I think it's happened in the last five years, when I decided to leave home. And that was, like, a big scandal in the family. But it was worth it. It was worth all the hassle and everything, because now I can see what is happening, and being in the Party, I can share this with more people.

You know, there used to be only four choices for the Puerto Rican woman—housewife, prostitute, or drug addict, and then, when the society needed more labor for its sweatshops, she would become a worker.

Now there's a new choice open to her that threatens the existence of the family and the state itself: The Revolution.

"America should never have taught us to read, she should never have given us eyes to see."

by Felipe Luciano

The first ten years of my life were spent in the projects. Long, long, vertical buildings, shit-encrusted walls—there were no rats and roaches, but it was its own prison. It's always reminded me of a mental institution—people closed in, not allowed to expand at all. I grew up there like most of the other Puerto Rican Black brothers and sisters in *El Barrio*.

When I went to public school, I was a bright student, very bright, but I was always a behavior problem—that's what the teachers told me. I rebelled against everything. There was something that I was always looking for as a child. I always knew that I had to do something, as romantic and as weird as this may sound. What that thing was, I didn't really know. I had images and dreams of becoming a doctor, becoming a social worker. Of course before any of those very legitimate dreams, I wanted to be a cowboy on a horse, riding through the plains in my big sombrero. I read *Cowboy Sam* and *Curious George* and Dr. Seuss—very, very entranced. My world was expanded because I was able to read a lot at a very early age.

We were very, very poor. My mother was separated from my father when she was three months pregnant with my sister. They had been married for about three years, and had had one baby right after the other. We went through the welfare scene—the welfare syndrome as I call it—always waiting for that check, anticipating that check, heart beating, mouth dry, arguing with each other. My brother, sister and myself used to fight each other for scraps of food on the table. When that welfare check was supposed to come, we used to run downstairs, open that mailbox. You played a game with yourself—you turned the key very slowly and peeked in the box very slowly, and if that welfare check wasn't there, there were two reactions you used to have. Like when we wanted to be cruel, when we wanted to get back at my mother for a beating she'd given us, we used to go and tell her the check had come and then we'd tell her it hadn't. Otherwise we'd come up with morose-looking faces and say "The check didn't come." I remember those days, I remember almost begging for food.

You resign yourself to poverty—my mother did this. Your face is rubbed in shit so much that you begin to accept that shit as a reality.

You've never seen anything else. Like the only thing we knew was that block. You never went out of that block. I didn't know there was a Museum of Modern Art. I didn't know that there were people who were living much, much better. I didn't know about racism. I mean we were just on that block—and that block was our home, it was all we knew.

The images of that poverty. . . . My stomach rumbling. My mother beating me when I knew it was because of my father—you know, they just had an argument where he almost hit her. The welfare investigator cursing out my mother because what she wants is spring clothing for her children and he's telling her how she just can't have it—when I read in the magazines that people—you know, other people—had spring clothes. Why couldn't we have clothes for Easter? And he's telling her, like, in a sense, "Fuck you." And I remember images of my saying, "When I grow up I'm gonna kill every welfare investigator I see, every one of them—you know, strangle them."

There's nothing extraordinary you know in my childhood—maybe just that I learned very early how to become accepted, how to rise above and beyond, as they say. Even at that point we knew that to the extent that we became white—we would advance in school. To the extent that we spoke properly—we would get Satisfactory or Excellent on our report cards. To the extent that we conformed—we were accepted. And since I read well, and I spoke well, I rose in terms of classes. And I remember the teachers always saying, when I hit a teacher or would throw a chair through a window, or would lead a group of cats through a riot in the cafeteria—a near-riot in the fourth or fifth grade—the teachers grabbed me by the side, grabbed me by my ear, you know. Wrenching my ear and saying, "You know you have so much potential. Why do you act like that? I mean look at your marks—you have so much potential. . . ." That thing went through all my school life—those words were uttered time and time again: "You have so much potential." Of course, what they considered potential was certainly not what I later became.

And my mother was very frustrated also. She couldn't get a job, she wanted to get off welfare. I never looked upon my mother as a woman; she was always my mother. I never looked upon her as a Black Puerto Rican woman who was oppressed—she was just Mommy. She's fat, she is a *bear*, you know, and I remember snuggling between her neck and . . . peace, you know it's peace, 'cause nobody can hurt you when you're with Mommy, 'cause Mommy's the big protector. Not Daddy, but Mommy—Daddy wasn't ever there. And she too wanted to get out, but she didn't know how. You know, she always wanted me to do something, since I was the first born. I was getting into a lot of trouble. But she had these images of me becoming something.

Finally we moved to California to get away from New York and because my mother wanted to go back to my grandmother. California was such an enlightening experience because I saw all these people—Japanese, Chinese, white people—they lived together without the kind of separation that you see in New York. And it was sunny all the time, like there was no snow, you know—just eighty-five-degree weather all the motherfuckin' time. I got *black*; I got black as the sun, man, and I got fat and healthy. I entered the fourth grade and got good grades in school. We had fields—this was in Wilmington, California, before they industrialized—we had fields that we used to run through. After school that's all we'd be doing. I got into track because I always wanted to do that, but I didn't have the chance to do it in New York. I had a lot of happiness, a lot of fun there because the environment was completely different. There were trees, there were horses, which I had never seen. They had a corral, a stable just a block away from the house. Just to see a horse, just to touch him was like another kind of world for me.

But it wasn't to last long. We stayed there only four months. My father was supposed to send us money in a legal separation. But he didn't send it. He got very bitter when my mother took us away, it seems. And though he hadn't done a motherfucking thing for us—remember that when I say that, I'm just remembering the bitterness of my younger years, because I really don't hate him—at that point, he felt my mother had slighted him by taking the kids away. Without the money from him we couldn't survive because my grandmother couldn't take the burden. So we had to go back. And we had to ask the welfare in Wilmington for the money. I remember the very degrading experience of my mother having to go there and be insulted three, four times during that week.

We only had enough money to pay our train fare; we had no money for food. So my grandmother, in a little handkerchief, tied up all of the coins she had. Of course, it didn't last us beyond Union Station in L.A. But we left, and I'll never forget, man, we were starving, you know, literally starving on that train coming back. Big, plush train and no food. We would look at people—you learn how to look at a person to let him know that you're hungry—and they'd give us a little tidbit, but it wasn't much. And I was very concerned for my mother, because throughout the whole trip she held her head in her hands. And it was traumatic, it was horrible, having to see my mother go through shit like that. I felt so responsible for her that I felt like a little man, since I was the oldest. And I was always to my mother lover, confidant, trustee, everything rolled into one.

On that train, hungry as we were, the only thing that saved us were some Black brothers working in the kitchen, and they saw us and we would walk in, we sat down and had some water in front of us. My mother with those little pennies bought some pastries and some coffee and tea because she couldn't afford any more. And the cats knew we were starving, I don't know how they knew, but they just started bringing things to us—burnt blueberry pie, I'll never forget it was burnt, but it was all they could afford, and they gave it to us. And that's how we survived—by them giving us little things. I don't know where they are, man, but all power to them wherever they are. I mean they saved us, I don't know how we would have gotten through that trip without them, 'cause I would've started robbin' or something.

Anyway, we got to New York and we ended up living right back on 112th Street, but in a different project. And for three years we lived there. I went to another school, and again, the same shit. I was, as my mother says, fucking up. I was still into my thing.

At that stage I was living a double life. On the one hand I was going with my mother to church. I grew up in the Puerto Rican Pentecostal Church, which is a scene unto itself—I mean it's a different world. The Holy Spirit, speaking tongues, body contortions, jumping on the floor, vomiting out demons, people entering trances—*vahilias*, as we call them in Spanish—which are just seances almost, that are held overnight . . . all those things I was very involved in. Man, I was a *fervent* church-goer. Even with all the streetfighting I was getting into. That's not unusual. We find in our community—the Puerto Rican community—that things are compatible. For instance, people have Catholic saints and at the same time they'll have a Voodoo doll, you know, or a piece of bread above the door so that the evil spirits can eat that and leave in peace.

So I made the church and the fighting compatible, you know. I would always just shut up about the fighting. I would never tell her. After church or before church she would talk about people beating up each other and be condemning them for it. I might be coming in from a fight myself, but I'd be coming in goodie-goodie and go to church with her, right. And so I just led that kind of a double life.

In school, the same kind of thing happened. I happened to *love* to read.

In fact I just raped books. I used to go to the library, get ten at a time, and just shut myself in my room, because that was my way of escape. Like getting into another world—with horses and trees and flowers, and fighting and adventures—going up on a mountain, and doing all those things that, you know, white folks do.

There were only a very few people that you could talk to about it. I mean, we still hadn't gotten to the point where we were that close to each other. But I had one or two friends—Big Ben, Richard as we called him, and June Bug, right, and we used to sit down and say, "Man, you know, Mount Everest is the highest mountain. I wish we could climb that one, man." We used to talk about riding horses, we used to talk about, oh, so many things.

But at the same time, I was of the street. I had to prove to my friends that I was just as bad as they were. I was always into fighting and scullies—Crack-top as we called it—using spinning tops to crack another guy's top. . . . That's really a ghetto game. Whoever couldn't spin his top had to put his in the middle, and all of us would take turns trying to crack his top—and yet each one cost fifteen cents, and for us that was a lot of money, right. Hot Peas and Butter, that's another game we played. Whoever is It takes a belt, and screams "Hot Peas and Butter," and goes around and whips the *hell* out of whoever he catches. Very violent games on *each other*. . . . We laugh about it now, but it was very rough, as you begin to think about it, how we murdered each other every day. I was vicious when it came to fighting, simply because I didn't want to be considered a schoolboy, you know.

When I was in eighth grade, I had a teacher—I'll never forget her—Mrs. Shapiro—she introduced us to Shakespeare. Here we were in eight-two, which is, of course, a step below eight-one, and they had told her she'd never be able to have us accept Shakespeare—but we loved it, you know. I was Puck in *A Midsummer Night's Dream*. We read *Twelfth Night*. We did *Romeo and Juliet*, which I thought was corn shit, and all kinds of things—but we began to enjoy Shakespeare.

And again I had to lead that double life. I enjoyed the fighting, you know. I enjoyed it—it was a release for all of us from whatever we were running from. We had our gang, we had our identity, we had our own community. We didn't realize it then—that the oppressor had taken away our community. What America has done is cause groups to fight each other to keep them from seeing the *real* cause of oppression. We didn't understand that then, man, we just understood that as far as we were concerned, you know, we wanted to be together. And we were very close to one another, and we used to goose each other—of course, had you called us homosexuals then, we would have just had a *fit*, but it was. . . . I mean, it's a natural stage for young cats to go through. And that was another factor involved in it. . . .

Oppression binds you together, sometimes in a negative manner, because you have nothing else to look at. You bind yourselves in locales, and one locale will fight against another. All of the energy that we had against the oppressor was perpetrated on our own people. . . . If I just begin to add up the number of brothers and sisters who had lye thrown in their faces—'cause we used to mix red lye in Pepsi-Cola and throw it in a cat's face—the number of brothers who are now crippled, the number of brothers who are *dead* because of those gang fights, it would number into the thousands.

There are very, very few survivors. Big Ben is a dope fiend, Charlie is a dope fiend. . . . June Big is a very frustrated man—he was brilliant, brilliant as a child, brilliant mind, so was Big Ben, by the way. June Bug ended up as a hospital orderly, and that's what he's doing now. Peachhead is on drugs. Leon, his brother, was shot in the streets and died. The others have died in Viet Nam, or are out on drugs now. One, Angelo, is in Harvard—no, he went to MIT—but he's now working for anti-poverty and lost to the world.

And for me I saw no future. College was to me like a dream, I could never get there. I think that's one of the things—that fear—that led me into, you know, like, vicious, man, vicious fighting. Not knowing what to do with your life, even though you've been taught the American Dream. America has sown her own seeds of destruction, because she's made oppressed people eat that dream up hook, line and sinker and when they found it shattered, they decided that the only way to begin to build that dream for themselves—interpret it for all oppressed people—is to shatter it, shatter the reality that is ugly, and begin to build a new one. America should never have taught us how to read, she should never have given us eyes to see.

BAYAMINIÑA*
by Pedro Juan Soto

From a distance, if one judged only by the colorful front, it was a cute little cart standing on a corner of 116th Street. It had blue, red and yellow stripes and the box on top—full of codfish fritters, sausages and *alcapurrias*—had glass on all four sides. A closer look, however, revealed that the cuteness was only a facade which covered up the wear and tear and the rottenness which devoured it from the wheels to the pushing bar. On a piece of tin nailed to the front, one could read in red uneven letters: BAYAMINIÑA.

But no one was paying any attention to the cart. The attention of the crowd was fixed on the argument between the vendor and the policeman. The black women moving towards Lennox Avenue would stop the quick swinging of their hips to watch the outcome of what was going on. The customers of the nearby bar had left their drinks and TV in order to follow the argument through the glass window. Even the people on cars and buses passing by would turn to stare.

I no pay more—the vendor was saying tensely—*I pay las' year other fine . . .*

But the policeman just shook his head as he finished scribbling on his notebook.

This has nothing to do with last year, buddy.

I got no money. I no pay more.

And the fine you'll have to pay next year will be a bigger one, if you don't get rid of that thing there.

You're killing me—said the vendor—*Why you do this?*

The Department of Health . . .

Okay, you gimme a job an' I . . .

. . . is after all you guys.

I have to eat—said the vendor—*Don't gimme no fine, gimme a job.*

I have nothing to do with that—said the policeman. He put the ticket in one of the vendor's shirt pockets and added—*You keep that . . . And remember to go to court.*

---

*Translator's note: Bayaminiña means literally "Go ahead, my little girl". The correct spelling is *vaya mi niña*. The use of the formal *usted* (*vaya* instead of *ve*) is common in some instances when a parent is addressing his child. Latin American drivers often give their vehicles a name expressive of their feelings for it.

Angrily, the vendor took the ticket out of his pocket and tried to read it, but he could not understand anything but the numbers.

All right, break it up—the policeman told the crowd. And turning to the vendor—*And you get going before I lose my patience.*

The vendor turned towards the school boys, thin and dark-faced like himself.

Ehtos abusadores—he mumbled—*!Sia la madre d'ehtos policías!*

C'mon—said the policeman—*Get the hell out of here.*

Suddenly, the vendor leaned down, picked up the stone which served as a brake for the little cart, and stood up with it in his fist. Already his face was ravaged by the first tears.

Gimme a job, saramanbich!

You'd better get your ass out of this neighborhood before I throw you in jail!—said the policeman with his eyes fixed on the threatening fist and raising his hand towards his holster.

The vendor hesitated, made an angry grimace, then turned around and threw himself against the cart. Kirilin! the glasses, and pon! pon! the wood. And all the time he screamed:

Gimme a job, saramanbich, gimme a job!

And the piece of tin—clan!clan!—where it read BAYAMINIÑA, already stained with blood and tears, was ridding itself of nails and recovering its true shape of junk.

Beyond Survival: Por que Sequiremos Siendo Puertorriqueños*

Frank Bonilla

One of the burdens of the wealthy is that they must from time to time take stock of their possessions. Thus, when a people become the simple possession of another, one of the experiences the colonized must face is to periodically see themselves and all that is theirs coldly assessed by various agents of the overlord. In Puerto Rico this process began very soon after the arrival of the first U.S. occupying force. In March of 1899 Acting Secretary of War, G.D. Meiklejohn, called on Department commanders in Cuba, Puerto Rico and the Philippines to report "upon the existing state of the inhabitants and the national resources of the islands." A sizeable outline of required information was provided which was to be transmitted "together with general observations as to opportunities for investment." [1] Reporting from Arecibo to Brigadier General George W. Davis, the military governor of Puerto Rico, a certain Captain Macomb wrote in that year:

> But the people—and I discuss the poor, working class—are, upon the whole, a
> gentle, patient, uncomplaining lot, living in ignorance and penury, generally polite,

*This essay was originally delivered as a lecture by Professor Bonilla at a lecture series sponsored by the Institute of Puerto Rican Studies of Brooklyn College in the spring of 1971. The lectures delivered during the series are available in a pamphlet published by the Institute, *A New Look at the Puerto Ricans and Their Society*. The essay is reprinted here with the permission of the author and the Institute of Puerto Rican Studies of Brooklyn College.

and willing to work in a plodding, undemonstrative way. Their very gentleness has permitted the unjust scale of wages they receive to become the custom. [2]

The captain dutifully went on to note that "In the United States general education and the newspapers and labor unions forever prevent such abuse." In the nearby district of Aguadilla a fellow officer, Captain Dentler, found things much the same.

> The people seem willing to work, even at starvation wages, and they seem to be docile and grateful for anything done for them. They are emotional, apt to make idols of some one of their number, and to be led about by him only to pull him to pieces later on. [3]

Across the island in Ponce, Lt. Blunt had apparently come upon slightly more stubborn human material.

> The natives are lazy and dirty, but are very sharp and cunning, and the introduction of American ideas disturbs them little, they being indifferent to the advantages offered. [4]

However, Blunt's premonitions about the unresponsiveness of the natives to the virtues of things American were not widely shared. The more affirmative view stated forthrightly by the aforementioned Capt. Dentler was that, "When American ideas are once inculcated into the people, they will never let go of them and will benefit from them." [5]

What are we to make of the fact that 70 years of increasingly elaborate social science research on Puerto Rico and its mainland offshoals have added practically nothing to the imagery of the Puerto Rican current among our U.S. overseers that could not readily be inferred or extrapolated from the 1900 impressions of the Dentlers and the Blunts. Are Puerto Ricans as a people so transparent, uniform and unchanging that our essential qualities could have been captured so quickly, once and for all, by the untrained eye of the first American occupation force? The obvious answer to this question in my view is that neither Lt. Blunt's appraisals nor much of the subsequent formal research have a great deal to do with the questions to which Puerto Ricans really require answers. These depictions are, on the contrary, successive salvos in a mind-warping exchange that has disfigured and scarred mentalities among both rulers and ruled. This fragmentary and distorted self-knowledge constitutes a crippling heritage from which, I believe, none of us has so far achieved more than partial deliverance.

Puerto Rican Inferiority

The case for Puerto Rican inferiority has many strands and all have been subsequently embellished since the turn of the century. Many of these recurrent themes would seem on the surface to have little to do with politics. Yet the way in which such issues are posed, the rationales that are appealed to in explaining alleged shortcomings, and the paths pointed to as solutions have enormous political consequences. All individuous stereotyping, however hackneyed and timeworn, has political content and overtones.[6] We do not need to dwell very long here on the more obvious forms of social rejection implicit in such crude forms of labelling. Are Puerto Ricans by nature and choice noisy, foul-mouthed, garish in dress, truculent and oversexed? These may be taken as good reasons to avoid Puerto Ricans as neighbors and workmates and to remove one's own from schools frequented by Puerto Rican children. But such images have an adverse political effect chiefly when Puerto Ricans themselves begin to believe they have something to gain by fleeing from their own kind. The more corrosive features of the legend are thus those that destroy the bases of solidarity among a people, that undermine their political confidence, that systematically throw into question their capacity for self-government, and that arbitrarily close off to them desired features. The essential components of the carefully cultivated myth of Puerto Rican political inferiority have been handed down practically unchanged since their appearance in their most ingenuous form in the War Department report that has been cited.[7] The Puerto Rican, we have been told in countless ways since then, is by disposition docile and submissive. His political impulses and capabilities are primitive (as measured against a falsely idealized mainland standard). He is dependent on outside (U.S.) leadership and models to break the hold of poverty and injustice on his society.

This net of constraining and defeating ideas encumbers our vision and action wherever we find ourselves. Whether on the island or in New York, breaking out of this confining encirclement is a first step toward that space in which we may take a liberating breath. Oppression lies wherever these ideas reign; our freedom is to be found wherever they can be exposed as a mere rationale for denying a people full manhood. What then stands between ourselves and freedom? Chiefly the difference between recognizing the repressive content in ideas and fully understanding what gives them power over us and lends strength to those who wield them against us. More specifically we have before us the unfinished work of sorting out that part of our oppression that is subjective and that which rests on more material factors and therefore requires more than a cleansing of minds in order to be overcome.

The pervasiveness of the notion of Puerto Rican passivity and submissiveness is not to be denied. "... there is hardly any area of Puerto Rican society," we have been told by René Marqués, "in which just a light scratching will not reveal docility as a constant and determinant feature."[8] Marqués certainly demonstrates that the theme is a recurrent one in Puerto Rican literature and that the Puerto Ricans have generated a rich and graphic vocabulary to express their consciousness of being a subjected people. His essay is at once a scathing, pained and painful exposé of the colonized mentality and the devices by which the oppressed seek to live with the humiliation of long felt powerlessness. This fact lends added weight to his argument. His is an authoritative and literarily informed view from the inside. Therefore, it not only collects and echoes but sets off reverberations of its own. Marqués's thesis has to be taken seriously not only with respect to the psychological and literary ground that he defines for himself but with respect to the many political inferences that he makes along the way.

The official rhetoric has come to celebrate Puerto Ricans as a democratic, tolerant, and peace-loving people. In days when we were more honest and more candid with each other, affirms Marqués, we acknowledged that these terms mean fatalistic, resigned, supine ("ñangotado," i.e., content to remain on our haunches as regards matters of the spirit). The commonwealth is a perfect political expression of this mentality. A Puerto Rican solution is one in which what looks inevitable is transformed into a national project. Our political violence, he affirms, is not revolutionary or revealing of heightened political consciousness but a heroism of despair. The nationalist movement is the maximum expression of a deeply ingrained suicidal impulse (the island, in fact, has a very high suicide rate). The statehood option reflects an equivalent impulse to extinction on a cultural plane. The rebel, middle class writer and intellectual is celebrated but absorbed; he relieves tensions but changes no one. In this bleak panorama Marqués provides a single ray of hope, his suggestion that the Puerto Rican in New York, as he loses the stain of his tropical origins ("la mancha del plátano") may eventually throw off the impulse to self-effacement and obliteration.

What Marqués chronicles with considerably more effect and detail than the sketch just given reveals is the psychological damage and cultural mayhem worked on Puerto Ricans by centuries of exploitation. He exposes the violence of colonialism but falls short in the apparent presumption that the colonized will indefinitely turn the destructive forces thus generated against themselves. The dialectic of impotence and stubborn resistance, however covert and diffuse, is perceived as a grinding friction shredding individuals and social ties but is denied any prospect of political resolution. We are, perhaps, developing a dangerous virtuosity in documenting the prostration, insecurity, ambivalences, and ideological bafflement within our ranks and assigning too little value to the contrary signs that point to a remarkable capacity for survival in a context of prolonged and radical ambiguity. Few people have been forced to move about the world for so long under such false (externally imposed), discordant and provisional (incompletely realized) identities. What can Puerto Ricans anywhere, most of us still passing through this mind-rending experience, ask or expect of each other?

This is a permanent, underlying question in most of what I want to review here. It is, of course, a question that never arises in the observations of the Dentlers, Blunts and their successors with more scientific pretensions. They are not searching passionately for meaningful commitments and viable paths to the advancement of Puerto Rican goals. They are content to document what they perceive as political bankruptcy, the fantasied superiority and invincibility of mainland political designs and the need, therefore, of extending U.S. tutelage indefinitely, however it may be mediated. Yet what kind of political bonds, commitments, and thrust can in fact be maintained in such adverse contexts? When individual lives on a massive scale are blasted by the impossibility of living up to the most private commitments to loved persons, where is the work of social reconnection to begin? If it is within a man's reach only momentarily and with great sacrifice to create and mount an idealized situation of abundance of conviviality for his family or friends, does he need a psychologist to tell him he is giving in to impulses or an anthropologist to inform him he is caught in a fiesta complex? When stability can be found in a galling accommodation to a low-keyed, routined existence, will some not lash out rebelliously against something they know needs to be destroyed? When the enemy is elusive and a fantastic price is paid for striking out against him, will not bizarre modes of copping out be invented or more accessible victims be found to be immolated in his place?[9] This of course will only certify a proneness to erratic behavior and more serious mental disturbances. Then, of course, intellectuals will reproach the mass for being politically inert and unresponsive to political ideals. They will credit to the exemplary action of a few leaders the survival of the independence ideal and the stubborn resilence of a culture surviving against tremendous odds.[10] By contrast the politics of personalism, of social work, of the poverty warriors, and the bootstrap will be seen to flourish. On the island and in mainland ghettoes the practical politicians, who understand how to manipulate "bread & butter" issues, will announce that they have saved their people from a corrosive nationalism and taught them to place economic solutions and speedy assimilation before vague political aspirations or the survival of cherished lifeways. With this they round out and hammer home the legend of Puerto Rico's conformity and purchased submission to an externally defined second-rate status.[11] While the subculture of prostitution and sexual exploitation flourishing in the island backwaters of dependent capitalism and New York slums is minutely recorded as a prototype of what is Puerto Rican, political leaders speak of Operation Serenity. While Puerto Rican young men are conscripted to brutalize others and give their lives in the undeclared wars of another nation, island statisticians tally the value to the economy of the remitted earnings and the social benefits that accrue on the island as the price of this military service. No wonder then that the legend comes back to mock us as in the words of an acute observer, the historian Richard Morse.

> Within this longer perspective, Puerto Rican political formulations take on a hollow ring. They seem designed for a people which is 'shopping' for status . . . No one would deny that voluntary political change should obey, among other things, broad economic considerations. But it is surprising that a people which prides itself on a Hispanic 'soul' should translate them into dollars and cents reckoning carried to the last decimal point.[12]

Such a remark may be intensive and characteristically omits any details concerning the nature of the market in which a nation is brought to trade its pride and integrity for survival. Still it captures a fragment of truth of which we are all painfully conscious. On another plane altogether is the main conclusion of a more recent and professedly "sympathetic" study of student politics at the University of Puerto Rico.

> Contemporary Puerto Rican students, the children of their fathers, have disproved a maxim that has characterized nationalist movements in many areas of the world.

Puerto Ricans, including their fathers, have shown that man *can* live by bread alone. (italics in the original).[13]

Se le olvidó notar a este joven científico que el pan con que se imagine le han llenado las bocas a los puertorriqueños ha sido poco, duro, y muy bien cobrado.

The Politics of Migration

Migration itself is thus transformed into a suspect act. Does it represent a massive capitulation, a sellout, escape, or suicide? Is there really no alternative open to Puerto Ricans, whether here or on the island, except full Americanization, a slow extinction and absorption into the underclass of decaying cities? Under what conditions can Puerto Ricans not merely survive but grow affirmatively as a culturally integrated and distinctive collectivity in the mainland context? If we are trying to throw off one set of destructive lies or partial truths, we gain nothing by simply improvising a more congenial set of premises about ourselves or our future prospects. Let it be clear that we are talking about an unprecedented job of psychological and cultural reconstitution and construction that must rest on a very special political and economic infra-structure. If we are unable to imagine outcomes that would satisfy our aspirations, how can we know when we are making or losing ground?

Between 1960 and 1970 the Puerto Rican population in New York shot to over a million. Over that decade the numbers of New York-born Puerto Ricans grew by 150 per cent while those born on the island and living in the States grew by only nineteen per cent.[14] This population overall is extremely young, averaging about 21 years in 1960. The eventual predominance of the mainland born is a significant fact, for the way in which they relate to their putative Americanness will prove decisive in terms of the community's future. As one of the older members of this so-called second generation, I feel a special responsibility to make explicit some of the political implications of choices that lie before us. There are certain core realities that we need to face up to and that we ourselves often conspire to mask or dissemble.

In the first place we are a captured people and remain captives. Formal rights of citizenship and apparent freedom of movement within the country's borders notwithstanding, we remain in a situation that is alien and not of our making. Our parents could not give us any citizenship other than that which, in a watered down form, was imposed on them.

Secondly, the amalgam of U.S. and island cultures and its mainland transplants has, from the Puerto Rican side, never been seen as a simple fusion. Puerto Ricans are not culturally Americans, and we must have the courage to speak up and affirm that we do not wish to be Americans if we are honestly committed to building on our Puerto Rican roots. Even the most ardent proponents of statehood or other forms of political association with the United States have been at pains to make clear that the island intended to remain true to its Hispanic and Antillean traditions. This fact has not passed unnoticed though it has elicited primarily sardonic comment.

> From the Puerto Rican point of view, this eventual society is perhaps not best described as 'bi-cultural.' For indeed, it is the Hispanic tradition that will supply the 'culture' while the United States will merely supply methods, technics, organizational charts, money for pump priming, and a market of 180 million people.[15]

As frequently occurs in such appraisals, the terms here become subtly inverted. Puerto Rico is depicted as ready to exploit the U.S. market while being neurotically standoffish about U.S. culture or unrealistic about the consequences of accepting certain technologies. The economic facts, of course, are exactly the reverse. The tiny island is one of the United States' largest and most lucrative export markets. Puerto Rican exports to the mainland market of 180 million are almost entirely the output of U.S. producers taking advantage of cheap labor and other benefits of the off-shore, commonwealth location. As regards the cultural argument, the Puerto Rican position has simply never been, as is insinuated, that U.S. technology could be appropriated without an impact on social organization or lifeways though defenses have in fact been inadequate.

I think we have to recognize in this long-standing rejection of a quick transfer of identity a profoundly political act that is decidedly life affirming and nonsuicidal. Within the most recent flow of migrants, a current that now seems to move directly from rural island settings to eastern seaboard cities, this awareness and search for a viable design for survival remains very much alive. Recent research in Boston reports that the most characteristic group accepts neither isolation nor assimilation.[16] This search for a space within which Puerto Ricans may live and grow in full freedom has been a constant in the fifty years or more that we have been a visible presence in U.S. cities. It is the counterpoint to the rejection in U.S. culture of all groups that are racially distinct or racially suspect. Speaking of Blacks, American Indians, Chicanos, and Puerto Ricans, Eduardo Seda has written:

> These groups have failed to adapt to the American melting pot because they are differentiated on the basis of racial criteria and in assimilating into the dominant American culture, these groups internalize the stigma and the self hatred ingrained in that culture against the people of color. In order to avoid the stigma inherent in the internalization of American culture these groups must maintain their own cultural identity as a separate entity in a pluralistic social scheme.[17]

Over the last decade, as the nature of the U.S. role abroad has been incontestably exposed at home, to become fully American has come to mean as well accepting the stigma and mission of the oppressor of others seeking liberation. To shrink from embracing this identity is hardly to be seen as an act of mere malcontents or cranks, neurotically attached to a failing culture.

The history of the Puerto Rican migration has yet to be written. The 1910 census registered some 1,500 Puerto Ricans born in the continental United States. This number had risen to 53,000 by 1930 and 70,000 by 1940. By 1950 the quarter million mark was close, and two decades later we number more than a million, nearly a third of all those with identifiable Puerto Rican parentage under U.S. jurisdiction. Because this movement has been chronicled chiefly by demographers and migration specialists, most of what we know has to do with a few characteristics of this population and small changes in these that signal gains in or obstacles to "assimilation."[18] By the late 1960's small "advances" could be documented for second generation Puerto Ricans as against their island born neighbors: They were not only more youthful but had more years of schooling, higher status jobs, larger incomes, married early and more often outside their group, and had fewer children. A newly noted trend was the shift in migration away from New York City which was said to augur a "diaspora" in which the second generation would spread throughout the nation. The growth of ethnic defense organizations and the penetration by some Puerto Ricans into the higher levels of the local party structure and municipal bureaucracy is also hailed as a sign of accelerating assimilation. The fact that, vis-a-vis other victimized groups, Puerto Ricans remain significantly at a disadvantage on every count (housing, education, income, jobs, health), is rarely mentioned in such accounts. Other groups have paid a similar price of admission for their place in the city and nation. After all, too, Puerto Ricans arrived inopportunely and with some grave handicaps (i.e., ambiguous Spanish-African antecedents, stubborn attachment to a foreign language, a strange variant of Catholicism, what looked like an irregularly bestowed citizenship, and brazenly stated doubts about the wish to be American).

I want to use the rest of my time here to argue further that this kind of celebration of Puerto Rican assimilation or integration is premature and in error. These gains in education skills, earning power and geographic mobility do not signal a simple siphoning off of tensions and a shearing off of individuals into some imaginary American mainstream. Placed against the backdrop of other events and trends here and on the island, they have to be seen as potentially providing a wholly new level of awareness and leadership arising from the depths of a community still imprisoned in poverty and continuously renewed by newcomers entering at the most exploited level. These small successes are also to be seen against the backdrop of the proportions of this youthful generation who are hostages of the society in other settings—who are in schools that teach nothing, without jobs or in dead end jobs, fighting a war in which none believe, crammed into the nation's cell blocks. All of these settings—the streets, the high schools and colleges, the prison—have become radicalizing contexts intensifying awareness, sharpening political skills, stimulating reflection and analysis, generating new commitment.

The present system operates so destructively and arbitrarily that talented and thoughtful youth may wind up as readily behind prison walls as in the college classroom. I want to read briefly from a couple of letters from men in Soledad prison in California. I find these letters remarkable because Puerto Ricans in that prison are few and most have been separated from their community for many years since early adolescence.

> I know that it seems as if people are not able to hold together very long. But we who can get together must stay together and struggle that much harder for the freedom, justice and equality which we as oppressed people have never seen. As everyone who recognizes the struggle for what it really is knows, it's time to unite.

> I want to help our people . . . I've been doing a lot of thinking about forming a Puerto Rican Awareness Group . . . Our people, Black, Brown, Red, Yellow people (brothers) are in need of unity. I understand that there's always a new idea and new minds that get together for our cause. I sure would love to contribute my ideas and my brotherhood and love to the brothers who are trying very hard to bring in a better life for our people.

As the inmates are the first to say "not every brother inside the joint is a soldier." Nevertheless, the prisons like the schools and other institutions that up till very recently had served largely to shake and obliterate individuality and Puerto Rican identity, have somehow been in part turned around. Puerto Rican men in prison are defining for *themselves* the condition for their reconnection to society and doing so in terms of a politically informed concern for their own. The prisons have become a front of concern and action as vital to our community as housing, jobs, or schools.

From this perspective the fact that in the city university system alone there are today more than eight thousand Puerto Rican students will prove significant chiefly to the extent that the colleges and universities are also turned into contexts of liberating work. That liberating work involves not only casting off the blinders of a colonializing education which explains only our inferiority and impotence but developing counter values that thwart cooptation and elitism. Four fifths of employed Puerto Ricans are blue collar workers.[19] We will gain nothing by penetrating the university unless those who enter are an advance party with working lifelines to the street, the community, the prison, the island and every other setting in which things important to mainland Puerto Ricans as a collectivity are occurring.

This may seem like a heavy burden to place on young people going into a new and complex milieu that is unprepared for them and reluctant to accept new definitions of its functions. University administrators are quick to respond to such formulations with charges that we are seeking to polarize, politicize, subvert, and fragment institutions and academic traditions. "What will majors in Puerto Rican studies find to do?" they ask, while cheerfully passing out undergraduate degrees in 18th century French drama and medieval history. This is, of course, a defensive screen, for they would like us to be seen as irresponsible radicals, hustlers, and interlopers ready to box our young into a meaningless academic dead end just to have a base in a corner of the academy. In point of fact our needs are fairly modest though impossible to realize within the framework of the universities as now constituted. We are, after all, not preparing our youth to administer an empire, manage global wars, travel to the moon, or control restive minorities. We do need to undo the work of a deforming education, to vitalize and take command of our own process of cultural construction, and to understand the economic and political requirements for our survival as a community.

One additional statistic concerning the New York Puerto Rican population requires comment. In the 1960 census 96 per cent of that population was classified as white. Who is kidding whom? What is the extent of Puerto Rican complicity in this numerical charade? Are Puerto Rican social standards of race really so relaxed that all but a few qualify as white? Are we simply refusing to play the racial numbers game according to mainland rules? I want to repeat here a few remarks I have made often before. We live in a society that knows only black and white. Puerto Rican complacency and equivocation with respect to race and even our more genuine accommodations of racial differences have little place here. As we have discovered, here one is black, white, or a non-something. Still Puerto Ricans—white or black—have little comprehension of the deep racial animosities that divide mainland Americans. Many are understandably reluctant to become part of a fight that is to them ugly and meaningless. But we cannot continue to pretend to be an island of civility and racial harmony untouched by the storm of racial conflict that surrounds us. Again we must acknowledge that our culture—like all others dominated by Europeans—has taught us to experience blackness as misfortune. Our escapism and lack of realism with respect to race issues is as much grounded in such fears and self-doubts as in any affirmative principles of equality. If the Puerto Rican approach to race is really more humane, we have to prove it here. And the only convincing proof of moral strength in this connection is to stand up as proudly for what is black in us as individuals and for what is black in our community as we do for our Puerto-Ricanness.

Beyond Survival

According to all going theories of history, culture, and collective psychology, Puerto Ricans do not exist or are bound to disappear. We are said to have no real institutions, distinctive culture, or secure identity. Whatever fragments of such unifying ideals and sentiments we may have scraped together in the past are only a weak shield against the overwhelming onslaught of the dominant culture with its power to penetrate and engulf the alien. I believe we have to acknowledge the silence, surface submission, and non-militancy that has marked much of our past. But we need also to see beyond that to the tenacity and capacity for survival contained in the resolute avoidance of a capitulation on the cultural front. This is part of the mystery to be unraveled and turned now to surer political purpose. The option to struggle for full sovereignty in the island and power over our own mainland communities remains very much alive. Part of the success of the colonizer lies in having pitted Puerto Ricans against Puerto Ricans in part of that contention. But this only accentuates the ultimate contradictions and heightens our awareness of what threatens; the powerful have nothing to give us except death and now the prospect of fratricide.

But what content are we to give abstract ideas such as pluralism and power in the complex and conflict-ridden context of U.S. cities? What kind of culture can be built on such shallow economic and political under-pinnings? In the past we have mainly been offered theories and designs pointing to easily won, bright futures. The bootstrap image is a case in point; a prodigious feat defying natural laws but implying a soothing economy of effort. We have before us the first Puerto Rican generation an important part of which sees heroic struggle as its destiny. They correctly insist on keeping attention riveted on the everyday reality of the deprivation endured by Puerto Ricans. But we do need some future vision of a state of the world satisfactory to us. This does not mean a quest for grand theories or scientific truths, but a systematic probing for politically significant truths. If we choose life, we have to understand survival as a community, then our creativity must be fed by a collective vision that reaches out to Puerto Ricans everywhere. When people ask in what way Puerto Ricans differ from earlier immigrants, we must be ready with the true answer which is that we are a displaced offshoot of a people and a land that have yet to be liberated and whose freedom is our own.

NOTES

1. *Puerto Rico*, embracing the Report of Brig. Gen. Geo. W. Davis, Military Governor, U.S. War Dept., Division of Customs and Insular Affairs, 1899, p. 3.

2. Ibid., p. 44.

3. Ibid., p. 45.

4. Ibid., p. 47.

5. Ibid., p. 45.

6. Among the scores of reviews of Oscar Lewis' *La Vida* (Random House, 1968) only that by Barrington Moore, Jr. *(New York Review of Books*, June 15, 1967) deals in a serious way

with the political implications of the culture of poverty thesis as it applies to Puerto Rico, even though Moore was among the few to disclaim any special knowledge of the Puerto Rican case.

7. Americans were not the first to attribute docility to Puerto Ricans. Similar observations had been made by Spaniards and Puerto Ricans before the U.S. invasion.

8. René Marqués. "El Puertorriqueño Dócil", *Revista de Ciencias Sociales*, Vol. VII, Nos. 1-2, 1963, p. 78.

9. The initiated will recognize in these remarks some of the 70 interrelated traits of the culture of poverty (Oscar Lewis, *A Study of Slum Culture*, New York: Random House, 1968.)

10. An otherwise highly useful and compact overview of nationalist thought and action in Puerto Rico has been called to task on this score. See Manuel Maldonado Denis, *Puerto Rico*, Siglo Veintiuno, 1969, and his "The Puerto Ricans: Protest or Submission," in the *Annals*, March 1969. The critique appears in *La Escalera*, Vol. IV, No. 1, June, 1970 (Gervasio Garcia, "Apuntes Sobre Una Interpretación de la Realidad Puertorriqueña").

11. On the progressive deflation of the commonwealth idea and its architects see Luis Nieves Falcón, "El Futuro Ideológico del Partido Popular Democrático," *Revista de Ciencias Sociales*, Vol. IX, No. 3, September 1965.

12. Richard M. Morse, "The Deceptive Transformation of Puerto Rico," paper delivered at a Conference on the Social Sciences in Historical Study, University of Michigan, May, 1959.

13. Arthur Liebman, *The Politics of Puerto Rican University Students*, University of Texas Press, 1970, p. 150.

14. *Puerto Ricans in New York State*, 1960-69, New York State Division of Human Rights, No. date.

15. Richard Morse, "The Deceptive Transformation," p. 30.

16. Manuel Teruel, *Puerto Ricans in Transition, Social Relations*, Honors Thesis, Harvard University, 1969.

17. Eduardo Seda Bonilla, "Ethnic Studies, Cultural Pluralism and Power," paper presented at the annual meeting of the Society for Applied Anthropology, University of Colorado, April, 1970, p. 1.

18. See especially "The Puerto Rican Experience on the U.S. Mainland," a special issue of the International Migration Review, Vol. II, Spring, 1968.

19. New York State Division of Human Rights, *Puerto Ricans*, p. 19.

BIOGRAPHICAL ESSAYS

Puerto Rico:
Toward a New Consciousness*

Gordon K. Lewis

Karl Wagenheim, *Puerto Rico: A Profile*. Praeger, New York, 1970.

Manuel Maldonado Denis, *Puerto Rico: Una Interpretación histórico-social. Siglo XXI editores*, México, 1969; and the English version, *Puerto Rico: A Socio-historic interpretation*. Random House, New York, 1972.

Juan Angel Silén, *Hacia una visión positiva del puertorriqueño*. Editorial Edil, Río Piedras, Puerto Rico, 1970; and the English version, *We, the Puerto Rican People. A story of oppression and resistance*. Monthly Review Press, New York and London, 1971.

Rafael L. Ramírez, Barry B. Levine and Carlos Buitrago Ortiz, *Problemas de Desigualdad Social en Puerto Rico*. Ediciones Libería Internacional, Río Piedras, Puerto Rico, 1972; and the English version, by the same publishers, *Problems of Social Inequality in Puerto Rico*.

Historically, it is a cardinal feature of colonialism everywhere that it generates in its subject-peoples not only economic and political depend-

*Reprinted from *Latin American Review of Books*, Vol. 1, No. 1 (Spring, 1973), pp. 147-158, with the permission of the author.

ency, but also a secondary intellectual and ideological dependency. The colonial educated class, trained in the respective metropolitan centres of learning, absorbs the metropolitan cultural bias and thought-patterns. The metropolitan scholarship thus becomes, in Maunier's phrase, the *instituteur social* of the colonial person, trapping him within a framework of reference that only too often is comically inappropriate to the problems of the colonial or neo-colonial society. The colonial thus becomes converted into his own executioner; first, in the struggle for national independence and, after that, in the struggle to build up a viable cultural identity, his capacity to interpret and understand his world is gravely compromised by his instinctive temptation to see it all in terms of metropolitan values, norms and priorites.

This habit of intellectual colonialism has notoriously been a disease endemic throughout the entire Caribbean region. It is heartening, then, to note—as these books testify—that a new wave of younger Puerto Rican social scientists is beginning to challenge all that, and, more particularly, to break the monopoly of North American social scientists whose books on Puerto Rico over the years have revealed cultural bias, intellectual condescension and academic pedantry. This new literature, at once radical and scholarly, thus breaks the pattern of the ponderous socio-anthropological study on the one hand, and, on the other, the tourist brochure composed with breathless enthusiasm by some self-elected 'friend of Puerto Rico'.

The Silén and Maldonado Denis volumes are indignant assaults upon the imperialist enemy, first Spain and then the United States; and one of their greatest virtues is that they recognize, in contrast to the traditional *insularismo* of the older Puerto Rican nationalist intelligentsia, the urgent need to construct a united front between the island forces and the great Puerto Rican pockets of the colonial *diaspora* in Manhattan and the Bronx. The volume of essays edited by Ramírez, Levine and Buitrago Ortiz looks at the mass poverty of the island society from a fresh viewpoint, at once avoiding the tendency of North American anthropologists to concentrate on the merely 'exotic' elements of rural poverty, and the temptation of others, as notably in Oscar Lewis's widely acclaimed *La Vida*, to indulge in a sort of peephole sociology that gravely exaggerates the more pornographic aspects of San Juan slum life. The Wagenheim book, finally, though composed by a Continental (i.e. from the US mainland), is written with fine sympathy for Puerto Rican realities, and succeeds in being an effective popularisation (in the best sense of the word), of those realities, for the benefit of journalists, students, the more open-minded Continental residents and the more serious-minded tourists.

All in all, the books reflect the astonishing intellectual ferment that has grown up in Puerto Rico society over the last five years, one measure of which is the fact, fascinating in itself, that the world 'socialism', albeit with Scandinavian rather than Cuban overtones, has become, through the medium of the rising *Partido Independentista Puertorriqueño*, a respectable term in the territorial political debate.

What is the portrait of modern Puerto Rico that emerges from these books? It is, to begin with, a transformed industrial economy, with the old rural society almost wholly destroyed, as indeed capitalism everywhere destroys the native economies. This has led, on the one hand, to massive proletarianisation of the poor as a rapid rural depopulation process brings the unemployed into the new urban slum districts. Avoiding rhetoric or polemic, the *Problemas de Desigualdad Social* volume chillingly describes the results: chronic poverty and increased levels of both absolute and relative income inequality, with one out of every four Puerto Rican families barely surviving on the *mantengo* (the Federal welfare handout). The transformation of land-ownership patterns means that the country laborer has been supplanted by the city middle-class dweller building his country week-end retreat, so that living in the countryside has become—as in England—a luxury for the city commuter, making him into a new parasitic class and reinforcing a typical feature of the Caribbean colonial economics—the stranglehold of the main city over the small towns and hamlets of the rest of the island. All this is a dreadful indictment of the classical model of economic growth embodied in the 'Operation Bootstrap' theories of the Puerto Rican planners. That the statistics for the growth of poverty are not even more startling is only due to the fact that, as Buitrago points out, the colony has in effect exported its unemployment problem by means of the massive migratory movement to the mainland, where the uprooted Puerto Rican laborer comes to constitute the new lumpenproletariat of the huge metropolitan slums, and the scandalously squalid large-scale capitalist fruit farms, from California to New Jersey. All this, in turn, leads to the erosion of traditional values and customs, embodied in the truly tragic figure of the returning Puerto Rican, embittered by his mainland exposure to a racist society, culturally schizoid, hating the *gringo* yet at the same time bearing with him notions of the 'superiority' of the North American life-style.

On the other hand, there has been an equally profound transformation in the character of the top Puerto Rican social layers. All over the Caribbean area, as indeed throughout the Americas as a whole, the social aristocracies based on land and/or trade have been decimated by new factors—the rise of the creole black and mulatto dictatorships, as in Haiti and Santo Domingo, the growth of the new modernising oligarchies, as in Puerto Rico itself, and, of course, the Cuban Revolution. The real inheritors of that change in the Puerto Rican case are the new capital-oriented meritocracy, whose members crowd the new executive suites, government agencies, law offices and banking headquarters in the glass-concrete structures of San Juan and Santurce. They have been reinforced by two minor streams: that of the San Juan-based Continentals, and that of the Cuban refugee group, both of whom exhibit a contemptuous hostility, only thinly disguised, for the Puerto Rican cultural tradition. Mariano Muñoz Hernández's essay—*Hacia un Análisis de la Clase Media en Puerto Rico*—in the Ramínez-Levine-Buitrago volume constitutes an illuminating portrait of this new middle group. It is not an attractive picture. They are the *nouveaux-riches*, only a brief generation away from the cane fields. They are desperately anxious to forget that background, terribly afraid that at any moment they may relapse back into it. They are profoundly class-conscious; they hate and fear the poor; they evince attitudes of extreme servility to those above them in the social scale; they estimate everybody in terms of their material possessions; they almost literally wallow in a life-style of vulgar conspicuous consumption; everything admirable or desirable bears the stamp of being made in the United States. They see education for their children not as an intellectually emancipating experience but as a mechanism of social mobility. They are politically reactionary. Above all, they are ideologically parasitical, for they see everything they possess as coming from the largesse of the American metropolis; in Muñoz Hernández' phrase, they have a sort of Santa Claus vision of social reality, believing good behavior will bring the gift of prosperity, bad behavior the punishment of poverty. This is a class, that is to say, that is neither the classic Marxian bourgeoisie, characterised by its relationship to the means of production, nor the classic Weberian middle class, characterised by comforting attitudes of social status. It is, rather, a vulgarized, bogus middle class.

An English observer of all this is reminded of Matthew Arnold's castigation of the cultural philistinism of the Bounderbys and the Gradgrinds of the rising Victorian middle class. The comparison is apposite. For what is taking place in Puerto Rico, as in many other non-

European societies, is a replica of the Victorian Industrial Revolution. But there is a fundamental difference: the industrialising process takes place today within the framework of a neo-colonialist system dominated by the North Atlantic system of monopoly capitalism, along with its basically expansionist and imperialist drive. The Victorian bourgeoisie was its own master. Its members knew, without a shadow of doubt, that they were, in Kiernan's book title, the lords of human kind. Its contemporary Third World counterparts are located in an entirely different socio-historical situation. They constitute, as it were, a second-level échelon to the real power group, the officialdom, of the American and Canadian transnational corporations that control the local econo-mies, and their immediate local allies. In this sense, to quote Norman Manley's observation with reference to the Jamaican situation, there is no real ruling class in these subordinate economies, only a dependent client-class beholden to the corporate organization men of the metropoli-tan head offices. The politico-administrative counterparts of these faceless business executives are the members of all the federal govern-ment agencies—the relevant regulatory commissions, the armed forces, the FBI, Congress itself—that control so many vital aspects of Puerto Rican life, constituting what one earlier writer on the American colonial-ist régime termed an 'oligarchy of strangers'. It is small wonder that so much of the Puerto Rican collective mentality is dependent-oriented, always looking to Americans to do things, obsessed to a paranoid degree with the Washington psycho-complex. In no single society of the modern world, perhaps, is it so terribly clear to see how the imperial Uncle Sam creates the colonial Uncle Tom.

Yet all this—the meek acceptance by the colonised of the value patterns of the coloniser—is by no means the whole story. It is the chief merit of the Silén and the Maldonado Denis books that they demonstrate, with ample documentation, how in recent years there has grown up a new, refreshing *risorgimento* of Puerto Rican cultural and political nation-alism openly challenging, for the first time since the abortive Nationalist Party movement of the 1930s, the entire apparatus of American rule. They describe how the revitalised nationalist parties have managed to radicalise whole new groups in the society—the masses of the urban slums; the forgotten poor of the small interior towns; the high school and college youth; the new industrial working class of the *Fomento* factories engaged in the militant strike activities of the present period; the homeless poor who have unleashed a new, aggressive land squatter movement; the small native shopkeeper-class, driven to the wall by the consumer-capitalist power of the American-based supermarket chains. There is, furthermore, the struggle of the youth against compulsory military service in the US armed forces, the revolt of the schoolteacher-class against the continuing use of the public school as an instrument of pro-American ideology, the emergence of a radical nativist clergy fighting both a complacent Catholic hierarchy and an Americanised Protestant Church (almost as if, in Silén's acid comment, Christ had been born in Bethlehem, Pennsylvania).

There are two things to note about all this. Firstly, it represents a real shift away from the traditional Puerto Rican national movement. That older movement centered around the literary intelligentsia with a distinctly élitist bias. Its tone was Hispanist, genteel, romantically utopian. It pitted the virtues of *hispanidad* against vulgarising American democracy; and ideologically it had much about it of the conservatism of Ortega, Unamuno, and Santayana. The new movement is ideologically far more radical, nourished by Marx, Lenin, Debray, Mao, and, of course, the Ché cult. It is, then, in the second place, resolutely internationalist in its outlook. Maldonado Denis' book thus sees the issue as a struggle of patriotic liberation, linking itself with such struggles everywhere; and the enemy is not so much an American democratic spirit that threatens the island neo-Hispanic order as it is the global American empire that has lost its democratic roots. This is indeed a new note; and its significance may be gauged by the fact, damning enough, that not one single leader of the island Establishment parties has ever dared utter a murmur of protest against the evil shame of the Vietnam war.

Third, and finally, the whole movement is solidly based on a deep sense of cultural nationalism. For Puerto Rico, culturally, is a nation. It has most, if not all, the ingredients necessary to national independence which Renan listed in his celebrated essay. In this sense, Wagenheim's book serves a useful purpose in pointing out, among much else, that the American-Yanqui stereotype of Puerto Rican nationalism as a terrorist movement of arson, violence, and attempted assassination of American Presidents is dangerously wrong. There is, in fact, a more subterranean, more gentle nationalism that permeates every corner of the Puerto Rican collective psyche and transcends orthodox political alignments and party groupings, thus constituting a powerful cultural basis for independence. It is for that reason, beyond doubt, that the ruling Statehood-Republican party in San Juan has not pushed energetically for statehood. They must instinctively know that for many Puerto Ricans, perhaps the majority, statehood would appear as cultural genocide, with the native base being eroded (as has happened in Hawaii). Statehood, indeed, would undoubtedly engender an open separatist movement of no mean proportions; and in such a situation it is not fanciful to imagine that Puerto Rico could become the American Ulster.

It is urgent, of course, to place all this in its proper perspective. There are two pitfalls into which such *independentista* literature falls, thus leading to incorrect theoretical analyses. The first is the temptation to indulge in historical romanticism, to offset the present with an idealised version of the past. Traditionally, this has taken the form of a romanticised view of the *jíbaro*, the Puerto Rican peasant type, in terms of a fatalistic vision of his life-style that was incorrigibly nostalgic. Neither Silén nor Maldonado Denis, it is true, would accept this view. But they do tend to retain some of it, so that Silén, for example, sees the hero, not as the *jíbaro* but as the original Indian aboriginal, whose occasional uprisings against the Spanish settlers are seen as the first note of the independence struggle (in much the same way as the new Russian nationalism has been tempted to see Peter the Great as the first member of the Russian Communist Party). Again, not only does Silén exaggerate Spanish oppression, so that he says practically nothing of the various reform steps taken in the interests of the *provincias de ultramar* by the occasional republican-liberal elements in nineteenth-century Spain; he manages to suggest that early Puerto Rico was some sort of Paradise Lost, in much the same way that the Catholic historians of Victorian England wrote of a Merrie England that, as they saw it, had been destroyed by Henry Tudor and his advisors in the sixteenth century. This is clearly inaccurate historical interpretation, however much it may have its sentimental roots in the consuming rage that the young Puerto Rican militant feels as he looks at what the Americanising process has done to his island home.

The second temptation is to exaggerate the extent of the present-day anti-American movement. Maldonado Denis is surely correct in insisting that Puerto Rico is neither a 'showcase of democracy', advertising the worth of America, nor a servile people afraid to challenge American rule, but a society and culture placed, by historical accident, under the rule of the most powerful empire in history. Silén, again, is surely right to expose the myth of the famous Puerto Rican 'docility'. It is enough merely to read the recently published anthology of another young Puerto Rican social scientist* to be reminded how the Puerto Rican dockworker and canecutters fought valiantly against the new American sugarcane and freight companies in the 1920s and 1930s, and at the same time helped produce a socialist pamphlet literature by now almost forgotten.

At the same time, with all this admitted, the answer to one myth is not to fashion another one: the image of a vast popular movement rising up against the Americans. It is surely misleading to quote the electoral voting figures gained by the *independentista* groups without informing the reader that it is a miniscule minority vote, and that the two major parties—the *Populares* and the government Statehood-Republican party, both of them actively pro-American collaborationist groups—continue to command the support of the electoral majority. The new strength of the national patriotic movement is indisputable; there is hardly a Puerto Rican schoolchild who has not heard the vibrant 'Yankee go home' slogan and does not know what it means; and the success of the movement is testified to by the panic-stricken response of the governmental forces, as they mount a new repressive policy, with police and intelligence agents, against the movement. But this hardly means that the moment of truth has arrived. The movement must face perhaps a further generation of struggle before it can hope to reap the fruits of victory.

It is of supreme importance and interest to ask how Americans themselves view all of this. Speaking now of academic America, it has not been an impressive record. The mainland anthropologists who put together the 1956 study, *The People of Puerto Rico*, were so obsessed with the 'little community' thesis that they concluded, erroneously, that there existed 'no common core of shared behaviour' in Puerto Rico, but only four 'subcultures' based on the economic foundations of the tobacco, coffee and sugar-growing areas, along with a class of urban 'prominent families'. They could not see the wood for the trees.

Later academic mandarins have compounded the error. Those of them, for example, who wrote advisory briefs for the 1965 Status Commission employed a vulgarised thesis of cultural diffusionism to prove, at least to their own satisfaction, that Puerto Rico could not claim to possess its own cultural idiosyncrasy; as if the fact that Puerto Ricans eat Danish ham or drive American automobiles or use transistor radios made in Japan

---

*Angel Quintero Rivera, *Lucha Obrera en Puerto Rico: Antología de Grandes Documentos de la Historia Obrera Puertorriqueña* (Rio Piedreas, Puerto Rico, CEREP, 1970).

precludes any effort at nationalist assertion. The argument, of course, failed to appreciate that in a world increasingly internationalist in its technology the nationalist assertion is most likely to flourish in the areas of culture, literature, and the arts.

Finally, Professor Henry Wells' book—*The Modernization of Puerto Rico* (Harvard University Press, 1969)—tries to argue that what has taken place in Puerto Rico since 1940 is not Americanisation but modernisation, which, by definition, is at once ideologically neutral and technically irreversible. But this is at best a half-truth only. It is, much of it, certainly, a modernizing process; but it is modernization passed through the filter of the American capitalist acquisitive society, which is an entirely different thing. It carries, then, all of the characteristics of that society: its cupidity, its paranoid preoccupation with material possessions, its growth mania, its mad consumerism, its belief that "promotion" will fix anything.

The 'modernization' argument is defective on a number of counts. It overlooks the crucial fact that the enforced bilateralism with the American economy compels Puerto Rico to buy everything through the States, thus inhibiting the growth of more healthy, multilateral relationships with, say, Europe or Latin America. It adopts the jejune argument that this is what people want, without seeing that, under the advertising pressures of capitalist mass media, people do not so much get what they want as want what they get. The absurd distortions of supply and demand that this enforced dependency on the American market produce—the fact that, to take only one example recently noted by a Puerto Rican columnist, peasant mothers in the interior valley hamlets will receive every Mother's Day greeting cards from their daughters in San Juan written in English and inscribed with the maudlin verses of some Midwestern lyricist—are thus made to appear as a natural part of an inevitable 'progress'. Yet this, surely, is not the socially controlled modernisation undertaken by a modern responsible welfare state. It is the rampant, barbaric commercialization of a whole life-style. It is small wonder that increasingly large numbers of Puerto Ricans who may not even be *autonomista* or *independentista* in any sense are beginning to echo the *cri de coeur* of one of their earlier leaders, Matienzo Cintrón, that 'yesterday we were a people, today we are only a crowd'.

Many socially-conscious Continentals are also feeling their way to similar conclusions. It is the attractive merit of the Wagenheim book that it finely reflects that spirit. He is the American liberal at his best. He perceives things acutely; he knows Puerto Rico intimately; he has a compassionate sympathy for the individual Puerto Rican. He can see what American cultural pollution has done; how, for instance, casino-based tourism has converted the once-pleasing Condado section of San Juan into a vulgar and ugly tourist-hotel strip.

Yet, for all that, the book is ultimately disappointing. That is, most certainly, because he writes from the limited viewpoint of the American liberal tradition. He identifies symptoms, but fails to perceive their underlying structural causes in the character of American society. He thus notes correctly that the new Puerto Rican business and managerial types are driven by what he calls the 'success syndrome'; but he fails to appreciate what that really means, or why it is so. He quotes the sad remarks of disillusioned government economic advisors on the continuing problem of chronic poverty in the economy; he does not see that this is not simply a lapse of policy or a 'mistake', but rather the necessary consequence of a business economy that contains the dichotomy of private affluence and mass poverty as a structural ingredient of its total character.

Above all, he cannot quite being himself to see that independence and, after independence, socialism are the only way out of all this. He accepts the associated status of the territory because 'public opinion' wants it, as shown in successive election results. He fails to see how that 'public opinion' has been manufactured. Manufactured, indeed, throughout the whole, long history of the colony: no less a person than the prestigious Director of the Institute of Puerto Rican Culture has pointed out how, for centuries, the Puerto Rican masses have been kept in their places by carefully conducted fear campaigns on the part of their rulers: fear of the English pirates in the sixteenth century, of the Dutch marauders in the seventeenth century, of the democratic ideas of the young American republic in the nineteenth century, and of 'Communist totalitarianism' at the present moment. The 1972 elections have once again demonstrated how easy it is to frighten the Puerto Rican elector with the McCarthyite tactic of identifying any sort of dissent with Cuba, Castro and Communism.

What explains this chronic inability of the American liberal to fully comprehend the real character of the colonial problem? In part, it is the character of American liberalism itself. It s ingrained pragmatism makes it incapable of thinking in terms of fundamental principle. It cannot take the long view of any situation; it thinks always of manoeuvre and adjustment to the given factors of the immediate situation. In its academic presentation, it believes in 'objectivity', which really means that one carefully draws up a balance sheet tabulating all the arguments for and against a particular thesis, and then abdicates any responsibility for arriving at a conclusive opinion one way or the other. This mode of argumentation thus confuses liberalism with neutrality. It is spiritually sterile. It leaves no room for moral indignation. It makes a hopelessly indecisive person of the author. All in all, it is a moral defect summed up in the acute observation of American wit Don Marquis on the figure of the Boston Brahmin George Endicott Peabody: he was determined to be a liberal if it killed him, so he never was a liberal, he was merely determined.

In part, again, it is a question of political naïveté. American today, as it has always been, is a startling combination of technological omnicompetence and old-fashioned ideology. Its thought-patterns are essentially nineteenth century; even its forces for change, like the Ralph Nader group, think only of replacing monopoly capitalism with competitive capitalism; and only in America is it possible today for a figure like Senator McGovern to be called a radical. That is eminently clear if a brief look is taken at a book recently published on the neighbouring US Vigrin Islands: Edward A. O'Neill, *Rape of the Virgin Islands* (New York, Praeger, Inc., 1972). The sad state of that other American colonial dependency is fully described. But, yet again, the indignation of the author is that of an American reformist liberal trapped within the prison of his own assumptions. For him, as the unlovely portrait emerges, it is a question, simply enough, of the beautiful tropical resources of the islands being destroyed by a gang of dishonest politicians and ruthless business tycoons, both Continental and native. It is the old story in American politics of the struggle between the evil 'bosses' and the pure-minded reformers. It is a simplistic morality play. It fails to see that the actors operate within a general system they sincerely accept and that they sincerely see themselves as honourable elements within that system. It fails to appreciate, accordingly, that it is not the agents, however distasteful they may be, who have to be analysed, but the system itself. It lacks a theoretical dialectic that makes particular phenomena understandable and explicable. Writers like Wagenheim and O'Neill thus end up as observers capable of analysing the symptoms without being able to identify the disease of which the symptoms are only a particular expression.

Yet there is more to it even than this. There seems to be something about the American temperament that makes it almost impossible for Americans to comprehend sympathetically other culture systems. The comparison with the English is instructive. The Englishman, traditionally, is an aristocrat; he regards the entry of new members into the club with distaste. The American, traditionally, is a democrat; he wants everybody to join the club. The American, then, cannot seem to stomach the fact that other peoples and cultures may not particularly want to join his club. So, even if he is free of racial pprejudice, he is full of cultural prejudice, founded on the conviction that there must be something naturally wrong with anybody who does not passionately desire a share of the American 'way oflife'. This explains the difference between the English and the American records in the Caribbean region. It was summed up a generation ago by an earlier American writer, noting the behaviour-patterns of his fellow Americans in the area. 'On first acquaintance', he wrote, 'we become warmly personal and paternal. The British are different. They are coldly impersonal; they go out to rule and nothing swerves them. In their code there is always socially an abyss between natives and rulers, yet they will die for each other. Time and time again, in our colonies, we have seen the American contact grow into something like a canker sore, a form of social indigestion, as it were, from too much sweetness.'[2] That is as true today as it was then. The result, in politico-constitutional terms, is independence in the English-speaking Caribbean, colonial tutelage still in the American Caribbean. The result, in economic terms, is a situation in which Puerto Ricans and Virgin Islanders become—in the phrase of one Puerto Rican writer—beggars at the back door of the White House. The result, in social terms, is the existence, both in Puerto Rico and the Virgins, of prestigious groups of American Continentals who have no desire to be genuinely assimilated, exhibit an attitude of condescending paternalism towards the local creole cultures and, in general, possess all the characteristic features of the expatriate mentality.

Perhaps the most important thing about most of the books under review, is that they demonstrate, with remarkable clarity, the general nature of modern American imperialism in the second half of the twentieth century. Puerto Rico is a classic case-study, from this viewpoint, of how that imperialism operates, and will increasingly operate in the future, to ensure its global supremacy. That imperialism, to begin with, is an expanding imperialism. All of the other imperialisms in the Caribbean region—English, Dutch, French—are contracting, they are on the way out. The result is that, today, every Caribbean society, whether formally independent or an associated state in some form or another with its respective metropolitan centre, is compelled to come to terms with the dark omnipresence of American power. The territories of the former British Empire have thus, in one way, simply moved out of the British frying pan into the American fire: and their emergent foreign policies revolve around that cardinal truth.

The methodology of American influence thus becomes something that has to be fully understood by every Caribbean nationalist force. Its major ingredients are apparent enough in the case of Puerto Rico. Grant the colony citizenship, but let it be a second-class citizenship, so that the colonials do not vote in the metropolitan elections, have no voice in the Congress, save that of a weak Resident Commissioner, must serve in the armed forces, frequently against their will, and cannot change their constitutional instruments except with the final consent of Washington. Let them travel freely within the United States, but deny them any independent power over customs, immigration, maritime services, interstate commerce, mails, and other matters. Let them elect their own chief executives and legislative branches, but deny them any real power over the business corporations that make astonishingly handsome profits on the basis of cheap Puerto Rican labour and generous tax-exemption development programs. Above all, deluge them, through American-style mass media advertising, with the promise of the material rewards of American materialist life: the house in the suburbs, the large automobile, all the household gimmicks of American technology. In this fashion, Puerto Rico becomes the perfumed colony, the kept woman of American imperialism. The appeal to economic greed and avarice thus works to dampen the spirit of political independence. Once this process is under way you do not need the method of CIA infiltration, as in the case of Guyana, or the method of naked military-naval intervention, as in the case of Cuba and Santo Domingo. In the Puerto Rican case the main instrument of all this is the device of the federal matching fund, which means that the territory receives annually anything between US $400 and 450 million; much of which is used to produce high-rise public-housing condominiums that destroy kinship and family ties, continental-style highways that accelerate a senseless automobilisation, urban renewal programs that bulldoze the slums instead of sensibly rehabilitating them, medical programs that benefit a local medical parasitical class rather than the individual patient. It all constitutes, in short, the pillage of the Third World. All over the world—Latin America, Africa, South East Asia—this process is rapidly developing. It is the leading feature of Puerto Rican "development" that here can be seen, in all of its brutal clarity, what the process really means. Here, remarkably concentrated, is a perfect example of the dependent Third World economy, that does not produce its own technology, adapted to the unique needs of the local environment, but rather imports an alien technology from the metropolitan centre.

What is the way out of all this? Both Silén and Maldonado Denis opt for the strategy of the armed struggle. Silén applauds the firebombing tactics of the minority clandestine group, Armed Commandos of Liberation; Maldonado Denis approvingly quotes the declaration of the same group that for each young Puerto Rican jailed for refusing to serve in the US armed forces they will execute one Yankee. Yet it is doubtful whether such a strategy of revolutionary violence corresponds—at the moment—to Puerto Rican realities. There is the fact, to begin with, that Puerto Rico is a deeply constitutionalist society. It possesses a viable apparatus of competing political parties, an independent press, an aggressive public opinion, and free elections. This is a far cry from the typical Caribbean *caudillo* tyrannies like Batista's Cuba, Duvalier's Haiti or Trujillo's Santo Domingo. Nor is this simply a matter of the imposition of an alien American system upon a colonial people, for the constitutionalist habit, along with the formation of parties, has its roots in the Spanish period, thus scotching the pleasing American myth that Americans after 1898 "gave" the party system to the new dependency.

There is the further fact that, as of today, the leading *independentista* groups accept that tradition, not as a sacred article of faith, but as a given concrete element within the total situation. They undertake, through their own newspapers, a vast educational program among the masses. They run their candidates in the electoral process. They recognise the limits of the tradition; but they also recognise that any revolutionary party must use the tools that are to hand, pushing them to the limits of their usefulness. There is, finally, the fact that very few of the preconditions of revolutionary insurrectionism listed by Lenin exist in present-day Puerto Rico: class consciousness raised to such a level that the masses are ready for the revolt; the existence of a trained cadre ready for the seizure of power; widespread alienation in the armed forces. To undertake insurrectionary activity in the absence of such conditions—as indeed the Jayuya uprising of 1950 in Puerto Rico itself shows—is to indulge in what Marx called "playing with revolution." Maldonado Denis invokes the image of urban guerrilla warfare. But no such movement has as yet succeeded in Latin America, where they proliferate, in bringing a single government to its knees. There may be far more valuable returns accruing from the alternative strategy of long-term, underground educational activity among the peasant masses, as is illustrated in Hugo Blanco's recently published book on the work of his group among the landless peasantry of the Peruvian high sierra. Terrorism, on the contrary, becomes Left-wing irresponsibility when a people is not ready for it. It leaves behind it, furthermore, a legacy of hatred that can mar a whole society for a generation; that, surely, is the lesson of the so-called *dialéctica de las pistolas* in the case of the Colombian *violencia*.

The Puerto Rican leadership, for the moment at least, is dedicated to the three-fold task of organisation, education and agitation. Nor are they likely to under-estimate the magnitude of their task. They have to wage war on two fronts: the nationalist struggle against the American Empire and the internal class struggle against the local pseudo-ruling class. They must accelerate the process of political polarisation between statehood and independence, and thus force every Puerto Rican into a final, irrevocable choice. They must learn how to deal with the opportunists, the parliamentary rhetoricians, the week-end *independentistas*. When they finally command a majority following they must confront the Americans with the demand for final separation, to be accompanied, ideally, by a treaty of separation that (1) enables the new Republic to pass through a period of economic transition by means of appropriate federal aid and (2) guarantees full reparations for the economic exploitation of the colony. If at that point Washington refuses, then the way will be opened for organized revolt. And for that, beyond any doubt, the American power will be morally responsible. But if the American ruling class is still capable of magnanimity, 1976 may well witness not merely the bicentennial anniversary of the American Republic but also the birth of the Puerto Rican Republic. This, clearly enough, is the agenda for the future.

Some of the Literature on Puerto Rico and Puerto Ricans in English

Adalberto López

In the decade of the 1960s, as minority groups became more vocal and militant in their struggle for social justice, young black and Chicano students pressured high schools and universities to create courses in black and Chicano history and culture and to establish Afro-American and Chicano studies programs. By the beginning of the 1970s such programs existed in dozens of universities and colleges where large numbers of black and Chicano students were concentrated. Puerto Rican students soon made demands similar to those of blacks and Chicanos, and today courses on Puerto Rican history and society are offered in several New York City public schools, and there are Puerto Rican studies programs in some New York City and State Universities.

The creation of new courses on black and Chicano history and culture and the establishment of Afro-American and Chicano studies programs suddenly created a widened market for publications to meet the needs of students and scholars. In the second half of the 1960s books on blacks and Chicanos were published in increasing numbers by publishers and university presses. In their rush to meet the needs of a growing market for such materials many writers—black, white, and Chicano—produced works whose scholarship and usefulness can be questioned. In their eagerness to exploit the new market, publishers were often indiscriminate in their choice of materials. Nonetheless, much of the material published on blacks and Chicanos since the mid-1960s has been both useful and of high quality.

Compared to black and Chicano studies programs, Puerto Rican studies programs are relatively new. Also relatively new are the growing enthusiasm of Puerto Rican students in the United States and the American reading public's widened interest in Puerto Rican history, culture and migration experience. Consequently, in the past few years the number of books published in English on Puerto Rico and Puerto Ricans has increased sharply. Nonetheless, more is still needed, and it might be useful now to pause and take stock of what is already available and reflect on what is still needed.

If we ignore, as we should, the vulgar apologies of Luis Muñoz Marín, governor of Puerto Rico from 1948 to 1964, and the "Puerto Rican economic miracle" he is claimed to have presided over, found in the works of Ralph Hancock, *Puerto Rico: A Success Story* (New York: D. Van Nostrand, 1960) and Earl Parker Hanson, *Puerto Rico: Land of Wonders* (New York: Alfred Knopf, 1960), the first work of merit published in English on Puerto Rico in the post-World War II period is Gordon K. Lewis, *Puerto Rico: Freedom and Power in the Caribbean*, (New York: Monthly Review Press, 1964), which appeared in an abridged paperback version by Harper and Row in 1968. The books deal primarily with Puerto Rican politics and society in the 20th century. Written from a highly sophisticated and balanced socialist point of view, it stresses the relentless "Americanization" of all facts of Puerto Rican society in the twentieth century, the economic dependence of Puerto Rico on the United States, the nature of the federal relationship between the island and the colonial metropolis, and the nature of Puerto Rican politics and contemporary society. It is a good and thoughtful book, but its prose is cumbersome and its arguments confusing to those who know little or nothing about Puerto Rico. Although the book has been of great value to area experts, most students on the U.S. mainland find it confusing, dull, and, therefore, of limited value.

Quite different from Lewis' book is the work by Juan Angel Silén, *We, the Puerto Rican People: A Story of Oppression and Resistance* (New York: Monthly Review Press, 1959). Silén is a young Puerto Rican Marxist who has been involved since the 1950s in the struggle for Puerto Rican independence. His book, which aims to expose the myth of the famous Puerto Rican "docility" by portraying continuing Puerto Rican resistance to the United States' presence on the island and North American exploitation of the Puerto Rican people, is short, well-organized, and readable. The book, however, presents a version of the history of Puerto Rico which is highly misleading. The author is much too infantile a Marxist. In his eagerness to fit the history of the island into a "scientific" Marxist framework and to convince the reader of the validity of his general thesis, he distorts—often beyond recognition—the history of Puerto Rico. Sections of the book are but a hodgepodge of infantilism, emotionalism, and poor history.

Much more useful to Puerto Rican students on the mainland and Americans interested in Puerto Rico are the books of Kal Wagenheim, *Puerto Rico: A Profile* (New York: Praeger Publishers, 1970), María Teresa Babín, *The Puerto Ricans' Spirit: Their History, Life, and Culture* (New York: Collier Books, 1972), and Manuel Maldonado-Denis, *Puerto Rico: A Socio-Historic Interpretation*, (New York: Random House, 1972). The work by Wagenheim, an *americano* who lived for many years in Puerto Rico as a journalist and was among the founders of the *Caribbean Review*, is a general introduction to Puerto Rican history and culture designed primarily for those in the United States who are uninformed about Puerto Rico. It includes, for example, short sections on Puerto Rican foods, holidays, literary figures, and politics. Of a more specialized nature is the book by Teresa Babín, a Puerto Rican who has devoted her scholarly career to the study of Puerto Rican literature, folklore, and culture. Although disorganized at times, the book is a fine, compact, readable cultural history of Puerto Rico revealing the Spanish, Indian, and African influences which shaped Puerto Rican culture. Like Wagenheim's book, hers is a general introduction to Puerto Rican culture designed more for the uninformed reader on the mainland than for area experts.

The book by Maldonado-Denis is one of the best which has been published on Puerto Rico in English so far. Originally published in Mexico in 1969, the English edition has been made more useful by the addition of an epilogue which brings the story of Puerto Rico up to 1970 and also a good interpretive essay on the Puerto Rican migration to the U.S. mainland. The boook exposes, as Gordon K. Lewis has pointed out, the unreality of the twin myths about Puerto Rico: that it is either a society of colonial servility or a "Showcase of Democracy." Like Silén, Maldonado-Denis is a Marxist historian and has been involved for decades in the struggle for Puerto Rican independence. But he is a more thoughtful historian and his Marxism is tempered by other theoretical influences as well as by the realization that Marx was not infallible. The work, which constitutes an indignant assault upon the imperialist enemy, is an interpretive essay based primarily on secondary sources and on the author's personal observations. Although it contains some errors of fact and omission, it is one of the most readable and balanced accounts available in English of Puerto Rican history and the Puerto Rican dilemma.

Also useful, but somewhat dangerous, is the book by Henry Wells, *The Modernization of Puerto Rico: A Political Study of Changing Values and Institutions* (Cambridge: Harvard University Press, 1969). Written by a political scientist rather than a historian, the work is less interpretive than Maldonado-Denis' but has far more factual information and therefore compliments nicely the latter's work. One of the major faults of the book, as Gordon K. Lewis has pointed out, is that it "tries to argue that what has taken place in Puerto Rico since 1940 is not Americanization but modernization, which, by definition, is at once ideologically neutral and technically irreversible." Wells fails to perceive that the "modernization" of Puerto Rico has taken place within a colonial context and has been directed by and on behalf of North American big business. Another major fault of the book is its tendency to downgrade the nationalist struggle and to eulogize, like many other North Americans who have written on Puerto Rico, the "modernizing" regime of Luis Muñoz Marín.

Useful as they both are, the books by Maldonado-Denis and Wells share an important shortcoming: Although their sections on the 20th century are good, both works concentrate primarily on the history and politics of Puerto Rico in the twentieth century and therefore unwittingly strengthen the assumption of many students that the history of the island before 1898 is uninteresting and of little consequence. At present the only book in English on Puerto Rican history before 1898 is Loida Figueroa's *History of Puerto Rico. From the Beginning to 1892* (New York: Anaya Book Company, 1972), a poorly translated version of the first two volumes of her history of Puerto Rico. One fault of this work is that the author's nationalism often leads her into erroneous conclusions about certain events in Puerto Rico before 1898. Also, the book is essentially a political history. There is still a need in English for a socio-economic study of Puerto Rico before 1898, especially the nineteenth century.

---

*Gordon K. Lewis, "Puerto Rico: Towards a New Consciousness," *Latin American Review of Books*, No. 1 (Spring, 1973), p. 153)

Another type of work which would be useful and which has not yet appeared in English is a documentary history of Puerto Rico. Karl and Olga Wagenheim (eds.), *The Puerto Ricans: A Documentary History* (New York: Praeger Publishers, 1973) pretends to be that. But that pretention is unwarranted and the title of the book highly misleading. Although the book includes several documents, it is primarily a collection of excerpts from various work on Puerto Rico arranged chronologically. One wonders in what sense the works of Richard Elman, Eric Williams, Dan Wakefield, Hubert Herring, Edward Rayan, and Karl Wagenheim himself constitute documents relevant to Puerto Rican history. Perhaps the Wagenheims have a weird conception of what a historical document is. Far more useful that what the Wagenheims have produced would have been an updated English translation of Eugenio Fernández Méndez (ed.), *Crónicas de Puerto Rico*, 2 volumes (San Juan: Biblioteca de Autores Puertorriqueños, 1959).

In addition to books of a general nature, there is still a need for more specialized monographs on Puerto Rican history and society. A few have already been published in English. There is, for example, Edward J. Barbusse, *The United States in Puerto Rico, 1898-1900* (Chapel Hill: University of North Carolina Press, 1966), a cumbersome but scholarly account of the events leading to the U.S. occupation of 1898, the first two years of American rule in Puerto Rico, and the background and provisions of the Foraker Act of 1900. Thomas G. Mathews's *Puerto Rican Politics and the New Deal* (Gainesville: University of Florida Press, 1960) is a good account of the social and economic crisis of the 1930s, the various attempts made by government agencies to cope with that crisis and Puerto Rican politics in the 1930s and early 1940s. Robert W. Anderson's *Party Politics in Puerto Rico* (Stanford: Stanford University Press, 1965) is a useful account of Puerto Rican politics in the twentieth century, especially in the period after 1940. The work by Charles T. Goodsell, *Administration of a Revolution* (Cambridge: Harvard University Press, 1965) is a dull but useful examination of administrative reforms in Puerto Rico between 1941 and 1946 with brief biographical sketches of some of the Puerto Ricans, like Jaime Benitez, who played an important role in those reforms. Finally, there is the book by Arthur Liebman, *The Politics of Puerto Rican University Students* (Austin: University of Texas Press, 1970), a modest sociological monograph based on questionnaires submitted to nearly 600 University of Puerto Rico students in 1964. Liebman's conclusion is that Puerto Rican students are not oriented to left-wing or nationalist movements and thus refute the popular image of the Latin American student. Given developments at the University of Puerto Rico and among Puerto Rican university students since Liebman carried out his study in 1964, this conclusion is perhaps no longer valid.

But these specialized monographs, most of which are out of print and all of which are unavailable in paperback and are, therefore, too costly to most Puerto Rican students in the United States, still fail to meet the needs of scholars and students in the English-speaking world. There is a need, for example, for an economic history of the Puerto Rican Nationalist Party and for a good political biography of Pedro Albizu Campos (1891-1965), Puerto Rico's most important nationalist leader in the twentieth century. The only work on Don Pedro available in English is Federico Ribes Tovar's *The Revolutionary* (New York: Plus Ultra Education Publishers, 1971), a disjointed and superficial account of Don Pedro's life. The book's only saving grace lies in the excellent photographs of the Nationalist leader, the Ponce Massacre of 1937 and the abortive revolt of 1950.

Also in need are books on the problems of poverty and inequality in contemporary Puerto Rico. Oscar Lewis's widely acclaimed *La Vida* (New York: Random House, 1965) certainly did not meet that need. As Gordon K. Lewis has so beautifully put it, the book is an exercise "in a sort of peephole sociology that gravely exaggerates the more pornographic aspects of San Juan slum life."* The book portrays poverty in a San Juan slum (*La Perla*) but does not go into an analysis of the sources of that poverty. It is a dirty book, a useless book, which, by concentrating on the life story of a family of prostitutes, has unwittingly strengthened the bigotry of North Americans, both on the island and on the mainland, who see Puerto Rican women as just so many whores.

A book which will appear in English soon and which will bring to the attention of the English-speaking world the problems of poverty and social inequality in contemporary Puerto Rico is *Problems of Social Inequality in Puerto Rico*, edited by Rafael L. Ramírez, Barry B. Levine, and Carlos Buitrago Ortiz. Avoiding rhetoric or polemic, the essays in this slender volume chillingly describe the results of the developmental program of the Popular Democratic Party under North American supervision: "chronic poverty and increased levels of both absolute and

*Ibid., p. 148

relative income inequality, with one out of every four Puerto Rican families barely surviving on the *mantengo* (the Federal welfare handout).''* That the statistics for the growth of poverty are not even greater is only due to the fact that, as is pointed out in Buitrago's essay in the collection, the colony has in effect exported its unemployment problem by means of the massive migratory movement to the mainland.

With a growing need for English language publications on Puerto Rico, scholars should seriously consider translating important Puerto Rican works now available only in Spanish. More works by important Puerto Rican literary figures like the playwright René Marqués and the novelist Pedro Juan Soto should be translated and published in English. Also useful would be translations of works such as Antonio Pedreira's *Insularismo* (Madrid: Tipografía Artística, 1934) and Tomás Blanco's *Prontuario Histórico de Puerto Rico* (San Juan: Biblioteca de Autores Puertorriqueños, 1943), two of the most important books of this century on Puerto Rico. Another work that should be translated and published in English is Angel Quintero Rivera's *Lucha Obrera en Puerto Rico* (Rio Piedras: CEREP, 1971), an excellent collection of documents dealing with the working class struggle in Puerto Rico. The book includes examples of some of the socialist literature that struggle produced during the first three decades of North American rule in the island, a literature which is now almost forgotten.

But if Puerto Rican students in the United States are interested in the history of Puerto Rico—just as blacks are interested in African history and Chicanos in Mexican history—they are primarily interested in the history of the Puerto Rican migration to the United States, in the history of the Puerto Rican communities in this country, and in the problems which continue to face those communities. Oscar Handlin's *The Newcomers: Negroes and Puerto Ricans in a Changing Metropolis* (Cambridge: Harvard University Press, 1959) has some useful information on the history of Puerto Ricans in New York City, but its main emphasis is on blacks. Clarence Senior's *Strangers then Neighbors: From Pilgrims to Puerto Ricans* (New York: Anti-Defamation League of B'Nai Brith, 1961) is a brief sociological study of the problems Puerto Ricans and other immigrants have faced in the United States. More useful is a work by C. Wright Mills, Clarence Senior, and Rose Kohn Goldsen, *The Puerto Rican Journey: New York's Newest Migrants* (New York:

---

*Ibid., p. 148.

Harper and Row, 1950). This work presents good insights into the causes of the Puerto Rican migration to the United States in the 1940s and the social and economic problems which overwhelmed Puerto Ricans in this country during that decade.

In the 1950s several works were published on Puerto Rican communities in New York City. One of the best of those books was Elena Padilla's *Up From Puerto Rico* (New York: Columbia University Press, 1958), the result of a study of New York Puerto Ricans made by a team of anthropologists. Dan Wakefield's *Island in the City: The World of Spanish Harlem* (Boston: Houghton Mifflin, 1959) is a reporter's readable account of life in Spanish Harlem ("El Barrio"), the largest Spanish-speaking community in the United States at the time the book was written and one of the country's worst ghettos. Similar to Wakefield's account is that of another reporter, Christopher Rand's *The Puerto Ricans* (Fair Lawn, New Jersey: Oxford University Press, 1958). Although the works by Wakefield and Rand are engagingly written and marked by a real sympathy for the problems afflicting Puerto Ricans in this country in the 1950s, both are marred by a tendency to play up the "colorful" and picturesque and overemphasize the more gaudy or sensational aspects of life in "El Barrio". Also, they were written by people who did not live in "El Barrio" and who, therefore, could have but an inkling of what ghetto life was all about.

Far more useful than Wakefield's and Rand's accounts of life in "El Barrio" is Patricia Sexton's *Spanish Harlem: Anatomy of Poverty* (New York: Harper and Row, 1965). Written by a sociologist who spent part of two years "getting acquainted" with East Harlem, this work does not gloss over the problems that confront many of the self-supporting, low-income dwellers of that section of Manhattan. It is a readable book, well-informed, and emphasizes the need for ghetto dwellers to work out their own destiny.

Much more recent are the works of Harold J. Alford, *The Proud Peoples* (New York: David McKay Company, 1972) and Bruce A Glasrud and Alan M. Smith, *Promises to Keep* (Chicago: Rand McNally, 1972). Alford's work claims to be a history of the Spanish speaking peoples of the United States, but is essentially a history of the Chicanos with a few passing references to Puerto Ricans and Cubans. The work by Glasrud and Smith is a two-volume collection of essays on non-whites in the United States, but of the 25 essays included in this work only one (written in 1950) deals with Pueto Ricans. Both of these works reflect a tendency by North American historians of ethnic groups to ignore Puerto Ricans. It is not unfair to conclude that both works are useless to Puerto Ricans and others in the United States who are interested in the history and experiences of Puerto Rican communities in this country.

Of the few works which have been published on Puerto Ricans in the United States recently, perhaps one of the most useful is Piri Thomas's *Down These Mean Streets* (New York: Alfred Knopf, 1967), a vivid and moving account of a Puerto Rican's childhood and adolescence in Spanish Harlem. Piri Thomas has followed this work with the recently published *Savior, Savior, Hold my Hand* (Garden City: Doubleday and Company, 1972), a good literary account which indicts white racism in Anglo suburbia and shows that in spite of the uproar of the 1960s, life in Spanish Harlem is worse than ever. Those interested in Puerto Rican ghetto life today and the new militancy among young Puerto Ricans will enjoy *Palante* (Hightstown, N.J.: McGraw Hill, 1971). Michael Abramson's collection of beautiful photographs of the Young Lords and their activities is introduced by a series of moving and down-to-earth essays by some of the Young Lords themselves. Also recent is Alfredo López's *The Puerto Rican Papers* (New York: The Bobbs-Merrill Company, 1973), a hodgepodge of poor history and emotionalism by a young Puerto Rican of the mainland who, like Juan Angel Silén, has pretentions to being a scientific Marxist. Finally, references should be made to Joseph P. Fitzpatrick's *The Puerto Rican Americans* (Englewood Cliffs, N.J.: Prentice Hall, 1971), the most up-to-date general account of the Puerto Rican migration to the United States and of the problems faced by Puerto Rican communities in this country, and to Francesco Cordasco's *Puerto Ricans on the United States Mainland* (Totowa, N.J.: Rowman and Littlefield, 1972), a very useful annotated bibliography of reports, doctoral dissertations, articles, and books on Puerto Ricans on the mainland.

But if works such as those of Piri Thomas, Joseph Fitzpatrick, Patricia Cayo, and Francesco Cordasco are useful, they still fail to meet the need for accounts—historical and sociological—of the Puerto Rican experience in the United States. Although there are plentiful figures on the numbers of Puerto Ricans who have migrated to the United States, there is a need for a scholarly and interpretive history of that migration both before and after World War II. Such a study must deal with questions about why Puerto Ricans migrated and from what social groups the migrants came. There is also a need for a comprehensive study of Puerto Rican communities in the United States, a study similar to that which Leo Grebler, Joan Moore, and Ralph C. Guzman prepared on the Chicanos (*The Mexican American People*. New York: The Free Press, 1970). Similarly, there is a need for a general history of Puerto Ricans in the United States, for an account of the Puerto Rican seasonal migrants, and for anthologies of literary works produced by Puerto Ricans living in this country. Until works of this sort become available and until the other needs which I have mentioned in this essay are met, the American public will continue to be ignorant about one of the nation's largest minorities, the Puerto Rican students in this country will continue to grope in the dark FOR an understanding of the land of their parents and of the Puerto Rican experience in the United States.

Bibliography

BIBLIOGRAPHIES, GENERAL, AND INTERPRETIVE WORKS

Babín, Maria Teresa. *The Puerto Ricans' Spirit: Their History, Life, and Culture.* New York: Collier-Macmillan, 1971.

Blanco, Tomás. *Prontuario Histórico de Puerto Rico.* San Juan: Biblioteca de Autores Puertorriqueños, 1946.

Cordasco, Francesco and Bucchioni, Eugene (eds.). *The Puerto Rican Experience: A Sociological Sourcebook.* Totowa, New Jersey: Towman and Littlefield, 1973.

Dessick, Jesse, ed. *Doctoral Research on Puerto Rico and Puerto Ricans.* New York: New York University Press, 1967.

Fernández Méndez, Eugenio. *Desarrollo distórico de la sociedad puertorriqueña.* San Juan: Instituto de Cultura Puertorriqueña, 1959.

Fernández Méndez, Eugenio. *The Sources of Puerto Rican Culture History: A Critical Appraisal.* San Juan: Ediciones El Cemi, 1967.

Figueroa, Loida. *History of Puerto Rico.* New York: Anaya Book Co., 1972.

Jones, Clarence and Picó, Rafael, eds. *Symposium on the Georgraphy of Puerto Rico.* Río Piedras: University of Puerto Rico Press, 1955.

Lewis, Gordon K. *Puerto Rico: Freedom and Power in the Caribbean.* New York: Monthly Review Press, 1963.

Maldonado-Denis, Manuel. *Puerto Rico: A Socio-Historic Interpretation.* New York: Random House, 1972.

Manrique Cabrera, Francisco. *Historia de la literatura puertorriqueña.* New York: Las Americas Publishing Co., 1956.

Pagán, Bolívar. *Historia de los partidos políticos puertorriqueños.* San Juan: Libreria Campos, 1959.

Pedreira, Antonio. *Insularismo: Ensayos de interpretación puertorriqueña.* San Juan: Biblioteca de Autores Puertorriqueños, 1934.

Puerto Rico Commission on the Status of Puerto Rico. *Status of Puerto Rico. Selected Background Studies Prepared for the United States-Puerto Rico*

Commission on the Status of Puerto Rico. Washington, D.C.: U.S. Government Printing Office, 1966.

Ramírez, Ramón. *La historia del movimiento libertador en la historia de Puerto Rico.* San Juan: Imprenta Borinquen, 1954.

Silén, Juan Angel. *We, the Puerto Rican People. A Story of Oppression and Resistance.* New York: Monthly Review Press, 1971.

The Puerto Ricans: A Documentary History, Edited by Karl Wagenheim and Olga Jimenez de Wagenheim. New York: Praeger, 1973.

Wells, Henry, *The Modernization of Puerto Rico: A Political Study of Changing Values and Institutions.* Cambridge, Mass.: Harvard University Press, 1969.

PUERTO RICO FROM 1493 TO 1898

Abad y Lasierra, Fray Iñigo, *Historia geográfica, civil y natural de la Isla de San Juan Bautista de Puerto Rico* [1788]. Río Piedras: Editorial Universitaria, 1959.

Alegria, Ricardo. *Discovery, Conquest and Colonization of Puerto Rico: 1493-1599.* San Juan: Colección de Estudios Puertorriqueños, 1971.

Alonso, Manuel, *El Gibaro. Cuadro de costumbres de la isla de Puerto Rico* [1849]. San Juan: Instituto de Cultural Puertorriqueña, 1967.

Atiles, Francisco del Valle. *El campesino puertorriqueño: sus condiciones fisicas, intelectuales y morales.* San Juan, 1887.

— Brau, Salvador. *La colonización de Puerto Rico.* San Juan: Instituto de Cultura Puertorriqueña, 1966.

— Brau, Salvador, *Las clases jornaleras de Puerto Rico.* San Juan, 1882.

Córdoba, Pedro Tomás de. *Memorias geográficas, históricas, económicas y estadísticas de la Isla de Puerto Rico.* San Juan: Oficina del Gobierno, 1831-1833.

Cruz Monclova, Lidio. *Historia de Puerto Rico en el siglo XIX,* 3 vols. Río Piedras: Editorial Universitaria, 1957-1964.

Fernández Méndez, Eugenio, ed. *Crónicas de Puerto Rico,* 2 vols. San Juan: Biblioteca de Autores Puertorriqueños, 1957.

Flinter, George. *An Account of the Present State of the Island of Puerto Rico.* London, 1834.

Gauthier Dapena, José A. *Trayectoria del pensamiento liberal puertorriqueño en el siglo XIX.* San Juan: Instituto de Cultura Puertorriqueñ, 1963.

Gómez Acevedo, Labor. *Organización y reglamentación del trabajo en el Puerto Rico del siglo XIX.* San Juan: Instituto de Cultura Puertorriqueña, 1970.

Morales Carrión, Arturo. *Historia del pueblo de Puerto Rico desde sus orígenes hasta el siglo XVIII.* San Juan: Departamento de Instrucción Publica, 1968.

Morales Carrión, Arturo, *Puerto Rico and the Non-Hispanic Caribbean.* Río Piedras: University of Puerto Rico Press, 1952.

Pedreira, Antonio. *Año terrible del 87.* San Juan: Biblioteca de Autores Puertorriqueños, 1964.

Suárez Díaz, Ada. *El Doctor Ramón Emeterio Betances, su vida y su obra.* San Juan: Ateneo Puertorriqueño, 1968.

Tapia y Rivera, A. *Mis memorias o Puerto Rico como lo encontré y como lo dejé.* San Juan, 1946.

PUERTO RICO SINCE 1898

Anderson, Robert W.. *Party Politics in Puerto Rico.* Stanford: Stanford University Press, 1965.

Andic, Eaut. *Distribution of Family Incomes in Puerto Rico.* Río Piedras: University of Puerto Rico Press, 1964.

Berbusse, Edward. *The United States in Puerto Rico: 1898-1900.* Chapel Hill: University of North Carolina Press, 1966.

Bourne, Dorothy and James. *Thirty Years of Change in Puerto Rico: A Case Study of Ten Selected Rural Areas.* New York: Praeger, 1966.

Brameld, Theodore. *The Remaking of a Culture: Life and Education in Puerto Rico.* New York: Harper and Row, 1959.

Clark, Victor S. et. al. *Porto Rico and its Problems.* Washington, D.C.: Brookings Institution, 1930.

Carreras, Juan, *Santiago Iglesias Pantín.* San Juan: Editorial Club de la Prensa, 1967.

Diffie, Bailey and Justine. *Porto Rico: A Broken Pledge.* New York: The Vanguard Press, 1931.

Dinwiddie, William. *Porto Rico. Its Conditions and Possibilities.* New York, 1899.

Epstein, Erwin H., ed. *Politics and Education in Puerto Rico: A Documentary History of the Language Issue.* Metuchen, N.J.: The Scarecrow Press, 1970.

Freyre, Jorge F. *External and Domestic Financing in the Economic Development of Puerto Rico.* Río Piedras: University of Puerto Rico Press, 1969.

Goodsell, Charles T. *Administration of a Revolution: Executive Reform in Puerto Rico Under Governor Tugwell, 1941-1946.* Cambridge, Mass.: Harvard University Press, 1965.

Howard University. *Symposium on Pueto Rico in the Year 2000.* Washington, D.C.: Howard University Press, 1968.

Mathews, Thomas G. *Puerto Rican Politics and the New Deal.* Gainesville: University of Florida Press, 1960.

Mintz, Sidney. *Worker in the Cane: A Puerto Rican Life History.* New Haven: Yale University Press, 1960.

Negrón de Montilla, Aida. *Americanization in Puerto Rico and the Public School System, 1900-1930.* Río Piedras: Editorial Edil, 1971.

Nieves Falcón, Luis. *Recruitment to Higher Education in Puerto Rico, 1940-1960.* Río Piedras: Editorial Universitaria, 1965.

Quintero Rivera, Angel, ed. *Lucha Obrera en Puerto Rico, antología de grandes documentos en las historia obrera puertorriqueña.* Río Piedras: CEREP, 1971.

Ramírez, Rafael, Levine, Barry, and Buitrago Ortíz, Carlos, eds. *Problemas de desigualdad social en Puerto Rico.* Río Piedras: Libreria Internacional, 1972.

Seda, Eduardo. *Los derechos civiles en las cultura puertorriqueña.* Pío Piedras: Editorial Universitaria, 1963.

Seda, Eduardo. *Social Change and Personality in a Puerto Rican Agrarian Reform Community.* Evanston: Northwestern University Press, 1973.

Stanford Research Institute. *Development of Tourism in the Commonwealth of Puerto Rico.* 7 vols. Souther Pasadena: Stanford Research Institute, 1968.

Steward, Julian et. al. *The People of Puerto Rico.* Urbana: University of Illinois Press, 1956.

Tugwell, Rexford Buy. *The Striken Land: The Story of Puerto Rico.* Garden City: Doubleday and Co., Inc., 1947.

Tumin, Melvin and Feldman, Arnold. *Social Class and Social Change in Puerto Rico.* Princeton, N.J.: Yale University Press, 1961.

Vázquez Calzada, José. *El desbalance entre recursos y población en Puerto Rico.* San Juan: Centro de Estudios Demograficos, 1966.

Villar Roces, Mario. *Puerto Rico y su reforma agraria.* Río Piedras: Editorial Edil, 1968.

PUERTO RICANS ON THE U.S. MAINLAND

Chenault, Lawrence. *The Puerto Rican Migrant in New York City.* New York: Columbia University Press, 1938.

Colón, Jesús. *A Puerto Rican in New York City.* New York: Mainstream Publisher, 1961.

Cordasco, Francesco, ed. *Puerto Rican Children in Mainland Schools.* Metuchen, N.J.: Scarecrow Press, 1968.

Cordasco, Francesco, ed. *Puerto Ricans on the United State Mainland: A*

Bibliography of Reports, Texts, Critical Studies and Related Material. Totowa, N.J.: Rowman and Littlefield, 1972.

Fitzpatrick, Joseph P. *Puerto Rican Americans: The Meaning of Migration to the Mainland.* Englewood Cliffs: Prentice Hall, 1971.

Handlin, Oscar. *The Newcomers: Negroes and Puerto Ricans in a Changing Metropolis.* Cambridge, Mass.: Harvard University Press, 1959.

Hernandez Alvarez, Jose. *Return Migration to Puerto Rico.* Berkeley: University of California Press, 1967.

Lopéz, Alfredo. *The Puerto Rican Papers: Notes on the Re-emergence of a Nation.* New York: Bobbs-Merrill, 1973.

Mills, C. Wright. *The Puerto Rican Journey.* New York: Columbia University Press, 1948.

Padilla, Elena. *Up From Puerto Rico.* New York: Columbia University Press, 1958.

Sexton, Patricia Cayo. *Spanish Harlem: Anatomy of Poverty.* New York, Harper and Row Publishers, 1965.

Soto, Pedro Juan. *Spiks.* 3rd. ed. Río Piedras: Editorial Cultural, 1970.

Thomas, Piri, *Down These Mean Street.* New York: Alfred Knopf, 1967.

Thomas, Piri, *Savior, Savior, Hold my Hand.* New York: Doubleday and Co., Inc., 1972.

Wakefield, Dan. *Island in the City: Puerto Ricans in New York.* New York: Houghton Mifflin, 1959.

Brief Chronology of Puerto Rican History

1493: Christopher Columbus discovers the island of Boriquén for Europe on November 19. He names it San Juan Bautista. (Later the island becomes known as Puerto Rico.)

1503: The Crown of Castille authorizes the shipping of black slaves to the New World.

1508: Juan Ponce de León begins the Spanish occupation of Boriquén and founds the settlement of Caparra.

1509: The Spaniards begin the evacuation of Caparra to the site where the city of San Juan stands today. Arrival of the first slaves in Puerto Rico.

1511: Under the leadership of Agüeybana II, the Taino inhabitants of Boriquén launch their first rebellion against the Spaniards. Agüeybana is killed and the rebellion is crushed. Many Tainos flee the island to neighboring islands.

1512: Alonso Manso, first bishop of Puerto Rico, arrives on the island. He returns to Spain in 1515.

1521: Ponce de León is wounded by local Indians while exploring the Florida Peninsula. He dies in Havana soon thereafter.

---

*Prepared by Adalberto López with the assistance of Pancho Moscoso and Richard Skurdall.

1530: Gold production in Puerto Rico declines rapidly. Many Spaniards leave the island to seek their fortunes elsewhere in the continent. Governor Manuel de Lando takes steps to stop the exodus. To replace a rapidly declining Indian labor force, more black slaves are introduced.

1531: Governor Lando describes Puerto Rico as "the key to the Indies."

1533: A watchtower to protect the port of San Juan is erected. The construction of *La Fortaleza* begins.

1539: The construction of El Morro fortress is authorized.

1565: Last Taino rebellion against the Spaniards.

1576: *La Fortaleza* becomes the official residence of the governors of Puerto Rico.

1582: Governor of Puerto Rico informs the king of Spain that only a few hundred Indians are left on the island.

1586: To cover the cost of administering and defending the island, the Mexican *situado* (subsidy) is introduced. It was not abolished until 1811.

1595: Francis Drake attacks San Juan in November, but is rebuffed.

1598: George Clifford, Count of Cumberland, attacks San Juan and holds on to it for 82 days (from June through November).

1603: Royal efforts are undertaken to cut down on the production of ginger.

1608: The Boquerón Fort, the bridge on the San Antonio channel and the Cañuelo Fort are built.

1625: A Dutch expedition, commanded by Boduin Hendrikson, attacks and takes San Juan. After occupying the city for almost two months, the Dutch burned most of it, then sailed away.

1635: The construction of a massive wall around San Juan is begun.

1647: Diego de Torres Vargas writes his *Descripción de la Isla y Ciudad de Puerto Rico.*

1700: Charles II of Spain dies after willing Spain and its empire to Philip of Anjou, grandson of Louis XIV of France. Soon thereafter the War of the Spanish Succession begins. It lasts until 1713.

1702: English attack near Arecibo is rebuffed.

1703: A Dutch invading force is repulsed near Guadianilla.

1714: The town of San Mateo de Cangrejos is founded.

1717: The town of Río Piedras is founded.

1723: The town of Guaynabo is founded.

1726: Coffee trees are introduced from the French Antilles.

1732: The town of Manatí is founded.

1735: The town of Guayama is founded.

1739: The town of Utuado is founded. Beginning of War of Jenkins' Ear between England and Spain.

1740: The town of Coamo is founded.

1745: The town of Toa Baja is founded.

1751: The town of Toa Alta is founded. José Campeche, well-known island painter, is born.

1752: The settlement of Ponce, on the south coast, officially becomes a town.

1753: Governor Felipe Ramírez de Estenos expels the English from the island of Vieques.

1756: The Real Compañia de Barcelona is created to carry on commerce with Puerto Rico and Hispaniola.

1757: Governor Ramírez de Estenos presents a plan for agrarian reform in the island. Juan Alejo Arizmendi is born in San Juan.

1760: The Town of Farjardo is founded.

1763: The town of Mayagüez, on the west coast, is founded.

1764: A new mail system is inaugurated between Spain and Cuba, and San Juan is an intermediate stop.

1765: Marshall Alejandro O'Reilly arrives in Puerto Rico. Census of the island's population: 44,833 persons of whom 5,037 are black slaves.

1771: The town of Cabo Rojo is founded.

1771: The town of Bayamón is founded.

1772: Founding of the towns of Pepino and Cayey.

1775: Founding of the towns of Caguas and Aguadilla. Ramorín Power y Giralt is born. Population of Puerto Rico is 70,250, including 6,467 black slaves.

1778: Arecibo, Coamo and Aguada attain official status as towns.

1782: The wall surrounding the main area of San Juan is completed.

1787: Exportation of tobacco to Holland is authorized. The Royal Mercantile Factory is established for the exporting of tobacco.

1793: The towns of Yabucoa and Humacao are founded.

1797: English attack Puerto Rico but are forced to withdraw. The towns of Juncos and Luquillo are founded. Spain authorizes commerce between Puerto Rico and neutral powers.

1803: Juan Alejo Arizmendi is appointed bishop of San Juan.

1807: The first printing press is brought to Puerto Rico. The island's first publication, *La Gaceta Oficial,* is printed. French troops begin to move into Spain.

1808: The Spanish people begin their war against the French armies of occupation. Soon thereafter a Junta Central is established to coordinate the anti-French war effort. The Junta calls for a meeting of the traditional Spanish Cortes (parliament) in the city of Cádiz.

1809: The Spanish American colonies are invited to elect deputies to the Cortes. The Puerto Rican creole elite chooses Ramón Power y Giralt to represent them.

1810: Wars of independence get underway in the Spanish American mainland.

1812: The Cortes of Cádiz enacts a constitution that gives the colonies some representation.

1814: Ferdinand VII, king of Spain, abolishes the Constitution of 1812 after the French armies have been forced out of Spain.

1815: Ferdinand VII grants Puerto Rico the *Cédula de Gracias.*

1820: Liberal revolt in Spain forces Ferdinand to reinstate Constitution of 1812. Puerto Rico is once again given the right to elect representatives to the Spanish Cortes. Public lighting is installed in San Juan.

1822: Román Baldorioty de Castro is born. Slaves revolt in Bayamón and Toa Baja.

1823: The liberal regime in Spain is overthrown. Ferdinand VII once again abolished the Constitution of 1812.

1825: José Julián Acosta is born.

1826: At a congress of representatives from several of the newly-created Spanish American republics, Simón Bolívar advocates the creation of an army to liberate Puerto Rico and Cuba. The United States opposes the plan. The town of Comerío is founded. Alejandro Tapia y Rivera is born.

1827: Ramón Emeterio Betances is born in Cabo Rojo.

1829: The town of Lares is founded. Julio L. Vizcarrondo and Segundo Ruiz Belvis are born.

1830: Simón Bolívar dies. The towns of Aibonito and Ceiba are founded.

1832: The Theological Seminary is officially opened in San Juan. Audiencia of Puerto Rico is created.

1837: Governor Miguel López Baños issues a decree known as *Bando de Policía y Buen Gobierno.*

1838: Andrés Vizcarrondo, Buenaventura Quiñones, Juan Quiñones and others plan an uprising to proclaim Puerto Rican independence. They are arrested when Governor López de Baños learns of the plan. Buenaventura Quiñones is discovered hanged in a cell in El Morro.

1839: Eugenio María de Hostos is born in Mayagüez.

1842: Salvador Brau is born.

1843: The *Aguinaldo Puertorriqueño* is published in San Juan.

1844: The *Album Puertorriqueño* is published in Barcelona.

1845: Spain finally gives in to British pressures and puts an end to the slave trade in Puerto Rico.

1848: Slave rebellions in Ponce and Vega Baja in Puerto Rico and in the neighboring island of Martinique lead Governor Juan Prim to issue the notorious *Bando Negro.*

1849: Governor Juan de la Pezuela introduces the system of passbooks (*libretas reglamentarias*). In Barcelona, Manuel A. Alonso's *El Gíbaro* is published.

1850: José Gautier Benítez and Cayetano Coll y Toste are born.

1854: Daniel de Rivera publishes his poem *Agüeybana el Bravo*. He is arrested by Governor Fernando Norzagaray. The School of Agriculture, Navigation, and Commerce is created. Román Baldorioty de Castro and José Julián Acosta, who had gone to Spain to study, return to Puerto Rico.

1855: Rosendo Matienzo Cintrón is born.

1857: Juan Morel Campos is born. So is José Celso Barbosa.

1859: Luis Muñoz Rivera is born.

1860: Ramón E. Betances is exiled from the island because of his pro-independence activities.

1862: Betances is once again exiled from Puerto Rico by the colonial authorities.

1863: Julio L. Vizcarrondo established in Madrid the Spanish Abolitionist Society.

1865: Cuban and Puerto Rican separatists establish a pro-independence Republican Society in New York City.

1866: José de Diego is born.

1867: Betances proclaims "The Ten Commandments of Free Men" in St. Thomas.

1868: On September 23, pro-independence groups take over the town of Lares and proclaim the creation of the Republic of Puerto Rico.

1869: The promulgation of a new constitution in Spain gives Puerto

Rico the right to elect deputies to the Spanish Cortes. The notorious *Guardia Civil* is introduced to Puerto Rico.

1870: The Liberal Reformist Party and the Conservative Party are founded.

1873: Slavery is abolished in Puerto Rico.

1874: The Spanish Federal Republic, which had been established in 1873, is overthrown by the Spanish military and the monarchy restored.

1878: New electoral law limits the size of the electorate in Puerto Rico to 2,000 persons (out of an adult male population of 374,640). Luis Lloréns Torres is born.

1879: The town of Culebra is founded on the island of the same name.

1880: A tramway from San Juan to Río Piedras is inaugurated.

1881: The Assimilist Party is founded.

1886: The *carretera militar* connecting San Juan to Ponce is completed.

1887: The Puerto Rican Autonomist Party is founded. Governor Romualdo Palacios launches reign of terror against the autonomists and reformists in general. Among those arrested and thrown into the dungeons of El Morro is Román Baldorioty de Castro.

1889: Baldorioty de Castro dies in Ponce.

1891: Pedro Albizu Campos is born in Ponce.

1892: The Cuban Revolutionary Party is founded in New York City by José Martí. A Puerto Rican Section of the party is organized.

1895: Cuban revolutionaries launch war of independence.

1897: Luis Muñoz Rivera, the most important autonomist leader on the island, betrays to the Spanish authorities in Puerto Rico a pro-independence plot in Yauco. Soon thereafter he travels to Spain to ask for autonomy for Puerto Rico. The regime of Sagasta in Spain grants Puerto Rico an Autonomous Charter.

1898: The United States goes to war against Spain. Spanish troops in Cuba are defeated. U.S. troops occupy the Philippines. In July, U.S. troops occupy Puerto Rico. In September, Spain and the United States sign the Treaty of Paris by virtue of which Spain ceded Puerto Rico to the United States. A U.S. general is named by Washington to govern the island. Luis Muñoz Marín is born.

1899: San Ciriaco hurricane devastates the island. General John Eaton is appointed Superintendent of Public Instruction. All newspapers published in Puerto Rico are placed under the direct control of the U.S. military government. The Puerto Rican Republican Party is founded.

1900: The Foraker Act sets up civil government. Charles H. Allen becomes the first civilian governor under U.S. colonial rule. The first Labor Congress is held.

1903: The University of Puerto Rico is established.

1904: The Unionist Party, led by Luis Muñoz Rivera, is founded.

1910: Under the leadership of Santiago Iglesias Pantín, la *Federación Libre de Trabajadores* is founded.

1911: The College of Agricultural and Engineering is established in Mayagüez.

1912: Matienzo Cintrón founds the Puerto Rican Independence Party.

1913: The Unionist Party eliminates statehood from its program. Matienzo Cintrón dies.

1915: The Puerto Rican Socialist Party (led by Santiago Iglesias) is founded.

1916: Luis Muñoz Rivera dies.

1917: The United States enters World War I. In March, the Jones Act is passed. The new act imposes U.S. citizenship on Puerto Ricans and makes them subject to the draft laws of the metropolis.

1918: The U.S. Supreme Court declares Puerto Rico an "unincorporated" territory belonging to but not forming part of the United States. José de Diego dies.

1919: Luis Muñoz Marín, son of Luis Muñoz Rivera, marries the American Mona Lee.

1921: Celso Barbosa dies.

1922: The Unionist Party eliminates independence as a goal from the party's platform. Antonio Barceló, leader of the Unionist Party, suggests the concept of the *Estado Libre Asociado*. Pro-independence Unionists leave the party, and under the leadership of José Coll y Cuchi found the Puerto Rican Nationalist Party.

1923: First radio station is established in Puerto Rico.

1924: Santiago Iglesias leads the Socialist Party (the party of the workers) into a pro-statehood alliance (the *Coalición*) with the Republican Party (the party of the rich).

1928: San Felipe hurricane hits the island.

1929: The Depression hits Puerto Rico. By 1930, 36% of the employable on the island were unemployed.

1930: Pedro Albizu Campos is elected president of the Nationalist Party.

1931: Luis Muñoz Marín returns to Puerto Rico after living for many years in the U.S.

1932: The Coalition of pro-statehood Republicans, sectors of the Unionist Party and sectors of the Socialist Party led by Santiago

Iglesias win the insular elections. Santiago Iglesias is elected Resident Commissioner to Washington. San Ciprián hurricane devastates the island.

1933: Cane workers at the South Porto Rico Sugar Company go on strike. They are joined in early 1934 by workers of the Fajardo Sugar Company and Central Aguirre Associates.

1934: Antonio S. Pedreira publishes his *Insularismo*.

1935: Nationalist militants are killed by police at the University of Puerto Rico.

1936: The chief of the insular police, Colonel Francis Riggs, is killed by two young Nationalists. Albizu Campos and several other Nationalists are arrested and tried for sedition. Albizu Campos is sentenced to the Federal Penitentiary in Atlanta, Georgia. Senator Tydings introduces the bill named after him that offers Puerto Rico its independence.

1937: At the commencement of a parade of the Nationalist Party in Ponce, the police opens fire and many Nationalists are killed. Thus the name "The Ponce Massacre."

1938: Luis Muñoz Marín and others leave the Liberal Party (formerly the Unionist Party) and found the Popular Democratic Party. Workers strike for 42 days on the water front in the Toa Baja-Dorado-Bayamón area. Antonio Barceló dies. Nationalists open fire on Governor Blanton Winship.

1939: Santiago Iglesias dies.

1940: The Popular Democratic Party of Luis Muñoz Marín wins a surprising and impressive electoral victory. Muñoz Marín becomes president of the insular sentate.

1941: Rexford Guy Tugwell is named the last North American governor of Puerto Rico.

1944: The Popular Democratic Party wins the election with 383,000 votes, compared to 208,000 of the combined opposition.

1946: President Truman names Jesús T. Piñero governor of Puerto Rico (the first Puerto Rican to occupy the post). The *Partido Independentista Puertorriqueño* (PIP) is founded in Bayamón.

1947: The insular legislative adopts the Industrial Incentives Act; Operation Bootstrap goes into effect. The goal is to attract foreign capital to the island. Albizu Campos returns to Puerto Rico after a 10-year prison term. President Truman signs the Crawford-Butler Act, permitting Puerto Ricans to elect their own governor.

1948: Students at the University of Puerto Rico go on strike. The Popular Democratic Party wins the election, with 392,000 votes against 346,000. Luis Muñoz Marín becomes the first elected governor in the history of Puerto Rico. The Catholic University in Ponce is founded.

1950: In July President Truman signs Public Law 600 permitting Puerto Rico to draft its own constitution within a colonial framework. In October a Nationalist revolt explodes in several parts of the island. Nationalists attack *La Fortaleza* in San Juan. On the mainland Nationalists try to kill Truman. In Puerto Rico the National Guard is mobilized to crush the revolt. Albizu Campos is arrested and once again sent to jail.

1951: A plebescite approves Law 600 by 75 per cent of the votes cast. Soon thereafter 92 delegates (the majority *populares*) are elected to a Constituent Convention to draw up the constitution of the Commonwealth of Puerto Rico or Associated Free State.

1952: On March 3, with 375,000 to 83,000 votes the constitution of the Commonwealth of Puerto Rico is approved.

1954: On March 1 four Nationalists open fire in the U.S. House of Representatives, wounding five congressmen.

1955: The Instituto de Cultura Puertorriqueña is established.

1956: The Popular Democratic Party wins 62 per cent of the total vote. The Statehood Republican Party doubles its 1952 total with 172,000 votes; the PIP drops to 85,000. The *Federacion Universitaria Pro-Independencia* (FUPI) is established.

1959: The U.S. Congress rejects the Fernos-Murray Bill, which aimed to amplify Puerto Rico's autonomy. The *Movimiento Pro-Independencia* (MPI) is founded.

1960: The Popular Democratic Party wins the elections with 58 per cent of the total votes cast. The FUPI launches a campaign against compulsory ROTC at the University of Puerto Rico.

1962: Muñoz Marín and President Kennedy exchange letters and arrange for the creation of a joint U.S.-Puerto Rico Status Commission to conduct studies on the status of the island.

1963: Cuba requests the inclusion of the Puerto Rican case in the agenda of the Committee of Twenty-Four (decoloniztion matters) of the United Nations.

1964: Muñoz Marín retires from the governorship. His handpicked successor, Roberto Sánchez Vilella, becomes the Popular Democratic Party candidate and easily wins the election.

1965: Pedro Albizu Campos dies.

1967: In a referendum on political status, the Commonwealth concept receives a majority of the votes, against statehood and independence. The C.A.L. (Commandos of Armed Liberation) is organized.

1968: A rift in the Popular Democratic Party causes Sánchez Vilella to leave the party. He forms his own People's Party. Luis Negrón López is the Popular Democratic candidate. Luis A. Ferré and the pro-statehood New Progressive Party (the heir of the old Republican Party) win by a narrow margin, interrupting 28 years of Popular Democratic Party rule.

1969: Senate minority leader Justo Méndez of the New Progressive Party tells the press that the Commonwealth is to be a "transitory" vehicle to statehood, reasoning that the 1968 election nullified the 1967 referendum.

1970: Governor Ferré and President Nixon agree on the formation of an *ad hoc* committee to discuss Ferré's request that Puerto Ricans be allowed to participate in presidential elections. Muñoz Marín retires from the Senate.

1971: The MPI changes its name to Puerto Rican Socialist Party and adopts Marxism-Leninism as its ideology.

1972: Rafael Hernández Colón of the Popular Democratic Party is elected governor of Puerto Rico. The Popular Democratic Party received 100,000 more votes than the New Progressive Party of Ferré.

1973: Waves of workers' strikes hit the island. The National Guard is mobilized to run certain enterprises paralyzed by these strikes. At an assembly of students at the University of Puerto Rico, the majority vote to strike for changes at the university. The university is forced to close.

DATE DUE

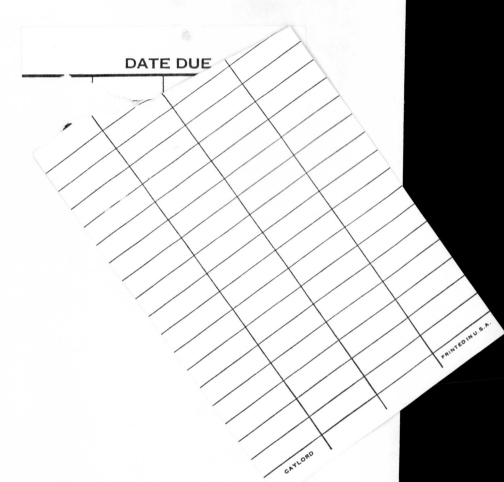

GAYLORD

PRINTED IN U.S.A.